CULTURAL DIFFERENCE AND ECONOMIC DISADVANTAGE IN REGIONAL HUMAN RIGHTS COURTS

CULTURAL DIFFERENCE AND ECONOMIC DISADVANTAGE IN REGIONAL HUMAN RIGHTS COURTS

An Integrated View

Valeska David

INTERSENTIA

Intersentia Ltd
8 Wellington Mews
Wellington Street | Cambridge
CB1 1HW | United Kingdom
Tel.: +44 1223 736 170
Email: mail@intersentia.co.uk
www.intersentia.com | www.intersentia.co.uk

Distribution for the UK and Ireland:
NBN International
Airport Business Centre, 10 Thornbury Road
Plymouth, PL6 7PP
United Kingdom
Tel.: +44 1752 202 301 | Fax: +44 1752 202 331
Email: orders@nbninternational.com

Distribution for Europe and all other countries:
Intersentia Publishing nv
Groenstraat 31
2640 Mortsel
Belgium
Tel.: +32 3 680 15 50 | Fax: +32 3 658 71 21
Email: mail@intersentia.be

Distribution for the USA and Canada:
Independent Publishers Group
Order Department
814 North Franklin Street
Chicago, IL 60610
USA
Tel.: +1 800 888 4741 (toll free) | Fax: +1 312 337 5985
Email: orders@ipgbook.com

Cultural Difference and Economic Disadvantage in Regional Human Rights Courts. An Integrated View

Artwork on cover: Lois Mailou Jones, Shapes and Colors – classicpaintings / Alamy Stock Photo

ISBN 978-1-78068-833-6
D/2020/7849/3
NUR 828

British Library Cataloguing in Publication Data. A catalogue record for this book is available from the British Library.

For Ander and Amanda

FOREWORD

Eva Brems

I had the pleasure of witnessing the genesis of this book, which is based on the author's Ph.D. thesis, written at Ghent University in the context of a broader research project on 'human rights integration'. Valeska David joined the team relatively late, as a result of which she had only three years to complete her doctoral work, instead of the four years that are common in Belgian law faculties. Many people in these circumstances would opt for a simple research design to maximize feasibility. While that may be a sensible thing to do, it does not match everybody's personality though. This researcher did not want external circumstances to interfere with her scholarly aspirations. And these were ambitious. She did not choose to focus on one supranational human rights jurisdiction, but rather opted for studying the two most important regional courts. Neither did she want to zoom in on one type of human rights violation, or to conduct her analysis from a single theoretical angle. This resulted in a very challenging research project, that Valeska was able to complete successfully thanks to her talent and dedication, as well as her versatile and creative intelligence.

1. HUMAN RIGHTS INTEGRATION FROM A RIGHTS HOLDERS' PERSPECTIVE

The project 'The Global Challenge of Human Rights Integration: Towards a Users' Perspective' (2012–2017), was sponsored as an Inter-University Attraction Pole (IAP) by the Belgian Science Policy Office (BELSPO). Research teams at five Belgian universities (Ghent University, Antwerp University, Vrije Universiteit Brussel, Université Libre de Bruxelles, and Université Saint Louis Bruxelles), as well as at Utrecht University in the Netherlands, collaborated in 'the study of human rights law as an integrated whole from a users' perspective'. The starting point of the research was the finding that both rights holders and duty bearers under human rights norms are confronted simultaneously with a multitude of human rights provisions differing as to their scope, focus, legal force and level of governance. This non-hierarchical accumulation of human rights provisions has resulted in a complex and uncoordinated legal architecture that may in some circumstances create obstacles for effective human rights protection. Valeska David's book can be seen as a keystone of this project, as it contributes to several of its central dimensions, and brings these to a higher level.

One of the objectives of the project was to develop theories describing and explaining the multi-layered nature of human rights law. These include legal pluralism[1] and network theory.[2] In addition, a few steps were made toward a pragmatic theory that would promote increased human rights integration in a manner that optimizes its benefits while avoiding potential pitfalls.[3] In her book, Valeska David provides an impressive and nuanced theoretical basis for a normative project of human rights integration, geared towards the combined consideration of cultural diversity and socio-economic inequality. Her herculean mixing and matching of theoretical concepts and frames points to the need for integration at the deeper level of theory as a necessary complement to human rights integration in judicial practice.

Another objective of the 'human rights integration' project was the building of bridges between layers of human rights law. This regards ways in which an integrated view of human rights may be envisaged, both as a project of normative development and as a matter of current procedural practice.[4] An attractive project in this regard concerned the 'rewriting' of supranational human rights decisions 'as if human rights law were one'.[5] This book project intended to show that even within the current fragmented landscape of international human rights law, it is possible to 'integrate' human rights to a significantly higher degree than is generally the case. To that end, it introduces concrete and innovative proposals for an integrated approach to supranational

---

1 Barbara Oomen, 'The application of socio-legal theories of legal pluralism to understanding the implementation and integration of human rights law,' *European Journal of Human Rights Law/Journal européen des droits de l'homme*, 2014(4), 471.

2 Antoine Bailleux, 'Human Rights in Network', *European Journal of Human Rights Law/ Journal européen des droits de l'homme*, 2014(3), 293.

3 Eva Brems, 'Should Pluriform Human Rights Become One ? Exploring the Benefits of Human Rights Integration', *European Journal of Human Rights/Journal européen des droits de l'homme*, 2014(4), 447; Eva Brems, 'Smart Human Rights Integration', in Eva Brems and Saïla Ouald Chaib (eds.), *Fragmentation and Integration in Human Rights Law: Users' Perspectives*, Edward Elgar Publishing 2018, 165.

4 See for example, the work of Dorothea Staes on the practice of the European Court of Human Rights of referring to 'sources' outside the European Convention on Human Rights, including to the case law of other bodies: 'When the European Court of Human Rights refers to external instruments. Mapping and justifications', Ph.D. thesis ULB, 2017. See also the work of Marijke De Pauw on a holistic interpretation of the rights of the elderly: 'International Human Rights Law: Between Fragmentation and Coordination – A case study on the emerging rights of older persons', Ph.D. thesis VUB- Université Saint Louis, 2017.

5 Eva Brems and Ellen Desmet, *Integrated human rights in practice, Rewriting human rights decisions*, Edward Elgar, 2017, p. 539.

human rights justice by redrafting crucial passages of landmark human rights judgments and decisions. In addition to the rewriting exercise, authors have outlined the methodology and/or theoretical framework that guided their approaches and explained how human rights monitoring bodies may adopt an integrated approach to human rights law. In that book, Valeska David contributed a chapter on an integrated approach to the rights of women and children in poverty.[6] 'Building bridges between layers of human rights law' can be a technical, even somewhat formal exercise, when it is focused on referencing relevant provisions and case law from across the international human rights landscape. Yet it is most meaningful when it is the expression of an integrated vision of the human rights issues that are at stake. Such a vision is precisely what Valeska David is building in the present book, as she analyzes case law through a rich theoretical prism.

The last feature of the 'human rights integration' project that I want to highlight here, is its focus on the perspectives of the 'users' of human rights law, i.e. the different actors that make human rights law.[7] When translated into a research agenda, this generally leads to field research involving methods such as interviews and observations with these actors.[8] These are of course very important, but are not possible or desirable for every legal research project. In the present book, Valeska David offers a method to put arguably the most important 'user' or actor of human rights law – the rights holder – at the center, in a desk-based research design. This in itself is a highly valuable contribution to human rights scholarship.

2. A TRIPLE FEAT OF COMPREHENSIVENESS

The preface and introduction to the present book explain its relationship to the phenomenon of fragmentation in international human rights law. This fragmentation is largely the result of specialization and of a drive toward tailoring rights protection to the realities on the ground. As such it is a necessary and valuable development, which is moreover far from completed. Indeed, justified calls continue to be made for new human rights instruments addressing violations vis-à-vis specific groups and/or new types of

---

6 Valeska David, 'Caring, rescuing or punishing? Rewriting RMS v Spain (ECtHR) from an integrated approach to the rights of women and children in poverty', in Eva Brems and Ellen Desmet, *Integrated human rights in practice, Rewriting human rights decisions*, Edward Elgar, 2017, p. 147.

7 Ellen Desmet, 'Analysing users' trajectories in human rights: a conceptual exploration and research agenda', *Human Rights & International Legal Discourse*, 2014, vol. 8, no. 2, 121.

8 E.g. Moritz Baumgärtel, *Demanding Rights. Europe's Supranational Courts and the Dilemma of Migrant Vulnerability*, Cambridge University Press, 2019.

human rights violations. At the same time, it is necessary, at this point in the development of international human rights law, to engender awareness of the potential pitfalls of fragmentation, and of the benefits of an integrative approach.

What I wish to point out in this section is that there has been a parallel development in human rights law scholarship. As an academic discipline, human rights law has in most institutions been recognized only since the last two decades of the twentieth century as separate from public international law or constitutional law. Even then, only few scholars used to identify themselves as exclusively focusing on human rights law. These numbers have grown fast, as human rights law courses were increasingly integrated in law school curricula, and research centers specializing in human rights law spread. Around the turn of the century, it was self-evident, at least in the context in which I operate, that a 'human rights law scholar' would attempt to follow up all developments in international human rights law, both regionally and at the UN level, in addition to developments in domestic law. Since then, the discipline has matured and witnessed both growth and increasing specialization. Given the proliferation of human rights norms, and the extensive output of some supranational human rights monitoring bodies, it is arguably not even possible today for a single scholar to be an expert in all aspects of international human rights law. Specialization of scholarship is therefore a logical and necessary development. Yet at the same time, it arguably becomes even more important that there should also be vibrant scholarly debates on transversal and overarching topics of human rights law. We need to know where we stand in the overall project of human rights law. We need to understand how different layers of human rights law interact, and how manifestations of injustice relate to the norms and procedures of human rights law in complex and imperfect ways. And we need to reflect on how the theoretical insights regarding specific types of injustice can be combined and translated into legal concepts and tools. In studying the trees, we should not forget to see the forest – or, for that matter, the complete ecosystem. This is challenging as, compared to single-issue scholarship, this requires the study of more institutions, more cases, more theories … and, in addition, it requires some courage, as in a broad research project, the impossibility of exhaustive knowledge renders the researcher vulnerable. This is why I applaud Valeska David in her choice of topic and research design. In this book, 'more is more', and complexity is of the essence. Her work is a triple feat of comprehensiveness.

First, there is of course the combination of a study of the case law of the European Court of Human Rights and that of the Inter-American Court of Human Rights. Despite similar institutional set-ups and human rights catalogues, these courts have developed quite different styles of argumentation. Part of the explanation for these differences lies most likely in the different contexts in which they operate, resulting amongst others in different types of cases and different stakeholder expectations, as well as different perceptions within the institutions themselves about the appropriate role of a regional human rights court. Part of the differences may be deliberate, and part may be accidental. The study of both courts within the same research design allows a focus on common challenges, and offers a richer resource for reflection on how to overcome these than single-court studies can. For scholars, a multiple-body study facilitates insights into the role of various context-dependent factors in legal human rights reasoning. For actors working with and within these bodies, such a study opens doors to alternative ways of reasoning, and to critical reflection on explicit or implicit choices in judicial practice.

Even more important is the substantive focus of the present book on a holistic view of human rights, that encompasses both issues of cultural diversity and challenges of socio-economic inequality. In rights scholarship, two 'integrative' or holistic concepts have received quite some attention. One is the indivisibility of human rights, a concept that is mobilized in international human rights law, chiefly to emphasize the need for joint consideration of economic and social rights with civil and political rights. The other is intersectionality, a concept in diversity studies, that is used chiefly to theorize the impact of intersections among identity traits that may give rise to discrimination and marginalization. In the context of human rights law, what indivisibility and intersectionality have in common is their pointing toward the need to be able to approach analytical legal categories in a flexible manner, in order to be able to comprehensively address real-life injustice. Yet the need to refine and integrate our insights into the realities of human rights violations and our approaches to remedy them, is much bigger than the scope of either intersectionality or indivisibility. In the present book, Valeska David thoroughly explores another context that calls for an integrated approach. While she provides profound theoretical backing for the specific combination of challenges regarding cultural diversity and socio-economic inequality, she also situates her findings in the broader project of striving for a legal framework that can do the best possible justice to all salient dimensions of human rights violations.

The third feat of comprehensiveness that Valeska David realizes in this book is the impressive combination of theoretical concepts and frameworks. Of course, it is perfectly acceptable for a scholar to choose a single theoretical framework to work with. Yet the effort Valeska put into engaging with multiple theories creates clear added value within her overall project of 'integration', as it offers anchor points for scholars who are familiar with different theoretical concepts. In addition, it contributes to facilitating conversations across theoretical silos.

In my opinion, both the research design and the analyses and insights presented in this book can offer a lot of inspiration, to both practitioners and scholars of human rights law.

PREFACE

Several considerations have led this author to analyse the supranational adjudication of claims concerning cultural and economic difference. These are claims that basically seek protection against social devaluation, disadvantage or exclusion on account of the applicants' cultural and economic particularities (hereinafter also referred to as cases of cultural and economic 'disadvantage', or cultural and economic 'diversity'). The first reason to examine these cases relates to the specific challenges they bring to human rights courts. Three main challenges are worth highlighting here. The first one has to do with the fact that cultural and economic criteria are usually accepted as rational, pertinent and legitimate grounds for social organisation. For example, in most areas of regulation (whether public or private), it appears quite reasonable to establish restrictions or duties regarding dress, hairstyle, language and cultural knowledge. The same holds for the observance of economic requirements such as payment of fees, being employed and having a certain income. The practical implication of assuming the legitimacy of all this is that rights claimants may have a hard time in demonstrating the injustice of norms and practices that rely on those cultural and economic criteria. Judges may actually be inclined to uphold them or to view them as harmless. This problem can be summed up as 'acute normalisation'. By this it is meant that cultural and economic differences and importantly, the set of privileges and disadvantages that accompany them, are internalised, accepted or otherwise presumed normal in a particularly acute way. Compared to other grounds of difference (e.g. gender, sex, race or nationality), the question may be seen as one of degree. While framing a claim as disadvantage based on gender, sex or race difference triggers some alarms, framing it as based on cultural or economic factors does not.

In the second place, questions of cultural and economic difference are often seen as something either too complex or too sensitive to be tackled by human rights courts. One line of argumentation emphasises that cultural and economic disadvantages are closely linked to complex structural, social and institutional issues. Complaints touching upon these issues should thus preferably be dealt with by means other than by seeking state liability in court, let alone in international courts. From another perspective, cultural and economic differences may be, respectively, an expression of deeply felt sentiments and traditions or particular histories and struggles. International courts should thus be careful about intruding into these areas, as they would be ill-placed and equipped to address such complex and sensitive matters. What usually follows from this is restraint or lenient reviews on the part of the judges examining claims of cultural and economic disadvantage. This second challenge can be described as an issue of 'restraint'.

In the third place, one may argue that complaints of cultural difference and economic disadvantage are so variable and changeable that they may take the law too far, requiring never-ending flexibility or even transformation of existing standards. Cultural and economic conditions vary from place to place and may imply different things for different people. Cultural and economic issues are actually typical sites of divergence among and across states, communities and individuals. Nearly everyone could claim any kind of right on the basis of cultural and economic circumstances. Yet, courts and human rights law could not be expected to be attentive to everyone's particularities, preferences or needs. Judges and other stakeholders may furthermore want to reduce divergent interpretations and solutions, for the sake of coherence and certainty. How many special or new rights can be granted; how many exceptions to the rule are allowed and whose cultural and economic claims are accommodated? These difficulties can be named as a question of 'limits.'

One might argue that issues of normalisation, restraint and limits are not exclusive of cultural and economic claims, as they would also manifest in the handling of other types of case involving issues of difference and inclusion. This is a fair point. But from the perspective of the people who see their rights or social inclusion compromised for cultural and/or economic reasons, those issues are significant challenges in their quest for redress. Also for judges, the simultaneous confluence of issues of acute normalisation, restraint and limits in a single case certainly adds pressure to their task. In understanding the challenges described above, it is also relevant to bear in mind that the field of cultural and economic rights is one of the least elaborated areas of human rights law, not least owing to their relatively recent and limited development through adjudication.[1] It thus comes as no surprise that the relationship between human rights law and cultural diversity, as well as that between human rights law and poverty, remain as current and contested subjects.

---

1 As regards cultural rights, see Rosemary J. Coombe, 'Legal Claims to Culture in and Against the Market: Neoliberalism and the Global Proliferation of Meaningful Difference', 1 *Law, Culture and the Humanities* (2005) 35, at 52; Yvonne M. Donders, *Human Rights: Eye for Cultural Diversity* (Amsterdam University Press, 2012). Inaugural Lecture delivered upon the appointment to the chair of Professor of International Human Rights and Cultural Diversity at the University of Amsterdam on 29 June 2012, at 16–18. As regards socio-economic rights, see e.g. Virginia Mantouvalou, 'The Case for Social Rights', *Georgetown Public Law Research Paper No. 10–18* (2010), at 13 (arguing that these rights appear vague and imprecise not because of something inherent in them but rather because they have not been developed by scholars, courts, advocates, etc.).

When one studies these two contested areas of rights claims, it appears furthermore intriguing the way they have been addressed. In particular, it is startling that issues of cultural and economic interests have often been examined by courts and scholars in a rather disaggregated manner. To start with, legal claims of cultural difference and economic disadvantage are rarely brought together in a single study.[2] Some human rights law scholars have focused on issues of cultural difference (or 'diversity') and inequality, while others have been concerned with questions of socio-economic disadvantage, poverty and economic rights. These two bodies of literature, however, rarely converge or talk to each other.[3] One nevertheless wonders why the discussions on Roma and Travellers' housing lifestyles or about religious accommodation in the workplace are rarely addressed from the perspective of social rights and structural inequalities. Why is it that problems of socio-economic disadvantage are seldom examined in terms of poverty-based discrimination or the use of harmful stereotypes, and not just in terms of states' socio-economic obligations? One also wonders why the applicants and other implicated parties in these cases are often defined from the perspective of their cultural or religious membership, on the one hand, or their socio-economic circumstances, on the other, as if these were the only relevant features that marked their experience. The question that arises then is how the analysis would change if all these cases were seen from the perspective of, for instance, gender, age and immigration background. And what if that holistic approach were also extended to rights? Many cases involving issues of cultural difference are certainly about culturally driven rights, just as many cases of economic disadvantage are about economically driven rights. But surely both sets of cases are not just about that. What if these cases were approached from the angle of rights and harms not immediately visible?

The underlying concern is how those claims and problems are legally framed.[4] At bottom, the book asks why not frame them differently, that is,

---

2 A notable exception is the study of whether and how fostering diversity (via multiculturalism, for example) decreases support or negatively affects policies of social welfare. See e.g. Jenny Phillimore, 'Diversity and social welfare. To restrict or include?', in Steven Vertovec (ed.), *Routledge International Handbook of Diversity Studies* (Routledge, 2015), at 245–253; Keith G. Banting, 'The Multicultural Welfare State: International Experience and North American Narratives', 39 *Social Policy and Administration* (2005) 98.

3 Note that here reference is mostly being made to legal studies. Unlike these, social theorists and sociologists have brought questions of cultural and economic difference together. See e.g. Terry Lovell (ed.), *(Mis)recognition, Social Inequality and Social Justice. Nancy Fraser and Pierre Bourdieu* (Routledge, 2007); Boaventura de Sousa Santos, 'Nuestra America reinventing a subaltern paradigm of recognition and redistribution', 18 *Theory, Culture & Society* (2001), at 192.

4 Framing is unavoidable. The issue is, however, to remain aware that 'every framing inevitably involves selection – if not pre-selection – through the conscious (and/or unconscious) placing of focus upon features or factors considered to be significant and/or valuable'.

more comprehensively, and whether doing so could enrich the legal analysis or illuminate useful avenues for tackling the challenges that come with those cases. But asking these questions requires considering how human rights law itself operates. Human rights law is supposed to rest on notions of indivisibility and interdependence, that is, on ideas of interconnection, unity and equal value across all rights. In practice, however, it is full of divisions: between types of right (civil and political rights, and economic, social and cultural rights), instruments (with differing binding force), organs, themes, regions and beneficiaries, among others. Human rights law has, in other words, fragmented.[5] Even within one general jurisdiction, such as that of the European and the Inter-American courts of human rights, divisions abound. Different parcels of standards and principles seem to apply depending on whether the applicant is defined as, for example, indigenous, a woman, a Roma, a member of a religious minority, an asylum seeker or a child; whether the issue is one of the public or private exercise of rights; whether it concerns positive or negative obligations; whether it is about equality or substantive liberties; and which line of case law it fits. This fragmentation is no bad thing, though. After all, it reflects serious efforts to fine-tune legal responses to different, traditionally overlooked types of problem and experience.

Arguably, what is problematic is that norms and standards sensitive to diversity (or to those marked as 'different') are often applied in a compartmentalised, isolated or unidimensional manner, cutting off relevant dimensions of the actors, norms or interests involved. This compartmentalised approach, which as noted above is quite common in the examination of cases concerning cultural and economic claims, carries several drawbacks. Besides failing to respond to the challenges posed by those cases, it may lead to a focus on abstract questions and to attribution of the problem to the difference or disadvantaged condition itself. This may, in turn, have two important effects: it may fail in making justice relate to people's lived experiences and it may leave the roots of the alleged violations unexamined.

Against this, the book turns to the idea of integration, that is, the idea that a more comprehensive approach to claims of cultural and economic difference is possible and useful. An integrated normative framework does not mean a general, abstract framework like that embodied in the Universal Declaration. By normative integration it is meant a normative framework that operates in a more holistic, interrelated and inclusive manner. For this, a point of

Anna Grear, '"Framing the Project" of international human rights law', in Conor Gearty and Costas Douzinas (eds.), *The Cambridge Companion to Human Rights Law* (Cambridge University Press, 2012), at 17.

5 See e.g. Carlos Iván Fuentes *et al.*, 'E Pluribus Unum – Bhinneka Tunggal Ika? Universal Human Rights and the Fragmentation of International Law', in René Provost and Colleen Sheppard, *Dialogues on Human Rights and Legal Pluralism* (Springer, 2013), at 52 and ff.

departure is the integrated approach to human rights proposed by Brems. She argues that such an integrated view has two implications. First, it implies 'a maximum widening of the range of human rights sources that are on the table'.[6] Second, an integrated view requires 'a maximum inclusion of human rights holders [...] whose rights are affected by a particular situation'.[7] As will be seen later, the integrated framework applied in this book builds upon and expands this notion of integration.

Using analytical and methodological insights provided by feminist theory and by cultural and critical legal studies more generally, Part I of the book on theoretical foundations develops an integrated and person-centred perspective that, put simply, strives to give practical effect to ideas of normative integration that are familiar to and yet underutilised in human rights law. These are the concepts of intersectionality, indivisibility and normative interdependence. To do so, Parts II and III of the book discuss more than 200 judgments and decisions from the European and the Inter-American courts of human rights.[8] These are cases that, in spite of their complexity, are often presented and resolved without due regard for those ideas of integration. Part II rethinks cultural difference from an integrated perspective and Chapter 2 focuses on cases mostly brought by Roma, Traveller and Muslim applicants before the European Court of Human Rights.[9] On the other side of the Atlantic, where the spectrum of claims of cultural diversity is substantially less varied and numerous, Chapter 3 of the book turns to cases submitted by indigenous and Afro-descendant individuals and communities to the Inter-American Court of Human Rights. Part III adopts an integrated view on claims of economic disadvantage. It examines cases where the litigants and/or the regional courts frame the problem as one about poverty and/or disadvantage in socio-economic welfare in several areas of social life (e.g. access to legal services, health, education, family welfare and social housing). Here again, the book addresses the work of both the European and the Inter-American courts of human rights (Chapters 4 and 5, respectively).

---

6 Eva Brems, 'Should Pluriform Human Rights Become One? Exploring the Benefits of Human Rights Integration', 4 *European Journal of Human Rights* (2014) 447, at 452.

7 Idem.

8 Although this sample may not be exhaustive, it is comprehensive enough for present purposes. The book furthermore draws on a number of cases from both regional courts which concern issues or applicants different from the ones that are the main focus of this book. Likewise, the author reviewed advisory opinions from the IACtHR and a number of rulings from other regional and international monitoring bodies. These are referenced when so deemed necessary for explanatory purposes.

9 The terms Roma and Traveller are used broadly to designate diverse groups and individuals that in the European Court's jurisprudence are generally referred to as 'Gypsies'. 'Roma' and 'Traveller' are taken as both a noun and a way to refer to a group. These terms and the way they are used in this book are by no means conveyed to deny the diversity within and across groups and individuals perceived or identified as Roma, Traveller or Gypsy.

The present book does not deal with the wide range of cultural and economic claims raised by those in non-hegemonic positions and the powerful alike. It only covers a relatively narrow segment of cases concerning cultural difference and economic disadvantage. And yet, the analysis undertaken here holds valuable potential for a large range of demands concerning difference and inclusion; from cases about adjustments for people with disabilities to claims for same-sex rights, to mention some. This is because most – if not all – forms of social division and exclusion encompass cultural and economic aspects.[10] It should also be noted that while the book focuses on litigation and the work of the judiciary, judges are not expected to do all the work required by human rights integration. As Chapter 6 reveals, other actors, such as lawyers, NGOs and third-party interveners can all play a crucial role in enriching the understanding of complex cases such those discussed here, although this issue is beyond the scope of this book.

Within these (and other) limitations, the book has two main aims. It seeks, firstly, to reveal whether and how prevailing judicial approaches to claims of cultural and economic difference may foreclose useful avenues for dealing with them and with the challenges they bring. Secondly, the book aims at providing guidelines for litigants and courts dealing with those matters to make their legal analysis more integrated, with a view to both making justice relate to people's lived reality and interrogating structural inequalities.

---

10 See e.g. Nancy Fraser, 'Social Justice in the Age of Identity Politics: Redistribution, Recognition, and Participation', in Nancy Fraser and Axel Honneth, *Redistribution or Recognition? A Political-Philosophical Exchange* (Verso, 2003), at 16–26; Sandra Fredman, 'Redistribution and Recognition: Reconciling Inequalities', 23(2) *South African Journal of Human Rights* (2007) 214, at 215; Seyla Benhabib, *The Claims of Culture. Equality and Diversity in the Global Era* (Princeton University Press, 2002), at 17. See also Chapter 1, sections 3, 4 and 5.

ACKNOWLEDGEMENTS

Writing this book has been a challenging and exciting journey that, luckily, I have not walked alone. I have made this journey thanks to many people. I know, and I hope all those who I am addressing now know, these words of gratitude will fall short of conveying what I actually feel.

This book would not have been possible without the precious advice and support given to me by Eva Brems. You have been more than a mentor to me, and I will always feel proud of and grateful for having worked with you. Likewise, I owe a big debt to Ellen Desmet and Koen De Feyter for their helpful comments and encouragement. Further, I would like to thank the energy and ideas shared by my colleagues from the Human Rights Centre of Ghent University and from the IAP Project. My gratitude also goes to the admirable experts who reviewed my work. Among them, Prof. Janneke Gerards, Prof. Laurence Burgorgue-Larsen, Prof. Paulo Pinto de Albuquerque, Prof. Dirk Heirbaut, Prof. Toon Moonen and the anonymous readers of the book manuscript. This book has greatly benefited from their insightful suggestions and critiques. This project is the result of doctoral research undertaken within the framework of an Inter-University Attraction Pole (IAP) research project called 'The Global Challenge of Human Rights Integration: Toward a Users' Perspective,' funded by the Interuniversity Attraction Poles Programme initiated by the Belgian Science Policy Office (Belspo).[1]

My deepest thanks go to Ander Marañón Zabalza. I have no words to thank you for all the love, help and enthusiasm, not just with this, but with everything I do. I am indebted to your generosity, sense of humour and wisdom. This book is dedicated to him and to our daughter, Amanda, who was born just before the completion of this project and made the greatest difference in my life.

Finally, I am grateful to my family and friends for their unconditional support and to Intersentia for making this book real. Special mention to Ahmed Hegazi for the professional and dedicated editorial work.

---

1 A major premise of this project is that the multi-layered experience of human rights norms has produced tension between divergence and coherence in human rights law in theory and practice. The project's 'work package' in which this book originates focused on the adjudication of questions of cultural and economic difference, which are reflective of contemporary tensions between universality and diversity in human rights law while being sites of contestation and divergent interpretations. Human Rights Integration Project Proposal 2012–2017, Contract P7/27, at 21 (on file with the author). Further information on the IAP's 'The Global Challenge of Human Rights Integration: Towards a Users' Perspective' can be found at <www.hrintegration.be>.

CONTENTS

LIST OF CASES

EUROPEAN COURT OF HUMAN RIGHTS AND FORMER COMMISSION

CASES CONCERNING MUSLIMS

CASES CONCERNING ROMA AND TRAVELLERS

CASES CONCERNING ECONOMIC DISADVANTAGE

OTHER CASES

INTER-AMERICAN COURT OF HUMAN RIGHTS

CASES CONCERNING INDIGENOUS AND AFRO-DESCENDANTS

CASES CONCERNING ECONOMIC DISADVANTAGE

OTHER CASES AND ADVISORY OPINIONS

INTER-AMERICAN COMMISSION ON HUMAN RIGHTS

EUROPEAN COURT OF JUSTICE

EUROPEAN COMMITTEE OF SOCIAL RIGHTS

HUMAN RIGHTS COMMITTEE

COMMITTEE ON ECONOMIC SOCIAL AND CULTURAL RIGHTS

COMMITTEE ON THE ELIMINATION OF THE DISCRIMINATION AGAINST WOMEN

COMMITTEE ON THE ELIMINATION OF RACIAL DISCRIMINATION

COMMITTEE ON THE RIGHTS OF THE CHILD

COMMITTEE ON THE RIGHTS OF PERSONS WITH DISABILITIES

INTRODUCTION

1. SETTING THE SCENE: A FRAGMENTED LAW FOR A COMPLEX WORLD

Plurality and inequality are features of many of today's societies. In this context, globalisation has made us very aware of growing divides not just between regions and states, but also among people. Differences along the lines of, for example, ethnic origin, religion, economic background, sex and sexual orientation, morals and lifestyles seem to have multiplied or become more visible. All this 'diversity', as it is usually labelled, has generated anxiety and concern, particularly in the last two or three decades. The concerns are largely motivated by the strong political and legal mobilisation that questions of social difference generate, as these differences translate into differences in power. As such, they give rise to claims of injustice, inequality, exclusion and disadvantage.[1] This is where human rights, the prime language of political and legal mobilisation,[2] come into play. Whether from the viewpoint of emancipation or legitimacy, human rights law has been used and criticised for (not) dealing with issues of difference or diversity.

Both states and individuals, especially those in non-hegemonic positions, expect human rights law to reflect and respond to their specific interests, values and needs. States have typically requested leeway to adapt human rights standards to their particular cultural, political and economic contexts. One body of literature has thus dealt with the relationship between human rights law and the so-called 'non-Western' states.[3] But within states, individuals and groups have

---

1 See e.g. Meena K. Bhamra, *The Challenge of Justice in Diverse Societies. Constitutionalism and Pluralism* (Ashgate, 2011), at 16 (arguing that 'the goal of justice is a key imperative behind the need to understand our new diversities and pluralities'); Tariq Modood, 'Difference, Multi and Equality', in Michel Seymour (ed.), *The Plural States of Recognition* (Palgrave Macmillan, 2010), at 153–155, 161–163 and 166; Davina Cooper, *Challenging Diversity. Rethinking Equality and the Value of Difference* (Cambridge University Press, 2004), at 7–8.

2 Ben Golder, 'Beyond Redemption? Problematising the Critique of Human Rights in Contemporary International Legal Thought', 77 *London Review of International Law* (2014) 2, at 2; Michael Ignatieff, *Human Rights as Politics and Idolatry* (Princeton University Press, 2003), at 53.

3 The discussion mostly refers to governments' assertion of culture as regards Islam and 'Asian values'. See e.g. Karen Engle, 'Culture and Human Rights: The Asian Values Debate in Context', 32 *International Law and Politics* (2000) 291, at 312–333; Eva Brems, 'Reconciling Universality and Diversity in International Human Rights: A Theoretical and Methodological Framework and Its Application in the Context of Islam', 5 *Human Rights Review* (2004) 5, at 5–12.

made similar demands. People claim that their rights are violated because their particularities are both taken and not taken into account in decision-making, in accessing social services or in the distribution of burdens and resources. The present book is situated at this level of analysis.

It is argued that human rights law, particularly as regards the human protected by it, 'simply does not do justice to the full complexity, the sheer fleshy variability and multiple forms, colours, shapes and sex/genders of the embodied human personality in all its vulnerability'.[4] For the universal and abstract subject of the Universal Declaration of Human Rights (UNDHR) was the projection of those with power. This is to say that the interests and concerns of mainly Western middle-class, heterosexual, Christian, body-able men determined, to a large extent, what counted as a human rights issue.[5] Still, those who do not represent the universal, but the particular or 'the different' (i.e. women, ethnic and religious minorities, those living in poverty, etc.), continually resort to human rights law and its mechanisms. They bring claims of all sorts to national and international courts: rights claims to exemptions, to recognition, to 'special protection', to 'new' rights, to be protected against discrimination, to have access to resources or to have them distributed differently. Exclusion has thereby been fought by seeking inclusion in 'the house of human rights'.[6] Human rights law has not remained indifferent, though. It has responded by diversifying itself. New treaties and standards multiply and identity/group-based 'compartments' of norms strive to serve the interests of women, indigenous peoples, persons with disabilities, and so on. Yet, the challenges continue, and the demands of difference do not cease.[7]

As with governments' discourses of difference in the face of human rights law, it appears that the realm of cultural difference is one of the most contested

---

4 Anna Grear, '"Framing the Project" of international human rights law', in Conor Gearty and Costas Douzinas (eds.), *The Cambridge Companion to Human Rights Law* (Cambridge University Press, 2012), at 32.

5 Ibid., at 28–29. This issue has been at the heart of most contemporary critiques of human rights. See *inter alia*, Frédéric Mégret, 'Where Does the Critique of International Human Rights Stand? An Exploration in 18 Vignettes', in Jose Maria Beneyto and David Kennedy (eds.), *New Approaches to International Law. The European and the American Experiences* (TMC Asser Press, 2012), at 3–40; Marie-Bénédicte Dembour, 'Critiques', in Daniel Moeckli *et al.* (eds.), *International Human Rights Law* (Oxford University Press, 2014), at 60–71; William Twining (ed.), *Human Rights: Southern Voices: Francis Deng, Abdullahi An-Na'im, Yash Ghai, Upendra Baxi* (Cambridge University Press, 2009); Hilary Charlesworth, 'Feminist Critiques of International Law and Their Critics', 13(1) *Third World Legal Studies* (1994) 1.

6 Frédéric Mégret, 'Where Does the Critique of International Human Rights Stand? An Exploration in 18 Vignettes', in Jose Maria Beneyto and David Kennedy (eds.), *New Approaches to International Law. The European and the American Experiences* (TMC Asser Press, 2012), at 28.

7 Costas Douzinas, 'The poverty of (rights) jurisprudence', in Conor Gearty and Costas Douzinas (eds.), *The Cambridge Companion to Human Rights Law* (Cambridge University Press, 2012), at 74–75.

when it comes to people's rights. From believers complaining against dismissal or restrictions for dressing according to their religion; travellers wanting to live in their caravans and to have a place to park them; indigenous and other rural communities claiming collective land rights; to members of fox-hunting associations requesting protection of their way of life, to mention just some examples – they have all brought their cases to human rights courts. Discussions then proliferate as to whether and how human rights courts (ought to) protect people's cultural identity; whose identity and practices are recognised; what are the limits of accommodation; what is implied by neutrality, equality, secularism and national identity; to mention some. On the other hand, it appears that states and human rights courts also struggle with rights claims touching upon economic disparities, which, to be sure, have deepened.[8] People living in poverty oppose the removal of their children on account of their lack of money. In view of their precariousness, they also claim a right to have legal assistance in civil matters, to be exempted from fees to access services and to be accorded 'special' consideration. Asylum seekers and other persons challenge the indifference of state agencies to their destitution. Others complain about discrimination on account of their impoverishment and claim protection against slave-like work.

Interestingly, while these claims also relate to social differences, exclusions and inequalities, they are seldom discussed as part of the 'diversity and human rights' trope like similar claims from (impoverished) states are. Admittedly, this has to do with the way issues of diversity or difference have come to be understood.[9] Inasmuch as they are bound up to identity, self-assertion and group-based recognition, it is clear why debates about people's diversity and human rights do not include 'economic difference'. Those who live in poverty or have a low income are rarely seen as a group and they want to see their difference – their poverty – not recognised, but eliminated. Even so, the fact remains that these people draw attention to their specific circumstances and demand 'special protection', exemptions, protection against discrimination, 'new' rights, and so on, through human rights law. Therefore, here also human rights courts face difficult questions. Are people living in poverty a category entitled to 'special rights' or exemptions? Do convention rights entail redistribution or duties to provide? How far can the European and the Inter-American Courts of Human Rights go on matters of socio-economic policy? Should they apply a standard of 'reasonability', a 'minimum core' or another standard of review?

---

8 Ibid., at 74 (noting that the promise of socio-economic rights remains rhetorical in the face of extreme material differentiation and poverty, which are the driving forces of capitalism).

9 Rosaura Sánchez, 'On a Critical Realist Theory of Identity', in Linda Martín Alcoff *et al.* (eds.), *Identity Politics Reconsidered* (Palgrave Macmillan, 2006), at 35 (noting that in the last three decades it has not been fashionable to talk about class and that this implies displacing a central fact of social life. 'This retreat from class [...] is prevalent among [...] proponents of a "politics of difference" who [...] often fail to link particular differences with social location').

A common approach to deal with these questions is to attempt an *a priori* demarcation of how to respond to claims of accommodation or flexibility in the name of cultural and economic difference. Another alternative though is to revise the way claims are framed and adjudicated. Perhaps prevailing approaches to cultural and economic claims are adding to instead of alleviating the difficulties surrounding their resolution. In fact, it is submitted that one particular problem worth examination is the compartmentalised or disaggregated way in which litigants and courts often address them.

Though perhaps for different reasons and in different ways, cases defined by discourses of 'cultural' and 'economic' difference or disadvantage are prone to fall into several 'compartments'. As will be further examined in subsequent chapters, legal arguments about cultural difference or disadvantage usually map onto one particular group (e.g. one religious or ethno-cultural group), one defined cultural or ethnic identity, one type of interest or harm (typically symbolic or related to people's spirituality and lifestyle) and thus one relatively narrow set of rights. Legal arguments concerning economic differences and disadvantages, on the other hand, are also seen as dealing with one separate, bounded sphere (that of economy and markets), one particular kind of interest or harm (normally material provision and a lack thereof), one line of case law (e.g. that concerning social policy) and one specific type of right, namely, socio-economic rights. And if rights claims of economic difference are examined from the perspective of identity groups, the hypothesis is that most of the time only one identity or group will be considered.

Admittedly, such a compartmentalised line of reasoning seems to be part of the growing specialisation (fragmentation) undergone by human rights law. Over the years human rights law, as part and parcel of international law, has fragmented. Instruments and monitoring bodies have multiplied, each of them governing – with different normative force – diverse subject matters, geographic regions and groups of people. Among the most prominent divides we find, on the one side, a major separation of civil and political rights from economic, social and cultural rights. On the other side, group-based rights usually target those historically excluded or discriminated against. As Mégret notes, 'one of the defining phenomena of the human rights project today is its increasing fragmentation along group lines (women, children, persons with disabilities, migrant workers, indigenous peoples, sexual minorities, etc.)'.[10]

In this context, human rights courts such as the Inter-American and European courts of human rights may appear to be placed in a less disaggregated

10 Frédéric Mégret, 'The Human Rights of Older Persons: A Growing Challenge', 11(1) *Human Rights Law Review* (2011) 37, at 39 (adding that 'this fragmentation is not only functional it is often qualitative, suggesting subtle but often significant differences in which the rights of various groups should be treated').

legal landscape. They oversee general human rights treaties with respect to groups of countries belonging to the same region. They can rule on a broad range of matters and are not bound to focus on one particular group or issue. Nevertheless, these two courts, unlike the one created in the African system, are almost exclusively concerned with civil and political rights. Most social and economic rights are, by contrast, outside their jurisdiction (or were until very recently, as in the case of the IACtHR). In addition, even if their competence is not confined to any particular category of beneficiaries, in practice these courts have developed differentiated standards based on, for example, identity and group vulnerability. The courts' rulings have furthermore given rise to diverse lines of case law (e.g. on discrimination, indigenous rights, foreseeable risks to life and health, and socio-economic policy). And each of these, though based on the same treaty, comes with its own subset of principles.

It is submitted that this fragmentation is not *per se* problematic. Yet, the question that arises is whether and how this compartmentalised normative landscape is being usefully applied to deal with a world of complex social relations and inequalities. The complexity lies, *inter alia*, in the fact that people belong to more than one group and are defined by multiple identities and roles. Further, a person may be disadvantaged in one dimension and quite privileged in another. We are no longer bound to our state of birth, nor do we necessarily recognise states as the main source of authority. Public power has come to be confused with or even eclipsed by private power and the national has become transnational. Norms and regulations interact and multiply in every field. Meanwhile, outward exclusion and discrimination are in retreat. Inequalities operate in inextricable ways while being usually clothed in neutrality and reasonability. What is more, it seems increasingly difficult to trace violations and disadvantages to individualised, isolated wrongdoings. Many are, rather, rooted in networks of widely accepted institutions, values and social practices.

Against this background, the present book explores whether acknowledging this complexity, at least in part, in cases that are thought in cultural and economic terms could add something to their resolution. With a view to that, this book develops and applies a normative framework to approach such cases in a comprehensive and non-compartmentalised way. This implies recognising that, for example, a case may not just be about the preservation of a cultural lifestyle, but rather about a family of Travellers claiming a right to live in their caravan while having land security and access to schools for their children in a context of public good's privatisation and prejudice against Travellers. Likewise, what may look like a case of socio-economic provision and social policy-making may also be about a single mother or a migrant man complaining against autonomy denial and negative stereotypes stemming from social policies aimed at improving theirs and others' living conditions. As will be seen in Chapter 1, there are some notable differences in the way privileges and disadvantages accorded on cultural and economic grounds are confronted and remedied in law.

The idea posed here is not to deny this. Rather, it is to consider whether and how an integrated approach to human rights can be helpful in questioning and addressing claims about what is typically regarded as either 'cultural' or 'economic'. Doing so, however, requires revisiting the 'compartmentalisation' prevailing in our legal thinking.

The idea of approaching such cases in a more holistic fashion is not entirely alien to human rights law, as further discussed in Chapter 1. One may note, for example, that the most recent human rights treaties dealing with claims of difference (i.e. with the needs and concerns of the non-hegemonic) take a more comprehensive, integrated approach than previous, traditional human rights treaties. Think of the Convention on the Rights of Persons with Disabilities.[11] Its novelty lies in bringing civil and political rights together with economic, social and cultural rights; considering multiple forms of discrimination as well as social and cultural barriers; acknowledging the fluidity of the category 'disability' and having regard to the fact that the majority of persons with disabilities live in conditions of poverty; encompassing different types of state obligation; and also cutting across other legal divides.[12] This may suggest that there is increasing awareness of the need to capture the complexity of claims of difference and inclusion by looking at human rights law more holistically. But how could this be accomplished in the adjudicatory work of the European and the Inter-American Courts of Human Rights?[13] This is one of the main issues explored in this book. The question is relevant because these two regional courts appear better placed for, and at the same time more in need of, an integrated approach to rights than their African counterpart and most UN treaty bodies.[14]

---

11 Convention on the Rights of Persons with Disabilities, adopted by the General Assembly, 24 January 2007, A/RES/61/106.

12 Frédéric Mégret, 'The Disabilities Convention: Towards a Holistic Concept of Rights', 12 *International Journal of Human Rights* (2008) 261, at 261–277. See further discussion under Chapter 1, section 5.2.3.

13 As will be further discussed later, it is important to keep in mind that the main treaty law enforced by both courts, albeit 'customised' to their region, is very much inspired by the UDHR and does not make explicit reference to the specific concerns or interests of groups affected by structural discrimination. Further, both the European Convention on Human Rights and the American Convention on Human Rights are largely confined to the protection of civil and political rights.

14 Many UN treaty bodies, save for the Human Rights Committee (HRC) and lately also the Committee on Economic Social and Cultural Rights (CESCR), receive individual communications under instruments dealing with one subject matter or with one target group, which would mean that they are less suited than the ECtHR and the IACtHR to adopting an integrated approach to human rights. At the same time, though, a number of these UN treaties, especially the most recent ones, are framed in a rather holistic fashion. That is, unlike the ECHR and the ACHR, they integrate economic, social and cultural rights with civil and political rights. They also regulate areas typically defined as public and private and some even require the consideration of multiple or complex forms of discrimination. On the other hand, it also appears that the need for an integrated perspective, particularly in the field of cultural and economic differences, is considerably less pressing in the case of the

2. A MORE INTEGRATED VIEW OF CULTURAL AND ECONOMIC CASES

To address the concerns outlined above, this book combines a literature review (across disciplines)[15] and case law analysis. The book examines about 230 judgments and decisions from both regional courts, selected on the basis of substantive and formal criteria. From a substantive point of view, the focus is on cases concerning cultural and economic interests and which rely on categories such as cultural and religious identity, group-based differences of culture or lifestyle, on the one hand; and poverty and socio-economic welfare, on the other. More specifically, these are cases in which arguments of ethno-cultural difference and economic disadvantage generally aim at increasing social participation, rather than at being protected against state-sponsored acts of criminalisation and bodily injury.[16] A key guiding principle has also been the identification of cultural and economic cases for which an integrated approach to human rights law could have the most added value. Part II: 'Rethinking cultural difference from an integrated perspective on human rights' thus deals with cases mostly brought by Roma, Travellers and Muslims, at the side of the European Court, and by Indigenous and Afro-descendant applicants, at the side of the Inter-American Court. Part III: 'Rethinking economic

---

African Court of Human and Peoples' Rights which enjoys by far the most comprehensive *ratione materiae* jurisdiction. As Mutua puts it, 'among the major human rights instruments, only the African Charter on Human and Peoples Rights attempts the comprehensive unification of these conflicting notions of community, individual rights, and duties to the family, the community and the state.' See Makau Mutua, *Human Rights: A Political and Cultural Critique* (University of Pennsylvania Press, 2002), at 66. Protocol to the African Charter on Human and Peoples' Rights on the Establishment of an African Court on Human and Peoples' Rights, Article 3(1). The provision reads: 'The jurisdiction of the Court shall extend to all cases and disputes submitted to it concerning the interpretation and application of the Charter, this Protocol and any other relevant Human Rights instrument ratified by the States concerned.'

15 This is mostly reflected in the use of non-legal doctrine and the application of unconventional legal methods inspired by fields of studies that, as seen below, include but are not limited to law. Inspiration was taken from political and social theory, particularly from debates on identity politics and multiculturalism, recognition and redistribution and on social inequality more generally. For further details, see the scholarship discussed in Chapter 1, which elaborates on the theoretical basis of the book.

16 So, for example, the book does not include cases concerning cultural or religious motivated persecution or alleged acts of torture against Muslims and persons of Roma origin. Nor does it study cases that focus on the religious or cultural autonomy of organisations. Similarly, cases concerning summary executions, enforced disappearances and acts of torture against members of indigenous communities or persons identified as belonging to tribal groups have not been analysed. However, as it will be seen later, the book does analyse some cases concerning acts of violence leading to forced displacement and loss of land of (indigenous or tribal) rural communities, given their relevance to issues under examination. A notable example of this is the case of *The Moiwana Community v. Suriname*, Judgment of 15 June 2005.

disadvantage from an integrated perspective on human rights' focuses on cases brought by persons living in poverty or socio-economic disadvantage before the two courts. From a formal point of view, the sample of cases includes decisions, 'routine' judgments and high-profile judgments, delivered by both supranational courts up until March 2019.[17] The question then is how to take a more integrated view of these cases. In other words, what are the main analytical insights used to approach the selected case law in an integrated, relational and inclusive manner? The answer can be found in frames of analysis of feminist studies as well as cultural and critical legal theory, which have shaped the integrated view of human rights law underpinning this book.

From feminist studies, the book borrows from intersectionality, relationality and practical, inclusive thinking. As intersectionality is further discussed below, for now it suffices to point out the basics. Intersectionality is a theory and a method of analysis that helps law to be responsive to real life's complexity, since it captures the fact that people's experiences are not compartmentalised, whether from the perspective of gender, race, age, body-ability, cultural background, class or any other source of social hierarchy. In the words of Mackinnon 'intersectionality [is] a method for fitting law to reality, rather than reality to law'.[18] Relationality, for its part, is very much connected to intersectionality in that it rejects binary (either/or) thinking to focus instead on interconnections.[19] This can be applied to all kinds of social entity: individuals, institutions and, of course, the law. They all work through relations while at the same time structuring further relations.[20] As will become clearer in following chapters, the book's normative framework builds upon this assumption that neither people

---

17 To identify the relevant rulings from the ECtHR via the Court's database HUDOC <https://hudoc.echr.coe.int/eng> the author used keywords (such as 'lifestyle', 'poverty', 'financial means', 'financial hardship', 'afford', 'social disadvantage') and a snowball search system. The book also benefited from some ECtHR factsheets, such as the ECtHR's factsheets on 'Roma and Travellers' from July 2015 and January 2017 as well as the factsheet on 'Religious symbols and clothing' from November 2015. All of them available at <http://www.echr.coe.int/Pages/home.aspx?p=press/factsheets&c>. Identification of ECtHR cases was also possible thanks to biweekly meetings (led by Prof. Brems at Ghent University) in which fellow researchers and the author used to discuss the recent jurisprudence of the European Court of Human Rights. In order to identify the relevant IACtHR case law, by contrast, a review of all existing judgments was feasible.

18 Catharine A. Mackinnon, 'Intersectionality as a Method: A Note', 38(4) *Signs* (2013) 1019, at 1024.

19 Patricia Hill Collins and Sirma Bilge, *Intersectionality* (Polity Press, 2016), at 27.

20 As Nedelsky puts it, 'each individual is in basic ways constituted by networks of relationships of which they are part – networks that range from intimate relations with parents, friends, or lovers to relations between student and teacher, welfare recipients and case workers, citizen and state, to being participants in a global economy, migrants in a world of gross economic inequality, inhabitants of a world shaped by global warming'. Jennifer Nedelsky, *Law's Relations. A Relational Theory of Self, Autonomy, and the Law* (Oxford University Press, 2011), at 19.

(rights holders) nor laws (human rights norms) stand in isolation. Rather, they are all interconnected. Finally, feminist-inspired practical reasoning requires, for one thing, paying close attention to the actual interests that are at stake in a case and to the effects of laws and practices over formal and *a priori* judgment.[21] For another, it implies being inclusive and value the multiple perspectives and tensions generated by new, unique contexts as a source for decision-making.[22] This book is animated by this pragmatic and inclusive drive, as it is interested in having as full as possible a picture when it comes to deciding the complaints under examination.[23]

The tools from feminist legal studies summarised above converge with elements of literary and critical legal theories, taken as part of the broader field of cultural studies of law,[24] which have also inspired the analysis presented in the following chapters. Particularly helpful have been the understanding of law as a narrative or discursive process and the adoption of a critical view of it from a rights holders' perspective.[25] According to the former, law does not just respond to societal problems and demands. It also constitutes them; it shapes them.[26]

21 In this vein, see e.g. Robin West, *Narrative, Authority, and the Law* (The University of Michigan Press, 1993), at 175 ('I believe we should criticize acts of power not by reference to their rationality, or their coherency, or their integrity, but by reference to their motivation and their effects.').

22 Katharine T. Bartlett, 'Feminist Legal Methods', 103(4) *Harvard Law Review* (1990) 829, at 853–854, 857–858 and 862–863.

23 The commitment to inclusion and the consideration of competing views is in turn related to a specific approach to the production of knowledge namely, positionality. This is a feminist epistemological stance that brings about awareness of the incompleteness and partiality of our experiences and perspectives. It invites self-criticism and correction by considering the perspectives of those who do not think like us. See Katharine T. Bartlett, 'Feminist Legal Methods', 103(4) *Harvard Law Review* (1990) 829, at 880–887. A similar epistemological stance has been associated with 'transversal politics.' See Nira Yuval-Davis, 'What is Transversal Politics', 12 *Soundings* (1999) 94, at 94–95. ('Transversal politics […] recognises that from each positioning the world is seen differently, and thus that any knowledge based on just one positioning is "unfinished".')

24 Guyora Binder and Robert Weisberg, *Literary Criticism of Law* (Princeton University Press, 2000), at 209 and 487. For a cultural understanding of law, see e.g. Lawrense Rose, *Law as Culture: An Invitation* (Princeton University Press, 2006).

25 On law as narrative, see Monika Fludernik, 'A Narratology of the Law? Narratives in Legal Discourse', 1(1) *Critical Analysis of Law* (2014) 87–109; Peter Brooks, 'Narrative in and of the Law', in James Phelan and Peter J. Rabinowitz (eds.), *A Companion to Narrative Theory* (Blackwell Publishing, 2005), at 415; Robin West, *Narrative, Authority, and the Law* (The University of Michigan Press, 1993), at 345–418 (regarding jurisprudence as narrative). The use of a rights holder's perspective is further discussed below. On the link between law as discourse and a critical legal analysis of it, see Marianne Jorgensen and Louise J. Phillips, *Discourse Analysis as a Theory and Method* (Sage, 2002), at 61.

26 Guyora Binder and Robert Weisberg, *Literary Criticism of Law* (Princeton University Press, 2000), at 18–19, 209 and 487–489. These authors provide an illuminating example of how the law constitutes social meanings and identities. They explain how the persecution faced by Jesuits in England (from Protestants) led Catholics to negotiate their religious affiliation within a social context marked by laws that persecuted them. Jesuits basically developed

Furthermore, thinking of law as narrative reveals its flexibility and capacity for change and empathy,[27] which is also relevant for the integrated normative framework advanced here. On the other hand, this book has deliberately opted for a framework of analysis that starts by looking at *rights holders* instead of norms or legal categories, which provides a critical, person-centred perspective. But from all the analytical frameworks summarised thus far, two lie at the very heart of the case law analysis, meriting separate attention. These are (1) intersectionality reformulated as 'cross-thinking' and (2) the rights holders' approach.

2.1. CROSS-THINKING

Taking intersectionality as a method of analysis, Matsuda proposes to 'ask the other question'. She explains:

> The way I try to understand the interconnection of all forms of subordination is through a method I call "ask the other question". When I see something that looks racist, I ask, "Where is the patriarchy in this?" When I see something that looks sexist, I ask, "Where is the heterosexism in this?" When I see something that looks homophobic, I ask, "Where are the class interests in this?"[28]

Building upon this understanding of intersectionality, the book proposes to examine the selected case law through what can be called 'cross-thinking'. In short, this is like 'to ask the other question' but over a wider set of issues. To explore who rights holders are, what harms are at stake and which norms are implicated in any given case, it uses one dimension of them to interrogate another. Thus, if the applicant's experience in a case seems to be constructed by courts or by litigants through the prism of one single identity or status (say, ethnic origin or cultural background), the book considers whether other

strategies that 'could at once hide and inwardly reaffirm their religious faith without violating Catholic ethics'. Catholics then played with mental reservation and language ambiguity. They 'subverted the state by constructing private selves that could pass undetected.' [...] 'Dissembling came to constitute the very Catholicism. The result was Catholic religious identity reconstructed in protestant terms, as a private and internal matter.'

27 See e.g. Robin West, *Narrative, Authority, and the Law* (The University of Michigan Press, 1993), at 327, 330–331 (on the idea that narrative facilitates the empathy by which judges can put themselves in the litigants' shoes).

28 Mari Matsuda, 'Beside My Sister, Facing the Enemy: Legal Theory Out of Coalition', 43 *Stanford Law Review* (1991) 1183, at 1189 (arguing that intersectionality works as a method by enabling researchers to 'ask the other question'). Similar, complementary methods include 'asking the woman question' and 'asking the male question'. See Katharine T. Bartlett, 'Feminist Legal Methods', 103(4) *Harvard Law Review* (1990) 829, at 837; Simone Cusack and Lisa Pusey, 'CEDAW and the Rights to Non-Discrimination and Equality', 14 *Melbourne Journal of International Law* (2013) 1, at 35.

possible identities compounded her experience (e.g. gender and class). But in addition, where cases are mainly read as an instance of interference with one type of harm or right (say, cultural disrespect and the right to private life), the book also looks at other types of harm and right that may be at stake as well (e.g. maldistribution, or political marginalisation and socio-economic rights). Cross-thinking thus allows us to look at cases beyond legal divides and categorisations that are too often taken for granted. In so doing, it helps us to consider the situation presented to us as a whole.

2.2. SHIFTING ATTENTION TOWARD RIGHTS HOLDERS

Most legal analyses start from the perspective of norms or legal categories. Instead, this book situates rights holders as the first step of normative inquiry, thus taking a perspective that is often under-theorised.[29] As will be seen in Chapters 2 to 5, the integrated normative framework applied to cases of cultural difference and economic disadvantage starts by considering the experience of claimants – as expressed by their arguments before human rights courts – and that of other rights holders, their social positions, interests and autonomy as well as the way the respective court – the IACtHR and the ECtHR – engages with those issues.[30] By taking rights holders as a point of departure, this book seeks to provide elements for a more critical and transformative view of human rights law. In fact, a focus on state obligations and legal categories does not necessarily challenge pre-existing inequalities.[31] The reason is that the analysis of state obligations and other legal categories starts from the *status quo*. Inequalities, however, tend to exist prior to laws.

Thus, if ethno-cultural minorities, such as Travellers, seek adjustments in planning/land regulations so as to be able to have security of tenure while living in caravans, a convention right/state obligation approach will translate this as

29 The common point of departure of legal scholarship in the field of integration and fragmentation and diversity is that of states' obligations, convention provisions, limitation clauses and norm conflicts. See literature on the fragmentation of international law referred to in Chapter 1, section 4.3. For a conceptualisation of a users' perspective in human rights, see Ellen Desmet, 'Analysing Users' Trajectories in Human Rights. A Conceptual Exploration and Research Agenda', 8(2) *Human Rights and International Legal Discourse* (2014) 121, at 123–124.

30 For this purpose, this book mostly relies on the information provided by the judgments. Only in some cases does it additionally examine the written observations submitted by the parties and by third-party interveners.

31 In a similar vein, Alan David Freeman, 'Legitimizing Racial Discrimination Through Antidiscrimination Law: A Critical Review of Supreme Court Doctrine', 62 *Minnesota Law Review* (1978) 1049 (arguing that the problem of discrimination law is that this is 'hopelessly embedded in the perpetrator perspective', while indifferent to the victim's perspective).

a request for a positive obligation to provide (i.e. allocate land, housing) or to grant special treatment (i.e. exemptions, accommodation). If we start instead from the perspective of the rights holders' experience, the framing of the issue changes. The same claim would rather appear as an obligation to remedy or put an end to the systematic exclusion of people whose needs and interests were not considered in planning regulations in the first place. Hence, as Porter argues, 'shifting the focus of legal analysis from the nature of claimants' rights to the nature of state obligations may often serve to cover up systemic patterns of injustice which are only apparent from the claimant's perspective'.[32]

By a similar token, analysing normative concepts at the expense of the claimants' perspective may easily lead judges to reason in a rather abstract, disaggregated manner, which is the opposite of what human rights integration is about. Note, for example, that judicial and scholarly debates on cases about poverty or socio-economic disadvantage often lack a rights holder approach. Many of these concern the scope of a state's obligations in the face of economic constraints; how poverty is defined; specific legal categories applicable to economic, social and cultural rights, such as 'reasonability', 'minimum core'; or abstract questions of social policy and resource allocation.[33] By focusing on these categories and leaving aside the perspective of rights claimants we may easily overlook what a concrete person is asking for in a certain context at a particular place and time. A purely normative inquiry may, in other words, pass over issues of context, structural inequalities and practical questions, such as individual circumstances and the actual interests that are at stake in a particular case.

The integrated approach to the case law presented in this book reflects all the insights summarised above. In fact, the case law analysis proceeds in the following comprehensive and relational way. First, it starts by looking at rights holders.

---

32 Bruce Porter, 'The Crisis of ESC Rights and Strategies for Addressing It', in John Squires *et al.* (eds.), *The Road to a Remedy: Current Issues in the Litigation of Economic, Social and Cultural Rights* (UNSW Press, 2005), at 55 (the author adds at 56: 'In the field of disability rights, for example, the obligations typology would tend to place the obligation of the state to install wheelchair ramps and elevators in public buildings as an obligation to provide. People with disabilities, however, will point out that this 'provision' is only made necessary by the fact that buildings were designed as if people with disabilities did not exist. Defining the right only in terms of the nature of the state obligation to provide does not challenge the pattern of social exclusion that lies behind the need for positive measures to provide'). See also Gerard Quinn and Anna Arstein-Kerslake, 'Restoring the "human" in "human rights": Personhood and doctrinal innovation in the UN disability convention', in Conor Gearty and Costas Douzinas (eds.), *The Cambridge Companion to Human Rights Law* (Cambridge University Press, 2012), at 36–38 and 53 (arguing for 'recovering the human' in human rights and noting that what makes the Convention on the Rights of People with Disabilities revolutionary is that 'it resolutely starts first with what it means to be human and then only secondly with the rights that can enable flourishing').

33 Bruce Porter, 'The Crisis of ESC Rights and Strategies for Addressing It', in John Squires *et al.* (eds.), *The Road to a Remedy: Current Issues in the Litigation of Economic, Social and Cultural Rights* (UNSW Press, 2005), at 49–51.

Here, the book suggests considering not only applicants, but also other persons potentially affected by the issue contested in the case. Then, in appreciating who these rights holders are and how they are presented, the analysis takes into account their multiple identities and social positions, avoiding a fragmented or divisive view of them. But since legal discourses, especially in the context of the ECtHR's case law, have often conceived of people's autonomy in a similarly dichotomic way, the book also promotes a more integrated approach to rights holders' autonomy. This accounts for the fact that in real life people are not fully autonomous, self-made individuals; neither are they fully constrained or dependants. Rather, agency is evolving and shaped by social relations and structures, which has important consequences for the case at hand and for other cases as well.

When it comes to examining the norms involved in the case law, a similar logic of analysis is applied. In identifying the relevant norms, one needs to ask oneself whether besides the harms and rights immediately associated with the dominant legal narrative of the case, other harms and rights may be implicated too. Thus, if a case is presented as concerning the accommodation of a particular lifestyle and an alleged disrespect for cultural identity and private life, one would also consider whether social rights, discrimination and socio-economic exclusion are involved. Further, because human rights norms are part of a broader normative environment at both the national and international levels, the book encourages 'pluralism awareness'. That is, having regard for related sources of norms, i.e. human rights norms from specialised treaties or from other monitoring bodies, as well relevant state and non-state regulations.

The reader will find this line of reasoning throughout Chapters 2 to 5 (Parts II and III), which deal with the European and the Inter-American case law concerning cultural difference and economic disadvantage, respectively. The theoretical and normative bases of this discussion are explored in Part I, Chapter 1. Toward the end, the book's final reflections are devoted to its findings as well as the opportunities and limitations of an integrated perspective to human rights law if this were to be implemented by the ECtHR and IACtHR.

PART I
THEORETICAL FOUNDATIONS

This first part of the book introduces its theoretical and normative foundations. It situates the complexity posed by typical cultural and economic human rights cases against the backdrop of increasing plurality and social differentiation. Chapter 1 addresses the legal and political mobilisation of claims of difference, including those based on cultural and economic grounds, its links with so-called identity politics and the criticism directed against it. On that basis, the discussion moves on to examine how human rights law has dealt with issues of diversity, identity and group-based inequality, and the way that this relates to both fragmentation and integration. Taking a broad understanding of fragmentation, the analysis problematises what it calls 'fragmentory' or 'compartmentalised' legal thinking, as well as the normative divides underlying it. The discussion thus turns to the search for integrated frameworks, both in theory and practice. Towards the end, this first part of the book attempts to place the ECtHR and the IACtHR in their regional and international context, shedding light on their opportunities and limitations for taking a more integrated view of cultural and economic cases. The normative and conceptual foundations elaborated in this first part are subsequently taken to analyse the courts' case law.

CHAPTER 1
A CONCEPTUAL AND NORMATIVE EXPLORATION

Human Rights are better approached and defended in an integrated rather than a disparate fashion. The rights must fit the people, not the people the rights. This requires looking at rights and their violations from a person-centred rather than a formula-based position, and analyzing them contextually rather than abstractly.

Albie Sachs[1]

Clearly, our curiosity is selective and, obviously, this selection is political. The way we frame the problem and think about the law protects the dominant beliefs or practices that conform with them, the norm .... Who or what kind of human rights do we thus see and which rights are obscured?

Susanne Baer[2]

1. INTRODUCTION: EMBEDDED DIFFERENCES AND SOCIAL EXCLUSION

It is clear that we inhabit a world of differences. We are crossed by and live among distinct identities and cultural values, as our societies are more plural than ever. Furthermore, social inequality divides us across and within regions, since the world never had so much wealth concentrated in so few hands.[3] We are increasingly aware of our differences in terms of religion, ethnicity, culture, sexual and gender identity, body-ability and economic resources, among many others. Globalisation processes characterised by (neo)liberalisation trends and increased flows of ideas and persons are some of the factors which have rendered

1 Justice Albie Sachs, *National Coalition for Gay and Lesbian Equality v. Minister of Justice* [1998] South African Constitutional Court- CCT11/98: 9 October 1998, 1999 (1) SA 6 (CC); 1998 (1) BCLR 1517 (CC), para. 112.

2 Susanne Baer, 'Privatizing Religion. Legal Groupism, No-Go-Areas and the Public-Private-Ideology in Human Rights Politics', 20 *Constellations* (2013) 68, at 73.

3 United Nations Development Programme, 'Humanity Divided: Confronting Inequality in Developing Countries' (UNDP, 2013), at 1; Oxfam, 'Wealth: Having It All and Wanting More', Issue Briefing (Oxfam, 2015), at 2–3.

liberal democracies more diverse or have made diversity more visible. Either way, both cultural and socio-economic disparities have widened. What is more, many claim that being singled out as different and having their difference overlooked both have the effect of excluding them from the socio-economic, cultural and political life of their communities. These claims have, for a while already, been expressed as issues of difference, identity and human rights. As such, they have reached not only domestic courts and political bodies, but also international human rights courts. The European Court of Human Rights (ECtHR) and the Inter-American Court of Human Rights (IACtHR) both have to deal with a growing number of such legal claims.

The above has taken place against the background of decades during which the language of difference and diversity gained currency while multiculturalism was widely embraced in Europe and the Americas.[4] More recently, however, the general context is also one of retreat.[5] Some argue that multiculturalist efforts have failed, that the accommodation of differences went too far and that we live in fractured societies. On the left-liberal side of the spectrum, critics point out that too much celebration of diversity undermines solidarity among the oppressed, diverts attention from economic injustice and destabilises the welfare state.[6] On the right side, claims of social unity and cohesion have been increasingly mobilised against several daunting threats, usually embodied in

---

4 See, by way of example, Will Kymlicka and Wayne Norman, *Citizenship in Diverse Societies* (Oxford University Press, 2000); Gideon Calder and Emanuela Ceva, *Diversity in Europe. Dilemmas of differential treatment in theory and practice* (Routledge, 2001); Meena K. Bhamra, *The Challenges of Justice in Diverse Societies. Constitutionalism and Pluralism* (Ashgate, 2011); András Sajó, *Human Rights with Modesty: The Problem of Universalism* (Springer, 2004); Council of Europe, *Institutional accommodation and the citizen: Legal and political interaction in a pluralist society*, Trends in Social Cohesion No. 21 (Council of Europe, 2009); David Goodhart, 'Too Diverse?', *Prospect*, February (2004).

5 Dominic Mcgoldrick, 'Multiculturalism and Its Discontents', 5 *Human Rights Law Review* (2005) 27, at 29–31 and 36–47. Anne Phillips, *Multiculturalism without Culture* (Princeton University Press, 2007), at 4–8; Rogers Brubaker, 'The Return of Assimilation? Changing Perspectives on Immigration and Its Sequels in France, Germany, and the United States', 24(4) *Ethnic & Racial Studies* (2001) 531, at 531. Kymlicka, however, argues that 'post-multiculturalists' tend to exaggerate and over-generalise the retreat from multiculturalism. See Will Kymlicka, 'The Rise and Fall of Multiculturalism? New Debates on Inclusion and Accommodation in Diverse Societies', 97 *International Social Science Journal* (2010) 199, at 103–105.

6 See *inter alia*, Brian Barry, *Culture and Equality: An Egalitarian Critique of Multiculturalism* (Polity Press, 2001), at 11–12 and 321; Keith G. Banting, 'The Multicultural Welfare State: International Experience and North American Narratives', 39(2) *Social Policy & Administration* (2005) 98, at 98–115. Underlying this concern is the idea that social citizenship, as developed by T. H. Marshall, is premised on a 'sense of community membership based on loyalty to a civilisation that is a common possession'. Thomas H. Marshall, 'Citizenship and social class', in Thomas H. Marshall and Tom Bottomore (eds.), *Citizenship and Social Class* (Pluto Press, 1950), at 8.

immigrants, and capitalised by growing xenophobic political forces.[7] But the political and social divisions around questions of diversity have not just added complexity to the debate. Claims for the protection and/or accommodation of distinctive groups or identities pursuing a myriad of interests multiply – from, for example, religious believers struggling to have a place in educational and professional settings, to LGBTI individuals dissatisfied with family welfare regulations, to parents in poverty, indigenous people and even fox-hunting communities demanding recognition and support for their livelihoods. Courts, in turn, wonder how far they can go in their responses; where to draw the line in defining protected identities and 'deserving' groups; which grounds of differentiation are problematic and why. In this regard, claims based on cultural and economic difference are particularly challenging, as explained in the Introduction. Can people living in poverty or irregular immigrants be portrayed as sharing an identity or as being a 'discrete minority' that deserves protection? Which cultural expressions are to be accommodated and why? How can human rights courts object to seemingly reasonable cultural and economic criteria? Should human rights protect our distinctiveness to the extent that this is socially valuable? If not, how should human rights deal with claims about differences and social exclusion?

Most of this chapter aims at exploring the conceptual and normative basis for the questions posed above. In doing so, the idea is advanced that part of the complexity posed by claims of cultural and economic difference could be addressed by moving away from fragmentary frames of analysis. But before discussing all this, the following section will first provide some clarification as to which differences matter and why.

This book is primarily concerned with *embedded*, rather than *embodied*, differences. These two concepts, borrowed from Martha Fineman,[8] serve to point out that beyond the way individual embodiment differs, it is relevant to enquire how we are differently situated in social relations and institutions.[9] Being different from others – those others who are implicitly our point of reference – usually makes us think that the difference is in us.[10] Yet, differences become salient and important insofar as formal and informal social structures

---

7 See as a way of example, Anton Pelinka, 'Right-wing Populism: Concept and Typology', in Ruth Wodak *et al.* (eds.), *Right-Wing Populism in Europe. Politics and Discourse* (Bloomsbury, 2013), at 8–9; Human Rights Council, Report of the Special Rapporteur on contemporary forms of racism, racial discrimination, xenophobia and related intolerance, Githu Muigai, A/HRC/14/43, 30 March 2010, paras. 5–23.

8 Martha Albertson Fineman, 'Equality and Difference – The Restrained State', 66(3) *Alabama Law Review* (2015) 609, at 619–622.

9 Ibid., at 621.

10 Marta Minow, *Making All the Difference. Inclusion, Exclusion and American Law* (Cornell University Press, 1990), at 22–23.

rely on them to determine who is accorded or denied a certain right, good or service.[11] So in order to understand why and how rights claims about social difference emerge, it is important to recall that the distribution of symbolic and material goods in society occurs on the basis of 'rules about membership and access'.[12] In fact, goods such as education, healthcare, employment, land, housing, family and social protection are usually allocated or differently attained depending on the social location of the person concerned (e.g. whether one is a member of an ethnic minority, a single mother, or disabled; whether one lives in a rural community, in a privileged urban centre or in a context of high marginalisation).[13] In this context, economic and cultural criteria are important factors of social differentiation. They frequently govern or determine (formally and informally) the enjoyment of employment, education, access to justice and to other services or spaces of social interaction.

Rules of institutional differentiation are not only explicit, though. They also consist of unstated prescriptions about what is normal or acceptable to the exclusion and differentiation of those who cannot fit the norm.[14] But who defines what is normal or acceptable? Usually people in positions of power who project their own experiences and values as neutral and universal.[15] These are typically identified with the experiences and values of a Western, self-sufficient, white, middle-class man, who has been the subject traditionally protected by law, including human rights law.[16] Whether those norms are implicit or explicit, the point is that most claims of difference and identity do not emerge from the mere

---

11 Ibid., 80–84.

12 Naila Kabeer, 'Social Exclusion, Poverty and Discrimination. Towards an Analytical Framework', 31(4) *Institute of Development Studies Bulletin* (2000) 83, at 87. Rules of membership and institutional differentiation tend to proliferate in Welfare capitalism, as this encourages the formation of corporate group identities, that is, identities recognised by the state and by virtue of which their members are granted some rights and privileges. See Seyla Benhabib, *The Claims of Culture. Equality and Diversity in the Global Era* (Princeton University Press, 2002), at 71–72.

13 Discrimination in this field is in fact prevalent and particularly harmful, as noted in Council of Europe, Living together. Combining diversity and freedom in 21st-century Europe – Report of the Group of Eminent Persons of the Council of Europe (Council of Europe, 2011), at 18.

14 In this vein, Iris Marion Young, 'Structural Injustice and the Politics of Difference', in Emily Grabham *et al.* (eds.), *Intersectionality and Beyond. Law, power and the politics of location* (Routledge Cavendish, 2009), at 278–279.

15 Sandra Fredman, 'Facing the Future: Substantive Equality Under the Spotlight', *Oxford University Legal Research Series, Paper No. 57* (2010), at 4 ('formal equality is premised on an abstract and universal individual … the abstract individual is clothed with the characteristics of the dominant group, which are then asserted as if they were universal'); Iris Marion Young, *Justice and the Politics of the Difference* (Princeton University Press, 2011), at 123.

16 Anna Grear, '"Framing the Project" of international human rights law', in Conor Gearty and Costas Douzinas (eds.), *The Cambridge Companion to Human Rights Law* (Cambridge University Press, 2012), at 28–29; Wendy O'Brien, 'Can International Human Rights Law Accommodate Bodily Diversity?', 15 *Human Rights Law Review* (2015) 1, at 9 and ff; Iris Marion Young, *Justice and the Politics of Difference* (Princeton University Press, 2011), at 110. ('The universal citizen is disembodied, dispassionate (male) reason … is also white and bourgeois'.)

fact of diversity; they rather arise from their designation as deviation and from their attendant disadvantage. Claims about individual and group differences are therefore intimately connected to problems of inequality and exclusion.

Although social exclusion has traditionally been equated with questions of socio-economic disadvantage,[17] its link with the lack of opportunities to participate fully in society in meaningful ways has been widely acknowledged. The notion of social exclusion has thus evolved to encompass aspects of material deprivation as well as deprivation in the form of marginalisation from social interaction.[18] In this broader account, the concept appears connected, on the one hand, to inequalities and discrimination based on gender, ethnicity, migration background, religious affiliation, disability, race, class and other grounds.[19] On the other hand, the concept of social exclusion allows thinking about the relational causations of a given deprivation, as pointed out by Sen.[20] This implies that the idea of social exclusion additionally draws attention to the way social attitudes, institutions and conventions create an environment where some people are placed at a disadvantage while others retain the resources and power to define the terms producing the former's subordination. Viewed in this light, the idea of inclusion – the remedy to exclusion – can be understood as meaning more than providing access to entitlements and spaces denied to the excluded.[21] Inclusion would rather mean full social participation, which requires challenging and transforming the institutional norms governing the distribution of goods and benefits.[22]

---

17 See Fernanda Doz Costa, 'Poverty and Human Rights: From Rhetoric to Legal Obligations, a Critical Account of Conceptual Frameworks', 9 *Sur – International Journal of Human Rights* (2008) 81, at 84.

18 See e.g. Council of the European Union, Joint Report by the Commission and the Council on Social Inclusion, 7101/04, 5 March 2004, at 7; Amartya Sen, 'Social Exclusion: Concept, Application, and Scrutiny', *Social Development Papers No. 1* (Asian Development Bank, 2000), at 3–5. See also Hugh Collins, 'Discrimination, Equality and Social Inclusion', 66 *The Modern Law Review* (2003) 16, at 23. (Explaining that under a social inclusion approach 'essential elements of "well-being" include material goods such as food and shelter, but also include opportunities to participate in meaningful ways in social life'.)

19 On social inclusion as a key justification for anti-discrimination laws, see Hugh Collins, 'Discrimination, Equality and Social Inclusion', 66 *The Modern Law Review* (2003) 16, at 21 and ff.

20 Amartya Sen, 'Social Exclusion: Concept, Application, and Scrutiny', *Social Development Papers No. 1* (Asian Development Bank, 2000), at 7–10.

21 For a critical account of inclusion and an exploration of alternative meanings, see Yuvraj Joshi, 'The Trouble with Inclusion', 21 *Virginia Journal of Social Policy & the Law* (2014) 207, at 213 and 215–216.

22 Rita Dhamoon, *Identity/Difference Politics. How Difference is Produced, and Why It Matters* (UBC Press, Vancouver, 2009), at 37. In a similar vein, Colleen Sheppard, '"Bread and Roses": Economic Justice and Constitutional Rights', 5(1) *Oñati Socio-Legal Series* (2015) 225, at 240. ('One recurrent theme is the need to focus not only on the substantive provision of goods and services, but as well on a reshaping of the governance processes of a reimagined social welfare state.'; referring to Giddens, 1998.)

The claims of cultural and economic differences discussed in this book should be seen against this background. They are politically and legally relevant insofar as they reflect problems of exclusion and demands for inclusion. Responding to these claims, however, is no easy task. While some forms of discrimination have given rise to significant political and legal interventions, thus aiding the combat against exclusion, that has not been the case for discrimination grounded in cultural and economic factors. As further discussed in subsequent chapters, political and legal responses tend to be more evasive for such claims. In addition, seeking inclusion by way of defying cultural and economic norms is quite a challenge, as noted in the general introduction, for such norms are highly internalised and accepted. Moreover, the multiple actors, types of right and obligations involved in complaints concerning cultural and economic differences are also likely to make their resolution complex and contested.

2. TERMINOLOGICAL CHOICES

2.1. DIFFERENCE, DISADVANTAGE AND DIVERSITY

The cases examined in this study could well be described as cases about diversity. Actually, most of the issues they bring to court are normally discussed in terms of the relationship between diversity and human rights law. And yet, throughout this book the words 'difference' and 'disadvantage' are used far more than the term 'diversity.' Why is that? To speak of difference or disadvantage has some advantages for the purpose of this study. First, these terms can aptly capture the fact that the complaints analysed here are not simply about cultural and economic variety. Rather, they are about people whose cultural and economic roles or characteristics are somehow associated with deviance. Because 'they are different', they are ascribed some form of disadvantage while others are accorded privileges. In other words, to speak of difference reminds us that what is legally relevant about cultural, economic or any other ground of social differentiation is not just a particular feature of people.[23] What matters is the way in which society, through its norms and structures, identifies some as less valued and less

[23] In this vein, see e.g. Tariq Modood, 'Difference, Multi and Equality', in Michel Seymour (ed.), *The Plural States of Recognition* (Palgrave Macmillan, 2010), at 153 (in discussing whether to use the language of difference or of culture: 'to speak of difference rather than culture allows recognizing that the difference in question is not just constituted from inside but also from the outside, from the representations and treatment of the minorities in question.'); Iris Marion Young, 'Structural Injustice and the Politics of Difference', in Emily Grabham *et al.* (eds.), *Intersectionality and Beyond. Law, power and the politics of location* (Routledge Cavendish, 2009), at 275–276 (speaking of 'positional difference').

able to participate in society and exercise rights than others.[24] Talking about difference or disadvantage furthermore entails a relational dimension (different/ disadvantaged from what or whom?) that draws attention to those whose position is unmarked and privileged.

Second, the terms difference and disadvantage, while closely related to diversity, are relatively free from some important criticism directed against the latter. To make a long story short, speaking of diversity may have some drawbacks. Notably, diversity tends to be used in a rather decontextualised and politically neutral manner.[25] Although the term is broad enough, it generally describes a state of heterogeneity often perceived as positive. It thus conveys recognition or valuation of differences and identities without addressing underlying issues of inequality and injustice, such as racism, sexism and economic oppression.[26] In addition, diversity 'increasingly comes to stand for "cultural diversity" in public debate'.[27] Though the term has been progressively associated with gender, sexual and other differences, its scope still seems to be relatively narrow. Class or socio-economic differences, for example, are usually out of the political and legal reflection inspired by those who use the language of diversity.

2.2. THE CULTURAL AND THE ECONOMIC

Given the ambivalences and contestations surrounding any determination of what is 'cultural' and 'economic', a brief clarification is nonetheless in order.

---

24 See e.g. Marta Minow, *Making All the Difference. Inclusion, Exclusion and American Law* (Cornell University Press, 1990), at 80–84; Christine A. Littleton, 'Reconstructing Sexual Equality', in Diana Tietjens Meyers (ed.), *Feminist Social Thought: A Reader* (Routledge, 1997), at 722 ('What makes pregnancy a disability rather than, say, an additional ability, is the structure of work, not reproduction. Normal pregnancy may make a woman unable to "work" for days, weeks or months, but it also makes her able to reproduce. From what viewpoint is the work that she cannot do "work" and the work that she is doing *not* work? Certainly not from hers.'); Martha Albertson Fineman, 'Equality and Difference – The Restrained State', 66(3) *Alabama Law Review* (2015) 609, at 621–622. For further discussion, see Chapter 1, section 1.

25 See e.g. Julie Ringelheim, 'Diversity and equality: an ambiguous relationship', in Gavan Titley and Alana Lentin (eds.), *The politics of diversity in Europe* (Council of Europe, 2008), at 36–39; Charles R. Lawrence III, 'Each Other's Harvest: Diversity's Deeper Meaning', 31 *University of San Francisco Law Review* (1997), at 765 (criticising the decoupling between diversity and the remediation of racism in the US debate on affirmative actions aimed at 'diversity' in education: 'I argue that diversity cannot be an end in itself – it is substanceless. It has no inherent meaning and cannot be a compelling interest unless we ask the prior question: diversity to what purpose?').

26 Alana Lentin and Gavan Titley, 'More Benetton than barricades? The politics of diversity in Europe', in Gavan Titley and Alana Lentin (eds.), *The politics of diversity in Europe* (Council of Europe, 2008), at 13 (arguing that diversity, especially in Europe, entails a 'decontextualized and deliberately ambiguous imaginary' that is shaped by consumer societies. Diversity can be understood as 'an attempt to re-brand multiculturalism while refusing to address the foundational problems of culture, race and socio-political power').

27 Idem.

The present book does not endorse a folk or essentialist understanding of culture. In other words, it does not support a view that reduces culture to religion, language, dress, food, dance or other topical representations of traditions and ways of life. Instead, it subscribes to a fluid, boundless and dynamic conception of culture.[28] Notwithstanding this, the book examines claims of cultural difference in a rather narrow sense. The cases analysed concern, in fact, questions of tradition, way of life, religion, custom and the like. But the reason for this focus is not that these cases are seen as being 'the cultural cases' par excellence. In fact, indigenous or religious rights claims are not seen as more 'authentically cultural' than those contesting prevailing values about women, LGBTI persons or people with disabilities.[29] The book addresses 'typical cultural cases' because cases of this kind are often addressed through discourses of cultural difference and identity rights, even if other normative frames are available (e.g. racism, gender inequality, socio-economic rights or political marginalisation). Hence, against this, one may wonder what if these cases were examined through a more comprehensive, inclusive and relational approach?

A somewhat similar caveat applies to the understanding of cases dealing with economic disadvantage. Most rights claims concerning social differentiation and exclusion have an economic dimension. Thus, besides claims grounded in class or economic status, those based on gender, ethnic background or body-ability, for example, can also be analysed from the perspective of their economic implications. Cases concerning domestic violence, inaccessibility of buildings and services, or harmful stereotypes all involve questions of economic disadvantage or difference. The present book, however, does not analyse such a broad range of cases concerning economic disadvantage. Nor is this discussion intended to undertake the usual examination of case law and legal frameworks potentially relevant to questions of poverty or conceptual debates on whether poverty constitutes a human rights violation in itself, a denial of rights in general, or rather the cause and consequence of violations.[30] Nevertheless, the

---

28 Sally Engle Merry, 'Human Rights Law and the Demonization of Culture (and Anthropology along the Way)', 26(1) *Political and Legal Anthropology Review* (2003) 55, at 67 ('Over the last two decades, anthropology has elaborated a conception of culture as unbounded, contested, and connected to relations of power. … Its boundaries are fluid, meanings are contested, and meaning is produced by institutional arrangements and political economy …').

29 All these claims are connected to divergent valuations as well as to different systems of signification and representation. To different degrees, they all deviate from some values, meanings and institutions prevailing in the larger society. Insofar as they seek to change those values, meanings and institutions, their claims are also cultural claims. In this vein, see Ruth Lisbeth, '(Mis)recognition, Social Inequality and Social Justice: a critical social policy perspective', in Terry Lovell (ed.), *(Mis)recognition, Social Inequality and Social Justice: Nancy Fraser and Pierre Bourdieu* (Routledge, 2007), at 161 (referring to the work of Tom Shakespeare on the disability movement); Bhikhu Parekh, *Rethinking Multiculturalism. Cultural Diversity and Political Theory* (Palgrave Macmillan, 2006), at 3–4.

30 For such a discussion, see e.g. Johannes Gerds, 'Human rights of people experiencing poverty in Europe: standards, obstacles and perspectives of protection in Council of Europe

book's relatively narrow focus is not motivated by a reductionist understanding of economic issues. The point is that since those claims are usually viewed as being about socio-economic hardship, social welfare and economic rights, it is worth reflecting on what may be missed by the use of this sort of narrative and what could be gained by viewing those claims in a more holistic fashion.

2.3. INTEGRATION AND FRAGMENTATION

A second important clarification concerns the use of the terms 'integration' and 'fragmentation'. It has already been mentioned that this study gives both notions a quite singular connotation compared to those prevailing in constitutional and international law. Now it is convenient to elaborate a bit further on this point. In both constitutional and international law, questions of integration and fragmentation have arisen against the backdrop of diversity or plurality. In constitutional law, the concern often revolves around the existence of different political communities as well as diverse cultural and group-based demands within the same constitutional space.[31] In this context, integrationists are supposed to stand in opposition to those advocating fragmentation, also known as supporters of accommodation. To put it simply, the latter would subscribe to the political and legal recognition of multiple identities and different ethno-cultural communities. The former, by contrast, would tend to be blind to difference and promote a common public identity.[32] In international law, the

instruments', in Council of Europe, *Redefining and combating poverty: Human rights, democracy and common goods in today's Europe* (Council of Europe, 2012), at 115–150; Colm O'Cinneide, 'A modest proposal: destitution, state responsibility and the European Convention on Human Rights', 5 *European Human Rights Law Review* (2008) 583; Fernando A. Chinchilla *et al.*, 'Pobreza y Derechos Humanos: hacia la definición de parámetros conceptuales desde la doctrina y acciones del sistema interamericano' in Instituto Interamericano de Derechos Humanos, *¿Quién Responde por los Derechos Humanos de las poblaciones más pobres en América Latina y El Caribe? Democracia Vs Desigualdad (2007-2011)* (Instituto Interamericano de Derechos Humanos, 2012), at 13–155; Laurens Lavrysen, 'Strengthening the protection of human rights of persons living in poverty under the ECHR', 33(3) *Netherlands Quarterly of Human Rights* (2015) 293; Fernanda Doz Costa, 'Poverty and human rights: From rhetoric to legal obligations: a critical account of conceptual frameworks', 9 *Sur – International Journal of Human Rights* (2008) 81; Ariel E. Dulitzky, 'Pobreza y derechos humanos en el sistema interamericano. Algunas aproximaciones preliminares', 48 *Revista Instituto Interamericano de Derechos Humanos* (2008) 107, at 107–134; Thomas Pogge, 'Are We Violating the Human Rights of the World's Poor?', 14(2) *Yale Human Rights & Development Law Journal* (2011) 1.

31 In this vein, Sujit Choudhry, 'Bridging comparative politics and comparative constitutional law: Constitutional design in divided societies', in Sujit Choudhry (ed.), *Constitutional Design for Divided Societies: Integration or Accommodation?* (Oxford University Press, 2008), at 3–14.

32 Ibid., at 27. See also, John McGarry *et al.*, 'Integration or accommodation? The enduring debate in conflict regulation', in Sujit Choudhry (ed.), *Constitutional Design for Divided Societies: Integration or Accommodation?* (Oxford University Press, 2008), at 41 and ff.

integration and fragmentation debate goes along similar lines. The former aims at cohesion and unity in the face of an international law increasingly fragmented into separate compartments.[33] Here, integration is often seen as a way to resolve the conflicts and the lack of coordination generated by the coexistence and simultaneous operation of diverse normative regimes, systems, organs, etc.

This book addresses some, but certainly not all, of the above aspects involved in discussions of integration and fragmentation. To start with, this book is limited to human rights law and thus does not elaborate on the fragmentation of international law in general. It does, however, start from a reality of global legal pluralism.[34] Nevertheless, the concepts of fragmentation and similar terms such as 'compartmentalisation' are not only used in relation to the several specialised sub-regimes of human rights law. They also serve to describe a way of thinking and analysing rights claims. When rights claims are interpreted and resolved by the manner in which they fit certain 'boxes' typically defined by group-based legal categories or by typologies of rights and other normative divides, then the study speaks of fragmentation or compartmentalisation.[35]

Integration, in this context, is therefore not so much about unifying the diverse sub-fields of human rights law. Its main concern is not delivering similar normative responses across different human rights laws and bodies. The integrated perspective to human rights applied in this book, rather, designates a methodological and normative stance for examining legal claims (for present purposes, those of cultural and economic difference) more holistically. As a substantive stance, it designates a normative practice that aspires to do justice to the lived reality of people and to the ideals of indivisibility and interdependence of rights. This is particularly desirable in the adjudication of complex cases or in areas that are prone to being examined through abstract or unidimensional

33 See e.g. Carlos Iván Fuentes *et al.*, 'E Pluribus Unum – Bhinneka Tunggal Ika? Universal Human Rights and the Fragmentation of International Law', in René Provost and Colleen Sheppard (eds.), *Dialogues on Human Rights and Legal Pluralism* (Springer, 2013), at 52–53 and 63 (analysing the proliferation of 'pockets of law'); International Law Commission, Fragmentation of International Law: Difficulties Arising from the Diversification and Expansion of International Law, Report of the Study Group of the International Law Commission, Finalised by Martti Koskenniemi, A/CN.4/L.682, 13 April 2006, paras. 7–13. For further discussion, see Chapter 1, section 4.3.

34 Paul Schiff Berman, 'Global Legal Pluralism', 80 *Southern California Law Review* (2007) 1155, at 1159 ('arguing that the global legal system is an interlocking web of jurisdictional assertions by state, international, and non-state normative communities'); Barbara Oomen, 'The application of socio-legal theories of legal pluralism to understanding the implementation and integration of human rights law', 4 *European Journal of Human Rights* (2014) 471, at 479 and 493 (referring to an international 'multi-layered' normative order with a wide variety of regimes and actors constitute human rights law while being constituted by it).

35 In the way the book uses the word 'compartmentalisation', inspiration has been taken from Janneke Gerards, 'The ECtHR's Response to Fundamental Rights Issue Related to Financial and Economic Difficulties. The Problem of Compartmentalisation', 33(3) *Netherlands Quarterly of Human Rights* (2015) 274, at 275. For further discussion, see Chapter 1, section 4.3.

legal categories. As a method, integration provides guidance on how to approach human rights cases in order to get there.[36] This basically implies an interest in understanding the multidimensionality of cases concerning cultural and economic difference. As explained below, this integrated perspective starts from the position of rights holders, whose lived experiences of identity, rights and social participation is complex and compounded, not fragmented.

3. THE POLITICAL AND LEGAL MOBILISATION OF DIFFERENCE

Claiming difference has political and legal traction. As mentioned earlier, many social movements and interest groups articulate their demands through self-assertion of their distinctive identities and experiences. This is, generally speaking, what is referred to as a politics of difference.[37] Relying on this form of mobilisation, many feminists, cultural and ethnic minorities, LGBTI and religious groups as well as disability rights movements advance a positive account of their identity and a concern about hegemonic cultural values, exclusion and distinctiveness. That is why a politics of difference is commonly equated with a politics of identity, culture or recognition.[38] Commonalities notwithstanding, for the sake of conceptual clarity, the following lines will attempt to further demarcate the normative implications of a politics of recognition, identity and difference in order to identify the theoretical framework that is best suited to the present book.

3.1. RECOGNITION, IDENTITY POLITICS AND CULTURE

Recognition, as construed in the work of, notably, Charles Taylor and Axel Honneth, is an intersubjective process by which our own sense of self, our identity, depends on acknowledgement from others. Recognition, identity and

---

[36] On the relationship of method and substance, see Katharine T. Bartlett, 'Feminist Legal Methods', 103(4) *Harvard Law Review* (1990) 829, at 844–846 (arguing that all legal methods shape substance and that what matters is whether the relationship between method and substance is proper or justifiable). Method and substance are intimately connected in law. See also Owen Fiss, 'The Forms of Justice', 93 *Harvard Law Review* (1979) 1, at 17 and ff (discussing the relationship between the form of adjudication and the type of justice delivered).

[37] See e.g. Sion Thompson, *The Political Theory of Recognition: A Critical Introduction* (Polity Press, 2006) (analysing recognition in Charles Taylor, Axel Honneth and Nancy Fraser); Iris Marion Young, *Justice and the Politics of the Difference* (Princeton University Press, 2011), at 157; Tariq Modood, 'Difference, Multi and Equality', in Michel Seymour (ed.), *The Plural States of Recognition* (Palgrave Macmillan, 2010), at 153.

[38] Simon Thompson and Majid Yar, *The Politics of Misrecognition* (Routledge, 2011), at 3.

self-realisation are therefore closely tied. The harm or oppression resulting from misrecognition operates, so goes the argument, by 'imprisoning someone in a false, distorted and reduced mode of being'.[39] This not only illuminates the connection between identity, self-esteem and respect, on the one side,[40] but also that between a politics of recognition and difference, on the other. So long as recognition has to do with what makes us authentic and unique, it is also about what makes us different from others.[41] Building upon similar reasoning, identity politics can be understood as a form of political mobilisation whereby marginalised groups seek emancipation from the demeaning way others – in dominant positions – define their identity and burden them with living according to imposed values.[42] These oppressed groups also assert their identity positively, deploying pride and revaluing despised attributes or characteristics associated with their identity.[43] The negative and positive invocation of identity is therefore linked to experiences of subordination. As Young argues, dominant groups occupy an unmarked position that makes it unnecessary to raise consciousness about their group identity. By contrast, oppressed groups, the victims of cultural imperialism, cannot forget their identity.[44]

The normative correlate of a politics of recognition is thus a theory of justice that focuses on the injustice produced by the cultural devaluation of and social disrespect for the identities and lifestyles of certain groups.[45] A politics of identity or recognition accordingly advocates for differentiated or special treatment for such groups. It furthermore highlights both the cultural roots of their subordination and the pivotal place of people's affiliations or attachments to specific modes of living which may deviate from those of the majority.[46]

39 Charles Taylor, 'The Politics of Recognition', in Charles Taylor, *Philosophical Arguments* (Harvard University Press, 1995), at 225.

40 Avigail Eisenberg, *Reasons of Identity. A Normative Guide to the Political & Legal Assessment of Identity Claims* (Oxford University Press, 2009), at 20.

41 Charles Taylor, 'The Politics of Recognition', in Charles Taylor, *Philosophical Arguments* (Harvard University Press, 1995), at 233; Simon Thompson, *The Political Theory of Recognition: A Critical Introduction* (Polity Press, 2006), at 55.

42 Bikhu Parekh, *A New Politics of Identity. Political Principles for an Interdependent World* (Palgrave Macmillan, 2008), at 32.

43 Idem. See also, Tariq Modood, 'Difference, Multi and Equality', in Michel Seymour (ed.), *The Plural States of Recognition* (Palgrave Macmillan, 2010), at 153.

44 Iris Marion Young, *Justice and the Politics of the Difference* (Princeton University Press, 2011), at 123.

45 Charles Taylor, 'The Politics of Recognition', in Charles Taylor, *Philosophical Arguments* (Harvard University Press, 1995); Axel Honneth, 'Grounding Recognition: A Rejoinder to Critical Questions', 45(2) *Inquiry* 499, at 499–519; Nancy Fraser and Axel Honneth, *Redistribution or Recognition? A Political-Philosophical Exchange* (Verso, 2003), at 125–189; Simon Thompson, *The Political Theory of Recognition: A Critical Introduction* (Polity Press, 2006).

46 Iris Marion Young, *Justice and the Politics of the Difference* (Princeton University Press, 2011), at 159–160.

Not surprisingly, therefore, notions of group identity and culture are at the forefront of this politics.

What culture and identity are, however, remains uncertain and contested. Eisenberg argues that 'identity refers to the attachments that people have to particular communities, ways of life, sets of beliefs, or practices that play a central role in their self-conception or self-understanding'.[47] But in fact a wide range of practices, values and activities may be regarded as meaningful in the construction of who we are. And since people appeal to their identity in very different contexts and with an infinitude of aims, the task of determining what constitutes an identity is fraught with complexity. Moreover, whereas it seems that beliefs and ways of life that are typically labelled as 'cultural' – such as language, religion and dress – have special salience in shaping identity,[48] in practice culture and identity are often used as interchangeable terms. As Seila Benhabib argues, 'culture' has become a ubiquitous synonym of identity.[49] And the reference to culture does not shed more light either. In fact, what sociologists and anthropologists have taught us in recent decades is that culture, like identity, is dynamic, multi-vocal and ever-changing.[50]

Within all this conceptual volatility, however, at least three things seem relatively clear. First, the all-encompassing and dynamic character of culture unveils the cultural character of human rights law. As such, it is not surprising that instances of legal recognition by way of new/specific rights play a relevant part in creating and reconfiguring identities, culture and groups.[51] Second, culture is a concept mostly invoked in relation to traditions or lifestyles and thus, to a specific context. As an embodiment of the particular, it is not hard to see why culture is usually situated in opposition to human rights and to equality, which are the hallmarks of universal ideals. Third, a remarkable feature of identity and culture is their capacity to express normative commitment, which

---

47 Avigail Eisenberg, *Reasons of Identity. A Normative Guide to the Political & Legal Assessment of Identity Claims* (Oxford University Press, 2009), at 18.

48 Ali Mazrui, for instance, argues that one of the functions of culture is to be a basis of people's identity. See Ali Mazrui, *Cultural Forces in World Politics* (James Currey, 1990), at 7 cited by Abdullahi A. An-Na'im, *Cultural Transformation and Human Rights* (Zed Books, 2002), at 23.

49 Seyla Benhabib, *The Claims of Culture. Equality and Diversity in the Global Era* (Princeton University Press, 2002), at 1.

50 Toon van Meijl, 'Anthropological Perspectives on Identity: From Sameness to Difference', in Margaret Wetherell and Chandra Talpade Mohanty (eds.), *The SAGE Handbook of Identities* (SAGE Publications, 2010), at 63–71.

51 See e.g. Sujit Choudhry, 'Distribution vs. Recognition: The Case of Antidiscrimination Laws', 9 *George Mason Law Review* (2000) 145, at 170–171; Barbara Oomen, 'The application of socio-legal theories of legal pluralism to understanding the implementation and integration of human rights law', 4 *European Journal of Human Rights* (2014) 471, at 475 (arguing that the customs of indigenous people are shaped by the interaction with human rights law and its conceptualisation of indigenous laws while human rights law, in turn, is shaped by the claims made by indigenous people).

explains their widespread utilisation via rights claims. According to Waldron, identity claims are put forward as versions of rights. Such claims, like rights claims, are usually presented as non-negotiable: They represent *who I am*, which cannot be sacrificed for the benefit of others. Identity claims are 'reservations which one is entitled to insist on for oneself and which others have to recognise as constraints'.[52] Moreover, as pointed out by Dembour and Wilson, these claims are likely to carry more weight in litigation, and thus they are used to ground not only typical cultural interests, but also political and socio-economic claims such as access to land, education, environmental protection and employment.[53] Possibly, this is facilitated by the flexibility of notions such as 'cultural rights' and 'culture' more generally, which makes their use especially apt for bringing onto the human rights agenda issues that would otherwise not easily fit. Almost any human right, it has been asserted, could be linked to culture and there is still no agreed definition or list of cultural rights.[54] Indeed, it is argued that the field of cultural rights remains one of the least elaborated by international human rights law. This opens up possibilities for claims that contest prevailing understandings of social, political, cultural and economic life.[55]

And thus, an ever-increasing multitude of actors uses the human rights discourse and norms to claim entitlements, resources and benefits that are deemed indispensable for the protection of one or more aspects of their identity or cultural specificity. This includes not only claims from disempowered groups pushing for causes branded as 'progressive'. It also includes rather reactionary claims from states, nationalist groups and other actors in more hegemonic positions.[56]

There can be no doubt then that identity and the language of culture is a powerful device. The so-called 'cultural turn' prompted by identity politics has impacted profoundly on the political and legal debates of liberal democracies. Having one's own sense of self distorted or disrespected is, with good reason,

---

52 Jeremy Waldron, 'Cultural Identity and Civic Responsibility', in Will Kymlicka and Wayne Norman, *Citizenship in Diverse Societies* (Oxford University Press, 2000), at 158.

53 Jane K. Cowan *et al.* (eds.), *Culture and Rights. Anthropological Perspectives* (Cambridge University Press, 2001), at 9.

54 Yvonne M. Donders, *Human Rights: Eye for Cultural Diversity* (Amsterdam University Press, 2012). Inaugural Lecture delivered upon the appointment to the chair of Professor of International Human Rights and Cultural Diversity at the University of Amsterdam on 29 June 2012, at 16.

55 Rosemary J. Coombe, 'Legal Claims to Culture in and Against the Market: Neoliberalism and the Global Proliferation of Meaningful Difference', 1(1) *Law Culture and the Humanities* (2005) 35, at 52.

56 Reeta Toivanen, 'Is Multiculturalism bad for the fight against discrimination?', in Martin Scheinin and Reetta Toivanen (eds.), *Rethinking Non-Discrimination and Minority Rights* (Institute for Human Rights Abo Akademi University, 2004), at 188.

taken more seriously, as is our cultural belonging.[57] In fact, identity injury and cultural disrespect in the form of stigma, shame and forced assimilation can all provoke serious harm that may encroach upon human rights, such as the right to health, the right to integrity, equality and the right to private life. And yet, from a normative viewpoint the tendency to equate recognition with identity affirmation and to focus on cultural or group identity injury, as prompted by identity politics, should be treated with caution.

3.2. PROBLEMATISING THE CENTRALITY OF CULTURE AND GROUP IDENTITY

The emphasis on identity harm and the centrality accorded to culture have been criticised on a number of grounds. Notably, this focus would go hand in hand with the reification of culture, fixed identity group boundaries and erasures of gender, race, class and other grounds of social stratification. Probably the best-known weakness of identity politics is its inclination towards essentialism or reification. This criticism, already introduced in section 2.1, basically points to the reductionism of conceiving groups and cultures as bounded entities whose members can be identified by reference to certain traits which also define the group or culture itself. Put briefly, it is argued that these essentialising views, even in their progressive strategic deployments, risk reifying identity, erecting artificial group boundaries and side-lining some voices and forms of oppression.[58]

Anne Phillips usefully distinguishes four forms of essentialism.[59] The first is 'the attribution of certain characteristics to everyone subsumed within a particular category'.[60] This is the kind of essentialism deployed when we make generalisations, such as 'women are caring', 'indigenous persons are rural-oriented' or 'welfare recipients are lazy'. It is the type of essentialism that rapidly

57 See e.g. Ruth Lister, '(Mis)recognition, social inequality and social justice. A critical social policy perspective', in Nancy Fraser and Pierre Bourdieu, *(Mis)recognition, Social Inequality and Social Justice* (Routledge, 2007), at 165–166; Avigail Eisenberg, *Reasons of Identity: A Normative Guide to the Political & Legal Assessment of Identity Claims* (Oxford University Press, 2009), at 19–20 (noting the relationship between identity, self-understanding and self-esteem and discussing how, on the basis of this relationship, several authors argue that identity ought to be taken seriously).

58 Angela P. Harris, 'Race and Essentialism in Feminist Legal Theory', 42 *Stanford Law Review* (1990) 581, at 588–590; Seyla Benhabib, *The Claims of Culture* (Princeton University Press, 2002), at 4. More recently, see Colleen Sheppard, 'Constitutional Recognition of Diversity in Canada', 30 *Vermont Law Review* (2006) 463, at 482–484; Anne Phillips, 'What's wrong with essentialism?', 11(1) *Distinktion: Scandinavian journal of social theory* (2010) 47.

59 Anne Phillips, 'What's wrong with essentialism?', 11(1) *Distinktion: Scandinavian journal of social theory* (2010) 47.

60 Ibid., at 50–51.

turns into stereotypes, that is, as explained by Cook and Cusack, generalised views or preconceptions about the attributes of members of a particular group or about the roles they should perform in society.[61] The second type of essentialism described by Phillips consists of the reification of a social category by attributing certain characteristics to it.[62] This is at play when we perceive groups as different and try to explain their difference by reference to characteristics deemed essential to each group. These attributes can be regarded as biological (e.g. body-able/disabled) or cultural (e.g. Muslim/Christian). By doing this, we naturalise what are mostly socially constructed differences and hierarchies,[63] or, to use the nomenclature proposed above, we see embedded differences as embodied.

The third kind of essentialism takes place when the group or collective entity is presented as relatively homogeneous for the purposes of political action or contestation.[64] This is quite familiar to rights rhetoric, especially to that of applicants who turn to courts and increasingly resort to groups' vindications and identity grounds in seeking protection. Such a move leads to the paradox that Minow calls the 'dilemma of difference': by using essentialism strategically to combat the stereotypes it has produced, the same difference that is targeted for elimination is reproduced.[65] The fourth kind of essentialism pointed out by Phillips operates by determining who belongs to the group or culture. Membership is controlled by verifying whether the individual exhibits the traits that supposedly define the group. This appears to be a common exercise undertaken by courts when they decide who fits a certain category. However, this is also done by insiders who claim to speak from within the collectivity. Phillips argues that this essentialism is the least visible of the four, possibly because it is more openly grounded in the socially constructed character of the attribute. In fact, this reasoning is regularly used with regard to culturally defined groups. It is to be noted that when recognition is reduced to identity celebration or cultural protection through the law, the latter indeed appears to have to define what constitutes a given identity, group or culture. On that basis, judges will accord

---

61 Rebeca J. Cook and Simone Cusack, *Gender Stereotyping: Transnational Legal Perspectives* (University of Pennsylvania Press, 2010), at 9–13.

62 Anne Phillips, 'What's wrong with essentialism?', 11(1) *Distinktion: Scandinavian journal of social theory* (2010) 47, at 53–54.

63 Ibid., at 54. In a similar vein, De Santos Sousa argues that one of the logics through which a certain entity is discredited or rendered invisible is the logic of social classification based on the 'monoculture' of 'naturalisation of differences'. It consists in distributing populations according to categories that naturalise hierarchies. Boaventura De Sousa Santos, 'Public Sphere and Epistemologies of the South', 37(1) *Africa Development* (2012) 43, at 53.

64 Anne Phillips, 'What's wrong with essentialism?', 11(1) *Distinktion: Scandinavian journal of social theory* (2010) 47, at 53–56.

65 Martha Minow, *Making All the Difference. Inclusion, Exclusion and American Law* (Cornell University Press, 1990), at 20. Also called 'the constitutive paradox of feminism' Joan Scott, referred to by Anne Phillips, 'What's wrong with essentialism?', 11(1) *Distinktion: Scandinavian journal of social theory* (2010) 47, at 55.

rights and deliver protection. This raises a number of difficulties that are more closely examined *infra* section 3.4.

But the politics of identity faces further objections, as already pointed out.[66] One of these is the concealment of other differences and the role of social barriers. As discussed earlier, a key aspect of processes of differentiation is their embeddedness in social relations and institutions. Yet, legal and political discourses usually reduce social identities to a matter of personal characteristics, something that simply lies with each person. Fineman, however, reminds that 'social identities are manufactured within institutional relationships and prevalent ideologies, not found in the designation of attributes associated with individual characteristics, actions, or affiliations, such as race, sex, religion, or sexual orientation'.[67] What matters, then, is how social institutions and relations working through those socially defined identities distribute power and disadvantage.[68] This feature also implies that notions of culture, recognition and identity can hardly be seen in isolation from those relations and institutions, including those that shape socio-economic arrangements. The place of this structural dimension, however, remains rather contested in the conceptualisation of the politics of recognition or identity, which has been charged with downplaying the role of social barriers and power imbalances.[69]

A good account of this concern is provided by Young's late work. In her view, the politics of cultural difference focuses too much on questions of cultural expression and toleration while at the same time bringing in a normalising discourse. In so doing, she argues, the politics of cultural difference obscures issues of structural inequality, such as racism.[70] As an example, she considers how the debates concerning the accommodation of Muslims in a multicultural Europe emphasise issues of cultural difference, while overlooking underlying structural inequalities.

---

66 For an overview of the variety of responses confronted by identity politics, see Austin Sarat and Thomas R. Kearns, *Cultural Pluralism, Identity Politics, and the Law* (The University of Michigan Press, 2001), at 4–7; Bikhu Parekh, 'Redistribution or recognition: a misguided debate', in Stephen May *et al.* (eds.), *Ethnicity, Nationalism and Minority Rights* (Cambridge University Press, 2004), at 201.

67 Martha Albertson Fineman, 'Equality and Difference – The Restrained State', 66(3) *Alabama Law Review* (2015) 609, at 613.

68 Idem.

69 Lois McNay, *Against Recognition* (Polity Press, 2008), at 8–9. Wendy Brown, for instance, argues that 'the culturalization of politics analytically vanquishes political economy, states, history, and international and transnational relations. It eliminates colonialism, capital, caste or class stratification, and external political domination from accounts of political conflict or instability.' Wendy Brown, *Regulating Aversion: Tolerance in the Age of Identity and Empire* (Princeton University Press, 2006), at 20.

70 Iris Marion Young, 'Structural Injustice and the Politics of Difference', in Emily Grabham *et al.* (eds.), *Intersectionality and Beyond. Law, power and the politics of location* (Routledge Cavendish, 2009), at 291 and 294–295.

> The claims of such Muslims that they should have the freedom to wear headscarves or make their prayer calls in the public square in the European cities where they live should not be divorced from this context of broad and entrenched structural privilege of majorities and social and economic disadvantage of minorities.[71]

Young furthermore contrasts such a politics with what she calls a politics of 'positional difference'.[72] This stance, similar to that adopted by Minow and Fineman, is concerned with groups constituted by social interactions and structures that distinguish between people and place them in hierarchies.

From a constitutional law perspective, Susanne Baer also criticises what she terms 'groupism', that is, basically, to 'construct human rights conflicts as group issues'[73] whereby rights are posited as claims about one's culture. She observes several problems with this strategy, particularly in the context of religious pluralism. Besides stereotyping and the issue of elitism – in the sense of who defines the collective claims at stake – she argues that groupism in human rights requires people to conform to standards that human rights should be able to challenge.[74] Furthermore, this group focus may trump the individual rights of minorities within minorities, as well as the rights of those who are identified with non-majoritarian cultures. In her view, 'groupism' works to shield sexism and racism while also 'othering' inequalities.[75]

Dhamoon has a similar concern about the centrality accorded to identity and culture in the analysis of tensions and conflicts that trouble Western multicultural societies. She argues that the preoccupation with culture diverts attention from questions of power, as expressed in racism, Islamophobia, poverty, ableism[76]

---

71 Ibid., at 291.

72 Ibid., at 275–276. ('This approach theorizes social groups as constituted through interactions that make categorical distinctions among people in hierarchies of status or privilege.')

73 Susanne Baer, 'Privatizing Religion. Legal Groupism, No-Go-Areas, and the Public-Private-Ideology in Human Rights Politics' 20(1) *Constellations* (2013) 68, at 75. She relies on Brubaker's work on 'groupism'. See Rogers Brubaker, *Ethnicity without Groups* (Harvard University Press, 2004).

74 Susanne Baer, 'A Closer Look at Law: Human Rights as Multi-Level Sites of Struggles Over Multi-Dimensional Equality', 6(2) *Utrecht Law Review* (2010) 56, at 59–60.

75 Susanne Baer, 'Privatizing Religion. Legal Groupism, No-Go-Areas, and the Public-Private-Ideology in Human Rights Politics', 20(1) *Constellations* (2013) 68, at 74–75. ('When sexism is practiced in the name of religion, it is shielded from the very reach of human rights, since religion employs the well-known strategy of insulating its private sphere from intervention'); Susanne Baer, 'A Closer Look at Law: Human Rights as Multi-Level Sites of Struggles Over Multi-Dimensional Equality', 6(2) *Utrecht Law Review* (2010) 56, at 61–62. (As an example, she refers to multicultural politics that focus on gendered violence in Muslim or other 'immigrant' families only. By 'othering sex inequality' majorities protect themselves 'from challenges to the normalcy of privilege'.)

76 According to Campbell, ableism refers to 'a network of beliefs, processes and practices that produces a particular kind of self and body (the corporeal standard) that is projected as the perfect, species-typical and therefore essential and fully human. Disability then is cast as a diminished state of being human.' Fiona Kumari Campbell, *Contours*

and homophobia.[77] The consequence of adopting a focus on identities and differences themselves, instead of taking a relational view of how differences and identities are produced and signified, is that problems of structural or material difference go disregarded.[78] Moreover, she argues that the overemphasis on culture promotes a 'unidimensional analysis of difference' whereby cultural forms of identification are prioritised, while its interaction with other axes of difference gets obscured.[79]

In a similar vein, it is argued that restricting legal protection to identity-based claims or grounds may have the additional problem of working against those in the most subordinated positions. Being able to organise around any given identity and make it visible presupposes favourable conditions and resources for identity recognition and mobilisation. As such, not all those who are disadvantaged would be in a position to mobilise in that way.[80] Those struggling with poverty, for example, would have much more difficulty in doing so.

A similar line of thought seems to drive redistributionist perspectives insofar as these worry about the oppression resulting from socio-economic structures. They admit that arguments about class and socio-economic equality have lost their appeal, while cultural difference and identity have become the new idiom of social justice.[81] Yet, advocates of redistribution argue that identity-centred politics and the emphasis on difference tend to displace legitimate concerns over maldistribution and economic disadvantage.[82] In an era of stark poverty and globalised inequalities, that would constitute a serious flaw. Nonetheless,

of Ableism: The Production of Disability and Abledness (Palgrave Macmillan, 2009), at 9, cited in Carol Thomas, 'Disability and diversity', in Steven Vertovec (ed.), *Routledge International Handbook of Diversity Studies* (Routledge, 2014), at 47.

77 Rita Dhamoon, *Identity/Difference Politics. How Difference is Produced, and Why It Matters* (UBC Press, 2009), at 2 and 6–8.

78 Ibid., at 9. This applies to progressive as well as to non-progressive identity politics. In this vein, but in the US context, see Martha T. McCluskey, 'How Equality Became Elitist: The Cultural Politics of Economics from the Court to the "Nanny Wars"', 35(4) *Seton Hall Law Review* (2005) 1291, at 1292. ('By fueling the "culture wars," the right helps deflect the problem of "class warfare" away from right-wing economic policies and onto egalitarian social policies.')

79 Rita Dhamoon, *Identity/Difference Politics. How Difference is Produced, and Why It Matters* (UBC Press, 2009), at 35–36.

80 In this vein, Jessica Eisen, 'On Shaky Grounds: Poverty and Analogous Grounds under the Charter', 2(2) *Canadian Journal of Poverty Law* (2013) 1, at 12.

81 On the shift from redistribution to recognition see, Nancy Fraser, 'Social Justice in the Age of Identity Politics: Redistribution, Recognition, and Participation', in Nancy Fraser and Axel Honneth, *Redistribution or Recognition? A Political-Philosophical Exchange* (Verso, 2003), at 89–93.

82 Brian Barry, *Culture and Equality: An Egalitarian Critique of Multiculturalism* (Polity Press, 2001), at 64; Richard Rorty, 'Is "Cultural Recognition" a Useful Notion for Leftist Politics?', 1(1) *Critical Horizons* (2001) 7, at 13–18; Simon Thompson, *The Political Theory of Recognition: A Critical Introduction* (Polity Press, 2006), at 103–104.

this kind of criticism does not need to reject recognition politics altogether, as Nancy Fraser shows. In fact, her writings challenge the division between recognition and redistribution, or more broadly, the separation between the cultural and the economic, the symbolic and the material. The dislocation of recognition from redistribution would be reflected, *inter alia*, in the types of collectivity and harm that are paradigmatically at the heart of each realm. While recognition appears concerned with groups defined by (cultural) identity, redistribution would deal with groups determined by their class position. The former would suffer from cultural or identity domination and the latter, from maldistribution.[83] Against this, Fraser argues that virtually all collectivities are bivalent in the sense that they are defined by both cultural and economic forces while being harmed on both grounds.[84] At the heart of her theory lies the affirmation of a mutual imbrication between recognition and redistribution and a reconceptualisation of justice as recognition.

3.3. FROM IDENTITY AFFIRMATION TO SOCIAL PARTICIPATION

While mindful of the psychological, social and legal relevance of collective identity and culture, it is submitted that normative analysis should pay more attention to embedded difference and social recognition, that is, to an understanding of recognition grounded more in social participation than in identity injury. The importance of moving away from a view of recognition centred on group identity to one based on social standing is illuminated by the integrated theory of justice propounded by Fraser. Importantly, she frames recognition not as a question of identity or intersubjective valuation, but as a matter of justice concerning social status.[85] Thus, unlike the conceptualisation of misrecognition articulated by Taylor and Honneth, misrecognition for Fraser consists of being rendered as inferior, invisible or in any other way less than a full partner in social interaction through institutionalised patterns of cultural value.[86]

By using this framework, it is possible to analyse the lack of recognition experienced by those who would hardly be able to mobilise an identity-based

83 Nancy Fraser, 'Social Justice in the Age of Identity Politics: Redistribution, Recognition, and Participation', in Nancy Fraser and Axel Honneth, *Redistribution or Recognition? A Political-Philosophical Exchange* (Verso, 2003), at 13–15.

84 Ibid., at 25. See also Meena K. Bhamra, *The Challenges of Justice in Diverse Societies. Constitutionalism and Pluralism* (Ashgate, 2011), at 19 (arguing that identities should be viewed as two-dimensional, encompassing both status and class).

85 Nancy Fraser and Axel Honneth, *Redistribution or Recognition? A Political-Philosophical Exchange* (Verso, 2003), at 29.

86 Ibid., at 29 and 221.

framework of protection, for example, people living in poverty.[87] In addition, viewing recognition as an issue of equal social participation suggests that the harms involved in cases of misrecognition will frequently go beyond identity injury or devaluation. They will often encompass, for instance, questions of socio-economic exclusion and political marginalisation. Finally, this approach makes it easier to avoid essentialist impulses while emphasising that differences, in the sense that matters here, are defined not merely by personal (cultural or identity) features, but primarily by an external environment that dictates who are different from, and thus less equal than, others.[88] This is not to say, however, that identity and culture are of secondary importance or that debates about them can be circumvented. People care about what they regard as their identity and culture and these questions hold a central place in current political and legal battles, which is unlikely to recede in the near future. What is nonetheless suggested is that rights claims concerning recognition or difference should not be resolved by focusing merely on cultural groups or on identity injury. Neither should those claims be divorced from interlocking social categories and structures of privilege and disadvantage. This implies, among other things, taking a point of view that integrates issues of both recognition and redistribution.

3.4. RECOGNITION, REDISTRIBUTION AND INTERACTIONS IN THEORY AND PRACTICE

Politically speaking, Fraser explains typical 'recognition' claims as those which mainly oppose patterns of social representation, communication and cultural oppression, that is, cultural domination. Redistribution claims, on the other hand, archetypally aim at combating marginalisation, destitution and exploitation, that is, socio-economic domination.[89] In social theory terms, Fraser relates redistribution claims to forms of subordination arising from a class structure that institutionalises economic mechanisms that impede some from taking part in social life. Recognition claims, in turn, would respond to subordination arising from a status order. This status order is hierarchical and operates by institutionalising 'patterns of cultural value that pervasively deny

87 Ruth Lister, '(Mis)recognition, social inequality and social justice. A critical social policy perspective', in Nancy Fraser and Pierre Bourdieu, *(Mis)recognition, Social Inequality and Social Justice* (Routledge, 2007), at 164.

88 Tariq Modood, 'Difference, Multi and Equality', in Michel Seymour (ed.), *The Plural States of Recognition* (Palgrave Macmillan, 2010), at 153.

89 Nancy Fraser, 'Social Justice in the Age of Identity Politics: Redistribution, Recognition, and Participation', in Nancy Fraser and Axel Honneth, *Redistribution or Recognition? A Political-Philosophical Exchange* (Verso, 2003), at 48.

some members the recognition they need in order to be full, participating partners in social interaction'.[90] Fraser and other scholars regret that these two spheres of justice appear to be divorced in political and legal thinking. Such a stance obscures the fact that cultural subordination and socio-economic inequality are more often than not intertwined, and hence that oppression must be fought on both sides.[91]

As already pointed out, the way misrecognition and maldistribution are intertwined in practice is most obviously evident in the experience of people facing structural discrimination, who embody undervalued identities and are disproportionately socio-economic disadvantaged.[92] As a result of this interplay, reversing cultural devaluation and misrecognition may, depending on the context, open up opportunities to overcome socio-economic exclusion.[93] And conversely, socio-economic intervention may also assist in combating prejudice and cultural subordination.[94] At the same time, many socio-economic measures (e.g. pensions, education, housing and wages) turn a blind eye to cultural diversity, resulting in the exclusion of those who do not conform to the norm

---

90 Ibid., at 49.

91 Nancy Fraser, 'Distorted Beyond All Recognition: A Rejoinder to Axel Honneth', in Nancy Fraser and Axel Honneth, *Redistribution or Recognition? A Political-Philosophical Exchange* (Verso, 2003), at 214–217; Bhikhu Parekh, 'Redistribution or recognition? A misguided debate', in Stephen May *et al.* (eds.), *Ethnicity, Nationalism and Minority Rights* (Cambridge University Press, 2004), at 202–209; Sandra Fredman, 'Redistribution and Recognition: Reconciling Inequalities', 23(2) *South African Journal of Human Rights* (2007) 214, at 215; Boaventura de Sousa Santos, 'Nuestra America reinventing a subaltern paradigm of recognition and redistribution', 18 *Theory, Culture & Society* (2001) 185, at 192; Seyla Benhabib, *The Claims of Culture. Equality and Diversity in the Global Era* (Princeton University Press, 2002), at 17. See also Lisa Duggan, *The Twilight of Equality? Neoliberalism, Cultural Politics and the Attack on Democracy* (Beacon Press, 2003), at 3 (Discussing United States politics, she argues: 'Neoliberalism was constructed in and through cultural and identity politics and cannot be undone by a movement without constituencies and analyses that respond directly to that fact. Nor will it be possible to build a new social movement that might be strong, creative, and diverse enough to engage the work of reinventing global politics for the new millennium as long as cultural and identity issues are separated, analytically and organizationally, from the political economy in which they are embedded.').

92 That is, people who as a result of complex cultural, political, economic and institutional processes are systematically placed at a disadvantage in most aspects of social life. See e.g. Olivier De Schutter and Annelies Verstichel, 'The Role of the Union in Integrating the Roma: Present and Possible Future', 2 *European Diversity and Autonomy Papers (EDAP)* (2005), at 27. Roberto Saba '(Des)igualdad estructural', 11 *Derecho y Humanidades* (2005) 123, at 4.

93 For instance, combating patterns of representations associated with heteronormativity is likely to improve the situation of LGBT people concerning paid work and social protection. Likewise, eliminating discrimination against the Roma may increase their educational opportunities and access to housing.

94 Ruth Lister, '(Mis)recognition, social inequality and social justice. A critical social policy perspective', in Terry Lovell (ed.), *(Mis)recognition, Social Inequality and Social Justice. Nancy Fraser and Pierre Bourdieu* (Routledge, 2007), at 167–168.

or the reinforcement of their stigmatisation.[95] On the other hand, overlooking socio-economic aspects may strengthen misrecognition. This is due to the fact that socio-economic inequalities tend to generate more homogeneous societies that misrecognise or disrespect (culturally) non-dominant groups. A recent report on inequalities from the United Nations Development Programme explains this dynamic:

> As dominant groups benefit from better access to resources, they have an incentive to maintain the conditions of inequality that benefit them [reference omitted]. For this, they rely on crafting inequality-justifying ideologies. These ideologies are translated into stereotypes and norms that define the ways in which groups supposedly differ and embed these beliefs into social interactions as well as into legal and cultural institutions.[96]

Moreover, financial crises have contributed to deepening group identity inequality and social exclusion.[97]

In spite of these interactions, it is all too common to insulate each of these dimensions of justice. Mapping onto the separation between the cultural and the economic, politically and legally the divide reproduces itself as one between group identity and socio-economic justice. To understand the acceptance of the division, some scholars note the different logics that underpin each realm. Individual and group differences, especially in terms of race, gender, disability and sex, are usually seen as embodied, monolithic and immutable, while socio-economic conditions are not.[98] Socio-economic arrangements are

---

95 Sandra Fredman, 'Positive Duties and Socio-Economic Disadvantage: Bringing Disadvantage onto the Equality Agenda', 55 *University of Oxford Legal Research Paper Series* (2010), at 3–4. It may also be the case that policies committed to ensuring enjoyment of socio-economic rights may pose a sort of trade-off that requires some groups to surrender certain rights as a price for having those goods and services. In this vein, Luke Clements and Janet Read, 'The Dog that Didn't Bark: The Issue of Access to Rights Under the European Convention on Human Rights by Disabled People', in Anna Lawson and Caroline Gooding (eds.), *Disability Rights in Europe. From Theory to Practice: Essays in European Law* (Hart Publishing, 2005), at 26.

96 United Nations Development Programme (UNDP), *Humanity Divided: Confronting Inequality in Developing Countries* (UNDP, 2013), at 264. In the same vein, Bhikhu Parekh, 'Redistribution or recognition? A misguided debate', in Stephen May *et al.* (eds.), *Ethnicity, Nationalism and Minority Rights* (Cambridge University Press, 2004), at 202.

97 In this vein, Speech of Mr Thorbjørn Jagland, Secretary General of the Council of Europe Civil society fórum; 'Living together. Combining diversity and freedom in 21st century Europe' Strasbourg, 14 November 2011, Council of Europe Portal, <www.coe.int/en/web/secretary-general/speeches-2011/>.

98 Angela P. Harris, 'Theorizing Class, Gender, and the Law: Three Approaches', 72(4) *Law and Contemporary Problems* (2009) 37, at 39. In the same vein, but in the specific legal context of the United States, see Mario Barnes and Erwin Chemerinsky, 'The Disparate Treatment of Race and Class in Constitutional Jurisprudence', 72(4) *Law and Contemporary Problems* (2009) 109, at 121–122.

constructed around the idea of equality of opportunity; they are perceived as neutral and give the impression of being governed by individuals' free choices.[99] None of them are thus seen as imposed, nor are they unchangeable aspects of individuals. Individuals' choices, rationality and objectivity actually hold an important place in how we understand socio-economic arrangements and also in explaining socio-economic differences.[100] These elements are, by contrast, out of the question when the difference is perceived as 'inner' or immutable. And when the marker of difference is not regarded as unchangeable – as happens with religious or other 'cultural' markers – they are associated with subjectivity, volatility or even coercion, in contrast to the objective and stable character of socio-economic matters. Being different is furthermore often equated with deviance, while socio-economic conditions are rarely seen as a matter of difference or deviation. Rather, they tend to represent the status quo, which is somehow a given.

From a normative perspective, Fredman identifies the above divide with the two main facets of inequality. One is the impairment of 'status-based' equality (which includes issues of accommodation of different identities). The other impinges on 'socio-economic' equality.[101] While the first has easily translated into legal rights, usually through anti-discrimination laws, socio-economic equality tends to be located in the terrain of social policy and welfare. Status-based equality claims have often been identified with negative obligations – to refrain from something. Socio-economic equality claims, by contrast, have been seen as paradigmatic examples of positive obligations – duties to provide. It therefore comes as no surprise that courts have typically been more open to adjudicating status-based than socio-economic equality claims. By the same token, 'courts operating within a traditional human rights model have rejected attempts to reformulate socio-economic inequality as a status-based wrong'.[102] Even when the two perspectives are brought together in a case, under a substantive notion of equality, for example, they do not sit comfortably together. In fact, tackling one may often result in overshadowing the other.[103] Finally, when it comes to the normative responses expected for claims of identity-based and socio-economic

99 Anne Phillips, 'Equality, Pluralism, Universality: Current Concerns in Normative Theory', 2 *British Journal of Politics and International Relations* (2000) 237, at 243–244; Athena D. Mutua, 'Introducing ClassCrits: From Class Blindness to a Critical Legal Analysis of Economic Inequality', 56(4) *Buffalo Law Review* (2008) 859, at 866 and 881.

100 In this vein, Martha Minow, *Making All the Difference. Inclusion, Exclusion and American Law* (Cornell University Press, 1990), at 70–73 (arguing that 'social arrangements are assumed to be neutral', thus 'not forced on anyone' so that 'individuals are free to make choices and to assume responsibility for those choices').

101 Sandra Fredman, 'Redistribution and Recognition: Reconciling Inequalities', 23 *South African Journal on Human Rights* (2007) 214, at 214–218.

102 Ibid., at 217.

103 Ibid., at 219.

difference, further divergence arises. While the paradigmatic ideal of justice in the socio-economic field seeks to erase group differentials and to emphasise equality, the ideal of justice advanced with regard to questions of identity difference, especially in recent decades, promotes the recognition and valuation of distinctive identities and cultures.

The tension and mutual imbrication between recognition and redistribution, as well as the implications that follow from that, also find expression in human rights law. While in principle human rights law holds the promise to be instrumental in combating both cultural and socio-economic injustice, human rights law itself has been challenged on both cultural and economic grounds. Moreover, as seen below, both dimensions often remain split in rights talk and practice.

4. DIVERSITY AND FRAGMENTATION IN HUMAN RIGHTS LAW

4.1. THE CULTURAL AND ECONOMIC CRITIQUE(S) OF HUMAN RIGHTS

Post-modern feminism and post-colonial perspectives, in particular, have usefully tied cultural and economic concerns together in their critiques of human rights law. By deconstructing identity categories such as gender and sex, the former has demonstrated that it is not enough to denounce the male orientation of human rights. Given that there is no such thing as an overarching female identity or experience, we need to enquire whether human rights are able to capture the needs of concrete women situated in different cultural and economic contexts, especially of those in less powerful positions.[104] In that respect, human rights – with its 'false universalisms' – has appeared to be insufficiently responsive to, for example, poor black women and indigenous rural women, whose needs and concerns differ from those of white middle-class women.[105]

From a post-colonial point of view, cultural critics usually point to the civilising, Eurocentric and imperialist *ethos* of universal human rights norms.[106]

104 Marie-Bénédicte Dembour, *Who Believes in Human Rights? Reflections on the European Convention* (Cambridge University Press, 2006), at 211 (analysing the post-modern feminist critique).

105 Dana Collins *et al.*, 'New Directions in Feminism and Human Rights. An Introduction', 12 *International Feminist Journal of Politics* (2010) 298, at 308; Annie Bunting, 'Theorizing Women's Cultural Diversity in Feminist International Human Rights Strategies', 20 *Journal of Law and Society* (1993) 6, at 7–10.

106 In this vein, Marie-Bénédicte Dembour, 'Critiques to Human Rights', in Daniel Moeckli *et al.* (eds.), *International Human Rights Law* (Oxford University Press, 2014).

With Europe and America as their point of reference, they argue that human rights law has built upon secularism, capitalism and political democracy. It has accordingly disregarded certain values, such as solidarity, while assuming, for example, the elevation of the individual and the devaluation of collectivities.[107] In addition to problems of cultural bias, they say that the Eurocentric and liberal human rights agenda tends to neglect issues of inequality and poverty.[108] As a corollary, human rights law would be unable to account for the needs and concerns of those enduring socio-economic subordination.[109] The second rank of social and economic rights would be the most blatant, albeit not the only, evidence of human rights' ambivalence in the face of inequality. A further indication of this would be that human rights law remains somewhat aloof from 'private violence', meaning that it fails to protect the most disadvantaged against both powerful private actors and market forces.[110]

In addition to questioning the responsiveness of human rights law to 'private' issues, to collectivities, to poverty and to specific cultural contexts, both strands of criticism also coincide in advocating the need to reject the conception of individual autonomy underlying liberalism and human rights, which specifies a free, rational, self-reliant agent who owns what he does and has.[111] This image denies the social embeddedness of all human beings. It thus fails to acknowledge how individuals' choices may be structurally constrained, either because of

---

107 Makau Mutua, 'Human Rights in Africa: The Limited Promise of Liberalism', 51(1) *African Studies Review* (2008) 17, at 31; Anatoly Kovler, 'Human Rights in a Contemporary Society and European Values: Critique of Eurocentrism', *1 EU-Russia Paper*, Center for EU-Russia Studies, University of Tartu (2011), at 14–15 (regarding the need to consider non-European approaches and address the 'tyranny of individualism').

108 Makau Mutua, 'Human Rights in Africa: The Limited Promise of Liberalism', 51(1) *African Studies Review* (2008) 17, at 31–32; Balakrishnan Rajagopal, 'Counter-Hegemonic International Law: Rethinking Human Rights and Development as a Third World Strategy', 27(5) *Third World Quarterly* (2006) 767; Tamara Relis, 'Human Rights and Southern Realities', 33(2) *Human Rights Quarterly* (2011) 509; Julia Suárez-Krabbe, 'Race, Social Struggles, and "Human" Rights: Contributions from the Global South', 6 *Journal of Critical Globalisation Studies* (2013) 78.

109 See e.g. Jaya Ramji-Nogales, 'Undocumented Migrants and the Failure of Universal Individualism', 47 *Vanderbilt Journal of Transnational Law* (2014) 699, at 710–712.

110 Balakrishnan Rajagopal, *International Law from Below: Development, Social Movements, and Third World Resistance* (Cambridge University Press, 2003), at 195; Bhupinder S. Chimni, 'Third World Approaches to International Law: A Manifesto', 8 *International Community Law Review* (2006) 3, at 9–11 and 17–18; Urs Marti, 'Social Rights in a Global Economy', in Jean-Christophe Merle (ed.), *Spheres of Global Justice – Volume 2: Fair Distribution. Global Economic, Social and Intergenerational Justice* (Springer, 2013), at 476–477.

111 Jennifer Nedelsky, *Law's Relations. A Relational Theory of Self, Autonomy, and the Law* (Oxford University Press, 2011) at 120; Ratna Kapur, 'Human Rights in the 21st Century: Take a Walk on the Dark Side', 28 *Sydney Law Review* (2006) 665, at 675; Annie Bunting, 'Theorizing Women's Cultural Diversity in Feminist International Human Rights Strategies', 20 *Journal of Law and Society* (1993) 6, at 7–8. See also, Jeanne M. Woods, 'Justiciable Social Rights as a Critique of the Liberal Paradigm', 38 *Texas International Law Journal* (2003) 763, at 768–770.

broader social and material conditions or because their choices are frequently the result of entrenched value patterns that condition their behaviour and opportunities.[112]

Underlying these critiques about who qualifies as a bearer of human rights and what qualifies as a human right are several challenges to the normative assumptions of the universality of human rights.

4.2. DIVERSITY AND UNIVERSALITY

This brings us to the by-now familiar story of diversity and universality in human rights. For quite a while this was a story of rivalry, particularly during the decades that followed the American Anthropological Association Statement on the Universal Declaration of Human Rights (UNDHR).[113] The ensuing cultural critiques pointed to the genealogy of human rights law. Because this was the historical, cultural and ideological by-product of certain dominant actors,[114] human rights were said to be limited in their legitimacy and/or utility. These limitations were usually characterised by reference to the foundational role of liberalism and its accent on the autonomous individual, his property and formal equality (the use of 'his' is deliberate).[115] They likewise pointed to the narrow range of interests and experiences that moulded the ideal of the human to be protected and which found expression in the themes and areas covered by human rights law. The latter would, for example, oversee the public, not the private sphere; the political, not the economic arena. And yet, human rights norms have been extensively used to assert what was originally left out from their reach. Marginalised voices (e.g. women, ethnic minorities, people with disability, people living in poverty and many others) have increasingly used human rights law to advance a varied range of demands. Along the way, human rights law has become increasingly attentive to group rights, cultural claims and

---

112 Martha Minow, *Making All the Difference. Inclusion, Exclusion and American Law* (Cornell University Press, 1990), at 73.

113 Executive Board, American Anthropological Association (AAA), 'Statement on Human Rights', 49(4) *American Anthropologist* (1947) 539. On the AAA's position, see e.g. Karen Engle, 'From Skepticism to Embrace: Human Rights and the American Anthropological Association from 1947–1999', 23(3) *Human Rights Quarterly* (2001) 536, at 536–559. The AAA statement inaugurated the 'cultural relativist' critique of human rights. These are usually identified with critiques coming from the 'Asian value debate', as well as from African and Islamic particularist views. For an analysis of these, see Eva Brems, *Human Rights: Universality and Diversity* (Martinus Nijhoff, 2001), at 33–90, 91–181 and 183–290.

114 David Kennedy, 'The International Human Rights Movement: Part of the Problem?', 15 *Harvard Human Rights Journal* (2002) 101, at 114.

115 For a critique of the implications of liberalism for social rights, see Jeanne M. Woods, 'Justiciable Social Rights as a Critique of the Liberal Paradigm', 38 *Texas International Law Journal* (2003) 763.

other demands for identity recognition.[116] In other words, human rights law itself has diversified. Thus, the narratives of diversity and human rights have come closer.

But coming closer is not the same as becoming one. Tension between both discourses persists, particularly with respect to cultural diversity. Merry observes that human rights discourses tend to view culture as backward, static and as an obstacle to progress.[117] Meanwhile, scholars keep worrying about the dangers of cultural practices that appear at odds with human rights.[118] At the same time, though, notions of human rights that are receptive of culture and diversity, and vice versa, have been on the rise, as this link is seen as a precondition for the local effectiveness of rights.[119] So while the tension may not have been fully resolved, both narratives have converged in important ways. The mixing of the diversity and universality 'genres' is well illustrated in headings such as 'relative universality',[120] 'inclusive universality',[121] 'differentiated universalism'[122] and 'culturalization of human rights'.[123] They summarise the generally accepted idea that if human rights are to live up to their promise for everyone, they must be attuned to specific and distinct contexts.[124] Human rights should and can be

---

116 In this vein, Helen Stacy, 'International Human Rights in a Fragmenting World', in András Sajó (ed.), *Human Rights with Modesty. The Problem of Universalism* (Martinus Nijhoff Publishers, 2004), at 165.

117 Sally Engle Merry, 'Human Rights Law and the Demonization of Culture (and Anthropology Along the Way)', 26(1) *Political and Legal Anthropology Review* (2003) 55, at 58–60.

118 Yvonne M. Donders, *Human Rights: Eye for Cultural Diversity* (Amsterdam University Press, 2012). Inaugural Lecture delivered upon the appointment to the chair of Professor of International Human Rights and Cultural Diversity at the University of Amsterdam on 29 June 2012, at 6–7; Federico Lenzerini, *The Culturalization of Human Rights Law* (Oxford University Press 2014), at 226–227.

119 Koen De Feyter, 'Localizing Human Rights', 2 *Discussion Paper*, Institute of Development Policy and Management, University of Antwerp (2006), at 5–6 and 9–11.

120 Jack Donnelly, 'The Relative Universality of Human Rights', 29(2) *Human Rights Quarterly* (2007) 281.

121 Eva Brems, 'Reconciling Universality and Diversity in International Human Rights: A Theoretical and Methodological Framework and Its Application in the Context of Islam', 5(3) *Human Rights Review* (2004) 5, at 11–19.

122 Ruth Lister, 'Citizenship: Towards a Feminist Synthesis', 57(1) *Feminist Review* (1997) 28, at 39. Similar notions, such as 'diversity in universality' and 'universality in diversity', have been used not only in academic but also political-legal discussions. By way of example, see UN Human Rights Council; Report of the High Commissioner containing the conclusion of the 15th Workshop on Regional Cooperation for the Promotion and Protection of Human Rights in the Asia-Pacific Region (21 to 23 April 2010), A/HRC/15/39, 3 August 2010, paras. 15–16.

123 Federico Lenzerini, *The Culturalization of Human Rights Law* (Oxford University Press, 2014).

124 Jack Donnelly, 'The Relative Universality of Human Rights' 29 *Human Rights Quarterly* (2007) 281, at 299–300; Eva Brems, 'Accommodating Diversity in International Human Rights: Legal Techniques', in Paul Meerts (ed.), *Culture and International Law* (Hague Academic Press, 2008), at 63–65; Felipe Gómez Isa, 'Cultural Diversity, Legal Pluralism, and Human Rights from an Indigenous Perspective: The Approach by the Colombian Constitutional Court and the Inter-American Court of Human Rights', 36(4) *Human Rights Quarterly* (2014) 722, at 733–734; Abdullahi A. An-Na'im, *Cultural Transformation and Human Rights in Africa* (Zed Books, 2002).

hospitable to a varied range of values, concerns and experiences. From this perspective, it becomes clearer that the basis of human rights' universalism resides in its emancipatory potential and not in its moral truth or philosophical transcendence.[125] On this basis, it is submitted that diversity, multiculturalism and human rights have important common grounds. They notably share narratives about the exclusion and marginalisation of powerless groups or minorities; the valuing and/or protection of cultural distinctiveness; and a concern with the management of diversity.

While this certainly creates an enriched or more integrated story, it is important to observe that some versions of these narratives may foster a too fragmentary or incomplete understanding of the common concerns referred to above. One of these is the tendency of some discourses to concentrate primarily on identifying protected groups, casting them in terms of discrete identities and seeing cultures as bounded. A second is the prioritisation of certain identity traits or cultural problems over others, especially those of ethnic ascendancy, while overlooking other intertwined markers of inequality which are also expressed in cultural patterns and disadvantage (e.g. gender, disability, sexuality and class). A third is the framing of cultural problems and identity differences as value issues that stand in parallel to structural considerations of power and socio-economic inequality.[126]

A significant part of the theorising and policy-making on diversity and human rights has been driven by an ethnic and cultural focus. This is unsurprising considering that Kymlicka, one of the most authoritative voices on multiculturalism, regards the latter as dealing with 'ethno-cultural minorities'.[127] Of course, there are good reasons for this focus. But there are also good reasons to enquire to what extent questions of diversity might be constructed too

125 Michael Goodhart, 'Neither Relative nor Universal: A Response to Donnelly', 30 *Human Rights Quarterly* (2008) 183, 191–193. Similarly, Eva Brems, 'Reconciling Universality and Diversity in International Law', in András Sajó (ed.), *Human Rights with Modesty. The Problem of Universalism* (Martinus Nijhoff Publishers, 2004), at 215–216.

126 The importance of reviewing these aspects is illuminated by insights from feminist multiculturalism. For an overview of these, albeit in the Canadian context, see Barbara Arneil, 'Recognizing Difference/Achieving Equality: Multiculturalism and Gender Justice', Paper Global Centre for Pluralism, Expert Roundtable on Canada's Experience with Pluralism (2008), at 4–10. See also, Rita Dhamoon, *Identity/Difference Politics. How Difference is Produced, and Why It Matters* (UBC Press, 2009), at 21–28 and 31–36. See further the discussion *infra* section 4.5.

127 See Will Kymlicka and Wayne Norman, *Citizenship in Diverse Societies* (Oxford University Press, 2000), at 2 and 18–19. While Modood and Parekh adopt a broader approach, their multiculturalism focuses, respectively, on extra-European/non-white groups and on long-established and self-conscious communities living by their own different systems of beliefs and practices. See Tariq Modood, 'Difference, Multi and Equality', in Michel Seymour (ed.), *The Plural States of Recognition* (Palgrave Macmillan, 2010), at 154; Bhikhu Parekh, *Rethinking Multiculturalism. Cultural Diversity and Political Theory* (Palgrave Macmillan, 2006), at 3–5.

narrowly in certain cases and what effects would follow from that. Emphasising the cultural preservation of specific group identities alone, for example, appears to risk disaggregation on at least two counts. In the first place, it may reinforce the contested idea that cultures and identities are somehow bounded entities, which easily translates in essentialism,[128] a problem already examined in this chapter.[129] As explained, conceiving of cultures and groups as identifiable wholes erases the complexity of the human experience by turning overlapping identity facets and social roles into a monolithic self. Additionally, it may increase the chance of losing sight of particular social, political and economic contexts that condition the claims made in the name of culture or identity difference.[130]

What has just been said does not amount to arguing that gender, class, race and other sources of social categorisation, alongside their respective systems of subordination (patriarchy, racism, etc.), always go disregarded in normative discourses about difference or diversity. To the contrary, these categories are indeed important for those working in the diversity field. Rather, the assertion advanced here is that, all in all, problems of social difference and inequality are often insulated or, we may say, compartmentalised.

4.3. FRAGMENTATION IN THEORY AND LAW

Thus, even when other forms of differentiation, such as those based on gender, sex, disability, class and race, may occupy a relevant place in discourses on diversity and human rights, there is a certain tendency to place them along parallel lines to ethno-cultural differences. At one end of the spectrum, we often find that one line of thought and norm articulation concentrates on sex, gender, race, body-ability and other 'inner' or embodied differences. At the other end, questions of cultural identity, such as those related to religion and the lifestyle of ethnic communities, are frequently grouped under another conceptual and legal framework.[131] This separation, even when analytically helpful, may convey the (misleading) message that only the second set of differences is socially

---

128 In short, this is the belief that a certain essence imbues members of a presumed group and defines their common identity. On the concept of essentialism, see e.g. Andrew Sayer, 'Essentialism, social constructionism, and beyond', 44(3) *The Sociological Review* (1997) 453, at 456–460.

129 See *supra* section 3.3.

130 Rita Dhamoon, *Identity/Difference Politics. How Difference is Produced, and Why It Matters* (UBC Press, 2009), at 9 and 34–35.

131 In this vein, Neus Torbisco Casals, *Groups Rights as Human Rights* (Springer, 2006), at 65–69 (distinguishing between 'social' and 'cultural' minorities and regarding the latter as the main concern of multiculturalists and defendants of accommodation); John Wrench, 'Diversity management', in Steven Vertovec (ed.), *Routledge International Handbook of Diversity Studies* (Routledge, 2015), at 255 (distinguishing between primary and secondary dimensions of diversity, according to their (un)changeable character).

constructed, while leaving under-examined the interplay between them, and between these and broader societal factors.

The literature provides interesting illustrations of the above separations. For instance, it is not rare to find that discussions of indigenous land claims, of complaints brought by Roma and Travellers which concern housing and planning, as well as of other cases involving demands from cultural minorities in areas such as education, the workplace and social security, are somehow bifurcated. While a set of scholarly work examines those cases as instances of cultural identity struggles for accommodation,[132] another set takes them to analyse what are seen as normative developments in the field of socio-economic rights, such as the rights to land, housing and social security.[133] The interplay between both dimensions is, however, rarely discussed.[134] Similarly, a number of debates on the rights of religious minorities in plural societies, even when considered in the context of the workplace or the educational system, seem to engage primarily with the question of recognising and valuing religion or group identity, whereas the impact of losing one's job or the opportunity of quality education is accorded little attention.[135] Furthermore, a number of writings have

---

132 See e.g. Ralph Sandland, 'Developing a Jurisprudence of Difference: The Protection of the Human Rights of Travelling Peoples by the European Court of Human Rights', 8(3) *Human Rights Law Review* (2008) 475–516; Felipe Gómez Isa, 'Cultural Diversity, Legal Pluralism, and Human Rights from an Indigenous Perspective: The Approach by the Colombian Constitutional Court and the Inter-American Court of Human Rights', 36(4) *Human Rights Quarterly* (2014) 722–755; Julie Ringelheim, 'Chapman redux: the European Court of Human Rights and Roma Traditional Lifestyle', in Eva Brems (ed.), *Diversity and European human rights: rewriting judgments of the ECHR* (Cambridge University Press, 2012); Michael Addo, 'Practice of United Nations Human Rights Treaty Bodies in the Reconciliation of Cultural Diversity with Universal Respect for Human Rights', 32 *Human Rights Quarterly* (2010) 601–664.

133 See e.g. Malcolm Langford (ed.), *Social Rights Jurisprudence: Emerging Trends in International and Comparative Law* (Cambridge University Press, 2009); Ellie Palmer, 'Protecting Socio-Economic Rights through the European Convention on Human Rights: Trends and Developments in the European Court of Human Rights', 2 *Erasmus Law Review* (2009) 397, at 415–418. Literature concerning socioeconomic rights and poverty generally discusses legal categories and strategies to tackle problems of justiciability and enforcement. See e.g. Marius Pieterse, 'Coming to Terms with Judicial Enforcement of Socio-Economic Rights', 20(3) *South African Journal on Human Rights* (2004) 383; David Marcus, 'The Normative Development of Socio-Economic Rights Through Supranational Adjudication', 42 *Stanford Journal of International Law* (2006) 53–102; June Sinclair, 'Poverty: Giving Meaning to the Right to Social Assistance', 2 *Stellenbosch Law Review* (2012) 191–224; Fernanda Doz Costa, 'Poverty and Human Rights: From Rhetoric to Legal Obligations, a Critical Account of Conceptual Frameworks', 5(9) *Sur – International Journal of Human Rights* (2008) 81–107.

134 This is to say that often the writings that focus on diversity and identity-rights issues do not deal with socio-economic questions, while those which deal with poverty and socio-economic rights rarely address questions of identity and cultural diversity.

135 Pascale Fournier and Gökçe Yurdakul, 'Unveiling distribution: Muslim women with headscarves in France and Germany', in Y. Michal Bodemann and Gökçe Yurdakul (eds.), *Migration, citizenship, ethnos* (Palgrave Macmillan, 2006), at 167–184.

adopted a single-identity focus. They address the rights of the groups 'women', 'persons with disabilities', 'indigenous peoples', 'LGTBI people' and so forth.[136] The diversity within and across these groups is, however, often overlooked. Meanwhile, some strands of diversity are far more absent from public and academic reflection. Lister, for instance, argues that discourses of difference have tended to marginalise social class.[137]

There may be good reason to retain some divisions in terms of types of group, identity and harm for analytical purposes. This actually seems to be part of a wider phenomenon of specialisation whose epistemological benefits cannot be denied. But the extent to which we engage – or do so only occasionally or not at all – in cross-cutting thinking is also reflective of how we account for and seek solutions to questions of difference and exclusion. In this vein, it is submitted that too much of a division obscures an understanding of how the law, and human rights law in particular, may be part of both the problem and the solution for inclusionary deficits in our diverse and unequal societies. Put differently, the diversity-human rights stories need to contain more complexity, be more integrated. There are several scholars and practitioners on diversity and human rights, as well as theorists of social policy, that have adopted more integrated approaches, as underscored below. Nevertheless, compartmentalised approaches seem to be prevalent in our normative thinking.

If we look at human rights law itself, it appears that this has embraced a relatively disaggregated group identity focus. First, the catalogue of rights holders and entitlements has progressively expanded through new specific instruments and specialised bodies to monitor state compliance. Notably, a growing number of human rights instruments target the rights of women, children, indigenous peoples, persons with disabilities, etc.[138] Second, in doing so, human rights law has fragmented. In the words of Mégret, the increasing demands for inclusion made by various groups in the form of societal acceptance of a diversity of ways of being human:

> has led to a fragmentation of international human rights law. Women, indigenous peoples, sexual minorities, migrants, persons with disabilities have sought to claim

136 Lisa García Bedolla, 'Intersections of Inequality: Understanding Marginalization and Privilege in the Post-Civil Rights Era', 3(2) *Politics & Gender* (2007) 232, at 237 (arguing that many analyses 'only focus on one line of marginality – race, gender, and or/class – rather than any sort of intersection among them').

137 Ruth Lister, 'A politics of recognition and respect: involving people with experience of poverty in decision-making that affects their lives', in John Andersen and Birte Siim (eds.), *The Politics of Inclusion and Empowerment. Gender, Class and Citizenship* (Palgrave Macmillan, 2004), at 122.

138 See e.g. International Convention on the Elimination of All Forms of Racial Discrimination [1966] UKTS 77 1969 (1966); Convention on the Elimination of All Forms of Discrimination Against Women, New York, [1986] IETS 1986; Convention on the Rights of the Child [1989] UKTS 44 1992 (1989); Convention on the Rights of Persons with Disabilities [2007] UKTS 13919 (2007); United Nations Declaration on the Rights of Indigenous Peoples A/RES/61/295 (2007).

> their rights in specific instruments they have insisted on reframing what human rights mean for them. More than merely about inclusion within the liberal house of rights, [they demand that] this house be fundamentally remodeled to accommodate a rich diversity of life-worlds – or indeed that it no longer be a single house at all.[139]

While human rights law evokes a sense of integrity or unity premised on the universality of human rights and the equal dignity of every person,[140] in reality the picture is one of dispersion. This picture is usually described as fragmentation within a global context of legal pluralism.[141] Human rights as law, Brems argues, 'are fragmented: found in a multitude of different legal sources, several of which have their own monitoring bodies, each with their own dynamic'.[142] To be sure, this is not something exclusive to human rights law. It is international law in general that has fragmented, although it is doubtful whether international law was ever a unified body outside lawyers' imagination.[143] Human rights law thus stands alongside the law of the sea, humanitarian law, trade law, environmental law, criminal law and the many other normative strands into which international public law has divided. Each has its own set of rules, principles, organs and specialised professionals.[144] Whether or not a reflection of post-modernist anxieties (as Koskenniemi puts it), the fact remains that concerns over fragmentation revolve around norm interactions. More precisely, the 'fragmentation debate' about human rights law, as in other areas of international law, is marked by questions of conflict of norms and divergent normative practices.[145] Pointing this out is important because the present book,

---

139 Frédéric Mégret, 'Where does the Critique of International Human Rights Stand? An Exploration in 18 Vignettes', in Jose Maria Beneyto and David Kennedy, *New Approaches to International Law. The European and the American Experiences* (TMC Asser Press, 2012), at 28.

140 See e.g. Marjan Ajevski, 'Fragmentation in International Human Rights Law – Beyond Conflict of Laws', 32(2) *Nordic Journal of Human Rights* (2014) 87, at 90 (arguing that 'there is a presumption of normative unity in IHR, to a large extent stemming from its shared commitment to the Universal Declaration on Human Rights'); Eva Brems, 'Introduction: rewriting decisions from a perspective of human rights integration', in Eva Brems and Ellen Desmet (eds.), *Integrated Human Rights in Practice. Rewriting Human Rights Decisions* (Edward Elgar, 2017), at 1.

141 Paul Schiff Berman, 'Global Legal Pluralism', 80 *Southern California Law Review* (2007) 1155, at 1159 and 1175.

142 Eva Brems, 'Introduction: rewriting decisions from a perspective of human rights integration', in Eva Brems and Ellen Desmet (eds.), *Integrated Human Rights in Practice. Rewriting Human Rights Decisions* (Edward Elgar, 2017), at 1.

143 Martti Koskenniemi and Päivi Leino, 'Fragmentation of International Law? Postmodern Anxieties', 15 *Leiden Journal of International Law* (2002) 553, at 556–559.

144 UN International Law Commission; Fragmentation of International Law: Difficulties arising from the Diversification and Expansion of International Law – Report of the Study Group of the International Law Commission, Finalized by Martti Koskenniemi, A/CN.4/L.682, 13 April 2006, para. 8.

145 Ibid., paras. 15–26. See also, Marjan Ajevski, 'Fragmentation in International Human Rights Law – Beyond Conflict of Laws', 32(2) *Nordic Journal of Human Rights* (2014) 87, at 89–90 (discussing 'the conflict bias').

while starting from this reality of legal pluralism and norm interaction, uses the idea of fragmentation in a broader way.

This book takes the word fragmentation to denote the way legal thinking and practice is articulated in, so to speak, 'boxes'.[146] By this it is meant that, in the first place, human rights law, even within one regional realm (say that of the ECtHR or the IACtHR) is applied through different, separated 'compartments'. Normative divides or 'boxes' run across, *inter alia*, different beneficiaries, types of right and lines of case law. This is the likely result of the co-existence, and thus the influence, of a number of global and regional human rights instruments each focused on a specific subject matter or right (e.g. prohibition of torture, enforced disappearance) and, notably for our purposes, on different categories of rights (civil and political, socio-economic) and groups of rights holders (e.g. rights of women, children, indigenous peoples). This book especially takes issue with this last kind of compartmentalisation, as this provides some of the most salient categorisations used in political and legal debates over difference and inclusion.[147] In fact, this idea of fragmentation not only applies to international human rights norms themselves. It may also be extended to the way human rights courts envision rights holders. When it comes to determining who are affected by a rights-restrictive measure in a given case, there is a tendency towards compartmentalised thinking too. Dividing lines separate applicants from other affected rights holders, while each is also split by an either/or view of, for example, their identity, social position and autonomy. In other words, rights holders are often seen and construed in a rather fragmented fashion.

---

146 The metaphor is also used by the 2006 International Law Commission report on Fragmentation of International Law. It is employed to signal 'the splitting up of the law into highly specialized "boxes" that claim relative autonomy from each other and from the general law'. In saying this, the Commission aims at addressing the relationship between different regimes or branches of international law, such as human rights law, environmental law and trade law. Each of these is seen as one 'box' of specialised norms that claim relative autonomy from each other. See UN International Law Commission; Fragmentation of International Law: Difficulties arising from the Diversification and Expansion of International Law – Report of the Study Group of the International Law Commission, Finalized by Martti Koskenniemi, A/CN.4/L.682, 13April 2006, para. 13. As will later become clear, this book extends the metaphor of 'boxes' and the idea of fragmentation to further dimensions of the praxis of human rights law.

147 In this vein, Nira Yuval-Davis *et al.*, 'Secure borders, safe haven and the gendered politics of belonging: Beyond social cohesion', 28(3) *Ethnic and Racial Studies* (2005) 513, at 531. ('In existing legislation, different aspects of human rights or equality mechanisms are treated separately, and different aspects of human identity such as sex discrimination, race equality and disability rights are addressed by separate laws and organizations. Some of us have been arguing for the need to integrate them and cross reference them but this need not be interpreted as the abolition of groups who are formulated around each of these as long as action and politics is coordinated: i.e. mechanisms are needed for the pulling together of these.')

Further 'boxes' may in fact be at play in adjudication, for their use is related to the legal categorisation needed to apply general legal precepts to particular facts.[148] Examining the ECtHR's case law dealing with economic justifications and austerity measures, Gerards observes that 'the Court's case law is, to a large extent, fragmented and compartmentalised'.[149] She argues that 'differences in approach can be explained by the Court's reliance on traditional dividing lines between the different Convention rights, between socio-economic and civil and political rights, and between the different "categories" or "compartments" of cases decided under their scope'.[150] Others have similarly argued that most human rights mechanisms, at the national and international levels, have 'tended to compartmentalise human rights violations into discrete categories, as much as the policy arrangements and institutions tended to separate the promotion and protection of human rights into different sectors'.[151] Another form of fragmentary thinking is often at play in the adjudication of socio-economic rights, as Porter observes. One of the main problems he identifies in this field is that domestic and international jurisprudence on such rights has 'associated legal enforceability with a project of disaggregating rights into components'.[152] In seeking immunity from the principle of progressive realisation, the adjudication of socio-economic rights has been too focused on abstract and universal categories such as 'minimum core' and types of state obligations. These 'components', as Porter calls them, tend to be assessed independently of socio-historical factors, individual circumstances, subjective interests, state context and the competing rights of other groups.[153]

The disaggregation in legal analysis may additionally be fostered by further conceptual divides. Principles and norms which are the basis of constitutional and human rights law claims of difference and inclusion are often interpreted in dichotomic ways, as the following debates attest.

---

148 In this vein, e.g. Sandra Liebengerg, 'Engaging the paradoxes of the universal and particular in human rights adjudication: The possibilities and pitfalls of "meaningful engagement"', 12 *African Human Rights Law Journal* (2012) 1, at 6; Sujit Choudhry, 'Distribution vs. Recognition: The Case of Antidiscrimination Laws', 9(1) *George Mason Law Review* (2000) 145, at 168.

149 Janneke Gerards, 'The ECtHR's Response to Fundamental Rights Issue related to Financial and Economic Difficulties. The Problem of Compartmentalisation', 33(3) *Netherlands Quarterly of Human Rights* (2015) 274, at 275.

150 Ibid., at 289.

151 Johanne Bouchard and Patrice Meyer-Bisch, 'Intersectionality and Interdependence of Human Rights: Same or Different?', 16 *The Equal Rights Review* (2016) 186, at 190.

152 Bruce Porter, 'The Crises of ESC Rights and Strategies for addressing it', in John Squires *et al.* (eds.), *The Road to a Remedy: Current Issues in the Litigation of Economic, Social and Cultural Rights* (UNSW Press, 2005), at 48.

153 Ibid., at 49–56.

4.4. EQUALITY, DIFFERENCE AND OTHER DIVIDES

It is commonplace to position issues of justice concerning social difference by reference to a so-called tension between equality and difference. Said tension furthermore traces a number of other dichotomies, such as those between equality and freedom, neutrality and accommodation, or universalism and particularism. As happens with most binary thinking, it will be seen that such oppositions are less irreconcilable than they pretend to be. Partly, this is due to the constant contestation and reformulation of those same politically loaded concepts. It is submitted that reviewing some of the analytical shifts surrounding these ideas is quite useful for understanding how human rights law has come to deal with claims about difference and social inclusion, what challenges have arisen as a result, and which normative avenues may offer a way out.

4.4.1. Formal Equality, Neutrality and Difference

The normative attention devoted to difference relates to the 'rise' of a substantive notion of equality. To appreciate the latter, it is useful to recall briefly the classical ideal of equality against which it emerged: formal equality. The classical idea of equality is 'formal' insofar as it is concerned with the fairness of treatment among individuals as defined by a rational relationship between means and ends. Through the prohibition of discrimination, it enquires whether individuals are selected or accorded rights and benefits on the basis of grounds that are deemed functionally related to the purported aim.[154] Personal merit, for example, is the kind of supposedly objective and reasonable criterion that passes the test posed by this equation. Typically, then, a norm that prevents women from gaining access to a certain professional position is considered arbitrary and therefore, discriminatory, inasmuch as sex cannot be rationally connected with the achievement of a legitimate goal, such as merit or productivity. In this framework, the complainant needs to be positioned against a comparator (in the example, women would be compared to men) and the impermissibility of the criterion employed operates symmetrically. This is to say that it is as bad to distinguish on the basis of being a woman as on the basis of being a man. The procedural and comparative character of formal equality is in line with Aristotle's formula of treating like cases alike, while treating unlike cases in an unlike manner.[155] Equality of treatment is nonetheless always preferred and

---

[154] Owen Fiss, 'Another Equality', 2(1) *Issues in Legal Scholarship*. Symposium: The Origins and Fate of Antisubordination Theory (2004), at 1.

[155] Robin West, *Re-Imagining Justice: Progressive Interpretations of Formal Equality, Rights, and the Rule of Law* (Ashgate, 2003), at 107.

presumed legitimate, whereas differences in treatment need to be justified by compelling reasons.[156]

Because the ideal here is to provide legal protection to everyone regardless of their differences, the formal equality norm is premised on a universal subject that is disconnected from particular circumstances; it is as abstract as the law.[157] So understood, equality goes hand in hand with ideals of impartiality and neutrality. Both principles commit governments not to endorse or favour any particular view of the good life so as to ensure that people are treated in equality.[158] One of the ways in which states seek to secure neutrality is through secularism, the assumption being that separating the state from the church and religion from the law allows states to be neutral.[159] This basically means securing a neutral public space, while religions and other minority cultural expressions are then confined to the private sphere.[160] Neutrality and secularism in turn would support tolerance, as they would generate the preconditions of mutual respect for human diversity.[161]

However, it is argued that while such abstraction reflects a move against former regulations that explicitly denied many people the quality of subjects of law, it is yet a projection of, and a call to conform to, the viewpoint of some, who are usually those in dominant positions.[162] Hence, this equality carries an assimilationist force. Taking a metaphor used by Calabresi, such equality works

---

156 On the dissimilar structure of the two sub-mandates contained in Aristotle's rule, see Robert Alexy, *Teoría de los derechos fundamentales* (Centro de Estudios Políticos y Constitucionales, 2008), at 362–363. The application of a relatively intense review of rationality/proportionality to distinctions among people has translated into requiring states to provide so-called weighty or very weighty reasons.

157 Martha Albertson Fineman, 'Equality and Difference – The Restrained State', 66(3) *Alabama Law Review* (2015) 609, at 616–617.

158 Ronald Dworkin, *Sovereign Virtue. The Theory and Practice of Equality* (Harvard University Press, 2002), at 281–284.

159 Wendy Brown, 'Civilizational Delusions: Secularism, Tolerance, Equality', 15(2) *Theory & Event* (2012) (analysing the assumptions operating in articulations and practices of modern Western secularism. The first of these reads: 'Secularism generates religious neutrality'. The author contests this and other assumptions); Peter G. Danchin, 'Islam in the Secular Nomos of the European Court of Human Rigths', 32(4) *Michigan Journal of International Law* (2011) 663, at 674.

160 Wendy Brown, 'Civilizational Delusions: Secularism, Tolerance, Equality', 152 *Theory & Event* (2012).

161 Ibid., (referring to the third assumption: 'secularism generates tolerance as mutual respect among religions.').

162 Idem. See also, Will Kymlicka and Wayne Norman, *Citizenship in Diverse Societies* (Oxford University Press, 2000), at 4; Timo Makkonen, 'Is Multiculturalism Bad for the Fight Against Discrimination?', in Martin Scheinin and Reetta Toivanen (eds.), *Rethinking Non-Discrimination and Minority Rights* (Institute for Human Rights Åbo Akademi University, 2004), at 172; Sandra Fredman, 'Disability Equality and the Existing Paradigm', in Anna Lawson and Caroline Gooding (eds.), *Disability Rights in Europe. From Theory to Practice* (Hart Publishing, 2005), at 201.

through the logic of the 'melting pot': 'equality will not be granted until the group which seeks equality is melted into the pot'.[163] In other words, equality comes at the price of embracing the values of and behaving like the dominant group.[164] Women 'only' need to show that they are just like men, gays and lesbians like straights, or Muslims like Christians. Along these lines, neutrality has also gradually fallen out of favour. It is argued that most governments, in one way or another, reflect or uphold majoritarian or historically rooted cultural values.[165] Furthermore, neutrality is grounded in a non-realistic account of society that ignores asymmetries of power among distinct segments of the population. As a consequence, it burdens some more than others.[166] Similarly, the idea of tolerance has been criticised for naturalising hierarchically organised social differences and for constituting an act of power by which the deviant other is admitted and regulated.[167]

4.4.2. *Equality and Liberty*

It is also worth noting that the division drawn between equality and difference somewhat echoes the longstanding, and usually overstated, tension between equality and liberty. In this opposition, equality is viewed as being inclined towards uniformity or homogeneity, particularly when it is displayed in the name of its redistributive goals. Liberty, in contrast, is viewed as enabling an unconstrained human flourishing, which leads to diverse and unique forms of living.[168] Those who follow this reasoning, therefore, worry about the sacrificing of liberty, archetypally represented by individual rights, as the cost of ensuring material equality. This would be the case, for instance, where welfare policies provide material support on condition that certain human rights are given up.

---

163 Guido Calabresi, *Ideals, Beliefs, Attitudes and the Law. Private Law Perspectives on a Public Law Problem* (Syracuse University Press, 1985), at 28.

164 Robin West, *Re-Imagining Justice: Progressive Interpretations of Formal Equality, Rights, and the Rule of Law* (Ashgate, 2003), at 124–125 (explaining how the comparator gets normalised and universalised).

165 See *inter alia*, Tariq Modood, 'Difference, Multi and Equality', in Michel Seymour (ed.), *The Plural States of Recognition* (Palgrave Macmillan, 2010), at 163; Iris Marion Young, *Justice and the Politics of the Difference* (Princeton University Press, 2011), at 114–115; Peter G. Danchin, 'Islam in the Secular Nomos of the European Court of Human Rights', 32(4) *Michigan Journal of International Law* (2011) 663, at 670–671; Malcolm Evans and Peter Petkoff, 'A Separation of Convenience? The Concept of Neutrality in the Jurisprudence of the European Court of Human Rights', 36 *Religion, State and Society* (2008) 205, at 214–215.

166 Roland Pierik and Wibren Van der Burg, 'What Is Neutrality?', 27 *Ratio Juris* (2014) 496, at 504–505.

167 Gail Lewis, 'Welcome to the margins: Diversity, tolerance, and policies of exclusion', 28(3) *Ethnic and Racial Studies* (2005) 536, at 540; Wendy Brown, *Regulating Aversion Tolerance in the Age of Identity and Empire* (Princeton University Press, 2008), at 26–29.

168 Norberto Bobbio, *Igualdad y Libertad* (Paidós Ibérica, 1993), at 90–91.

In addition, liberty and equality have also been portrayed as standing in a strained relationship with recognition and identity struggles. Thus, where group-based egalitarian demands seek societal respect and accommodation of their particularities, libertarians may object that such an enterprise tends to disregard the liberties – the rights and freedoms – of others who are forced to show acceptance of the group or its values, even against their own convictions. An example of this conflict can be found in religious objections to endorsing or supporting same-sex marriage legislation.[169] In other instances, some of which are reflected in the case law discussed in the following chapters, claims about difference and inclusion seem to be framed in such a way that liberty (individual rights) and equality (the prohibition of discrimination) are an either/or issue.

Some of the debates that have taken place in the context of the United States Supreme Court concerning LGBT rights are illuminating in this regard. One line of argument posits that equality, rather than liberty, is the right normative framework for litigating LGBT cases. One of the reasons for this is that equality allows a more comprehensive analysis than that provided by a fragmentary liberty-based approach. As Gerken puts it, the liberty paradigm:

> seems to require members of the LGBT community to litigate pieces of their humanity, one by one. First they assert their right as human beings to have intimate relations with another person. Then they assert the right to marry or to have a family. To work. To serve their country. These are all fine things. But it seems to me they do not capture the essence of what is at stake in these debates, which is to recognize not the parts of personhood [...] but to acknowledge the entire person before us whether we share anything or not.[170]

A different standpoint is offered by Yoshino, who sees more benefits than drawbacks in the move from (group-based) equality analysis towards one that is liberty-based.[171] He contends that this move fosters a more universalistic and less essentialising form of protection. It diminishes the 'pluralism anxiety' of courts (i.e. the concern with endless groups claiming protection), while still embracing egalitarian considerations.[172]

The oppositional forces between equality and difference or between equality and liberty are not, however, restricted to what the 'external' dimension of a group demands from the state or mainstream society. The difficulty also arises

---

169 For an interesting view on this debate, see John Corvino, '"Bake Me a Cake": Three Paths for Balancing Liberty and Equality', Guest Post in *What's Wrong?*, 15 October 2015, <whatswrongcvsp.com/2015/10/15/guest-post-from-john-corvino-bake-me-a-cake-three-paths-for-balancing-liberty-and-equality/>.

170 Heather K. Gerken, 'Larry and Lawrence', 42 *Tulsa Law Review* (2006) 843, at 851 (adding that the liberty paradigm also casts the analysis of LGBT cases more abstract).

171 Kenji Yoshino, 'The New Equal Protection', 124 *Harvard Law Review* (2011) 747, at 776–791.

172 Ibid., at 792–794.

with respect to intra-group relations whereby one or some members complain against practices or norms validated by the group. This tension is typically exemplified by reference to women (or others in their name) who vindicate equality rights against the freedom of their religious community to maintain rules which restrict women's rights or participation.

4.4.3. From Form to Substance

To be sure, formal equality operationalised through anti-discrimination measures works well in some contexts. Today, it may serve to address cases of blatant under-inclusion, just as it did in the past. Nonetheless, the problem that unfolded with the traditional view of equality is that its formal assessment of treatment among individuals is not able to tackle the use of seemingly neutral and rational criteria which, however, entail great detrimental impact on some people.[173] Think, for instance, of a norm that subjects social benefits to the performance of a full-time job or a company's regulation that requires employees to work on Saturday. The first norm would probably put a higher burden on women, especially on those living in precarious socio-economic circumstances. The second norm in turn is likely to impact more negatively on Seventh-day Adventists. This is what we now know as indirect discrimination: the inability of minorities or disempowered populations to meet ostensibly neutral and 'objective' criteria based on majoritarian or dominant parameters. But perhaps more critically, formal equality does not grasp the inequality entrenched in wider patterns of exclusion and disadvantage that do not fit the mould of direct or indirect discrimination cases.[174] Consider, for example, the problem of institutional passivity in the face of violence against women or the pervasive exclusion of people with disabilities, who are impeded from accessing buildings and using services. This is to say that formal equality fails to tackle structural biases.[175]

The formal anti-discrimination ideal has also proved to be an obstacle to taking action in favour of those sectors of the population that remained, in practice, historically disadvantaged in most spheres of social life. This is because the suspicion of irrationality embodied in certain identity markers applies all across the board, casting as illegitimate even those distinctions that attempt to provide 'preferential' treatment for, or improve the situation of, those who are unable to take part in social interaction on an equal footing. 'Affirmative' or 'positive' action, as well as 'special measures' – terms used to describe those

---

173 Colm O'Cinneide, 'The Right to Equality: A Substantive Legal Norm or Vacuous Rhetoric?', 1 *UCL Human Rights Review* (2008) 80, at 86; Owen M. Fiss, 'Groups and the Equal Protection Clause', 5(2) *Philosophy & Public Affairs* (1976) 107, at 107–117.

174 Catharine A MacKinnon, 'Substantive Equality: A Perspective', 96 *Minnesota Law Review* (2011) 1, at 8–9.

175 On structural biases see also *infra* section 5.2.3.

attempts to further effective equality – to redress inequalities experienced by, say, women, racialised people, indigenous people or persons with disabilities, can easily be frustrated under a formal equality framework.

But why is it that formal equality falls short when it comes to addressing factual inequalities and claims for social differences to be taken on board? After all, it is widely admitted that Aristotelian equality not only mandates equal treatment for those similarly situated, but also requires different treatment for the dissimilar.[176] Is not this part of equality quite enough to respond to demands of accommodation and other justice challenges in diverse and unequal societies? At first glance, it might look like that. However, delivering equality for the equals and difference for the dissimilar is not very promising. Such a principle does not say anything about where to draw the line for comparison and which perspective defines who are viewed as alike and who as unalike.[177] Nor does it provide any substantive criteria for ascertaining those factors. Ignoring this question leads us to accept judgments on whether people are similar or different according to socially entrenched views about identities and roles. By doing so, we fail to see how the problem may stem from institutionalised and internalised norms that produce those views of difference and similarity in the first place.

All these considerations have prompted the reformulation of classic equality. A substantive or anti-subordination approach to equality has been advanced as a way to overcome the drawbacks of formal equality pointed out above. Unlike the latter, substantive equality abandons a blind-justice paradigm in order to see and recognise differences among individuals and social groups, so as to redress power imbalances and subordination.[178] This equality distances itself from the individual accent of its formal counterpart and becomes specifically responsive to group subordination.[179] It is, therefore, attentive to context and is reconciled with differential treatment as this may serve to remedy the disadvantaged position of oppressed groups. It might be argued that this is not something

176 Aristotle, *The Politics* (Penguin, 1962), at 195–196 (cited in Colm O'Cinneide, 'The Right to Equality: A Substantive Legal Norm or Vacuous Rhetoric?', 1 *UCL Human Rights Review* (2008) 80, at 85.

177 In this vein, Catharine A MacKinnon, 'Substantive Equality: A Perspective', 96 *Minnesota Law Review* (2011) 1, at 5.

178 Emmanuelle Bribosia and Isabelle Rovire, *Reasonable Accommodation Beyond Disability in Europe?* (European Commission, 2013), at 5; Frédérique Ast, 'European legal frameworks responding to diversity and the need for institutional change. Indirect Discrimination as a means of protecting pluralism: challenges and limits', in Council of Europe, *Institutional accommodation and the citizen: legal and political interaction in a pluralist society* (Council of Europe, 2009), at 88–89; Owen M. Fiss, 'Groups and the Equal Protection Clause', 5(2) *Philosophy & Public Affairs* (1976) 107.

179 Anne Smith and Eithne McLaughlin, 'Delivering Equality: Equality Mainstreaming and Constitutionalisation of Socio-Economic Rights', 61(2) *Northern Ireland Legal Quarterly* (2010) 93, at 97–98; Owen M. Fiss, 'Groups and the Equal Protection Clause', 5(2) *Philosophy & Public Affairs* (1976) 107.

unique about substantive equality, since even under a formal equality inquiry there is a group-based element. This is so by virtue of the prohibited grounds of discrimination, which refer to personal characteristics historically used to marginalise those who appear to share them. Nonetheless, it is argued that the novelty of the attention to group identity paid by substantive equality is that it allows the tracing of social disadvantage,[180] looking at groups asymmetrically and placing their disadvantage in a more social or collective framework.

Some clarifications need to be introduced into this analysis, however, as substantive equality, like all normative concepts, has more than one interpretation. Notably, the group aspect involved in substantive equality facilitates the reduction of this concept to the recognition of distinctive identities and the promotion of disadvantaged groups, thus treating different people differently.[181] However, substantive equality may mean more than that and more than opposition to indirect discrimination. Substantive equality is also interpreted as a call to undo the way social norms and structures define and entrench our differences by disadvantaging those who occupy certain social positions or 'identities'.[182] And under this prism, the key aspect is not group or cultural identity, but changing the roots of subordination or, in the words of Mackinnon, of hierarchy.[183] It is in this light that substantive equality allows us to acknowledge how societies have been premised on the vantage point of a few. As a consequence, those who do not share the dominant traits and experiences are prevented from interacting in society on an equal footing. This is why instead of focusing on celebrating or eliminating group differences and identities, substantive equality aims at

---

180 In a similar vein, see Avigail Eisenberg, 'Rights in the Age of Identity Politics', 50 *Osgoode Hall Law Journal* (2013) 609, at 616–619. (Without referring to substantive equality, the author explains how the identity-based approach often used in antidiscrimination analysis allows social exclusion and historical injustice toward minority groups to be traced. She argues that such approach nonetheless carries risks.)

181 The politics of identity and multiculturalism have been influential in placing the recognition of difference and group disadvantage at the heart of substantive equality. See e.g. Nicholas Bamforth *et al.*, *Discrimination Law: Theory and Context. Text and Materials* (Sweet and Maxwell, 2008), at 208; Kristin Henrard, Equal Rights versus Special Rights?: Minority Protection and the Prohibition of Discrimination, Report prepared for the European Commission (2007), at 13 (discussing substantive equality mainly in terms of differential treatment).

182 See *inter alia*, Martha Albertson Fineman, 'Equality and Difference – The Restrained State', 66 *Alabama Law Review* (2015) 609, at 621; Marius Pieterse, 'Finding for the Applicant? Individual Equality Plaintiffs and Group-based Disadvantage', 24 *South African Journal of Human Rights* (2008) 397, at 413; Sandra Fredman, 'Substantive equality revisited', 14(3) *International Journal of Constitutional Law* (2016) 712, at 719–720 and 733–734.

183 Catherine A. MacKinnon, 'Substantive Equality: A Perspective', 96 *Minnesota Law Review* (2011) 1, at 10–15; Martha Albertson Fineman, 'Equality and Difference – The Restrained State', 66 *Alabama Law Review* (2015) 609, at 621. (Exemplifying this point by reference to the disadvantage associated with care work. She argues that it is the social role and societal structures that define them, not the sex of the caretaker, that bring disadvantage, so if men become caretakers they also suffer economically and professionally.)

removing the hierarchies and disadvantages constructed around them.[184] Herein resides the greatest potential of substantive equality to supplement the use of formal equality.

In any case, it is not only the principle of equality that has undergone transformation. It should be observed that the idea of neutrality is being refashioned too. Pierik and Van Der Burg, for example, argue that neutrality does not need to be understood solely in its narrow liberal conception of hands-off or as what they call 'exclusive neutrality'. For it may be conceived also as 'inclusive neutrality'.[185] So reconstructed, neutrality takes account of and includes different cultures, religions and worldviews in the public sphere and in its debates. Governments not only allow people to organise around and express their particular identities. They may even support and accommodate such expressions. What is more, while in some contexts this neutrality primarily needs to take issue with the representation of minority groups, in other contexts it may need to go further and even take structural inequalities on board.[186]

Similarly, the language of toleration has been replaced by that of accommodation, which is generally seen as one type of differential treatment backed by substantive equality.[187] Moreover, so long as substantive equality is viewed as a vehicle for challenging and changing the norms underlying structures of inequality, accommodation is gradually ceding space to a language of 'transformation'.[188] For some, this would reflect a sort of 'universal' turn in equality.[189]

---

184 In this vein, Sandra Fredman, 'Redistribution and Recognition: Reconciling Inequalities', 23(2) *South African Journal of Human Rights* (2007) 214, at 216.

185 Roland Pierik and Wibren Van der Burg, 'What Is Neutrality?', 27 *Ratio Juris* (2014) 496, at 498–499.

186 Ibid., at 500–502.

187 Kristin Henrard, 'Fundamental Rights and Minorities', in Steven Vertovec (ed.), *Routledge International Handbook of Diversity Studies* (Routledge, 2015), at 225. As later discussed in this chapter, in international human rights law duties of accommodation have been explicitly endorsed only in the field of disability rights.

188 And substantive equality is viewed as encompassing a transformative equality that 'transforms' the underlying norms and structures of inequality. See Simone Cusack and Lisa Pusey, 'CEDAW and the Rights to Non-Discrimination and Equality', 14 *Melbourne Journal of International Law* (2013) 1, at 11 (explaining that the CEDAW Committee has tended to view transformative equality as part of substantive equality); Sandra Fredman, 'Beyond the Dichotomy of Formal and Substantive Equality: Towards a New Definition of Equal Rights', in Ineke Boerefijn *et al.* (eds.), *Temporary Special Measures: Accelerating De Facto Equality of Women under Article 4(1) UN Convention on the Elimination of All Forms of Discrimination Against Women* (Intersentia, 2003), at 115.

189 Sandra Fredman, 'Disability Equality: A Challenge to the Existing Anti-Discrimination Paradigm?', in Anna Lawson and Caroline Gooding (eds.), *Disability Rights in Europe. From Theory to Practice, Essays in European Law* (Hart Publishing, 2005), at 206–207. For a critique of the 'universal turn' in the context of sexual harassment and anti-bullying regulations in the workplace in the US, see Jessica A. Clarke, 'Beyond Equality? Against the Universal Turn in Workplace Protections', 86 *Indiana Law Journal* (2011) 1219.

4.4.4. *Equality Divided: From Substance to Socio-Economic Equality?*

Thus far, the discussion of distinct paradigms of equality has underlined the question of *who* is the subject of an equality inquiry? It was stated that while formal approaches to equality put the accent on individual harms and wrongs, substantive visions of equality focus on disadvantaged groups or minorities. But the issue of the equality/difference of *what* also merits some consideration, if only to find that normative thinking is divided on this as well.

One clear area of concern for achieving equality is ensuring dignity and respect. To do so, measures promoting equality seek to combat prejudice as well as stereotypes that diminish and insult people, especially those belonging to historically disadvantaged groups. Along these lines, we can discern the recognition side of equality. Nonetheless, equality measures are also concerned with questions of socio-economic justice. That is their redistribution side. The link between equality and socio-economic justice traces back to the resource-distribution approach taken by influential egalitarians such as Dworkin and Rawls.[190] Mindful of the arbitrariness of birth and the unfair consequences derived from an inherited social class, they draw attention to what individuals deserve and which inequalities are the result of injustice and misfortune.

The accent on the individual associated with resource equality and the attention devoted to groups by the ideal of equal recognition/respect suggest a sort of correspondence between substantive equality and identity or recognition politics, on the one hand, and between formal equality and redistributive accounts of justice, on the other.[191] However, some nuances are required. It was explained above that substantive equality is not just about granting different treatment to different groups. To that extent, there is no straightforward equivalence between substantive equality and identity politics. Likewise, socio-economic concerns are not exclusive of formal equality. In fact, the nexus between equality and socio-economic justice strengthens the closer we get to substantive equality, as this presupposes an active state and a commitment to redressing group disparities.[192] This contrasts with the anti-discrimination paradigm, which is charged with rendering socio-economic inequalities invisible.[193] Thus, according to Fredman,

---

190 Ronald Dworkin, 'What is equality? Part 1: Equality of welfare', 10(3) *Philosophy & Public Affairs* (1981) 185; John Rawls, *A Theory of Justice* (Harvard University Press, 1971).

191 In this vein, Davina Cooper, *Challenging Diversity. Rethinking Equality and the Value of Difference* (Cambridge University Press, 2004), at 74 ('while resource equality largely focuses on the individual, the paramount concern of much writing on equal recognition is the group or collectivity.').

192 Gwen Brodsky and Shelagh Day, 'Beyond the Social and Economic Rights Debate: Substantive Equality Speaks to Poverty', 14 *Canadian Journal of Women and the Law* (2002) 184, at 205–206.

193 Mark Bell, 'Promoting Equality Through Social Inclusion: Case Studies from the European Social Charter', in Tonia Novitz and David Mangan (eds.), *The Role of Labour Standards in Sustainable Development: Theory in Practice* (British Academy and Oxford University Press, 2011), at 79–80, <hdl.handle.net/2381/10109>.

substantive equality 'moves the anti-discrimination agenda into areas often inhabited by anti-poverty, welfare, or social inclusion'.[194] And the link goes beyond theoretical reflection. Material equality has been an important *leitmotiv* in egalitarian struggles, such as those undertaken by Afro-descendant and gay liberation movements.[195] Porter, for instance, explains how more than 20 years ago equality seekers in Canada conceived the substantive equality provision in the Constitution as encompassing socio-economic rights.[196]

And yet, the prevailing normative approaches see non-discrimination as an issue divorced from socio-economic equality. Equality is fragmented between identity-based and socio-economic equality.[197] Anti-discrimination measures are confined to combating expressions of prejudice or disrespect on the basis of group attributes, while usually remaining alien to socio-economic disadvantage. Socio-economic equality issues, on the other hand, are seen as a matter of social policy and needs.[198] In this account, non-discrimination has little to say about the fact that certain segments of the population are socio-economically disadvantaged or that these are disproportionally deprived of their rights. Furthermore, even stereotypes related to socio-economic conditions and measures that have a disparate impact on socio-economically disadvantaged people are rarely scrutinised under the prohibition of discrimination.[199] This is

---

194 Sandra Fredman, 'Providing Equality: Substantive Equality and the Positive Duty to Provide', 21(2) *South African Journal on Human Rights* (2005) 163, at 166. See also, Sandra Fredman, 'The Potential and Limits of an Equal Rights Paradigm in Addressing Poverty', 3 *Stellenbosch Law Review* (2011) 566, at 577.

195 See, *inter alia*, Carol Anderson, *Eyes Off the Prize: the UN and the African American Struggle for Human Rights* (Cambridge University Press, 2003), at 5, 8 and 276; Natalie Oswin, 'Producing Homonormativity in Neoliberal South Africa: Recognition, Redistribution, and the Equality Project', 32(3) *Signs* (2007) 649, at 662–665.

196 Bruce Porter, 'Expectations of Equality', 33(2) *Supreme Court Law Review* (2006) 23, at 27.

197 As Anne Phillips observes: 'The work on equality has, however, bifurcated in a startling way, with most of the writing on economic equality focusing on the principles that should regulate the distribution of goods between individuals, and most of the writing on social equality addressing patterns of oppression that regulate the relationship between marginal and dominant groups.' What is more, they seem not to talk very often to each other. See Anne Phillips, 'Equality, Pluralism, Universality: Current Concerns in Normative Theory', 2(2) *British Journal of Politics & International Relations* (2000) 237, at 240 and 246. Similarly, Equal Rights Trust seeks 'to overcome the fragmentation which has occurred between equality and human rights, and between identity-based equality and socio-economic equality. Tolerance and Non-discrimination requires the adoption of a unified approach to equality, focused on the complex and complementary relationship between different types of discrimination and inequality.' See The Equal Rights Trust, *Our Purpose*, The Equal Rights Trust, <www.equalrightstrust.org/content/our-purpose> and The Equal Rights Trust, 'Statement from the Equal Rights Trust: Tolerance and Non-discrimination', a written submission to the OSCE Review Conference on Tolerance and Non-discrimination, 11 October 2010.

198 Sandra Fredman, 'Redistribution and Recognition: Reconciling Inequalities', 23 *South African Journal on Human Rights* (2007) 214, at 217.

199 In the US Constitutional Context, see Julia A. Nice, 'No Scrutiny Whatsoever: Deconstitutionalization of Poverty Law, Dual Rules of Law, and Dialogic Default', 35(3)

further examined in Chapters 4 and 5. In any event, the fragmentation is unfortunate in the face of societies marked by multiple and intersecting inequalities.

Of course, the above are not the only divides and compartments prevailing in human rights law. Some, such as those between civil/political and socio-economic rights, as well as the split of rights holders' identities and agency, were mentioned earlier and will be further problematised below. But there are other important separations worth mentioning. One is the well-known public/private dichotomy, a longstanding target of feminist critiques. In spite of the progress made on women's rights, the divide persists in the practice of human rights courts.[200] Another outstanding split is that separating individual rights from collective or group rights, which emerges from the idea that human rights are geared towards individuals only. As some authors have argued, while these compartmentalisations may be instrumental for certain (powerful) agendas, looking at the lived experiences of people exposes their artificial and untenable character.[201]

Now, admitting the value of group-based approaches to violations, as a substantive notion of equality reveals, it is also necessary to recapitulate why too much of a focus on groups and identities can be problematic. As already stated, this is one notable driver of fragmentation in human rights. The following sections deal with this question, as well as with the difficulties posed by other forms of compartmentalised thinking.

4.5. A CAUTIOUS APPROACH TO GROUP IDENTITY AND OTHER COMPARTMENTS IN HUMAN RIGHTS LAW

It was pointed out above that human rights law has evolved with a remarkable group-identity orientation. This should not be conflated with a proliferation of

---

Fordham Urban Law Journal (2008) 629, at 629; Mario L. Barnes and Erwin Chemerinsky, 'The Disparate Treatment of Race and Class in Constitutional Jurisprudence,' 72(4) *Law and Contemporary Problems* (2009) 109, at 119 and ff. For a discussion of the need to include socio-economic disadvantage as a ground of discrimination to address the stigmatising aspects of poverty (mainly in the context of domestic jurisdictions), see Sandra Fredman, 'The Potential and Limits of an Equal Rights Paradigm in Addressing Poverty', 3 *Stellenbosch Law Review* (2011) 566, at 581–584.

200 For example, the freedom of religion and conscience appears fractured along the lines of private and public exercise of the right. See e.g. Peter G. Danchin, 'Islam in the Secular Nomos of the European Court of Human Rights', 32(4) *Michigan Journal of International Law* (2011) 663, at 707–712.

201 Dana Collins *et al.*, 'New Directions in Feminism and Human Rights. An Introduction', 12 *International Feminist Journal of Politics* (2010) 298, at 309 (discussing the collective rights v. individual rights divide).

collective rights or rights accorded to collective right holders.[202] To be clear, the individual rights framework remains the dominant paradigm within human rights law. But while protection continues to be afforded mainly to individuals, great importance is attached to individual membership in a collectivity affirming a certain identity or experiencing exclusion and cultural devaluation. Not only do specialised human rights instruments attest to this, but also the work of (quasi)judicial human rights organs. Human rights courts are, for instance, increasingly vocal in protecting people against violations affecting core aspects of their identity. Likewise, concepts such as 'cultural identity' and 'vulnerable group' have gained leverage,[203] particularly when they serve to justify special rights or differentiated treatments, such as exemptions or additional support not available to the majority. Against this backdrop, it is convenient to recall the problems this group identity lens may bring along. The arguments of political theory and legal practice reviewed in the previous sections suggest the following difficulties.

Firstly, too much of an emphasis on group identity or culture may lead to a restrictive framing of the claims and interests at stake. This follows from the unidimensional analysis that such an approach promotes, which easily obscures overlapping identities and rights as well as issues of socio-economic disadvantage. Secondly, the identity group 'compartment' invites judges and legislators to define the identity or the group in question. The complexity of such an enterprise seems obvious when we think of how to answer the question of what is Islam or indigeneity? Or who is a Roma or a Rastafari? Equally challenging is, however, to define groups and identities that do not appear to be typically 'cultural' – a fact that only reinforces the fluidity and socially constructed character of all identity markers. Thus, if we take the cases of disability and gender or sex, we will find that courts and legislative bodies encounter a great deal of definitional trouble. Are fat people disabled? Are people with fertility problems disabled? Is womanhood determined by having female genitals or by feeling oneself to be a woman? As can be expected, from the moment courts answer those questions, essentialism enters the stage. The group or identity in question is defined by reference to certain attributes that are imagined to constitute the whole. As a result, judges may reify people and practices as well as take a stance on the values and merits of a given culture or identity. So, thirdly, going down this road risks relegating insiders' voices while taking courts far away from the ideal of neutrality they normally seek to uphold. Fourthly, the exercise of identity demarcation carries a double-edged sword for litigants. Basically, they are left with the choice of either

202 Different accounts of what group rights are can be seen in Neus Torbisco Casals, *Group Rights as Human Rights* (Springer, 2006).

203 On the concept of vulnerability before human rights courts, see Lourdes Peroni and Alexandra Timmer, 'Vulnerable Groups: The Promise of an Emerging Concept in European Human Rights Convention Law', 11(4) *International Journal of Constitutional Law* (2013) 1056;

showing that they belong to the group, share its identity and thus conform to the norm according to which the identity or group is defined, or risking being left unprotected.[204] Finally, under an identity group analysis, it is disquieting that judges are invited to identify and situate social groups prior to the relations and institutions producing inequality. This conceals how social categorisations and groups may actually be the result of those relations. As argued by Cooper, such an approach can 'produce excessively fragmented accounts which neglect more systematic connections' to understanding relations of oppression and privilege.[205]

While this book is particularly interested in the identity group framework – because of its prominence in claims of difference and inclusion – it is clear that this is not the only form of normative disaggregation deserving attention. It has been argued that strategies for the adjudication of socio-economic rights that focus on abstract categories such as minimum core and types of state obligations are both counter-productive and unhelpful.[206] Counter-productive because a focus on those legal categories tends to divorce the rights claims from their specific circumstances, giving judges the impression that they have to decide on universal entitlements or abstract questions, which of course they are reluctant to do. This is related to the challenges of limits and restraint highlighted in the general introduction. When courts perceive that they are being asked to rule on general duties of socio-economic assistance or on socio-economic entitlements for everyone, they will likely conduct a very lenient review of the actual claims at hand. At the same time, a categorical thinking revolving around types of obligations is not helpful. The reason is that in practice most

---

Romina I. Sijniensky, 'From the Non-Discrimination Clause to the Concept of Vulnerability in International Human Rights Law. Advancing the Needs for Special Protection of Certain Groups and Individuals', in Yves Haeck *et al.* (eds.), *The Realisation of Human Rights: When Theory Meets Practice. Studies in Honour of Leo Zwaak* (Intersentia, 2013). On the legal mobilisation of culture and cultural identity, see e.g. Marco Odello, 'Indigenous peoples' rights and cultural identity in the Inter-American context', 16(1) *The International Journal of Human Rights* (2012) 25–50; Juliet Hooker, 'Indigenous Inclusion/Black Exclusion: Race, Ethnicity and Multicultural Citizenship in Latin America', 37 *Journal of Latin American Studies* (2005) 285–310; Federico Lenzerini, *The Culturalization of Human Rights Law* (Oxford University Press, 2014), at 116–208; Yvonne M. Donders, *Human Rights: Eye for Cultural Diversity* (Amsterdam University Press, 2012). Inaugural Lecture delivered upon the appointment to the chair of Professor of International Human Rights and Cultural Diversity at the University of Amsterdam on 29 June 2012, at 18–25.

204 Marius Pieterse, 'Finding for the Applicant? Individual Equality Plaintiffs and Group-Based Disadvantage', 24 *South African Journal on Human Rights* (2008) 397, at 413–414; Sandra Fredman, 'Facing the Future: Substantive Equality under the Spotlight', *Oxford University Legal Studies Research Series Paper No. 57/2010* (2010), at 5.

205 Davina Cooper, *Challenging Diversity. Rethinking Equality and the Value of Difference* (Cambridge University Press, 2004), at 50.

206 See *supra* section 4.3, discussing the work of Porter.

social rights claims bring together and combine different categories of state obligations.[207] In the context of the ECtHR, Gerards also contends that the Court's compartmentalised view in cases involving budgetary justifications is problematic. In the first place, a focus on types of right and lines of case law leads to different standards of protection and different outcomes to substantially similar types of claims, without a principled justification. In the second place, and even if such analysis seems understandable from the perspective of the structure of the Convention, doing so runs against the effective and equal protection of all Convention rights. It undermines the interdependence and indivisibility of human rights.

While legal categorisation and fragmentation may be inevitable, finding ways to lessen their perils is not straightforward. To that end, looking at more integrated frameworks of normative analysis could reveal helpful insights.

5. IN SEARCH OF FURTHER INTEGRATION

In the previous sections it was highlighted how our increasingly plural and unequal societies generate multiple and cross-cutting forms of exclusion that operate through institutionalised norms that distinguish between people. In this vein, Fraser observes that the contemporary status order has become more complex and so has its modes of subordination.[208] The boundaries between cultures are no longer clear and societies encompass a range of sub-cultures with divergent values. People are not locked into one single status; rather, they occupy and move across multiple axes of subordination and privilege, which are in turn not only part of the status order of cultural values, but also of the economic realm.[209] The question then arises as to which normative approaches are useful to dealing with all this complexity.

5.1. A FEW THEORETICAL AND NORMATIVE PROPOSALS

Fraser's normative response is guided by a single moral principle that integrates both dimensions of justice – redistribution and recognition. Such a principle, namely 'parity of participation', requires that social arrangements allow all

207 Bruce Porter, 'The Crises of ESC Rights and Strategies for Addressing It', in John Squires *et al.* (eds.), *The Road to a Remedy: Current Issues in the Litigation of Economic, Social and Cultural Rights* (UNSW Press, 2005), at 52 and 57.

208 Nancy Fraser, 'Social Justice in the Age of Identity Politics: Redistribution, Recognition, and Participation', in Nancy Fraser and Axel Honneth, *Redistribution or Recognition? A Political-Philosophical Exchange* (Verso, 2003), at 55–57.

209 Ibid., at 57–58.

(adult) members of society to interact with one another as peers.[210] Parity of participation is therefore a substantive standard for evaluating claims of both redistribution and recognition. But there is more: the standard also has a procedural character. It provides a parameter for deliberating and deciding on both kinds of claims. When it comes to status – value pattern – subordination, for instance, parity of participation determines the conditions under which decisions will be made on whether and how people are to be recognised. The conditions are those of a democratic public dialogue that permits the full, free intervention of all implicated parties.[211]

Several scholars, including some aligned with multiculturalism, have similarly underlined the need for more integrated frames to help grasp, for example, the complementarity between the cultural and economic, or between recognition and redistribution.[212] These are, in fact, increasingly perceived as entangled dimensions of justice, or more precisely, of equality. According to de Sousa Santos, 'we have the right to be equal whenever difference diminishes us; we have the right to be different whenever equality decharacterizes us'.[213] In a similar vein, but from another doctrinal tradition, Fredman argues that substantive equality encompasses recognition, redistribution, and more. She advocates for a multidimensional notion of substantive equality, in which she integrates four distinct aims: recognition, redistribution, transformation and participation.[214] The recognition strand of equality tackles stigma, stereotyping, humiliation and violence. The redistribution aspect seeks to remedy social and material disadvantage. The third component aims at transforming the norms underlying structures and institutions instead of requesting conformity with them. Finally, participation requires hearing and responding to the voices of those experiencing inequality. Importantly, these four dimensions are viewed in constant interaction and therefore all of them should be considered when evaluating laws and policies.[215]

---

210 Ibid., at 36.

211 Ibid., at 43–44.

212 See *inter alia*, Will Kymlicka, 'The Rise and Fall of Multiculturalism? New Debates on Inclusion and Accommodation in Diverse Societies', 199 *International Social Science Journal* (2010) 97, at 102 (arguing that multiculturalism for indigenous peoples, national minorities and immigrant groups combine cultural recognition, economic redistribution and political participation); Bikhu Parekh, 'Redistribution or recognition: a misguided debate', in Stephen May *et al.* (eds.), *Ethnicity, Nationalism and Minority Rights* (Cambridge University Press, 2004), at 209–210.

213 Boaventura De Sousa Santos, 'Nuestra America: Reinventing a Subaltern Paradigm of Recognition and Redistribution', 18 *Theory, Culture & Society* (2001) 185, at 193.

214 Sandra Fredman, *Antidiscrimination Law* (Oxford University Press, 2011), at 25–33.

215 Sandra Fredman and Beth Goldblatt, 'Gender Equality and Human Rights', 4 *Women Discussion Paper Series* (2014), at 7.

From a constitutional law perspective, Baer also proposes a more holistic understanding of how fundamental rights work. Her proposal rests on a triangular relationship between equality, liberty and dignity.[216] Instead of colliding or standing in isolation, as they are usually presented and applied to legal disputes, these three rights should be seen as interdependent and as enriching each other.[217] In so doing, they provide a framework that is more attentive to context and thus, more apt for dealing with complex cases, that is, the kind of case that involves multidimensional inequalities. These are cases that, in other words, cannot be understood as being about sex, ethnicity or disability alone, for they are 'shaped by interdependent inequalities, in specific contexts and with specific effects'.[218] In the context of economic, social and cultural rights advocacy, Porter similarly promotes 'a holistic, rather than a disaggregating approach to rights'.[219] By this, he does not simply mean the integration of civil/political rights with socio-economic rights. Rather, he means looking at obligations, standards of review and other legal categories 'from the standpoint of particular claimants in particular circumstances and through a purposive approach to the right that is to be protected'.[220] Such an approach is necessarily sensitive to context and to the interdependence of rights.[221]

Pragmatic reasoning also favours a more integrated view of cases involving claims about difference and social inclusion. Notably, adopting a compartmentalised approach does not shed light on the real difficulties in responding to a given claim. For instance, the controversies regarding LGBTI claims to be entitled to benefit from social protection, inheritance rights or health services are hardly separable from the challenge they pose to dominant value systems concerning the family and gender and sexual binaries. Similarly, it is quite difficult to explain the resistance encountered by claims about cultural identity and ways of life if we ignore the fact that they are made in the context of challenging spatial planning policies, claiming access to land, gaining employment or having access to other resources. Arguably, many responses to those claims would not be the same if at stake were something different or of a different nature.[222]

---

216 Susanne Baer, 'Dignity, liberty, equality: A fundamental rights triangle of constitutionalism', 59(4) *The University of Toronto Law Journal* (2009) 418.

217 Ibid., at 418–423. The author applies her argument to a number of cases decided by courts to demonstrate convincingly the potential of her triangular view of equality, liberty and dignity.

218 Ibid., at 425.

219 Bruce Porter, 'The Crises of ESC Rights and Strategies for Addressing It', in John Squires *et al.* (eds.), *The Road to a Remedy: Current Issues in the Litigation of Economic, Social and Cultural Rights* (UNSW Press, 2005), at 56.

220 Idem.

221 Idem.

222 In a similar vein, see Martha Minow, *Making All the Difference. Inclusion, Exclusion and American Law* (Cornell University Press, 1990), at 355–356 (discussing the importance of debating what is the purpose of litigation for the Mashpee people, rather than reducing the judicial inquiry to the question are the Mashpee a federal tribe?).

5.2. INTEGRATED FRAMEWORKS IN HUMAN RIGHTS LAW

The search for more integrated frameworks that may cope with the complexity exposed above also has resonance in human rights law. There are three themes that express the aspiration to foster integration and reduce fragmentation/compartmentalisation within human rights law. The first is the concept of intersectionality, which maps onto the problems of essentialism and the prioritisation of some identities over others. The second is the notion of indivisibility, which counterbalances the tendency to displace socio-economic issues and connects identity-based violations with those that are redistribution-driven. The third is the social model of disability, which is the most serious effort by human rights law to unveil the way social institutions and relations embed (body-ability) differences while dealing with them in a comprehensive manner. Drawing on these three integrated models, a rights holder-centred and integrated approach to human rights law is suggested towards the end.

5.2.1. *Integration as Intersectionality*

The notion of intersectionality arose in response to the problems of identity politics, particularly essentialism and its erasure of 'intragroup differences'.[223] Pushed from within critical race theory and feminist studies, intersectionality first came to contest the monolithic representation of women. It was argued that the category of women actually spoke for a subset of them: white middle-class women. Meanwhile, black women were side-lined and neither the category of race nor the category of gender could fully grasp their experiences.[224] According to Crenshaw, 'sex and race discrimination have come to be defined in terms of the experiences of those who are privileged *but for* their racial or sexual characteristics'.[225] This focus marginalised those who were disadvantaged on multiple grounds. In response, intersectionality challenged the idea that discrimination had to do with discrete forms of subordination and that identity was a matter of 'either/or'.[226] In law, this claim mainly pointed

---

223 Jennifer C. Nash, 'Re-thinking intersectionality', 89 *Feminist Review* (2008) 1, at 2–3.

224 Kimberle Crenshaw; 'Demarginalizing the Intersection of Race and Sex: A Black Feminist Critique of Antidiscrimination Doctrine, Feminist Theory and Antiracist Politics', 140 *University of Chicago Legal Forum* (1989) 139; Kimberle Crenshaw; 'Mapping the Margins: Intersectionality, Identity Politics and Violence Against Women of Color', 43(6) *Stanford Law Review* (1991) 1241, at 1241–1245.

225 Kimberle Crenshaw, 'Demarginalizing the Intersection of Race and Sex: A Black Feminist Critique of Antidiscrimination Doctrine, Feminist Theory and Antiracist Politics', 140 *University of Chicago Legal Forum* (1989) 139, at 151.

226 Kimberle Crenshaw; 'Mapping the Margins: Intersectionality, Identity Politics and Violence Against Women of Color', 43(6) *Stanford Law Review* (1991) 1241, at 1242.

to the insufficiencies of anti-discrimination frameworks, which relied on a single-axis scheme of protection. It was then suggested that experiences at the intersections be recognised, acknowledging the multidimensionality of the individual and taking account of the fluidity and contingency of our identities. This implied, in other words, overcoming 'the fragmenting of identity by legal analysis'.[227]

Soon this analysis extended beyond the markers of race and gender to encompass other identity locations, such as those of disability, sexuality and so forth.[228] In this way, intersectionality has come to be interwoven with identity. In its most extended usage, it is a theory and methodology that focuses on the particular disadvantages produced by the interaction of multiple identities. The benefits of such approach are obvious. Not in vain is intersectionality considered to be one of the most crucial contributions made by feminist theory.[229] And yet, conceiving of intersectionality purely in terms of overlapping identity might still fall short of dealing with questions of difference and social exclusion. Joanne Conaghan, for example, argues that intersectionality 'tells us little about the wider context in which such experiences are produced, mediated and expressed'.[230] Put differently, so long as intersectionality is bound up with questions of identity formation, it tends to neglect the social relations and structures from which identity divisions and intersections derive. Conaghan explains:

> Issues of identity are but an aspect, not a substitute for, fuller investigation into the operation of gender and race within inequality regimes within which identities are formed, navigated and resisted. In addition, the concept of identity is less suited to certain kinds of analysis. Take, for example, the uneasy status of class in intersectionality discourse.[231]

Moreover, as a matter of identity, intersectionality has also been branded as 'separatist' or 'fragmentary'. Intersectionality allegedly 'breaks groups into

---

227 Trina Grillo, 'Anti-Essentialism and Intersectionality: Tools to Dismantle the Master's House', 10 *Berkeley Women's Law Journal* (1995) 16, at 17.

228 See, *inter alia*, Sirma Bilge Sirma, 'Developing Intersectional Solidarities: A Plea for Queer Intersectionality', in Malinda Smith and Fatima Jafer (eds.), *Beyond the Queer Alphabet: Conversations on Gender, Sexuality and Intersectionality* (Canadian Federation for the Humanities and Social Science, 2012), <the-menace.s3.amazonaws.com/uploads/Beyond_the_Queer_Alphabet_20March2012-F.pdf>; Sumi Cho, 'Post-Intersectionality. The Curious Reception of Intersectionality in Legal Scholarship', 10(2) *Du Bois Review* (2013) 385, at 391.

229 Leslie McCall, 'The Complexity of Intersectionality', 30(3) *Signs* (2005) 1771, at 1771.

230 Joanne Conaghan, 'Intersectionality and the Feminist Project in Law', in Emily Grabham *et al.* (eds.), *Law, Power and the Politics of Subjectivity. Intersectionality and Beyond* (Routledge Cavendish, 2008), at 29.

231 Idem.

ever smaller sub-groups'.[232] So understood, intersectionality would produce the opposite effect to integration.[233]

While the criticism of identity politics is warranted, equating intersectionality with identity politics seems misplaced. Since its very origins, intersectionality has been conceived as encompassing more than composite identities. A crucial part of intersectionality concerns social structure.[234] When Crenshaw elaborated what she termed 'structural intersectionality', she analysed the need to account for multiple grounds of identity in view of their imbrication with 'systems' of domination. In that framework, Crenshaw explained, for example, how shelters serving women who suffered from domestic violence and immigration regulations were unresponsive to poor immigrant women, especially black women, as these institutions overlooked disadvantages compounded by, for example, poverty, child-care responsibilities, employment and housing practices, lack of access to resources, and cultural barriers.[235] Later, McCall explicitly engaged with an intersectional approach, though from a non-legal perspective, to explore questions of multiple social categories and structural inequality.[236] And more recently, Smith has claimed that 'intersectionality is a tool which can be used for precisely the examination of the root causes of inequality [...] [and that] the language of identity is just the way that the inquiry into the power structures operating beneath discrimination is articulated'.[237]

---

232 Patricia Hill Collins and Sirma Bilge, *Intersectionality* (Polity Press, 2016), at 127 (referring to Ehrenreich who criticised intersectionality on the basis of the 'infinite regress problem'. See Nancy Ehrenreich, 'Subordination and Symbiosis: Mechanisms of Mutual Support Between Subordination Systems', 71(2) *UMKC Law Review* (2002) 251.

233 For further criticism of intersectionality, see Sumi Cho, 'Post-Intersectionality. The Curious Reception of Intersectionality in Legal Scholarship', 10(2) *Du Bois Review* (2013) 385, at 389–393. Critiques other than those indicated above and which are not examined in this book include: the alleged categorical hegemony of race and gender and the charge of not being coalitional enough.

234 See e.g. Patricia Hill Collins and Sirma Bilge, *Intersectionality* (Polity, 2016), at 15. (Arguing that intersectionality as an analytical tool can foster a better understanding of global inequality. 'Rather than seeing the wealth gap as unconnected to categories such as race, gender, age and citizenship, differences in wealth reflect structures intersecting power relations.')

235 Kimberle Crenshaw, 'Mapping the Margins: Intersectionality, Identity Politics, and Violence Against Women of Color', 43(6) *Stanford Law Review* (1991) 1241, at 1245–1251. See also her analysis of sexual violence against black women in Kimberle Crenshaw, 'Demarginalizing the Intersection of Race and Sex: A Black Feminist Critique of Antidiscrimination Doctrine, Feminist Theory, and Antiracist Politics', 140 *University of Chicago Legal Forum* (1989) 139, at 158–159.

236 Leslie McCall, 'The Complexity of Intersectionality', 30(3) *Signs* (2005) 1771, at 1784–1792. Her methodology starts from the premise (at 1785) that 'there are relationships of inequality among already constituted social groups, as imperfect and ever changing as they are, and takes those relationships as the center of the analysis'.

237 Ben Smith, 'Intersectional Discrimination and Substantive Equality: A Comparative and Theoretical Perspective', 16 *The Equal Rights Review* (2016) 73, at 77.

Intersectionality has been introduced gradually into international law and human rights bodies are showing a growing interest in it.[238] As in domestic jurisdictions, anti-discrimination and equality treaty provisions are the main vehicles for operationalising it. Terms such as 'multiple discrimination' or 'intersectional discrimination' are thus used to capture those situations in which different grounds of discrimination operate simultaneously and intermingle. Unlike the additive approach of 'multiple discrimination',[239] intersectionality helps identify the unique types of violation occurring at the interface of an array of systems of inequality.[240] It illuminates the way hierarchies and power structures create the experiences associated with the grounds of discrimination.[241] In doing so, intersectionality avoids not just the reification of such categories along a single axis, but also their treatment as compartments dislodged from the social forces that define them.[242] Given the incremental purchase of intersectionality within human rights law and its aptitude for ensuring that experiences of oppression and privilege are not compartmentalised, it is a concept worth

238 See e.g. Patricia Hill Collins and Sirma Bilge, *Intersectionality* (Polity, 2016), at 92 (referring to the 2001 World Conference against Racism in Durban). Further, the Convention on the Rights of Persons with Disabilities expressly recognises the intersectional discrimination experienced by these persons, including on grounds such as 'social origin', 'property' and 'other status'. Preamble (p) Convention on the Rights of Persons with Disabilities. See also, CESCR, General Comment No. 20: Non-discrimination in economic, social and cultural rights (art. 2, para. 2, of the International Covenant on Economic, Social and Cultural Rights), E/C.12/GC/20, 2 July 2009, paras. 17 and 27; CEDAW Committee, General Recommendation No. 28 on the Core Obligations of States Parties under Article 2 of Convention on the Elimination of All Forms of Discrimination against Women, CEDAW/C/GC/28, 16 December 2010, para. 18; CERD, General Recommendation No. 32: The meaning and scope of special measures in the International Convention on the Elimination of All Forms Racial Discrimination, CERD/C/GC/32, 24 September 2009, at para. 7. See also, UN Human Rights Council; Complementary International Standards: Compilation of Conclusions and Recommendations of the Study by the Five Experts on the Content and Scope of Substantive Gaps in the Existing International Instruments to Combat Racism Racial Discrimination, Xenophobia and Related Intolerance, A/HRC/AC.1/1/ CRP.4, 18 February 2008; and UN Human Rights Council; Complementary International Standards: Compilation of Conclusions and Recommendations of the Study by the Five Experts on the Content and Scope of Substantive Gaps in the Existing International Instruments to Combat Racism Racial Discrimination, Xenophobia and Related Intolerance, A/HRC/4/WG.3/6, 27 August 2007, paras. 48–49, 111 (underlining the need for the CERD Committee to analyse the issue of multiple discrimination, including that of race and religion).

239 Nicholas Bamforth *et al.*, *Discrimination Law: Theory and Context. Text and Materials* (Sweet and Maxwell, 2008), at 541.

240 Johanna E. Bond, 'International Intersectionality: A Theoretical and Pragmatic Exploration of Women's International Human Rights Violations', 52 *Emory Law Journal* (2003) 71, at 157–158.

241 Catharine Mackinnon, 'Intersectionality as a Method: A Note', 38(4) *Signs* (2013) 2019, at 2023–2024; Ben Smith, 'Intersectional Discrimination and Substantive Equality: A Comparative and Theoretical Perspective', 16 *The Equal Rights Review* (2016) 73, at 77; Martha Albertson Fineman, 'The Vulnerable Subject: Anchoring Equality in the Human Condition', 20(1) *Yale Journal of Law & Feminism* (2008) 1, at 16.

242 Catharine Mackinnon, 'Intersectionality as a Method: A Note', 38(4) *Signs* (2013) 2019, at 2023.

retaining for this book. It enables us to enquire whether and how human rights bodies take account of the way socio-economic, cultural and other differences structure social relations and institutions such as land, family and housing regulations, welfare measures, educational policies and the workplace. In doing so, intersectionality helps to account for the complexity of human experience. In this way, we may also come closer to appreciating rights holders as a whole.

5.2.2. Integration as Indivisibility and Interdependence

The premise that human rights are indivisible, as well as interdependent and interrelated, is a well-known dogma of human rights law. Scholars in the field of human rights history situate the impetus for indivisibility in post-colonial efforts to revise the human rights project, that is, across the 1950s and 1960s, when newly independent states joined the United Nations.[243] During this time and for the two following decades, the basis of the idea of indivisibility appeared to be tied to claims for economic justice and development that attempted to situate socio-economic rights as a priority.[244] So what is often presented as a qualitative divide between both categories of rights and which has traditionally privileged civil and political rights is the result of ideological struggles. While these were mostly shaped by the Cold War, they were deepened during the 1980s, when the ideas promoted by the Washington Consensus eroded the State's capacity to create conditions of socio-economic security.[245] Indivisibility, conceived as a reunion of the 'universal' rights that were split into the two main covenants, would crystallise in the 1993 World Conference of Human Rights. The Vienna Declaration, which marks the official and broad endorsement of indivisibility, proclaimed: 'All human rights are universal, indivisible and interdependent and interrelated. The international community must treat human rights globally in a fair and equal manner, on the same footing, and with the same emphasis.'[246]

---

243 Daniel J. Whelan, *Indivisible Human Rights. A History* (University of Pennsylvania Press, 2010), at 137; Roland Burke, 'Confronting "Indivisibility" in the History of Economic and Social Rights: From Parity to Priority and Back Again', 12 *Human Rights and Human Welfare* (2012) 53, at 60.

244 Daniel J. Whelan, *Indivisible Human Rights. A History* (University of Pennsylvania Press, 2010), at 150–154.

245 Fernando A. Chinchilla *et al.*, 'Pobreza y Derechos Humanos: hacia la definición de parámetros conceptuales desde la doctrina y acciones del sistema interamericano', in Instituto Interamericano de Derechos Humanos, *¿Quién responde por los derechos humanos de las poblaciones más pobres en América Latina y El Caribe? Democracia vs desigualdad 2007–2011* (Instituto Interamericano de Derechos Humanos, 2012), at 22.

246 Vienna Declaration and Programme of Action, U.N. GAOR, World Conf. on Hum. Rts., 48th Sess., 22d plen. mtg., part I, 5, U.N. Doc. A/CONF.157/24 (1993), *reprinted in* 32 I.L.M. 1661 (1993).

Though efforts have been made to distinguish indivisibility, interdependence and interrelatedness,[247] the three concepts are frequently invoked as a single package. Definitional precision in this respect is beyond the scope of this work, so this section will limit itself to flagging the normative force behind the idea of indivisibility and its implications. Put simply and broadly, indivisibility expresses the unity and mutually reinforcing character of human rights, with particular reference to the integration of civil and political rights with social, economic and cultural rights. This idea of unity is mostly predicated with regard to the implementation of rights, with socio-economic rights being declared to be as justiciable as civil and political rights, and with regard to the equal importance of both categories of rights. More recently, Quane also asserts indivisibility and interdependence in terms of the content of rights, pointing to existing rights overlaps that blur the boundaries between the content of different kinds of rights.[248] In addition, indivisibility has been interpreted as having deeper implications. Crooms, for instance, posits that to characterise international human rights as indivisible is to recognise that oppression is caused by interlocking and interdependent institutions, in a way that echoes the operation of Collin's 'matrix of domination'.[249]

Despite divergences in the scope and impact attributed to indivisibility, it is relatively safe to affirm that this principle seeks to depart from a fragmented understanding of human rights and to promote a more holistic view across themes, types of right and other divisions in human rights law. In other words, indivisibility bolsters human rights integration.[250] Here resides the relevance of this concept for the book. One of the methods conceived to give legal effect to indivisibility and interdependence is in fact called the 'integrated or holistic approach to human rights'.[251] This approach, which is closely related to the

---

247 James W. Nickel, 'Rethinking indivisibility: Towards a theory of supporting relations between human rights', 30(4) *Human Rights Quarterly* (2008) 984, at 987. In his view, 'indivisibility is a very strong form of interdependence (or bidirectional support)'.

248 Helen Quane, 'A Further Dimension to the Interdependence and Indivisibility of Human Rights?: Recent Developments Concerning the Rights of Indigenous Peoples', 25 *Harvard Human Rights Journal* (2012) 49, at 51–54 and 58–65.

249 Lisa A. Crooms, 'Indivisible Rights and Intersectional Identities or, What Do Women's Human Rights Have to Do with the Race Convention', 40(3) *Howard Law Journal* (1996) 619, at 626. The 'matrix of domination' as conceptualised by Patricia Hill Collins 'refers to how these intersecting oppressions [of race and gender and so on] are actually organized. Regardless of the particular intersections involved, structural, disciplinary, hegemonic, and interpersonal domains of power reappear across quite different forms of oppression.' Patricia Hill Collins, *Black Feminist Thought: Knowledge, Consciousness, and the Politics of Empowerment* (Routledge, 2000), at 18.

250 Eva Brems, 'Should Pluriform Human Rights Become One? Exploring the Benefits of Human Rights Integration', 4 *European Journal of Human Rights* (2014) 447, at 466–467; Rosalind P. Petchesky, 'Human Rights, Reproductive Health and Economic Justice: Why They Are Indivisible', 8(15) Reproductive Health Matters (2000) 12, at 12–13.

251 Virginia Mantouvalou, 'Work and Private Life: Sidabras and Dziautas v. Lithuania', 30 *European Law Review* (2005) 573, at 574.

'permeability' doctrine, is based on the idea that civil and political rights have socio-economic dimensions. As such, the latter can be adjudicated via civil and political rights. At the same time, though, it has been argued that 'in spite of the formal acceptance of universality, indivisibility and interdependence as foundational human rights principles, there is no common agreement as to how they should be operationalised in policies or in the legal work of the UN'.[252] Hence, the need to find mechanisms to implement these principles seems to remain.

5.2.3. *Integration by Shifting to Social Structures: The Social Model of Disability*

For a long time, disability was not seen as a human rights issue. Its official incorporation into mainstream human rights took place through the United Nations Convention on the Rights of Persons with Disabilities (CRPD).[253] The treaty has brought about a paradigm shift, not just on account of enlarging the subject protected by human rights law, but also on a number of other grounds. One of them is the endorsement of a social model of disability.[254] According to this, disability is not a matter of individual impairment, but rather a social construct. It is the way we have structured our society and social relations that renders a person unable to participate in the political, economic and socio-cultural life of a community.[255] As such, the understanding of disability has been reconfigured, moving away from an individualised medical conceptualisation of disability as a health issue of physical or mental impairment.[256] Focusing instead on social relations, cultural meanings and institutions, this model reveals how dominant notions of body-ability are the tacit norm against which people with disabilities have been depicted as *abnormal*.[257] It also demonstrates that social

252 Johanne Bouchard and Patrice Meyer-Bisch, 'Intersectionality and Interdependence of Human Rights: Same or Different?', 16 *Equal Rights Review* (2016) 186, at 188.

253 United Nations Convention on the Rights of Persons with Disabilities, adopted on 13 December 2006 during the sixty-first session of the General Assembly by resolution A/RES/61/106.

254 Convention on the Rights of People with Disability, Preamble, para. (e): 'Recognizing that disability is an evolving concept and that disability results from the interaction between persons with impairments and attitudinal and environmental barriers that hinders their full and effective participation in society on an equal basis with others.'

255 United Nations, Office of the High Commissioner for Human Rights, *Monitoring the Convention on the Rights of Persons with Disabilities, Guidance for Human Rights Monitors*, Professional training series No. 17, HR/P/PT/17, New York and Geneva, at 8.

256 Idem.; Rosemary Kayess and Philip French, 'Out of Darkness into Light? Introducing the Convention on the Rights of Persons with Disabilities', 8(1) *Human Rights Law Review* (2008) 1, at 6; Ravi Malhotra and Morgan Rowe, *Exploring Disability Identity and Disability Rights through Narratives. Finding a Voice of Their Own* (Routledge, 2014), at 2.

257 Carol Thomas, 'Disability and diversity', in Steven Vertovec (ed.), *Routledge International Handbook of Diversity Studies* (Routledge, 2014), at 47. She situates the awareness of discourses on what is normal and abnormal in the context of contributions made by post-structuralist/post-modernist scholars.

barriers are not inevitable; they can be removed. This reminds us of Minow's work, in which, as discussed earlier, she argues that social differences are not *in* people, but are rather dictated by a social environment constructed upon unstated norms of what is normal and acceptable.

This approach is matched by further normative innovations. Indeed, the CRPD also endorses a substantive view of equality which includes a commitment to achieving *de facto* equality and a state duty to ensure reasonable accommodation.[258] Reasonable accommodation conveys the idea that equality requires being responsive to peoples' differences. It is linked to the adoption of special or positive measures directed towards 'protected' minority groups or categories.[259] Underlying this duty is the acknowledgement that society has been premised on the basis of able-body experiences. Supposedly neutral regulations and arrangements which would otherwise burden or exclude people with disabilities should therefore be adjusted so as to incorporate their needs and concerns, allowing their social participation. Yet, the duty of reasonable accommodation has an individualised nature and its potential impact is curtailed by the requirement not to impose a disproportionate burden on the actor providing the service in question.[260]

Notwithstanding its observed group-based orientations, the Convention simultaneously makes a significant turn towards more 'universal' strategies. This is most clearly reflected in requirements of accessibility and universal design.[261] Both notions envisage an environment that operates with the widest range of users in mind, thereby avoiding 'separate' or 'special' solutions which may carry stigmatisation.[262]

---

258 CRPD, Article 5. Article 2 defines reasonable accommodation as 'necessary and appropriate modification and adjustments not imposing a disproportionate or undue burden, where needed in a particular case, to ensure to persons with disabilities the enjoyment or exercise on an equal basis with others of all human rights and fundamental freedoms'. On the link between reasonable accommodation and substantive equality, albeit in the European context, see Emmanuelle Bribosia and Isabelle Rorive, *Reasonable Accommodation beyond Disability in Europe?* (European Commission, 2013).

259 Interights, *Non-Discrimination in International Law. A Handbook for Practitioners* (Interights, 2011), at 97; Rosemary Kayess and Phillip French, 'Out of Darkness into Light? Introducing the Convention on the Rights of Persons with Disabilities', 8(1) *Human Rights Law Review* (2008) 1, at 9.

260 Rosemary Kayess and Phillip French, 'Out of Darkness into Light? Introducing the Convention on the Rights of Persons with Disabilities', 8(1) *Human Rights Law Review* (2008) 1, at 9; Olivier De Schutter and Annelies Verstichel, 'The Role of the Union in Integrating the Roma: Present and Possible Future', 2 *European Diversity and Autonomy Papers (EDAP)* (2005), at 19.

261 CRPD, Article 2 defines 'Universal design' as 'the design of products, environments, programmes and services to be usable by all people, to the greatest extent possible, without the need for adaptation or specialized design. "Universal design" shall not exclude assistive devices for particular groups of persons with disabilities where this is needed.' On Accessibility see Articles 3 (f) and 9.

262 Colin Barnes, 'Understanding Disability and the Importance of Design for All', 1(1) *Journal of Accessibility and Design for All* (2011) 55, at 68–69.

The novelties sketched above are part of an overall revision of the mainstream conception of human rights. As pointed out by Mégret, what is remarkable about the CRPD is how this treaty challenges, more than any other convention, important biases and dichotomies underlying the whole body of human rights law.[263] Notably, the Convention takes significant steps towards bridging the divides inherent in the dichotomies of, for example, civil/political rights v. socio-economic rights, individual v. community and state v. society.[264] The treaty brings together socio-economic and civil and political rights while also combining the standards of review typically applied to each set of rights.[265] The Convention also takes account of the socio-economic disadvantage usually faced by people with disabilities and recognises 'the critical need to address the negative impact of poverty'.[266] It furthermore acknowledges the fluidity of disability, insofar as it regards it as an 'evolving concept'.[267] At the same time, the treaty takes heed of the intersectional experience of most people with disabilities, 'who are subject to multiple or aggravated forms of discrimination'.[268]

These normative changes attempt, in sum, to deal with rights claims related to the experience of disability through a more integrated view of human rights. Importantly, such a holistic framework holds promise for dealing with social differences in general. In fact, there is nothing peculiar about disability that could preclude looking through similar lenses at other human rights issues concerning difference and exclusion. This follows from the socially constructed character of all markers of difference and the fluidity of and the interaction among identities, as well as their institutional embeddedness. One may then wonder whether the premises of the social model will be able to travel further within the human rights law edifice to make it less disaggregated and better suited to dealing more comprehensively with claims about difference and exclusion.[269]

---

263 Frédéric Mégret, 'The Disabilities Convention : Towards a Holistic Concept of Rights', 12(2) *The International Journal of Human Rights* (2008) 261.

264 Ibid., at 265–268.

265 Besides classical civil and political rights, several provisions of the Convention incorporate social, economic and cultural rights, while others stipulate rights that are rather mixed in nature. See, for example, CRPD, Articles 24–28, and Article 30; as well as Articles 4(2), 16, 19–20 and 23. The right to education in Article 24 seems to combine immediate and gradual obligations. In this vein, see Frédéric Mégret, 'The Disabilities Convention: Towards a Holistic Concept of Rights', 12(2) *The International Journal of Human Rights* (2008) 261, at 270.

266 CRPD, Preamble, letter (t).

267 CRPD, Preamble, letter (e).

268 CRPD, Preamble, letters (p)(q)(r); Articles 6 and 7.

269 The concept has already travelled across different layers of law. In domestic jurisdictions, the duty of reasonable accommodation was originally confined to religious diversity and disability, but in some cases it has been extended to all grounds of discrimination. In the international context, until the CRPD reasonable accommodation was limited to the area of employment (e.g. EU, Employment Equality Directive 2000/78/EC), while now it applies to all areas of service provision. Further expansion seems to be feasible.

It is worth noting that the integrated approach to human rights law adopted in this book draws on the three integrated legal perspectives discussed above. As will become clearer in subsequent chapters, the insight of intersectionality is most clearly reflected in the first layer of integrated analysis proposed here namely, looking at rights holders as a whole. For its part, the idea of integration as indivisibility and interdependence is a core aspect of the second layer of integrated analysis used in this book. This is a normative stance that promotes 'cross thinking' about harms and norms while encouraging awareness of legal pluralism. Finally, it is submitted that using these two layers of legal analysis in a relational manner may help to redirect attention to social barriers and structural inequalities. In fact, having a fuller understanding of rights holders and the norms and harms at stake in a given case tends to shift the focus away from the group or individual concerned and from predefined normative categories. This paves the way for looking at social constructs or unstated norms and trying to make human rights work within a complex reality.

But how much complexity and comprehensiveness can human rights courts take on board?

6. A FEW WORDS ON THE (IM)POSSIBILITIES OF HUMAN RIGHTS LAW AND ITS COURTS

This book is fundamentally concerned with the way supranational courts of human rights address cases involving claims about difference and social inclusion. It therefore studies legal claims in adjudication settings. Pointing this out is important because significant limitations to the adoption of a more integrated framework for dealing with those claims may appear, in principle, inherent to law and to the adjudication task performed by human rights courts.

6.1. SOME LIMITATIONS AND POSSIBILITIES WITHIN A PLURAL LEGAL ENVIRONMENT

On the one hand, human rights courts, like many other courts, confront important difficulties in grappling with the complexity of people's lived experiences. Crucial among the obstacles is the seemingly inevitable task of categorisation that courts undertake. Law works with abstract concepts and judges try to determine who or what falls within them.[270] So when a claimant raises issues

---

270 Jane K. Cowan *et al.* (eds.), *Culture and Rights. Anthropological Perspectives* (Cambridge University Press, 2001), at 10; Martha Albertson Fineman, 'Equality and Difference – The Restrained State', 66 *Alabama Law Review* (2015) 609, at 616 ('Law relies on broad categories that are rather entrenched within the law as it has developed over centuries as a coercive tool of the state …').

of discrimination, accommodation or otherwise special treatment, the court will inquire whether the complainant fits a protected category or belongs to a 'vulnerable' group. Is the complainant a woman, an indigenous person, a person with a disability, a national, a Roma, a Christian? To the extent that courts engage in this process of categorisation, the meaning of those categories will tend to be essentialised.[271] Furthermore, as stated earlier, 'cultures' and 'identities' may be shaped or formed as a result of that process. Yet, though categorisation may be inherent to law and to adjudication, the expectation that the law should be able to capture the lived experiences of people and the complexities of inequality is not senseless. After all, public confidence in the law as a governing mechanism relies, to an important extent, on the belief in its capacity to respond to and regulate an intricate social life.[272] This justifies the insistence on conceptual and normative frameworks that could help in building that capacity.

On the other hand, when it comes to assessing specific cultural and economic circumstances and arrangements, courts in general and human rights courts in particular find themselves in an uncomfortable position. Claims based on particular cultural and economic realities unsettle the universal validity and abstraction of human rights norms, and thus, the courts' ability to deal with them. Moreover, the structural nature of some of the underlying problems, such as widespread prejudice and unfair institutional design, challenges the adjudicatory model set up by human rights treaties. In particular, under an individual justice model of adjudication, human rights courts are ill-equipped to deal with structural violations.[273] In other words, the ECtHR and IACtHR are

---

271 Sujit Choudhry, 'Distribution vs. Recognition: The Case of Anti-Discriminations Laws', 9 *George Mason Law Review* (2000) 145, at 168.

272 Joanne Conaghan, 'Intersectionality and the Feminist Project in Law', in Emily Grabham *et al.* (eds.), *Intersectionality and Beyond. Law, Power and the Politics of Subjectivity* (Routledge Cavendish, 2008), at 28.

273 Structural violations are understood as violations which cannot easily be attributed to individual wrongdoings and which are, rather, systemic in nature. They are rooted in the institutional and social fabric of a community and rely on an inequitable distribution of power. These definitional elements can be found in the work of Kathleen Ho, 'Structural Violence as a Human Rights Violation', 4(2) *Essex Human Rights Review* (2007) 1; Roberto Saba, '(Des)igualdad estructural', 11 *Derecho y Humanidades* (2005) 123, at 139–146. Similarly, Víctor Abramovich discusses how the Inter-American System has increasingly dealt with structural patterns of violation. Without defining these, this author characterises them mainly in terms of inequality and the exclusion of systemically discriminated groups. Víctor Abramovich, 'From Massive Violations to Structural Patterns: New Approaches and Classic Tensions in the Inter-American Human Rights System', 6(11) *SUR International Journal on Human Rights* (2009) 7, at 16–22. In the context of the ECHR, see Wojciech Sadurski, 'Partnering with Strasbourg: Constitutionalization of the European Court of Human Rights, the Accession of Central and East European States to the Council of Europe, and the Idea of Pilot Judgments', 9(3) *Human Rights Law Review* (2009) 397, at 414 and ff (discussing how in the last decade the Court has, through the 'pilot procedure', come to deal with systematic and structural violations); Jacco Bomhoff, '"The Rights and Freedoms of Others": The ECHR and its Peculiar Category of Conflicts between Individual Fundamental Rights', in Eva Brems (ed.),

not only constrained by the cultural background and the legal culture in which they are embedded, but also by their legal mandate and the type of justice they are supposed to deliver.

When comparing one type of claim to another, human rights law, as well as courts, seem better suited to addressing recognition-driven claims (identity-based difference) than those involving redistribution issues (socio-economic difference). The elasticity of identity and cultural rights,[274] the use of equality and non-discrimination and the whole group-based development of human rights facilitate the handling of complaints dealing with cultural or identity differences. Coping with challenges to socio-economic arrangements is trickier. Setting aside restrictions on adjudicating socio-economic rights or social policy issues, and assuming that courts may be able/willing to intrude into this arena, the question remains whether human rights norms are flexible enough to address violations grounded in socio-economic disparities. In this respect, the liberalist imprint of human rights has led to scepticism. Golder's position is quite illustrative. In his opinion, 'the context of global capitalism sets a limit to the contingency of human rights such that any dissident vision of what it means to be human that seriously challenges the operation of market systems appears simply unintelligible or unrealizable'.[275]

As will be seen later, the above-mentioned constraints have triggered interesting normative strategies. For instance, the ECtHR has adopted the principle that when sensitive cultural matters are at stake, it will preferably defer to states, which will enjoy a broad latitude ('margin of appreciation') to resolve the matter.

Conflicts Between Fundamental Rights (Intersentia, 2008), at 644 (discussing the lack of a structural perspective in the context of conflicting rights. He argues that the ECtHR's jurisdiction is exclusively rights-based and neglects issues of structures, which is problematic insofar as it contributes 'to an overvaluation of the importance of effects on individuals in specific cases and to an undervaluation of critical scrutiny of the wider aims pursued by, and of effects to be expected from, governmental action.').

274 On the flexibility of cultural rights claims and the opportunities they may open up, see e.g. Yvonne M. Donders, *Human Rights: Eye for Cultural Diversity* (Amsterdam University Press, 2012). Inaugural Lecture delivered upon the appointment to the chair of Professor of International Human Rights and Cultural Diversity at the University of Amsterdam on 29 June 2012, at 16, Rosemary J. Coombe, 'Legal Claims to Culture in and Against the Market: Neoliberalism and the Global Proliferation of Meaningful Difference', 1 *Law Culture & the Human* (2005) 35, at 52; Balakrishnan Rajagopal, *International Law from Below: Development, Social Movements, and Third World Resistance* (Cambridge University Press, 2003), at 166 and 170.

275 Ben Golder, 'Beyond Redemption? Problematizing the critique of human rights in contemporary legal thought', 2(1) *London Review of International Law* (2014) 77, at 111–112. See also Karen Engle, 'On Fragile Architecture', 22(1) *European Journal of International Law* (2011) 141, at 160. A more optimistic variant of this scepticism can be found in Paul O'Connell, 'On Reconciling Irreconcilables: Neo-Liberal Globalisation and Human Rights', 7 *Human Rights Law Review* (2007) 483, at 507 (arguing that human rights and neoliberalism are ontologically irreconcilable: 'the neo-liberal globalisation is inconsistent with the protection of human rights not only in theory, but also in practice ... human rights will only be realised against the dominant form of globalization and not within it.').

And the same goes for cases posing questions of socio-economic policy. For similar reasons, courts may also be inclined to rule on both types of claim on the basis of procedural rather than substantive grounds. Underlying human rights courts' reluctance to intrude into both culturally and socio-economically sensitive terrain is also the subsidiary – and at best, complementary – role of supranational adjudicatory bodies. They are far away from and insufficiently familiar with the social reality in which rights violations take place.[276]

But the analysis of the normative responses provided by the ECtHR and the IACtHR requires us, additionally, to be attentive to the particular conditions determining whether and how rights are interpreted and adjudicated by each court. These conditions are given by, for example, the institutional, historical, cultural and political context of the courts as well as the type of litigation taking place before them.[277] While many of these aspects differ significantly for each regional court, as seen below, there is one common circumstance that offers not just challenges but also some interesting opportunities, that is, a multi-layered legal environment. Neither the European nor the Inter-American Court of Human Rights sits in isolation and both oversee legal regimes that are far from being self-contained. Rather, they are part of an international environment in which distinct actors, norms and institutions are in constant interaction, a context of global legal pluralism.[278]

Underlying complaints about difference, identity affiliation and social inclusion there is usually a normative landscape marked by legal overlaps and competing authorities. They disclose a normative plurality made up of interactions between, for example, government legislation and policies, local development plans, constitutional norms, human rights law, private actors' practices and norms arising from ethnic, religious and cultural affiliations.[279]

---

276 On the 'better placed argument' in the ECtHR and its importance for tackling cultural and economic sensitive matters, see Janneke Gerards, 'Pluralism, deference and the margin of appreciation doctrine', 17(1) *European Law Journal* (2011) 80, at 110–11.

277 Christopher McCrudden, 'The Pluralism of Human Rights Adjudication', University of Michigan Public Law Research Paper 1, at 14, available at <ssrn.com/abstract=2474206> (Chapter 1 in Liora Lazarus, Christopher McCrudden and Nigel Bowles (eds.), *Reasoning Rights. Comparative Judidical Engagement* (Hart Publishing, 2014).

278 Eva Brems, 'Should Pluriform Human Rights Become One? Exploring the Benefits of Human Rights Integration', 4 *European Journal of Human Rights* (2014) 447, at 448–451; Carlos Iván Fuentes *et al.*, 'E Pluribus Unum – Bhinneka Tunggal Ika? Universal Human Rights and the Fragmentation of International Law', in René Provost and Colleen Sheppard (eds.), *Dialogues on Human Rights and Legal Pluralism* (Springer, 2013), at 69; Barbara Oomen, 'The application of socio-legal theories of legal pluralism to understanding the implementation and integration of human rights law', 4 *European Journal of Human Rights* (2014) 471, at 493.

279 On how this plurality affects the implementation and adjudication of human rights standards, see Valeska David and Julie Fraser, 'A Legal Pluralist Approach to the Use of Cultural Perspectives in the Implementation and Adjudication of Human Rights Norms', 23 *Buffalo Human Rights Law Review* (2017) 75.

Taking a pluralist approach may favour, in the words of Berman, mechanisms and practices that expand the range of voices heard or considered, which, in turn, could potentially help to channel or tame normative conflict.[280] Sheppard, for her part, argues that the complexity and dynamic character of legal regulation (characterised by several socio-economic, cultural and political realities) has critical implications for the constitutional recognition of diverse social groups.[281] Any affirmation of related constitutional rights should therefore be assessed against that context.[282] Thus, while taking into account legal plurality may upset the idea of adjudicating *the* law[283] – i.e. the ECHR or the ACHR – doing so may provide some valuable opportunities. Notably, it may counterbalance the temptation to adopt compartmentalised views that reduce cases concerning recognition and social inclusion to, for example, cases primarily about a religion, a lifestyle *or* about pensions, welfare *or* about equality. Following Baer, the resolution of those disputes would be 'enriched by a larger pool of arguments'.[284] Whereas considering this is no easy task, 'the multiple levels of and the varieties in regulation which ensure human rights would allow us to reveal the inconsistencies of "law", of claims of "secularism", of "the right to religious freedom" or "the right to equality"'.[285] In other words, more integrated accounts of such cases not only presuppose thinking of situated rights holders as a whole, of interdependent rights and interacting forms of power. They also require us to think more broadly, more inclusively, about the law(s) that are relevant to adjudicating rights claims about difference and inclusion, such as those analysed in the subsequent chapters.

6.2. A QUICK OVERVIEW OF TWO REGIONAL COURTS

It is not possible to provide a detailed account of the history, functions and current practice of the two regional courts examined in this book. However, for the sake of contextualisation, the following lines will highlight a few key features of each court so as to give an idea of how and why they work the way they do.

---

280 Paul Schiff Berman, 'Global Legal Pluralism', 80 *Southern California Law Review* (2007) 1155, at 1166–1168.

281 Colleen Sheppard, 'Constitutional Recognition of Diversity in Canada', 30 *Vermont Law Review* (2006) 466, at 478–479.

282 Idem.

283 Legal pluralist scholars have long studied the legal hybridity occurring in a given social field. See e.g. Sally Falk Moore, 'Law and Social Change: The Semi-Autonomous Social Field as an Appropriate Subject of Study', 7(4) *Law & Society Review* (1973) 719, at 720.

284 Susanne Baer, 'A Closer Look at Law: Human Rights as Multi-Level Sites of Struggles over Multi-Dimensional Equality', 6(2) *Utrecht Law Review* (2010) 56, at 72 (speaking from a constitutional perspective).

285 Idem.

6.2.1. *The European Court of Human Rights*

The European Court of Human Rights was created under the auspices of the Council of Europe to oversee state compliance with the European Convention on Human Rights (ECHR), which was adopted in 1950 and entered into force in 1953. The ECHR was drafted by European governments in the post-war years in response to the atrocities of the Second World War and to the spread of Communism in Europe.[286] Albeit born at the time that saw the emergence of the welfare state, the Convention nonetheless reflects the divisions of the Cold War. Social and economic rights were thus largely left out of the Convention, which primarily protects a wide range of civil and political rights. It is important to point out that until 1998 the Court coexisted with the former European Commission of Human Rights (ECommHR). In this system, for a petition to reach the Court the Commission had to have declared it admissible and adopted a report on the merits. This is, as seen below, how supervision in the Inter-American system currently works. With Protocol No. 11, however, the ECommHR was replaced by the new permanent Court, which absorbed all the adjudicatory work with mandatory jurisdiction over all member states.[287] Since then, individuals have had direct access to the Court, which can rule on individual petitions and inter-state complaints.[288] Over the years, the ECtHR has become the most developed international adjudicatory body.[289] And the number of individual complaints, which can be submitted by individuals or groups of individuals and legal persons, has sky-rocketed.[290]

But in which conditions has the Court's extensive case law developed? It is said that the ECHR has

> been used primarily to raise questions of particular violations of human rights in states that basically conform to its requirements and are representative of "the common

---

286 David J. Harris *et al.*, *Law of the European Convention on Human Rights* (Oxford University Press, 2014), at 3.

287 Pieter Van Dijk *et al.* (eds.), *Theory and Practice of the European Convention on Human Rights* (Intersentia, 2006), at 35–36. See Protocol No. 11 to the Convention for the Protection of Human Rights and Fundamental Freedoms, Restructuring the Control Machinery Established Thereby, adopted on 11 May 1994 and entered into force on 1 November 1998.

288 ECHR, Articles 33 and 34 respectively.

289 In the sense that it has the largest experience in the judicial examination of international individual complaints and that it has generated more jurisprudence than any other international body. See Henry J. Steiner *et al.*, *International Human Rights in Context: Law, Politics, Morals* (Oxford University Press, 2007), at 933.

290 As recently as 2016, a total of 38,505 applications were decided (through a judgment or decision, or by being struck out of the list). By 31 December 2016, approximately 79,750 applications were pending before the Court. See ECtHR, The ECHR in facts & figures 2016, document prepared by the Public Relations Unit of the Court (March 2017), available at <www.echr.coe.int>.

> heritage of political traditions, ideals, freedoms and the rule of law" [...] or, in the case of post-communist member states [...] that committed themselves to move in this direction.[291]

The increase in member states that followed the fall of the Berlin wall brought about significant changes for the Court, especially for its workload and the types of case to be decided. Importantly, the Court started to deal more often (or more explicitly) with systematic and structural violations.[292] The emergence of the 'pilot judgement' procedure is the most remarkable effort it has made to deal with both structural violations and the exponential caseload.[293] While there is still debate over the extent to which the Strasbourg Court is confined to delivering retrospective individual justice or rather provides constitutional-like justice or both, other characteristics of the Court are more firmly established. For present purposes, it is relevant to highlight the Court's reliance on the doctrine of the margin of appreciation and the notion of normative consensus.[294] On the basis of the former the Court will, under certain circumstances, grant some latitude or defer to the solutions adopted by national authorities.[295] The margin will usually be wider in the absence of consensus among member states, that is, a common ground or shared approach across states as to the standards applicable to a given matter, especially those considered sensitive.[296] A further significant

---

291 David J. Harris *et al.*, *Law of the European Convention on Human Rights* (Oxford University Press, 2014), at 4. The Preamble of the ECHR refers to 'the governments of European countries which are like-minded and have a common heritage of political traditions, ideals, freedom and the rule of law' and which 'take the first steps for the collective enforcement of certain of the rights stated in the Universal Declaration'.

292 Wojciech Sadurski, 'Partnering with Strasbourg: Constitutionalization of the European Court of Human Rights, the Accession of Central and East European States to the Council of Europe, and the Idea of Pilot Judgments', 9(3) *Human Rights Law Review* (2009) 397, at 413–414.

293 Ibid., at 414 and ff. ECtHR, (GC) *Hutten-Czapska v. Poland*, App. No. 35014/97, Judgment of 19 June 2006, para. 233 (holding that '[t]his kind of adjudicative approach by the Court to systemic or structural problems in the national legal order has been described as a "pilot judgment procedure" ...'). Other important related reforms include Protocol No. 14 to the Convention for the Protection of Human Rights and Fundamental Freedoms, amending the control system of the Convention and which entered into force in 2010. (The changes introduced concern, *inter alia*, the petitions' admissibility criteria, the treatment of repetitive cases and the support provided to the Committee of Ministers in the execution of judgments.)

294 David J. Harris *et al.*, *Law of the European Convention on Human Rights* (Oxford University Press, 2014), at 10–12 and 14–17.

295 Several factors determine when and how much discretion is left to state parties. According to Janneke Gerards, these can be grouped into three main factors: 'the common ground factor', the 'better placed argument' and the nature of the affected right or interest. See Janneke Gerards, 'Pluralism, deference and the margin of appreciation doctrine', 17(1) *European Law Journal* (2011) 80, at 107–113.

296 Ibid., at 108–110; David J. Harris *et al.*, *Law of the European Convention on Human Rights* (Oxford University Press, 2014), at 10–12 and 14–17. On these tools and their relationship with the living instrument doctrine (which is also an important characteristic of the

feature is the fact that the ECtHR's remedial powers (outside pilot procedures) are very limited. Save for compensation and very occasional requests for restitution measures, the Committee of Ministers is the body entrusted with overseeing the execution of judgments (including all necessary steps to comply with them).

6.2.2. *The Inter-American Court of Human Rights*

It is not possible to start a conversation about this Court without referring to the Commission.[297] The Inter-American system, like the European system in its origins, rests upon two supervisory organs: the Inter-American Commission and the Inter-American Court of Human Rights. The Commission was the first of the two supervisory organs to be created. So, by the time the American Convention entered into force in 1978 and established the Court, the Commission had already been operating for about two decades.[298] The Commission's functions are broad. They comprise both contentious and promotional activities.[299] The latter include the preparation of country-based and thematic reports, the holding of general and thematic hearings with different stakeholders, the review of states' periodic reports on the implementation of human rights and the undertaking of on-site visits, among others. The breadth and flexibility of the Commission's promotional functions have allowed it, among other things, to deal with structural violations and complex policy matters, which are rather difficult to tackle via the adjudication of individual cases.[300] Even so, and because the Commission continues to intervene in the submission and substantiation of individual petitions before the Court, its views on those matters have influenced the Court's interpretation. The Court's powers, by contrast, are relatively limited. It delivers binding judgments in contentious cases submitted by the Commission or by state parties against (other) states that have accepted the Court's jurisdiction. The Court can also

Court's work), see also George Letsas, 'The ECHR as a living instrument: its meaning and its legitimacy', in Andreas Føllesdal *et al.* (eds.), *Constituting Europe. The European Court of Human Rights in a National, European and Global Context* (Cambridge University Press, 2013), at 112–122.

297 Cecilia Medina, 'Towards Effectiveness in the Protection of Human Rights in the Americas', 8(2) Transnational *Law and Contemporary Problems* (1998) 337, at 344 (arguing that 'standard-setting within the inter-American system has been carried out quite forcefully, with major input by the Commission').

298 The Commission was created in 1959 by Resolution of the Fifth Meeting of Consultation of Ministers of Foreign Affairs. OEA/Ser.C/II.5, Santiago, Chile, 1959.

299 ACHR, Articles 41–42. See also the Statute and the Rules of Procedure of the Commission, approved respectively in 1979 by resolution No. 447, and in 2009 during the 137th regular period of sessions, last modified in 2013.

300 Tara Melish, 'The Inter-American Commission on Human Rights. Defending Social Rights through Case-Based Petitions', in Malcolm Langford (ed.), *Social Rights Jurisprudence: Emerging Trends in Comparative and International Law* (Cambridge University Press, 2008), at 339–340.

issue advisory opinions requested by OAS member states and organs, including the Commission.[301] Unlike the European system, then, individuals do not have direct access to the Inter-American Court. Nevertheless, a number of reforms have improved the participation of alleged victims before it.[302]

To understand many of the procedural and substantive features of the Court, it is crucial to consider the context in which it has operated. The creation of the Court 'can be seen as a strong response to dictatorships and the appalling situation of human rights in many of the Organization of American States (OAS) Member States'.[303] Hence, unlike what happened in the European system, the Inter-American organs strove to secure democracy and respect for human rights across countries that largely ignored or were even hostile to both.[304] Albeit today the region is no longer under the rule of dictatorships, serious democratic deficits and inequalities persist. Deregulation, corruption, defective justice systems, acute socio-economic disparities, racial discrimination and other structural problems are still unresolved challenges for several American democracies. As a result, 'new' human rights issues have been brought to the Court's docket – such as equality claims from different groups, indigenous rights and freedom of speech. Nevertheless, it should be noted that a significant proportion of the Court's judgments continues to deal with gross and systematic violations such as disappearances, torture and summary executions.[305] Having to work for the promotion of and respect for human rights in these conditions has been a major driver for the Court's creative interpretations. The Court's 'quasi-constitutional' role,[306] its distance from the margin of appreciation

---

301 ACHR, Articles 61–62 and 64. From the 35 OAS member states, today only 20 accept the jurisdiction of the Court. In 2013 member states set in motion a new reform to 'strengthening the Inter-American system'. However, other stakeholders have seen this process as an attempt to undermine the system, particularly the Inter-American Commission's powers.

302 Since 2009, alleged victims have been considered the only party against which the state litigates. Accordingly, the debate and the evidential activity of the trial take place among them. This is to say that the Commission no longer acts as an intermediary or representative of alleged victims. On this and previous reforms regarding victims' participation before the Court see, Valeska David, 'The Inauguration of the Inter-American Defenders' Era: Reflections after the *Furlan* Case', 7 *Inter-American and European Human Rights Journal* (2014) 245, at 246–250.

303 Cecilia Medina, *The American Convention on Human Rights. Crucial Rights and Their Theory and Practice* (Intersentia, 2016), at 2.

304 Robert K. Goldman, 'History and Action: the Inter-American Human Rights System and the Role of the Inter-American Commission on Human Rights', 31 *Human Rights Quarterly* (2009) 856, at 866–867.

305 This is mainly due to the huge workload of the Commission and its lengthy ensuing delay in processing cases that concern atrocities from the 1980s and early 1990s.

306 Laurence Burgorgue-Larsen, 'La Corte Interamericana de Derechos Humanos como tribunal constitucional', in Héctor Fix-Fierro *et al.* (co-ords.), *Ius Constitutionale Commune en América Latina. Rasgos, potencialidades y desafíos* (UNAM, 2014), at 421–458; Ariel E. Dulitzky, 'An Inter-American Constitutional Court? The Invention of the Conventionality Control by the Inter-American Court of Human Rights', 50(1) *Texas International Law Journal* (2015) 45–93.

doctrine and broad remedial powers as well as several other aspects of its case law and working methods should be seen in this context. As a former judge observes, 'the Court has developed its case law with a view to finding the most appropriate solutions to the ailments of the people on the continent'.[307]

7. CONCLUDING REMARKS

It is beyond the scope of this book to fully explore the doctrinal debates addressed in this chapter and the way they have evolved up to the present. But the succinct review given above suffices for noting the following key points. Firstly, whereas in the past many would have asserted that people's differences should not matter, for quite some time now the point seems to have been exactly the opposite. Claims about identity, difference and social inclusion have attained political and legal salience and have generated a number of responses. In this context, and despite the complexity involved in such claims, they tend to be approached in rather dispersed ways. Notably, our normative thinking seems to favour a group-identity focus, the prioritisation of some identities or social positions over others and the inclination to disconnect identity-driven differences from socio-economic issues and from broader contextual questions in which the former take meaning. The attempt to reduce complex cases to the elucidation of what constitutes a certain identity and whether it is valuable, or to the application of certain abstract categories, makes it too problematic to justify who and what deserve protection. Arguably, the prevalence of these approaches adds considerable difficulty to the resolution of some legal claims, especially when they come before human rights courts such as the ECtHR and the IACtHR.

At the basis of this fragmentary thinking are, *inter alia*, doctrinal and political divides regarding the place of identity, culture, recognition, redistribution, etc.; the diversification and ensuing fragmentation of human rights law; and a number of competing narratives and dichotomies regarding key concepts such as equality, difference, neutrality, liberty and further normative divisions. Against this background, the message conveyed is not that collective identities and social groups are insignificant. They are indeed crucial elements in agency formation, solidarity, and legal and political mobilisation. Moreover, they provide useful insights into power differentials in society. The argument posited is rather that we nonetheless need to pay attention to the limitations of an identity- or group-centred legal analysis (as well as to the use of other 'compartments') for dealing with rights claims advanced in contexts of great diversity and inequality.

---

[307] Cecilia Medina, *The American Convention on Human Rights. Crucial Rights and Their Theory and Practice* (Intersentia, 2016), at 3.

What is more, we need to work with more integrated frameworks that help us to grasp the interactions between complex forms of inequality and exclusion.

One may therefore wonder: are there conceptual and normative tools that might help us to transition from that fragmentation to a more holistic outlook? A number of scholars resort to conceptual and normative devices such as parity of participation, multidimensional equality and an integrated view of human rights, all of which may assist a more comprehensive analysis. What is more, the problems highlighted above and the need for more integrated accounts have resonance in human rights law as well. Here, it is suggested that insights be taken from the notions of intersectionality, the indivisibility of human rights, the social model of disability and the overall normative environment of human rights courts. Building upon these insights, a rights-holder-centred and integrated framework is applied to the case law analysed in the following chapters.

PART II

RETHINKING CULTURAL DIFFERENCE FROM AN INTEGRATED PERSPECTIVE ON HUMAN RIGHTS

The assumption underlying this second part is that the ECtHR and the IACtHR have both in one way or another addressed several claims from persons belonging to non-dominant ethno-cultural groups through a relatively compartmentalised approach based on cultural difference. As such, it is submitted that the ECtHR and IACtHR could benefit from a more comprehensive analysis.

The interest in enriching existing legal narratives in ethno-cultural diversity cases has to do with the challenges that these pose to human rights courts. There are at least three challenges with which this book is particularly concerned. The first is how to avoid dealing with issues of cultural difference without displacing the concrete individual concerned or wider issues of social inequality. The second is how courts could escape what Minow calls 'the dilemma of difference'. That is, courts may recreate the 'stigma' of difference by both ignoring difference and by focusing on it.[1] The dilemma arises out of the fact that in both strategies the difference is always located in the minority raising the claim. The third hurdle holding particular relevance here is the growing difficulty in justifying who gets to enjoy 'special protection' or accommodation and when. Thus, while admitting that an integrated model of human rights can be beneficial to the adjudication of all kinds of rights complaints, the following discussion is particularly interested in what such a model may offer to the handling of cultural diversity cases and to the challenges they bring.

1 Martha Minow, *Making All the Difference. Inclusion, Exclusion and American Law* (Cornell University Press, 1990), at 20–25.

CHAPTER 2

AN INTEGRATED APPROACH TO CULTURAL DIFFERENCE IN THE EUROPEAN COURT OF HUMAN RIGHTS

1. INTRODUCTION

The European Court of Human Rights (ECtHR) has been confronted with an enormous volume of cases concerning questions of ethno-cultural diversity. The most direct avenues for advancing rights claims to recognition of cultural differences are Article 8 (right to respect for private and family life), Article 9 (freedom of thought, conscience and religion), Article 2 of Protocol No. 1 (right to education) and Article 10 (freedom of expression) of the European Convention on Human Rights (ECHR).[1] From the existing case law in this area, this chapter focuses on complaints brought by Roma and Travellers as well as Muslim applicants.[2] The former set of cases mainly relies on Article 8 ECHR, often accompanied by Articles 1 (right to property) and 2 (right to education) of Protocol No. 1. Muslim applicants, in turn, mainly invoke Article 9 ECHR, Article 2 Protocol 1 and Articles 10 and 11 ECHR. Both Roma/Travellers and Muslim applicants share the frequent invocation of the prohibition of discrimination (Article 14 ECHR).

---

1 ECtHR, Research Division; *Cultural rights in the case-law of the European Court of Human Rights* (Council of Europe, 2017), at 4.

2 The book does not examine complaints brought by religious organisations. As further clarified below, an important reason for this is that this book focuses on the claims made by (natural) persons who represent the culturally and economically 'different'. In doing so, it directs attention to persons in non-hegemonic positions seeking recognition and redress with a view to greater social participation. Further, the book focuses on claims that are sites of divergence and contestation. Religious organisations and churches do not fall within this scope. Not only do the types of claims they bring to the ECtHR deviate from the object of study, but also their litigation does not engender comparable debate. This can be attributed, among other reasons, to the fact that the ECtHR is quite responsive to the 'institutional' plights of such applicants. On this last point, see Javier Martínez-Torrón, 'The (Un) protection of individual religious identity in the Strasbourg case law', 1(2) *Oxford Journal of Law and Religion* (2012) 363.

Broadly speaking, in the cases studied Roma, Travellers and Muslims generally seek protection against discrimination; redress of disadvantages associated with their actual or perceived difference, and accommodation of cultural/religious aspects of their life. As will be seen below, these complaints are varied in scope and relate to different areas of social life, such as land planning and housing, education, the workplace, social protection, the use of public services and public spaces, political representation and participation in other spheres of power. As such, most of the cases reviewed not only concern the opportunity to live in accordance with one's cultural/religious identity. They also touch upon socio-economic and participation rights. In this context, and because this book is interested in what an integrated normative framework can offer to the adjudication of cases otherwise addressed through a relatively narrow approach, the present discussion will draw particular attention to those judgments and decisions where, despite the complexity and multidimensionality of the problems under review, emphasis is put on questions of ethno-cultural difference and competing group demands. In other words, this chapter will examine more closely the subset of rulings where the Court has adopted a normative approach mostly anchored in ethno-cultural and religious identity (i.e. being a 'Roma', being a 'Muslim'), as this focus is quite representative of a compartmentalised frame of analysis. In the case of Roma and Travellers, these are mostly cases dealing with a so-called 'Gypsy' way of life involving the occupation of caravans. For Muslims, a large part of such identity-based cases concerns the wearing of the Islamic veil (whether the *hijab* or *niqab*).

Rights claims for recognition of cultural differences, whether in the framework of substantive provisions such as Articles 8 and 9 or through the prohibition of discrimination (Article 14 ECHR), place the individual within a cultural or religious community. These individual complaints consequently have not only an individual but also a collective dimension. One of the Court's starting points in the examination of culturally-related cases is in fact the identification of the applicant's membership of an ethno-cultural or religious collectivity.[3] Moreover, the Court has observed, for example, that in contexts of religious plurality, the role of the state 'is not to remove the cause of tension by eliminating pluralism, but to ensure that the competing groups tolerate each other'.[4] This underscores the fact that cultural diversity cases also concern social relations among groups.

3 Usually the Court identifies the ethnic or religious affiliation of the individual applicant in its account of the circumstances of the case and/or at the outset of its legal analysis. It states, for instance, 'the applicant belongs to/is/considers herself to be a member of (Traveller, Muslim, Christian)'.

4 See e.g. ECtHR, (GC) *Leyla Şahin v. Turkey*, App. no. 44774/98, Judgment of 10 November 2005, para. 107; (GC) *S.A.S. v. France*, App. no. 43835/11, Judgment of 1 July 2014, para. 126; *Ebrahimian v. France*, App. no. 64846/11, Judgment of 26 November 2015, para. 55.

Quite often such relations are regarded as relations of inequality, usually between minorities and majorities, which is an important factor driving judicialisation. Still, one criticism that courts are prone to encountering is that they are too concerned with the individual, while disregarding group-based inequalities.[5] The point is, in other words, that the extent to which the outcome of litigation goes beyond the individual parties, as well as the framing of the case against a broader social context, does matter. The issue of group and cultural membership is therefore critical for the legal analysis of the cases examined here.

But does this require courts such as the ECtHR to focus on group identity and its definitional features as such? What opportunities and drawbacks are at play in that sort of categorisation? As these questions may suggest, the collective aspects that are of interest here do not concern corporate issues or otherwise institutionalised collective cultural expressions, such as places of worship and the organisational autonomy of culturally-based communities.[6] Rather, the questions explored in the following lines concern the Strasbourg Court's approach to 'the' social group to which the applicant allegedly belongs and which significantly shapes her social standing and rights claims.[7] How, then, does the Court conceive of Roma and Muslims and how does this affect the way the Court conceives of their rights claims and adjudicate them? As explained below, the Court has usually conceived of them as ethno-cultural/religious bounded groups whose claims relate to the handling of cultural/religious difference.[8]

---

5 Ellen Wiles, 'Headscarves, Human Rights, and Harmonious Multicultural Society: Implications of the French Ban for Interpretations of Equality', 41(3) *Law and Society Review* (2007) 699, at 713–717; Sandra Fredman and Beth Goldblatt, 'Gender Equality and Human Rights', 4 *UN Women Discussion Paper Series* (2014), at 9. Several scholars have criticised the centrality that human rights organs and constitutional courts accord to the individual retrospective model of justice. Many of them argue for more structural approaches to deliver group-oriented solutions. See e.g. Owen M. Fiss, 'The Forms of Justice', 93(1) *Harvard Law Review* (1979) 1, at 18 and ff; Owen M. Fiss, 'The Allure of Individualism', 78 *Iowa Law Review* (1993) 965; David Landau, 'The Reality of Social Rights Enforcement', 53(1) *Harvard International Law Journal* (2012) 189, at 404 and ff.

6 These aspects are especially salient in the field of religious diversity and are manifested, for instance, in the relationship between organised religious communities and the state, as well as in their association through religious institutions.

7 This author uses 'the' within quotation marks because courts tend to locate individual applicants in relation to one single social group. However, in practice, people belong simultaneously to several groups. For a fuller discussion of this issue, see *infra* sections 2 and 3.

8 The bounded view of social groups relates to the idea of 'groupism', as envisaged by Baer and Brubaker. This portrays some human rights conflicts as group issues and reduces people 'to specific characteristics that are then politicized, as boundaries, in the processes of othering.' See Susanne Baer, 'Privatizing Religion. Legal Groupism, No-Go-Areas, and the Public-Private-Ideology in Human Rights Politics', 20(1) *Constellations* (2013) 68, at 75 and Rogers Brubaker, 'Ethnicity without Groups', 43(2) *Archives Européennes de Sociologie* (2002) 163, at 164.

2. CULTURAL DIFFERENCE AS LEGAL COMPARTMENT

While this lens enables the Court to acknowledge the cultural embodiment of the applicants and guides it in determining the standards applicable to the case, the group cultural identity concern is quite unidimensional. It focuses only on the applicant and on others like her; it presents her as member of one group or culture/religion, and it draws attention to a limited repertoire of grievances and norms – those that are assumed to be immediately linked to the exercise of the culture/religion in question. It is submitted that by taking this road, other concerns easily fall out of sight, for example, other aspects of the applicants' identity and social location and the position of other rights holders, as well as a wider spectrum of relevant harms and norms.

The reduced line of sight has to do, at least in part, with the problems entailed by a focus on Culture 'with capital C', to use Anne Phillips's expression.[9] As she explains, this means to cast 'culture itself as protagonist. "Culture" becomes the explanation and people's activities the explanandum. This is a route that brings us to an essentialised version of culture.'[10] It is argued that the Court has actually taken this route in many of the cases studied. And in doing so, it has attempted to define and evaluate, often narrowly, the cultural identity and the problems faced by the collectivity in question. As these aspects of the judicial analysis are problematised below, we may consider the possibility and convenience of looking beyond cultural identity and crossing group boundaries.

2.1. THE ROMA WAY OF LIFE UNDER ARTICLE 8 ECHR

Two themes have been recurrent in the Court's narrative regarding the collective identity of Roma and Traveller people under Article 8 ECHR: the ethno-cultural specificity of the Roma/Travellers and their vulnerability. This chapter will start by examining the first: the ethno-cultural identity. The Court has underscored the applicants' membership in a group defined by its own history, traditions and values. This discourse of ethno-cultural distinctiveness has been a constant for the cases examined, whether they concern the recognition of Roma rites and beliefs;[11] the educational segregation of Roma children (although to a lesser extent);[12] or the planning regulations hindering the private and family life of

9 Anne Phillips, 'What's wrong with Essentialism?', 11(1) *Distinktion: Scandinavian Journal of Social Theory* (2010) 47, at 54.

10 Idem.

11 Such as in ECtHR, *Muñoz Díaz v. Spain*, App. no. 49151/07, Judgment of 8 December 2009.

12 See, *inter alia*, ECtHR, (GC) *D.H. and Others v. the Czech Republic*, App. no. 57325/00, Judgment of 13 November 2007; *Sampanis and Others v. Greece*, App. no. 32526/06, Judgment of 5 June 2008.

Roma and Traveller people.[13] It is probably in this last sphere, however, that the rhetoric of a Roma/Traveller cultural identity has been more prominent.

One may find it surprising that the aforementioned complaints concerning cultural-identity rights could rely on Article 8 ECHR (the right to private and family life) since, especially when compared to freedom of religion (Article 9 ECHR), the cultural dimension of Article 8 seems at best tenuous. However, this provision has been interpreted as comprising the protection of a way of life and a minority identity. This goes back to the time when the former European Commission of Human Rights examined indigenous peoples' complaints against European Nordic countries.[14] The Saami claimed property over lands they had traditionally used for reindeer herding, hunting and fishing in Norway. But the Commission reframed their property claim as an issue of private life under Article 8 ECHR. And within that framework, it stated that minorities were, in principle, entitled to claim the right to *respect for a particular way of life* which they could lead as private life, family life or home.[15] The applicants lost their case, but the above interpretation paved the way for the protection of ethno-cultural minorities and potentially for other people seeking protection of a particular lifestyle. Surprisingly, however, most developments in this field are not to be found in indigenous rights cases, which still remain relatively scarce within the Court's jurisprudence.[16] With only a few complaints about indigenous peoples' rights decided by the ECtHR on the merits, it has actually been in the framework of Roma's and Travellers' claims concerning the stationing of caravans that the protection of a minority way of life has evolved and gained leverage.

In fact, the idea of a 'Gypsy way of life' has evolved through a number of cases – mostly against the United Kingdom and France – dealing with evictions or threats of eviction of nomadic and sedentary Roma and Travellers who lived in caravans stationed in contravention of land-use regulations. Most infringements are grounded in visual amenity and environmental protection. In this context, and especially during the early phase of this jurisprudence, the Court defined what it has called a 'Gypsy way of life' mainly by reference to

---

13 See e.g. ECtHR, *Porter v. the United Kingdom*, App. no. 47953/99, Judgment of 30 January 2001; (GC) *Chapman v. the United Kingdom*, App. no. 27238/95, Judgment of 18 January 2001; *Horie v. the United Kingdom*, App. no. 31845/10, Decision of 1 February 2011; *Buckland v. the United Kingdom*, App. no. 40060/08, Judgment of 18 September 2012.

14 EComm.HR, *G. and E. v. Norway*, Application nos. 9278/81 and 9415/81, Decision of 3 October 1983.

15 Ibid., at 35 (emphasis added). The UN Human Rights Committee endorsed a similar interpretation on the basis of Article 27 of the International Covenant on Civil and Political Rights (ICCPR). See, *inter alia*, HRC, General Comment No. 23: Article 27 (Rights of Minorities), CCPR/C/21/Rev.1/Add.5, Adopted on 6 April 1994, para. 7.

16 See e.g. Timo Koivurova, 'Jurisprudence of the European Court of Human Rights Regarding Indigenous Peoples: Retrospect and Prospects', 18(1) *International Journal on Minority and Group Rights* (2011) 1, at 8–10.

living in caravans and in itinerancy. Since the Grand Chamber judgment in *Chapman* and the other judgments delivered along with it, the occupation of caravans has become an integral part of the Roma/Traveller identity protected under Article 8 ECHR. In the Court's view, this identity reflects the minority's long tradition of a travelling lifestyle, a tradition that persisted despite many Gypsies (as the Court calls them) having adopted a settled existence. This last remark notwithstanding, itinerancy gained salience as an 'essential' element of Roma culture. Even when at the time of those judgments the Court formally acknowledged that many Roma and Travellers no longer lived a nomadic life,[17] it still went on to conclude that those who appeared not to be pursuing an itinerant life any more fell outside 'the traditional itinerant Gypsy lifestyle'.[18] Accordingly, a narrow view of Roma lifestyle received protection.[19] Practical consequences would follow from this, some of which attest to the problems that the scholarship associates with essentialism.[20]

Referring to the situation of Roma and Travellers in the British context, Poulter has observed that 'by defining travellers by what they do (or by folkloric expectations of their behaviour), the state has retained the power to control their use of the land, differentiate their authentication and respond to the prejudices of the majority population'.[21] In the context of the Strasbourg Court, the depiction has had implications for the practices and the people granted legal protection. Recognising and protecting a Gypsy way of life to the extent that it is nomadic leaves sedentary Roma in a difficult situation. For one thing, the interest in matching the cultural identity that is offered greater legal protection is likely to push sedentary Roma into nomadism. This, however, exposes Gypsies and Travellers to a life that is no longer economically viable, one based on precarious and insecure occupations.[22] Such itinerancy could also carry further disadvantages, such as exclusion from access to services that require a

---

17 See e.g. ECtHR, GC Cases of 18 January 2001: *Chapman v. the United Kingdom*, App. no. 27238/95, para. 73; *Beard v. the United Kingdom*, App. no. 24882/94, para. 84; *Coster v. the United Kingdom*, App. no. 24876/94, para. 87.

18 ECtHR, (GC) *Chapman v. the United Kingdom*, App. no. 27238/95, Judgment of 18 January 2001, para. 105; (GC) *Beard v. the United Kingdom*, App. no. 24882/94, Judgment of 18 January 2001, para. 116; (GC) *Coster v. the United Kingdom*, App. no. 24876/94, Judgment of 18 January 2001, para. 119; (GC) *Lee v. the United Kingdom*, App. no. 25289/94, Judgment 18 January 2001, para. 107; *Clark and Others v. the United Kingdom*, App. no. 28575/95, Decision of 22 May 2001, at 11; *Harrison v. the United Kingdom*, App. no. 32263/96, Decision of 3 May 2001, at 12.

19 On related criticism, see e.g. Julie Ringelheim, 'Chapman redux: the European Court of Human Rights and Roma Traditional Lifestyle', in Eva Brems (ed.), *Diversity and European Human Rights. Rewriting Judgments of the ECHR* (Cambridge University Press, 2012), at 431–434.

20 See the discussion *supra* at Chapter 1, section 2.3 and 3.5.

21 Sebastian Poulter, *Ethnicity, Law, and Human Rights: the English experience* (Clarendon Press, 1998), at 541.

22 The Traveller Movement, *A Place to call home: Ethnicity, culture and planning for Traveller sites* (The Traveller Movement, 2014), at 3–4 and 8.

fixed residency, a problem well reflected in the experience of the applicant in *Connors*.[23] For another thing, the protection of a narrow Gypsy way of life made it harder for some Roma and Travellers to convince the Court, and arguably domestic authorities too, that they belonged to the protected minority and were entitled to redress. This is suggested by the fact that the Court had routinely found against applicants who did not appear to follow *the* traditional 'Gypsy lifestyle', like those in *Chapman*, *Coster*, *Clark* and others.[24]

With time though, the Court has shown greater awareness of these problems and moved away from its previous legal emphasis on nomadism. In *Connors v. The United Kingdom*, for instance, the Court points out that while many Gypsies remained nomadic just in spirit, the domestic law continued regarding nomadism the *raison d'être* of special regulations that allowed summary evictions from official sites.[25] The Court then criticised the United Kingdom for placing major obstacles in the way of those pursuing an itinerant lifestyle while also excluding from procedural protection those living a sedentary life. Furthermore, in more recent case law the sedentary lifestyle of Roma and Travellers, as marked by, for example, community life with strong family and social ties, has also received heightened protection under Article 8.[26] Though the reduction of a 'Gypsy' culture to itinerancy was abandoned by the Court, questions about group identity resurfaced in another fashion. In 2011, in deciding the admissibility of *Horie v. the United Kingdom*, the Court was of the opinion that unlike Romani Gypsies and Irish Travellers, 'New Travellers live a nomadic lifestyle through personal choice and not on account of being born into any ethnic or cultural group'.[27] The assertion was *obiter dicta*, but it disclosed another disquieting form of controlling and reinforcing group boundaries. The Traveller identity was defined by an ethnic origin physically determined. In other words, issues of behaviour and belief were attributed by the Court to biologically inherited characteristics. An outstanding implication of this approach is the potential disregard for rights claims associated with needs and concerns that are, by contrast, perceived as 'chosen'. As further discussed *infra* at section 3.2, both the premises and the consequences of this stance are problematic.

---

23 ECtHR, *Connors v. the United Kingdom*, App. no. 66746/01, Judgment of 27 May 2004, para. 35 (Mr Connors had no permanent address and he used his wife's address for postal purposes, including medical appointments).

24 See judgments and decision cited *supra* n. 18.

25 ECtHR, *Connors v. the United Kingdom*, App. no. 66746/01, Judgment of 27 May 2004, para. 93.

26 ECtHR, *Yordanova and Others v. Bulgaria*, App. no. 25446/06, Judgment of 24 April 2012, paras. 105, 121 and 131; *Winterstein and Others v. France*, App. no. 27013/07, Judgment of 17 October 2013, para. 71.

27 ECtHR, *Horie v. the United Kingdom*, App. no. 31845/10, Decision of 1 February 2011, paras. 28–29. On this case see also the post by Lourdes Peroni and Alexandra Timmer, 'Gypsy Way of Life "By Birth" or "By Choice"', *Strasbourg Observers*, 22 February 2011, <strasbourgobservers.com/category/cases/horie-v-uk/>.

But as will be seen below, the attempt to grasp the stakes of the case by focusing on a certain distinctive cultural identity is not exclusive to the Court's case law on Roma lifestyle under Article 8 ECHR. Contested judicial appraisals of culture and group boundaries take place as well in the context of religious diversity cases, such as those concerning Muslims and Islam. While these are discussed in the next subsection, it is important to keep in mind the question of whose and which interests and norms remain visible.

2.2. ISLAM DEFINED AND MUSLIMS' IDENTITY UNDER ARTICLE 9 ECHR

As already noted, while scholars consider the Court to be fairly attentive towards collective aspects of freedom of religion, such as those concerning the autonomy of religious communities,[28] a marked difference is evident in how the Court's discourse constructs the ethnic-religious groups to which applicants allegedly belong. In this respect, difficulties of essentialism and group boundaries are notably at issue in cases involving Islam, particularly those on state prohibitions of 'conspicuous' religious symbols and headscarves in schools, the parliament, universities, the workplace, the judiciary and in other contexts.[29] In order to rule these cases, the Court has put considerable emphasis on religious difference, mostly by focusing on the applicants' religious practice, set against state neutrality.[30]

A series of decisions and judgments issued by the Court on the wearing of the hijab in public settings provide a good overview of the Court's initial approach to Islam and Muslims, especially Muslim women. By attributing certain values and meanings to the Islamic veil, the Court has delineated the contours of Islam and Muslims' identity.[31] A number of definitional features were set out

28 See e.g. Julie Ringelheim, 'Rights, Religion and the Public Sphere: The European Court of Human Rights in Search of a Theory?', in Lorenzo Zucca and Camil Ungureanu (eds.), *Law, State and Religion in the New Europa: Debates and Dilemmas* (Cambridge University Press, 2012), at 287–288 and 295; Eva Brems, 'Human Rights as a framework for negotiating/protecting cultural differences: an exploration of the case-law of the European Court of Human Rights', in Marie-Claire Foblets *et al.* (eds.), *Cultural Diversity and the Law: State Responses Around the World* (Bruylant, 2010), at 680; Carolyn Evans, 'Individual and Group Religious Freedom in the European Court of Human Rights: Cracks in the Intellectual Architecture', 26 *Journal of Law & Religion* (2010) 321, at 335–343.

29 Other contexts include the wearing of religious garments in official photographs and public places. See, for example, EComm.HR, *Karaduman v. Turkey*, App. no. 16278/90, Decision of 3 May 1993 and ECtHR, ECtHR, (GC) *S.A.S. v. France*, App. no. 43835/11, Judgment of 1 July 2014.

30 See, for example, the case law summarised in ECtHR, *Dogru v. France*, App. no. 27058/05, Judgment of 4 December 2008, paras. 61–72.

31 To understand the use of the term religious identity in this context, it is helpful to recall the link between the notions of religion as identity and religion as a way of life. Gunn usefully explains that 'religion as identity emphasizes affiliation with a group. In this sense, identity

through cases dealing with restrictions and bans on veiling that were challenged by Muslim women and girls in the context of public educational institutions, such as *Karaduman*, *Dahlab*, *Sahin*, *Dogru* and *Kervanci*. First, the Court – and the Commission before it – was of the opinion that the hijab was a 'powerful' or ostentatious symbol which exerted pressure or had a proselytising effect.[32] Second, the Court presented it as coercive and contrary to gender equality, insofar as it appeared to be imposed on women by the *Qur'an*.[33] The hijab was thus situated in opposition to the tenets underlying the European Convention, inasmuch as it 'could not easily be reconciled with the message of tolerance, respect for others and, above all, equality and non-discrimination'.[34] Third, the aforementioned rulings, as well as those dealing with the discharge of Muslim men studying or working in the army on account of professing Islam, also connected their religious identity to radicalisation or fundamentalism and thus to intolerance and threats to public order.[35]

Though constructed mostly in the context of religious garments, the above value assessment of Islam persisted and even deepened with the Grand Chamber judgment on the constitutionality of the pro-Islam Welfare Party in Turkey.[36] The case concerns the decision of the Turkish Constitutional Court to dissolve an established political party, the Refah Party, for aiming at activities contrary to secularism. Additionally, six of its leaders were barred from taking part in

---

religion is experienced as something akin to family, ethnicity, race, or nationality … it is more likely to emphasize shared histories, cultures, ethnicity, and traditions.' See T. Jeremy Gunn, 'The Complexity of Religion and the Definition of "Religion" in International Law', 16 *Harvard Human Rights Journal* (2003) 189, at 201–205.

32 See e.g. EComm.HR, *Karaduman v. Turkey*, App. no. 16278/90, Decision of 3 May 1993, at 108; ECtHR, *Dahlab v. Switzerland*, App. no. 42393/98, Decision of 15 February 2001, at 2 and 13; (GC) *Leyla Şahin v. Turkey*, App. no. 44774/98, Judgment of 10 November 2005, para. 111; *Kervanci v. France*, App. no. 31645/04, Judgment of 4 December 2008, para. 71; *Dogru v. France*, App. no. 27058/05, Judgment of 4 December 2008; *Ebrahimian v. France*, App. no. 64846/11, Judgment of 26 November 2015, paras. 62 and 69.

33 ECtHR, *Dahlab v. Switzerland*, App. no. 42393/98, Decision of 15 February 2001, at 13; (GC) *Leyla Şahin v. Turkey*, App. no. 44774/98, Judgment of 10 November 2005, paras. 111 and 115.

34 ECtHR, *Dahlab v. Switzerland*, App. no. 42393/98, Decision of 15 February 2001, para. 13; (GC) *Leyla Şahin v. Turkey*, App. no. 44774/98, Judgment of 10 November 2005, para. 116 (here the Court used not the same wording, but a similar one).

35 In the context of the military career, EComm.HR, *Yanasik v. Turkey*, App. no. 14524/89, Decision of 6 January1993, at 23 and 27; ECtHR, *Kalaç v. Turkey*, App. no. 20704/92, Judgment of 1 July 1997, paras. 25 and 28. Regarding bans on religious garments, see EComm.HR, *Bulut v. Turkey*, App. no. 18783/91, Decision of 3 May 1993 ('… lorsqu'elles établissent les règles disciplinaires concernant la tenue vestimentaire des étudiants, peuvent veiller à ce que certains courants fondamentalistes religieux ne troublent l'ordre public …'); ECtHR, *Dahlab v. Switzerland*, App. no. 42393/98, Decision of 15 February 2001, at 11–13; (GC) *Leyla Şahin v. Turkey*, App. no. 44774/98, Judgment of 10 November 2005, para. 114. See also, Carolyn Evans, '"The Islamic Scarf' in the European Court of Human Rights', 7 *Melbourne Journal of International Law* (2006) 52, at 69–71.

36 ECtHR, (GC) *Refah Partisi (The Welfare Party) and Others v. Turkey*, Application nos. 41340/98, 41342/98, 41343/98 and 41344/98, Judgment of 13 February 2003.

political party activities for five years. In upholding the unconstitutionality of the party, the Grand Chamber, like the Chamber, found it

> difficult to declare one's respect for democracy and human rights while at the same time supporting a regime based on Sharia, which clearly diverges from Convention values, particularly with regard to its criminal law and criminal procedure, its rules on the legal status of women and the way it intervenes in all spheres of private and public life in accordance with religious precepts.[37]

Strikingly, the passage also refers to the 'stable and invariable' character of Sharia, an assertion that stands in open contradiction to the unbounded and changing character of cultures so repeatedly stressed by anthropologists elsewhere.[38] The Grand Chamber reasoned along similar lines in *Yiğit v. Turkey*, a case dealing with a widow who was unable to obtain a survivor pension as a result of having married under Islamic rites only.[39] Besides the importance Turkey accorded to the principle of secularism, the Court noted that the state party 'aimed to put an end to a marriage tradition which places women at a clear disadvantage, not to say in a situation of dependence and inferiority, compared to men'.[40] This line of reasoning has, unsurprisingly, attracted abundant criticism.[41]

Some relevant shifts, however, took place in the 2013 case of *S.A.S. v. France*. Here the Court examined the French blanket ban on the full-face veil (*niqab*) in public places. In this context, and unlike previous cases, the Court did not define Islam in terms of its alleged opposition to gender equality. It stated that 'a State Party cannot invoke gender equality in order to ban a practice that is defended by women'.[42] The full-face veiling was then considered 'the expression of a cultural identity which contributes to the pluralism that is inherent in democracy'.[43] The Court furthermore noted 'the variability of the notions of virtuousness and decency that are applied to the uncovering of the human body'.[44]

---

37 Ibid., para. 123.

38 See e.g. Sally Engle Merry, 'Human Rights Law and the Demonization of Culture (And Anthropology Along the Way)', 26(1) *Political and Legal Anthropology Review* (2003) 55, at 67; Toon van Meijl, 'Anthropological Perspectives on Identity: From Sameness to Difference', in Margaret Wetherell and Chandra Talpade Mohanty, *The SAGE Handbook of Identities* (SAGE Publications, 2010), at 63–71.

39 ECtHR, (GC) *Şerife Yiğit v. Turkey*, App. no. 3976/05, Judgment of 2 November 2010.

40 Ibid., para. 81. The Court assessed the state's refusal to recognise religious marriages in light of, for example, the prohibition of polygamy and respect for gender equality.

41 Eva Brems, 'Human Rights as a framework for negotiating/protecting cultural differences: an exploration of the case-law of the European Court of Human Rights', in Marie-Claire Foblets *et al.* (eds.), *Cultural Diversity and the Law: State Responses Around the World* (Bruylant, 2010), at 678 (stating that it represents 'a worrying tendency too of an outsider interpretation of religious symbols which barely rises above the level of prejudice').

42 ECtHR, (GC) *S.A.S. v. France*, App. no. 43835/11, Judgment of 1 July 2014, para. 119.

43 Ibid., para. 120.

44 Idem.

Ultimately, however, the Court accepted the ban, this time on the basis of the extra-conventional ground invoked by France of preserving the conditions of 'living together'.[45] While the association between Islam and fundamentalism also receded within public order considerations, the full-face veil appeared to compromise security and social cohesion due to the importance of individuals' faces for identification and social interaction. However, as discussed below, evidence as to how a face veil could make social life impossible or as to the likelihood that the ban would improve social interaction was lacking in the judgment. For the dissenting judges, the majority's decision built on uneasiness and fears around Islam and the full-face veil, the sources of which are the philosophical and symbolic meanings attributed to them.[46] This last observation may find support in the fact that, although the ban is general and not addressed to anyone in particular, so far only the covering of the face inspired by Islam, and no other forms of face concealment that occur in our societies, has engendered so much debate and unsettledness that it has been found necessary to enact a blanket ban.

Although the same line of reasoning of *S.A.S.* was restated in the 2017 cases of *Dakir v. Belgium* and *Belcacemi and Oussar v. Belgium*,[47] some judgments between the three offer a different discourse, one in which the focus on the distinctiveness of Islam appears mitigated. In *Ebrahimian v. France*, a case brought by a social worker of the psychiatric ward of a public hospital whose contract was not renewed because she wore the *hijab*, the Court's analysis does not revolve so much around the characteristics attributed to the *hijab* or to Islam. Instead, most of the Court's reasoning concerns public servants' duty of neutrality and the centrality of secularism in the French context. Yet, it is interesting to observe that the *hijab* was still regarded as an outward symbol inherently conflicting with the equal treatment and impartiality owed to all users of public services.[48] At the same time, while the reasoning seems to abandon the emphasis on Islam and religious identity, it does move somewhat towards a normative analysis of French identity as expressed in neutrality and secularism. This alerts us to movement from a normative framework centred on one narrow category, say that of group identity, to one centred on another, in this case, the collective identity of the state. In both scenarios, the risks of keeping the analysis at a fragmented and abstract level, losing sight of the multiple identities of rights holders and of the whole range of affected rights, are quite similar. As Minow noted decades ago, 'the use of a specific notion of identity to resolve a

---

45 ECtHR, (GC) *S.A.S. v. France*, App. no. 43835/11, Judgment of 1 July 2014, paras. 121–122.

46 ECtHR, (GC) *S.A.S. v. France*, App. no. 43835/11, Judgment of 1 July 2014, Joint partly dissenting opinion of Judges Nussberger and Jäderblom, para. 6.

47 ECtHR, *Dakir v. Belgium*, App. no. 4619/12, Judgment of 11 July 2017; *Belcacemi and Oussar v. Belgium*, App. no. 37798/13, Judgment of 11 July 2017.

48 ECtHR, *Ebrahimian v. France*, App. no. 64846/11, Judgment of 26 November 2015, paras. 62–63 and 67–71.

legal dispute can obscure the complexity of lived experiences while imposing the force of the state behind the selected notion of identity'.[49]

It should be noted though that the adjudication of other cases involving Muslims' religious practices has been largely devoid of group identity and religious determinations. Cases of religious exemption from school lessons such as *Hasan and Eylem v. Turkey* and *Osmanoğlu and Kocabaş v. Switzerland* are examples.[50] In the former, two parents unsuccessfully requested the school authorities to exempt her daughter from lessons on religious culture and ethics since their content was based on the Sunni understanding of Islam, while the applicants were adherents of the Alevi faith, a minority branch of Islam. The case of *Osmanoğlu and Kocabaş*, in turn, concerned a request from Muslim parents to exempt their daughter from compulsory mixed-gender swimming classes on religious grounds. Likewise, another normative approach can be seen in a case concerning the wearing of Islam-related attire in the public space but which, unlike the cases discussed above, involved male Muslims.[51] What these cases show is that their resolution did not require the Court to endorse a normative analysis reduced to questions of religious difference and group identity. Actually, to different degrees, these judgments took heed of the specific situation of the applicants and other rights holders, bearing in mind who they were and in which contexts the restrictions applied. I will return to these judgments below.

Given the Court's emphasis on the (negative) appraisal of Islam and Islamic veiling in particular, the perils of cultural essentialism displayed in some cases involving Muslims and Islam may seem evident by now. Former Judge Tulkens noted some of them when dissenting in *Sahin*, a case brought by a medical student challenging a ban on the wearing of the Islamic headscarf in universities and other state educational institutions in Turkey. The judge argued that

> it is not the Court's role to make an appraisal of this type – in this instance a unilateral and negative one – of a religion or religious practice, just as it is not its role to determine in a general and abstract way the signification of wearing the headscarf or to impose its viewpoint on the applicant.[52]

Against the background of prevailing (Christian-based) notions of secularism and religion understood as 'privatised belief',[53] the impact of the Court's assumptions

---

49 Martha Minow, 'Identities', 3 *Yale Journal of Law & the Humanities* (1991) 97, at 111.

50 ECtHR, *Hasan and Eylem v. Turkey*, App. no. 1448/04, Judgment of 9 October 2007; *Osmanoğlu and Kocabaş v. Switzerland*, App. no. 29086/12, Judgment of 10 January 2017.

51 ECtHR, *Ahmet Arslan and Others v. Turkey*, Application no. 41135/98, Judgment of 23 February 2010.

52 ECtHR, (GC) *Leyla Şahin v. Turkey*, App. no. 44774/98, Judgment of 10 November 2005, Dissenting opinion of Judge Tulkens, para. 11.

53 Peter G. Danchin, 'Islam in the Secular Nomos of the European Court of Human Rigths', 32(4) *Michigan Journal of International Law* (2011) 663, at 672 (noting how Christian

about Islam and Muslims' way of life upon the application of Article 9 ECHR should not be underestimated. Framing the normative inquiry as one about what is accepted or permitted for a 'different' religious tradition characterised by outward manifestation, pressure, fundamentalism and threats to equality is likely to predetermine any subsequent analysis, whether in relation to the state's margin of appreciation, the protection of public order or the rights of others. Moreover, as further discussed below, a discourse too concerned with a distinctive identity or religious practice – for example, the wearing of headscarves – feeds a quite unidimensional way of understanding who the persons affected are and what the harms at stake in the cases are. Note, for example, how in the cases discussed earlier the analysis focuses on veiled Muslim women and those who might be negatively affected by an exposure to them. It also examines how such practice undermines the agency of those persons; how to deal with the religious injury of banning headscarves, and with threats to gender equality, to social cohesion and to neutrality and secularism. Viewed this way, several dimensions of the cases seem to be side-lined, as will be seen later.

2.3. ROMA'S VULNERABILITY AND MUSLIMS' INVULNERABILITY

As stated at the outset, in several cases reviewed here the Court has emphasised that Roma people constitute a vulnerable group. In characterising the Roma as a minority in a vulnerable position, the Court has notably relied on Council of Europe recommendations.[54] These contend, *inter alia*, that Gypsies are 'a true European minority' who 'greatly contribute to the cultural diversity of

narratives have shaped the Court's understanding of secularism and religious subjectivity, the latter being understood as something internal. He also argues that 'the tacit background assumptions shaping the public-private divide-religion as primarily a matter of belief or conscience whose proper place is in the private sphere become more visible when it is a Muslim who seeks to manifest a non-Christian belief or practice in the public sphere'); T. Jeremy Gunn, 'The Complexity of Religion and the Definition of "Religion" in International Law', 16 *Harvard Human Rights Journal* (2003) 189, at 200 and 204 (noting that a conception of religion that has at its core the idea of religion as belief corresponds to a modern privatised Christian view of religion).

54 See PACE, Recommendation 1203 (1993) on Gypsies in Europe, Adopted on 2 February 1993; Recommendation 1557 (2002) on the Legal Situation of Roma in Europe, Adopted on 25 April 2002; EU COCEN; Recommendation on the Situation of Roma in the Candidate Countries: Background Document – Guiding Principles for Improving the Situation of the Roma based on the Recommendations of the Council of Europe's Specialist Group of Roma/Gipsy and on the Recommendation of the OSCE High Commissioner on National Minorities, Adopted by the European Union (COCEN group) at the Tampere Summit, December 1999. The Court has also referred to PACE recommendations on combating discrimination and social exclusion of the Roma, such as Resolution 1740 (2010) on the situation of Roma in Europe and relevant activities of the Council of Europe, Adopted on 22 June 2010.

Europe (...) be it by language and music or by their trades and crafts'.[55] Such recommendations also situate their group vulnerability in relation to 'a double minority status', as the Roma belong to an ethnic community and to some of the most socially disadvantaged groups.[56] The Court has also linked this vulnerability to a history of discrimination and social exclusion widely acknowledged by the Council of Europe and by several human rights monitoring bodies.[57] Though not as salient as the Gypsy way of life, group vulnerability also shapes in significant ways the framing and outcome of the cases.

Spelling out the legal consequences of group vulnerability, the Court has held that 'the vulnerable position of Roma/Gypsies means that special consideration should be given to their needs and their different lifestyle, both in the relevant regulatory framework and in reaching decisions in particular cases'.[58] A positive obligation to facilitate the 'Gypsy way of life' has thereby been imposed on states.[59] This does not go as far as to exempt Roma people from the application of general laws. But it does make of their minority and vulnerable status an element to be considered by the state when crafting regulations and implementing them.[60] It also narrows the state's margin of appreciation,[61] not a minor effect in cases dealing with cultural and social policy matters. In fact, states have been granted a wide margin of discretion on social issues such as planning, housing and educational policies (typically challenged by Roma and

55 PACE, Recommendation 1203 (1993) on Gypsies in Europe, Adopted on 2 February 1993, paras. 1–3.

56 PACE, Recommendation 1557 (2002) on the Legal Situation of Roma in Europe, Adopted on 25 April 2002, para. 4.

57 See, for example, the Council of Europe's material referenced by the Court in ECtHR, *Yordanova and Others v. Bulgaria*, App. no. 25446/06, Judgment of 24 April 2012, paras. 73–79. Following a similar approach, in cases such as *D.H. and Others* and *Oršuš and Others*, the Court has stated that 'as a result of their history' the Roma 'has become a specific type of disadvantaged and vulnerable minority' in need of special protection. ECtHR, (GC) *D.H. and Others v. the Czech Republic*, App. no. 57325/00, Judgment of 13 November 2007, para. 182; ECtHR, (GC) *Oršuš and Others v. Croatia*, App. no. 15766/03, Judgment of 16 March 2010, para. 147.

58 ECtHR, (GC) *Chapman v. the United Kingdom*, App. no. 27238/95, Judgment of 18 January 2001, para. 96; *Connors v. the United Kingdom*, App. no. 66746/01, Judgment of 27 May 2004, para. 84; *Horie v. the United Kingdom*, App. no. 31845/10, Decision of 1 February 2011, para. 26; (GC) *D.H. and Others v. the Czech Republic*, App. no. 57325/00, Judgment of 13 November 2007, para. 181; (GC) *Oršuš and Others v. Croatia*, App. no. 15766/03, Judgment of 16 March 2010, para. 148; *Horváth and Kiss v. Hungary*, App. no. 11146/11, Judgment of 29 January 2013, para. 102; *Winterstein and Others v. France*, App. no. 27013/07, Judgment of 17 October 2013, para. 88; *Muñoz Díaz v. Spain*, App. no. 49151/07, Judgment of 8 December 2009, para. 61.

59 See e.g. ECtHR, (GC) *Chapman v. the United Kingdom*, App. no. 27238/95, Judgment of 18 January 2001, para. 96; (GC) *Beard v. the United Kingdom*, App. no. 24882/94, Judgment of 18 January 2001, para. 107; (GC) *Coster v. the United Kingdom*, App. no. 24876/94, Judgment of 18 January 2001, para. 110; (GC) *Lee v. the United Kingdom*, App. no. 25289/94, Judgment 18 January 2001, para. 98.

60 See *supra* notes 58 and 59 and the references therein.

61 ECtHR, *Alajos Kiss v. Hungary*, App. no. 38832/06, Judgment of 20 May 2010, para. 42.

Traveller complaints), especially where they involve a multitude of local actors or where there is significant diversity of practices across member states.[62] The special protection afforded to Roma/Travellers as a vulnerable group has thus extended to different fields, including education, planning and housing. In the judgments on educational segregation of Roma children, for example, the status of vulnerable group was linked to a specific form of disadvantage related to longstanding prejudice and discrimination.[63] In practice, however, the incidence of group vulnerability was quite limited in most cases concerning the stationing of caravans.[64] Or at least it was until the 2013 case of *Winterstein v. France*, a judgment dealing with the eviction faced by mostly settled Travellers living in mobile homes *de facto* tolerated by the authorities. Here the Court found for the applicants on the ground that the state had failed to take into account the needs of evicted Travellers seeking relocation in family plots.[65] According to the Court, the vulnerability and lifestyle of the group had a role to play not only when assessing the proportionality of eviction, but also when deciding on the specific arrangements applicable in the event of removal, including timing and alternative shelter.[66]

The Court's interest in coming to grips with the disadvantaged ('vulnerable') situation of the Roma as a group seems not only justified, but also potentially beneficial for the protection of human rights in a number of cases. Qualifying this and other groups as vulnerable might help in unveiling group asymmetries and social barriers, placing individual disadvantages – cultural or otherwise – within a social context.[67] A few examples of these opportunities have already

---

62 See, *inter alia*, ECtHR, (CG) *Chapman v. the United Kingdom*, App. no. 27238/95, Judgment of 18 January 2001, para. 92; (GC) *Beard v. the United Kingdom*, App. no. 24882/94, Judgment of 18 January 2001, para. 103; *Yordanova and Others v. Bulgaria*, App. no. 25446/06, Judgment of 24 April 2012, para. 118(1); *Winterstein and Others v. France*, App. no. 27013/07, Judgment of 17 October 2013, para. 76 (α); *Horváth and Kiss v. Hungary*, App. no. 11146/11, Judgment of 29 January 2013, para. 103; *Dakir v. Belgium*, App. no. 4619/12, Judgment of 11 July 2017, para. 54.

63 ECRtHR, (GC) *D.H. and Others v. the Czech Republic*, App. no. 57325/00, Judgment of 13 November 2007, paras. 54–80, 182; *Horváth and Kiss v. Hungary*, App. no. 11146/11, Judgment of 29 January 2013, paras. 102 and 110.

64 ECtHR, (GC) *Chapman v. the United Kingdom*, App. no. 27238/95, Judgment of 18 January 2001, Joint Dissenting Opinion of Judges Pastor Ridruejo, Bonello, Tulkens, Strážnická, Lorenzen, Fischbach and Casadevall, paras. 1 and 3–4 and Separate Opinion of Judge Bonello, para. 6. Moreover, virtually all Roma/Traveller cases involving the stationing of caravans in which the Court recognised their group vulnerability, with the notable exception of Connors, Buckland and Winterstein, either dismissed the applicants' claims or found against them.

65 ECtHR, *Winterstein and Others v. France*, App. no. 27013/07, Judgment of 17 October 2013, paras. 90–94.

66 Ibid., para. 88. (Following ECtHR, *Yordanova and Others v. Bulgaria*, App. no. 25446/06, Judgment of 24 April 2012.)

67 This reading of vulnerability, tied to substantive equality, is propounded by Lourdes Peroni in the context of the Court's case law on group vulnerability. She argues that group vulnerability not only 'switches the attention from the individual to the environment that puts her

been introduced. Take, for instance, the way in which vulnerability gave rise to the state's procedural obligation to facilitate the Gypsy way of life. This may increase the participation of Roma people in the design and enforcement of institutions (e.g. development plans, housing policies, education programmes) usually crafted without their involvement. This obligation also has the potential to set out a duty to accommodate their needs and practices, so far largely disregarded in most European countries. Another illustration is provided by the Court's finding of indirect discrimination in cases of systematic placement of Roma children in separate classes or separate schools, which was based on an analysis of the group's *de facto* social exclusion.[68]

Yet, and bearing in mind that it is beyond the scope of this book to unpack fully the notion of vulnerability or its effects,[69] there are some risks in adopting the group vulnerability frame as applied in the cases studied. First, group vulnerability, especially when it operates more as an identity attribute than as something contingent, may overshadow the specific circumstances of its members as well as the social structures that are a source of vulnerability. This could explain, for example, the fact that despite the recognition of Roma's vulnerability, the Court has not in practice accorded much weight to the intersecting vulnerabilities experienced by some applicants or the constraints they faced as a result of housing and planning policies, which are further examined below.[70] A second difficulty is, as pointed out by Peroni and Timmer, the possibility of portraying some groups, and hence their members, as inherently vulnerable,

at disadvantage'. It also asks 'how the same environment that is disadvantaging some is simultaneously privileging others'. See Lourdes Peroni, *Opening Up the European Convention Human Rights Subject: An Inclusive Multilayered Framework for Adjudicating Religious and Cultural Claims*, PhD Dissertation (Ghent University, 2014), at 100. The doctrine of group vulnerability may also come close to the notion of group subordination articulated by Fiss within the framework of equality and non-discrimination back in the late 1970s. See Owen M. Fiss, 'Groups and the Equal Protection Clause', 5(2) *Philosophy & Public Affairs* (1976) 107. A similar but more recent account of group subordination can be seen in Roberto Saba, '(Des)Igualdad Estructural', 11 *Derecho y Humanidades* (2005) 123.

68 ECtHR, (GC) *D.H. and Others v. the Czech Republic*, App. no. 57325/00, Judgment of 13 November 2007. See further discussion *infra* section 3.1.1.

69 For this, see Martha Albertson Fineman, 'The Vulnerable Subject: Anchoring Equality in the Human Condition', 20 *Yale Journal of Law & Feminism* (2008) 1; Lourdes Peroni and Alexandra Timmer, 'Vulnerable Groups: The Promise of an Emerging Concept in European Human Rights Convention Law', 11(4) *International Journal of Constitutional Law* (2013) 1056. For an analysis of group vulnerability in the Inter-American Court, see Romina I. Sijniensky, 'From the Non-Discrimination Clause to the Concept of Vulnerability in International Human Rights Law. Advancing the Needs for Special Protection of Certain Groups and Individuals', in Yves Haeck *et al.* (eds.), *The Realisation of Human Rights: When Theory Meets Practice. Studies in Honour of Leo Zwaak* (Intersentia, 2013), at 259–272. See also Chapter 3, sections 2 and 3 and Chapter 5, sections 2 and 3.

70 This issue is discussed *infra* section 3.1.1.

which may undermine their agency and empowerment.[71] As further analysed below, this may also reduce the Court's understanding of the case. A third risk to consider, also noted by the same authors, is the adoption of a fixed view of 'what is allowed to fall under the vulnerable-group concept'[72] in a way that 'unduly limits the application of group-vulnerability reasoning'.[73] Possibly grounded in the belief that group protection concerns 'discrete insular minorities',[74] this may foster the perception that only some groups are vulnerable. It is as if the vulnerable groups were 'out there' awaiting judicial recognition. The Roma appear to be one of those 'true' minority groups, Muslims do not. In contrast to the rulings dealing with the Roma, the judicial discourse on Muslims and Islam evolved, in the cases studied, without any allusion to group vulnerability. But if group vulnerability has something to do with social disadvantage, widespread prejudice or a history of discrimination, then it is quite surprising – to say the least – that the Court has not considered this religious group through the prism of vulnerability. There is, in fact, abundant material within and beyond the Council of Europe documenting the exclusion, discrimination and stereotyping of Muslims (especially women).[75] And recognition of vulnerability in the Court's case law is not trivial. As explained with regard to the Roma, it does affect the course of adjudication.

2.4. CROSSING GROUP BOUNDARIES AND MOVING DOWN TO THE REAL-LIFE HUMAN

A legal focus on group boundaries, whether fixed around ethno-cultural and religious identity or around vulnerability, may reduce the visual range of the

---

71 Lourdes Peroni and Alexandra Timmer, 'Vulnerable Groups: The Promise of an Emerging Concept in European Human Rights Convention Law', 11 *International Journal of Constitutional Law* (2013) 1056, at 1072–1073. These authors also analyse this problem, which they explore in terms of 'stigmatisation' and 'paternalism'.

72 Ibid., at 1072.

73 Idem.

74 This concept is at the core of minority protection and anti-discrimination doctrines, including the application of 'suspect categories'. Its origin lies with the Supreme Court of the United States, more concretely, with footnote 4 of its judgment in Supreme Court of the United States, *United States v. Carolene Products Co.*, 304 U.S. 144, Decision adopted on 25 April 1938.

75 See, e.g. PACE, Resolution 1743 (2010) on Islam, Islamism and Islamophobia in Europe, Adopted on 23 June 2010, at 1; Irene Zempi and Neil Chakraborti, *Islamophobia, Victimization and the Veil* (Palgrave Macmillan, 2014); Council of Europe, Living Together: Combining diversity and Freedom in 21st-century Europe – Report of the Group of Eminent Persons of the Council of Europe (Council of Europe, 2011), at 15–16; UN Human Rights Council, Report of the Special Rapporteur on freedom of religion or belief on his mission to Denmark, Heiner Bielefeldt, A/HRC/34/50/Add.1, 28 December 2016, paras. 28–35 and Report of the Special Rapporteur on freedom of religion or belief on her mission to France, Asma Jahangir, E/CN.4/2006/5/Add.4, 8 March 2006, paras. 63, 67 and 101–104.

Court in a number of ways. A first difficulty to note has to do with the centrality that cultural/religious difference acquires within the overall judicial discourse. This may lead the Court, and indeed it is argued it has done so, to overemphasise a group identity represented by cultural symbols (such as the wearing of headscarves) and traditional practices (such as living in itinerant caravans) at the expense of the specific needs and interests of applicants and other rights holders.[76] What is more, so long as such an emphasis locates the social conflicts underlying the cases within one culture/religion or group, then the culture/religion or group itself becomes the reason for the dispute. When this happens, it is more likely that the Court will pass over broader issues of power imbalance, such as widespread discrimination, poverty, racism, islamophobia and so on. This could be one of the reasons why, as will be seen below, little attention has been accorded to racial discrimination and socio-economic inequality in the so-called 'caravan cases'. A similar concern goes for the so-called 'headscarf cases'. In these cases, the emphasis on religious difference and identity is in reverse proportion to the analysis of discrimination and islamophobia.[77] At the same time, that emphasis has come with several abstract questions such as the meaning of neutrality, secularism and pluralism.

A second problem, which is further examined below, is that besides giving rise to stereotypes about the collectivity and its cultural identity, the reification of a social group also mobilises stereotypes about its members. Besides compromising equality and non-discrimination norms, such stereotypes operate as a way of controlling, once again, the boundaries of the group. In the cases studied, these stereotypes of Muslims and Roma furthermore tended to obscure the actual experience of the applicants before the Court. As a consequence, stereotypes made it easier to adjudicate on the basis of abstract considerations instead of evidence regarding the specific interests and harms experienced by rights holders.

A third problem relates to the group identity assessment carried out by the Court, which carries implications beyond the cases discussed above. Why are some cultures or groups more deserving than others and whose viewpoint is taken into account in coming to that decision? There is certainly something troubling

---

76 In this vein, see also Lourdes Peroni, *Opening Up the European Convention Human Rights Subject: An Inclusive Multilayered Framework for Adjudicating Religious and Cultural Claims*, PhD Dissertation (Ghent University, 2014), at 206–214 (discussing a number of cases in which stereotypes and naturalisations push the applicant to the background).

77 Issues of racism and widespread discrimination were nonetheless addressed by the Court in cases dealing with the school segregation of Roma children. To a lesser extent, the Court also referred to discrimination concerns in the case of *S.A.S. v. France* on the full-face covering ban, although without normative consequences for the case. Nonetheless, it should also be noted that in these cases the Court's normative analysis was less concerned with defining the cultural/religious identities in question. The Court's approach in these cases is further discussed *infra* sections 3.1.3 and 4.1.1.

about restricting protection or accommodation to practices representative of cultures or identities deemed worthy enough of judicial approval.[78] Besides the problems enumerated above, the positive or negative assessment of any given culture or identity risks undermining the ideal of judicial neutrality, understood as impartiality and fairness. Indeed, charges of possible bias and double standards have already been voiced against the Court, particularly with regard to its case law involving Islam.[79] Former Judge Kovler critically raised this point: 'on the one hand, the Court recognised the specific character of Romas' way of life and the necessity of its protection (...) on the other side, in some cases the Court manifested a certain hostility in respect of Islamic values and institutions.'[80]

This question holds special relevance for a Court that is actually called on to rule on a wide range of culturally driven claims.[81] So long as the Court faces more claims for accommodation or for 'special' rights from a growing range of culturally-defined groups, there is greater pressure to elucidate the grounds on which the Court takes such decisions. This scenario should incentivise the Court to look beyond cultural identity and group boundaries for the purposes of justification. An integrated normative framework like the one developed in this chapter is therefore equally useful for setting limits to the flexibility of human rights law. Consider, for example, the case of individuals and a countryside association from the United Kingdom which invoked Article 8 ECHR and the protection of their lifestyle and cultural traditions as rural 'hunting communities' to challenge a state ban on fox and other animal hunting with dogs.[82] One main reason adduced by the Court to declare the complaint inadmissible was that the applicants did not belong to a 'discrete minority group' like an ethnic or national minority.[83] While this conclusion might appear self-evident here, the line-drawing is likely to be much more debatable in a number of other cases. As such,

---

78 For a discussion on the judicial protection of 'respectable' beliefs and its dangers, see Lucy Vickers, 'Religious Discrimination in the Workplace: An Emerging Hierarchy?', 12(3) *Ecclesiastical Law Journal* (2010) 280, at 284–285.

79 See *inter alia*, Turan Kayaoglu, 'Trying Islam: Muslims before the European Court of Human Rights', 34(4) *Journal of Muslim Minority Affairs* (2014) 345, at 346 and 354–360; Carolyn Evans, '"The Islamic Scarf" in the European Court of Human Rights', 7 *Melbourne Journal of International Law* (2006) 52, at 70–71; Yasin Aktay, 'European Values and the Muslim World: Turkish Cases at the European Court of Human Rights', 20(1) *Global Change Peace & Security* (2008) 99, at 99–108.

80 Anatoly Kovler, 'Human Rights in a Contemporary Society and European Values: Critique of Eurocentrism', *1 EU-Russia Paper*, Center for EU-Russia Studies, University of Tartu (2011), at 8.

81 For a general overview of the variety of culture-based claims brought to the Court, see European Court of Human Rights, Research Division, *Cultural rights in the case-law of the European Court of Human Rights* (Council of Europe, 2017).

82 ECtHR, *Friend and The Countryside Alliance and Others v. the United Kingdom*, Application nos. 16072/06 and 27809/08, Decision of 24 November 2009, paras. 36–38.

83 Ibid., para. 44. The Court also argued at para. 43 that the private life limb of Article 8 does not cover activities that are essentially public, such as hunting.

the other – more crucial – considerations provided by the Court with respect to the harm actually experienced by the applicants were very much warranted. Notably, the Court argued that the ban did not take away their employment, nor did it stigmatise them in the eyes of society.[84] These constitute legitimate and relevant normative grounds for denying the special protection sought by the applicants in that case.

Hence, moving away from normative approaches entailing judicial determinations of the sort criticised here is desirable. And, importantly, it is feasible too. The adjudication of rights claims related to cultural difference does not need to set culture or group identity as the protagonist. This does not mean denying the relevance of individuals' cultural attachments and collective identities, let alone that of group inequalities. It does mean, however, that the Court should be wary of forgetting that culture is dynamic, that people embody several identities and that cultural/religious rights are usually only part of the problem brought before the Court. In sum, a range of reasons call for courts like the ECtHR to remain aware of the fluidity of culture while also acknowledging group heterogeneity. And since group heterogeneity stems from the fact that groups are composed of people who are simultaneously members of several groups, a first step in that direction is to pay greater attention to intersectionality. The next section turns to this and to other aspects of individuals' complexity.

3. WHOLE HUMANS: LOOKING THROUGH AND ACROSS RIGHTS HOLDERS

As we have seen, cases dealing with questions of ethno-cultural diversity tend to bring one aspect of individual applicants to the forefront: their cultural or ethnic affiliation. This appears quite reasonable. The litigants' strategic choices, the categorisation inherent to adjudication and the prevalence of a one-sided view of discrimination claims all reinforce the salience of individuals' cultural attachment. Yet, in real life, individuals are more than that; considered as a whole, their experience is more complex. That is why this section builds upon an intersectional framework. To borrow the words of Hill Collins and Bilge: 'Intersectionality is a way of understanding and analysing the complexity in the world, in people, and in human experience.'[85] Complexity flows from people's multiple affiliations or 'identities' and, more crucially, from the set of social relationships in which they are embedded. Hence, a first question arises: does the Court integrate facets of individual identity and social location other than

---

84 Ibid., para. 45. These considerations were also articulated within the framework of Article 8 ECHR, but in its limb of respect for one's home.

85 Patricia Hill Collins and Sirma Bilge, *Intersectionality* (Polity Press, 2016), at 25.

culture and ethnicity into its adjudication of these cases? And how can taking this on board contribute to the handling of these or other cases? This is the first issue to be explored here.

Still connected to life complexity, the two other issues discussed in this section also relate to another important feature of intersectionality. As the same authors referred to above remind us, intersectionality is grounded in 'relational thinking'.[86] This kind of thinking rejects 'either/or' binary rationales and focuses instead on relationships. From this perspective the Court's approach to individual autonomy will be examined, a feature of rights holders quite often debated in the adjudication of the cases studied. Does the Court take into account that autonomy unfolds across intricate relationships? Does it acknowledge that, like individuals' affiliations, autonomy is not an 'either/or' issue? Lastly, a final layer of complexity and relationality is worth noting. Because people do not stand in isolation from others and from social relations, usually a wider range of rights holders are affected by the measure allegedly hindering cultural or religious aspects of applicants. Some of these individuals concur with the applicant, and some, instead, compete with her. This is the third issue addressed below. It will be seen that whether the Court acknowledges or overlooks all this complexity has important normative consequences.

3.1. LOOKING BEYOND THE CULTURAL IDENTITIES OF RIGHTS HOLDERS

3.1.1. A More Integrated View of Roma and Traveller Applicants

The majority of the complaints brought by Roma and Travellers struggling with the stationing of caravans and eviction threats posited an allegation of violation of Article 14 ECHR. Regardless of the exact framing employed, they mainly pointed to indirect discrimination. The allegation was basically this: despite the ostensible neutrality of planning regulations, they disadvantaged Gypsies and Travellers, whose lifestyle deviated from that of the majority population. The state, in sum, failed to accommodate their specific needs.[87] The Court, however, having decided on Article 8 ECHR, routinely found that there was either no violation or no further issue to examine under Article 14.[88] For a while, the

86 Ibid., at 27.

87 See e.g. ECtHR, (GC) *Beard v. the United Kingdom*, App. no. 24882/94, Judgment of 18 January 2001, para. 130; *Wells v. The United Kingdom*, App. no. 37794/05, Decision of 16 January 2007, at 7 and 10.

88 See e.g. ECtHR, (GC) *Lee v. the United Kingdom*, App. no. 25289/94, Judgment of 18 January 2001, para. 129; (GC) *Chapman v. the United Kingdom*, App. no. 27238/95, Judgment of 18 January 2001, paras. 129–130; *Smith v. the United Kingdom*, App. no. 40435/98, Decision

Court's response was that affording different treatment to Gypsies would raise an issue of discrimination against the non-Gypsy population. The applicants, in its opinion, were 'not worse than any non-gypsy who wants to live in a caravan and finds it disagreeable to live in a house'.[89] But who were those 'Gypsy' applicants and how was their experience so comparable with those 'non-gypsies'?

A closer look at the cases discussing Roma/Traveller lifestyles reveals that most of them were brought by women, either single or in a couple, living with their children. The applicants' view on their rights deprivation was therefore marked by that experience. For example, in *Buckley*, *Chapman* and its twin judgments (as well as in subsequent cases) the cultural claim was accompanied by concerns such as 'to provide a safe and stable environment for her children and to be near to the school they were attending'.[90] This last concern explains the allegations of violation of the right to education (Article 2 Protocol 1 ECHR) in such cases, a claim that the Court barely addressed. In cases such as *Smith*, *Easton* and *Connors* (all against the United Kingdom), the applicants also invoked issues of caring and family health concerns.[91] At the same time, it is not hard to appreciate that most Roma applicants, men and women, had a deprived economic situation and that this too informed their plight. In several rulings, including those in the line of *Chapman*, the Court did not only require attention

of 30 January 2001, at 15; *Linda Porter v. the United Kingdom*, App. no. 47953/99, Decision of 30 January 2001, at 10; *Connors v. the United Kingdom*, App. no. 66746/01, Judgment of 27 May 2004, para. 97; *Codona v. the United Kingdom*, App. no. 485/05, Decision of 7 February 2006, at 13–14; and *Wells v. the United Kingdom*, App. no. 37794/05, Decision of 16 January 2007, at 11. This was the case even where the problem appeared to be more about direct than indirect discrimination. ECtHR, *Harrison v. the United Kingdom*, App. no. 32263/96, Decision of 3 May 2001, at 14–15. In this case, the applicant complained about the different treatment received compared to persons involved in development projects who did obtain planning permission.

89 See cases cited *supra* note 88. See also ECtHR, (GC) *Coster v. the United Kingdom*, App. no. 24876/94, Judgment of 18 January 2001, paras. 110–111; (GC) *Beard v. the United Kingdom*, App. no. 24882/94, Judgment of 18 January 2001, para. 108.

90 EComm.HR, *Buckley v. the United Kingdom*, App. no. 20348/92, Report of 11 January 1995, paras. 23, 61 and 66; ECtHR, (GC) *Chapman v. the United Kingdom*, App. no. 27238/95, Judgment of 18 January 2001, para. 64. Where the claim was not formulated explicitly by the applicant, it was nonetheless present in the background of the case. For instance, in ECtHR, (GC) *Beard v. the United Kingdom*, App. no. 24882/94, Judgment of 18 January 2001, para. 62, reference was made to research according to which: 'Of the 50 gypsy site applicants interviewed, for most acquiring permission for their own land was an important factor in improving the quality of life, gaining independence and providing security. For many, the education of their children was another important reason for private site application.' See also the claims in ECtHR, *Winterstein and Others v. France*, App. no. 27013/07, Judgment of 17 October 2013, paras. 8, 28, 39 and 48.

91 ECtHR, *Smith v. the United Kingdom*, App. no. 40435/98, Decision of 30 January 2001, at 2–3; *Eatson v. the United Kingdom*, App. no. 39664/98, Decision of 30 January 2001, at 4 and 10; *Connors v. the United Kingdom*, App. no. 66746/01, Judgment of 27 May 2004, paras. 76 and 85.

(on grounds of group-vulnerability) to their 'different lifestyle', but also to their needs; and it even mentioned humanitarian considerations.[92] However, although this suggests awareness of the social precariousness experienced by Roma and Travellers, it does not seem that the Court had ascertained whether and how their general destitution materialised in the case of the applicants, particularly in the light of their eviction.[93]

Already in *Buckley v. the United Kingdom*, the first judgment of its kind, the Court's approach to the applicant appeared quite fragmented. A 'Gypsy' woman claimed that the prohibition of living in her caravan on her own land, coupled with the actual unavailability of alternative sites, constituted a disproportionate interference with her right to private and family life and to respect for her home. She asserted a right to settle on a safe and stable site and a right to live in a caravan and keep travelling (according to her Gypsy lifestyle) when possible. The Court turned down the Commission's finding of an Article 8 violation. And the partly dissenting Judge Repik precisely criticised the majority for not considering the impact of eviction on the applicant 'given her financial and family situation'.[94] Along these lines, Dembour argues that by overlooking these facets of the applicants' experience the Court disappoints those who may expect it 'to become more attuned and responsive to women's positions as carers'.[95] Equally disappointing is that not only in this case but also in similar subsequent cases the Court had assumed the applicant's freedom to move somewhere else, notably, to private sites. It stated that 'in principle gypsies are at liberty to camp on any caravan site which has planning permission; there has been no suggestion that permissions exclude *gypsies as a group*'.[96] The Court reached that conclusion in spite of the documented incidents of violence and other safety issues that Ms Buckley, and other applicants like her, had experienced.[97] The Court also forgot that no freedom to move to private sites existed for those Roma

---

92 See e.g. ECtHR, (GC) *Chapman v. the United Kingdom*, App. no. 27238/95, Judgment of 18 January 2001, paras. 96 and 115; *Harrison v. the United Kingdom*, App. no. 32263/96, Decision of 3 May 2001, at 12–13.

93 A different approach has however been adopted in more recent cases such as ECtHR, *Yordanova and Others v. Bulgaria*, Application no. 25446/06, Judgment of 24 April 2012, paras. 13, 85 and 90; and *Winterstein and Others v. France*, App. no. 27013/07, Judgment of 17 October 2013, paras. 88–94.

94 ECtHR, *Buckley v. the United Kingdom*, App. no. 20348/92, Judgment of 29 September 1996, at 23.

95 Marie-Bénédicte Dembour, *Who Believes in Human Rights? Reflections on the European Convention* (Cambridge University Press, 2006), at 197–201.

96 ECtHR, (GC) *Chapman v. the United Kingdom*, App. no. 27238/95, Judgment of 18 January 2001, para. 97; (GC) *Beard v. the United Kingdom*, App. no. 24882/94, Judgment of 18 January 2001, para. 108; (GC) *Lee v. the United Kingdom*, App. no. 25289/94, Judgment of 18 January 2001, para. 99; (GC) *Coster v. the United Kingdom*, App. no. 24876/94, Judgment of 18 January 2001, para. 111 [emphasis added].

97 Similar suitability issues were invoked by applicants in other cases. See, for example, ECtHR, *Smith v. the United Kingdom*, App. no. 40435/98, Decision of 30 January 2001, at 2.

applicants who could not afford them or were rejected on the basis of entrenched prejudice.[98] A similar oversight of compounded socio-economic disadvantage is observable in *Wells*.[99] In this case, the domestic courts regarded the applicant's precarious circumstances and the fact he had nowhere else to go as irrelevant to justifying his 'incapacity' to comply with an enforcement notice. The ECtHR limited itself to endorsing the domestic court's finding to that effect and observed that many other persons were not able to continue residing on sites or houses 'attractive' to them.[100]

But there are some exceptions to this compartmentalised line of reasoning. A notable example is *Yordanova and Others v. Bulgaria*. In this case, which concerned the forcible eviction of Roma families living in an informal settlement and is further discussed below, the Court is explicitly sensitive to the socio-economic hardship of Roma applicants. Interestingly, however, this is a case where the argument of ethno-cultural difference, unlike the aforementioned cases, does not play a significant role in the applicant's submissions or in the Court's analysis. In fact, the Court appears to place much emphasis on the applicants belonging to a socially disadvantaged group 'regardless of the ethnic origin of their members'.[101]

Intersectional lenses can also illuminate cases such as *Muñoz Díaz v. Spain* and *Yiğit v. Turkey*.[102] Both concerned the denial of a survivor pension to the applicants, widows and mothers of six, on account of the lack of legal validity of their marriages, which were performed according to Romani and Islamic rites, respectively. Irrespective of the important factual differences between the cases (e.g. that Spain, unlike Turkey, had recognised the validity of certain religious marriages performed in good faith), it is relevant to observe that their ethno-cultural attachments were not the only sources of disadvantage. Gender, and thus the power asymmetries constructed around it, were also at issue. This was not really so because only women were granted survivor pensions – which actually did not appear to be the case. Rather, it was because gender relations were constructed in such a way within the applicants' religious and

98 In this vein, see ECtHR, (GC) *Chapman v. The United Kingdom*, App. no. 27238/95, Judgment of 18 January 2001, Joint dissenting opinion of judges Pastor Ridruejo, Bonello, Tulkens, Strážnická, Lorenzen, Fischbach and Casadevall, para. 6. ('The reference by the majority to the alleged liberty of Gypsies to camp on any caravan site with planning permission … ignores the reality that Gypsies are not welcome on private residential sites which are, in any event, often prohibitively expensive'.)

99 ECtHR, *Wells v. the United Kingdom*, App. no. 37794/05, Decision of 16 January 2007.

100 ECtHR, *Wells v. the United Kingdom*, App. no. 37794/05, Decision of 16 January 2007, para. 10.

101 ECtHR, *Yordanova and Others v. Bulgaria*, App. no. 25446/06, Judgment of 24 April 2012, para. 129.

102 ECtHR, *Muñoz Díaz v. Spain*, App. no. 49151/07, Judgment of 8 December 2009; (GC) *Şerife Yiğit v. Turkey*, App. no. 3976/05, Judgment of 2 November 2010.

ethnic communities (and also within the broader society) that both devoted most of their lives to caring for their children. And as they did not take part in remunerated work, or did so only partially, economic deprivation was likely to follow without their husbands. The particular way in which the non-recognition of their cultural marriages for the purpose of a survival pension burdened the applicants is what intersectionality exposes. Part of this concern was reflected in the Court's regard for the specific life circumstances of Ms Muñoz Díaz. Alongside her ethnic and community affiliation, the Court recalled that the social benefits already granted by the state recognised the applicant as 'a wife and the mother of a large family, this situation being regarded as particularly worthy of assistance'.[103] It is unclear, however, how the Court weighted these factors in the case of Mrs Yiğit, who was ultimately denied access to social security rights after having taken care of the home, the deceased spouse and six children. In this case, much of the Court's analysis focused instead on the importance Turkey accorded to the principle of secularism and on its view of Islam and its marriage tradition.[104]

The Court has, however, come closer to an intersectional perspective in cases concerning the school segregation of Roma children, such as *D.H. v. Czech Republic*, *Sampanis v. Greece*, *Oršuš and Others v. Croatia* and *Horváth and Kiss v. Hungary*. In the landmark judgment *D.H. v. Czech Republic*, the Grand Chamber relied on extensive statistics and reports to hold that the special educational system provided for Roma children amounted to indirect discrimination on the basis of ethnic origin (in violation of Article 14 ECHR jointly with Article 2 of Protocol No. 1).[105] Although the finding rested on the situation of the applicants as members of the Roma community, the Court assessed the seriousness of the interference with the right to education in view of the fact that the 'applicants were minor children for whom the right to education was of paramount importance'.[106] However, this intersectional starting point did not really unfold by, for example, incorporating into the analysis specific standards tailored to the children's needs or by further assessing their experience in that position. In this vein, one author notes critically that the Court was too focused on the Roma

---

103 ECtHR, *Muñoz Díaz v. Spain*, App. no. 49151/07, Judgment of 8 December 2009, para. 62.

104 ECtHR, (GC) *Şerife Yiğit v. Turkey*, App. no. 3976/05, Judgment of 2 November 2010, para. 81.

105 These materials basically documented how Roma children were systematically assigned to segregated schools on the basis of racial or ethnic and cultural grounds, rather than on the basis of intellectual capability. According to the data submitted, 'overall, a Roma child was more than twenty-seven times more likely than a similarly situated non-Roma child to be assigned to a special school'. ECtHR, (GC) *D.H. and Others v. the Czech Republic*, App. no. 57325/00, Judgment of 13 November 2007, para. 134.

106 ECtHR, (GC) *D.H. and Others v. the Czech Republic*, App. no. 57325/00, Judgment of 13 November 2007, para. 182 *in fine*. See also, (GC) *Oršuš and Others v. Croatia*, App. no. 15766/03, Judgment of 16 March 2010, para. 147.

as a disadvantaged ethnic group and on the parents' consent, while remaining quite detached from the interests of the applicants as children.[107] Additionally, it should be noted that the risk of being placed in a segregated school in *D.H.* had to do with the applicants' socio-economic position too. Third-party interveners in the case actually drew the Court's attention to the situation of Roma children from vulnerable families. They argued that 'the Czech Republic was notable for its placement of children in segregated settings because of "social disadvantage"'.[108] Yet, this dimension of the applicants' experience was not included in the Court's analysis.[109]

In the similar cases that followed, the Court paid greater attention to the applicants' circumstances as children. In *Horváth and Kiss v. Hungary*, the Court also made some links between the applicants' ethno-cultural specificity and their socio-economic condition. The applicants had explicitly situated the misdiagnosing of Roma children within their context of social deprivation and cultural distinctiveness. They stated that 'the definition of mental disability as comprising social deprivation and/or having a minority culture amounted to bias and prejudice'.[110] The Court findings, as in previous cases, were limited to indirect discrimination on the grounds of ethnic origin or race. Nonetheless, this time the Court at least considered the applicants' social deprivation for the purposes of explaining the operation of the educational misplacement of children and how this reinforced their social exclusion.[111]

---

107 Sia Spiliopoulou Åkermark, 'Images of children in education: a critical reading of D.H. and Others v. Czech Republic', in Eva Brems (ed.), *Diversity and European Human Rights. Rewriting Judgments of the ECHR* (Cambridge University Press, 2013), at 52–53. At 59, the author even concludes that 'in situations of multiple diversities, or intersectionality, the Court seems to be giving precedence to racial or ethnic ascription over other aspects of diversity and vulnerability, such as gender or age'. On related criticism, see also the dissenting opinion of Judge Borrego in *D.H. and Others v. the Czech Republic* cited above.

108 ECtHR, (GC) *D.H. and Others v. the Czech Republic*, App. no. 57325/00, Judgment of 13 November 2007, paras. 169–170 (referring to the intervention of the International Step by Step Association, the Roma Education Fund and the European Early Childhood Education Research Association).

109 The Grand Chamber's considerations in this respect were limited to a reference to the PACE, Recommendation 1557 (2002) on the Legal Situation of Roma in Europe, Adopted on 25 April 2002, according to which the Roma are 'an ethnic community and most of them belong to the socially disadvantaged groups of society'. The Court also alluded to the social disadvantage of the children's parents in its analysis of their alleged waiving of rights. However, the latter resulted in a very paternalistic stance. See paras. 58 and 203 of the judgment.

110 ECtHR, *Horváth and Kiss v. Hungary*, App. no. 11146/11, Judgment of 29 January 2013, para. 91.

111 Ibid., para. 115. The Court referred to a report indicating that children were 'misdiagnosed because of socio-economic disadvantage or cultural differences. These children are unlikely to break out of this system of inferior education, resulting in their lower educational achievement and poorer prospects of employment.'

3.1.2. *A More Integrated View of Muslim Applicants*

Turning to Muslims' rights claims regarding religious attire, reflections inspired by a richer view of rights holders are equally in order. Not all people who feel attached to a religion can exercise their freedom of religion and other rights in the same manner. Crucial dimensions of the cases dealing with religious expression and Islamic veils would be missed without an intersectional approach. They can only be captured once we appreciate that applicants are, for example, Muslim women and girls (many with a migrant background) studying or working as teachers in public primary and secondary education; women who went into a court room as a party or as a lawyer, who want to take office in parliament or walk in public places while wearing a *hijab* or a *niqab*.[112] Several applicants argued that the contested bans on covering constituted discrimination in violation of Article 9 and/or other provisions in conjunction with Article 14 ECHR. But their claim was not only one of religious discrimination. It was also one of discrimination based on sex and even on ethnic origin. In some cases they contrasted their situation with that of, for example, Muslim men and boys, with Muslim women who chose not to wear the veil, and with Christians who could conceal their faces with masks or dress the way they wanted during Christian festivities.[113] Thus, the point was that other religious women and Muslim men were able to work, to study and to enter public spaces without being subjected to any form of prohibition or exclusion. Although here, in contrast to the aforementioned Roma/Traveller cases, the claim of intersectionality (violations based on inequalities attached to religion and gender and/or ethnic origin combined) appears relatively clear in the applicants' arguments, the Court did not take it up either.

While in cases involving prohibitions of conspicuous religious symbols the Court devoted a not insignificant number of paragraphs to the religious practice of Muslim women, it rapidly ruled out discrimination because the measures

---

112 On women's complaints about being expelled from the courtroom and/or otherwise sanctioned for wearing the veil in that context, see ECtHR, cases of *Lachiri v. Belgium*, App. no. 3413/09, Communicated on 9 October 2015; *Hamidović v. Bosnia and Herzegovina*, App. no. 57792/15, Communicated on 24 March 2016 (At the time of writing no judgment had been issued on these complaints). See also ECtHR, *Barik Edidi v. Spain*, App. no. 21780/13, Decision of 26 April 2016. (This complaint was declared inadmissible. The ECtHR found that the lack of examination of the merits of the case by the domestic courts were attributable to the applicant's conduct and therefore it did not examine any of the claims based on Articles 8, 9 and protocol 12 ECHR.)

113 ECtHR, *Dahlab v. Switzerland*, App. no. 42393/98, Decision of 15 February 2001, at 7 and 13; *Köse and 93 Others v. Turkey*, App. no. 26625/02, Decision of 24 January 2006, at 8; *Araç v. Turkey*, App. no 9907/02, Decision of 19 September 2006, at 2–3; (GC) *S.A.S. v. France*, App. no. 43835/11, Judgment of 1 July 2014, paras. 3 and 80 (this last one on grounds of sex, religion and ethnic origin).

were supposedly 'not directed at' or 'unrelated to' the applicant's religion.[114] They were rather aimed at ensuring neutrality and secularism in the public sphere. A similar answer was provided in cases in which Muslim women claimed sex discrimination.[115] The reasoning was furthermore reinforced by the argument that, in any case, the measure applied equally to a whole category of persons. That is, the ban 'could also be applied to a man who, in similar circumstances, wore clothing that clearly identified him as a member of a different faith'.[116] It follows, then, that the Court's main concern was the (non)existence of formal direct discrimination. The issue was, in other words, whether the state openly targeted one personal trait or one group defined by one common characteristic. Underlying this was the formal and single-ground comparator-based inquiry so typical of anti-discrimination law.[117] This line of reasoning does not lend itself well to assessing the allegations of real-life experiences of discrimination discussed here. For one thing, the formula seems to fit blatant forms of discrimination typical of past times, when people's characteristics were openly singled out by laws and regulations disfavouring them. For another, as further explained below, the reasoning behind formal discrimination is blind to compounded experiences. Looking at complaints against veil and face covering bans through the perspective of the individuals concerned exposes how they were affected as both women and Muslim believers. As such, they shared some experiences with both Muslim men and women from other faiths. Yet they also confronted a unique and specific form of violation.

In the Grand Chamber judgment in *S.A.S. v. France* as well as in the recent cases of *Dakir and Belcacemi and Oussar v. Belgium*, the Court conceded that it was 'aware of the fact that the impugned ban mainly affects Muslim women who wish to wear the full-face veil'.[118] Yet, it downplayed the implications of this conclusion by saying that it 'finds it to be of *some significance* that the ban is

114 ECtHR, (GC) *Leyla Şahin v. Turkey*, App. no. 44774/98, Judgment of 10 November 2005, para. 165; *Kurtulmuş v. Turkey*, App. no. 65500/01, Decision of 24 January 2006, at 9; (GC) *S.A.S. v. France*, App. no. 43835/11, Judgment of 1 July 2014, para. 151.

115 ECtHR, *Kurtulmuş v. Turkey*, App. no. 65500/01, Decision of 24 January 2006, at 9; *Köse and 93 Others v. Turkey*, App. no. 26625/02, Decision of 24 January 2006, at 8; *Araç v. Turkey*, App. no. 9907/02, Decision of 19 September 2006, at 5 (referring not to neutrality or secularism, but to an objective measure namely, 'a simple means of identification'); (GC) *S.A.S. v. France*, App. no. 43835/11, Judgment of 1 July 2014, para. 161.

116 ECtHR, *Dahlab v. Switzerland*, App. no. 42393/98, Decision of 15 February 2001, at 14.

117 On formal equality and direct discrimination see *supra* Chapter 1, section 3.4. The use of a comparator for establishing a prima facie case of discrimination can be seen already in the Belgian Linguistics case (ECtHR, *'Relating to certain aspects of the laws on the use of languages in education in Belgium' v. Belgium*, Application nos. 1474/62, 1677/62, 1691/62, 1769/63, 1994/63 and 2126/64, Judgment of 23 July 1968), where the ECtHR held that different treatment is improper only if it exists between individuals in relatively similar situations.

118 ECtHR, (CG) *S.A.S. v. France*, App. no. 43835/11, Judgment of 1 July 2014, para. 149; *Dakir v. Belgium*, App. no. 461/12, Judgment of 11 July 2017, para. 55; *Belcacemi and Oussar v. Belgium*, App. no. 37798/13, Judgment of 11 July 2017, para. 52.

not expressly based on the religious connotation of the clothing in question but solely on the fact that it conceals the face'.[119] 'Some significance' actually made all the difference because the Court simply returned to the direct discrimination logic. Since the ban was based on the concealing of the face, it could not be discrimination. Interestingly, in the *S.A.S.* case the Court for the first time raised concerns about Islamophobia and 'the risk of contributing to the consolidation of the stereotypes which affect certain categories of the population'.[120] However, these concerns were not connected to the decision on the case at hand.

The human rights implications of the intersection between religion and gender did not totally escape the Court's analysis, though. The latter did identify, in most of the cases reviewed, a worrisome interplay to the extent that it showed concern about the way religion may endorse oppressive gender roles burdening mostly women. But did the Court recognise that nearly all religions and cultures, and thus pretty much everyone involved in them – not only some – take part in that?[121] And was the Court ready to explore the stereotypical views based on religion, gender and ethnic origin that could be assumed or promoted by the contested bans? For the most part, the Court failed to scrutinise this issue closely or to explore the implications that the impugned restrictions had for the lives of the women and girls concerned. In this regard, it is worth noting that similarly to the educational segregation cases commented on above, in *S.A.S. v. France* as well as in *Dakir* and *Belcacemi and Oussar v. Belgium* third-party interveners also provided relevant insights as to the lived reality of women like the applicant.[122] This could have assisted the Court to approach rights holders

---

119 ECtHR, (CG) *S.A.S. v. France*, App. no. 43835/11, Judgment of 1 July 2014, para. 151 (emphasis added). Similarly, *Dakir v. Belgium*, App. no. 461/12, Judgment of 11 July 2017, para. 58.

120 ECtHR, (CG) *S.A.S. v. France*, App. no. 43835/11, Judgment of 1 July 2014, para. 149. Similarly, *Dakir and Belcacemi and Oussar v. Belgium*, Apps. no. 461/12 and 37798/13, Judgments of 11 July 2017, paras. 55 and 52, respectively. In these last cases, the Court does not speak of Islamophobia, but it does recognise the risk of contributing to stereotyping and intolerance while also restricting the scope of pluralism.

121 In this connection, Dolores Morondo Taramundi argues that even though the full veil is gendered and not free from patriarchal meaning and relations, it is discriminatory to target only some women (a sub-group of Muslim women) and oblige them to go beyond any other women in the challenge to patriarchy and the upholding of equality. See Dolores Morondo Taramundi, 'El principio de igualdad entre mujeres y hombres frente a la prohibición del velo islámico integral', 30 *Anuario de Filosofía del Derecho* (2014) 291, at 302.

122 The Human Rights Centre of the Law Faculty of Ghent University, for example, submitted findings from empirical research on the views of women wearing face veils. On the basis of that material, it invited the Grand Chamber to incorporate their experiences into its assessment, instead of upholding common assumptions and stereotypes about those women, their religion and their approach to social interaction in the public space. See the written comments submitted to both cases at <www.hrc.ugent.be/third-party-interventions-before-ecthr/>. For a broader discussion of the need to incorporate the actual perspectives of face veil wearers in policy-making concerning face-covering bans so as to avoid this proceeding in disregard of the lived reality of the women concerned, see Eva Brems (ed.), *The Experiences of Face Veil Wearers in Europe and the Law* (Cambridge University Press, 2014).

in a more integrated fashion. However, the Court did not incorporate those insights into the legal analysis.

Reflecting upon the specific experience of the affected rights holders should lead the Court not only to consider their identity, but also their social positions. The latter should be understood in a broad way and not limited to socio-economic position. Since an intersectional perspective is interested in who the concrete applicants are, it is important to distinguish how the restriction in question affects them and is tied to their particular circumstances. For example, in many 'headscarf cases', the Muslim women negatively affected were public servants. This is not the same as experiencing the ban as a child/adult student (as in *Dogru, Sahin* and others), or as a private party seeking access to the justice system or to public spaces (as in *S.A.S.*, *Dakir and Belcacemi and Oussar*, on the one hand, and *Lachiri v. Belgium*, on the other).[123]

An examination and distinction of these circumstances has been largely absent in cases concerning the wearing of the *hijab*, despite the fact that such analysis is not alien to the ECtHR. It has done so in *Ahmet Arslan and Others*, where it declared the disproportionality of the Turkish ban on religious attire in light of the fact that the Muslim men concerned were mere citizens, not public servants, making use of the public space.[124] Similar reasoning can be found in the 2017 case of *Hamidović v. Bosnia and Herzegovina*.[125] Here the Court rightly emphasised that since the applicant (a Muslim man summoned to remove his skullcap) was a private person called to testify in court, his situation had to be distinguished from that of public officials wearing religious clothing at the workplace. Notably, the latter could be under duties of discretion and neutrality not applicable to the former.[126] As regards Muslim women wearing the *hijab* though, as recently as 2018 the Court engaged, for the first time, in this kind of analysis. It did it in *Lachiri v. Belgium*, concerning the complaint of a Muslim woman who was a civil party to a criminal case and was excluded from the courtroom because she refused to remove her *hijab*.[127] The Court observed that Mrs Lachiri was not a representative of the state, but a mere citizen. As such, she could not be bound by a duty of discretion in the public expression of her religious beliefs.[128] It is nonetheless intriguing that unlike the stance taken in

123 ECtHR, (GC) *S.A.S. v. France*, App. no. 43835/11, Judgment of 1 July 2014; *Dakir v. Belgium*, App. no. 4619/12, Judgment of 11 July 2017; *Belcacemi and Oussar v. Belgium*, App. no. 37798/13, Judgment of 11 July 2017; and *Lachiri v. Belgium*, App. no. 3413/09, Judgment of 18 September 2018.

124 ECtHR, *Ahmet Arslan and Others v. Turkey*, App. no. 41135/98, Judgment of 23 February 2010, paras. 48–49.

125 ECtHR, *Hamidović v. Bosnia and Herzegovina*, App. no. 57792/15, Judgment of 5 December 2017.

126 Ibid., para. 40.

127 ECtHR, *Lachiri v. Belgium*, App. no. 3413/09, Judgment of 18 September 2018.

128 Ibid., para. 44.

the case of *Hamidović* referred to above, in *Lachiri* the Court seems to suggest that had the applicant been excluded on account of the state aim of maintaining secularism or neutrality in the public arena (instead of maintaining public order), the restriction could have been justified. This appears at odds with the Court's own considerations regarding the specific circumstances of the applicants in both cases. In fact, even if the aim of state neutrality were invoked, it is far from clear how a private citizen, by the sole fact of her appearance in court (or in other public premises), could be in a position to compromise the court's neutrality.

3.1.3. Intersectionality within the Antidiscrimination Review: Indirect Discrimination and Stereotypes

Regulations or practices that uphold harmful stereotypes, even when unintended, raise issues of discrimination and, particularly, of indirect discrimination. Moreover, as mentioned earlier, this dynamic works in a circular way. The stereotypes assigned to members of the group confirm the reification of the group or religion itself, thus reinforcing the group/cultural boundaries and hierarchies discussed in the previous section.[129] Assumptions such as 'Muslim women are victimised and subordinated' while 'Muslim men are oppressors and fundamentalists' are clear examples of compounded stereotypes, that is, stereotypes made up of two or more stereotypes combined that assign attributes to members of sub-groups.[130] Importantly, as we have seen in cases involving the Islamic veil (whether the *hijab* or *niqab*), the use or upholding of stereotypes obfuscated the real-life experience of the specific applicants concerned.[131] Intersectionality then helps by bringing the individual, her interests and the harms experienced back into the analysis. Something similar goes for

---

129 Rebecca J. Cook and Simone Cusack, *Gender Stereotyping: Transnational Legal Perspectives* (University of Pennsylvania Press, 2010), at 715–716; Valorie K. Vojdik, 'Politics of the Headscarf in Turkey: Masculinities, Feminism, and the Construction of Collective Identities', 33 *Harvard Journal of Law and Gender* (2010) 661, at 676 (noting that '[c]olonialists seized upon the veil as the "most visible marker of the differentness and inferiority of Islamic societies"', a symbol of both the degradation of Islamic women and the backwardness of Islamic men). See also Anne Phillips, 'What's wrong with Essentialism?', 11(1) *Distinktion: Scandinavian Journal of Social Theory* (2010) 47, at 51–52 (referring to the way in which essentialised discourses of coercive minority cultures have combined with an essentialised discourse of the victimised young women from minority groups).

130 Rebeca J. Cook and Simone Cusack, *Gender Stereotyping: Transnational Legal Perspectives* (University of Pennsylvania Press, 2010), at 29–31.

131 Discussing how the concrete applicants were obscured in the so-called 'headscarf cases', see e.g. Valorie K. Vojdik, 'Politics of the Headscarf in Turkey: Masculinities, Feminism, and the Construction of Collective Identities', 33 *Harvard Journal of Law and Gender* (2010) 661, at 672; see Carolyn Evans, 'Individual and group religious freedom in the European Court of Human Rights: Cracks in the intellectual architecture', 26 *Journal of Law and Religion* (2010–2011) 321, at 330–331.

stereotypes such as 'Gypsies are nomads' or 'Gypsies are born Gypsies'. Albeit the merit evaluation and forms of 'authentication' are different in both types of case, the consequences are similarly problematic.[132] In the Roma/Traveller cases discussed, the overlapping identities and the specific gender, economic and other concerns of the applicants tended to fade from the Court's proportionality analysis.

As explained in Chapter 1 and further demonstrated here, intersectionality usually goes hand in hand with questions of discrimination. This is reflected in several allegations discussed above which relied on Article 14 ECHR. Regrettably, too often the Court has not even examined the merits of the complaint. And when it has done so, the judicial query has been limited to direct discrimination. To the extent that the Court confines itself to asking whether the measures challenged by applicants distinguish on the basis of one personal characteristic or targeted one particular group of people, intersectionality is bound to fade, at least from the discrimination analysis. Conversely, the prohibition of indirect discrimination constitutes an important tool for tackling intersectional violations. This, however, presupposes a move towards a substantive conception of equality. Recall that according to this conception and in contrast to formal equality, what matters is not so much the comparator or the instrumentality of the treatment. What matters is the concrete effect of the restriction measured by a substantive standard: disadvantage in the enjoyment of rights or dignity.[133]

Thus, a first reason for synergy between intersectionality and indirect discrimination is evident. Direct discrimination does not work for intersectionality. The formalism and single-ground comparator focus of the former do not leave space for the latter. But a second and important link between intersectionality and indirect discrimination is that, by tackling measures couched in neutral terms, indirect discrimination is suitable for dealing with the use of proxies for discrimination.[134] That is, indirect discrimination can interrogate regulations based on 'relevant' and 'objective' criteria which, in certain contexts,

---

132 For a detailed account of the impact of these stereotypes and 'naturalisations' within and beyond the adjudicated cases, see Lourdes Peroni, *Opening Up the European Convention Human Rights Subject: An Inclusive Multilayered Framework for Adjudicating Religious and Cultural Claims*, PhD Dissertation (Ghent University, 2014), at 203–217.

133 Interights, *Non-Discrimination in International Law: A Handbook for Practitioners* (Interights, 2011), at 105. For a fuller discussion on substantive and formal equality in *supra* Chapter 1, section 3.4.3.

134 Generally speaking, discrimination by proxy arises out of classifications that do not rely on a prohibited ground but on a usually rational and objective ground that in practice impacts on significant numbers of those who are identified with the prohibited ground. Typical examples discussed in the literature are employers' policies rejecting applicants with all-braided hairstyles, which in practice mean screening out a large proportion of black women. For a discussion of discrimination by proxy in the context of the United States, see e.g. Camille Gear Rich, 'Performing Racial and Ethnic Identity: Discrimination by Proxy and the Future of Title VII', 79 *N.Y.U. Law Review* (2004) 1134.

may nonetheless translate into unacceptable exclusions of persons who would otherwise be identified with one, or more protected categories (e.g. race, sex, religion). As we have seen, a primary education system based on language and psycho-intellectual tests may result, despite their neutrality and reasonability at face value, in the exclusion of Roma children. Likewise, dress codes that forbid the covering of the hair or the face in public institutions or in public places may marginalise Muslim women as well as women and men from religions not rooted in the Christian tradition. When the people who are disfavoured by regulations based on language or dress style or any other allegedly neutral, rational criterion are, in practice, nearly indistinguishable from those who would be disfavoured if the measure were to rely on sex and ethnic origin and/or religion, for example, then there is a strong indication that those social locations or identities have become too intertwined for their attendant disadvantage to be captured by a single ground.

To be sure, claiming or making a finding of indirect discrimination can be based on one single identity. This is in fact usually the case, as reflected in the complaints and judgments discussed above. Most of these relied on ethnic origin or religion. Framed in this way, indirect discrimination would not make visible the intersecting identities and social positions of the applicants. However, since the one-sided perspective is not the only flaw in the classical conception of anti-discrimination law, the question of how many identity grounds are used is not so decisive for the Court's ability to adopt an intersectional analysis. Crenshaw, who is credited with devising intersectionality, argued that an additional problem of anti-discrimination law was the way each discrimination ground was conceived of. Each category tends to be constructed as reflecting the experience of those who are more privileged therein.[135] Thus, if the claim is one of gender discrimination, implicitly the lenses for all the other social positions of the woman in question are those of privilege. As Fredman explains, 'this assumes that all her other characteristics are on the privileged side of the relationship. In other words, she is assumed to be a white, able-bodied, heterosexual woman, of the dominant religion or belief (which could include secularism) etc'.[136] And the same goes for a claim based on race, religion and so forth. The result is that those who are most disadvantaged go unnoticed.[137] This reminds us that intersectionality is not simply a question of identifying overlapping identities.

---

[135] Kimberle Crenshaw, 'Demarginalizing the Intersection of Race and Sex: A Black Feminist Critique of Antidiscrimination Doctrine, Feminist Theory and Antiracist Politics', 1 *The University of Chicago Legal Forum* (1989) 139, at 151 ('sex and race discrimination have come to be defined in terms of the experiences of those who are privileged *but for* their racial or sexual characteristics').

[136] Sandra Fredman, Intersectional discrimination in EU gender equality and non-discrimination law, Report prepared for the European Commission (2016), at 31.

[137] Ibid., at 31.

Rather, it is about identifying rights violations which are more likely to affect those who are at the intersections of systems of inequalities.

As such, Fredman argues that even when the examination of discrimination focuses on a single ground (say, religion or ethnic origin), it is still possible to engage with intersectionality. To do so, she proposes 'a capacious approach to the discrimination grounds'.[138] By an extensive interpretation of each ground, she means that 'all aspects of an individual's identity should be taken into account even within one identity ground'.[139] Coming back to the previous example, this is to say that the category woman should cover all women, in all their diversity (e.g. black, Muslim, poor, young women). Looking at the cases studied through this perspective, one could argue that the Court went in this direction in *D.H. and Others v. the Czech Republic* and in similar subsequent judgments. In fact, although the Court in such cases mainly deals with the discrimination ground of ethnic origin, it does so in a manner that is inclusive of the experience of those who may be less visible within the Roma community, namely children and, to a lesser extent, the poor among them.

3.1.4. Intersectionality Beyond the Antidiscrimination Review

Building upon the above suggestion, it is submitted that a similar intersectional perspective could be used outside the confines of discrimination grounds. It may well be extended to the interpretation of other Convention provisions. For example, whose experience or vantage point is used for interpreting who is a 'believer' or a 'Muslim' under Article 9 ECHR? Or who is the reference point to construe the follower of a 'Gypsy way of life' or 'the Traveller' in Article 8 ECHR? Thinking of them as if they are women, children, poor, sedentary, etc. makes these norms reflective of a wider array of human experiences. This is another way of moving in the direction of intersectionality and challenging the unstated norms that marginalise those who are at the crossroads of several identities and power differentials.

All in all, the case law discussed thus far demonstrates that in order to capture what was at stake for the applicants it was not enough to take account of their Roma origin or cultural/religious traditions. The interplay between several identities and social locations (e.g. gender, socio-economic position, age) can play an important role in the adjudication of ethnic diversity cases. But this role does not need to be confined to the application of anti-discrimination clauses. Anti-discrimination is certainly the best-known tool for operationalising intersectionality in law. And possibly, assuming the availability of evidence, some of the discrimination complaints reviewed above could also have been grounded in the combined effect

---

138 Ibid., at 35–36, 69 and ff.

139 Ibid., at 69.

of ethnic origin, religion and social origin and/or gender. Yet, conceived as an analytical and normative framework – as it is in this book – an intersectional approach may provide a broader set of normative insights.

Notably, on account of its incidence in defining the point of view adopted to appreciate the relevant norms and the way these are interpreted, intersectionality holds relevance for the framing of the case. As demonstrated by the cases discussed above, intersectionality may shape the proportionality review of rights interferences, since it sheds light on the importance and impact of the restriction on the rights of the concrete individuals affected. Accordingly, an intersectional perspective can affect the width of the state's margin of appreciation too. One of the factors shaping the scope of the margin of discretion enjoyed by states is the nature of the right restricted, its importance for the individual and the intensity of the restriction.[140] Identifying the multiple identities and social positions of the applicant makes it possible to give appropriate weight to these aspects. Finally, accounting for those who are subjected to multiple disadvantages not only makes law more responsive to them, but also serves to identify the type of diversity that requires legal intervention.[141]

3.2. PROBLEMATISING THE 'EITHER/OR' VIEW OF INDIVIDUALS' AUTONOMY AND CHOICE

Another way of ignoring individuals' complexity is to reduce their agency to a zero-sum game whereby they are viewed as either fully autonomous or as deprived of agency. Both understandings disregard how individuals are embedded in social relations and structures and how their agency therefore unfolds in a continuum rather than in an all or nothing fashion.[142] An integrated approach to rights holders acknowledges this as part of their lived experience.

---

140 See e.g. Janneke Gerards, 'Pluralism, deference and the margin of appreciation doctrine', 17(1) *European Law Journal* (2011) 80, at 112–113 (and cases cited therein).

141 In this vein, Barbara Tomlinson, 'To Tell the Truth and Not Get Trapped: Desire, Distance, and Intersectionality at the Scene of Argument', 38 *Signs* (2013) 993, at 1012 (arguing that if understood in terms of power instead of mere overlapping identity, intersectionality reveals which differences carry normative significance).

142 Jennifer Nedelsky, 'Reconceiving Autonomy: Sources, Thoughts and Reflections', 1 *Yale Journal of Law and Feminism* (1989) 7, at 11–20 (arguing that the concept of autonomy 'has inherent tensions between the idea of autonomy as both originating with oneself and being conditioned and shaped by one's social context'. Further, she notes that this dichotomy maps onto a number of other dichotomies, namely those between the individual and the collective as well as between the private and the public). See also, Kathleen Lynch and Judy Walsh, 'Love, Care and Solidarity: What Is and Is Not Commodifiable', in Kathleen Lynch *et al.* (eds.), *Affective Equality. Love, Care and Injustice* (Palgrave Macmillan, 2009), at 41 ('people live in varying states of dependency and interdependency. And each care reality is intersectionally connected to the other, moving along a fluid continuum from care-full-ness to care-less-ness').

Moreover, as this approach avoids assigning a meaning to their identities, so it avoids assigning a meaning to their choices. The question of how we understand individuals' autonomy may seem a mere theoretical issue, but it is not. Important normative consequences follow from it. The following discussion starts by exploring those related to the first extreme of the spectrum: the judicial construction of an unencumbered subject.

3.2.1. The Autonomous, Unconstrained Side of Rights Holders

The way in which the understanding of individuals' autonomy has shaped the scope of protection afforded to rights holders in cultural diversity cases can be appreciated in the examination of questions such as (1) whether the personal characteristic in question was out of people's control (such as race or ethnic origin) or chosen and changeable (such as culture and religion), and (2) whether the interference complained of could be attributed to the individual's choices and autonomy. As will be seen below, when the personal trait was perceived as having been chosen or when she or he was regarded as having unconstrained choices, the Court tended to see her or him as less deserving of protection.[143] The issue of choice appears particularly salient in cases involving Article 9 ECHR.[144]

143 As a way of example, see the ECtHR's approach in its admissibility decision in *Horie v. the United Kingdom*, App. no. 31845/10, Decision of 1 February 2011, discussed *supra* section 2. The issue of choice also played an important role in the case of *Codona v. the United Kingdom*. Following eviction and having applied for accommodation as a homeless person, the applicant had been offered bricks and mortar accommodation, which she refused. In her view, this was not respectful of her lifestyle. For the Court, however, 'the applicant's refusal of such accommodation was anything other than a choice for the consequences of which the respondent State is not responsible'. ECtHR, *Codona v. the United Kingdom*, App. no. 485/05, Decision of 7 February 2006, at 12. The problem of what protection is afforded to 'chosen' traits or conducts has also arisen in other international tribunals and in domestic courts, in the context not only of substantive rights but also of the prohibition of discrimination. In domestic legal orders see, *inter alia*, Marius Pieterse, 'Finding for the Applicant? Individual Equality Plaintiffs and Group-Based Disadvantage', 24 *South African Journal on Human Rights* (2008) 397, at 410; Kenji Yoshino, 'The New Equal Protection', 124 *Harvard Law Review* (2011) 747, at 762–763, fn. 104 (and sources cited therein); Lucy Vickers, 'Promoting Equality or Fostering Resentment? The Public Sector Equality Duty and Religion and Belief', 31 *Legal Studies* (2011) 135, at 138–139.

144 See the cases concerning Muslim applicants discussed hereunder, where the Court emphasised that they had chosen a certain job or career, or had chosen to keep wearing the *hijab*. See also, Peter W. Edge, 'Religious rights and choice under the European Convention on Human Rights', 3 *Web Journal of Current Legal Issues* (2000), <www.bailii.org/uk/other/journals/WebJCLI/2000/issue3/edge3.html>. In the context of the ECJ, see the opinions of the Advocates General Kokott and Sharpston before the ECJ in the cases of *Achbita and Bougnaoui* (ECJ, *Samira Achbita, Centrum voor gelijkheid van kansen en voor racismebestrijding v. G4S Secure Solutions NV*, Case C-157/15, Request for a preliminary ruling from the Hof van Cassatie (Belgium), Lodged on 3 April 2015). For a comment on this see Lucy Vickers, 'ECJ headscarf series (2): the role of choice; and the margin of appreciation', *Strasbourg Observers*, 8 September 2016, <strasbourgobservers.com/2016/09/08/blog-series-the-role-of-choice-and-the-margin-of-appreciation/>.

In fact, in several of the cases studied the ECtHR not only narrowly defined rights holders in terms of a certain cultural or religious script. It also did so by considering their standing as one of fully autonomous free-will subjects. This was particularly so for some Roma/Travellers and for most Muslim applicants. In short: these applicants appeared to be endowed with plenty of free choices. Looking back, they could have chosen not to accept a job or position which required them to give up what they claimed as their right. They could have chosen not to keep breaching the regulation restricting their cultural or religious expression and accept the 'inconvenience'. Looking forward, they usually had the choice of finding another job, studying somewhere else or moving and living elsewhere, depending on the case. The existence of these unconstrained choices had the effect of reducing or denying legal protection.

Illustrative of this logic are some of the Roma and Traveller cases where the Court downplayed the applicants' grief in view of their alleged autonomy to move with their caravans to private sites, although, as outlined above, for many that was not a real option.[145] Likewise, in *Muñoz Díaz v. Spain* and *Yiğit v. Turkey* one of the arguments raised by the respondent states was precisely that both women had had the choice to contract a civil marriage. In *Muñoz Díaz*, the Court appropriately rejected the argument. It held:

> The prohibition of discrimination enshrined in Article 14 of the Convention is meaningful only if, in each particular case, the applicant's personal situation in relation to the criteria listed in that provision is taken into account exactly as it stands. To proceed otherwise in dismissing the victim's claims on the ground that he or she could have avoided the discrimination by altering one of the factors in question – for example, by entering into a civil marriage – would render Article 14 devoid of substance.[146]

However, the unconstrained autonomy reasoning has often played out in the Court's rejection of minority claims of religious accommodation and protection against discrimination.[147] In the cases studied here, we may note that in contrast to *Muñoz Díaz*, the Grand Chamber in *Yiğit v. Turkey* found that the applicant was aware of her situation and had had sufficiently long time (26 years) to

---

145 See *supra* section 3.1.1.

146 ECtHR, *Muñoz Díaz v. Spain*, App. no. 49151/07, Judgment of 8 December 2009, para. 70.

147 See e.g. EComm.HR, *Konttinen v. Finland*, App. no. 24949/94, Decision of 3 December 1996, at 68; *Stedman v. the United Kingdom*, App. no. 29107/95, Decision of 9 April 1997. See also, Julie Ringelheim, 'Rights, Religion and the Public Sphere: The European Court of Human Rights in Search of a Theory?', in Lorenzo Zucca and Camil Ungureanu (eds.), *Law, State and Religion in the New Europa: Debates and Dilemmas* (Cambridge University Press, 2012), at 296–297; Turan Kayaoglu, 'Trying Islam: Muslims before the European Court of Human Rights', 34(4) *Journal of Muslim Minority Affairs* (2014) 345, at 350–351 (referring to Non-Christian religions in general).

contract a civil marriage.[148] Returning to the former Commission, a Muslim teacher who complained that the state school in which he worked had refused to arrange his timetable so as to enable him to take 45 minutes off for praying on Fridays at the mosque was found to be free to resign.[149] Muslim men in the Turkish army who were discharged encountered a similar response. It was their choice to pursue a military career and accept a system of military discipline which could entail the restriction of their rights.[150] The trend continued with the so-called 'headscarf ban' cases. In *Karaduman* and *Bulut* (both concerning university students who were prevented from obtaining a degree certificate in Turkey for refusing to provide an identity photograph without a headscarf) as well as in *Kurtulmuş* (regarding the dismissal of a Turkish university professor on account of wearing the headscarf), the applicants' choice to study or work in public educational institutions governed by secularism was a reason to conclude that their freedom of religion was not even restricted.[151] In later cases involving female students covering their hair in public schools – several of them against France – the Court observed that pupils were free to attend the school provided that they complied with the prohibition on conspicuous religious symbols. The Court furthermore noted that pupils had the chance to keep studying by correspondence. The normative consequence was the same.[152]

---

148 ECtHR, (GC) *Şerife Yiğit v. Turkey*, App. no. 3976/05, Judgment of 2 November 2010, paras. 84–86. The Court, in distinguishing the case from *Muñoz Díaz*, recalled that in the latter, the applicant had married according to Roma rites and traditions at a time when it was not possible in Spain, except by making a prior declaration of apostasy or of affiliation to a different faith, to be married otherwise than in accordance with the rites of the Catholic Church.

149 EComm.HR, *X. v. United Kingdom*, App. no. 8160/78, Decision of 12 March 1981, paras. 9 and 15 (The Commission found that the applicant voluntarily accepted teaching obligations under his contract with the school and remained free to resign if he found that these duties conflicted with his religious duties).

150 EComm.HR, *Yanasik v. Turkey*, App. no. 14524/89, Decision of 6 January 1993, at 27. See also, ECtHR, *Kalaç v. Turkey*, App. no. 20704/92, Judgment of 1 July 1997, para. 28.

151 EComm.HR, *Karaduman v. Turkey*, App. no. 16278/90, at 108 and *Bulut v. Turkey*, App. no. 18783/91, at 5 both decisions of 3 May 1993. (The Commission found no interference with her Article 9 right because 'by choosing to pursue her higher education in a secular university a student submits to those university rules, which may make the freedom of students to manifest their religion subject to restrictions ...); ECtHR, *Kurtulmuş v. Turkey*, App. no. 65500/01, Decision of 24 January 2006, at 6. ('There is no doubt that the applicant assumed the status of a public servant of her own free will ... she could not have been unaware of the rules requiring her not to express her religious beliefs in public in an ostentatious manner.')

152 See ECtHR, *Köse and 93 Others v. Turkey*, App. no. 26625/02, Decision of 24 January 2006, at 14. In dismissing an infringement on the right set out in the second sentence of Article 2 of Protocol No. 1 ('In the exercise of any functions which it assumes in relation to education and to teaching, the State shall respect the right of parents to ensure such education and teaching in conformity with their own religious and philosophical convictions.') the Court noted, *inter alia*, 'that both the parents and the pupils were informed of the consequences of not obeying the rules (...) the pupils are free to continue to attend the schools provided they comply with the rules on dress.' See also, ECtHR, *Kervanci v. France*, App. no. 31645/04 and *Dogru v. France*, App. no. 27058/05, both judgments of 4 December 2008, paras. 73 and 76 (concerning two Muslim girls who had

Against this backdrop, the Court's shift in the 2013 *Eweida and Others* case is remarkable. This case did not concern Muslims or Roma people, but it is highly relevant to the present discussion. One of the applicants, a practising Christian woman, was prevented by her employer, British Airways, from wearing a visible necklace with a cross, as was required by the company's uniform code. The Court moved away from the idea of a free choice to resign or find a job elsewhere. Instead of holding that the possibility of changing jobs would negate any interference with the applicant's right to manifest her religion, the Court stated that 'the better approach would be to weigh that possibility in the overall balance when considering whether or not the restriction was proportionate'.[153] It then found the proportionality requirement unmet, as too much weight had been given to the corporate image of British Airways, which in any case was not a right protected under the Convention.[154]

3.2.2. *The Constrained, Passive Side of Rights Holders*

A sceptical stance towards the free choice of applicants, to the point of depriving them of agency, can be found in *D.H. v. Czech Republic* and the other similar cases of school segregation of Roma children. The state argued that parents had consented to the placement of their children in special schools and the fact that these children had not pursued secondary or higher education was the result of their choices, not of their special education.[155] The Court disagreed, as it was 'not satisfied that the parents of the Roma children, who were members of a disadvantaged community and often poorly educated, were capable of weighing up all the aspects of the situation and the consequences of giving their consent'.[156]

---

been expelled from school because they refused to take off their headscarves during sports classes but who had proposed replacing it with a cap). The Court took into account, among other factors to dismiss, a violation of Article 9: 'the penalty imposed is merely the consequence of the applicant's refusal to comply with the rules applicable on the school premises' and the fact that 'the applicant was able to continue her schooling by correspondence classes'. In the same vein, see ECtHR, *Aktas v. France*, App. no. 43563/08, Decision of 30 June 2009; *Bayrak v. France*, App. no. 14308/08, Decision of 30 June 2009; *Gamaleddyn v. France*, App. no. 18527/08, Decision of 30 June 2009 and *Ghazal v. France*, App. no. 29134/08, Decision of 30 June 2009, decisions of inadmissibility of 2009. These cases concerned the expulsion of girls from school for wearing a headscarf or kerchief in breach of the 2004 French act prohibiting the wearing of all conspicuous signs of religious faith during lessons.

153 ECtHR, *Eweida and Others v. the United Kingdom*, App. nos. 48420/10, 59842/10, 51671/10 and 36516/10, Judgment of 15 January 2013, para. 83.

154 ECtHR, *Eweida and Others v. the United Kingdom*, App. nos. 48420/10, 59842/10, 51671/10 and 36516/10, Judgment of 15 January 2013, para. 94.

155 ECtHR, (GC) *D.H. and Others v. the Czech Republic*, App. no. 57325/00, Judgment of 13 November 2007, paras. 153–158.

156 ECtHR, (GC) *D.H. and Others v. the Czech Republic*, App. no. 57325/00, Judgment of 13 November 2007, para. 203. In a more agency-friendly note, the Court also suggested that a choice between mainstream education in which children risked isolation and ostracism, and special schools where the majority of the pupils were Roma, was not that much of a choice.

The result was certainly responsive to the applicant's plight, but at the cost of the Court's paternalism.

Likewise, the rhetoric of autonomous individuals was strongly mitigated or absent when the Court examined whether the restriction of the applicants' religious manifestation was necessary to secure 'the rights of others' adversely affected by the applicants' exercise of rights.[157] Thus, against the rights of female applicants prevented from wearing a headscarf in the workplace and in educational institutions, the Court considered the rights of other women, other girls and their parents whose agency appeared impaired or threatened. In *Dahlab*, for example, the Court examined the impact produced by 'such a powerful external symbol' 'on the freedom of conscience and religion of very young children' (aged between four and eight), who are 'more easily influenced than older pupils'.[158] Similarly, the Court recalled in *Köse* the need 'to protect adolescents when they are at an impressionable age'.[159] In *Sahin*, the Court stated that 'it must be borne in mind the impact which wearing such a symbol [...] may have on those who choose not to wear it'.[160] And in the recent case of *Ebrahimian*, the Court weighed the applicant's freedom to manifest her religion against the state of fragility and dependency of the patients and users with whom the applicant was in contact.[161] The Court appeared generally sympathetic towards the interests of these other rights holders.

Concerns about exposure to pressure or greater dependency limiting the autonomy of individuals may appear well placed in some cases. For example, they seem justified when the Court worries about the impact of the headscarf worn by a Muslim teacher upon pupils aged between four and eight in *Dahlab*. The same could be argued about the Court's concerns regarding psychiatric patients in *Ebrahimian*. Nevertheless, the more grown-up and the least psychologically and physically impaired people are, the less convincing it appears to treat them as fragile, passive or non-autonomous. From this perspective, it is difficult to explain why the Court regards adolescents in *Kose* and adults in *Sahin* strongly malleable and constrained. Viewed in this light, another question arises within the framework of the cases discussed. How can it be explained that while the autonomy of adults and adolescents whom the Court intended to protect was deemed so weakened, the applicants in those same cases were by contrast

157 This analysis takes place in the examination of permissible grounds for restricting human rights, which include 'the protection of the rights and freedom of others.' See e.g. Articles 8(2), 9(2) and 10(2) ECHR.

158 ECtHR, *Dahlab v. Switzerland*, App. no. 42393/98, Decision of 15 February 2001, at 13.

159 ECtHR, *Köse and 93 Others v. Turkey*, App. no. 26625/02, Decision of 24 January 2006, at 11.

160 ECtHR, (GC) *Leyla Şahin v. Turkey*, App. no. 44774/98, Judgment of 10 November 2005, para. 115.

161 ECtHR, *Ebrahimian v. France*, App. no. 64846/11, Judgment of 26 November 2015, paras. 61–62.

portrayed as fully endowed with autonomy and free choice? At the same time, in the cases where headscarf bans were justified by reference to gender equality and in which the Court perceived the veil to be 'imposed' on women,[162] the kind of women who were regarded as fully autonomous to avoid the interference were suddenly stripped of agency and regarded as subordinated. Thus, at one extreme, Muslim women appeared endowed with plenty of choices. At the other extreme, they had none. How can sense be made of this?

Without any pretension of exhaustion, it is submitted that looking at the issue with respect to which individuals were positioned may illuminate the difference. Note that individuals were seen as constrained when positioned against culture or religion. They were, however, seen as unencumbered with regard to socio-economic matters, such as education, employment or social security. This suggests the need to revise the lines commonly drawn between the cultural and material realms. Scholars have pointed out that socio-economic arrangements are usually perceived as neutral and governed by individual free choice, whereas the opposite occurs with ethnic and cultural aspects.[163] The latter are either viewed as embodied and out of our control, as is the case of race and ethnic origin, or they are conceived as intricately subjective or coercive, as happens with religions and cultures (especially with some). As the examples above demonstrate, the dichotomy is not only artificial, but also ideological.

3.2.3. *Integrating the Autonomous and the Constrained Sides of Rights Holders*

Some of the cases discussed above suggest that the Court has failed to capture the lived reality of an individual autonomy which runs across a spectrum, instead of being expressed in an either/or formula. To that extent it has fallen short of acknowledging the social reality of individuals and its effect on their choices.[164] In fact, agency changes with time and circumstance. And there are,

---

162 See cases discussed *supra* section 2. See also, Carolyn Evans, '"The Islamic Scarf" in the European Court of Human Rights', 7 *Melbourne Journal of International Law* (2006) 52, at 65–69.

163 Angela P. Harris, 'Theorizing Class, Gender, and the Law: Three Approaches', 72 *Law and Contemporary Problems* (2009) 37, at 39. In the same vein, but in the specific legal context of the United States, see Mario L. Barnes and Erwin Chemerinsky, 'The Disparate Treatment of Race and Class in Constitutional Jurisprudence', 72(4) *Law and Contemporary Problems* (2009) 109, at 121–122; Anne Phillips, 'Equality, Pluralism, Universality: Current Concerns in Normative Theory', 2(2) *British Journal of Politics & International Relations* (2000) 237, at 243–244.

164 Peroni also criticises the ECtHR's dual representation of 'cultural subjects': while some are viewed as wholly autonomous, others are depicted as determined or oppressed. She argues that each of these stances corresponds to two versions of 'an invulnerable subject'. See Lourdes Peroni, *Opening Up the European Convention Human Rights Subject: An Inclusive Multilayered Framework for Adjudicating Religious and Cultural Claims*, PhD Dissertation (Ghent University, 2014), at 92–98.

by definition, no areas in which individuals are fully autonomous and others in which they are passive recipients.[165]

Whether in the context of substantive provisions alone or in combination with anti-discrimination clauses, it is important to realise that the individual free-will rationale is not a given. Using that argument not to interfere with the *status quo* is actually a normative choice. It has purchase because it resonates with the familiar liberal idea that the state should refrain from intervening with the choices made by autonomous individuals.[166] Yet, as revealed by the cases examined in this book, the argument is problematic in several respects. Firstly, it takes for granted that there are immutable and mutable personal traits, ignoring the great extent to which all of them are socially constructed.[167] Secondly, it introduces an 'assimilationist bias' into the normative analysis, insofar as the scale is, from the beginning, inclined towards conforming to the norm.[168] Moreover, as pointed out by Ringelheim, to present the issue as one of individual free choice obscures the legal background against which the facts take place. That is, the legislation usually reflects and protects the cultural concerns of the majority.[169] And since the law is but one manifestation of larger social structures and institutions, thinking of individuals as unencumbered in fact conceals the

165 Ruth Lister, 'Citizenship: Towards a Feminist Synthesis', 57 *Feminist Review* (1997) 28, at 35. ('People can be, at the same time, both the subordinate objects of hierarchical power relations and subjects who are agents in their own lives, capable of exercising power in the 'generative' sense of self-actualization'.)

166 On liberal ideals and autonomous free choice, see e.g. Anita L. Allen, 'Coercing Privacy', 40(3) *William & Mary Law Review* (1999) 723, at 753; Jennifer Nedelsky, 'Reconceiving Autonomy: Sources, Thoughts and Reflections', 1 *Yale Journal of Law and Feminism* (1989) 7, at 8 ('The image of humans as self-determining creatures nevertheless remains one of the most powerful dimensions of liberal thought'.).

167 Johanna E. Bond, 'International Intersectionality: A Theoretical and Pragmatic Exploration of Women's International Human Rights Violations', 52 *Emory Law Journal* (2003) 71, at 103, 109–119; Patricia Hill Collins, *Black Feminist Thought: Knowledge, Consciousness, and the Politics of Empowerment* (Routledge, 2000), at 15; Kenji Yoshino, 'Assimilationist Bias in Equal Protection: The Visibility Presumption and the Case of Don't Ask, Don't Tell', 108(3) *The Yale Law Journal* (1998) 485, at 496, fn. 35.

168 Kenji Yoshino, 'Assimilationist Bias in Equal Protection: The Visibility Presumption and the Case of Don't Ask, Don't Tell', 108(3) *The Yale Law Journal* (1998) 485, at 500–519 (explaining the 'assimilationist bias' inherent in the immutability and visibility criteria and criticising this prerequisite for heightened protection in the jurisprudence of the United States Supreme Court).

169 Julie Ringelheim, 'Rights, Religion and the Public Sphere: The European Court of Human Rights in Search of a Theory?', in Lorenzo Zucca and Camil Ungureanu (eds.), *Law, State and Religion in the New Europa: Debates and Dilemmas* (Cambridge University Press, 2012), at 293–294 (referring to the EComm.HR case of *X. v. United Kingdom*, App. no. 8160/78, Decision of 12 March 1981, she argues that 'the Commission thus presents the issue as one of free choice, obscuring the legal background against which the facts take place: the legislation guarantees workers the right not to work on Sunday, but does not provide any protection to those wishing to take time off for religious reasons on a different day. The applicant was not in a position to negotiate his work schedule: he could only accept it or resign').

many limitations imposed by markets, patterns of discrimination, material inequality, etc. This is why the Court should not simply assume that the past and future choices of applicants are unconstrained, nor should it ascribe them any unequivocal meaning.[170] This reinforces the need to pay attention to the social context in which cultural differences acquire salience (as discussed in Chapter 1) and adopt an integrated perspective on the cases.

3.3. A BROAD VIEW OF RIGHTS HOLDERS

As the above discussion demonstrates, grasping the complexity of who and whose rights are at stake in a case goes beyond the applicants' experience. Following Brems, the applicants in a case are the most visible right holders, but not the only ones. 'The human rights of other, less visible, rights holders are equally important as a matter of principle and need to be respected, protected and fulfilled equally.'[171] Most of the cases examined here provide a clear example of how these other rights holders include both those who are affected in a similar way to the applicant and those whose interests, rather, oppose those of the applicant.[172] As we have seen, the Court often looks at this last kind of rights holder. It notably does so when it examines the state aim of safeguarding 'the rights of others'. In most of the 'religious cases' referenced above, the Court examined the applicants' complaints against competing claims of equal treatment for other women, men, pupils and public service users. Incorporating these competing rights holders into the story constitutes a necessary and healthy exercise. But the fact that the Court does not always integrate all the relevant rights holders into the picture or that it is inconsistent in doing so in some cases can be problematic.

It is submitted that the integration of other affected rights holders should be inclusive and non-selective.[173] Consequently, the Court should pay equal attention to individuals who, like the applicant, are negatively affected by the measure contested. As argued by Brems with regard to the *Dahlab* case, assessing the impact of a headscarf ban at educational institutions requires the rights of other students and teachers covering their hair to be taken into account. One would therefore need to consider that those pupils 'may experience

170 For a similar approach but in the context of the South African Constitutional Court case law, see Marius Pieterse, 'Finding for the Applicant? Individual Equality Plaintiffs and Group-Based Disadvantage', 24 *South African Journal on Human Rights* (2008) 397, at 411–412.

171 Eva Brems, 'Should Pluriform Human Rights Become One? Exploring the Benefits of Human Rights Integration', 4 *European Journal of Human Rights* (2014) 447, at 458.

172 Ibid., at 458–461 (referring to 'conflicting rights' and 'competing rights').

173 Eva Brems, 'Should Pluriform Human Rights Become One? Exploring the Benefits of Human Rights Integration', 4 *European Journal of Human Rights* (2014) 447, at 458.

stigmatisation and pressure due to such a measure'.[174] Similarly, this reasoning required the Court to pay attention to the rights and needs of the children and other dependents living with the applicants in *Buckley*, *Chapman* and the other similar cases regarding Roma and Traveller people. However, these other rights holders, who were, like the applicants, directly and negatively affected by the eviction threats, were hardly mentioned by the Court, which noticed them and the interference with their rights only in passing.

Another example of the added value of a comprehensive view of the rights holders is provided by *S.A.S. v. France* and subsequent similar cases brought against Belgium. In these cases, the full-face covering ban in question did not target any religion, as the governments and the Court observed, but just the covering of the face in public places. On account of this, it is plausible to think that several kinds of rights holder besides the applicant and Muslim women like her were exposed to criminalisation. One can imagine that women and men with tattoos concealing their faces, motorcycle riders or runners wearing a balaclava could all be affected.[175] An examination of whether and how their rights were restricted by the face-covering ban could have further illuminated the Court's analysis of the proportionality (necessity) of the measure as well as its compatibility with equality and non-discrimination.

A more integrated approach to rights holders was in fact taken by the Court in the recent case of *Osmanoğlu and Kocabaş v. Switzerland.* The applicants, Muslim parents, requested the authorities to exempt their two daughters – who were under the age of puberty – from compulsory mixed swimming lessons. The Court partly supported its finding of non-violation of Article 9 ECHR by reference to the situation of similarly situated children who were nonetheless less socially privileged that those of the applicants. In responding to the applicants' argument that their daughters were taking private swimming lessons, the Court not only regarded school lessons as a vehicle for the development and social integration of the children.[176] It also held that allowing exemptions on the basis

174 Ibid., at 461. In the same vein see CRC, Concluding observations: Germany, CRC/C/15/Add.226, 26 February 2004, para. 30.

175 Yvonne M. Donders, for example, asks: 'is communication with a woman wearing a face veil more difficult than, for instance, with a person whose face is fully covered with tattoos?' See Yvonne M. Donders, *Human Rights: Eye for Cultural Diversity* (Amsterdam University Press, 2012). Inaugural Lecture delivered upon the appointment to the chair of Professor of International Human Rights and Cultural Diversity at the University of Amsterdam on 29 June 2012, at 25 (reflecting on the basis of an empirical study by Annelies Moors, *Gezichtssluiers. Draagsters en Debatten*, Amsterdam School for Social Science Research, 31 January 2009).

176 Despite the assimilationist tone used by the Court – which defined successful social integration as done 'according to the local customs' – it is noteworthy that significant weight was accorded to the interests of potentially affected children who were not the applicants' children. See ECtHR, *Osmanoğlu and Kocabaş v. Switzerland*, App. no. 29086/12, Judgment of 10 January 2017, paras. 97–98.

of the possibility to have private lessons would create an unacceptable inequality for children whose parents did not have the financial means to afford them.[177]

Finally, it is important to observe that whether the complexity and the whole range of individuals affected is acknowledged or not has consequences beyond the issues identified above. Notably, it may also provide important insights as to the sorts of harm at stake, which, in turn, may return us to the norms potentially applicable to the case at hand. Identifying, for instance, individuals' identities and social locations may reveal community or other non-state norms to which individuals feel bound. Furthermore, an intersectional perspective can lead judges to have regard for specific international norms governing the rights of, for example, children, women, indigenous peoples, ethnic minorities and so forth. In addition, overcoming the reduction of individuals to an unencumbered self-sufficient being paves the way towards integrating structural disadvantages and harms that could otherwise go unnoticed, such as exclusion from employment, structural discrimination and restrictions of socio-economic rights. These normative aspects of the cases are discussed in the following sections.

4. INTEGRATED RIGHTS: CROSS-THINKING ABOUT HARMS AND NORMS

As happens with rights holders, when it comes to the harms and norms at stake in a case the picture is often more complex than it might first appear. Many complaints dealing with minority cultural and religious claims emphasise harms such as stereotype, disrespect and lack of accommodation of certain beliefs and modes of living. Most of these harms, which may be labelled 'recognition harms',[178] are examined by the Court through Articles 8 and 9 ECHR. Very occasionally they are addressed via Article 14 ECHR too. Nevertheless, further grievances are usually involved, and applicants put them forward. In some instances, people's political participation is injured too. But perhaps more notably for our purposes, a large proportion of the cases studied also touch upon what we may call 'redistribution harms'.[179] Indeed, applicants lost their jobs, were excluded from schools and universities, found themselves unable to access social security or were evicted from their lands and homes. The question then is whether and how these harms were integrated by the Court and through which norms? To put it in human rights law language: how much did the Court engage with the indivisibility and interdependence of human rights when adjudicating claims concerning ethno-cultural difference?

---

177 Ibid., para. 100.

178 The terminology is borrowed from Nancy Fraser and is used in the light of the discussion in Chapter 1, section 2.4.

179 Idem.

4.1. INTEGRATING REDISTRIBUTION AND STRUCTURAL ISSUES INTO RECOGNITION WRONGS

By virtue of its mandate, the Court cannot apply the whole range of human rights which would arguably capture all the kinds of violations posed by a case. One notorious limitation in this respect is that most rights set forth in the ECHR and its protocols falling within the Court's jurisdiction correspond to those that are commonly regarded as civil and political. The exception includes a few social rights – often invoked by applicants in the cases studied – such as the right to property (Article 1 Protocol 1) and the right to education (Article 2 Protocol 1) ECHR. The latter is relevant in both its limbs of 'access to educational institutions existing at a given time' (para. 1) and respect for 'the right of parents to ensure such education and teaching in conformity with their own religious and philosophical convictions' (para. 2). As will be seen below, only in a few instances has the Court made use of these provisions to scrutinise in relative detail the restrictions placed on the property or education rights of applicants.

Meanwhile, some cases disclose important restrictions on other social rights that are not found in the Convention, such as the right to work and to social security. While these rights are not enshrined in the ECHR or in its protocols, some of them have found protection indirectly via other Convention provisions, such as Article 1 Protocol 1 and Article 8 ECHR. Examples are the cases of *Muñoz Díaz v. Spain* and *Yiğit v. Turkey*, which concerned not only a lack of recognition of the applicants' cultural and religious marriages but also their inability to obtain a survivor's pension and social security benefits based on the entitlements of their deceased spouses. Here, the Court explored the applicants' socio-economic distress by analysing the right to property in conjunction with the prohibition of discrimination.[180] The Court's analysis of work-related rights, however, has been more limited, at least in cases involving Islam and Muslim women.

4.1.1. *Indivisibility or Invisibility in Cases Involving Muslims*

In the Grand Chamber judgment in *Sahin v. Turkey*, the Court had to deal with the right to education (Article 2 Protocol 1 ECHR). However, it simply transposed its considerations under freedom of religion to the allegations concerning the

[180] ECtHR, *Muñoz Díaz v. Spain*, App. no. 49151/07, Judgment of 8 December 2009, paras. 42–71; (GC) *Şerife Yiğit v. Turkey*, App. no. 3976/05, Judgment of 2 November 2010, paras. 57–86. It is to be noted that in *Şerife Yiğit* the Court additionally grappled with the material interests protected by the right to family life. However, it did not go down to the specific situation of the applicant as it did in *Muñoz Díaz v. Spain*, in spite of the fact that the applicant in *Şerife Yiğit* also lacked access to social security rights after having taken care of the home, the deceased spouse and six children.

right to education.[181] The Court noted that the applicant could reasonably have foreseen the risk she ran if she continued to wear the headscarf in defiance of the prohibition. 'Consequently, the restriction in question did not impair the very essence of the applicant's right to education.'[182] No concrete assessment was carried out by the Court in terms of the actual impossibility of finishing her medical studies in Turkey, the fact that she had to move abroad to study and the alleged difficulties with following her profession in Turkey. Similarly, the Court's decision in *Dogru* limited itself to reaffirming that the right to education does not preclude the imposition of penalties, while finding no separate issue to address apart from freedom of religion.[183] The way in which the schooling of girls covering their hair was impaired (the girls were expelled and had to resume their studies through correspondence) hardly received attention. Recently, however, the Court adopted a more integrated stance in the aforementioned case of *Osmanoğlu and Kocabaş v. Switzerland*. Although in this case, which concerned a school's religious exemption, the respondent state was not a party to Protocol 1 ECHR, the Court nonetheless decided to consider Article 2 of this Protocol (right to education). It did so 'for the sake of completeness', because the Convention had to be read as a whole and Article 2(2) Protocol 1 (child education in conformity with the parents' religious convictions) was *lex specialis* regarding Article 9.[184]

The integration of socio-economic harms and structural barriers has been especially meagre in the context of labour rights. Consider, for example, the inadmissibility decision in *Dahlab v. Switzerland*, which dealt with a headscarf ban applied to public schools on account of which the applicant was fired. An issue disputed by the parties was whether teaching in private schools remained an option open to the applicant. For the applicant, effective access to those schools was doubtful, for the state practically had a monopoly on infant classes and the few private schools left were non-denominational or were affiliated to religions other than that of the applicant.[185] This meant that the applicant – and other teachers like her – was virtually prevented from working in her professional capacity at all. Despite the seriousness of the alleged harm, the Court's decision

---

181 ECtHR, (GC) *Leyla Şahin v. Turkey*, App. no. 44774/98, Judgment of 10 November 2005, para. 157.

182 ECtHR, (GC) *Leyla Şahin v. Turkey*, App. no. 44774/98, Judgment of 10 November 2005, para. 161.

183 ECtHR, *Dogru v. France*, App. no. 27058/05, Judgment of 4 December 2008, paras. 83–84.

184 ECtHR, *Osmanoğlu and Kocabaş v. Switzerland*, Application no. 29086/12, Judgment of 10 January 2017, para. 90. The original text in French reads: 'Dans le souci d'être complet [...] la Cour juge néanmoins utile de rappeler les principes pertinents applicables sous l'angle de l'article 2 du Protocole no 1, étant donné que la Convention doit être lue comme un tout et que la dernière disposition constitue, du moins s'agissant de sa seconde phrase, la lex specialis par rapport à l'article 9 en matière d'éducation et d'enseignement, matière dont relève la présente affaire.'

185 ECtHR, *Dahlab v. Switzerland*, App. no. 42393/98, Decision of 15 February 2001, at 8 and 10.

did not even examine these allegations. In *Kurtulmus*, a Muslim teacher complained that her dismissal had deprived her of her sole source of income and of access to social security benefits, in violation of Article 1 Protocol 1. But the Court's response was brief and formal. It simply pointed out that since an amnesty had been applied, the applicant was able to seek reinstatement to her teaching post. It also added that a public servant's removal from office and the resultant loss of future income did not affect his or her 'possessions'.[186]

The lack of attention to the actual effects of losing one's job and to existing barriers to engaging in certain occupations may be seen as an extension of the fragmented view of rights holders' autonomy discussed earlier, or as an extension of what Ouald Chaib calls the 'freedom to resign' doctrine in cases involving religious rights claims.[187] The doctrine arises out of a number of cases in which the Court argued that where an employee had freely entered into a labour contract and had knowingly deviated from the conditions imposed by it (e.g. by breaching a dress code or working schedules on religious grounds), a dismissal would not amount to interference with his or her freedom of religion. This perspective presents as reasonable the setting aside of the (self-inflicted) socio-economic harm suffered by the dismissed applicant from the balancing or proportionality analysis undertaken by the Court.

Needless to say, the Court cannot be expected to adjudicate on the right to work or the right to social security. Institutional constraints cannot be ignored. But we know, because the Court made it clear long ago in the *Airey* case,[188] that the Court should not simply ignore socio-economic harms. Actually, some engagement with the interdependence and indivisibility of all human rights is possible. One way of doing so is by assessing socio-economic injuries in the proportionality analysis conducted by the Court when weighing the legitimacy of state restrictions of Convention rights. This is precisely what the Court did in the previously mentioned *Eweida* case. Here, the first applicant, a Christian woman prevented from wearing a cross at work, alleged that the enforcement of the uniform code was not only 'deeply humiliating and offensive; in addition, the loss of her salary for four months created significant financial hardship'.[189] Protection of her religious freedom, so went the argument, could not be requested at the expense of her job. Similarly, the fourth applicant, a practising Christian man who claimed – unsuccessfully – a religious exemption from his duties as a psycho-sexual counsellor, underlined the severity of the harm resulting from

---

186 ECtHR, *Kurtulmuş v. Turkey*, App. no. 65500/01, Decision of 24 January 2006, at 9.

187 Saïla Ouald Chaib, *Belief in Justice. Towards More Inclusivity in and through the Freedom of Religion Case Law of the European Court of Human Rights*, PhD Dissertation (Ghent University, 2015), at 136–139.

188 ECtHR, *Airey v. Ireland*, App. no. 6289/73, Judgment of 9 October 1979, para. 26.

189 ECtHR, *Eweida and Others v. the United Kingdom*, Application nos. 48420/10, 59842/10, 51671/10 and 36516/10, Judgment of 15 January 2013, para. 65.

employment dismissal.[190] While in previous case law the Court had had regard to the consequences of being excluded from a range of jobs, it had done so in response to an explicit prohibition from engaging in certain occupations and for contextual reasons other than cultural/religious ones.[191] Hence, *Eweida* stands as the first case of its kind in which the Court rightly took into account the seriousness of losing one's job as well as the possibility of changing jobs in its proportionality analysis under Article 9 ECHR.[192]

This kind of engagement with the indivisibility of rights is especially needed when the applicant is not only facing dismissal or non-renewal of contract, but also a virtual bar on finding a job in a whole field (e.g. public service) or in a whole area of expertise (e.g. employment as a teacher). From this perspective, it is difficult to understand why no traces of the *Eweida* approach are to be found in the 2015 case of *Ebrahimian v. France*, an omission underscored by the concurring-dissenting judge.[193] In this last case the Court accepted that a strict implementation of the principles of neutrality and secularism consisting of a ban on religious garments could hold not just for public servants in the education field, as it had ruled in previous cases, but also for all kinds of civil servant. As a result, the non-renewal of the applicant's contract on account of wearing a headscarf was found legitimate. Although the Court referred to the specific functions performed by the applicant (a social assistant in the psychiatric unit of a public hospital), to the particular circumstances of the patients with whom the applicant was in contact (persons in a state of relative fragility as a result of their psychiatric condition) and to the absence of complaints of pressure or

---

190 Ibid., para. 74.

191 A notable example is the case of *Sidabras and Dziautas v. Lithuania*, which deals with a ban imposed on former KGB officers from being employed in some public and private sector jobs. According to the Court, their exclusion from certain types of private sector employment fell within their right to private life since it is 'in the course of their working lives that the majority of people have a significant, if not the greatest, opportunity of developing relationships with the outside world under the right to private life'. The prohibition from engaging in the occupation of the applicants' choice had a significant impact upon their opportunity to develop relationships with the outside world and created serious difficulties for 'earning their living', which added to stigmatisation suffered by the applicants (as former KGB agents). Examining Article 8 taken jointly with Article 14 ECHR, the Court found that the ban was disproportional. Notably, the impugned law contained no definition of the specific jobs, functions or tasks which the applicants were barred from holding, which prevented the Court from ascertaining the link with the means chosen to achieve the aims sought by the ban. See ECtHR, *Sidabras and Džiautas v. Lithuania*, App. nos. 55480/00 and 59330/00, Judgment of 27 July 2004, paras. 44 and 48–49.

192 ECtHR, *Eweida and Others v. the United Kingdom*, Application nos. 48420/10, 59842/10, 51671/10 and 36516/10, Judgment of 15 January 2013, para. 83, *in fine*. The Court also took this stance with respect to the third and fourth applicants. See paras. 106 and 109. The overall shift should be seen in light of the argumentation offered by the applicants, who, notably, elaborated on this point. See paras. 65 and 74.

193 ECtHR, *Ebrahimian v. France*, App. no. 64846/11, Judgment of 26 November 2015, Partly Concurring and Partly Dissenting Opinion Judge O'Leary, para. 37.

proselytism against the applicant,[194] the Court's conclusion was determined primarily by rather abstract reasoning based on the concepts of secularism and neutrality.[195]

The legitimacy of a general ban on religious symbols, especially those outwardly visible, among all public officials is derived in *Ebrahimian* from two main grounds. The first is from the place that secularism and neutrality holds in the French constitution.[196] The second is the legitimacy that flows from the wide margin of appreciation granted to the state given the 'profound differences' on religious issues that exist within democratic societies.[197] The Court's review ends up being deferential and abstract. In its proportionality review it simply defers to that undertaken by the domestic authorities and relies on taken-for-granted notions of secularism and neutrality. In so doing, the Court also fails to assess the applicant's loss of employment, as well as further obstacles to employability. As noted by Brems, the interpretation adopted in *Ebrahimian* basically left the applicant without a chance of working in the entire French public sector.[198] And yet, this element finds no place in the judgment. It is therefore regrettable that serious socio-economic issues and even a growing context of structural discrimination in the form of Islamophobia were obscured by a focus on neutrality, secularism, religious difference and French identity.[199] All the above supports the view advanced by scholars that casting the rights claims of Muslim women as a matter of religious difference and identity, neutrality or secularism tends to ignore the socio-economic aspects of their lives and the role of the state in ensuring their socio-economic integration.[200]

---

194 Ibid., paras. 62–69.

195 See ibid., Dissenting Opinion of Judge Gaetano, at 39 (holding that '[t]he thrust of the judgment is to the effect that the abstract principle of laïcité or secularism of the State requires a blanket prohibition on the wearing by a public official at work of any symbol denoting his or her religious belief').

196 Note that the constitutional status of the principle of secularism may be seen as a precondition for accepting that the protection of such principle falls within the ambit of 'the protection of the rights and freedoms of others'. In this vein, see ECtHR, *Hamidović v. Bosnia and Herzegovina*, App. no. 57792/15, Judgment of 5 December 2017, Concurring Opinion of Judge de Gaetano, para. 4.

197 Ibid., paras. 55–70.

198 In this vein, see Eva Brems, 'Ebrahimian v. France: headscarf ban upheld for entire public sector', *Strasbourg Observers*, 27 November 2015, <strasbourgobservers.com/2015/11/27/ebrahimian-v-france-headscarf-ban-upheld-for-entire-public-sector/>.

199 On the wider context of Islamophobia in Europe see, *inter alia*, Amnesty International, *Choice and Prejudice: Discrimination Against Muslims in Europe* (Amnesty International, 2012); European Monitoring Centre on Racism and Xenophobia, *Muslims in the European Union: Discrimination and Islamophobia* (EUMC, 2006), at 73–75 (on the situation in France).

200 Pascale Fournier and Gökçe Yurdakul, 'Unveiling distribution: Muslim women with headscarves in France and Germany', in Michal Bodemann and Gökçe Yurdakul (eds.), *Migration, citizenship, ethnos* (Palgrave Macmillan, 2006), at 178. See also Iris Marion Young, 'Structural Injustice and the Politics of Difference', in Emily Grabham *et al.* (eds.), *Intersectionality and Beyond. Law, power and the politics of location* (Routledge Cavendish, 2009), at 291.

The fact that *Eweida* dealt with a private company and *Ebrahimian* with a public service can make a difference, given the particular roles of public officials and the place of neutrality in the state's policies. But the specificity of each context does not release the Court from the need to consider the socio-economic harm faced by the applicant and the wider context of exclusion at play in *Ebrahimian*. It remains to be seen, though, how the ECtHR will respond if confronted with a neutrality policy banning the wearing of visible religious symbols in the private workplace. In the light of *Eweida*, it is hard to imagine that the Court could take a similar stance to that adopted in *Ebrahimian*. After all, most of the abstract reasoning on neutrality, secularism and French *laïcité* advanced by the Court in this case does not hold for private companies.

The question appears particularly interesting against the backdrop of the recent rulings of the European Court of Justice (ECJ) in the cases of *Achbita* and *Bougnaoui*, both concerning the manifestation of beliefs in the private workplace.[201] In both cases Muslim women employees working in private companies had been dismissed on account of wearing a headscarf. While in *Bougnaoui* the ECJ finds discrimination and rejects the possibility that customers' preferences could justify an encroachment of the employees' right to manifest their religion and beliefs,[202] in *Achbita* this position is accepted as long as it is grounded in a general policy of (corporate) neutrality. One of the disquieting issues about the ECJ's reasoning in this last case – besides the narrow understanding of direct discrimination and the generous interpretation of the freedom to conduct a business – is the scant regard for the applicant's employability and the job market reality.[203] In this respect, the ECJ limits itself to evaluating whether it had been possible to offer the applicant a post without visual contact with customers.[204] However, no assessment is made of what this would mean in practice and what socio-economic opportunities were being curtailed for the applicant and others like her. Several concrete questions about what was at stake in *Achbita* and about what the private policy of neutrality was for were thus overlooked. It is yet to be seen whether, in the event of the

---

201 ECJ, *Samira Achbita, Centrum voor gelijkheid van kansen en voor racismebestrijding v. G4S Secure Solutions NV*, Case C-157/15, Request for a preliminary ruling from the Hof van Cassatie (Belgium), Lodged on 3 April 2015; (GC) *Asma Bougnaoui, Association de défense des droits de l'homme (ADDH) v. Micropole SA*, Case C-188/15, Judgment of 14 March 2017.

202 ECJ, (GC) *Asma Bougnaoui, Association de défense des droits de l'homme (ADDH) v. Micropole SA*, Case C-188/15, Judgment of 14 March 2017, para. 41.

203 In this vein, see Saïla Ouald Chaib and Valeska David, 'European Court of Justice keeps the door to religious discrimination in the private workplace opened. The European Court of Human Rights could close it', *Strasbourg Observers*, 27 March 2017, <strasbourgobservers.com/2017/03/27/european-court-of-justice-keeps-the-door-to-religious-discrimination-in-the-private-workplace-opened-the-european-court-of-human-rights-could-close-it/>.

204 ECJ, *Samira Achbita, Centrum voor gelijkheid van kansen en voor racismebestrijding v. G4S Secure Solutions NV*, Case C-157/15, Request for a preliminary ruling from the Hof van Cassatie (Belgium), Lodged on 3 April 2015, para. 43.

ECtHR ruling on a similar case, questions of this kind are integrated into any considerations of religious difference and neutrality.

4.1.2. *Indivisibility or Invisibility in Cases Involving Roma and Travellers*

As regards Roma applicants in cases involving questions of cultural difference, the Court has also addressed violations to the right to education enshrined in Protocol 1 to the ECHR. Notably, it has done so in the series of cases dealing with the school segregation of Roma children.[205] Yet, a thorough review of allegations of violations of this right has not been the rule; and, as noted above, the same can be said about claims concerning the right to property. In several cases the Court conducted a rather superficial examination of Articles 1 and 2 Protocol 1 ECHR (rights to property and education, respectively), despite being empowered to do otherwise. That was the case with regard to the right to education claim raised by a number of Roma and Travellers in 'Gypsy lifestyle' cases. One of their main concerns was that the school attendance of their children was disrupted every time the applicants were forced to move as the result of an eviction order. The Court, however, barely reacted to that argument and often concluded that such complaints were insufficiently substantiated.[206] Likewise, Roma applicants occupying land that was not their property denounced the removal and destruction of their belongings when evicted, in violation of their possession rights (Article 1 Protocol 1). However, the claim did not attract a thorough review from the Court.[207]

The Court has nonetheless fared better when assessing the impact of losing one's home. This is reflected in a number of judgments concerning Roma

---

[205] See, for example, ECtHR, (GC) *D.H. and Others v. the Czech Republic*, App. no. 57325/00, Judgment of 13 November 2007; (GC) *Oršuš and Others v. Croatia*, App. no. 15766/03, Judgment of 16 March 2010. Article 2 Protocol 1 has also been at the core of other cases and so has been examined in detail, i.e. in cases concerning requests for exemption of pupils from school lessons on religious grounds. See e.g. ECtHR, *Hasan and Eylem Zegin v. Turkey*, App. no. 1448/04, Judgment of 9 October 2007 and *Osmanoğlu and Kocabaş v. Switzerland*, Application no. 29086/12, Judgment of 10 January 2017.

[206] ECtHR, (GC) *Coster v. the United Kingdom*, App. no. 24876/94, Judgment of 18 January 2001, para. 137; (GC) *Lee v. the United Kingdom*, App. no. 25289/94, Judgment of 18 January 2001, para. 125; *Harrison v. the United Kingdom*, App. no. 10721/02, Judgment of 17 July 2008, para. 2, at 14; *Clark and Others v. the United Kingdom*, App. no. 28575/95, Decision of 22 May 2001, para. 3, at 13; *Beatrice and John Smith v. the United Kingdom*, App. no. 34334/96, Decision of 3 May 2001, at 14–15.

[207] ECtHR, *Connors v. the United Kingdom*, App. no. 66746/01, Judgment of 27 May 2004, paras. 99–100. For further discussion on this, see Chapter 4, section 4.3.1. In the cases decided in 2001 applicants also claimed a violation of their right to property but on account of being denied the right to live on their own land. In fact, according to state regulations, they were not allowed to station their caravans on the land of their property. In none of them did the Court examine this claim separately from Article 8 ECHR. In this respect, it should be noted that some applicants explicitly accepted a dismissal of their property claim in case of a finding of violation of Article 8 ECHR.

and Travellers. The starting point was to recognise that caravans belonging to the Roma and Travellers are 'homes' within the scope of Article 8 ECHR.[208] Initially, the Court was of the view that Article 8 ECHR does not comprise a right to be provided with a home or require the state to provide a number of suitable sites for Gypsies.[209] In the context of the wide margin of appreciation enjoyed by the state in planning and housing matters, the Court furthermore adopted a formal approach to evaluating the availability of suitable sites for Gypsies and Travellers.[210] Later, however, the stance progressively changed. The Court applied procedural safeguards against the (threats of) evictions faced by Roma and Travellers and even conceded that a duty to provide (suitable) housing for particularly vulnerable individuals could indeed flow from Article 8 ECHR.[211]

Connors, the first successful judgment for Roma struggling with land planning regulations, was a pioneer in the application of procedural housing safeguards. Applying a procedural review, the Court challenged the summary eviction procedure that affected the applicants and examined the socio-economic policies in place.[212] What is more, in this judgment the Court also weighed the risk of homelessness faced by the applicants. The case concerned the application of a summary eviction procedure justified by the state on the ground that accommodation of Roma and Travellers' needs (consistent with their nomadic lifestyle) required authorities to be flexible in the management of site provision. As a result, the applicant had been deprived of guarantees enjoyed by tenants living in conventional housing and in other mobile homes. So, it is noteworthy that the problem in this case was not so much the lack of accommodation of

---

208 ECtHR, *Buckley v. the United Kingdom*, App. no. 20348/92, Judgment of 29 September 1996, para. 54.

209 See e.g. ECtHR, (GC) *Chapman and Others*, App. no. 27238/95, Judgment of 18 January 2001, paras. 98–99; (GC) *Coster v. the United Kingdom*, App. no. 24876/94, Judgment of 18 January 2001, para. 113.

210 ECtHR, (GC) *Chapman and Others*, App. no. 27238/95, Judgment of 18 January 2001, paras. 102 and 111 (attaching great weight to the illegality of the occupation, while downplaying the fact that no public sites were available either in the district or in the county as a whole).

211 ECtHR, *Yordanova and Others v. Bulgaria*, App. no. 25446/06, Judgment of 24 April 2012, para. 130. Following *Chapman*, the Court would admit that 'Article 8 could impose a positive obligation on the authorities to provide accommodation for a homeless gypsy' but would continue to be cautious and restrict the scope of this obligation. See ECtHR, *Codona v. the United Kingdom*, App. no. 485/05, Decision of 7 February 2006, at 10.

212 The Court made in *Connors* a more comprehensive and less formalistic examination of the domestic legal framework. For instance, it examined closely whether the summary eviction really accomplished its purported aims. Furthermore, it addressed the policies in place. It took into account, *inter alia*, that 70 per cent of local authorities did not have any written Gypsy/Traveller accommodation policy, that there was almost no increase in the number of local authority pitches and that no special allowances were made for gypsies in the planning criteria applied by authorities in deciding on the stationing of caravans on private sites. ECtHR, *Connors v. the United Kingdom*, App. no. 66746/01, Judgment of 27 May 2004, para. 85.

a nomadic *Gypsy way of life*, as in previous Roma/Traveller cases. The issue in *Connors* was rather that the state, in implementing such accommodation, had deprived the applicants of the security of tenure enjoyed by other tenants. This might suggest that it was easier for the Court to unpack the socio-economic dimension of Article 8 when the culturally based claim for accommodation of a distinct minority lifestyle (the so-called Roma cultural identity) was not so salient. The subsequent case of *Buckland*, which was similar to *Connors*, was also decided on procedural housing rights.[213]

The safeguards applied in this area were further expanded in cases such as *Yordanova* and *Winterstein*.[214] These judgments, unlike most of the previous land planning cases, dealt with the eviction of Roma and Traveller communities of a hundred or more people who had resided for decades in *de facto* tolerated settlements in Bulgaria and France, respectively. In these judgments the Court held that any person facing the risk of losing her home has the right to have the reasonableness and proportionality of the measure reviewed by an independent tribunal. This involved a number of steps on the part of the state, including giving adequate reasons in response to arguments raised in opposition to the eviction and consideration to the risk of homelessness and the social disadvantage of the applicants.[215] As further discussed below, this interpretation was backed by existing regional and international standards for socio-economic rights.[216] By virtue of this socio-economic permeation of Article 8, stronger protection of tenure was provided to sedentary Roma and Travellers.

Overall, however, the Court's engagement with the indivisibility of human rights in the cases reviewed was limited, particularly where arguments over cultural and religious identity stood out. Integrating elements of socio-economic rights does not mean that a violation should be found. It does mean, however, that cases should not be decided as if they were mostly or only about cultural difference. It implies acknowledging that the cases studied are also about specific individuals facing concrete hurdles, including material ones. The importance of this point is reaffirmed by the patterns of socio-economic exclusion affecting ethno-cultural minorities. Well known is the precarious situation of the Roma

---

213 ECtHR, *Buckland v. the United Kingdom*, App. no. 40060/08, Judgment of 18 September 2012, paras. 68–70.

214 ECtHR, *Yordanova and Others v. Bulgaria*, App. no. 25446/06, Judgment of 24 April 2012 and *Winterstein and Others v. France*, App. no. 27013/07, Judgment of 17 October 2013.

215 ECtHR, *Yordanova and Others v. Bulgaria*, App. no. 25446/06, Judgment of 24 April 2012, paras. 118, 124–126 and 132; *Winterstein and Others v. France*, App. no. 27013/07, Judgment of 17 October 2013, paras. 83–88.

216 In this vein, see also, Adélaïde Remiche, 'Yordanova and others v Bulgaria: the Influence of the Social Right to Adequate Housing on the Interpretation of the Civil Right to Respect for one's Home', 12(4) *Human Rights Law Review* (2012) 787, at 794.

in Europe. The Council of Europe (CoE) has repeatedly invited member states to take steps to remedy their disadvantage.[217] And while many concerns regarding Muslims may revolve around Islam, security threats associated with it and with 'their' cultural difference, there is much reason to worry about their socio-economic exclusion. Studies indicate that in several member states Muslims face particularly high rates of disadvantage in the labour market and in other areas of social life such as income, housing and health,[218] not to mention the compounded disadvantages experienced by Muslim women. Hence, the risk of rendering invisible the socio-economic stakes of culturally defined cases deserves to be taken seriously.

4.2. AVOIDING NORM REDUCTIONISM AND PROMOTING AWARENESS OF LEGAL PLURALISM

Working with notions of indivisibility and interdependence is one way of adopting a relational view of human rights norms. But it is not the only one. Human rights norms do not stand in isolation. This holds true within and outside the Convention. Looking from within the Convention, a first aspect that is startling about the judgments reviewed here is that despite the normative complexity posed by the cases, many rulings took one Convention provision as *the* predominant legal framework. These are Articles 8 and 9 ECHR. This happened even though applicants often resorted to several other provisions, such as equality and non-discrimination, freedom of expression, the right to education, property, due process, free elections and freedom of assembly. As already mentioned, when the Court did not decline the examination of these other provisions, it frequently conducted a rather superficial analysis of them. This may be attributed, at least partially, to the argumentation offered by litigants. At the same time, one convention provision may admittedly be at the core of a given case. And yet, for the reasons explained below, it is important to be careful not to incur too far into norm reductionism.

217 See e.g. Council of Europe, Commissioner of Human Rights Report, *Human rights of Roma and Travellers in Europe* (Council of Europe, 2012); PACE, Resolution 1740 (2010) on the situation of Roma in Europe and relevant activities of the Council of Europe, Adopted on 22 June 2010; PACE, Recommendation 1203 (1993) on Gypsies in Europe, Adopted on 2 February 1993; PACE, Recommendation 1557 (2002) on the Legal Situation of Roma in Europe, Adopted on 25 April 2002.

218 Tufyal Choudhury, 'Muslims and Discrimination', in Samir Amghar *et al.* (eds.), *European Islam: Challenges for Public Policy and Society* (Center for European Policy Studies, 2007), at 78–92; Gökçe Yurdakul and Pascale Fournier, 'Unveiling Distribution: Muslim Women with Headscarves in France and Germany', in Y. Michal Bodemann and Gökçe Yurdakul (eds.), *Migration, Citizenship, Ethnos* (Palgrave Macmillan, 2006), at 175–177.

4.2.1. *A More Comprehensive Approach to Convention Norms*

From the perspective of the Convention provisions, over-reliance on a single norm may be counter-productive. Notably, using a single normative lens may overstate one aspect of the case or of the applicant's experience at the expense of other interlocked issues. One may wonder, for instance, to what extent an exclusive focus on Article 9 in cases concerning veil bans eclipses the applicants' experiences as women, as well as their problems in terms of educational and employment opportunities. Reducing the normative analysis to that provision may also foster the view that headscarves are a matter of religion only. And this, in turn, facilitates the external attribution of one essentialised meaning to the practice. On the other hand, adding freedom of speech (Article 10 ECHR), for example, opens up other kinds of argument. Under Article 10, the premise is that the wider the tools and resources for enriching public debate the better and that the state should facilitate the participation of those who have fewer chances of engaging in it. Then, neither the content of the expression nor state neutrality (which in any case should be enabling instead of constraining) appear as strong as under the prevailing reading of Article 9.[219] Similar considerations can be posited with regard to the centrality of Article 8 in Roma cases regarding planning regulations. Concerns may arise, particularly to the extent that much emphasis is put on a particular lifestyle to the neglect of property rights, education and equality. In this vein, one may critically point at the Court's general refusal to examine Muslims' and Roma's cases from the viewpoint of the prohibition of discrimination for the sole reason of having addressed the allegation of violation of religious freedom (Article 9 ECHR) or private life (Article 8). The question of inequality, which is not necessarily implied in restrictions to religious or cultural rights, is thus left unexplored. The problem is, in other words, that certain harms may be obscured and normative insights for addressing them may be lost. Cases may thus end up very narrowly defined as a matter of 'a gypsy way of life', a 'headscarf', and so on.

Looking from outside the Convention, a second aspect to consider in grasping the normative complexity posed by the cases studied is that the Convention's provisions are part of a dynamic and multilayered system of laws, as pointed out in the Introduction and Chapter 1 Thus, a relational view of the applicable norms in the cases studied requires not losing sight of the range of

---

219 It is interesting to note that in the case of the first applicant in *Eweida and Others* (concerning her dismissal from British Airways for wearing a cross), part of the Court's argumentation somewhat resembles this freedom of expression rationale. It held that 'a healthy democratic society needs to tolerate and *sustain* pluralism and diversity; but also because of the value to an individual who has made religion a central tenet of his or her life to *be able to communicate that belief to others*'. ECtHR, *Eweida and Others v. the United Kingdom*, App. nos. 48420/10, 59842/10, 51671/10 and 36516/10, Judgment of 15 January 2013, para. 94.

norms involved domestically and internationally. We will start by examining the implications of this suggestion, which may be called 'legal pluralism awareness'. This is not unfamiliar to the Court. Several of its judgments recount the 'relevant international law and practice' and incorporate domestic regulations when examining the 'background of the case'. Moreover, these are relevant factors when the Court examines the existence of a 'consensus' among member states. Whether and how much of this normative plurality is integrated seems especially relevant for adjudicating cases dealing with cultural diversity. Why? Because these cases, more often than not, are inserted within a vast, complex and interacting legal landscape.

4.2.2. *Integrating Domestic and International Norms through Evolutive Interpretation and Consensus*

The idea that the ECHR is a 'living instrument' to be interpreted and applied in 'present day conditions' emerged very early in the Court's jurisprudence, and it came to stay.[220] This principle not only entails that the Convention should be read with flexibility and with eyes open to change, in keeping with social and cultural transformations. It furthermore conveys the idea that the Court should be 'influenced by the developments and commonly accepted standards in […] the member States of the Council of Europe'.[221] It is thus not uncommon for the Court to bring into its judgments comparative law from the Council of Europe (and even beyond), as well as international instruments of many kinds. This dynamic interpretation, which takes into account international and domestic normative developments, including those reflecting a European consensus, is also present in the cases studied in this chapter. It should be noted, though, that while in some judgments this normative review is relatively exhaustive, in others it is nearly absent.

The European legal context referred to by the Court for the purposes of identifying a regional consensus comprises not only domestic legislation and case law. It also encompasses sources from a myriad of bodies within the Council of Europe. The degree to which one or another is to be considered seems variable, though. For example, in those religious difference cases studied here in which the Court addressed the issue of consensus (in many, it did not), the focus was largely on comparative law. However, in cases concerning Roma and Traveller caravans and informal occupation, as well as in those dealing with educational segregation, the Court reviewed more extensively the standards laid down in European instruments and in decisions from regional monitoring bodies. Among these were the European Framework Convention for the Protection of

220 ECtHR, *Tyrer v. the United Kingdom*, App. no. 5856/72, Judgment of 25 April 1978, para. 31.
221 Idem.

National Minorities, the European Social Charter, decisions from the European Committee of Social Rights and the European Commission against Racism and Intolerance, as well as Resolutions and Recommendations of the Committee of Ministers and of the Parliamentary Assembly of the Council of Europe. As many of these bodies and instruments are mainly concerned with the protection of human rights, it is not strange that their inclusion may yield a 'common approach' that is actually more rights-protective than the one provided by the laws of the respondent state or of several member states.

What is more, such a set of regional standards has proven to be, in a number of respects, usefully tailored to the rights holders and the stakes of the cases at hand. In cases such as *D.H.*, *Sampanis*, *Oršuš*, and *Horváth and Kiss*, for instance, the Court took into account standards on the situation of Roma children from the perspective of their right to education, the prohibition of racism and other forms of discrimination, and their social and economic integration within the respondent state.[222] In cases such as *Yordanova* and *Winterstein*, the European normative review incorporated specific standards on housing rights (i.e. safeguards in case of eviction) and non-discrimination, among others. Moreover, it is to be noted that in all these cases the Court eventually echoed the findings of other European supervisory mechanisms which, in similar cases, had found a breach of human rights obligations. As discussed below, the impact of normative developments from other human rights instruments and bodies can be amplified by the inclusion of sources outside the regional system. In the cases of *Yordanova* and *Winterstein*, for example, the Court not only considered decisions from the European Committee of Social Rights (ECSR), but also General Comments of the UN Committee on Economic, Social and Cultural Rights (UN CommESCR).[223] Importantly, these sources provide specific standards on the right to housing and, particularly, on forced eviction. These include consultation with the community or individual concerned, reasonable notice, provision of information, a guarantee that the eviction will be carried out in a reasonable manner and alternative housing measures. This might explain the Court's emphasis, in both cases, on procedural guarantees for securing respect for the home.

---

[222] ECtHR, (GC) *D.H. and Others v. the Czech Republic*, App. no. 57325/00, Judgment of 13 November 2007, paras. 195–200 and 205–207; *Sampanis and Others v. Greece*, App. no. 32526/05, Judgment of 5 June 2008, paras. 77–83 and 95–97; *Horváth and Kiss v. Hungary*, App. no. 11146/11, Judgment of 29 January 2013, paras. 115–128.

[223] In *Yordanova* the Court listed these instruments and decisions as 'relevant international material' (paras. 73–83), whereas in *Winterstein* it included them in its analysis on the merits (para. 87). Some of the specific sources referenced in these judgments are: Committee of Ministers of the Council of Europe, Recommendation 2005 on improving the housing conditions of Roma and Recommendation 2008 on policies for Roma and/or Travellers in Europe; CESCR, General Comment No. 7: The right to adequate housing (art. 11), E/1998/22, 20 May 1997; and ECSR, *European Roma Rights Centre v. Bulgaria*, Collective complaint no. 31/2005, Decision on the merits of 18 October 2006.

Now, irrespective of the norms that are brought into the European common ground, it is well known that whether there is or there is no consensus does matter. Notably, there is an inverse relationship between the consensus and the margin of appreciation granted to the state. In short: the less the consensus, the wider the state discretion. Yet, the cases studied do not show a consistent judicial analysis of this matter. In most cases dealing with Roma claims, the Court identified an 'emerging international consensus amongst the Contracting States of the Council of Europe recognising the special needs of minorities and an obligation to protect their security, identity and lifestyle'.[224] However, while in some cases (notably, those dealing with the 'gypsy way of life') the Court found that such an emerging consensus was not clear enough to derive any concrete guidance, in others (notably, those concerning educational segregation) the Court was ready to follow that same consensus. But not only the conditions – regarding specificity or otherwise – under which a given consensus could be applied have turned out to be opaque. There has also been a lack of clarity in determining the existence of consensus, whether emerging or firmly established, particularly when the normative landscape was one of non-regulation. Some judgments concerning Muslims' religious expressions attest to this difficulty.

A case in point is *S.A.S. v. France*, in which the Court concluded that 'there is no European consensus against a ban (on a full-face veil in public)'.[225] At the same time, however, the Court admitted that France was 'very much in a minority position in Europe: except for Belgium, no other member State of the Council of Europe has, to date, opted for such a measure'.[226] How could there then not be a consensus against such a ban? The Court justified this paradox by referring to the fact that a number of member states had been *debating* the question of the wearing of the full-face veil. But can the consensus be more

[224] ECtHR, see e.g. (GC) *Beard v. the United Kingdom*, App. no. 24882/94, Judgment of 18 January 2001, para. 104; (GC) *Chapman v. the United Kingdom*, App. no. 27238/95, Judgment of 18 January 2001, para. 93; (GC) *Coster v. the United Kingdom*, App. no. 24876/94, Judgment of 18 January 2001, para. 107; (GC) *Lee v. the United Kingdom*, App. no. 25289/94, Judgment of 18 January 2001, para. 95; *Eatson v. the United Kingdom*, App. no. 39664/98, Decision of 30 January 2001, at 7; *Smith v. the United Kingdom*, App. no. 40435/98, Decision of 30 January 2001, at 7; *Beatrice and John Smith v. the United Kingdom*, App. no. 34334/96, Decision of 3 May 2001, at 10; *Clark and Others v. the United Kingdom*, App. no. 28575/95, Decision of 22 May 2001, at 9; (GC) *D.H. and Others v. the Czech Republic*, App. no. 57325/00, Judgment of 13 November 2007, para. 181; *Sampanis and Others v. Greece*, App. no. 32526/05, Judgment of 5 June 2008, para. 73; *Muñoz Díaz v. Spain*, App. no. 49151/07, Judgment of 8 December 2009, para. 60; (GC) *Oršuš and Others v. Croatia*, App. no. 15766/03, Judgment of 16 March 2010, para. 148.

[225] ECtHR, (GC) *S.A.S. v. France*, App. no. 43835/11, Judgment of 1 July 2014, para. 156. In the same vein, see *Dakir and Belcacemi and Oussar v. Belgium*, App. nos. 4619/12 and 37798/13, Judgments of 11 July 2017, paras. 59 and 55, respectively ('there is still no consensus within the member States of the Council of Europe as to whether or not there should be a blanket ban on the wearing of the full-face veil in public places').

[226] Idem., para. 156.

determined by public debate about norms than by norms themselves?[227] In any event, this singular approach was not new. The Court reached a similar conclusion in *Sahin*, where no consensus was derived from an overwhelming lack of regulation across member states of the wearing of religious symbols in university education.[228] The same line of reasoning resurfaced recently, though more implicitly, in *Ebrahimian v. France*. In this judgment the issue of consensus was additionally confusing because of the area of regulation examined by the Court. While the case concerned a ban intended for the entire public sector, the Court relied on its previous findings of non-consensus regarding religious attire in the field of education.[229]

The above inconsistencies draw attention to the way the Court formulates the normative inquiry, which seems to predetermine the conclusion as to the existence and scope of consensus.[230] It does not seem the same to ask whether other member states have in place bans on religious attire in a given area, as to ask whether there are such bans or similar ones in any other area. Nor are these questions equivalent to asking (as the Court suggested in *Sahin* and *Ebrahimian*) whether there is a uniform *conception of the significance* of religion in society. Further, the existence of debate in and on itself (unlike the issue of its quality, which is quite important) does not say much either. After all, policies that substantially curtail fundamental rights are always likely to be debated. Moreover, rights claims from unpopular groups or minorities are likely to engender a great deal of debate and societal opposition. In this vein, and whenever a consensus argument may appear linked to public support, account should also be taken of the constitutive role of the law. This means that, for example, to the extent that a state's law disapproves of characteristics or practices identified with certain ethno-cultural groups, public opposition will likely be reinforced. As such, courts such as the ECtHR should be careful not to evaluate society's preferences and debates as if the state – and its laws – would play no role in shaping them. Finally, the Court should also avoid being selective in the identification of normative affairs. The decision to regulate something and the decision to leave it unregulated are both normatively relevant.

---

227 On the position that the norms as they stood at the material time were reflective of a European consensus against the ban, see the joint partly dissenting opinion of Judges Nussberger and Jäderblom, para. 156. See also Human Rights Centre, Ghent University; Third Party Interventions <www.hrc.ugent.be/third-party-interventions-before-ecthr/>.

228 See Dissenting Opinion of Judge Tulkens in ECtHR, (GC) *Leyla Şahin v. Turkey*, App. no. 44774/98, Judgment of 10 November 2005, para. 3. See para. 55 of the judgment, which states that alongside Turkey, Azerbaijan and Albania were the only member states to have introduced regulations on wearing the Islamic headscarf in universities.

229 ECtHR, *Ebrahimian v. France*, App. no. 64846/11, Judgment of 26 November 2015, para. 56.

230 In this vein, see Carolyn Evans, 'Individual and group religious freedom in the European Court of Human Rights: Cracks in the intellectual architecture', 26 *Journal of Law and Religion* (2010) 321, at 333–334.

But the review of relevant norms does not end there. As already mentioned, the Court's account of its legal environment is not confined to Europe. It is also guided by several international human rights treaties and the standards set by different monitoring bodies. In the cases studied, this practice has been incremental and more notorious in the last decade. In the segregation cases mentioned above and in *Yordanova* and *Winterstein*,[231] as well as in the full-face veil case of *S.A.S. v. France*,[232] the Court referred to several UN instruments and bodies. These include, *inter alia*, the International Covenant on Civil and Political Rights (ICCPR) and the Human Rights Committee; the International Covenant on Economic, Social and Cultural Rights (ICESCR) and its supervisory Committee; the Convention on the Elimination of Racial Discrimination (CERD) and its respective Committee; and the Convention on the Rights of the Child (CRC). And, as was the case with European bodies previously mentioned, the Court took into account quite specific guidelines and interpretations (regarding housing rights, equality, child rights, etc.) adopted in the framework of general comments and individual complaints. Also, the Court referred to rulings adopted in similar cases, including those which significantly differed from those held by the Court. In the aforesaid *S.A.S.* case, for example, the Court recalled that the Human Rights Committee had decided a case against Uzbekistan which was very similar to *Sahin*. There, the Committee, in contrast to the Court, held that the expulsion of a female student from university for refusing to comply with a headscarf prohibition violated her freedom of religion.[233]

How did this divergence play out in *S.A.S.* and in subsequent similar cases? In *S.A.S.* the Grand Chamber appeared to disregard the interpretation adopted by the Committee as irrelevant. It pointed out that the Committee had 'not yet ruled on the question of a blanket ban on the wearing of the full-face veil in public places'.[234] Surprisingly, however, when a few years later the Court was again confronted – in *Ebrahimian* – with the wearing of the veil (not a full-face veil) in a public institution (not a university, but a public hospital), no reference was made to those views of the Human Rights Committee. To attribute the omission to the different field addressed in each case (*Sahin*, like *Hudoyberganova*, was

---

231 ECtHR, (GC) *D.H. and Others v. the Czech Republic*, App. no. 57325/00, Judgment of 13 November 2007, paras. 92–102; (GC) *Oršuš and Others v. Croatia*, App. no. 15766/03, Judgment of 16 March 2010; *Yordanova and Others v. Bulgaria*, App. no. 25446/06, Judgment of 24 April 2012, para. 83; *Winterstein and Others v. France*, App. no. 27013/07, Judgment of 17 October 2013, para. 87.

232 ECtHR, (GC) *S.A.S. v. France*, App. no. 43835/11, Judgment of 1 July 2014, paras. 38–39.

233 HRC, *Hudoyberganova v. Uzbekistan*, Communication no. 931/2000, Views adopted on 5 November 2004. For a brief commentary on this decision and its contrast with the position adopted by the ECtHR, see Martin Scheinin, 'International Human Rights Law and the Islamic Headscarf: A Short Note on the Position of the European Court of Human Rights and the Human Rights Committee', in W. Cole Durhman Jr. *et al.* (eds.), *Islam, Europe and Emerging Legal Issues* (Ashgate, 2012), at 83–86.

234 ECtHR, (GC) *S.A.S. v. France*, App. no. 43835/11, Judgment of 1 July 2014, para. 39.

about education institutions, while *Ebrahimian* concerned a hospital) is not convincing particularly since the judgment in *Ebrahimian* mostly relied on standards developed in the context of public education.

Nevertheless, there are a number of grounds for suggesting that the Court cannot simply do away with the rulings of other international human rights bodies in similar cases, particularly if they enhance or increase protection. First, as pointed out by Brems, the state's margin of discretion 'remains circumscribed by its other human rights obligations, amongst others emanating from UN treaties'.[235] Indeed, Article 53 ECHR explicitly requires states to prioritise the most right-protective interpretation of the Convention Rights.[236] Second, the Court's remark in *S.A.S.* and its eventual alignment with the approach adopted by the European Committee of Social Rights in Roma cases concerning housing lends some practical credence to that principle. Third, when it comes to specific UN human rights instruments and treaties, there is a place for the principle of *lex specialis* to play out.[237] Finally, on a more substantive note it can be argued that cases involving ethno-cultural minorities may posit additional grounds for deviation from local solutions in favour of progressive international standards. Inasmuch as the interests of disenfranchised minorities are likely to be absent from domestic policy-making and even from judicial processes, there are greater reasons for seeing supranational control as a last avenue to compensate for that.

It is interesting to observe that to the extent that the 'living instrument' doctrine and, more notably, the notion of consensus appeal to common normative developments, a strong imprint of homogeneity and *status quo* appear in them. This can be problematic from the perspective of the claims put forward by applicants in minority or non-dominant positions. However, the use of those tools is regarded as enabling both continuity and deviation *vis à vis* the common normative approach and the cultural and normative setting prevailing in the respondent state.[238]

---

235 Eva Brems, 'Should Pluriform Human Rights become One? Exploring the benefits of Human Rights Integration', 4 *European Journal of Human Rights* (2014) 447, at 463.

236 ECHR, Article 50: 'Nothing in this Convention shall be construed as limiting or derogating from any of the human rights and fundamental freedoms which may be ensured under the laws of any High Contracting Party or under any other agreement to which it is a party.'

237 Eva Brems, 'Should Pluriform Human Rights Become One? Exploring the Benefits of Human Rights Integration', 4 *European Journal of Human Rights* (2014) 447, at 463.

238 This holds true well beyond the ambit of the case law discussed in this chapter. See George Letsas, 'The ECHR as a living instrument: its meaning and its legitimacy', in Andreas Føllesdal *et al.* (eds.), *Constituting Europe. The European Court of Human Rights in a National, European and Global Context* (Cambridge University Press, 2013), 106, at 112 (referring to the third pattern disclosed by the Court's early case law when portraying the Convention as a living instrument. The author regards the use of present-day developments in the Council of Europe as a counterweight to the moral climate prevailing on the respondent state as 'the central feature of evolutive interpretation as applied by the old Court').

4.2.3. *Integration of Informal and Tradition-Based Laws*

As discussed above, diverse state laws have been considered by the Court with relative regularity. However, another form of domestic normativity should not be forgotten. This evolves within organisations and among communities through a myriad of formal and informal regulations, including tradition-based laws. This layer of normativity, present in several cases analysed here, comprises the religious and cultural commitments governing the lives of applicants with ethnic, religious and cultural affiliations.[239] Drawing on Tamanaha's categorisation, such commitments reflect customary normative orders as well as community/cultural normative systems.[240] In the words of Malik, these are 'minority legal orders'.[241] Additionally, informal norms regulating dress, food and working habits, as well as modes of using lands and homes, exist – prior to or sometimes in parallel with state regulations – in municipalities, schools, hospitals, neighbourhoods, private business and so forth.

Does the Court take this normativity into account and how does that matter for the cases reviewed here? While this is the layer of normativity that, compared to the ones addressed above, has attracted more limited attention from the Court, it has not been totally absent from its reasoning. Among the range of community or customary norms we could think of, we should bear in mind that those expressing religious prescriptions or practices enjoy specific protection under Article 9 ECHR. Their normative force is actually one of the reasons militating in favour of the accommodation of religious manifestations. As such, when confronted with cases involving Article 9 ECHR, such as the ones discussed previously, the Court has regularly recognised and accorded weight to what applicants claim as being required by their religion. Still, in the context of the Court's case law involving Islamic veils, it is interesting to observe the critical view of some authors, for whom it is possible to note 'a certain reluctance to

239 For instance, many have questioned their subjection to 'general laws and policies [which] failed to accommodate their particular needs arising from their tradition of living and travelling in caravans'. See ECtHR, (GC) *Beard v. the United Kingdom*, App. no. 24882/94, Judgment of 18 January 2001, para. 130; (GC) *Chapman v. the United Kingdom*, App. no. 27238/95, Judgment of 18 January 2001; (GC) *Coster v. the United Kingdom*, App. no. 24876/94, Judgment of 18 January 2001, para. 139; (GC) *Lee v. the United Kingdom*, App. no. 25289/94, Judgment of 18 January 2001, para. 127. According to Acton, Caffrey and Mundy, different normative systems are appropriate for different lifestyles amongst the Roma. Thomas Acton *et al.*, 'Theorizing Gypsy Law', 45 *American Journal of Comparative Law* (1997) 237, at 237, 244 and 248–249.

240 Brian Tamanaha, 'Understanding Legal Pluralism: Past to Present, Local to Global', 30 *Sydney Law Review* (2008) 375, at 397–399.

241 Maleiha Malik, 'Religion and Minority Legal Orders', in Jean L. Cohen and Cécile Laborde (eds.), *Religion, Secularism and Constitutional Democracy* (Columbia University Press, 2016), at 358–360.

acknowledge the value and religious importance of the wearing of a headscarf, as if the Court [were] not entirely convinced it is required by Islam'.[242]

The Court's recognition of other, non-religious community norms, however, has been more uneven. For example, with regard to Roma's cultural normativity, the Court has regarded the cultural commitments of applicants like Ms Chapman as the preferences of individuals.[243] Yet, the Court deployed a much more appropriate stance in *Muñoz Díaz*. Here, the Court emphasised 'the importance of the beliefs that the applicant derives from belonging to the Roma community – a community which has its own values that are well established and deeply rooted in Spanish society'.[244] The Court then even went to say that 'the force of the collective beliefs of a community that is well-defined culturally cannot be ignored'.[245] It is argued that this approach should be maintained and applied consistently across different cases.

In fact, ignoring non-state norms, such as customary or community laws, can be problematic. As the aforementioned cases suggest, one of the difficulties of ignoring these norms is that the Court may end up mischaracterising what is at stake. This also holds true for decentralised layers of normativity.[246] A good example of this can be found in cases concerning religious attire, such as bans on religious manifestation in public institutions. In fact, what is at stake in such cases will be judged differently if the contested prohibitions are accompanied by, say, similar formal or informal bans operating in other fields of social life, for example in private organisations and recreational centres such as swimming pools, gyms and restaurants. What might in principle be viewed as limitations on the religious expressions of the staff working in one public institution might, once viewed within the whole normative context, start looking like sex and religious segregation.

To be sure, going along with this normative plurality is a difficult endeavour. Judges and lawyers have neither the training nor the institutional capacity to adjudicate so many levels of normativity. Nevertheless, to differing degrees they

---

242 Saïla Ouald Chaib, *Belief in Justice. Towards More Inclusivity in and through the Freedom of Religion Case Law of the European Court of Human Rights*, PhD Dissertation (Ghent University, 2015), at 115 (citing Carolyn Evans, '"The Islamic Scarf" in the European Court of Human Rights', 7(1) *Melbourne Journal of International Law* (2006) 52, at 55–56).

243 ECtHR, (GC) *Chapman v. the United Kingdom*, App. no. 27238/95, Judgment of 18 January 2001, para. 113. See also, ECtHR, (GC) *Beard v. the United Kingdom*, App. no. 24882/94, Judgment of 18 January 2001, para. 125; (GC) *Coster v. the United Kingdom*, App. no. 24876/94, Judgment of 18 January 2001, para. 126; (GC) *Lee v. the United Kingdom*, App. no. 25289/94, Judgment of 18 January 2001, para. 114; *Wells v. the United Kingdom*, App. no. 37794/05, Decision of 16 January 2007, at 10.

244 ECtHR, *Muñoz Díaz v. Spain*, App. no. 49151/07, Judgment of 8 December 2009, para. 56.

245 Ibid., para. 59.

246 In this vein, see Pascale Fournier, 'Headscarf and burqa controversies at the crossroad of politics, society and law', 19(6) *Social Identities* (2013) 689, at 694.

can – and actually do – take into account diverse and even competing norms. Moreover, applicants and third-party interveners can play an important role in providing the Court with the material required to take into account a wider range of norms. As the discussion above demonstrates, something important about the cases studied will surely be missed if their normative spectrum is too reduced. As Baer puts it, at the very least 'one simply misses the richness of legally-based arguments which are available'.[247]

5. CONCLUDING REMARKS

The cases reviewed in this book are all reflective of the challenges and difficulties posed by legal discourses of cultural difference. They include, among others, whether to accommodate and to whom; whether to intrude into social and economic policies; how to deal with competing religious and cultural views in the face of prevailing notions of neutrality and secularism; and how to ensure inclusion and equality for those culturally 'different'. In the cases concerning caravans and the 'Gypsy' lifestyle, as well as in the cases involving Islamic veils, a discourse of cultural difference has been prevalent among the parties and in the ECtHR. In cases regarding the educational segregation of Roma children, in turn, the discourse of cultural difference has been more present in the parties' arguments than in the Court's analysis. Also more tenuous appears to be the issue of cultural difference in cases of eviction from informal settlements as well as in Islam-related cases concerning curricular exemptions and male religious dress style.

In cases defined by cultural and religious difference, the Court's approach places great emphasis on group identity and on culture or religion, particularly as expressed in symbols and practices. This has been accompanied by attempts to define the boundaries of the cultural/religious group or identity in question. In the light of scholarly criticism, it is not so surprising to note some ensuing difficulties, such as essentialism, stereotypes and a tendency to displace other aspects that are important for the adjudication of the case. While the group vulnerability framework used in some cases holds more potential for a more flexible, comprehensive analysis, in practice some of the difficulties associated with cultural and religious identity boundaries seem to have re-emerged in that context.

As the application of an integrated approach to human rights law reveals, such a fragmented view of the cases has in fact overlooked several dimensions of the rights holders and the harms and norms at stake. Some concrete experiences

[247] Susanne Baer, 'A Closer Look at Law: Human Rights as Multi-Level Sites of Struggles over Multi-Dimensional Equality', 6(2) *Utrecht Law Review* (2010) 56, at 71.

of the applicants, especially in relation to gender, socio-economic status and migration background, have been side-lined. The application of the integrated framework proposed in this book shows that the Court could have derived some useful normative insights had it considered rights holders as a whole. Examining the applicants' multiple identities and social positions, for instance, could have affected the proportionality analysis or the width of the margin of appreciation, as well as the admissibility and outcome of discrimination claims. Nevertheless, the Court has only occasionally tackled allegations of discrimination. When this happened, the Court, with the notable exception of cases of child educational segregation, generally endorsed a rather formalistic and single-ground review. As a result, it quickly dismissed claims of compounded (multiple or intersectional) discrimination.

Likewise, in a number of cases the Court has adopted a divisive view of the rights holders' agency whereby they are portrayed either as fully autonomous and endowed with choices or as passive and constrained. At the same time, its responses have varied depending on the meaning attributed to people's choices. In addition, the Court has paid limited attention to some rights holders other than the applicants who are also affected by the measures contested. Furthermore, in most cases where the lens of cultural/religious difference or identity was salient, several interlocked harms and norms were displaced. This was especially so for socio-economic harms related to rights not enshrined in the Convention and for issues of structural inequality.

At times, the Court focused not on the religious identity or group of the applicant but on categories associated with societal/national identity, such as *laïcité*, secularism and neutrality. When this happened, it was seen that some of the problems of the group identity framework are nonetheless reproduced. A compartmentalisation-like issue arose to the extent that an overemphasis on those categories leads to an abstract judicial review, detached from the specific persons and interests at stake in the case at hand.

An integrated perspective also shows that, especially in cases with a focus on cultural/religious difference, the analysis usually focuses on one Convention provision, missing the opportunity to explore a larger array of legal arguments. While the Court's stance towards regional and international norms has been richer, the lack of consistency in their incorporation has also added difficulties to the handling of contested cases of cultural difference. This is particularly evidenced by the varying criteria applied by the Court as to what normative aspects are relevant to the issue of consensus and under what conditions there is consensus. Also, it was seen that the Court has not always clarified when to depart from relevant international standards and why. Further, although the Court had limited regard to informal and tradition-based norms, a more serious engagement with this layer of normativity could also have provided useful insights for dealing with the cases under study.

Finally, it is interesting to observe that cultural rights claims seem to encounter more resistance and be less likely to be considered from an integrated perspective when they are perceived as being positive claims of accommodation, exemption or provision. A reflection of this can be found in cases defined as (positive) recognition of cultural or religious difference, which rarely incorporate redistributive or socio-economic issues. By contrast, cases challenging 'negative difference' (stigma and exclusion), such as those concerning school segregation, appear to fare better in the integration of socio-economic aspects.

In the light of all the above, this chapter has highlighted a need to revise the use of compartmentalised legal thinking and to consider the use of an integrated approach to human rights law. The chapter that follows examines similar challenges and questions raised by cases dealing with cultural difference and inclusion, although in a very different context, namely that of the Inter-American Court of Human Rights. Who are indigenous and Afro-descendant applicants in the eyes of the Court and what place does it accord to legal categories of identity, culture and group vulnerability? How does all this affect the resolution of complex cases about cultural distinctiveness, legal recognition, collective rights and access to resources? To what extent does the Inter-American Court of Human Rights adopt an integrated perspective on the rights holders and the norms involved in such cases? These are some of the questions discussed in Chapter 3.

CHAPTER 3

AN INTEGRATED APPROACH TO CULTURAL DIFFERENCE IN THE INTER-AMERICAN COURT OF HUMAN RIGHTS

1. INTRODUCTION

Despite the cultural and religious diversity of the Americas, the Inter-American Court of Human Rights (IACtHR or 'the Court') has so far been confronted with a relatively limited spectrum of cases explicitly dealing with issues of cultural difference. All of them concern indigenous and Afro-descendant communities and/or their members. Their complaints are inscribed within a history of struggles against multiple forms of political and social marginalisation, dispossession and cultural assimilation across the American region. This has given rise to significant mobilisation, mainly under the auspices of cultural-based arguments, at the domestic and international levels. The bulk of the cases that have thereby reached the Court involve indigenous or tribal communal claims of restitution of and control over lands and resources. The background to these cases is generally one of lack of recognition of their collective land rights, failure to delimit, title, and protect their territories and/or the authorisation of private exploitation of part of their lands and resources. These are the cases with the strongest emphasis on cultural difference and identity, a normative approach that is sustained by Article 21 ACHR (the right to property). In a few other cases, individuals and/or groups have raised issues of political participation, use of a minority language and discriminatory treatment in access to identity documents and services. Another group of judgments relates to massacres and other acts of violence against indigenous and Afro-descendant populations. Most of them have not been thoroughly examined in this book, although some have been included and referenced when needed. It is nonetheless worth mentioning that most of these judgments have considered the cultural impact of those crimes in the reparations awards.

Though the American Convention rights holder is the individual (or it was until recently),[1] the Court's judgments in the aforementioned cases place great emphasis on the group. Obviously, this is even more so in community-based complaints. Now, as discussed in the context of the European Court's case law, one may wonder how does the Inter-American Court conceive of the group and what place does it accord to this in its legal analysis? It is submitted that indigenous and Afro-descendant peoples are mainly portrayed as relatively bounded groups defined by a distinctive cultural identity. In a more limited fashion, they have also been seen through the prism of vulnerability. Both normative frames (group cultural identity and vulnerability) have shaped in significant ways the legal analysis and the resolution of the cases.

2. CULTURAL DIFFERENCE AS LEGAL COMPARTMENT

That legal arguments on cultural identity hold a central place in the Court's adjudication of indigenous rights claims should not come as a surprise. Group identity mobilisation has achieved a great deal in the legal protection of fundamental rights.[2] And indigenous peoples have probably been the most successful in advancing their rights claims through a cultural identity approach.[3] After all, the idea of the social group as a bounded entity with a certain identity or common experience,[4] just like that of cultural belonging, is suited well to

---

1 This remained so until the 2012 judgment in the *Sarayaku* case, when the Court appeared to accept for the first time that indigenous communities, as collectivities, were holders of Convention rights. This is further discussed *infra* section 3.3.2.

2 See e.g. Frédéric Mégret, 'The Human Rights of Older Persons: A Growing Challenge', 11(1) *Human Rights Law Review* (2011) 37, at 39. In the constitutional context, see William N. Eskridge Jr., 'Some Effects of Identity-Based Social Movements on Constitutional Law in the Twentieth Century', 100 *Michigan Law Review* (2002) 2062.

3 See e.g. Karen Engle, 'On Fragile Architecture: The UN Declaration on the Rights of Indigenous Peoples in the Context of Human Rights', 22(1) *The European Journal of International Law* (2011) 141, at 142. Thomas M. Antkowiak, 'Rights, resources, and rhetoric: indigenous peoples and the Inter-American Court', 35(1) *University of Pennsylvania Journal of International Law* (2013) 113, at 136 ('the indigenous human rights movement has enjoyed much more success than minority rights frameworks in general, to the extent that such groups are seeking to portray themselves as "indigenous" to obtain the expanding rights and protections associated with that status'); Benedict Kingsbury, 'Reconciling Five Competing Conceptual Structures of Indigenous Peoples' Claims in International and Comparative Law', 34 *New York University Journal of International Law and Politics* (2001) 189, at 233 (referring to the success of indigenous peoples' rights compared to those of minorities in general).

4 This is the kind of notion of social group propounded by Owen M. Fiss with respect to African-Americans with a view to constructing his notion of equality as group anti-subordination. See Owen M. Fiss, 'Groups and the Equal Protection Clause', 5(2) *Philosophy and Public Affairs* (1976) 107, at 148 ('a social group is more than a collection of individuals [...] A social group, as I use the term, has two other characteristics. (1) It is an entity [...] This means that the group has a distinct existence apart from its members, and also that it has an identity. [...]

indigenous peoples. However, as discussed in Chapter 2 when arguments about collective culture or identity take too much prominence in legal discourse, it is likely that courts will focus on them, missing the chance of going down the road of a comprehensive approach to the case. The following discussion will thus explore the Court's understanding of indigenous and Afro-descendant cultural distinctiveness, the importance attached to it and the relationship between this and an integrated model for adjudicating claims of difference and inclusion.

2.1. INDIGENOUS AND AFRO-DESCENDANT CULTURE UNDER ARTICLE 21 ACHR

Questions of collective culture and group belonging have a long history in the Court's jurisprudence on indigenous people's rights. Even before the judgment in the famous *Awas Tingni* case,[5] the Court had shown interest in a normative approach sensitive to the cultural particularities of ethnic groups.[6] But it is certainly within the context of collective land claims that indigenous culture, anchored in an expanded right to property (Article 21 ACHR), translated into a set of practices and beliefs worth legal protection. The basis of this protection lies with the special and collective attachment of indigenous peoples to their ancestral territories. In the words of the Court, 'the close ties of indigenous people with the land must be recognized and understood as the fundamental basis of their cultures, their spiritual life, their integrity, and their economic survival'.[7] For indigenous communities, 'relations to the land are not merely a matter of possession and production but a material and spiritual element which they must fully enjoy, so that it may preserve their cultural legacy and transmit it to future generations'.[8] Importantly, 'the spiritual and material basis for indigenous

(2) There is also a condition of inter-dependence. The identity and well-being of the members of the group and the identity and well-being of the group are linked.').

5 IACtHR, *The Mayagna (Sumo) Awas Tingni Community v. Nicaragua*, Judgment of 31 August 2001. The case concerned an indigenous community of the Atlantic Coast of Nicaragua who had no ownership title to the ancestral territory it claimed. The state authorities had authorised, without the community's consent, a private corporation to log on their lands. Other indigenous communities also had competing claims over part of those lands.

6 During the 1990s, the reparation judgment in the *Aloeboetoe* case, brought on behalf of members of a tribal Afro-rural community in Suriname, had already signalled the importance the Court would attach to the culture of indigenous and tribal peoples. IACtHR, *Aloeboetoe et al. v. Suriname*, Judgment of 4 December 1991 and *Aloeboetoe et al. v. Suriname*, Judgment of 10 September 1993. This case is further discussed *infra* section 3.1.1.

7 IACtHR, *The Mayagna (Sumo) Awas Tingni Community v. Nicaragua*, Judgment of 31 August 2001, para. 149.

8 IACtHR, *The Mayagna (Sumo) Awas Tingni Community v. Nicaragua*, Judgment of 31 August 2001, para. 149; *The Moiwana Community v. Suriname*, Judgment of 15 June 2005, para. 131; *The Xákmok Kásek Indigenous Community v. Paraguay*, Judgment of 24 August 2010, para. 86;

identity is mainly supported by their unique relationship with their traditional lands. As long as said relationship exists, the right to claim lands is enforceable, otherwise, it will lapse.'[9] The Court has stressed the importance of indigenous land rights for the 'reproduction of their culture'[10] and for 'preserving cultural identities in a democratic and pluralist society'.[11] The salience of this element also crystallised in a right to cultural identity not envisaged by the ACHR and which has nonetheless been enforced on the basis of Article 21 ACHR.[12] But what is the indigenous culture whose preservation warrants specific rights and safeguards?

The Court has attempted to define it as follows:

> The culture of the members of the indigenous communities directly relates to a specific way of being, seeing, and acting in the world, developed on the basis of their close relationship with their traditional territories and the resources therein, not only because they are their main means of subsistence, but also because they are part of their worldview, their religiosity, and therefore, of their cultural identity.[13]

Along these lines, the Court has repeatedly emphasised indigenous traditions. Examples include ceremonial activities, languages, arts and rituals, practices in connection with nature, customary law, dress, seasonal or nomadic hunting, fishing or gathering, and use of natural resources associated with their customs or other elements characteristic of their culture.[14] In this portrayal of traditional

The Garifuna Punta Piedra Community and its Members v. Honduras, Judgment of 8 October 2015, para. 166.

9 IACtHR, *The Sawhoyamaxa Indigenous Community v. Paraguay*, Judgment of 29 March 2006, para. 131; *The Xákmok Kásek Indigenous Community v. Paraguay*, Judgment of 24 August 2010, para. 112.

10 IACtHR, *The Yakye Axa Indigenous Community v. Paraguay*, Judgment of 17 June 2005, para. 146. In a similar vein, IACtHR, *The Afro-descendant communities displaced from the Cacarica River Basin (Operation Genesis) v. Colombia*, Judgment of 20 November 2013, para. 254; *The Garifuna Punta Piedra Community and its Members v. Honduras*, Judgment of 8 October 2015, para. 167.

11 IACtHR, *The Yakye Axa Indigenous Community v. Paraguay*, Judgment of 17 June 2005, para. 148.

12 IACtHR, *Kichwa Indigenous People of Sarayaku v. Ecuador*, Judgment of 27 June 2012, paras. 213, 217 and 220; *The Kaliña and Lokono Peoples v. Suriname*, Judgment of 25 November 2015, para. 198.

13 IACtHR, *The Yakye Axa Indigenous Community v. Paraguay*, Judgment of 17 June 2005, para. 135; *The Kuna Indigenous People of Madungandí and the Emberá Indigenous People of Bayano and their Members v. Panama*, Judgment of 14 October 2014, para. 112; *The Garífuna Punta Piedra Community and its Members v. Honduras*, Judgment of 8 October 2015, para. 166.

14 See e.g. IACtHR, *The Yakye Axa Indigenous Community v. Paraguay*, Judgment of 17 June 2005, para. 154; *The Sawhoyamaxa Indigenous Community v. Paraguay*, Judgment of 29 March 2006, para. 131; *The Kichwa Indigenous People of Sarayaku v. Ecuador*, Judgment of 27 June 2012, para. 148; *The Kuna Indigenous People of Madungandí and the Emberá Indigenous People of Bayano and their Members v. Panama*, Judgment of 14 October 2014, para. 58.

customs and uses, indigenous culture seems rather static or even romanticised. Such a view has important consequences. Notably, it determines (in a narrow manner) who does or does not qualify as a member of the group, and what does or does not count as part of the protected identity. As discussed earlier (in the context of the previous chapter), the route of cultural essentialism (i.e. trying to fix the content of 'Culture' and the borders of group identity) is indeed problematic. This holds true even if the characterisation in question has a positive or idealised tone.

On the basis of the cases analysed here, a number of potential and actual drawbacks to a normative approach marked by the protection of indigenous groups and their cultural identity deserve attention. The first is the risk of unnecessarily limiting the economic and political empowerment of indigenous communities and thus, the range of activities that may qualify for legal protection. In fact, the case law suggests that lands and natural resources are protected only to the extent that they have been used in accordance with those cultural traditions.[15] As some scholars have argued, this depiction of indigenous identity/culture forecloses opportunities for communities who may wish to benefit from 'non-traditional' practices or techniques for managing or exploiting their natural resources.[16] Think, for instance, of mining, hydrocarbon production or tourism, to mention some less 'traditional' and more market-oriented activities. Pushing indigenous peoples away from these kinds of activity may, at the same time, severely hamper their wellbeing, as traditional activities may no longer provide adequate sustenance.[17] One recent judgment – *Kaliña and Lokono Peoples v. Suriname* – might nonetheless suggest that the Court is more aware of these problems. Underlining the full guarantees that indigenous peoples should enjoy over the lands and resources traditionally used to carry on their way of life, the Court also considered 'other complementary or additional traditional areas to which they have had access for their traditional or subsistence activities (*which may have other purposes*)'.[18] It is unclear whether

15 See e.g. IACtHR, *The Sawhoyamaxa Indigenous Community v. Paraguay*, Judgment of 29 March 2006, paras. 131–132; *The Saramaka People. v. Suriname*, Judgment of 28 November 2007, para. 155. For a critique, see Thomas M. Antkowiak, 'Rights, Resources, and Rhetoric: Indigenous Peoples and the Inter-American Court', 35(1) *University of Pennsylvania Journal of International Law* (2013) 113, at 167.

16 Ariel E. Dulitzky, 'When Afro-Descendants Became "Tribal Peoples": The Inter-American Human Rights System and Rural Black Communities', 1 *UCLA Journal of International Law and Foreign Affairs* (2010) 29, at 47–48; Thomas M. Antkowiak, 'Rights, Resources, and Rhetoric: Indigenous Peoples and the Inter-American Court', 35(1) *University of Pennsylvania Journal of International Law* (2013) 113, at 161.

17 In this vein, see Karen Engle, *The Elusive Promise of Indigenous Development: Rights, Culture, Strategy* (Duke University Press, 2010), at 196.

18 IACtHR, *The Kaliña and Lokono Peoples v. Suriname*, Judgment of 25 November 2015, para. 139 (emphasis added).

this last remark could leave the door open to the protection of practices which do not necessarily fit a folk view of indigenous identity. In principle, it seems a first step in that direction, although it is yet something to be seen.

A second drawback of an essentialist approach to indigenous and tribal culture is the upholding of rigid group boundaries regarding the beneficiaries of legal protection. It should be noted that while the Court's interpretation of Article 21 ACHR has not really been controverted by states' parties, they have contested the qualification of indigenous peoples. In *Saramaka*, for example, Suriname argued that the Saramaka people had lost their cultural specificity as they had immersed themselves in 'modern society'.[19] In response, the Court reaffirmed the qualification of the Saramaka peoples as a tribal group and contended that the deviation of some individual members from Saramaka customs did not change the cultural distinctiveness of the group. Recently, Honduras claimed that the *Garífuna Punta Piedra Community* was not indigenous to the country or the region and that thus they had no more rights than any other resident in the area.[20] The Court did not examine the merits of this allegation (made at the public hearing of the case) as it dismissed it for being extemporaneous and contrary to the principles of estoppel and good faith.[21] Similarly, in *Kaliña and Lokono* the state invoked the community's 'acculturation' to exclude them from the management of natural reserves established in their ancestral territory.[22] It follows that the Court's essentialist view of indigenous and tribal identity offers a space for strong contestation. This may result in denying protection to people claiming indigenous rights just because they do not fit the judicial cultural script of what it means to be indigenous.

In cases where the 'indigeneity' of the applicants has not been straightforward, the Court has proceeded to verify whether they could fall under the broader category of 'tribal' people. The Court has so far taken this path with regard to members of Afro-descendant rural populations from Central America. This can be seen in the cases of *Moiwana* and *Saramaka*, both against Suriname, as well as the *Operation Genesis* case against Colombia. The applicants in these cases were

---

19 IACtHR, *The Saramaka People. v. Suriname*, Judgment of 28 November 2007, para. 164. This case involved the state granting of logging and mining concessions on lands traditionally used and occupied by the Saramaka.

20 IACtHR, *The Garífuna Punta Piedra Community and its Members v. Honduras*, Judgment of 8 October 2015, para. 51.

21 Ibid., paras. 55–56. Generally speaking, the international law principle of estoppel prevents a party from going back on its acts or allegations when its previous conduct or allegations have induced reliance by or detriment to others. In the case at hand, the principle barred the state from benefiting from an allegation that had not been made earlier, also in view of its own conduct throughout the case.

22 IACtHR, *The Kaliña and Lokono Peoples v. Suriname*, Judgment of 25 November 2015, note 234 ('the Kaliña and Lokono peoples are undergoing a process of acculturation and are more interested in modern activities than in traditional knowledge. Therefore, they are unable to adapt to changes in nature, such as floods and winds.').

descendants of African slaves forcibly taken to Suriname and Colombia, who settled in the areas concerned in the 17th and 19th centuries.[23] They all claimed a right to communal property in land and other entitlements to the natural resources therein. The Court, having found that they constituted (Maroon) tribal peoples, granted them indigenous rights. The conclusion was based on the applicants' distinctive cultural, social and economic characteristics as expressed in their connection with the land and their customary norms. Meeting a specific indigenous cultural code was therefore crucial for belonging and qualifying for protection under Article 21 ACHR. For example, in *Moiwana* the Court stated that while the applicants were not indigenous to the region, for around a century 'the community members lived in the area *in strict adherence* to N'djuka custom'.[24] A similar approach was taken in *Saramaka*, where the Court asserted the indigenous-like culture of the applicants by referring to a set of customs and beliefs reflective of their 'social, ancestral, and spiritual essence'.[25]

Whereas the interpretation adopted by the Court has been progressive and beneficial for many Afro-descendant peoples, one may wonder whether it has somehow eclipsed part of their specific needs and concerns. In fact, as discussed in Chapters 1 and 2, a group identity normative approach often entails the danger of obscuring the situation of group members and varied forms of overlapping disadvantages. In the framework of its promotional and supervisory role, the Inter-American Commission has called upon states to bear in mind 'that the needs of the Afro-descendant population in the Americas cannot be completely subsumed within policies for indigenous peoples'.[26] What is more, Afro-descendant civil society organisations themselves argue that 'one of the invisibility mechanisms [obscuring the needs, culture and current obstacles of Afro-descendant people] has been precisely to subsume or compare their needs with those of other groups affected by discrimination'.[27]

The benefits of the solution applied to Afro-descendant rural communities in the above cases are apparent. They were granted the broad set of rights that the Inter-American Court has so far recognised for indigenous and tribal peoples. Nevertheless, making these rights conditional to the extent that a certain cultural script is met implies that many (Afro-descendants and others) will perhaps not be able to live up to the cultural tradition legally recognised.

23 IACtHR, *The Moiwana Community v. Suriname*, Judgment of 15 June 2005, para. 132; *The Saramaka People v. Suriname*, Judgment of 28 November 2007, para. 80; *The Afro-descendant communities displaced from the Cacarica River Basin (Operation Genesis) v. Colombia*, Judgment of 20 November 2013, paras. 85 and 345.

24 IACtHR, *The Moiwana Community v. Suriname*, Judgment of 15 June 2005, para. 132 (emphasis added).

25 IACtHR, *The Saramaka People. v. Suriname*, Judgment of 28 November 2007, para. 82.

26 IACommHR, The situation of the people of African descent in the Americas, OEA/Ser.L/V/II. Doc. 62, 5 December 2011, para. 77.

27 Ibid., para. 78.

To avoid exclusion, they will have to overstate their cultural adherence. This can have serious consequences for many indigenous and tribal populations who, for a variety of reasons, may lead a life that differs from *the* indigenous way of life. But additionally, the normative use of such a cultural code poses difficulties for other populations who may understandably seek indigenous-like forms of legal protection. An example is precisely those Afro-communities who may not be able to mobilise the cultural identity discourse applied to indigenous peoples.

Moreover, insofar as the Court extends collective rights to Afro-descendants on condition of fitting an indigenous/tribal way of life, it reinforces the exclusion of Afro-Latinos from state reforms enshrining collective rights. In this vein, Hooker asked why Afro-Latinos have not been as successful in winning collective rights, at the domestic level, as indigenous people, despite common experiences of racial discrimination and social exclusion? And she has found that the main reason is that 'such rights are awarded based on the perceived possession of a distinct cultural group identity, not a history of political exclusion or racial discrimination.'[28] What is more, her study shows that this criterion, rather than being required by legal commitments, is the result of the distinct way in which 'blacks and indians have historically been racialised in Latin America.'[29] While the latter are perceived as having contributed to the *mestizaje* (hybridity) that forged the national political community, the place of the former is far more ambiguous. It is against this backdrop that national elites have been more receptive to a narrative of distinctive cultural identity than to one based on racism and exclusion.[30] For our purposes, this analysis illuminates how problematic it is taking for granted these distinctions between groups and identities as well as assuming their normative legitimacy. As such, similar questions to those raised in regard to Afro-rural populations can be extended to other groups. Could peasants, pastoralists and landless communities in Latin America, for example, benefit from collective land rights and other safeguards granted to indigenous and tribal peoples? Many of those people also have communitarian ways of life and also suffer from discrimination, dispossession and insecurity in land tenure. And yet, they may not easily gain access to those rights if they have to fit the cultural characteristics that define indigenous peoples according to the Court's case law.[31]

---

28 Juliet Hooker, 'Indigenous Inclusion/Black Exclusion: Race, Ethnicity and Multicultural Citizenship in Latin America', 37 *Journal of Latin American Studies* (2005) 285, at 296, 291–300.

29 Ibid., at 301.

30 Ibid., at 303–305.

31 The former UN Special Rapporteur on the right to food, for instance, has addressed this point with regard to pastoralists, fishermen and peasants. He has called for the protection to be extended at least to certain traditional communities that entertain a similar relationship with their ancestral lands, centred on the community rather than on the individual. UN General Assembly, Report of the Special Rapporteur on the Right to Food,

Of course, one could argue that human rights law provided for a rights regime specifically envisaged for indigenous peoples only. And still, the Inter-American Court does not have direct material competence over a regime sufficiently specific to justify a normative response limited to indigenous peoples only. Moreover, upon interrogation of the reasons and aims underlying the indigenous legal framework, one may legitimately contest whether (the lack of) alignment with a certain cultural imprint suffices to justify the denial of relevant similar entitlements to other people. After all, human rights law's primary concern is people's equal enjoyment of rights, rather than the preservation of any cultural or identity code in itself.

To be sure, though, the question of who is entitled to 'special' safeguards is not only relevant with a view to extending legal protection. The question holds equal importance for setting limits to the flexibility of human rights law. In other words, assuming that the Court could not accommodate all the demands of collective or otherwise 'special' rights, the following question arises: does the issue of group identity or cultural belonging constitute sufficient ground for the Court to justify the refusal of accommodation, resource redistribution or the non-imposition of specific duties upon states? So far, the Court has been called upon to answer this question only with regard to indigenous and Afro-descendant rural individuals and communities. However, it is likely that in the future the Court will, like its European counterpart, be confronted with a much wider range of culturally based claims. Unless the Court opts to make extensive value appraisals of cultures to decide which ones merit preservation, it should look for justifications beyond the issue of group identity. Admittedly, some degree of essentialism may be unavoidable in adjudication. Yet, a more careful stance in this respect is nonetheless possible, as already discussed. One way of doing so is by adopting an integrated approach to the adjudication of cultural diversity cases and examining in an inclusive, non-selective and relational manner the elements discussed in the sections 3 and 4 below.

Moreover, a comprehensive view of the cases discussed here may also draw attention to two further dangers of the identity-based normative framework described above. One is the risk of confirming or promoting general

---

Olivier De Schutter, A/65/281, 11 August 2010, paras. 13 and 26. In the Inter-American context, Ariel E. Dulitzky criticises the Inter-American Court's approach in cases involving massacres in rural areas which caused the displacement of peasants' families. He points out that in these cases, in contrast to very similar cases concerning Afro-descendant (tribal) and indigenous communities, 'the Court has made no special consideration with respect to the protection of these territories'. See Ariel E. Dulitzky, 'When Afro-Descendants Became "Tribal Peoples": The Inter-American Human Rights System and Rural Black Communities', 29 *UCLA Journal of International Law and Foreign Affairs* (2010) 29, at 45, fn. 68 (referring to the cases of IACtHR, *"Mapiripán Massacre" v. Colombia*, Judgment of 15 September 2005; IACtHR, *Pueblo Bello Massacre v. Colombia*, Judgment of 31 January 2006; and *Ituango Massacres v. Colombia*, Judgment of 1 July 2006.

assumptions about indigenous people which, by extension, may also affect Afro-descendant people. On account of the cultural identity that supposedly defines them, the group and its members are likely to be stereotyped as rural-oriented, anchored in traditional or 'non-modern' activities, guided by spiritual motivations and lacking in knowledge or abilities to manage 'modern business'. The vicious cycle of reification may impact not only on the Court's merits analysis of claims to, for example, land, resources, benefit sharing and access to services. It may also have an effect on the Court's award of reparations, as further discussed *infra* section 3.2. In addition, implicit in the group identity focus adopted by the Court is the risk of leaving untouched the roots of the violations experienced by most indigenous and tribal peoples, that is, racism, economic inequality and political marginalisation.[32]

But before turning to the application of the integrated framework followed in this book, this section will conclude by exploring another criterion that has guided the Court's normative approach to ethno-cultural diversity cases.

2.2. INDIGENOUS PEOPLE AND AFRO-DESCENDANTS AS GROUPS IN VULNERABLE SITUATIONS

Alongside cultural identity, the collective experience of indigenous and Afro-descendant people is often characterised in terms of vulnerability. For the Court, the differences between indigenous and ethnic minorities, on the one hand, and majority populations, on the other, are given by, *inter alia*, cultural particularities and social difficulties which keep the former in a situation of vulnerability.[33] In this context, the Court, unlike the Strasbourg Court, consistently speaks of a 'situation' or 'condition' of vulnerability, instead of 'vulnerable groups'.[34] Moreover, in doing so the Inter-American Court has

---

32 Karen Engle, 'On Fragile Architecture: The UN Declaration on the Rights of Indigenous Peoples in the Context of Human Rights', 22 (1) *The European Journal of International Law* (2011) 141, at 142, 157 and ff.

33 See e.g. IACtHR, *Yatama v. Nicaragua*, Judgment of 23 June 2005, para. 202; *The Kichwa Indigenous People of Sarayaku v. Ecuador*, Judgment of 27 June 2012, para. 81; *The Kuna Indigenous People of Madungandí and the Emberá Indigenous People of Bayano and their Members v. Panama*, Judgment of 14 October 2014, para. 167; *The Community Garifuna Triunfo de la Cruz & its Members v. Honduras*, Judgment of 8 October 2015, paras. 228 and 238.

34 See e.g. IACtHR, *The Mayagna (Sumo) Awas Tingni Community v. Nicaragua*, Judgment of 31 August 2001, para. 62; *Yatama v. Nicaragua*, Judgment of 23 June 2005, para. 202; *The Girls Yean and Bosico v. Dominican Republic*, Judgment of 8 September 2005, paras. 67–72; *The Yakye Axa Indigenous Community v. Paraguay*, Judgment of 17 June 2005, paras. 162–163 and 167; *The Sawhoyamaxa Indigenous Community v. Paraguay*, Judgment of 29 March 2006, paras. 80, 85 and 88; *The Saramaka People. v. Suriname*, Judgment of 28 November 2007, paras. 173 and 178; *The Xákmok Kásek Indigenous Community v. Paraguay*, Judgment of

frequently indicated that those situations of vulnerability have been imposed on the group or individuals concerned, thus rendering them vulnerable. The difference in wording may seem minor, merely rhetorical. But it is not. Language is powerful and the words chosen make a difference. Denoting the situational character of vulnerability gives the concept more flexibility and contingency. Indeed, the term is mostly employed to pinpoint the 'special' or 'extreme' risks (threats to physical integrity and risks of suffering rights violations in general), as well as a history of discrimination or exclusion faced by certain ethno-cultural groups and individuals, rather than to signal an attribute of them.[35] This use of vulnerability holds an interesting potential inasmuch as it seems to lessen the dangers of essentialism already discussed.

From a normative point of view, categorising people as being in a situation of vulnerability entails relatively similar effects to those studied in the context of the European Court. Notably, for the Inter-American Court the condition of vulnerability of indigenous and Afro-descendant people (and peoples) subjects the state to stricter obligations, which require it to have 'special' regard for their needs and concerns as well as to secure specific protection to make their rights effective. Additionally, the Court has taken into account in its reparations orders the vulnerability experienced by the applicants.[36] As further explained below, the concept of vulnerability applied in this case law also appears as an alternative but closely related framework to that of equality and non-discrimination. Moreover, the Court has also drawn attention to overlapping forms of vulnerability related to the rights holder's identity and socio-economic condition. In this sense, the notion of vulnerability seems to enable a relatively comprehensive view of the human rights situation of the

---

24 August 2010, paras. 227 and 246; *The Kichwa Indigenous People of Sarayaku v. Ecuador*, Judgment of 27 June 2012, para. 81; *The Afro-descendant communities displaced from the Cacarica River Basin (Operation Genesis) v. Colombia*, Judgment of 20 November 2013, paras. 315 and 327–329; *The Kuna Indigenous People of Madungandí and the Emberá Indigenous People of Bayano and their Members v. Panama*, Judgment of 14 October 2014, para. 167; *The Community Garifuna Triunfo de la Cruz & its Members v. Honduras*, Judgment of 8 October 2015, para. 228. Rather exceptionally, the Court in *Yean and Bosico* also characterised the applicants as members of 'a vulnerable social group in the Dominican Republic'. See IACtHR, *The Girls Yean and Bosico v. Dominican Republic*, Judgment of 8 September 2005, para. 109(9).

35 Idem. These are the connotations that vulnerability has taken in the cases of ethno-cultural difference examined here. But it should be noted that in other areas of the Court's case law (such as those involving children and persons with disabilities), the concept of vulnerability seems to designate a condition intrinsic to a group. See Romina I. Sijniensky, 'From the Non-Discrimination Clause to the Concept of Vulnerability in International Human Rights Law. Advancing the Needs for Special Protection of Certain Groups and Individuals', in Yves Haeck *et al.* (eds.), *The Realisation of Human Rights: When Theory Meets Practice. Studies in Honour of Leo Zwaak* (Intersentia, 2013), at 267–268.

36 See e.g. IACtHR, *The Girls Yean and Bosico v. Dominican Republic*, Judgment of 8 September 2005, para. 204.

groups and individuals concerned. On account of this, we will return to vulnerability in some of the sections below.

Thus far, it has been argued that legal determinations of group boundaries, cultural identity, traditional practices and the like may yield a fragile ground upon which to found judicial rulings. The problem is not just the questionable appraisals that courts undertake within that framework. A discourse too concerned with group identity and culture may also obscure the richness of normatively relevant elements for addressing the case. Crucial among them are the particular rights holders affected and their specific interests and needs. While ethno-cultural membership is itself the expression of an embodied and relational notion of human beings, it is but one part of the whole. The next section therefore enquires whether and how the Inter-American Court recognises the complexity within and across categories of rights holders, as well as the normative consequences that follow from it.

3. WHOLE HUMANS: LOOKING THROUGH AND ACROSS RIGHTS HOLDERS

To explore this question, it is useful to distinguish between two kinds of ethno-cultural diversity cases submitted to the Court. On the one hand, there are the cases litigated from the perspective of indigenous and Afro-descendant communities, which mostly concern land-related rights claims. The majority of the case law reviewed falls within this category, which is, as already explained, more noticeably based on cultural difference and identity arguments. On the other hand, there are a few cases that concern individuals' rights claims, which do not relate to land and natural resources. In these cases, the Court's normative approach has been attentive to group identity but not confined to cultural characteristics. The distinction between these cases holds special relevance for the analysis conducted in this section. Indeed, each set of cases poses different challenges for a legal framework inspired by intersectionality and hence interested in the specific positioning of rights holders.

Collective land judgments largely focus on the situation of indigenous and Afro-descendant communities. As such, the specific concerns and grievances of individual members are often absent from the Court's legal analysis in such cases. But this makes sense. The prioritisation of the collective over the individual has responded to the arguments put forward by the applicants and the Commission, which were usually grounded in collective values and needs. In fact, although until recently the bearer of rights under the ACHR as interpreted by the Court had been the individual or any group of individuals, indigenous rights claims have frequently sought some recognition of their collective personality and, as such, entitlement to collective rights. This group-oriented focus may explain the fact that many land-related judgments provide limited information on who the individual members of the affected communities were and how the alleged violations might have impacted differently upon them. This in itself changes the questions that an integrated approach to rights holders could ask. An intersectional perspective to collective indigenous land cases would thus be wary of passing over the situation of individual members whose circumstances might guide the resolution of the case and/or the remedies devised. This is one of the first issues discussed below. The discussion then moves to the Court's approach to the agency of rights holders, a matter that is also shaped in interesting ways by the collective orientation of many judgments. Finally, the situation of other rights holders who may be affected by the restrictions debated in the judgments, particularly those who advance claims that stand in tension with those of indigenous/tribal communities, needs to be examined. This broad view of rights holders will furthermore pay attention to the legal subjectivity accorded to indigenous peoples collectively, as this would represent an enlargement of the rights holders traditionally seen in the Inter-American adjudication.

3.1. LOOKING BEYOND THE COLLECTIVE AND CULTURAL IDENTITIES OF RIGHTS HOLDERS

We should bear in mind that while the Court may consider it unnecessary to engage with the experience of the individual applicants in the merits analysis of collective cases, it may, however, need to do so in its analysis of reparations. This situation arises every time there are individualised violations and requests for individualised remedies. However, it is in this sphere – in the Court's awards of reparations – that one may notice that some community-oriented judgments have overlooked, to differing degrees, the individual members. The most extreme expression of this problem consisted of displacing the individual altogether. Where the Court, in contrast, did not leave community members out of the assessment of reparations, issues arose as to the extent to which the Court could or should have considered their specific identities and social locations when devising its remedial orders. The discussion below will subsequently address the limited sample of collective cases in which the Court examined, in its merits analysis, the circumstances and overlapping identities of community members. It will be seen that it was in the context of an individual case not argued from the perspective of cultural difference that the Court took questions of intersectionality more into account.

3.1.1. Integrating Collective and Individual Remedies

Individuals faded against the collectivity in cases in which, the Court having declared individualised violations and community members having requested individualised compensation, only the community was awarded reparations. The case of *Yakye Axa* is one example.[37] During the 1990s the *Yakye Axa* community started reclaiming its ancestral lands and, in the meantime, settled along a public road. But there they had no access to their means of subsistence or to basic services. Extreme destitution, harassment and disease followed. The Court found a violation of Articles 4, 8 and 25 and 21 ACHR – rights to life (interpreted as conditions enabling a dignified existence), access to justice and property, respectively. The applicants requested compensation for the moral damage suffered by the community and its members, who had endured inhuman living conditions, threats and diseases for years. Yet, only collective remedies for the community (monetary and non-monetary) were awarded.[38] The merits analysis of this case, however, did pay more attention to different circumstances and needs across community members. This is further discussed below.

The case of *Yatama v. Nicaragua* provides another example of individuals being erased from the reparations.[39] Unlike most indigenous cases, this one concerned the state's refusal to register and allow candidates from an indigenous regional political party (*Yapti Tasba Masraka Nanih Asla Takanka* – YATAMA) to run for municipal elections. The refusal was based on legislation according to which only candidates from political parties presenting candidatures in at least 80 per cent of the municipalities were entitled to stand for elections. The Court declared as discriminatory the character of the restriction, which imposed onerous requirements and a form of political organisation alien to indigenous peoples. It thus found violations of the rights to political participation, equality and access to justice of both the individuals who were prevented from standing for election and of the indigenous communities they represented.[40] Nevertheless, the excluded candidates did not receive compensation, for either the moral or the pecuniary damage they had claimed. Again, the Court only envisaged reparations for the collectivity.[41] In his analysis of the Court's reparations, Anthowiak notes further instances in which individual members of indigenous communities were 'forgotten'. He also observes critically that in indigenous community cases, individuals received little economic compensation.[42]

---

37 IACtHR, *The Yakye Axa Indigenous Community v. Paraguay*, Judgment of 17 June 2005.

38 Ibid., para. 197 (a), (b). The refusal to grant compensation to the next of kin of the community members who died is understandable in view of the Court's conclusion that the state could not be held responsible for such deaths. However, with respect to the moral damage claimed by the individuals whose rights to a dignified life, access to justice and property had been violated, it is unclear why the Court did not grant them compensation.

39 IACtHR, *Yatama v. Nicaragua*, Judgment of 23 June 2005.

40 Ibid., para. 275.

41 It is interesting to observe that the Court had made some remarks about the harm experienced by the candidates. It mentioned, for example, their frustration and the special significance of representing their indigenous community.

42 Ibid., at 64–70.

But, as mentioned above, there are collective-oriented judgments where the individual was not entirely left out of the picture. The overlapping identities and disadvantages faced by some community members then had a role to play. Consider, for example, the reparation judgment in the *Aloeboetoe* case. The case concerned the detention and killing of several male, unarmed Maroons (Afro-descendants who belonged to the Saramaka). They were detained and murdered by state agents on suspicion of belonging to a subversive group. In 1991, Suriname acknowledged its responsibility for the violations, the Court issued a judgment taking note of the acknowledgement and deferred its ruling on reparations. The Commission requested that in defining the beneficiaries of reparations for pecuniary damages, the Court should 'take into account the family structure of the Maroons' – which was largely matrilineal and practised polygamy.[43] Thus, in applying Article 63(1) ACHR on reparations awards,[44] the Court had to consider the deceased victims, all adult men, and their heirs: 'relatives in the ascending line', 'spouses' and 'children'. To define which spouses and children were awarded compensation, the Court eventually decided to take into account Saramaka customs, including the reality of polygamy. This is a remarkable example of integration of customary norms, as further discussed below. But here it is relevant to draw attention to the reasons provided for the Court for doing so and to the added value of an intersectional approach.

The Court decided this reparation issue on the basis of a single concern: 'The only question of importance here is whether the laws of Suriname in the area of family law apply to the Saramaka tribe. [...] The members of the tribe are unaware of it and adhere to their own rules.'[45] While the cultural sensitivity of the Court in its approach to reparations is outstanding, it is interesting to observe that its language remained gender neutral. The Court simply did not mention how paramount was the issue of considering or ignoring the *Saramaka* cultural practices for *Saramaka* women in particular. Limiting compensation to only one wife for each victim would have rendered several *Saramaka* women, possibly along with their children, vulnerable and destitute. In reality, the entire issue of reparations was above all pivotal for *Saramaka* women, given their specific position within their community. As research indicates, in practice *Saramaka* women are mainly dependent on their spouse for their material

43 IACtHR, *Aloeboetoe et al. v. Suriname*, Judgment of 10 September 1993, para. 17.

44 Article 63(1) ACHR reads as follows: 'If the Court finds that there has been a violation of a right or freedom protected by this Convention, the Court shall rule that the injured party be ensured the enjoyment of his right or freedom that was violated. It shall also rule, if appropriate, that the consequences of the measure or situation that constituted the breach of such right or freedom be remedied and that fair compensation be paid to the injured party.'

45 IACtHR, *Aloeboetoe et al. v. Suriname*, Judgment of 10 September 1993, para. 58.

subsistence and not, as one might assume for a matrilineal system of descent, on their maternal brother.[46]

In light of the foregoing, an intersectional approach to reparations would have been valuable. It would have assisted the Court in identifying the specific disadvantages and harms risked by *Saramaka* women and children as rights holders and relatives of the deceased victims. The gender inequality that would have resulted from a disregard for the cultural practices of the *Saramaka* provided not just an additional ground for the Court's decision to consider it, but actually quite a strong one. As such, the reasoning holds relevance for states too. Indeed, state parties may question whether the mere ineffectiveness of their laws over certain populations authorises international courts to do away with them. Against that, due regard for the vulnerable position of ethnic minority women and their children adds an important argument to the question of what the law was in practice and even to the question of cultural difference in itself.

A gendered view of the consequences of the violations experienced by tribal/Afro-descendant women was explicitly requested in the case of *Operation Genesis v. Colombia*. This case dealt with the forced displacement of Afro-descendant communities from the Cacarica River basin in Colombia and the killing of one community member. As a result of the displacement, many families split up. In this connection, the applicants requested a gender-differentiated measure of reparation.[47] They asked for 'financial subsidies to be granted to the women heads of household in recognition of the loss of their husbands or companions in Operation Genesis or, if they were already heads of household, owing to the difficulties suffered'.[48] The Court emphasised that taking 'into account the position of the women among the members of the family or other differentiated aspects, such as whether the land and other means of production are owned collectively' was required for administrative reparations to be legitimate.[49] Eventually, however, the applicants' request was not addressed by the Court. Owing to the administrative reparations put in place by the government within the framework of its transitional justice programme, the Court concluded that it was not for it to order additional measures.[50]

---

46 Marisol Molestina, 'La Sentencia de Reparaciones del Caso Aloeboetoe y Otros: Un Punto de Vista Antropológico', 25 *Revista IIDH*, Comentarios sobre la práctica de los órganos del sistema interamericano de protección de los derechos humanos (1998) 109, at 122.

47 For a gendered analysis of reparations in international human rights law, see Ruth Rubio-Marin (ed.), *The Gender of Reparations. Unsettling Sexual Hierarchies While Redressing Human Rights Violations* (Cambridge University Press, 2009).

48 IACtHR, *The Afro-descendant communities displaced from the Cacarica River Basin (Operation Genesis) v. Colombia*, Judgment of 20 November 2013, para. 468.

49 Ibid., para. 470.

50 Ibid., paras. 470–474.

Traces of an intersectional perspective have not been exclusively confined to the Court's pronouncements on reparations, though. Relevant insights can be found in the merits analysis of a few collective cases. This is the next question examined.

3.1.2. Integrating Individuals' Multiple Positioning into the Merits Analysis

Interestingly, the collective-oriented judgments that display a more comprehensive view of indigenous community members are those which did not rely as heavily as others on the cultural identity framework of Article 21 ACHR. These cases have the particularity of having been mainly addressed through an alternative framework, one based on Article 4 ACHR concerning the right to life. Within this framework, identity cultural arguments were present but were not as salient as in the other collective land cases.

Illustrative are the judgments issued in the aforementioned Paraguayan cases of *Yakye Axa*, *Sawhoyamaxa* and *Xákmok Kásek*. These are part of a series of cases concerning indigenous communities from the Paraguayan Chaco, a large region bordering Brazil and Bolivia whose occupation during the 19th century resulted in, for example, lands being sold on the London stock exchange and in an Anglican 'pacification' of the indigenous population.[51] The first two communities seeking restitution ended up settling beside public routes, where they could not cater for their needs or access water, medical care, sanitation and other services. The case of *Xákmok Kásek* originated in the same occupation of the Paraguayan Chaco and the indigenous peoples affected also had their territorial claims pending for decades. In the meantime, their lands were also sold to private companies. In this case, however, instead of being forced to settle outside their ancestral territory, the community remained within a reduced part of it, where their activities, access to resources and mobility were severely restricted by the private owners of the land. As a result, the members of the *Xákmok Kásek* community faced appalling living conditions as well.

Besides taking into account the extreme poverty experienced by all the community members who found themselves unable to practise their land-related subsistence activities and without access to basic services,[52] the Court scrutinised the impact this had on the children, the elderly and the pregnant women of the community. With regard to both elderly people and pregnant women, the Court required additional steps from the state to

51 IACtHR, *The Yakye Axa Indigenous Community v. Paraguay*, Judgment of 17 June 2005, para. 50.

52 Ibid., para. 164; IACtHR, *The Sawhoyamaxa Indigenous Community v. Paraguay*, Judgment of 29 March 2006, paras. 73(61)–(72) and 168–170; *The Xákmok Kásek Indigenous Community v. Paraguay*, Judgment of 24 August 2010, paras. 189 and ff.

secure their access to adequate medical care.[53] Likewise, in *Sawhoyamaxa* and *Xákmok Kásek* the Court examined the early death, lack of medical assistance and malnutrition of the boys and girls of the community.[54] Also of note, in *Xákmok Kásek* the Court addressed the death of indigenous women who had no access to maternal care, a situation which the Court also connected to their experience of poverty.[55]

The Court in *Yakye Axa* also interpreted the right to life of indigenous children in light of Article 19 ACHR (rights of the child).[56] In this vein, it should be noted that the very existence of this specific provision within the ACHR is remarkable from an intersectional perspective. It places the Court under the obligation to have due regard for the situation of children. On this basis (Article 4 and 19 ACHR), the Court in *Yakye Axa* held that the state had to ensure that indigenous children's wellbeing and life project would not be disrupted as a result of the situation faced by their community.[57] In *Xákmok Kásek*, a violation of children's rights (Article 19 ACHR) was additionally found on account of 'the loss of traditional practices, such as male and female initiation rites and the Community's languages [...]', which affected more severely the identity and development of indigenous children.[58] The consequences of children's separation from their ancestral lands were also examined on the basis of Article 19 ACHR and the existing international *corpus juris* on children's rights when displacements were caused by internal armed conflict. The *Operation Genesis v. Colombia* case is illustrative.[59]

---

53 IACtHR, *The Yakye Axa Indigenous Community v. Paraguay*, Judgment of 17 June 2005, para. 175 (regarding the elderly members of the community. The Court also drew attention to their particular role within the community, as they were the main persons responsible for the oral transmission of the culture); *The Sawhoyamaxa Indigenous Community v. Paraguay*, Judgment of 29 March 2006, para. 177 (regarding the pregnant women of the community).

54 IACtHR, *The Sawhoyamaxa Indigenous Community v. Paraguay*, Judgment of 29 March 2006, para. 171; *The Xákmok Kásek Indigenous Community v. Paraguay*, Judgment of 24 August 2010, paras. 259–260.

55 IACtHR, *The Xákmok Kásek Indigenous Community v. Paraguay*, Judgment of 24 August 2010, paras. 231–234.

56 Article 19 ACHR ('rights of the child') reads as follows: 'Every minor child has the right to the measures of protection required by his condition as a minor on the part of his family, society, and the state.'

57 IACtHR, *The Yakye Axa Indigenous Community v. Paraguay*, Judgment of 17 June 2005, para. 172.

58 IACtHR, *The Xákmok Kásek Indigenous Community v. Paraguay*, Judgment of 24 August 2010, paras. 260–264.

59 While here the accent was put on the heightened vulnerability of any child who faces armed conflict and displacement, such vulnerability was also described by reference to the children's separation from their ancestral lands. See IACtHR, *The Afro-descendant communities displaced from the Cacarica River Basin (Operation Genesis) v. Colombia*, Judgment of 20 November 2013, paras. 330–331 (the children's vulnerability was also characterised in terms of their lack of access to education, healthcare and adequate nutrition and to their deprived living conditions).

Thus, while the Court mainly approached the situation of all those individuals from the perspective of indigenous membership, it did conceive of this as comprising other non-privileged identities. In this vein, the Court's efforts in acknowledging the different social positions of community members in the Paraguayan cases somewhat resemble the 'capacious approach' to intersectionality proposed by Fredman.[60] In fact, their experience as indigenous persons was inclusive of indigenous children, indigenous women and the elderly living in poverty, an approach taken in the context of substantive provisions and not of discrimination grounds. It is worth noting that more recently, in the case of *The Members of the village of Chichupac and neighbouring communities*,[61] the Court undertook a similar comprehensive analysis whereby it acknowledged the 'differentiated impact' that some violations had had on indigenous women and children. But this case is not so much about collective land rights and related cultural particularities. Rather, it concerns the effects of the massacres, extrajudicial executions, torture, forced disappearances and rapes perpetrated against Maya indigenous people in Guatemala, concretely, those of the village of Chichupac and neighbouring communities in the Municipality of Rabinal.[62]

The judgment nonetheless addresses the loss of lands and the impossibility of returning to ancestral territory, although in the context of the communities' forced displacement and the ensuing violation of their freedom of movement and residence (Article 22 ACHR). Within the scope of this provision, the Court examined the differentiated impact of the forced displacement upon the women and children of the communities.[63] Women had to become the heads of household while coping with the effects of the violence endured, including the killing of their family members. Further, many of them were raped and had become pregnant as a consequence, while also being stigmatised and excluded as a result. The Court additionally noted the particular vulnerability to which children were exposed, including those who were born out of rape.[64]

60 See *supra* Chapter 2, section 3.1.3.

61 IACtHR, *The Members of the village of Chichupac and neighboring communities of the Municipality of Rabinal v. Guatemala*, Judgment of 30 November 2016.

62 This is not the first case in which the Court had to deal with this kind of event. The cases of the Río Negro and Plan de Sánchez massacres also concern similar gross violations against members of the Maya Achí peoples who resided in the Rabinal Municipality in Guatemala. See IACtHR, *The Río Negro Massacres v. Guatemala*, Judgment of 4 September 2012; and *The Plan de Sánchez Massacre v. Guatemala*, Judgment of 29 April 2004.

63 The Court had similarly drawn attention to the differentiated impact of the violations on indigenous children in IACtHR, *The Río Negro Massacres v. Guatemala*, Judgment of 4 September 2012, paras. 142–143.

64 IACtHR, *The Members of the village of Chichupac and neighboring communities of the Municipality of Rabinal v. Guatemala*, Judgment of 30 November 2016, paras. 198–202.

From the few judgments litigated on behalf of Afro-descendant/indigenous individuals instead of collectivities, one – the case of *Yean and Bosico v. Dominican Republic*[65] – took some steps towards intersectionality. In this case, two girls of Haitian descent who were born in the Dominican Republic were denied a late birth registration. Prevented from obtaining Dominican nationality, they risked expulsion from the country and could not enrol at school or access other social services. Thus, while the case was framed as a case of violations tied to the ethno-cultural identity of the applicants, the issue was not, as in most indigenous cases, one of cultural identity protection. In practice, the Court examined the case within the overall social context of Haitians and Dominicans of Haitian origin in the Dominican Republic, who were in a 'particularly vulnerable situation' as a result of entrenched discrimination, poverty and residential isolation.[66] Owing to these circumstances, which prompted most Dominicans of Haitian origin to use the late birth declaration procedure, they were systematically prevented from obtaining nationality.

The interplay between ethnic origin, poverty and place of residence underpinned the Court's account of why most Dominican mothers of Haitian origin resorted to such late birth registration procedures. As the Court noted, they did so because they usually gave birth at home, given the difficulty of traveling to the hospitals in the cities, their limited financial resources, and out of fear of making themselves known to state officials and being deported.[67] The same compounded disadvantages also explained why most of those families could not provide the documents required to obtain nationality, as these included identity cards and marriage certificates that they did not have. The Court assessed the seriousness of the ensuing rights restrictions through the prism of the best interests of the child and of the special vulnerability of the applicants as girl children.[68] It thus examined all the allegations in light of Article 19 ACHR (rights of the child) and drew attention to the seriousness of hindering the girls' education.

While this emergent intersectional approach somewhat folded into a finding of direct discrimination, mainly on the basis of migration status,[69] it resurfaced in the Court's reference to the vulnerable situation of the applicants and in the reparation orders. In fact, the Court had described such vulnerability by virtue of the confluence of several disadvantages,[70] and not just on account of

---

65 IACtHR, *The Girls Yean and Bosico v. Dominican Republic*, Judgment of 8 September 2005.

66 Ibid., paras. 109(1)–(10).

67 Ibid., para. 109(10).

68 Ibid., para. 134.

69 Ibid., paras. 155–166. The Court noted that the different treatment accorded to the girls Yean and Bosico (whose situation fell within the regulation provided for children under the age of 13) was arbitrary and amounted to discrimination. It also pointed out that the prohibition of discrimination applies irrespective of a person's migratory status in a state.

70 Ibid., para. 168.

their ethnic origin or migration status. As to the reparations, the state was required to 'take into consideration the particularly vulnerable situation of Dominican children of Haitian origin' when regulating late birth registration.[71] The Court spelled this requirement out. Basically, the applicants and other children like them were entitled to a much more flexible system of birth registration. The documents required should be only those essential for establishing that the birth occurred in the Dominican Republic; the identification of the parents could not be restricted to the presentation of identity cards; and the whole procedure should be standardised so as to limit the discretion of state officials.[72] Interestingly, this remedial formula seems to be best suited to a finding of indirect – instead of direct – discrimination, since the Court went beyond demanding adherence to the legal framework within which the situation of the girls fell. It actually required flexibility and the introduction of some 'exceptions' to the general regulations on birth certificates. In this way, the Court attempted to tackle the specific violations arising from the applicants' intersecting identities and overlapping vulnerabilities.

Although the other case concerning an individual applicant, *Lopez Alvarez v. Honduras*,[73] addressed violations related to his ethno-cultural identity only, it is nonetheless possible to reflect upon the potential benefits of an intersectional perspective to cases like this. Mr Lopez Alvarez, who belonged to the Garifuna ethnic minority and was an activist for the rights of black and indigenous peoples, was charged with drug trafficking and remained deprived of his liberty for more than six years. While in prison, he was prevented from speaking in his mother tongue with other Garifuna inmates and visitors, for 'security reasons'. The judgment, which underlined the applicant's right to use a language constitutive of his identity, does not provide sufficient elements to explore the integration of an intersectional approach.[74] However, it is interesting to note that intersectionality is useful for illuminating the harsher law enforcement treatment encountered by men from ethnic minorities, like the applicant. This treatment, as well as their higher rates of detention, is very often expression of what scholars have called 'gendered racism'.[75] To put it

[71] Ibid., para. 240.
[72] Idem.
[73] IACtHR, *López Álvarez v. Honduras*, Judgment of 1 February 2006.
[74] The factual and legal issues discussed by the parties and the Court concerned the restrictions imposed on him as a Garifuna and the harm caused by preventing him from speaking in his mother tongue. The Court found that he had been discriminated against 'as a member of the Garifuna community' and that his freedom of expression (Article 13 ACHR) had been violated. The Court stressed the state duty to take into account the characteristics of indigenous community members that made up their cultural identity and which distinguish them from the rest. See paras. 169–172.
[75] See Athena D. Mutua, 'Multidimentionality is to Masculinities What Intersectionality is to Feminism', 13 *Nevada Law Journal* (2013) 341, at 346 (discussing in particular the operation of gendered racism in the context of racial profiling).

simply, this makes it possible to account for the fact that men from minority backgrounds may face interference with their rights not only by virtue of their ethnic origin, but also on account of gender insofar as it is their 'maleness' that is seen as, for example, dangerous and in need of restraint. In the case of Mr Lopez Alvarez, this was compounded by his position as a community leader and human rights defender, in retaliation for which he had been imprisoned.

Overall, the analysis made thus far provides us with a number of useful indications about the actual and potential implications of a more comprehensive approach to applicants in cultural diversity cases before the Inter-American Court. First, in indigenous community cases such a perspective draws attention to the situation of individual members who are likely to be side-lined by a collective and cultural identity approach to the case. Second, for both collective and individual cases, an intersectional perspective could offer: (a) a more accurate account of the causes of the rights interferences (as seen in *Yean and Bosico*); and (b) a normative ground for applying differentiated standards dictated by specific norms (such as children's rights and socio-economic rights in *Yakye Axa* and *Sawhoyamaxa*, or customary norms in *Aloeboetoe*) or by giving additional weight to certain harms and risks in the proportionality analysis (as happened with the lack of education, name and nationality in the case of girls *Yean and Bosico*). Finally, a more integrated view of rights holders would also facilitate (c) the devising of appropriate remedies for individual members and intra-group segments (as discussed in relation to *Aloeboetoe* and *Operation Genesis v. Colombia*).

Finally, it is interesting to observe that several of the aforementioned attempts to capture the multiple positioning of some indigenous/Afro-descendant community members take the form of an emphasis on sub-groups (e.g. indigenous children and indigenous women). Considering that the Court's case law on indigenous/tribal people also emphasises their group distinctiveness and 'special' characteristics, one may wonder whether the attention paid to subgroups in need of heightened protection reinforces an analysis too concerned with their own particularities. Such a view may fall short of challenging structural barriers and underlying inequalities, as propounded by intersectionality theory. In this vein, one may note, on the one hand, that the way the Court applies the notion of vulnerability to indigenous people, and to some members in particular, seems to lessen that risk. As discussed below, the Court has often associated the condition of vulnerability of indigenous communities and its members with exclusion, violence and institutional deficits. Moreover, it has addressed the specific or differentiated forms of violation encountered by some community members rather than simply pointing at their characteristics. On the other hand, however, it is puzzling that questions of structural discrimination have been little discussed in collective indigenous cases. Section 4.1.2 *infra* further explores this issue.

3.1.3. *An Intersectional Approach Beyond the Anti-Discrimination Review*

Having discussed the Court's overtures and closures in regard to the multiple identities and social locations of indigenous and Afro-descendant applicants, it is time to ask: what about the relationship between an intersectional approach and anti-discrimination law? As discussed in the context of the European Court, allegations pointing at multiple axes of disadvantage are likely to bring about issues of intersectional and indirect discrimination. However, in the ethno-cultural diversity cases examined by the Inter-American Court, that link has taken a singular fashion, that is, an analysis along the lines of vulnerability. It should be noted, to start with, that in cases concerning collective land claims, the role of equality and non-discrimination analysis has been rather limited. The restricted application of non-discrimination clauses, further discussed *infra* section 4.1.2, also holds true for the judgments in which the Court engaged with some intersectional reasoning. It was in individual cases that the Court elaborated more on equality and discrimination. And yet, only in *Yean and Bosico* was there an emergent intersectional approach, which nonetheless was addressed through single-ground discrimination. Overall, the move towards a more comprehensive understanding of the applicants' experience in both this case and in the few collective judgments examined above appears to be connected more to the notion of vulnerability than to equality and non-discrimination.

In fact, several of the Court's considerations on vulnerability situated applicants as facing heightened risks as a result of 'special' or 'extreme' vulnerability as well as overlapping sources of vulnerability. For this reason, the Court raised the standard of diligence required from the state, applied norms tailored to the specific identities and situations of the applicants and imposed special measures to redress those deemed most vulnerable. To differing degrees, all this resonates with intersectionality thinking in law. The decision to use the concept of vulnerability rather than non-discrimination as a vehicle for intersectionality considerations may have to do with the perception that vulnerability represents a closely related yet 'more comprehensive approach with respect to the prevalent discrimination theory'.[76] If the Court effectively resorts to vulnerability as a way to be freed from the constraints of group-identity grounds of discrimination and its difficulties in accounting for relations of privilege and disempowerment,[77] then it makes perfect sense to

---

76 Romina I. Sijniensky, 'From the Non-Discrimination Clause to the Concept of Vulnerability in International Human Rights Law. Advancing the Needs for Special Protection of Certain Groups and Individuals', in Yves Haeck *et al.* (eds.), *The Realisation of Human Rights: When Theory Meets Practice. Studies in Honour of Leo Zwaak* (Intersentia, 2013), at 262.

77 These are some of the main flaws that Fineman identifies in anti-discrimination law and which she proposes to overcome by her normative theory of vulnerability.

find intersectionality concerns clothed in the language of vulnerability. The move is surprising, though, since the Inter-American Court has distanced itself from the dominant formal paradigm of equality and non-discrimination to endorse a substantive/structural conception of this principle.[78] So long as such a conception is preoccupied with the actual subordination of some parts of the population, as well as with the social institutions and structural barriers that sustain it, it is well suited to engaging in intersectionality analysis. Nevertheless, as will be seen below, it is the equality and non-discrimination framework that is generally underused in the community-oriented cases studied here.

The discussion will now turn to a further dimension of individual rights holders which is often reduced in adjudication: their agency. As seen already, human complexity flows not only from people's multiple identities and social locations, but also from the way their agency and social embeddedness unfolds in real life. Put simply, viewing rights holders as fully autonomous in certain areas and as devoid of agency in others does not do justice to their lived experience. Most of the time, individuals' autonomy is somewhere in between, unfolding according to time and context. Ignoring this complexity could lead judges to paternalism, to attributing meanings to individual's choices, to reinforcing stereotypes or to taking misplaced normative stances. How much of this can be found in the Inter-American Court's case law regarding ethno-cultural difference?

3.2. PROBLEMATISING THE 'EITHER/OR' VIEW OF INDIVIDUALS' AUTONOMY AND CHOICE

Unlike some of the ECtHR's rulings previously examined, the general discourse of the Inter-American Court has not portrayed applicants or other rights holders as unencumbered subjects with regard to socio-economic or cultural matters. It has generally remained distant from the rhetoric of available choices for applicants to avoid or mitigate the rights interferences they have complained of. Its reasoning in cases such as *Yakye Axa* and *Sawhoyamaxa* is illustrative of this.[79] Yet, as explained earlier, acknowledging that individuals' autonomy is

---

See Martha Albertson Fineman, 'The Vulnerable Subject: Anchoring Equality in the Human Condition', 20(1) *Yale Journal of Law and Feminism* (2008) 1, at 1–3.

78 See e.g. Valeska David, 'The Inter-American Concept of Structural Equality and Discrimination', 2(2) *Anti-Discrimination Law Review* (2017) 5, at 12 and ff; Victor Abramovich, 'From Massive Violations to Structural Patterns: New Approaches and Classic Tensions in the Inter-American Human Rights System', 6(11) *Sur-International Journal of Human Rights* (2009) 7, at 17–22.

79 In both cases the state argued that the communities and their leaders had chosen to undergo the rights interferences they complained of, as they had put themselves at the

shaped or limited by social relations and structures should not lead to denial of their agency. Both conditions can, and actually do, often coexist within our human complexity. This is, however, an issue which the Inter-American Court has seemingly struggled with, particularly when it comes to economic matters.

In the context of its culturally sensitive interpretation of Article 21 ACHR, the Court has strongly defended the autonomy of indigenous communities. Throughout the cases studied, it has recognised their right to decide on matters that may affect them. Indigenous peoples should be given timely information and consulted and in some circumstances their consent is even required.[80] The Court has furthermore condemned the state's failure to recognise the collective legal personality of indigenous and tribal peoples (Article 3 ACHR).[81] Though it is argued that the Court, like many other international bodies, has fallen short of fully recognising indigenous peoples' right to (collective) self-determination,[82] it has certainly made significant steps in that direction. This is particularly apparent in the *Saramaka* judgment, in which it interpreted Article 21 as 'calling for the right of members of indigenous and tribal communities to freely determine and enjoy their own social, cultural and economic development'.[83] A similar reading along the lines of self-determination also features in most recent judgments, further discussed below, which

side of a road where they could not gather for their needs. The Court dismissed the claim. Basically, it found that the applicants had been propelled to take action to vindicate their lands and had legitimately refused the temporary solutions proposed by the state as they had not been consulted about those alternatives. It held: 'The Court considers that there were powerful reasons for the members of the Community to abandon the estates where they lived and worked, due to the extremely hard physical and labor conditions they had to endure [...] [nonetheless] this argument is not enough for the State to disregard its duty to protect and guarantee the right to life of the alleged victims.' See IACtHR, *The Yakye Axa Indigenous Community v. Paraguay*, Judgment of 17 June 2005, paras. 159 (d), 164 and 171; and *The Sawhoyamaxa Indigenous Community v. Paraguay*, Judgment of 29 March 2006, para. 163.

80 See e.g. IACtHR, *The Saramaka People v. Suriname*, Judgment of 28 November 2007, paras. 95 and 133–137; *The Kichwa Indigenous People of Sarayaku v. Ecuador*, Judgment of 27 June 2012, paras. 159–211; *The Garífuna Community of Triunfo de la Cruz and its Members v. Honduras*, Judgment of 8 October 2015, para. 156.

81 IACtHR, *The Saramaka People v. Suriname*, Judgment of 28 November 2007, paras. 167–175; *The Kaliña and Lokono Peoples v. Suriname*, Judgment of 25 November 2015, paras. 112–114. For the Court, recognition of their juridical personality is a precondition for these peoples to fully exercise these rights in a collective manner.

82 Thomas M. Antkowiak, 'Rights, Resources, and Rhetoric: Indigenous Peoples and the Inter-American Court', 35(1) *University of Pennsylvania Journal of International Law* (2013) 113, at 153. The author's analysis relies on the notion of self-determination propounded by Anaya, which comprises five dimensions: non-discrimination, cultural integrity, lands and resources, social welfare and development, and self-government. See James Anaya, *Indigenous Peoples in International Law* (Oxford University Press, 2004).

83 IACtHR, *The Saramaka People v. Suriname*, Judgment of 28 November 2007, para. 95.

elaborate on indigenous peoples' right to effective participation under Article 23 ('Right to Participate in Government').[84]

But against this backdrop, a sort of paradox can be discerned: the Court, at the same time, has found that indigenous applicants somehow lack the agency required to manage by themselves the reparations granted by the Court. In the Court's early jurisprudence on indigenous rights, the problem arose specifically with regard to one modality of reparation. This is the creation of a trust fund (as a remedy for collective moral damage or as a means of redressing both pecuniary and non-pecuniary damage) for developing educational, housing and other programmes for the benefit of the victims and their communities. In doing so, the Court provided a detailed scheme for its operation. Notably, it set up its managing committee while defining the exact fate of the resources.

The aforementioned reparation judgment in *Aloeboetoe* provides the most worrisome example of the tension between such a practice and recognition of the applicants' agency. In this case, the Court ordered the state to deposit its economic compensation in a trust fund composed of members appointed by the Court itself. Then, it instructed: '*the adult beneficiaries may withdraw up to* 25% (twenty-five percent) of the sum due to them at the time that the Government of Suriname makes the deposit. The trust fund for the adults shall be set up with the remaining funds [...] *semiannual withdrawals shall be permitted*.'[85] How is this remedial scheme to be reconciled with the individual autonomy of indigenous people? The Court's paternalist approach seems to convey a stereotyped view of indigenous adults, who are, under assumptions of inability or incapability, stripped of autonomy.[86] While this paternalism was certainly lessened in subsequent cases, for a while difficulties persisted.

In cases such as *Awas Tingni*, *Moiwana*, *Yakye Axa* and *Saramaka*, to mention just some, the Court again ordered similar community development funds. This time, the appointment of the fund's administrative committee was left to the parties.[87] Although the new system assured the victims of some degree

---

84 As will be seen below, the Court has recently interpreted Article 23 (Right to Participate in Government) as requiring the state to put in place mechanisms enabling indigenous communities to participate effectively in matters affecting their interests, including any development or conservation project that may affect them. They have the right to determine their own social, cultural and economic development. See e.g. IACtHR, *The Kaliña and Lokono Peoples v. Suriname*, Judgment of 25 November 2015, paras. 122–126, 196 and 203–206.

85 IACtHR, *Aloeboetoe et al. v. Suriname*, Judgment of 10 September 1993, para. 102 (emphasis added).

86 For a critic of the 'administrative and participatory paternalism' of the Court in its cases concerning indigenous peoples, see Ariel E. Dulitzky, 'When Afro-Descendants Became "Tribal Peoples": The Inter-American Human Rights System and Rural Black Communities', 1 *UCLA Journal of International Law and Foreign Affairs* (2010) 29, at 52–55.

87 IACtHR, *The Moiwana Community v. Suriname*, Judgment of 15 June 2005, paras. 213–215; *The Saramaka People v. Suriname*, Judgment of 28 November 2007, paras. 201–202.

of involvement, it fell short of the applicants' demands for intervention. They pledged to be informed, to cooperate with and to consent to the design and execution of the development programmes.[88] Yet, the Court only got close to that in *Saramaka*, where it held that the implementation committee 'shall *consult* with the Saramaka people before decisions are taken and implemented'.[89] This case aside, the fund scheme only recognised a limited legal capacity for the applicants to make decisions about their own reparations. Coupled with the Court's protection of 'traditional' activities, the Court's approach risked fostering stereotypes and differences between 'us' and 'them' as economic agents. Scholars have noted that before indigenous cases the fund mechanism had only been used for the compensation of children;[90] that in indigenous cases 'the Court's monetary reparations frequently disappoint';[91] and that individuals get little economic compensation.[92] Put together, this means that indigenous/Afro-descendant individuals have rarely had the option to dispose of their reparations as other victims of human rights violations do.

In this context, the Court's radical change of approach in the 2012 case of *Sarayaku* cannot but be welcome. The Court, remarkably, held that the sum awarded for non-pecuniary damage 'may be invested as the People see fit, in accordance with its own decision-making mechanisms and institutions'.[93] This position has since been maintained.[94]

See also *The Sawhoyamaxa Indigenous Community v. Paraguay*, Judgment of 29 March 2006, paras. 224–225.

88 IACtHR, *The Moiwana Community v. Suriname*, Judgment of 15 June 2005, para. 199.2(h); *The Sawhoyamaxa Indigenous Community v. Paraguay*, para. 202(g).

89 IACtHR, *The Saramaka People v. Suriname*, Judgment of 28 November 2007, para. 202 (emphasis added).

90 IACtHR, *Velasquez Rodriguez v. Honduras*, Judgment of 21 July 1989, para. 58 (cited in Ariel E. Dulitzky, 'When Afro-Descendants Became "Tribal Peoples": The Inter-American Human Rights System and Rural Black Communities', 15(1) *UCLA Journal of International Law and Foreign Affairs* (2010) 29, at 53 (noting that 'before *Aloeboetoe*, the Court had only created trust funds managed by the family itself, and only when reparations were ordered for minor children').

91 Thomas M. Antkowiak, 'A Dark Side of Virtue: The Inter-American Court and Reparations for Indigenous Peoples', 25 *Duke Journal of Comparative & International Law* (2014) 1, at 3.

92 Ibid., at 64–70.

93 IACtHR, *The Kichwa Indigenous People of Sarayaku v. Ecuador*, Judgment of 27 June 2012, para. 323. The Court added that the money would be 'for the implementation of educational, cultural, food security, health care and eco-tourism development projects or other community infrastructure projects or projects of collective interest that the People considers a priority'.

94 See e.g. IACtHR, *The Kuna Indigenous People of Madungandí and the Emberá Indigenous People of Bayano and their Members v. Panama*, Judgment of 14 October 2014, para. 240 (the amount had to be paid to the representatives of the communities so they could invest the money as they saw fit and in accordance with their institutions and decision-making mechanisms); *The Garífuna Punta Piedra Community and its Members v. Honduras*, Judgment of 8 October 2015, para. 334 (the Court provided that the applicants should appoint a representative to dialogue with the state and thus ensure that the fund is implemented

3.3. A BROAD VIEW OF RIGHTS HOLDERS

Up to this point, most of the discussion has revolved around applicants. But we know that they do not stand alone and that what they claim for themselves usually affects others. Most of the cases discussed here are no exception to this rule. As such, one may ask: which rights holders are seen by the Inter-American Court? Does it integrate in its analysis the situation of rights holders other than the applicants for the purposes of deciding the cases studied? And what would be gained by doing so?

3.3.1. Other Communities and Individuals Affected

The judgments dealing with individual allegations of ethno-cultural-based violations show a Court ready to see and consider other rights holders, in particular, those who are like the applicants. This is aptly demonstrated by the allusions to other children and adults of Haitian descent in the case of *Yean and Bosico*; and to the rights of other members of the Garifuna community who were imprisoned in *Lopez Alvarez*. In both cases, the seriousness of the interference was viewed in the light of the prejudicial effects it had on the dignity and inclusion of those other individuals. By contrast, the situation of rights holders whose interests stand in opposition to the interests of the applicants and others like them was not discussed. This made sense, though. There were no claims or evidence suggesting that granting nationality or allowing the use of a minority language would have severed the rights of other individuals or groups.

In judgments concerning collective rights claims, however, the rights of other rights holders have virtually always been at issue. But in these cases, where the applicants are the indigenous community and its individual members, the attention given to a larger array of rights holders has been incremental. In particular, there are two types of rights holder whose visibility has been progressively increased. In the first place, there are indigenous or rural and collective-oriented communities who have similar and yet competing rights claims to those of the applicants. Whether the Court has taken into account the way in which its interpretation or solution in a case would affect them is not always clear. By the time of *Awas Tingni*, this was already an issue. The state argued that finding for the applicants would set aside the interests of other indigenous communities living in the territories reclaimed. The Court succinctly responded to this argument by holding that the communal rights recognised

---

as the community saw fit. The Court also gave guidelines as to the areas of investment of the development projects, but on the basis of the explicit request from the applicants); *The Community Garifuna Triunfo de la Cruz & its Members v. Honduras*, Judgment of 8 October 2015, para. 297.

to the *Awas Tingni* community were 'without detriment to the rights of other indigenous communities'.[95] The statement fell short of explaining what that meant in practice. And eventually, conflicting rights claims from neighbouring communities proved to be a major challenge for the implementation of the Court's judgment.[96]

Greater consideration for those other rights holders, and even an attempt to anticipate conflict, would nonetheless be shown in subsequent cases. In *Moiwana*, the Court ordered the state, by way of reparation, to demarcate and title the applicant's ancestral lands with the full participation not only of the *Moiwana* community, but also of the neighbouring communities and villages.[97] In more recent cases, such as *Kaliña and Lokono* and *Garífuna Punta Piedra Community*, the Court elaborated further on this concern. It required the state to respect the rights of other indigenous and tribal communities living in the same area claimed by the applicants and to develop, in agreement with the communities concerned, rules for their peaceful coexistence in the territory.[98] Overall, when other indigenous communities are considered by the Court, this seems to impact on the implementation of the judgment rather than on the interpretation and findings of the Court.

In the second place, the rights of other individuals have often been at stake. These are private owners or users of the disputed ancestral lands. Typically, these rights holders would come into play when the Court analysed whether the interferences with ancestral lands were aimed at achieving a legitimate aim, such as protecting 'the rights of others'. But the threefold test of legality, legitimate aim and necessity has not always featured in indigenous land judgments.[99] In fact, attention to balancing was lacking in several judgments studied. Since *Yakye Axa*, however, the necessity test seems to have gradually gained application.[100]

---

95 IACtHR, *The Mayagna (Sumo) Awas Tingni Community v. Nicaragua*, Judgment of 31 August 2001, para. 153.

96 Leonardo J. Alvarado, 'Prospects and Challenges in the Implementation of Indigenous Peoples' Human Rights in International Law: Lessons from the Case of Awas Tingni v. Nicaragua', 24(3) *Arizona Journal of International & Comparative Law* (2007) 609, at 628 and ff; IACtHR, Order of the Inter-American Court of Human Rights of 3 April 2009 in the Case of *The Mayagna (Sumo) Awas Tingni Community v. Nicaragua* (Monitoring Compliance with Judgment), 3 April 2009, paras. 10 and ff.

97 IACtHR, *The Moiwana Community v. Suriname*, Judgment of 15 June 2005, paras. 209–210.

98 IACtHR, *The Kaliña and Lokono Peoples v. Suriname*, Judgment of 25 November 2015, para. 141; *The Garífuna Punta Piedra Community and its Members v. Honduras*, Judgment of 8 October 2015, para. 326.

99 Either because the state does not frame the restriction in those terms, or the facts of the case do not allow such a framing, or because the Court's reasoning stresses the applicable standard and whether the state met it or not, instead of following a necessity test approach.

100 IACtHR, *The Yakye Axa Indigenous Community v. Paraguay*, Judgment of 17 June 2005, para. 144; *The Saramaka People. v. Suriname*, Judgment of 28 November 2007, paras. 127–128; *The Kichwa Indigenous People of Sarayaku v. Ecuador*, Judgment 27 June 2012, paras. 156–157; *The Xucuru Indigenous People and its Members v. Brazil*, Judgment of 5 February 2017,

Over time, the Court has thereby taken into account the competing rights claims from third parties, who are normally non-indigenous. According to the Court, their private property deserves equal protection under Article 21 ACHR. Therefore, the land claims of indigenous communities have no priority *per se*. It is the state and not the Court that is called on to decide whose property rights are to prevail.[101] Accordingly, in the case of *The Xucuru Indigenous People*, the Court found that the applicants' collective ownership was to prevail over third parties' private property because Brazilian authorities and laws had accorded priority to the former.[102] The Court has also pointed out that existing private property is not a sufficient reason to deny restitution to indigenous peoples. At the same time, it has accepted the provision of alternative lands under certain circumstances, which include evidence that expropriation options have been seriously evaluated.[103] Still, the ultimate fate of the lands does not change the conclusion that when a state grants private titles to disputed lands while knowing of existing indigenous territorial claims, it will likely engage its international responsibility.[104]

Irrespective of the concrete standpoint taken by the judgments in dealing with the above questions, the examples reviewed demonstrate that regard for the situation of other affected rights holders provides a number of relevant insights for the resolution of the cases. For example, the fact that other indigenous or tribal communities could be prejudiced in the enjoyment of their land rights is a factor that may influence not only the reparations orders, but also the scope of the rights to be accorded. It may reshape the rights to delimitation and titling recognised for indigenous peoples (e.g. favouring flexible boundaries and usages, resembling customary practices). It may also lead the Court to apply participatory rights to these or other contested areas so as to secure a fair balance between the rights of the different indigenous communities; or it may provide a reason to defer to local solutions.

At the same time, making these other rights holders (members of other indigenous neighbouring communities) visible also means that their position

para. 125 (yet, the reference to elements of the proportionality test has not always been reflected throughout the Court's reasoning).

101 See e.g. IACtHR, *The Kuna Indigenous Community of Madungandí and the Emberá Indigenous Community of Bayano and their Members*, Judgment of 14 October 2014, para. 144; *The Kaliña and Lokono Peoples v. Suriname*, Judgment of 25 November 2015, para. 156.

102 IACtHR, *The Xucuru Indigenous People and its Members v. Brazil*, Judgment of 5 February 2017, para. 127.

103 IACtHR, *The Yakye Axa Indigenous Community v. Paraguay*, Judgment of 17 June 2005, para. 217; *The Garífuna Punta Piedra Community and its Members v. Honduras*, Judgment of 8 October 2015, paras. 324(d) and 325; *The Kaliña and Lokono Peoples v. Suriname*, Judgment of 25 November 2015, para. 158.

104 IACtHR, *The Kaliña and Lokono Peoples v. Suriname*, Judgment of 25 November 2015, paras. 153–160; *The Garífuna Community of Triunfo de la Cruz and its Members v. Honduras*, Judgment of 8 October 2015, para. 151.

will be distinguished from that of individual private owners or users. For the rights of the latter are not supplemented by any specific regime of rights, nor do they have ties or needs similar to those that indigenous peoples have with their ancestral lands. Nevertheless, the specific characteristics and situation of these third parties may also be a matter for consideration. One such example is whether they are families whose homes and livelihoods are located in the ancestral lands, as in the case of the *Garífuna Punta Piedra Community.*[105] Another is whether the occupation consists instead of holiday homes or hotels owned by private actors, as in *Kaliña and Lokono*,[106] or whether they are national or transnational corporations which have obtained rights to exploit indigenous territories, as in several of the cases reviewed. These are all circumstances that change what is at stake for those actors and thus, the norms that may assist them vary accordingly. In the first example, the families would be protected by, for instance, the right to a home and guarantees against eviction, which would not assist the other third parties. As it transpires from this analysis, regard for rights holders other than the applicant is consistent with an inclusive view of human rights and is helpful for resolving the cases at hand. While the Court has progressively taken heed of those rights holders, it is yet to fully unpack the insights that their integration brings to the adjudication task.

3.3.2. Seeing Collective Rights Holders

Finally, it is important to mention one last category of rights holders considered by the Court. This is the inclusion of indigenous peoples, collectively, among the bearers of Convention rights. Although this is something quite recent whose effects are yet to be clarified, its significance should not be understated. Until the *Sarayaku* case the Court had systematically confined the status of rights holders just to the individual members of indigenous communities. This followed from the wording of Article 1.2 ACHR (Obligation to Respect Rights): 'for the purposes of this Convention, "person" means every human being', which has been traditionally interpreted as referring to individuals. Although Judge Vio Grossi had argued otherwise in his separate opinion in *Xákmok Kásek*,[107]

105 IACtHR, *The Garífuna Punta Piedra Community and its Members v. Honduras*, Judgment of 8 October 2015, paras. 102–104. One of the main issues in this case was actually the community's lack of peaceful enjoyment of their titled lands as a result of the settlement of peasants, on which they had remained in dispute for decades. See paras. 86–110 of the judgment.

106 IACtHR, *The Kaliña and Lokono Peoples v. Suriname*, Judgment of 25 November 2015, para. 147.

107 IACtHR, *The Xákmok Kásek Indigenous Community v. Paraguay*, Judgment of 24 August 2010, Concurring vote of Judge Vío Grossi, para. 26 (arguing for 'a broader understanding of the provisions of Article 1 of the Convention, [reference omitted] so that the obligation to respect and ensure to all persons the exercise of the rights established in the Convention

for the majority of the Court the legal subjectivity remained with the community members. With *Sarayaku* and subsequent judgments, however, the Court appears to have extended legal subjectivity to indigenous communities as groups. The shift features in the context of the interpretation not of Article 1 ACHR, though, but of the notion of 'injured party' contained in Article 63(1) regarding reparations.[108] With a view to awarding reparations, the Court has since affirmed that the indigenous peoples concerned *and* their members are both to be considered the injured party.[109] Since an injured party is anyone who has been declared a victim of the violation of any right recognised in the Convention, it follows that only those who are holders of Convention rights can be an injured party.

If there was any doubt as to whether the above remarks actually amount to recognition of indigenous communities as collective bearers of Convention rights, this was recently clarified in an Advisory Opinion issued at the request of Panama.[110] This state asked the Court whether legal persons or non-governmental entities legally recognised could be considered persons under Article 1.2 ACHR for the purposes of submitting allegations of violations and exhausting domestic remedies. One of the issues of special interest in this regard was the situation of indigenous communities. In its response, the Court 'reiterates that it has already recognised indigenous and tribal communities as rights holders by virtue of the current evolution of international law on the matter'.[111] These communities, 'because of the particular situation in which they find themselves', must be regarded as holders of certain human rights, that is,

---

would also include the collectivities or communities, such as the indigenous peoples, to the extent that at least some of these rights extend to these entities. Rights that, consequently, the members may only enjoy and exercise through the collectivity and because they form part of it, which, all things considered, would imply that such rights are not merely of an individual nature.').

108 Article 63(1) ACHR reads as follows: 'If the Court finds that there has been a violation of a right or freedom protected by this Convention, the Court shall rule that the injured party be ensured the enjoyment of his right or freedom that was violated. It shall also rule, if appropriate, that the consequences of the measure or situation that constituted the breach of such right or freedom be remedied and that fair compensation be paid to the injured party.'

109 IACtHR, *The Kichwa Indigenous People of Sarayaku v. Ecuador*, Judgment of 27 June 2012, para. 231; *The Kuna Indigenous Community of Madungandí and the Emberá Indigenous Community of Bayano and their Members*, Judgment of 14 October 2014, para. 209; *The Kaliña and Lokono Peoples v. Suriname*, Judgment of 25 November 2015, para. 273 (emphasis added).

110 IACtHR, Advisory Opinion OC-22/16 on the Entitlement of legal entities to hold rights under the Inter-American human rights system (Interpretation and scope of Article 1(2), in relation to Articles 1(2), 8, 11(2), 13, 16, 21, 24, 25, 29, 30, 44, 46 and 62(3) of the American Convention on Human Rights, as well as of Article 8(1)(A) and (B) of the Protocol of San Salvador), Adopted on 26 February 2016.

111 Ibid., para. 82 (author's translation – no official English version available at the time of writing).

those whose enjoyment is necessarily collective.[112] They can therefore directly resort to the Inter-American system without it being necessary to individualise each of their members.[113] According this status to collective subjects such as indigenous communities represents an outstanding enlargement of the range of rights holders thus far acknowledged by the Court, and by international monitoring bodies in general. This is one of the most remarkable aspects of the integrated perspective to rights holders developed by the Court in the case law studied here.

But an integrated view of human rights law is not only about rights holders, as already noted in the previous chapters. It is also about the way one thinks of the harms and norms involved in any given case. For present purposes, it is submitted that approaching these in an interconnected – or more holistic – fashion may provide valuable insights for the handling of cases dealing with issues of cultural difference and inclusion. This is analysed below.

4. INTEGRATED RIGHTS: CROSS-THINKING ABOUT HARMS AND NORMS

4.1. INTEGRATING REDISTRIBUTION AND STRUCTURAL ISSUES TO RECOGNITION WRONGS

Since culture has been the main catalyser of the Court's adjudication in indigenous and Afro-descendant cases, it is not surprising that cultural harms hold special salience in its normative analyses. The Court has identified a broad range of 'recognition' issues: from injuries resulting from discriminatory treatment based on ethnic identity and national origin or migration status,[114] to a lack of recognition of legal personality,[115] and threats to the preservation of cultural practices, rituals and other elements.[116] While the Court's analysis

112 Ibid., para. 83 (author's translation – no official English version available at the time of writing).

113 Ibid., para. 84.

114 IACtHR, *López Álvarez v. Honduras*, Judgment of 1 February 2006, paras. 169–173; *The Girls Yean and Bosico v. Dominican Republic*, Judgment of 8 September 2005, paras. 152–168; *The Xákmok Kásek Indigenous Community v. Paraguay*, Judgment of 24 August 2010, paras. 273–274 (although no discrimination ground was indicated in this last case).

115 See e.g. IACtHR, *The Saramaka People v. Suriname*, Judgment of 28 November 2007, paras. 169–175.

116 See e.g. IACtHR, *The Xákmok Kásek Indigenous Community v. Paraguay*, Judgment of 24 August 2010, paras. 174–182; *The Kichwa Indigenous People of Sarayaku v. Ecuador*, Judgment of 27 June 2012, paras. 218–219. For a general overview of cultural-identity harms examined by the Court, see Marco Odello, 'Indigenous peoples' rights and cultural identity in the Inter-American context', 16(1) *The International Journal of Human Rights* (2012) 25, at 35–40.

of identity-related harms has striven to cater for the concerns of the applicants, it is clear that they did not exhaust the range of relevant grievances. Economic suffering was explicitly denounced by reference to public and private instances of land dispossession and exploitation.[117] Likewise, where investment projects on ancestral lands were accepted without the meaningful participation of the communities concerned, political marginalisation was involved. As previously explained in the context of the European Court, the aim of this section is to explore whether and how the Inter-American Court integrated those harms into its analysis. Thereafter, the discussion will turn to the way this integration (or lack thereof) shaped the Court's normative assessment of the cases.

4.1.1. *Indivisibility or Invisibility in Cases of Ethno-Cultural Difference*

Faced with a jurisprudence marked by questions of cultural recognition, to what extent has the Court accounted for what can be called 'redistribution' harms? In cases dealing with land claims, the Court has generally shown awareness of these harms. It has done so through two main avenues: its reparations awards and its merit analysis of violations of Article 4 ACHR (right to life). In terms of reparations, the Court has repeatedly ordered the state to return land, to grant titles and to ensure the communities' effective enjoyment of the land and its resources. The Court has also requested the implementation of development funds and, in cases of economic exploitation of indigenous territories, a reasonable sharing of benefits has been imposed. All of these measures certainly cater for the redistribution harms experienced by the applicants.

But while the socio-economic drive of reparations has been a constant, the socio-economic import of the Court's analysis on the merits has been uneven. For the case law prior to 2009, a likely explanation for this is that the Court found itself lacking contentious jurisdiction over socio-economic rights others than those for which the Additional Protocol to the American Convention on Human Rights in the Area of Economic, Social and Cultural Rights (hereinafter, 'the Protocol of San Salvador') explicitly granted it competence. These are Articles 8.1(a) and 13, which protect, respectively, the right to unionise and the right to education.[118] In this reading, Article 26 ACHR (on the progressive

117 The applicants in *Yakye Axa* put it in the following terms: '[…] protection of the right to life and integrity of the indigenous peoples cannot be disassociated from protection of economic, social, and cultural rights. Guaranteeing said rights is a necessary condition to comply with the requirement of decent living conditions, without which it is difficult, if not impossible, to develop flourishing life aspirations.' See IACtHR, *The Yakye Axa Indigenous Community v. Paraguay*, Judgment of 17 June 2005, para. 158 (f).

118 Additional Protocol to the American Convention on Human Rights in the Area of Economic, Social and Cultural Rights, 17 November 1988, entered into force 16 November 1999

development of economic, social and cultural rights) was supposedly not justiciable before the Court.[119]

Thus, in the 2005 case of *Yean and Bosico*, a core part of the case was that the girls were denied their right to education as a result of discriminatory practices that prevented them from obtaining the birth certificates required for their school enrolment. The applicants invoked Article 26 ACHR in their petition[120] (since the Dominican Republic was not a party to the Protocol of San Salvador). For the purposes of awarding compensation, the Court noted the harm caused to the girls by depriving them of the opportunity to access education.[121] In the merits analysis, however, the impairment of the girls' education was a side consideration in the context of the right to juridical personality (Article 3) and the right to a name (Article 18) ACHR. In this regard, Article 26 was taken in conjunction with Article 19 on children's rights for hermeneutic purposes only. Melish criticises the Court's decision in this case not to examine the violation of the right to education under Article 26 ACHR. She argues that this stance has a concrete adverse effect, namely, that while the Court required the reform of the procedures for the granting of birth certificates, 'it was silent on the necessary reforms to the regulatory norms governing public school registration'.[122] Similarly, when ruling on the indigenous land cases of *Yakye Axa* and *Xákmok Kásek*, the Court made an interpretative reference to a number of socio-economic rights enshrined in the Protocol of San Salvador (which are further analysed below).

('Protocol of San Salvador'). Article 19 (Means of protection) para. 6 reads: '6. Any instance in which the rights established in paragraph a) of Article 8 and in Article 13 are violated by action directly attributable to a State Party to this Protocol may give rise, through participation of the Inter-American Commission on Human Rights and, when applicable, of the Inter-American Court of Human Rights, to application of the system of individual petitions governed by Article 44 through 51 and 61 through 69 of the American Convention on Human Rights.'

119 As seen later, this is no longer the case for the Court has affirmed its competence to rule on the social rights protected by Article 26 ACHR. Prior to 2017, however, this was debated. For an argument in favour of the justiciability of Article 26 and for transcending the view of differentiated standards of review, see Tara Melish, 'The Inter-American Court of Human Rights. Beyond Progressivity', in Malcolm Langford, *Social Rights Jurisprudence: Emerging Trends in Comparative and International Law* (Cambridge University Press, 2008), at 24–29 and 61–65. For arguments against the justiciability of Article 26 ACHR, see Oswaldo Ruiz Chiriboga, 'The American Convention and the Protocol of San Salvador: Two Intertwined Treaties: Non-Enforceability of Economic, Social and Cultural Rights in the Inter-American System', 31(2) *Netherlands Quarterly of Human Rights* (2013) 159.

120 IACtHR, *The Girls Yean and Bosico v. Dominican Republic*, Judgment of 8 September 2005, para. 115 (b).

121 Ibid., para. 244.

122 Tara Melish, 'The Inter-American Commission on Human Rights. Defending Social Rights Through Case-Based Petitions', in Malcolm Langford (ed.), *Social Rights Jurisprudence: Emerging Trends in Comparative and International Law* (Cambridge University Press, 2008), at 406.

However, in 2009 the Court issued a first judgment (unrelated to indigenous peoples) affirming its jurisdiction over all provisions in the ACHR, including Article 26.[123] This arguably placed the Court in a position to examine allegations of violations of socio-economic rights on the basis of Article 26. Still, the Court remained rather reluctant to take this path in post-2009 land cases brought by indigenous peoples. In the case of *Sarayaku*, the applicants alleged a violation of Article 26 as well as of Article 23 (political rights) ACHR. The Court, however, refused to rule on those provisions and held that the alleged violations had been sufficiently analysed under the rights to communal property, consultation and cultural identity under Article 21 ACHR.[124] As will be seen in Chapter 5 the scope of application of Article 26 ACHR has been widely debated within the Court. Yet, very recent judgments unrelated to indigenous rights have eventually inclined the scale in favour of the justiciability of Article 26, which has thereby been applied by the Court.[125] It is therefore expected that future cases concerning indigenous and tribal people will have social rights claims adjudicated.

Thus, in the context of its merits analysis, Article 4 ACHR (right to life) emerged as the clearest pathway for indirectly capturing the socio-economic grievances complained of by indigenous and tribal communities and their members. But this route has only been taken in three collective land cases. These are *Yakye Axa*, *Sawhoyamaxa* and *Xákmok Kásek*, all of them involving indigenous communities from the Paraguayan Chaco. These cases were already introduced *supra* (section 3.1) and their factual circumstances were quite similar. Basically, indigenous communities of hundreds of people were either living on public roads or confined in a small part of their territory while awaiting the outcome of the proceedings they had initiated to reclaim their ancestral lands. Deprived of their lands and of their traditional means of subsistence, they all lived in extreme destitution and without access to the most basic services. The applicants alleged that members of the community had even died as a result. Besides the right to property, the Court examined the three cases under the right to life (Article 4 ACHR) reinterpreted as a right to dignified life or *vida digna*.[126]

---

123 IACtHR, *Acevedo Buendía et al. ('Discharged and Retired Employees of the Comptroller') v. Peru*, Judgment of 1 July 2009, paras. 19 and 92–106.

124 IACtHR, *The Kichwa Indigenous People of Sarayaku v. Ecuador*, Judgment of 27 June 2012, para. 230.

125 See IACtHR, *Lagos del Campo v. Peru*, Judgment of 31 August 2017; *Cuscul Pivaral et al. v. Guatemala*, Judgment of 23 August 2018; and *Muelle Flores v. Peru*, Judgment of 6 March 2019.

126 The provision (Article 4 ACHR) does not say anything about dignity. The relevant paragraph states: 'Every person has the right to have his life respected. This right shall be protected by law and, in general, from the moment of conception. No one shall be arbitrarily deprived of his life.'

In *Yakye Axa*, the Court argued that states were bound to 'generating minimum living conditions that are compatible with the dignity of the human person [...] [avoiding] creating conditions that hinder or impede it'.[127] Positive and concrete measures were required to fulfil this obligation, giving priority to those most vulnerable and at risk. Within this framework, the Court examined the applicant's lack of access to food, health, housing, water, sanitation and education.[128] Further, it connected these deprivations with a threat to the applicant's worldview and cultural identity.[129] The Court implied the unsuitability of the alternatives for relocation offered by the state and concluded that the latter had failed to undertake measures to correct the conditions preventing the community members from having a decent life.[130] In *Sawhoyamaxa*, the Court not only addressed the poor living conditions of the applicants (malnutrition, lack of medical care and of drinking water, etc.), but also accorded responsibility to the state for not preventing or avoiding the death of some community members, despite having been aware of the risks they were facing.[131]

The Court returned to the dignified life analysis in *Xákmok Kásek*. Here, the Court even provided a detailed account of minimum standards regarding water, food, health and education. These it translated as well into reparation measures consisting of the provision of goods and basic services.[132] The Court stressed that the lack of access to the community's traditional lands 'has led them to depend almost exclusively on State actions and be forced to live not only in a way that is different from their cultural patterns, but in squalor'.[133] The IACtHR also referred to the UN Committee on Economic Social and Cultural Rights' view on how poverty restricts the ability of individuals and groups to access and contribute to cultural life and enjoy their own culture.[134] Thus, even if only by focusing on minimum deliverables, the notion of *vida digna* proved to be a valuable avenue for capturing the socio-economic stakes of the cases.

---

127 IACtHR, *The Yakye Axa Indigenous Community v. Paraguay*, Judgment of 17 June 2005, para. 162.

128 Ibid., para. 163.

129 Ibid., para. 167. The Court noted that 'detriment to the right to health, and closely tied to this, detriment to the right to food and access to clean water, have a major impact on the right to a decent existence and basic conditions to exercise other human rights, such as the right to education or the right to cultural identity'.

130 Ibid., paras. 170–176.

131 IACtHR, *The Sawhoyamaxa Indigenous Community v. Paraguay*, Judgment of 29 March 2006, paras. 170–178.

132 IACtHR, *The Xákmok Kásek Indigenous Community v. Paraguay*, Judgment of 24 August 2010, para. 300.

133 Ibid., para. 115.

134 Ibid., para. 216; CESCR, General Comment No. 21: Right of everyone to take part in cultural life (Article 15, para. 1a of the Covenant on Economic, Social and Cultural Rights), E/C.12/GC/21, 21 December 2009, para. 38.

Also interesting about this approach is that it seems to integrate economic considerations without displacing cultural identity concerns. This is consistent with the premise that what a dignified existence requires necessarily varies across people, place and time.

Overall then, the Court has engaged with the socio-economic rights and structural issues involved in the cases more through its remedial orders than through its merits analysis. Moreover, while the Court has aptly used Article 4 ACHR – in a few cases – as a vehicle to reinforce the indivisibility of rights, the underutilisation of Article 26 ACHR that prevailed until recently, a normative basis which supposedly enables the Court to enforce socio-economic rights directly, could have brought more invisibility than indivisibility. As will be seen in the subsections below, other kinds of wrong have also found limited visibility in the Court's case law on indigenous communities.

4.1.2. Structural Inequalities and Non-Discrimination Clauses

Another potential avenue for tackling structural inequalities affecting indigenous and other communities regarded as culturally different, as argued for the cases studied, is the use of Articles 1.1 and 24 ACHR. These contain, respectively, a prohibition of discrimination in the enjoyment of Convention rights and a right to equal protection of the law that extends beyond Convention provisions.[135] The relevance of these provisions for the cases discussed is aptly reflected in the words of Anaya. As he explains, 'the right of indigenous peoples to maintain the integrity of their cultures is a simple matter of equality, of being free from historical and ongoing practices that have treated indigenous cultures as inferior to the dominant cultures'.[136] While the Court has viewed the experience of indigenous/Afro-descendant people from the perspective of patterns of discrimination and social inequality in individual cases,[137] that has been rare in its collective-oriented judgments. Nor have

135 Article 1(1) ACHR provides: 'The States Parties to this Convention undertake to respect the rights and freedoms recognized herein and to ensure to all persons subject to their jurisdiction the free and full exercise of those rights and freedoms, without any discrimination for reasons of race, color, sex, language, religion, political or other opinion, national or social origin, economic status, birth, or any other social condition.' Article 24 ACHR reads: 'All persons are equal before the law. Consequently, they are entitled, without discrimination, to equal protection of the law.'

136 See James Anaya, 'International Human Rights and Indigenous Peoples: The Move Toward the Multicultural State', 21 *Arizona Journal of International & Comparative Law* (2004) 13, at 16.

137 Besides the cases of *Yean and Bosico* and *López Alvarez* discussed above (IACtHR, *The Girls Yean and Bosico v. Dominican Republic*, Judgment of 8 September 2005, paras. 134–168; *López Álvarez v. Honduras*, Judgment of 1 February 2006, paras. 169–173), findings of discrimination in individual indigenous cases have notably been made with regard to denials of justice following acts of violence. See e.g. IACtHR, *Fernández Ortega et al. v. Mexico*,

applicants in such cases, at least until recently, frequently articulated their claims in terms of racial or other forms of discrimination.

Back in *Awas Tingni*, the Commission claimed, among other things, that 'non-recognition of the equality of property rights based on indigenous tradition is contrary to the principle of non-discrimination set forth in article 1(1) of the Convention'.[138] The Court, however, did not follow this road. Instead, as already mentioned, it elaborated on the need to protect the special cultural ties between indigenous communities and their ancestral lands. The communitarian tradition sustaining that relationship was recognised by the Court within the framework of Article 21 alone, a conclusion supported by reference to the Nicaraguan Constitution and indigenous customary laws.[139] The equality concern nonetheless resurfaced in the concurring vote of Judge García Ramírez. In his view, denying other ways of using and enjoying property would create inequality for millions of people, who would be left unprotected by the Convention.[140] A few years later, the Court did endorse an egalitarian approach to the indigenous claims raised in *Yakye Axa*, albeit only as a matter of 'prior considerations'.[141] In this context, the Court held that states must ensure, on an equal basis, full exercise and enjoyment of the rights of indigenous people. To do so, states 'must take into account the specific characteristics that differentiate the members of the indigenous peoples from the general population and that constitute their cultural identity'.[142] The Court furthermore bound itself to the same commitment for the purposes of interpreting and applying the Convention.[143]

The equality dimension was eventually incorporated into the analysis of the merits in the *Sawhoyamaxa* case, where the Court followed Judge García Ramírez's opinion in *Awas Tingni*. The Court, acknowledging that the communal property of indigenous peoples 'does not necessarily conform to the classic concept of property', asserted that this deserved equal protection under

---

Judgment of 30 August 2010, paras. 200–201; *Rosendo Cantú and other v. Mexico*, Judgment of 31 August 2010, paras. 184–185 (finding discrimination in their access to justice for lack of an interpreter who could assist them in presenting their criminal complaint and participate in the proceedings). In a similar vein, but in the context of reparation orders, see IACtHR, *Tiu Tojín v. Guatemala*, Judgment of 26 November 2008, paras. 92–100 (regarding obstacles to accessing justice faced by members of the Maya Ixil indigenous people, who sought justice for the enforced disappearance of their next of kin).

138 IACtHR, *The Mayagna (Sumo) Awas Tingni Community v. Nicaragua*, Judgment of 31 August 2001, para. 140 (b).

139 On the integration of extra conventional norms, see *infra* section 4.2.

140 IACtHR, *The Mayagna (Sumo) Awas Tingni Community v. Nicaragua*, Judgment of 31 August 2001, Concurring vote of Judge García Ramírez, para. 13.

141 IACtHR, *The Yakye Axa Indigenous Community v. Paraguay*, Judgment of 17 June 2005, para. 51.

142 Idem.

143 Idem.

Article 21 ACHR.[144] Why? The Court not only pointed to the cultural protection grounds advanced in previous cases. This time, it added egalitarian reasons to the equation:

> Disregard for specific versions of use and enjoyment of property, springing from the culture, uses, customs, and beliefs of each people, would be tantamount to holding that there is only one way of using and disposing of property, which, in turn, would render protection under Article 21 of the Convention illusory for millions of persons.[145]

In other words, if the protection afforded by the ACHR was to be equally effective and meaningful to everyone, a collective reading of the right to property needed to be accepted. Doing otherwise would make indigenous peoples – and potentially other persons and communities – less equal in rights. This is reinforced by the fact that it is hard to decouple the struggles of indigenous and Afro-descendant individuals and groups from longstanding forms of racial discrimination in the Americas.[146]

But equality and discrimination arguments have not travelled one way only. They have given rise to competing claims from states. Typically, the argument posits that securing the communal property rights of indigenous and tribal peoples would raise issues of discrimination for the rest of the population.[147] The Court has found this claim to be without merit. In *Saramaka*, referring to, for example, the ECtHR case of *Connors v. United Kingdom* discussed in Chapter 2, the Court held that 'unequal treatment towards persons in unequal situations does not necessarily amount to impermissible discrimination. Legislation that recognises said differences is therefore not necessarily discriminatory.'[148] The Court went further and asserted that equality sometimes requires differentiated treatment. It then recalled that 'special measures are necessary … in order to ensure [for indigenous and tribal peoples] their survival in accordance with their traditions and customs'.[149] The Court's use of the term 'special measures'

---

144 IACtHR, *The Sawhoyamaxa Indigenous Community v. Paraguay*, Judgment of 29 March 2006, para. 120.

145 Idem.

146 See e.g. Rodolfo Stavenhagen, *Peasants, Culture and Indigenous Peoples – Critical Issues* (Springer, 2013), at 58–59 and 74–79. In some cases submitted to the Court, the Commission has argued that racism or racial discrimination is at the root of the violations, but this has been argued more often with regard to Afro-descendants than to indigenous applicants. See, *inter alia*, IACtHR, *Aloeboetoe et al. v. Suriname*, Judgment of 10 September 1993, paras. 83–83; *The Afro-descendant communities displaced from the Cacarica River Basin (Operation Genesis) v. Colombia*, Judgment of 20 November 2013, para. 335; *Expelled Dominicans and Haitians v. Dominican Republic*, Judgment of 28 August 2014, para. 399.

147 IACtHR, *The Saramaka People v. Suriname*, Judgment of 28 November 2007, para. 99.

148 Ibid., para. 103.

149 Idem.

within the framework of equality reasoning, however, does not seem to mean temporary measures aimed at achieving *de facto* equality for structurally discriminated groups, in a way similar to affirmative action.[150] The reference appears, rather, to point to the positive steps that states should adopt to ensure that all human rights are effectively enjoyed by indigenous people, for which their particularities need to be taken into account.[151]

In spite of its egalitarian reflections, the Court has rarely examined a violation of equality and non-discrimination provisions in indigenous land cases. Only in the aforementioned case of *Xákmok Kásek* did the Court find such a violation, partly echoing the pleadings of the Commission and the representatives in that case. The Court emphasised that states must refrain from creating, even if indirectly, situations of *de jure* or *de facto* discrimination. Furthermore, they are under an obligation to 'adopt positive measures to reverse or change discriminatory situations that exist in their societies and that prejudice a specific group of people'.[152] For the Court, the situation of extreme vulnerability experienced by the community and the lack of institutional support and of socio-economic services in the area, alongside a system of ownership which privileged the rights of private owners over those of indigenous communities, revealed *de facto* discrimination (although no discrimination ground was specified).[153] Nevertheless, the interpretation did not last. In the 2014 case of the *Kuna and Emberá Indigenous People*, in a style reminiscent of its European counterpart, the IACtHR declined to pronounce on a similar allegation of violation of the right to equality under the law (Article 24 ACHR) and referred instead to its findings under the right to property and judicial protection.[154] It should be noted that the Commission has also asserted racial

150 On the difference between 'special measures' which resemble affirmative action and other types of positive measures for ensuring human rights, see e.g. CEDAW Committee, General Recommendation No. 25: Article 4, paragraph 1 of the Convention (temporary special measures), 18 August 2004, para. 19. 'The provision of general conditions in order to guarantee the civil, political, economic, social and cultural rights of women and the girl child, designed to ensure for them a life of dignity and non-discrimination, cannot be called temporary special measures.'

151 See, for example, the Court's references to 'special measures' in IACtHR, *The Saramaka People v. Suriname*, Judgment of 28 November 2007, paras. 91, 96, 103 and 172.

152 IACtHR, *The Xákmok Kásek Indigenous Community v. Paraguay*, Judgment of 24 August 2010, para. 271.

153 Ibid., paras. 273–275.

154 IACtHR, *The Kuna Indigenous People of Madungandí and the Emberá Indigenous People of Bayano and their Members v. Panama*, Judgment of 14 October 2014, paras. 203–204. Previously, in the *Operation Genesis* case the Court dismissed the examination of the equality and non-discrimination claims made by the applicants and the Commission. See IACtHR, *The Afro-descendant communities displaced from the Cacarica River Basin (Operation Genesis) v. Colombia*, Judgment of 20 November 2013, paras. 307–312 and 337.

discrimination in collective-oriented indigenous cases related to widespread acts of persecution and violence. However, the Court has not found itself in a position to agree with that (either because of material competence or because of lack of substantiation).[155]

Could collective complaints of land destitution and marginalisation that are currently discussed under the cultural frame of property be instead or in addition addressed through the equality and non-discrimination clauses? If Articles 1.1 and 24 ACHR were read from a classical formal comparator perspective, those rights claims could barely be translated into the language of discrimination. A normative approach along the lines of substantive equality, however, could be suited to the task. Recall that substantive equality, inasmuch as it is concerned with social context and with challenging subordination, may require difference to be accommodated, disadvantage to be redressed and institutions to be transformed.[156] This makes the underutilisation of equality arguments more intriguing in this context since, as noted earlier, the Inter-American Court has enthusiastically embraced a structural conception of equality.[157]

To the extent that this analysis is left underexplored, some opportunities could be missed. Notably, the equality prism might serve to capture an important part of the harm experienced by indigenous communities and their members which is not necessarily reflected in the protection of their culture or in the reparations awards, that is, harm related to structural inequality and racism. From another perspective, this line of reasoning could further clarify the reasons for and the limits of cultural accommodation within and beyond indigenous people's cases. The idea that some cultural practices should be respected and protected because doing otherwise would lead to exclusion and to further discrimination enriches significantly the legal discourse on cultural identity. It also decreases the risk of attributing both the problems and the solutions debated in these cases to any group or culture. The jurisprudence examined thus far suggests that the Court has been in a position to moving in that direction, and has actually done so to some extent. Yet, the integration of this normative approach remains elusive for land-related cases.

This attests to the importance of reviewing the comprehensiveness of the normative spectrum used by the Court to rule in ethno-cultural diversity cases. The following section aims at further problematising this matter.

---

155 IACtHR, *The Members of the village of Chichupac and neighboring communities of the Municipality of Rabinal v. Guatemala*, Judgment of 30 November 2016, paras. 206–207, 250 and 258.

156 For a discussion of substantive equality, see Chapter 1, section 4. 4.

157 See *supra* section 3.1.3, and references therein.

4.2. AVOIDING NORM REDUCTIONISM AND PROMOTING AWARENESS OF LEGAL PLURALISM

How rich was the Court's normative repertoire in the cases studied? As with the European Court, this question will be approached from the perspective of Convention and extra-Convention norms. From the perspective of the ACHR, it is convenient to distinguish again between cases brought by individuals and those litigated mainly on behalf of indigenous/Afro-descendant communities. In the latter, the range of Convention norms addressed by the Court appears to have been more limited.

4.2.1. A More Comprehensive Approach to Convention Norms

It is clear by now that the entry point for litigating cases dealing with the collective territorial claims of indigenous and Afro-descendant people has been Article 21 ACHR (right to property reconceptualised in the light of indigenous cultural identity). What is more, this is the normative umbrella under which the Court has addressed manifold rights allegations. This does not mean downplaying the examination frequently conducted by the Court from the viewpoint of Articles 8 and 25 ACHR (the rights to a fair trial and to an effective remedy, respectively).[158] Through these procedural provisions the Court has grappled with the general absence or inefficacy of domestic avenues for indigenous people(s) to seek land restitution and redress. Yet, the bulk of the substantive claims put forward by indigenous and Afro-descendant people(s) have fallen under Article 21 ACHR. Thus, similarly to the European case law discussed earlier, here too one Convention provision has become the protagonist of normatively complex cases.

The difficulties associated with a cultural frame have already been explored in the previous sections, so there is no need to restate them here. The centrality of the right to property, however, deserves a few words. Antkowiak draws attention to the pitfalls of a normative analysis reduced to property rights. In his view, in the current state of affairs this is a weak basis for protecting indigenous peoples.[159] He points to three main weaknesses. The first is the structure of the right itself: Article 21 ACHR authorises property deprivation and interference under a wide variety of circumstances. Secondly, other property-related cases (not concerning indigenous peoples) reveal a loose interpretation of the

[158] And where such judicial or administrative proceedings are available, these are often too long and burdensome.

[159] Thomas M. Antkowiak, 'Rights, resources, and rhetoric: indigenous peoples and the Inter-American Court', 35 *University of Pennsylvania Journal of International Law* (2013) 113, at 163.

legitimate conditions for restricting the right.[160] Finally, the author views the right to property as a framework that favours a 'minimalist' approach to the safeguards owed to indigenous peoples, one limited to ensuring their cultural and physical survival.[161]

What about other Convention provisions, then? The subsection above reviewed the normative roads not yet taken, or timidly explored, by the Court in indigenous collective cases. One is Article 26 ACHR on the progressive development of economic, social and cultural rights. The other is Article 1.1 and Article 24 on the right to equality and the prohibition of discrimination. It should be recalled, though, that the Court has tried out other normative frameworks in indigenous land cases.

One outstanding example, not least because of its multidimensional character, is the right to life (Article 4 ACHR), cast as dignified life (*vida digna*). As previously discussed, this normative construction enabled the Court to integrate both cultural and socio-economic harms and look beyond issues of traditional practices.[162] In addition, one may note the recent integration of the right to political participation (Article 23) into the Court's analysis,[163] a development that was preceded by the assertion of the indigenous communities' right to have their collective juridical personality recognised (under Article 3 ACHR).[164] In *Kaliña and Lokono v. Suriname*, the Court incorporated Article 23 by virtue of the *iura novit curia* principle to examine the exclusion of the applicants from the management of the nature reserves located in their ancestral territories.[165] The Court not only noted Suriname's

---

160 The case referenced by the author in this regard is IACtHR, *Salvador Chiriboga v. Ecuador*, Judgment of 6 May 2008, paras. 65–66.

161 Thomas M. Antkowiak, 'Rights, resources, and rhetoric: indigenous peoples and the Inter-American Court', 35 *University of Pennsylvania Journal of International Law* (2013) 113, at 163–171.

162 Also in this vein, see ibid., at 180–185.

163 Article 23 ACHR reads as follows:
Right to Participate in Government:
1. Every citizen shall enjoy the following rights and opportunities: a) to take part in the conduct of public affairs, directly or through freely chosen representatives; b) to vote and to be elected in genuine periodic elections, which shall be by universal and equal suffrage and by secret ballot that guarantees the free expression of the will of the voters; and c) to have access, under general conditions of equality, to the public service of his country.
2. The law may regulate the exercise of the rights and opportunities referred to in the preceding paragraph only on the basis of age, nationality, residence, language, education, civil and mental capacity, or sentencing by a competent court in criminal proceedings.

In its judgment the Court focuses on Article 23.1(a).

164 Article 3 ACHR reads: 'Every person has the right to recognition as a person before the law.' See IACtHR, *The Saramaka People v. Suriname*, Judgment of 28 November 2007, paras. 173–174; *The Kaliña and Lokono Peoples v. Suriname*, Judgment of 25 November 2015, paras. 107–109 and 114.

165 IACtHR, *The Kaliña and Lokono Peoples v. Suriname*, Judgment of 25 November 2015, para. 126.

continued failure to recognise indigenous collective land rights. It also found that the state had granted land titles to non-indigenous people, established three nature reserves and allowed mining on the *Kaliña* and *Lokono* ancestral territory. The Court justified the application of Article 23 in the following terms:

> the participation of the indigenous communities in the conservation of the environment is not only a matter of public interest, but also part of the exercise of their right as indigenous peoples "to participate in decision-making in matters which would affect their rights, [...] in accordance with their own procedures and [...] institutions".[166]

Article 23 thereby seems to come closer to the vindications of political autonomy usually made under the still contested right to self-determination,[167] albeit not without opposition.[168] The Court did not go as far, though. The violation finding was a procedural one. For the Court, 'no violation has been constituted by the lack of exclusive management and monitoring of the nature reserves by the indigenous peoples'.[169] A violation arose, however, from 'the absence of explicit mechanisms that guarantee the access, use and effective participation of the *Kaliña and Lokono* indigenous peoples in the conservation of the said nature reserves and the benefits these reserves yield'.[170] Still, this represents an interesting enlargement of the Court's normative sight. In fact, when indigenous peoples were concerned, the participation rights enshrined in Article 23 had been either absent or narrowly applied. At first, they had only been applied to restrictions on political participation *sensu stricto*, i.e. the impossibility of running for election in *Yatama v. Nicaragua*. And later, in *Sarayaku*, the Court refused to examine separately an allegation of violation of Article 23 in relation to their lack of participation in matters that affected the indigenous community.[171]

---

166 Ibid., para. 196.

167 Some aspects of the political and economic dimensions of the right to self-determination of indigenous peoples have been particularly subject to debate. As regards 'external' political autonomy, see e.g. Karen Engle, 'On Fragile Architecture: The UN Declaration on the Rights of Indigenous Peoples in the Context of Human Rights', 22 *European Journal of International Law* (2011) 141, at 152–157 (also noting at 148–149 that the discourse of cultural rights meant a displacement of self-determination). As regards challenges to the economic dimension of self-autonomy, see Alice Farmer, 'Towards a Meaningful Rebirth of Economic Self-Determination: Human Rights Realization in Resource-Rich Countries', 39 *International Law and Politics* (2006) 417; Stefaan Smis *et al.*, 'The Question of Land Grab in Africa and The Indigenous Peoples' Right to Traditional Lands, Territories and Resources', 35 *Loyola of Los Angeles International and Comparative Law Review* (2013) 493, at 514–515.

168 IACtHR, *The Kaliña and Lokono Peoples v. Suriname*, Judgment of 25 November 2015, dissenting opinion of Judge Pérez Pérez, paras. 17–23.

169 Ibid., para. 197.

170 Idem.

171 IACtHR, *The Kichwa Indigenous People of Sarayaku v. Ecuador*, Judgment of 27 June 2012, paras. 123 and 230.

The participation mechanisms protected on the basis of Article 23, as applied in *Kaliña and Lokono*, were directly linked with the right of indigenous people to prior informed consultation,[172] until then recognised on the grounds of the right to property (Article 21). The relevance of this normative move goes beyond legal technicalities. Grounding the right to consultation in the right to political participation enshrined in Article 23 may have important practical effects for indigenous communities and for other people. For indigenous communities and their members, such interpretation could provide a stronger basis for participation rights (including prior informed consultation or even consent) in the face of the weaknesses of Article 21 identified by Antkowiak. Of note, the effective participation of indigenous communities would no longer be confined to development projects affecting their (cultural) way of life within their ancestral territories. For groups and individuals other than indigenous people, in turn, the above reading of Article 23 could actually allow them to benefit from a right to consultation on matters that may affect them. This would mean, in other words, opening up consultation-like rights to potentially all kinds of people whose rights could be undermined by intrusive public or private projects, at least under certain conditions.

But if the Court's normative repertoire has been, at least for a while, relatively limited when it comes to the Convention rights applied in ethno-cultural difference cases, the opposite occurs with extra-Convention norms. The readiness of the Inter-American Court to resort to and use a wide range of 'external' norms to respond to ethno-cultural claims is perhaps one of the best-known features of this line of case law. Now it is time to elaborate on this point. How the Court justifies this practice, which weight it accords to extra-Convention laws and what problems and opportunities arise along the way are some of the questions explored below.

4.2.2. Integrating Domestic and International Norms through the Living Instrument and the Pro-Personae Principles

The *Awas Tingni* judgment, the first to address indigenous culturally motivated claims on the merits, yielded the basis of the Court's innovative interpretation of Article 21 ACHR. These are the living instrument doctrine and the *pro-personae* principle.[173] In *Awas Tingni v. Nicaragua*, the Court started by

172 IACtHR, *The Kaliña and Lokono Peoples v. Suriname*, Judgment of 25 November 2015, paras. 202–212.

173 This is also commonly known as the '*pro homine*' principle. The term '*pro personae*' is, however, preferred here as it represents a more gender-inclusive use of language. The principle appears to materialise the mandate set forth in Article 31(1) of the Vienna Convention, which requires that the object and purpose of the treaties be considered when interpreting them. Human rights treaties aim at the protection of individuals. Accordingly, the Court should

recalling that the drafters of the Convention decided to refer to the 'use and enjoyment of his property' instead of 'private property'.[174] Then it went on to hold that 'human rights treaties are *living instruments* whose interpretation must adapt to the evolution of the times and, specifically, to current living conditions'.[175] Importantly, the Court relied on Article 29(b) of the Convention. Pursuant to this, 'no provision may be interpreted as restricting the enjoyment or exercise of any right or freedom recognized by virtue of the laws of any State Party or by virtue of another convention to which one of the said states is a party'.[176] That is, the interpretation of human rights provisions had to be *pro-personae*. Nicaragua was not a party to ILO Convention No. 169 at the time and the United Nations Declaration on the Rights of Indigenous Peoples had not yet been adopted. The Court referred, however, to the Constitution of Nicaragua, which explicitly recognised the communal property of Atlantic Coastal Communities.[177] On this basis, the Court concluded that the right to property protected by Article 21 ACHR included the collective property of members of indigenous communities.

This interpretation of Article 21 was further developed and upheld regardless of whether national legislation enshrined the right of indigenous peoples to collective property. This was the case in *Moiwana v. Suriname*,[178] the judgment on tribal land rights that came after *Awas Tingni*. In finding for the applicants, the Court appeared to support its interpretation, on the one hand, by drawing on the idea that Article 21 ACHR had an autonomous meaning which included, since *Awas Tingni*, collective forms of use and ownership. On the other hand, and perhaps more notably, the Court relied on indigenous and tribal customary norms and traditional practices.[179] Later, in deciding the

always give preference to those interpretations that are more protective of rights holders. From this it also follows that 'the content and scope of rights must be interpreted broadly, while their restriction must itself require a restrained interpretation'. See Cecilia Medina, *The American Convention on Human Rights. Crucial Rights and Their Theory and Practice* (Intersentia, 2016), at 52. See also, IACtHR, *Matter of Viviana Gallardo et al. v. Costa Rica*, Decision of 13 November 1981, para. 16.

174 IACtHR, *The Mayagna (Sumo) Awas Tingni Community v. Nicaragua*, Judgment of 31 August 2001, para. 146.

175 Idem.

176 Ibid., para. 147. See Article 29 ACHR 'Restrictions Regarding Interpretation: No provision of this Convention shall be interpreted as: (b) restricting the enjoyment or exercise of any right or freedom recognized by virtue of the laws of any State Party or by virtue of another convention to which one of the said states is a party.'

177 IACtHR, *The Mayagna (Sumo) Awas Tingni Community v. Nicaragua*, Judgment of 31 August 2001, paras. 148 and 153. At the time of the judgment, Article 5 of the Constitution of Nicaragua was entitled 'Rights of the Atlantic Coastal Communities' and provided: 'The State recognises the communal land-tenure systems of the Atlantic Coast communities. It also recognises their right to enjoy, use and exploit the waters and forests on their communal lands.'

178 IACtHR, *The Moiwana Community v. Suriname*, Judgment of 15 June 2005.

179 Ibid., paras. 131–133.

cases of *Saramaka*[180] and *Kaliña and Lokono Peoples*,[181] both against Suriname, the Court took an additional path to support its conclusion that Suriname was under an obligation to recognise and secure the tribal peoples' collective land rights. It applied the *pro-personae* principle and resorted to general treaties ratified by Suriname, namely the International Covenant on Civil and Political Rights (ICCPR) and the International Covenant on Economic, Social and Cultural Rights (ICESCR).[182] The Court read Article 21 ACHR in the light of Article 1 common to both Covenants (right to self-determination) as well as of Article 27 ICCPR (minorities' rights).[183] By virtue of Article 29(b) ACHR, the Court found itself 'unable to interpret the provisions of Article 21 [ACHR] in a sense that would limit the enjoyment and exercise of the rights recognized by Suriname in these covenants'.[184]

Throughout the Court's case law, Article 29(b) ACHR and the living instrument doctrine have become general principles of interpretation.[185] Moreover, as Medina notes, 'dynamism and the pro persona rule provide judges with ample scope for a very creative interpretation'.[186] And indeed, both

---

180 IACtHR, *The Saramaka People v. Suriname*, Judgment of 28 November 2007.

181 IACtHR, *The Kaliña and Lokono Peoples v. Suriname*, Judgment of 25 November 2015.

182 International Covenant on Civil and Political Rights, 999 UNTS 171 (entered into force 23 March 1976) [ICCPR]; International Covenant on Economic, Social and Cultural Rights, 993 U.N.T.S 3 (entered into force on 3 January 1976) [ICESCR].

183 Article 1 common to the ICCPR and the ICESCR reads as follows:

1. All peoples have the right of self-determination. By virtue of that right they freely determine their political status and freely pursue their economic, social and cultural development.
2. All peoples may, for their own ends, freely dispose of their natural wealth and resources without prejudice to any obligations arising out of international economic co-operation, based upon the principle of mutual benefit, and international law. In no case may a people be deprived of its own means of subsistence.
3. The States Parties to the present Covenant, including those having responsibility for the administration of Non-Self-Governing and Trust Territories, shall promote the realization of the right of self-determination, and shall respect that right, in conformity with the provisions of the Charter of the United Nations.

Article 27 ICCPR provides:

In those States in which ethnic, religious or linguistic minorities exist, persons belonging to such minorities shall not be denied the right, in community with the other members of their group, to enjoy their own culture, to profess and practise their own religion, or to use their own language.

184 IACtHR, *The Kaliña and Lokono Peoples v. Suriname*, Judgment of 25 November 2015, paras. 122 and 124.

185 Cecilia Medina, *The American Convention on Human Rights. Crucial Rights and Their Theory and Practice* (Intersentia, 2016), at 52–53. It is interesting to note that the application of the living instrument doctrine in indigenous cases was supported by reference to, *inter alia*, the European Court of Human Rights. See IACtHR, *The Yakye Axa Indigenous Community v. Paraguay*, Judgment of 17 June 2005, para. 125. The Court referred to the ECtHR, *Tyrer v. the United Kingdom*, App. no. 5856/72, Judgment of 25 April 1978, para. 31.

186 Cecilia Medina, *The American Convention on Human Rights. Crucial Rights and Their Theory and Practice* (Intersentia, 2016), at 54.

principles combined, often identified with an 'evolutionary interpretation', enabled the Court to take on board not just the indigenous 'rights-protective' laws of state parties, but also international human rights instruments outside the Inter-American System. Among these are general treaties such as those mentioned above but also specific treaties such as ILO Convention No. 169, which the Court has used in several cases since *Yakye Axa*.[187] However, it is noteworthy that the Court does not limit its normative exploration to binding instruments ratified by the respondent state. The Court has additionally considered soft law, such as the UN Declaration on the Rights of Indigenous Peoples and the UN Guiding Principles on Business and Human Rights, to mention just two.[188]

Naturally, the integration of international sources has extended to the rulings and observations issued by the monitoring bodies overseeing the treaties in question.[189] The views of, for example, the Human Rights Committee, the UN Special Rapporteur on the situation of human rights and fundamental freedoms of indigenous people and the CERD Committee were particularly influential in the Court's approach to investment projects in indigenous lands, such as those discussed in *Saramaka v. Suriname*.[190] The three safeguards required by the Court to ensure that private concessions within indigenous ancestral territories do not undermine their subsistence (effective participation, benefit-sharing and impact assessment), as well as the obligation to ensure the free, prior and informed consent of indigenous communities to major development projects, were both attributed to the standards developed by those and other international bodies.[191] The numerous instruments, principles and decisions invoked by the Court have certainly been an important driving force for the recognition of specific rights and safeguards not provided for by the text

187 See e.g. IACtHR, *The Yakye Axa Indigenous Community v. Paraguay*, Judgment of 17 June 2005, paras. 136–137; *The Sawhoyamaxa Indigenous Community v. Paraguay*, Judgment of 29 March 2006, paras. 117–119; *The Kichwa Indigenous People of Sarayaku v. Ecuador*, Judgment of 27 June 2012, paras. 160–163; *The Community Garifuna Triunfo de la Cruz & its Members v. Honduras*, Judgment of 8 October 2015, paras. 103 and 122.

188 See e.g. IACtHR, *The Kuna Indigenous People of Madungandí and the Emberá Indigenous People of Bayano and their Members v. Panama*, Judgment of 14 October 2014, para. 118, fn. 204 (referring to the United Nations Declaration on the Rights of Indigenous Peoples); *The Kaliña and Lokono Peoples v. Suriname*, Judgment of 25 November 2015, fn. 235 (referring to the United Nations Declaration on the Rights of Indigenous Peoples) and paras. 224–225 (referring to the Guiding Principles on Business and Human Rights); *The Garífuna Punta Piedra Community and its Members v. Honduras*, Judgment of 8 October 2015, para. 174.

189 IACtHR, *The Saramaka People v. Suriname*, Judgment of 28 November 2007, paras. 130–140. See also, *The Garífuna Punta Piedra Community and its Members v. Honduras*, Judgment of 8 October 2015, paras. 175–176.

190 IACtHR, *the Saramaka People v. Suriname*, Judgment of 28 November 2007, paras. 130–140. See also, *Garífuna Punta Piedra Community and its Members v. Honduras*, Judgment of 8 October 2015, paras. 175–176.

191 IACtHR, *The Saramaka People v. Suriname*, Judgment of 28 November 2007, paras. 130–140.

of the ACHR. The most recent example of the normative impact of international sources upon the interpretation adopted by the Court is the extension of legal subjectivity to indigenous communities themselves. As already noted, for a long time the Court had only recognised individual community members as holders of Convention rights, although it frequently addressed the situation of the collective through its reparations.[192] The *Sarayaku* case, however, marked a turning point. Relying on Article 1 of the 2007 United Nations Declaration on the Rights of Indigenous Peoples, Article 3.1 of ILO Convention No. 169 and General Comments of the Economic Social and Cultural Rights,[193] the Court held:

> On previous occasions [...] the Court has declared violations to the detriment of the members of indigenous or tribal communities and peoples. However, *international law on indigenous or tribal communities and peoples recognizes rights to the peoples as collective subjects of international law* and not only as members of such communities or peoples. In view of the fact that indigenous or tribal communities and peoples, united by their particular ways of life and identity, exercise some rights recognized by the Convention on a collective basis, the Court points out that *the legal considerations expressed or indicated in this Judgment should be understood from that collective perspective.*[194]

It is submitted that the principle vested in Article 29(b) ACHR provides the Court with a strong ground for dismissing interpretations or solutions that are less rights-protective than those provided by other treaties ratified by the

---

192 See e.g. IACtHR, *The Moiwana Community v. Suriname*, Judgment of 15 June 2005, para. 194; *The Saramaka People v. Suriname*, Judgment of 28 November 2007, para. 189.

193 Article 1 of the 2007 United Nations Declaration on the Rights of Indigenous Peoples reads: 'Indigenous peoples have the right to the full enjoyment, as a collective or as individuals, of all human rights and fundamental freedoms recognized in the Charter of the United Nations, the Universal Declaration of Human Rights and international human rights law.' Article 3.1 of ILO Convention no. 169 states that: 'Indigenous and tribal peoples shall enjoy the full measure of human rights and fundamental freedoms, without hindrance or discrimination. The provisions of this Convention shall apply without discrimination to male and female members of these peoples.' The General Comments of the Committee on Economic, Social and Cultural Rights referenced by the Court were: General Comment no. 17: The right of everyone to benefit from the protection of the moral and material interests resulting from any scientific, literary or artistic production of which he or she is the author (Article 15, para. 1 (c), of the Covenant), E/C.12/GC/17, 12 January 2006, paras. 7, 8 and 32 (concerning the right to benefit from the protection of the moral and material interests resulting from scientific, literary or artistic production, which applies to indigenous peoples as collective subjects and not only to their members as individuals) and General Comment no. 21: Right of everyone to take part in cultural life (Article 15, para. 1a of the Covenant on Economic, Social and Cultural Rights), E/C.12/GC/21, 21 December 2009 (concerning the right of 'everyone' to take part in cultural life).

194 IACtHR, *The Kichwa Indigenous People of Sarayaku v. Ecuador*, Judgment of 27 June 2012, para. 231 (emphasis added).

respondent state, and by the monitoring bodies supervising those treaties. However, its use with regard to soft law instruments or decisions that are not binding upon the respondent state appears less convincing, especially when major normative consequences follow from it. Neuman, for example, is quite critical of the Court's general practice of considering an 'ever-expanding "corpus juris" of binding and non-binding norms' (beyond the case law on indigenous rights).[195] The reasons for his criticism are varied. One of them is the equal value the Court seems to attribute to all those norms for the purpose of defining the states' obligations under the ACHR. Another relevant problem he identifies is the way this practice has been accompanied by a disregard for the consent expressed by the regional community of states.[196] In his view, 'ignoring the role of the states raises issues both of legitimation and of effectiveness'.[197]

4.2.3. Disregarding Consensus?

To be sure, international standards are not the only extra-Convention norms considered by the Court. The normative systems of the American states have also had a place in the Court's case law on indigenous and Afro-descendant peoples, albeit in a more modest fashion. Besides examining the domestic laws of the respondent state, as the Court has done since *Awas Tingni*, the Court has incrementally looked at the laws of other states too. It did so, for instance, when examining the question of the obligation to consult indigenous peoples in *Sarayaku*. Note that this was one of the main issues debated in this case. The Kichwa of Sarayaku were recognised by Ecuador as indigenous peoples and granted collective land rights accordingly. Nevertheless, the state authorised oil concessions over part of their ancestral territories without, as argued by the applicants, their consent or consultation. Asserting that several OAS states had incorporated the ILO standards on consultation rights via legislation and high court rulings,[198] the Court referred to Argentina, Bolivia, Chile, Colombia, Mexico, Nicaragua, Paraguay, Peru and Venezuela.[199] The Court added that similar developments had taken place in countries which

---

195 Gerald L. Neuman, 'Import, Export and Regional Consent in the Inter-American Court of Human Rights', 19 *The European Journal of International Law* (2008) 101.

196 Ibid., at 114–115.

197 Ibid., at 115.

198 Of note, ILO Convention no. 169 'has been particularly influential in Latin American courts, [reference omitted] the region where it has the highest numbers of ratifications'. See Ben Saul, *Indigenous Peoples and Human Rights. International and Regional Jurisprudence* (Hart Publishing, 2016), at 6.

199 IACtHR, *The Kichwa Indigenous People of Sarayaku v. Ecuador*, Judgment of 27 June 2012, para. 164.

had not ratified ILO Convention no. 169, such as Canada, the United States and New Zealand. This indicated, so argued the Court, that 'the obligation to consult, in addition to being a treaty-based provision, is also a general principle of international law'.[200]

A similar approach was taken in *Kuna and Emberá*. Restitution of the communities' ancestral lands was not possible in this case as a result of the flooding caused by a hydroelectric dam constructed in their territory. Although Panama had undertaken to provide the applicants with alternative lands, the claimants argued that the state had failed to demarcate, title and protect such lands from occupation and illegal logging, which was confirmed by the Court. In this context, the Court referred to the laws of several OAS states under the jurisdiction of the Court that had, in some way, incorporated a state obligation to delimit, demarcate and title indigenous lands.[201] This, according to the Court, evidenced recognition of said obligations. Furthermore, this was in line with the UN Declaration on the Rights of Indigenous Peoples, which had been approved, the Court pointed out, by Panama.[202] Later in the same judgment, the Court resorted again to the laws of several countries of the region (save for one, the same states it had mentioned earlier), which included, in some way, the inalienability and imprescriptibility of indigenous lands.[203] Similar reasoning was adopted by the Court in the case of *Garífuna Punta Piedra Community and its Members v. Honduras*. Observing the lack of clear title of the indigenous community following the occupation of their lands by third parties, the Court even held that it had 'verified an *international consensus*' with respect to the inalienability and imprescriptibility of indigenous territories. The Court noted that regulations in that vein existed in a number of American states.[204] The norms and judicial decisions of these and other American states (most but not all of which were parties to the Convention) were once more considered by the Court to reaffirm the binding character of the obligation to consult indigenous peoples.[205]

The appeal to existing relevant norms in countries from the American region and the recent use of the term 'consensus' might remind us of the regional consensus inquiry applied by the European Court. Yet, on a closer look there is not so much resemblance. Although the Court's recent judgments show an increased interest in supporting its interpretations on the basis of domestic

---

200 Idem.

201 IACtHR, *The Kuna Indigenous People of Madungandí and the Emberá Indigenous People of Bayano and their Members v. Panama*, Judgment of 14 October 2014, para. 118.

202 Idem.

203 Ibid., para. 143.

204 IACtHR, *The Garífuna Punta Piedra Community and its Members v. Honduras*, Judgment of 8 October 2015, para. 179 (emphasis added).

205 Ibid., para. 223.

norms, the use of the term 'consensus' may still be far from a consistent attempt to embed Inter-American judgments in domestic legal systems.[206]

To start with, the concept of 'regional consensus' has so far remained alien to the Court's lexicon (at least in the cases reviewed). Secondly, there has been no indication as to whether and how the Court ascertains the varied scope and content of the cited regulations. In *Sarayaku*, for example, the laws and decisions referenced were quite varied in character. Some recognised a right of indigenous peoples to be consulted; others conferred a relatively vague right to participate or to have their views heard and considered, while they also differed in their ambit of application.[207] The Court simply summarised the normative diversity by saying that those laws and decisions 'refer to the importance of consultation or of communal property'.[208] The unaddressed variety among the regulations invoked in other cases is implied in the Court's assertion that such norms recognise or incorporate 'in some way' the standards in question. Thirdly, the comparative law review conducted by the Court appears rather unsystematic and selective. As the judgments discussed above demonstrate, the Court has brought together domestic norms from member states (most Latin American countries), from non-member states (the United States and Canada) and even from countries as distant as New Zealand.[209] And despite the differences, it is not clear what weight is accorded to each of them. More importantly, all of the Court's allusions to domestic laws and judicial decisions were aligned with the interpretation asserted by the Court. In other words, only those rulings and laws supporting a right to, for example, consultation and communal property in the terms defined by the Court were invoked. As Dulitzky critically shows, no account was taken of any domestic decision or

---

206 This would be unfortunate as it would not contribute to a two-way normative dialogue. On the part of most Latin American states, domestic courts 'frequently seek to embed their decisions in the human rights law of the region'. See Michael Freitas Mohallen, 'Horizontal Judicial Dialogue in South America', in Amrei Müller (ed.), *Judicial Dialogue and Human Rights* (Cambridge University Press, 2017), at 75–79.

207 Ibid., fn. 190–212.

208 IACtHR, *The Kichwa Indigenous People of Sarayaku v. Ecuador*, Judgment of 27 June 2012, para. 164.

209 It should be noted that, besides Belize, the countries of the CARICOM (the Caribbean Community) have been rather absent from the Court's references. Importantly, while all CARICOM states are members of the OAS, only two acceded to the Court's jurisdiction and one of them, Trinidad & Tobago, denounced the Convention and the Court's jurisdiction in 1998. The sub-region's lack of participation has to do, however, with a history of language exclusion since the creation of the Inter-American system of human rights. For an overview of this problem, see Margarette May Macaulay, 'The relationship of English-Speaking Caribbean and the Inter-American Legal System of Human Rights', in Sergio García Ramírez and Mireya Castañeda Hernández (eds.), *Recepción nacional del derecho internacional de los derechos humanos y admission de la competencia contenciosa de la Corte Interamericana* (Universidad Autónoma de México, 2009), at 151–155.

law militating against the Court's position. And the omission is not due to the absence of competing normative postulates at the domestic level.[210]

Finally, another element in assessing the Court's references to states' normative orders is that this Court, in contrast to the ECtHR, rarely displays any deference towards respondent states.[211] Instead of granting national actors any margin of discretion for being, in principle, better placed to assess the local implementation of human rights, the Court has developed the opposite doctrine, that is, the so-called 'Conventionality Control'. According to the latter, all public authorities in a state, especially judges, have a duty to verify *ex officio* the compatibility between domestic norms or practices and the American Convention. That exercise should result in the non-application or invalidation of norms and interpretations that deviate from the ACHR and the Court's interpretation thereof.[212] This is not an uncontested device. It has been both prised and criticised.[213] For present purposes, however, it has been used in just

---

210 Ariel E. Dulitzky, 'An Inter-American Constitutional Court? The Invention of the Conventionality Control by the Inter-American Court of Human Rights', 50 *Texas International Law Journal* (2015) 45, at 75 and fn. 204.

211 The notion of 'margin of appreciation' has hardly ever been used by the Inter-American Court. It has been applied a few times and not necessarily to grant some leeway to the state. The notion of a margin of discretion was used in its first ruling, the Advisory Opinion 4/84, when it had not yet decided any contentious case (the Advisory Opinion dealt with Costa Rica's legal framework concerning the naturalisation of foreigners and its compatibility with the rights to nationality and equality and non-discrimination). See IACtHR, Advisory Opinion OC-4/84 on the Proposed Amendments of the Naturalization Provisions of the Constitution of Costa Rica, Adopted on 19 January 1984, paras. 58–63. The Court has also invoked the margin of discretion in a contentious case dealing with the criminal conviction of a journalist on charges of defamation. But then the Court argued that states had a *reduced* margin for the restriction of political or public interest debates. See IACtHR, *Herrera Ulloa v. Costa Rica*, Judgment of 2 July 2004, para. 127 (see also para. 161 on the limited discretion enjoyed by states in the regulation of effective remedies). Former Judge Cançado Trindade has argued vehemently against the use of the margin of appreciation doctrine by the Inter-American Court. See Antonio Cançado Trindade, 'Reflexiones sobre el Futuro del Sistema Interamericano de Protección de los Derechos Humanos', in Juan E. Méndez and Francisco Cox (eds.), *El Futuro del Sistema Interamericano de Protección a los Derechos Humanos* (IIDH, 1998), at 582–583 and 593.

212 IACtHR, *Control de Convencionalidad*, Cuadernillo de Jurisprudencia de la Corte Inter-Americana de Derechos Humanos No. 7 (Inter-American Court of Human Rights, 2015). It should be noted that this doctrine emerged in the Court's case law concerning amnesty laws. See IACtHR, *Almonacid-Arellano et al. v. Chile*, Judgment of 26 September 2006, para. 124.

213 For an unproblematic or positive view, see Victor Bazán, 'El Control de convencionalidad: incógnitas, desafíos y perspectivas', in Víctor Bazán and Claudio Nash (eds.), *Justicia Constitucional y Derechos Fundamentales: El Control de Convencionalidad* (Fundación Konrad Adenauer, 2012), at 17–55; Néstor Pedro Sagüés, 'Obligaciones Internacionales y Control de Convencionalidad', 8(1) *Estudios Constitucionales* (2010) 117. For a critical view, see Ariel E. Dulitzky, 'An Inter-American Constitutional Court? The Invention of the Conventionality Control by the Inter-American Court of Human Rights', 50 *Texas International Law Journal* (2015) 45, at 60–69; Karlos A. Castilla Juárez, '¿Control Interno o

a few indigenous land cases and mainly for requesting, by way of reparations, changes in the content and application of domestic regulations on land and consultation rights.[214]

A thorough exploration of the Conventionality Control is beyond the scope of this book. Nor is this the place to discuss the desirability of importing a European-like consensus or margin of appreciation into the Inter-American system. Actually, several factors could explain the Court's vision of its virtual constitutional role and its caution or even scepticism about those devices.[215] Obviously, the history of the system and the context in which it operates have been decisive.[216] Also, to some degree the singular stance taken by the Court might be sustained by a mitigated sense of its own distance, as a supranational tribunal, from local reality. In fact, the Court's practice of conducting *in-situ* visits, its extensive fact-finding work and its reliance on numerous expert opinions, all very much present in indigenous and Afro-descendant cases, seem to contribute to the Court's inclination to dispense with normative insights from the regional community of states. What nonetheless calls for reflection here is the extent to which the Court's practices of normative integration might aim more at achieving uniformity under its lead than at openly engaging with the network of domestic norms governing the human rights matters decided in San José. More importantly, the question arises as to whether such a stance would be the most fitting and effective for dealing with complex cases such as the ones discussed here.

Difuso de Convencionalidad? Una Mejor Idea: la Garantía de Tratados', 13 *Anuario Mexicano de Derecho Internacional* (2013) 51.

214 In the case of the *Xákmok Kásek Indigenous Community v. Paraguay*, on the basis of the Conventionality Control the Court ordered Paraguay 'to take the measures necessary to ensure that Decree No. 11,804 [the decree declaring part of the land claimed by the members of the Community as a protected wooded area] is not an obstacle to returning the traditional land to the members of the Community'. See IACtHR, *The Xákmok Kásek Indigenous Community v. Paraguay*, Judgment of 24 August 2010, para. 311. In a similar vein, see IACtHR, *The Garífuna Punta Piedra Community and its Members v. Honduras*, Judgment of 8 October 2015, para. 346.

215 For example, the difficult regional context (e.g. widespread inequality, corruption, fragile rule of law or defective justice systems; although these problems may not be equally present across the region, they affect, to differing degrees, the human rights situation in several American states) and the types of case submitted to the Court (while lately the Court has not only examined cases of gross, massive and grave violations, these still represent a big part of the Court's jurisprudence).

216 Cecilia Medina, *The American Convention on Human Rights. Crucial Rights and Their Theory and Practice* (Intersentia, 2016), at 1–3 (referring to the widespread violations carried out by dictatorships and the economic and social disparities, rigid class distinctions, illiteracy, and other appalling conditions of the American continent. She also stresses how much this context has influenced the interpretations and solutions applied by the Court); Robert K. Goldman, 'History and Action: the Inter-American Human Rights System and the Role of the Inter-American Commission on Human Rights', 31 *Human Rights Quarterly* (2009) 856, at 866–867.

Having said this, the following section will turn to the last layer of normativity frequently integrated by the Court into cases concerning indigenous/Afro-descendant communities.

4.2.4. *Integration of Informal and Tradition-Based Laws*

Another remarkable feature of the cross-fertilisation practice of the Inter-American Court in the cases studied is its deference towards customary law. As the previous sections demonstrate, indigenous peoples' communal way of life, their specific modes of organisation, religious rites and social norms have been considered by the Court since the earliest cases. Recall how the Court determined the beneficiaries of remedies in its reparation judgment in *Aloeboetoe*. Applying Article 38(1)(c) of the Statute of the International Court of Justice, the Court noted that according to the rules generally accepted by most legal systems, a person's successors are her 'children', 'spouse' and 'relatives in the ascending line'.[217] These terms, the Court argued, should be interpreted according to local law. But since in practice Surinamese law was not effective in the locality of the victims, whose family relations were instead governed by Saramaka law, the Court decided to use the latter for its interpretation of the terms referred to above.[218] It thereby provided for the equal pecuniary compensation of more than one wife (in accordance with polygamy customs), regardless of the – lack of – marriage registration. In doing so, the Court also asserted limits to its accommodation. It stated that the Saramaka custom would be considered 'to the degree that it does not contradict the American Convention. Hence, in referring to 'relatives in the ascending line' the Court shall make no distinction as to sex, even if that might be contrary to Saramaka custom.'[219]

217 Article 38(1)(c) of the Statute of the International Court of Justice reads as follows: '1. The Court, whose function is to decide in accordance with international law such disputes as are submitted to it, shall apply: (b) international custom, as evidence of a general practice accepted as law.' The Statute of the International Court of Justice is annexed to the Charter of the United Nations, which was signed at San Francisco on 26 June 1945.

218 '[...] The only question of importance here is whether the laws of Suriname in the area of family law apply to the Saramaka tribe. On this issue, the evidence offered leads to the conclusion that Surinamese family law is not effective insofar as the Saramakas are concerned. The members of the tribe are unaware of it and adhere to their own rules. The State for its part does not provide the facilities necessary for the registration of births, marriages, and deaths, an essential requirement for the enforcement of Surinamese law. Furthermore, the Saramakas do not bring the conflicts that arise over such matters before the State's tribunals, whose role in these areas is practically non-existent with respect to the Saramakas. It should be pointed out that, in the instant case, Suriname recognized the existence of a Saramaka customary law.' IACtHR, *Aloeboetoe et al. v. Suriname*, Judgment of 10 September 1993, paras. 58 and 62.

219 IACtHR, *Aloeboetoe et al. v. Suriname*, Judgment of 10 September 1993, para. 62.

The references to customary law expanded in subsequent judgments. They were further used for defining the beneficiaries and modes of reparation under Article 63 of the Convention.[220] Later, customary law was also employed for interpreting Convention provisions in the merits analysis. Article 21 ACHR has been, as we have seen, the main 'receptor' of indigenous and tribal customary norms. The outcome of this line of reasoning is already known: the reconceptualisation of the right to property, now cast in collective terms, and its expansion through a set of sub-rights inspired by indigenous customary practices.[221] In this vein, one should also note that the state obligation to consult indigenous and tribal peoples or to obtain their consent is particularly instrumental for the continuing actualisation and incorporation of customary norms.

While the Court has referred abundantly to indigenous customary norms and has required states to accommodate it in the implementation of domestic and international law, it has not gone as far as to apply customary law as such. Giving legal force to unrecognised and non-titled indigenous property based exclusively on indigenous customs and uses is perhaps one of the few examples of a direct import of indigenous customs. In fact, as it transpires from the previous sections, the Court has not applied customary rules of succession in the context of reparations, or community rules regulating the possession and use of the land and its resources. Nonetheless, the Court's efforts to integrate indigenous normativity for interpretative purposes cannot be overstated.

The way this layer of normativity has been integrated offers relevant insights into the reasons for and the consequences of incorporating customary

---

220 See, for example, the judgment in *Moiwana*, where the Court considered the victims' suffering in light of N'djuka beliefs. IACtHR, *The Moiwana Community v. Suriname*, Judgment of 15 June 2005, para. 195.

221 These include, *inter alia*, recognition of the indigenous people's possession of land flowing from their uses and customs as equivalent to an official ownership title; a right to protection of their cultural identity; restitution of their ancestral lands and if alternative lands of equal extension and quality were to be assigned, their provision with the agreement of the concerned peoples, taking into account their customs, values and intended use of the land. Also, indigenous peoples have a right to be consulted on matters that may affect them and a limited right to free, prior and informed consent, which should also be implemented in accordance to their traditions and customs. I say this right is 'limited' because in *Saramaka v. Suriname* the Court restricted the right to free, prior and informed consent to 'large-scale development or invest projects.' See, IACtHR, *The Saramaka People v. Suriname*, Judgment of 28 November 2007, para. 134. As regards the other specific rights referred to above, see e.g. IACtHR, *The Mayagna (Sumo) Awas Tingni Community v. Nicaragua*, Judgment of 31 August 2001, paras. 151–153 and 164; *The Yakye Axa Indigenous Community v. Paraguay*, Judgment of 17 June 2005, paras. 138–149; *The Sawhoyamaxa Indigenous Community v. Paraguay*, Judgment of 29 March 2006, paras. 127–130; *The Xákmok Kásek Indigenous Community v. Paraguay*, Judgment of 24 August 2010, paras. 109–121; *The Kichwa Indigenous People of Sarayaku v. Ecuador*, Judgment of 27 June 2012, paras. 159 and ff.

norms in these cases. The why and how of the practice should first be placed in a regional context in which several American states formally recognise, in one way or another, indigenous customary laws. Actually, in many cases the Court's regard for indigenous customs has been grounded in the state recognition of customary norms and collective land rights. In the few cases in which this was not so, as happened in *Aloeboetoe* and in other cases against Suriname (which does not recognise Saramaka customary law in its domestic order), the Court contented itself with noting that the state did not deny the *existence* of indigenous customary norms.[222] Additionally, the Court's extensive reliance on expert evidence from anthropologists, sociologists and other professionals has certainly played a crucial role in facilitating the incorporation of tradition-based laws.[223] The consideration of the cultural norms and traditions of indigenous people has also been justified by reference to egalitarian considerations, namely, a reading of Article 21 that would not leave those people unprotected.[224]

As to the consequences, to the extent that cultural practices and claims were recognised as expressions of customary laws, these carried additional weight in the normative analysis. In other words, the customary law character of land-related modes of living constituted a relevant ground for their accommodation. The same goes for the finding of indirect discrimination in the *Yatama* case. The Court did not hesitate in rejecting the indirect imposition of modes of political organisation unfamiliar to those dictated by indigenous customs. Consideration of these norms also enabled the Court to make the Convention relevant to indigenous and Afro-descendant peoples. And as customary law was crucial for understanding the rights restrictions complained of and the implementation hurdles for the Court's rulings, regard for customary norms may assist in these respects too. But it has yet to be seen how the Court will deal with other kinds of community norms and informal regulations in other types of claims of ethno-cultural difference.

---

222 See e.g. IACtHR, *Aloeboetoe et al. v. Suriname*, Judgment of 10 September 1993, para. 58 *in fine*. The Court stated the following: 'It should be pointed out that, in the instant case, Suriname recognized the existence of a Saramaka customary law.'

223 See e.g. IACtHR, *The Mayagna (Sumo) Awas Tingni Community v. Nicaragua*, Judgment of 31 August 2001, para. 83 (c), (d), (j); *The Moiwana Community v. Suriname*, Judgment of 15 June 2005, paras. 79–80 and 193; *The Kichwa Indigenous People of Sarayaku v. Ecuador*, Judgment of 27 June 2012, paras. 154–155.

224 As already mentioned, *Sawhoyamaxa* advanced egalitarian reasons as a compelling ground for accommodating customary law. See IACtHR, *The Sawhoyamaxa Indigenous Community v. Paraguay*, Judgment of 29 March 2006, para. 120. This has been reiterated in subsequent cases: IACtHR, *The Kichwa Indigenous People of Sarayaku v. Ecuador*, Judgment of 27 June 2012, para. 161; *The Kuna Indigenous People of Madungandí and the Emberá Indigenous People of Bayano and their Members v. Panama*, Judgment of 14 October 2014, para. 111.

5. CONCLUDING REMARKS

From the set of judgments studied in this chapter, those involving collective land claims from indigenous and Afro-descendant rural communities are those most notably marked by discourses of ethno-cultural difference and identity. This has led to a normative approach that places emphasis on the traditional beliefs and practices of indigenous communities. While the Court has, on this basis, granted specific and even 'novel' rights that strive to cater for the needs and concerns of the people involved, this essentialism has also raised problems. Some of them are the potential socio-economic disempowerment of indigenous and tribal people and others who may want to benefit from the indigenous-rights framework; the potential exclusion, without sufficient justification, of other persons and groups who may seek similar legal protection; the risk of stereotyping those who are identified as indigenous or tribal; the glossing over of the specific concerns and disadvantages of some individuals and sub-groups; and the potential future difficulty of discerning which other cultural difference claims will be accommodated.

Looking at cases dealing with issues of ethno-cultural difference from an integrated perspective adds interesting insights. With regard to rights holders, it is possible to note that while the Court has taken significant steps towards redressing collective harm, individuals should not be forgotten when individualised harm has been claimed and proven. Nevertheless, the Court has adopted a more comprehensive view of people belonging to indigenous/tribal communities, especially in judgments that are not so reliant on Article 21 ACHR. Differentiated violations experienced by some indigenous members – notably women, children and the elderly – have occasionally been identified. A richer analysis of the positioning of indigenous and Afro-descendant applicants has also been facilitated by the notion of vulnerability, especially when applied in a compounded manner. As argued earlier, acknowledging the multiple positioning of applicants provides useful elements for, amongst others, the contextualisation of the violations, the proportionality analysis and the assessment of reparations.

In addition, it was seen that the Court only occasionally dealt with questions of individual autonomy for the purpose of adjudicating the cases studied. One possible reason for this is the Court's tendency to concentrate more on the group's socio-historical conditions than on individual circumstances. In any event, the Court has rejected the argument that applicants have autonomy and free choice to avoid or mitigate the impairment of their rights. Yet, consideration of the autonomy of indigenous communities was initially accompanied by a disregard for the agency of its members for the purpose of reparations. This has been rightly amended in more recent cases. For its part, the range of rights holders considered by the Court in the cases examined is varied. The Court has only incrementally incorporated into its analysis the situation of communities and individuals with competing claims. Whether these claims and the position of those groups and persons are taken into account or not holds relevance not only for the implementation of the judgment but also for the interpretations and solutions advanced therein. While the Court is yet to fully explore the potential normative insights arising from 'seeing' other affected rights holders, it has made a revolutionary enlargement of the range of rights holders to be considered. This is the recognition of indigenous/tribal communities, collectively, as Convention rights holders.

Also of note is the fact that the cultural identity line of case law has at its core the right to property (Article 21 ACHR), which has operated as an umbrella norm. Within a rather limited normative range of Convention norms guided by Article 21 ACHR, the socio-economic and discrimination dimensions of the cases have often been addressed through reparation measures, while underexplored in the merits analysis. Taking into account the applicants' economic grievances in its reparation awards is quite significant. But this does not mean that integrating this element into the merits analysis would be superfluous. Even if one thinks of reparations only, it should be recalled that any reparation award must always keep a direct relationship with the findings of violation. Analysing the case law from an integrated perspective also revealed that the right to a dignified life (Article 4 ACHR) proved to be a useful avenue for bringing in economic harms next to problems of cultural misrecognition. And while the Court's previous ambivalence towards the justiciability of socio-economic rights via Article 26 ACHR had shed uncertainty on how far the Court could go in realising the indivisibility of rights, the Court now appears to fully embrace this principle through the direct justiciability of social rights, which seems to be inaugurating a new jurisprudential era. In addition, recent case law has shown the relevance of (previously neglected) political rights, which are suited to grounding participation rights for indigenous and other people. Likewise, it appears necessary to consider the applicability of equality and non-discrimination, particularly with a view to exploring possible root causes of violations, such as racial and other forms of structural inequality.

But where the Court's affinity with a comprehensive perspective to human rights is perhaps most evident is at the level of normative integration of international and customary norms. Several international sources, of varied nature, have been integrated in the ethno-cultural cases reviewed here. Indigenous customary law has likewise attained weight in the merits and reparations analysis. These tradition-based norms have assisted the Court in defining the beneficiaries and scope of reparations, interpreting Convention rights, weighing cultural claims and foreseeing implementation hurdles. For this, an evolutionary and dynamic interpretation (identified with the living instrument doctrine and the *pro-personae* principle) has been material. As to domestic law and normative regional consensus, however, the assessment is more mixed. On the one hand, domestic legislation and judicial decisions have been progressively considered by the Court. On the other, though, the Court has not fully engaged with the normative reality of the region. Notably, its approach has been rather selective and not fully inclusive, which may not be instrumental for addressing the complexities and controversies underlying the cases. Many of the opportunities and limitations derived from the Court's discourse on ethno-cultural difference will probably be visible only once it gets to decide on claims concerning cultural identities and practices that are not as valued as those of indigenous people.

PART III

RETHINKING ECONOMIC DISADVANTAGE FROM AN INTEGRATED PERSPECTIVE ON HUMAN RIGHTS

This third part of the book will discuss a line of case law that offers a picture that is both similar and dissimilar to that examined in Part I. Similarly to the cases on ethno-cultural difference studied in Part I, one set of legal claims can be framed as a legal right to be protected against disadvantages unfairly accorded to a perceived or actual (socio-economic) difference. In some cases, this is formulated as protection against restrictions of substantive rights and/or as protection against discrimination on socio-economic grounds. Nevertheless, unlike cultural diversity cases, arguments about social relations among groups and about identity tend to be much more absent in poverty-related cases. In other words, poverty or socio-economic difference usually does not translate into a group-identity assertion.[1] Yet, as it will be seen later, this holds truer for the European than the Inter-American Court. In this connection, it is relevant to note that while the question of poverty-related violations has been a topical issue for some time in the Inter-American system,[2] in the context of the Council of Europe, the issue has gained attention in the last decade.[3]

---

1 On this issue, but in the context of the United States, see Athena D. Mutua, 'Introducing ClassCrits: From Class Blindness to a Critical Legal Analysis of Economic Inequality', 56(4) *Buffalo Law Review* (2008) 859, at 879. See also, Sarah Ganty and Maxime Vanderstraeten, 'Actualités de La Lutte Contre La Discrimination Dans Les Biens et Les Services, En Ce Compris L'enseignement', in Emmanuelle Bribosia *et al.* (eds.), *Droit de la Non-discrimination. Avancées et enjeux* (Bruylant, 2016), at 199.

2 During the 1980s and 1990s, the IACommHR had already issued a number of country reports addressing the human rights situation of people living in poverty. See e.g. IACommHR, Report on the Situation of Human Rights in El Salvador, OEA/Ser.L/V/II.46, 17 November 1978, Chapter XI – Economic, Social and Cultural Rights; Report on the Situation of Human Rights in Ecuador, OEA/Ser.L/V/II.96, 24 April 1997, Chapter II. B. In the 2000s, the Commission also devoted attention to this matter in its thematic reports and reports on the merits of individual complaints. The IACtHR, for its part, started to consider this question in contentious cases by the end of the 1990s. See e.g. IACtHR, *"Street Children" (Villagrán-Morales et al.) v. Guatemala*, Judgment of 19 November 1999, paras. 144 and 191.

3 This has been notably so in the aftermath of the 2008 economic crises. See e.g. Françoise Tulkens, *The European Convention on Human Rights and the economic crisis: The issue of poverty*, European University Institute Working Papers AEL 2013/08 (2013); Council of

It is also interesting to observe that so long as people living in poverty do not assert a positive right to live in accordance with a (poor) lifestyle, and because assertions of socio-economic disadvantage generally have little legal traction, it seems that human rights courts do not face the pressure, which they confront in culturally-based claims, to set limits to a potentially 'endless' list of claims for accommodation or special treatment. This would mean that courts do not have the 'pluralism anxiety' about which modes of living and 'special protections' should be accepted under human rights law. Nevertheless, these courts face another challenge that runs along somewhat parallel lines. This is the question of how far they should go in adjudicating issues of socio-economic assistance. There is a problem of limits here as well, but this takes the shape of a floodgate concern.[4] Basically, courts should be careful, so goes the argument, not to open a door into the state's budget by setting general duties of assistance or engaging in social policy-making.[5] The concern arises even in cases in which the main issue is not really, or not only one of access to economic resources.[6] As will be seen in Chapters 4 and 5, an important way to mitigate this concern is by appreciating the cases and the rights claims in a more integrated perspective. An integrated approach is furthermore needed because economic disadvantage is not randomly distributed in society. There are certain persons – e.g. indigenous and ethnic minorities, asylum seekers, women, single parents, persons with disabilities and children – who are more likely to experience rights violations for reasons of poverty. As Brodsky and Day note with regard to poverty-related litigation, failure to take into account these links 'results in an impoverished analysis of the nature and extent of the harms' produced by the contested regulations.[7] Yet, because of the way that human rights law and the regional courts tend to operate in this field, those and other interactions are often disaggregated.

Europe, Steering Committee for Human Rights (CDDH); The Impact of the economic crisis and austerity measures on human rights in Europe. Feasibility study, CDDH(2015)R84 Addendum IV, 11 December 2015.

4 This concern is quite common among jurisdictions that have to deal with rights claims grounded in socio-economic disadvantage. See e.g., Michelle Foster, 'Non-Refoulement on the Basis of Socio-Economic Deprivation: The Scope of Complementary Protection in International Human Rights Law', 2 *New Zealand Law Review* (2009) 257, at 296 and 308–309.

5 In the Strasbourg Court, Judge Sajó raised this concern in his partly dissenting opinion in the Grand Chamber case of *M.S.S. v. Belgium and Greece* ('There seems to be only a small step between the Court's present position and that of a general and unconditional positive obligation of the State to provide shelter and other material services to satisfy the basic needs of the "vulnerable"'). ECtHR, (GC) *M.S.S. v. Belgium and Greece*, App. no. 30696/09, Judgment of 21 January 2011, at 103. See also, Marc Bossuyt, 'Is the European Court of Human Rights on a slippery slope?', in Spyridon Flogaitis *et al.* (eds.), *The European Court of Human Rights and Its Discontents. Turning Criticism into Strength* (Edward Elgar, 2013), at 32–33.

6 Such as in cases concerning the use or promotion of stereotypes and stigmas attached to socio-economic deprivation. Some examples can be found in the cases discussed in Chapter 4, sections 3.2.1 and 3.2.2.

7 Gwen Brodsky and Shelagh Day, 'Poverty is a Human Rights Violation', paper prepared for the December 2001 consultation of The Poverty and Human Rights Project (Canada), at 12.

CHAPTER 4

AN INTEGRATED APPROACH TO ECONOMIC DISADVANTAGE IN THE EUROPEAN COURT OF HUMAN RIGHTS

1. INTRODUCTION

The question of how the European Court of Human Rights can deal with rights claims of poverty and socio-economic disadvantage has gained growing attention in the last decade. Following the most recent economic crisis, people living in European countries have seen an increase not just in the proportion of the population in and at risk of poverty, but also in income inequality, insecure living conditions and regressive social policies.[1] It is therefore not surprising that scholars and practitioners alike had shown renewed interest in what the ECtHR can offer to the protection of the rights of those experiencing poverty and social service cuts.[2] The present chapter can be seen as contributing to these efforts, but from a quite distinctive point of view. The chapter basically examines the complex ways in which people's experiences of socio-economic deprivation are interrelated with a range of rights, interests, harms, inequalities and social positions. Having regard to the fact that it is usually easier for a court like the ECtHR to embrace a categorical and fragmentary than a comprehensive and relational line of thought, the chapter analyses claims of socio-economic disadvantage from an integrated perspective. Within this framework, the chapter discusses different types of claim. Some are framed as protection against destitution (violations resulting from

---

1 See e.g. Council of Europe, *Living in dignity in the 21st century. Poverty and inequality in societies of human rights. The Paradox of democracies* (Council of Europe, 2013), at 7–27.

2 Françoise Tulkens, *The European Convention on Human Rights and the economic crisis: The issue of poverty*, European University Institute Working Papers AEL 2013/08 (2013); European Parliament, Directorate General for Internal Policies, Policy Department Citizens' Rights and Constitutional Affairs, *The Impact of the Crisis on Fundamental Rights across Member States of the EU: Comparative Analysis – Study for the LIBE Committee* (European Parliament, 2015); Council of Europe, *Redefining and Combating Poverty: Human Rights, Democracy and Common Goods in Today's Europe*, Trends in Social Cohesion, No. 25 (Council of Europe, 2012).

extreme poverty); others contest the detrimental effect imposed by certain regulations or practices which are insensitive to people's socio-economic situation (fees for courts and other services, housing regulations, denial of medical attention); others complain of excessive policing or interference with their rights because of poverty (family separation, prohibition of begging); while there are also claims of discrimination on poverty-related grounds.

Given that the ECHR does not contain a right to be free from poverty or other specific references to socio-economic disadvantage (save for Article 14's prohibition of discrimination on grounds of 'social origin' or 'other social status'), a relatively wide range of rights is mobilised in the cases examined. These include, *inter alia*, the right to life (Article 2); the prohibition of torture and degrading treatment (Article 3); the right to private and family life (Article 8); the prohibition of discrimination (Article 14); and the right to property (Article 1 Protocol No. 1) ECHR. The discussion proceeds as in previous chapters.

2. ECONOMIC DISADVANTAGE, GROUP IDENTITY QUESTIONS AND LEGAL COMPARTMENTS

2.1. DISADVANTAGE WITHOUT GROUP OR IDENTITY

A first interesting aspect of the case law examined in this chapter is that rights claims to be free from burdens or exclusions based on socio-economic disadvantage are not usually based on arguments about group and identity. This contrasts with an important part of the case law discussed in Chapters 2 and 3 The difference seems understandable, though. As Fraser argues, 'the last thing [the proletariat] needs is recognition of its difference'.[3] Poverty is, rather, viewed as something to overcome and with which people would rarely identify themselves. Further, people living in poverty are not, so it appears, one of those groups that attract the protection of the law. There may be several reasons for this. One common explanation points to the significant heterogeneity among the socio-economically disadvantaged[4] – a reason that is in itself problematic, since it presupposes that other social groups are homogeneous

3 Nancy Fraser, *Justice Interruptus: Critical reflections on the "postsocialist" condition* (Routledge, 1997), at 18, cited in Ruth Lister, '(Mis)recognition, social inequality and social justice. A critical social policy perspective' in Terry Lovell (ed.), *(Mis)recognition, Social Inequality and Social Justice. Nancy Fraser and Pierre Bourdieu* (Routledge, 2007), at 164.

4 See e.g. Colleen Sheppard, '"Bread and Roses": Economic Justice and Constitutional Rights', 5(1) *Oñati Socio-Legal Series* (2015) 225, at 236 (discussing Canadian judgments that found that people living in poverty 'include virtually everybody in our society', that the poor are an 'amorphous group' and that they are 'not defined by a common characteristic').

and coherent. Another factor preventing an identity approach may be the social stigma attached to poverty.[5] This stigma gives people little incentive to identify themselves as 'poor'. Of course, one may argue that legal visibility and responsiveness could equally be attained by addressing their situation from a group-based perspective, without having to deal with identity assertions. This could be done by, for example, regarding people living in poverty as a 'vulnerable group', whereby special attention is drawn to their needs and concerns. However, as further explained below, the ECtHR has so far been reluctant to do so.

But beyond the reasons we could think of for explaining that claims of socio-economic difference do not fall within a group or identity framework, attention will be focused on the normative implications of this position. One such implication is that it makes it easier for the Court to accept that the rights deficits involved in an experience of poverty are an individual matter only. This may downplay important relational aspects of the violations complained of. One such aspect concerns possible inequalities among groups. For example, advancing ethno-cultural claims from a group inequality perspective may draw attention to the way a certain regulation or norm disadvantages a minority while simultaneously privileging a cultural or religious majority. Although socio-economic disadvantage has to do with a reality of economic difference between the haves and have-nots, this element of social group difference is often absent from the ECtHR's case law.[6] Another, related consequence of thinking that poverty is not about relations between groups is that socio-economic deprivation appears to be an individual fault. In this regard, it will be noticed that the Court acknowledges the vulnerability of asylum seekers living in extreme poverty and other persons whose rights are restricted as a result of a situation of poverty over which they have little or no control. Yet, the Court does not seem to recognise people living in poverty, such as single parents living on welfare or persons on a low income, as a

---

5 Several scholars recall Adam Smith's idea of poverty as an impediment to 'the ability to appear in public without shame'. See e.g. Amartya Sen, *Inequality Reexamined* (Clarendon Press, 1992), at 115; Amartya Sen, 'Social Exclusion: Concept, Application, and Scrutiny', *Social Development Papers No. 1* (Asian Development Bank, 2000), at 4; Sandra Fredman, 'The Potential and Limits of an Equal Rights Paradigm in Addressing Poverty', 3 *Stellenbosch Law Review* (2011) 566, at 579 (citing Adam Smith, *An Inquiry Into The Nature And Causes Of The Wealth Of Nations* (Clarendon Press, 1975), at 351–352 and 1776).

6 Salomon argues that 'given its preoccupation with people who are left out, discriminated against, and marginalised, it is perhaps not surprising that human rights concerns around poverty are approached with a focus on the poor, not on the affluent, and not on the gap between them'. Margot E. Salomon, 'Why Should It Matter That Others Have More? Poverty, Inequality, and the Potential of International Human Rights Law', 15 *LSE Law, Society and Economy Working Papers* (2010) 1, at 2. In the context of adjudication and compared to other human rights claims such as those addressed in Chapters 2 and 3, one may argue that the issue of 'difference' or inequality is notably absent in poverty-related rights claims.

vulnerable group. What is more, the Court has not always challenged the idea, usually advanced by domestic authorities, that individuals' economic deprivation is simply the result of their own conduct.[7]

An additional, practical implication of the lack of a group or identity framework is that legal mobilisation around socio-economic disadvantage, unlike ethno-cultural and gender identity, is likely to be more limited.[8] In the case law examined here, this is suggested by the fact that applicants only occasionally invoke their economic deprivation or poverty as a basis for their normative claims. Sometimes they posit it just as a contextual circumstance to be additionally considered by the Court. On the part of the Court, the legal invisibility of socio-economic disadvantage also has to do, as will be seen below, with its careful stance on socio-economic matters and the particular normative approach that has developed in this field. Before turning to these questions, it is interesting to note that the avoidance or the erasing of people's socio-economic condition stands in contrast to the visibility of the socio-economic circumstances of respondent states, which are usually considered by the Court.

2.2. THE SOCIAL POLICY COMPARTMENT AND THE INVISIBILITY OF ECONOMIC DISADVANTAGE

Whereas it may be difficult, at least in the ECHR context, to present complaints related to poverty as a matter of identity or group difference, it is relatively easy to put them into the 'box' of welfare policies and socio-economic rights. As such, a question arises: what does this framing entail?

It was noted above that long ago, in the *Airey* case, the Court rejected watertight divisions separating social and economic rights from the civil and political rights covered by the Convention.[9] However, challenges to the divide between the two categories of rights have been met with resistance. In *Airey*, the Irish government advanced two kinds of concern that resurface time and again.

---

7 See cases references *infra* section 2.2.1.

8 In a similar vein, but from the perspective of legal discourses in the United Sates, see e.g. Martha R. Mahoney, 'Class and Status in American Law: Race, Interest, and the Anti-Transformation Cases', 76 *Southern California Law Review* (2003) 799, at 842 ('Since law more easily recognizes race and gender rather than class issues, the need to shape legally cognizable claims has also tended to diminish consciousness of and arguments about class.').

9 ECtHR, *Airey v. Ireland*, App. no. 6289/73, Judgment of 9 October 1979, para. 26, at 11. It is noteworthy that more recently the Court has at times inverted the emphasis of the *Airey* precedent by saying: 'Although many of the rights it contains have implications of a social or economic nature, the Convention is essentially directed at the protection of civil and political rights.' See (GC) *N. v. the United Kingdom*, App. no. 26565/05, (GC) Judgment of 27 May 2008, para. 44.

First, it argued that it was not the role of the Court to intrude into matters of socio-economic policy. These belonged to the state's political bodies, which had the capacity and legitimacy to seek progressive social development.[10] Second, the government advanced a 'floodgate' concern. Accepting Mrs Airey's claim would amount, so went the argument, to imposing an obligation to provide free legal aid in all cases concerning the determination of a 'civil right' under Article 6 ECHR. This line of objection was further elaborated by the Greek government and the separate opinion of Judge Sajó in *M.S.S.*, a 2013 case involving an asylum seeker living in extreme destitution. For the former, ruling in favour of the applicant 'would open the doors to countless similar applications from homeless persons and place an undue positive obligation on the States in terms of welfare policy'.[11] Similarly, Judge Sajó posited that 'there seems to be only a small step between the Court's present position and that of a general and unconditional positive obligation of the State to provide shelter and other material services to satisfy the basic needs of the "vulnerable"'.[12]

Against this hesitation about intruding into socio-economic terrain, the Court's attempt to 'contain' cases regarded as being about socio-economic policies or welfare issues appears understandable. This categorisation, however, often means adopting a rationale that promotes a partial or compartmentalised view of the case at hand.[13] Indeed, the Court frequently emphasises the wide margin of appreciation granted to states in crafting socio-economic policies and in balancing individual rights against the general interest.[14] In such cases, the Court's discourse also tends to say more about what rights do *not* provide for than about what they do.[15] A common consequence of using this framework of analysis is that a quite deferential review is applied. While this may not be perceived as *per se* problematic, here it is relevant to note one problematic

10 Idem. ('The Convention should not be interpreted so as to achieve social and economic developments in a Contracting State; such developments can only be progressive.')

11 ECtHR, (GC) *M.S.S. v. Belgium and Greece*, App. no. 30696/09, Judgment of 21 January 2011, para. 243.

12 Ibid., Partly concurring and partly dissenting opinion of Judge Sajó, at 103.

13 In this vein, see Janneke Gerards, 'The ECtHR's Response to Fundamental Rights Issue related to Financial and Economic Difficulties. The Problem of Compartmentalisation', 33(3) *Netherlands Quarterly of Human Rights* (2015) 274, at 277 (but referring to cases dealing with measures adopted in the context of the economic crisis).

14 See e.g. ECtHR, *Wells v. the United Kingdom*, App. no. 37794/05, Decision of 16 January 2007, at 9; *Bah v. the United Kingdom*, Judgment of 27 September 2011, para. 47; *Ponomaryovi v. Bulgaria*, App. no. 5335/05, Judgment of 21 June 2011, para. 52; *Garib v. the Netherlands*, App. no. 43494/09, Judgment of 23 February 2016, para. 116(a); *Bagdonavicius and Others v. Russia*, App. no. 19841/06, Judgment of 11 October 2016, para. 97.

15 It would say, for example, that the right to private life and respect for the home does not comprise a right to be provided with a home; while the right to property does not provide a right to obtain social benefits or similar socio-economic entitlements. See e.g. ECtHR, *Wells v. the United Kingdom*, App. no. 37794/05, Decision of 16 January 2007, at 9; *Bah v. the United Kingdom*, Judgment of 27 September 2011, para. 40.

implication, namely that the case analysis would mainly focus on the justification given for the general social policy underlying the case, while overlooking its concrete application to the applicant and the actual interests at stake.

A good example of this can be found in *Garib v. the Netherlands*, a case dealing with the refusal of a permit to a single mother living on social welfare to take up residence in a neighbouring area.[16] This followed from the application of legislation preventing 'newcomers' living on social welfare or below a certain level of income from settling in certain socioeconomically distressed areas. Both the Chamber and the Grand Chamber started from the broad discretion enjoyed by the state on issues of housing policy. On this basis, they applied an abstract review that accepted the legitimacy of virtually whatever the legislature deemed to best serve the public interest.[17] As discussed later in this chapter, the applicant's vulnerability as a single mother of two children, the level of interference with her autonomy under the right to choose one's residence (Article 2 Protocol 4), the fact that she was already living in the area and other crucial aspects of the specific case were not considered. The case could have been framed as discrimination based on poverty or on grounds of gender and race, or as a restriction to an autonomy right. But it was not. For the Court, the predominant framework was that of the state latitude when it comes to complex socio-economic policies and this, importantly, limited the comprehensiveness of the analysis.[18] In that sense, this framing operated as a normative compartment. Hence, while a judicial approach that is not too concerned with identity or groups seems to open up opportunities for a more comprehensive analysis, this does not mean that alternative forms of fragmentation may not be in play. In the types of case studied here, insulating the socio-economic realm in the way described above and erasing people's socio-economic disadvantage both take us back to fragmentary thinking.

Socio-economic disadvantage has often been side-lined by the Court and by litigants. Economic deprivation may be one of the most significant elements

---

16 ECtHR, *Garib v. the Netherlands*, App. no. 43494/09, Judgment of 23 February 2016 and (GC) Judgment of 6 November 2017.

17 Ibid., paras. 113 and 137, respectively.

18 For a criticism of the ensuing lack of engagement with the concrete reality of the case see ECtHR, (GC) *Garib v. the Netherlands*, App. no. 43494/09, Judgment of 6 November 2017, Dissenting Opinions of Judge Kūris, para. 4; Judges Pinto de Albuquerque and Vehabović, paras. 16–20, and Judges Tsotsoria and Geatano, paras. 2–4. See also Joint Third Party Intervention submitted by the Human Rights Centre of Ghent University and the Equality Law Clinic of the Université Libre de Bruxelles, (available at <www.hrc.ugent.be/wp-content/uploads/2017/01/Garib-tpi-hrc-ugent-ulb.pdf>; and Valeska David and Sarah Ganty, 'Strasbourg fails to protect the rights of people living in or at risk of poverty: the disappointing Grand Chamber judgment in *Garib v the Netherlands*', *Strasbourg Observers*, 16 November 2017 <strasbourgobservers.com/2017/11/16/strasbourg-fails-to-protect-the-rights-of-people-living-in-or-at-risk-of-poverty-the-disappointing-grand-chamber-judgment-in-garib-v-the-netherlands/>.

defining the applicant's experience and yet they may decide to leave this out of their allegations. It is likely, then, that the Court will respond accordingly, analysing the case in rather economically neutral terms. Consider *Lacatus v. Switzerland*, which has yet to be decided.[19] A criminal prohibition on begging was set up in Geneva, on the basis of which the applicant had been convicted and fined several times. One could barely imagine a measure more openly aimed at specifically regulating people living in poverty than a ban on begging. And yet the applicant frames her rights allegations, particularly those on discrimination, only by reference to her Roma origin. Her situation of poverty is an invisible aspect of her claims. From the questions the Court has posed to the parties in examining the case, it appears that, correspondingly, the Court is following an ethnic-only approach.

It is *a fortiori* less surprising that applicants do not highlight their economic situation in cases in which this aspect may be perceived as less central to their complaint. This is all the more so when other social locations, such as ethnic origin, nationality, gender and religion, may absorb the class component. Consider *Ponomaryovi v. Bulgaria*.[20] In this case, which concerned the imposition of fees for secondary education on certain categories of foreign nationals, the applicants – two brothers of Russian nationality – did not mobilise arguments about their inability to afford those fees. The whole problem was framed exclusively from the perspective of nationality. From the facts recounted in the judgment, however, it appears that they had no property or income and their mother had been out of work for many years, while her husband's small business had been shut down. The brothers actually had to take out a bank loan to raise money to pay for their residence permits.[21] Nevertheless, none of these aspects seem to have been incorporated into the presentation of their plight. And as one would expect, the Court did not take them into account either. The case was examined against the state's budgetary constraints, but without regard for the economic deprivation of the applicants, even though the Court had decided to focus explicitly on the applicants' personal circumstances.[22]

Another example is *Moser v. Austria*.[23] The applicant in this case lived in precarious conditions and since she did not have legal residence in Austria, she was not entitled to financial aid. In this context, her newborn baby was

---

19 ECtHR, *Lacatus v. Switzerland*, App. no. 14065/15, Communicated on 11 February 2016 (pending application as of April 2019).

20 ECtHR, *Ponomaryovi v. Bulgaria*, App. no. 5335/05, Judgment of 21 June 2011.

21 Ibid., paras. 12–15.

22 Ibid., para. 59. ('The Court does not need, in the very specific circumstances of this case, to determine whether the Bulgarian State is entitled to deprive all unlawfully residing aliens of educational benefits – such as free education – which it has agreed to provide to its nationals and certain limited categories of aliens. [...] The Court will therefore have regard primarily to the applicants' personal situation.')

23 ECtHR, *Moser v. Austria*, App. no. 12643/02, Judgment of 21 September 2006.

taken into care on account of her poverty and unclear residence status, while placement in a child-mother home was not offered. The applicant attributed the treatment she and her child received mainly to her Serbian nationality rather than to her destitution, and thus she claimed discrimination on the basis of nationality only. While the Court dismissed this allegation, it did note, in the framework of the right to family life (Article 8 ECHR), that child removal was based on both her poverty and her residential status, which in fact was explicitly acknowledged by the state.[24] In a similar case, where the applicant had also lost her daughter on account of her deprived socio-economic situation, she alleged discrimination on the basis of her culture, race and colour of skin.[25] The closest she got to depicting her economic status was a reference to her physical appearance and lifestyle. Her socio-economic position was, however, brought up and considered in the framework of her complaint under the right to family life.

At times, though, even when applicants position their socio-economic disadvantage as a significant element of their allegations, the Court may nonetheless set it aside in its legal assessment. This is particularly so when the applicant's destitution is not considered extreme. The oversight operates either by erasing the main ground of perceived disadvantage or by subsuming socio-economic status under another aspect of social difference. What losses may result from displacing the applicants' economic circumstances? Some case law suggests that ignoring this aspect may have at least two notable effects. First, it may distort the extent and type of harm experienced. Second, it may render invisible the element of difference and potential inequality involved in the case. Beyond the specifics of the cases at hand, economically neutral readings also perpetuate middle-class biases in legal and policy responses to rights violations and inequalities. The cases below attest to these problems.

In *Tolstoy Miloslavsky v. the United Kingdom*, the applicant sought to appeal an award of damages in a defamation case.[26] To do so, he was required to pay £124,900 as security for the respondent's costs. Unable to afford this, he claimed a denial of access to a court (in violation of Article 6.1 ECHR). His economic difficulties, however, were not really discussed in the judgment. In an abstract reasoning, the Court emphasised that it was legitimate to protect the other party from the respondent's legal costs and that overall, the applicant's case had been heard in the previous stages of the proceeding. The Court admitted that the sum requested was substantial, particularly as it had to be paid within 14 days. Strikingly, though, the only reference to the applicant's financial possibilities

---

24 Ibid., paras. 68–69. ('It was based solely on her lack of appropriate accommodation and financial means and her unclear residence status.')

25 ECtHR, *R.M.S. v. Spain*, App. no. 28775/12, Judgment of 18 June 2013, para. 95.

26 ECtHR, *Tolstoy Miloslavsky v. the United Kingdom*, App. no. 18139/91, Judgment of 13 July 1995.

was the following: 'nothing indicated that he would have been able to raise the money had he been given more time'.[27] His right to access the courts had not been violated.[28] In other words, since the applicant's financial difficulties were unsurmountable, nothing could have been done. The problem began and ended with the applicant. Questioning the system of fees for appeals given its impact upon the least privileged litigants was not even imagined by the Court.

Subsequently, however, the Court reached the opposite conclusion in *Aït-Mouhoub v. France*,[29] a somewhat similar case to *Tolstoy Miloslavsky*. Contesting the refusal of legal aid and the imposition of FRF 80,000 as security costs in the context of a criminal proceeding and a civil-party application, the Court found the amount 'disproportionate seeing that Mr Aït-Mouhoub [...] had no financial resources whatsoever'.[30] It is plausible to think that the different approach adopted in these two judgments had to do with the applicants' different degrees of economic hardship, which in *Aït-Mouhoub* was extreme: he had no income at all. But as the Court did not take on board the socio-economic position of the applicant in examining the proportionality of the court fees in *Tolstoy Miloslavsky*, the question remains open.

An economically abstract approach resurfaces in *Gnahoré v. France*.[31] This time, the claim of access to court concerned an appeal against the placement of the applicant's child. Care orders had been taken on grounds of abuse but after these charges had been dropped, they were renewed on account of the applicant's poverty and problems in the relationship with his child. Under Article 6 ECHR (right to a fair trial), the applicant, a Côte d'Ivoire national, complained against the refusal of legal aid, a decision founded on the lack of prospect of success for his appeal. For the Court, however, the refusal of legal aid only denied the applicant free assistance from a lawyer; it did not prevent him from pursuing his appeal.[32] Further, the Court noted that the procedure without compulsory representation was simpler and that legal aid mechanisms needed to select the cases on which public money was spent.[33] The assessment remained detached from what this design actually entailed for impoverished litigants with a migrant background like the applicant, who faced disadvantages not encountered by well-off litigants.

The cases above reveal, in the first place, how certain grievances are simply not seen and thus not assessed in the proportionality analysis. These consist in, for example, not being able to have one's case heard before a higher court, while

---

27 Ibid., para. 64.

28 Ibid., para. 67. Judge Jambrek's dissenting opinion precisely criticises the majority for its reasoning under Article 6 ECHR.

29 ECtHR, *Aït-Mouhoub v. France*, App. no. 22924/93, Judgment of 28 October 1998.

30 Ibid., paras. 57–62.

31 ECtHR, *Gnahoré v. France*, App. no. 40031/98, Judgment of 19 September 2000.

32 Ibid., para. 39.

33 Ibid., paras. 40–41.

others do; or having to pursue one's case under an unfavourable presumption that makes a loss in court more likely. And there is, of course, the feeling of being a second-class citizen whose interests are less worthy of protection. In the second place, and closely linked to the latter, to the extent that the applicant's socio-economic deprivation – her main ground of disadvantage – is left unexplored, so is the relative advantage of better-off rights holders. This is to say that the issue of difference and potential inequality escapes judicial review. The issue complained of is then more likely to be seen as an unfortunate situation, not as a human rights issue.

Some of these drawbacks were pointed out by the dissenting judges in *Gnahoré*. Looking from the perspective of the applicant, the dissenters argued that 'the system may be perceived as being inherently unfair by the least well-off appellants, as *they are the only ones* who have to show that they have a prima facie case on appeal'.[34] And even if they had managed to appeal after being refused legal aid, they 'will be disadvantaged *in comparison to* appellants who have not applied for legal aid' (since refusal of legal aid is based on a lack of strong grounds of appeal). In the eyes of the dissenters, 'the least well-off members of society *should not thereby be denied access to justice* [...] as guaranteed by Article 6 of the Convention'.[35] Also of note, these judges called into question the unavoidability of the burdens imposed on impoverished litigants by pointing to feasible alternatives for arranging the legal aid system. They asked why not, instead of spending money in a thorough examination of the prospects of appeal for deciding on the granting of legal aid, conduct that examination when the appeal on points of law was being considered. A line of reasoning like this has the value of casting doubt on the reasonableness of measures that may be perceived as 'normal' from a 'middle-class' perspective. This is an important move because if unveiling dominant biases based on culture, gender or other factors is already challenging, those based on socio-economic background are likely to remain even more hidden.

Encouraging the Court to be more attentive to economic hardship requires litigants to elaborate more on this aspect of their claim. This includes providing evidence regarding their socio-economic position, the link between this and their rights deprivations and the relative advantage of others. Perhaps this could explain the different stance taken in *Kreuz v. Poland*.[36] Unlike the aforementioned judgments, here the Court did engage with the applicant's financial limitations. It criticised the domestic courts for adopting a hypothetical view of the applicant's economic situation based on the idea that, as a businessman, he should have secured funds for the court fees required to pursue civil proceedings. The Court's conclusion that the fee was excessive for the applicant rested on his

34 Ibid., Dissenting Opinion of Judges Tulkens and Loucaides, at 1.

35 Ibid., Dissenting Opinion of Judges Tulkens and Loucaides, at 2.

36 ECtHR, *Kreuz v. Poland*, App. no. 28249/95, Judgment of 19 June 2001.

actual economic circumstances (he had invested all his savings, had losses and no income from his venture) and on the principle that access to court must be 'effective'. The Court further acknowledged the detrimental consequences faced by the applicant. Notably, he had to desist from his claim, 'his case never being heard by a court'.[37] Interestingly, though, the material distress faced by the applicant in this case was arguably somewhat less acute than what the Court had overlooked in previous cases.

There are some cases, however, where the applicants' socio-economic disadvantage is eclipsed (rather than totally erased) by other grounds of difference. Illustrative of this are complaints involving Roma and Travellers. Most judgments and decisions in these cases, at least those examined in this book, approached the applicants from the perspective of their race or ethnic origin only. This emphasis appears justified. Racial discrimination is at the core of the exclusion and rights deprivations experienced by Roma and Travellers in many fields;[38] although, to be clear, the judgments studied here rarely speak of racial discrimination.[39] The judgments nonetheless address the applicants' membership of a group defined by ethno-cultural characteristics, as seen in Chapter 2 which holds a prominent place in their legal analysis. At the same time, though, many inequalities ascribed to Roma and Travellers' ethnic origin are very much intertwined with their socio-economic disadvantage. Yet, this dimension was often overshadowed when not simply missing in the judicial reasoning. As discussed in the framework of Chapters 2 and 3, the applicants' destitution – like their gender – has often been ignored in rulings dealing with the stationing of caravans and eviction procedures against Roma and Travellers.[40] The Court held, for instance, that Roma/Traveller applicants facing evictions could simply camp on any caravan site which had planning permission.[41] No account was taken of the fact that stationing their mobile homes on public pitches or on their own land was the only real alternative for those applicants who could not afford private sites.

---

37 Ibid., paras. 60–66.

38 See e.g. European Union Agency for Fundamental Rights, Housing Conditions of Roma and Travellers in the European Union: Comparative report (FRA, 2009), at 6. ('It is clear from this report that one of the reasons for the bad housing conditions of Roma and Travellers is racial discrimination'); Malcolm Harrison *et al.*, *Migrants, Minorities and Housing: Exclusion, Discrimination and Anti-Discrimination in 15 Member States of the European Union* (European Monitoring Centre on Racism and Xenophobia, 2005), at 92–93 and 127–128.

39 With the notable exception of the judgments on the educational segregation of Roma children discussed in Chapter 2, section 1.1.

40 See also Chapter 2, section 3.1.1.

41 ECtHR, (GC) *Chapman v. the United Kingdom*, App. no. 27238/95, Judgment of 18 January 2001, para. 97; (GC) *Beard v. the United Kingdom*, App. no. 24882/94, Judgment of 18 January 2001, para. 108; (GC) *Lee v. the United Kingdom*, App. no. 25289/94, Judgment of 18 January 2001, para. 99; (GC) *Coster v. the United Kingdom*, App. no. 24876/94, Judgment of 18 January 2001, para. 111.

In other cases, economic constraints have been downplayed or left out from the inquiry into how domestic authorities took heed of the 'special needs' of 'Gypsy' applicants. The case of *Wells* is an example.[42] The applicant, who lived with his family in a caravan, opposed eviction on the basis of a statutory defence of incapacity because of personal circumstances.[43] He referred, *inter alia*, to his economic limitations and the fact that he and his family had nowhere else to go, as there was a shortfall of sites and he did not qualify for social housing. As the owner of a caravan, he was not deemed to be homeless and if he had sold it, he would have been deemed intentionally homeless. In both cases, local authority accommodation would not be made available for him. The domestic courts were eventually of the opinion that destitution and homelessness were irrelevant. Incapacity was simply about being physically able to leave the site. The applicant was convicted, fined GBP 1,500 and ordered to pay costs. The Court upheld the domestic courts' assessment, recalling that Article 8 ECHR did not give a right to home or provide for accommodation preferences. It noted further that 'gypsies must be regarded as in the same unfortunate position as many others who are not able to afford to continue to reside on sites or in houses attractive to them'.[44] In discarding the need to examine the applicant's discrimination complaint, the Court observed that 'his status as a gypsy was taken into account [...] and was reasonably regarded as not of decisive relevance'.[45] Nothing was said about the consideration (not) given to his situation of poverty.

All in all, the Roma and Traveller cases reviewed illustrate some of the normative consequences of side-lining the applicants' socio-economic disadvantage. Among others, the Court mischaracterised what was at stake for the applicants in some cases, as the intensity of the rights interference they faced was minimised. The scrutiny in terms of proportionality and non-discrimination has therefore been partial. What is more, the different ways in which material deprivation affected the enjoyment of human rights tended to be obfuscated. For example, it is clear that destitution imposes excessive burdens or aggravates the impact of land planning regulations affecting Roma and Travellers generally. But experiencing poverty may also be one of the root causes of violations. This was the case with Roma children's misdiagnosis, which seems to have rested on the stereotype according to which 'being a poor Romani child equals to having a mild mental disability'.[46]

---

42 See also Chapter 2, section 3.1.1.

43 ECtHR, *Wells v. the United Kingdom*, App. no. 37794/05, Decision of 16 January 2007.

44 Ibid., at 10.

45 Ibid., at. 11.

46 Lilla Farkas, Report on Discrimination of Roma Children in Education, Report prepared for the European Commission (2014), at 32.

The case law reviewed thus far provides a fair indication of how challenging it may be to conceive of class or economic disadvantage as something legally relevant, even in human rights law. The limited visibility of this aspect of people's lives in the rights discourse supports the view advanced by scholars that normative discussions about diversity and inclusion rarely include class or economic difference.[47] This is at odds with the fact that a range of measures and practices impinging upon human rights are grounded on economic hierarchies or have a disproportionate impact on those more at risk of socio-economic exclusion. The above examples also suggest that litigants themselves may overlook their socio-economic hardship, probably because this is not perceived as a source of strength for winning their cases. Because the litigants and/or the Court overlook questions of socio-economic difference, the result is a fragmented account of the case (and of rights holders, in particular), which, as seen above, leads to normative and practical problems. Considering that poverty is frequently discarded as a group characteristic or as an aspect of identity holding legal relevance, one may still ask whether it is considered as a source of vulnerability that triggers specific normative responses. Or, to follow the Court's nomenclature, the question is whether people living in poverty are considered to belong to a 'vulnerable group'. To this the discussion turns in what follows.

2.3. THE SOCIO-ECONOMICALLY DISADVANTAGED AS (IN)VULNERABLE

As noted in Chapter 2, the Court's judgment in *Yordanova*, a case concerning a Roma community living in an informal settlement and which is further discussed below, seems to link the applicant's vulnerability to their socio-economic precariousness. In view of their status as a socially disadvantaged group, and regardless of their ethnic origin, their needs deserved particular attention.[48] The Court similarly stressed the special protection owed to persons in vulnerable situations when examining the situation of the applicant in *Soares de Melo*, an impoverished mother who lost her children on account of poverty.[49] These judgments may suggest that the Court is heading towards

---

47 Rosaura Sánchez, 'On a Critical Realist Theory of Identity', in Linda Martín Alcoff *et al.* (eds.), *Identity Politics Reconsidered* (Palgrave Macmillan, 2006), at 35; Rita Dhamoon, *Identity/Difference Politics. How Difference is Produced, and Why It Matters* (UBC Press, 2009), at 8–9; Seyla Benhabib, *The Claims of Culture. Equality and Diversity in the Global Era* (Princeton University Press, 2002), at 17.

48 ECtHR, *Yordanova and Others v. Bulgaria*, App. no. 25446/06, Judgment of 24 April 2012, paras. 129–130.

49 ECtHR, *Soares de Melo v. Portugal*, App. no. 72850/14, Judgment of 16 February 2016, para. 106. See also, *Barnea and Caldararu v. Italy*, App no. 37931/15, Judgment of 22 June 2017, para. 72.

the recognition of people living in poverty as a vulnerable group. However, this is far from being settled. Judges López Guerra and Keller, dissenting in the recent case of *Garib v. the Netherlands*, precisely argued, *inter alia*, that 'the poor are a vulnerable group in and of themselves'.[50] A similar position appears advanced by Judge Pinto's dissenting opinion in the Grand Chamber judgment adopted in the same case.[51] Considering that people living in poverty have been and continue to be subject to prejudice, stereotyping and social exclusion, the argument is certainly tenable. Problems nonetheless arise once one thinks of the Court's ambivalences when determining who belongs to vulnerable groups.

While in principle the concept of vulnerability has the advantage of being flexible and sensitive to context, the second part of this book has shown that at times the Court takes it as something closer to an attribute of certain bounded, *a priori* disadvantaged groups. Roma and Travellers have it, for instance; Muslims (and Muslim women in particular) do not. Consider as well the dissenting opinion of Judge Sajó in *M.S.S.* In his view, asylum seekers 'cannot be unconditionally considered as a particularly vulnerable group, in the sense in which the jurisprudence of the Court uses the term'.[52] In support of this claim, he advances two main arguments. One is that asylum seekers are not a group as such. They are 'far from homogeneous' and 'not socially classified'. The other is that even if some asylum seekers are vulnerable, this does not hold for all the members of the 'class'.[53]

Read this way, the notion of vulnerable groups would only apply to relatively homogeneous social groups affected by long-lasting prejudice and exclusion provided that its consequences were suffered by all the members of the group. There is no need to elaborate why in this light people living in poverty are not suitable candidates for qualifying as a vulnerable group. Poverty and socio-economic disadvantage are contested concepts, as is the identification of those to whom they apply. One of the arguments posited by the government at the Grand Chamber hearing in *Garib v. the Netherlands* goes precisely along these lines. It contended that the concept of poverty was relative and that the fact that the applicant was living on social welfare did not allow the case to be framed as one about poverty and vulnerability.[54] As explained earlier in this

---

50 ECtHR, *Garib v. the Netherlands*, App. no. 43494/09, Judgment of 23 February 2016, Dissenting opinion of Judges López Guerra and Keller, para. 14.

51 ECtHR, (GC) *Garib v. the Netherlands*, App. no. 43494/09, Judgment of 6 November 2017, Dissenting opinion of Judge Pinto, paras. 13 and 29–30.

52 ECtHR, (GC) *M.S.S. v. Belgium and Greece*, App. no. 30696/09, Judgment of 21 January 2011, Partly concurring and partly dissenting opinion of Judge Sajó, at 101.

53 Ibid., at 102.

54 ECtHR, Grand Chamber hearing in *Garib v. the Netherlands*, held on 25 January 2017 (referred to the Grand Chamber on 12 September 2016). In this case, the Chamber and the Grand Chamber totally ignored the question of the applicant's vulnerability as a single mother living on social welfare.

book, conceiving of any social groups as bounded homogeneous entities is more an illusion than a reality. But for those who keep the illusion alive in law, diversity is particularly evident across people living in poverty.

This last point underscores the fact that while the law naturally aims at simplifying and categorising, appropriate legal responses sometimes require a comprehensive analysis. As the above reflections suggest, this is no less true for rights claims grounded in socio-economic disadvantage. Looking at the social institutions and relations in which individuals and their rights are embedded is a helpful way to appreciate the need for an integrated approach to human rights law in poverty-related cases. The following section thus attempts to examine what an integrated and relational normative analysis could reveal about these cases.

3. WHOLE HUMANS: LOOKING THROUGH AND ACROSS RIGHTS HOLDERS

In the previous chapter, when discussing what it means to approach rights holders as whole individuals in the adjudication of cases concerning ethno-cultural difference, the discussion started by identifying the single aspect of individuals that had most salience in the judicial setting, that is, the ethnic or cultural affiliation of applicants. It then explained that, without downplaying the relevance of this aspect, the individuals concerned were more than that. Other facets of their identity and social position should not be displaced, if judges (and of course, litigants as well) wanted to avoid mischaracterising the stakes of the case. In this chapter, however, the present discussion about the complexity of rights holders takes a different starting point. It cannot simply start by asking which facets of applicants other than their socio-economic position were considered by the Court, for this very aspect of the applicants' lives – economic disadvantage – was often missing, let alone salient, as seen above.

3.1. LOOKING BEYOND THE APPLICANTS' POVERTY

Against this backdrop, the discussion below examines those cases in which the economic hardship of rights holders was in some way taken into account by the Court. Section 3.1 analyses the indirect integration of the applicants' socio-economic disadvantage through other grounds of difference, such as ethnic origin or migration status. Section 3.2, for its part, discusses the integration of different experiences of poverty. Here, the main question will point to the extent to which the cases were framed (by the litigants and/or by the Court) as gender-neutral, disability-neutral and neutral from the perspective of the individuals' nationality, ethnicity/race, cultural background and other social locations. Importantly, the enquiry aims at elucidating whether and how such framings and understandings of the cases impoverish their legal analysis.

3.1.1. Socio-Economic Disadvantage through Other Grounds of Difference

It was seen above that in some cases concerning Roma and Travellers the applicants' experience of socio-economic disadvantage was obscured by a concern with their ethno-cultural identity. Yet, there were cases in which questions of socio-economic disadvantage, rather than being absorbed by other grounds of difference, were advanced through them. Cases dealing with the educational segregation of Roma children, which the Court has qualified as indirect discrimination on the ground of ethnic origin, are illustrative. Separate placement had not only to do with the children's ethnic origin, but also with their socio-economic disadvantage. As explained in Chapter 2, it was notably in *Horváth and Kiss* that the Court acknowledged the correlation between material deprivation and the misdiagnosis of Roma children.[55] The reference to social deprivation allowed the Court to explain how the educational misplacement of children worked and how their social exclusion was worsened. But this element was not reflected in the Court's finding of discrimination in relation to the right to education.

In Chapter 2 mention was also made of the judgment in *Yordanova*.[56] This stands out for, among other things, taking into account the socio-economic disadvantage of the Roma community concerned as an aspect related to its status of ethnic minority. The applicants, who lived in an informal settlement, in single-storey houses without basic sanitation services, were ordered to leave, as their houses were to be demolished. Having remained there for decades, they argued that 'for people as desperately poor and outcast as them the expectation that the inactivity would last was a basis to build lives on'.[57] The eviction order was, in their view, taken in disregard of those circumstances and of their risk of homelessness, being actually motivated by racist prejudices. On this basis, they alleged a violation of Articles 8 and 14 ECHR. The Court agreed that the applicants were part of an 'outcast community and one of the socially disadvantaged groups'.[58] Such a social group, 'regardless of the ethnic origin of its members may need assistance in order to be able effectively to

55 ECtHR, *Horváth and Kiss v. Hungary*, App. no. 11146/11, Judgment of 29 January 2013, para. 115. See further Chapter 2, section 3.1.1.

56 ECtHR, *Yordanova and Others v. Bulgaria*, App. no. 25446/06, Judgment of 24 April 2012.

57 Ibid., para. 85. See also para. 13 of the same judgment.

58 Ibid., para. 129.

enjoy the same rights as the majority population'.[59] The conclusion was that 'the disadvantaged position of the social group to which the applicants belong could and should have been taken into consideration'.[60] A similar approach was taken in *Winterstein*, in which the Court also elaborated on the applicants' socio-economic deprivation and risks of homelessness, albeit only within the framework of Article 8 ECHR.[61]

Important implications may follow from this interpretation. One is the potential recognition of impoverished and socially excluded people as a 'social group' to be considered in decision-making affecting them. Secondly, to the extent that the Court acknowledges that those persons may need assistance not available to the majority, poverty-related claims could also give rise to duties of accommodation. In a case like *Yordanova*, these could consist of exemptions from planning regulations, participation in the devising of solutions to their housing needs and even socio-economic assistance. It remains to be seen whether the Court will further develop this interpretation in somewhat similar pending cases communicated to Slovenia in 2015.[62] They also involve a community of Roma residents in an informal settlement, although the issue there is not eviction. Instead, the applicants, relying on Articles 3, 8 and 14 ECHR, seek access to basic infrastructure such as water, sanitation and electricity. The domestic authorities had refused, noting that the legislation does not allow for infrastructure to be provided to illegally constructed buildings. For the applicants, however, 'their disadvantaged position should have prompted the authorities to adjust their approach and ensure that they are able effectively to enjoy the same fundamental rights as the majority population'.[63] Notwithstanding this, it is interesting to note that while the Roma/Traveller cases of eviction with a focus on ethno-cultural identity (the so-called 'caravan cases' discussed earlier) have tended to downplay the issue of socio-economic disadvantage, the last Roma/Traveller eviction judgments that rely on a more socio-economic narrative (such as *Yordanova* and *Winterstein*) have for their part displaced the issue of racial discrimination.[64]

---

59 Idem. In this paragraph the Court also notably holds: 'In the context of Article 8, in cases such as the present one, the applicants' specificity as a social group and their needs must be one of the relevant factors in the proportionality assessment that the national authorities are under a duty to undertake.'

60 Ibid., para. 132.

61 ECtHR, *Winterstein and Others v. France*, App. no. 27013/07, Judgment of 17 October 2013.

62 ECtHR, *Hudorovič v. Slovenia* and *Novak and Others v. Slovenia*, App. nos. 24816/14 and 25140/14, Statement of facts and questions, Communicated on 8 April 2015 (pending applications as of April 2019).

63 Ibid., at 4. See also the Third Party Intervention submitted in this case by the Human Rights Centre of Ghent University, <www.hrc.ugent.be/third-party-interventions/>.

64 In both of them, the Court finds it unnecessary to examine the discrimination complaint under Article 14. Further, in *Yordanova* the applicants had explicitly alleged 'racial discrimination' and 'racial bias', but to no avail.

But the above are not the only sets of cases in which the applicants' economic position has been brought under other identities or social positions. The Court also partially subsumed their socio-economic hardship under another ground of difference in the 2010 case of *O'Donoghue and Others v. the United Kingdom*.[65] Here, the Court had to examine the imposition of fees restricting immigrants' right to marry through a scheme aimed at preventing sham marriages. Persons subject to immigration control who wanted to marry in the United Kingdom at the time needed either entry clearance or a certificate of approval. At first, approval was denied to all those who had no leave to remain, including asylum seekers such as Mr Iwu, a Nigerian national and Ms O'Donoghue's partner. Under this scheme the couple could not even apply for approval. A third version of the scheme opened up that possibility to them, but upon payment of a GBP 295 fee. None of these requirements applied to EEA nationals (nationals of countries of the European Economic Area) and to persons seeking to marry under the rites of the Church of England. As the couple was Catholic, had no resources to pay the fee (the first applicant was on social benefits and the second applicant was not allowed to work) and did not obtain an exemption, they could not marry until friends raised funds for them. The applicants alleged a violation of their rights to marry and found a family (Article 12), freedom of religion (Article 9) and to family life (Article 8), both severally and in conjunction with Article 14 (prohibition of discrimination). As further discussed below, the applicants' claims included arguments based on their socio-economic disadvantage, alongside disadvantage on the basis of nationality and other traits. In particular, they alleged discrimination on the grounds of 'religion, nationality and poverty'.[66] The Court, however, found discrimination only in respect of the right to marry on the basis of religion.[67] It condemned direct discrimination against persons who professed no religion or a non-Anglican faith and wanted to marry. Their economic situation, like their migration status, was, however, displaced.

The above conclusion reached in *O'Donoghue and Others* is sound and yet incomplete. In fact, out of all those who did not wish to marry in accordance with Anglicanism, only those under immigration control were negatively affected by the scheme.[68] Moreover, within this pool those who could not afford

---

65 ECtHR, *O'Donoghue and Others v. the United Kingdom*, App. no. 34848/07, Judgment of 14 December 2010.

66 Ibid., para. 98. The applicants also alleged discrimination in connection with their Convention rights to private and family life (Article 8) and to freedom of religion (Article 9).

67 Ibid., paras. 102–105. The Court additionally found a separate violation on account of a discriminatory restriction of freedom of religion (Article 9 in conjunction with Article 14 ECHR). Ibid., para. 110.

68 The Court seemed to accept this when it considered that the second applicant could not marry as he 'was both unwilling (on account of his religious beliefs) and unable (on account of his residence in Northern Ireland) to enter into such a marriage'. Notwithstanding the

the permission fee were the most disadvantaged. By declining to examine whether the scheme was discriminatory on account of nationality (or migration status, as the Court pointed out) and poverty, the Court left unexplored the issue of compounded discrimination against a subgroup of immigrants.[69] It should be noted that it was a certain category of immigrants – those who were from a non-European background and poor – who were regarded with suspicion and deterred or prevented from freely marrying and leading their family life in the receiving country. Leaving this question out of the picture therefore failed to interrogate the incidence of possible compounded assumptions or stereotypes, something that section 3.2.1 *infra* addresses in more depth. The Article 14 reasoning in this case also suggests that only a disadvantage on the basis of religion raises an issue of inequality, while the unfavourable treatment accorded to migration and socio-economic status does not.

By contrast, while the right to marry (Article 12 ECHR alone) was mostly examined from the perspective of migration status and nationality, the Court incorporated therein the question of economic disadvantage. According to the applicants, the scheme 'failed to take account of the different personal circumstances which could affect different individuals'.[70] The fee was too high and admitted no exemption. It was 'beyond the means of most of the immigrant population' and not just of 'the poorest of the poor'.[71] Considering that 'many persons who are subject to immigration control will either be unable to work' or 'will fall into the lower income bracket', the Court concluded that the fee impaired their right to marry (Article 12 ECHR).[72] It thereby acknowledged the applicants' socio-economic precariousness and its close link with their immigration status. The Court did not further examine the disparate effect that such an economic requirement had, as a matter of equality, on the non-European immigrant population. Nevertheless, its analysis under Article 12 ECHR put into question a migratory regulation that only allowed for the legal admission and entitlement of better-off, usually highly skilled non-Europeans. This reveals that from a social policy perspective, concealing

reference to the applicant's residence status, the Court confined its discrimination finding solely to religion. See ibid., para. 102.

69 The Court's recounting of the third-party interveners' argumentation includes one concern that resonates with indirect discrimination language. ECtHR, *O'Donoghue and Others v. the United Kingdom*, App. no. 34848/07, Judgment of 14 December 2010, para. 78. (According to the Equality and Human Rights Commission, 'the fee levied was disproportionate and excessively high. This had a particularly harsh impact on the affected group, many of whom had not been in the United Kingdom for a long time and had not had an opportunity to build up their financial resources.')

70 Ibid., para. 65.

71 Idem.

72 Ibid., para. 90.

the socio-economic dimension of legal claims may help to perpetuate the use of institutions and rules that, whether in the field of migration or ethno-cultural integration, tend to serve only the better-off segments of migrants and minorities.

While tackling the claims reviewed above from the viewpoint of ethno-cultural disadvantage, migration status, gender or other axes of exclusion is worthwhile, obscuring the class component may perpetuate laws and policies that are not responsive to minorities, foreigners and women who live in poverty. The cases discussed above are not isolated examples. Scholars have noted, for example, how issues that are primarily defined as gender issues, such as childcare or more flexible, part-time work, continue to overlook the experience of poor women. They cannot afford childcare services that are regulated from a distinctly middle-class perspective. Nor can they benefit from part-time work when they cannot live on a part-time salary.[73]

Still, there are other ways in which rights holders tend to be disaggregated in poverty-related complaints. The following section explores the fragmentation resulting from the disentangling of class or poverty from other social locations.

3.1.2. Integrating the Different Faces of Poverty

People who experience socio-economic disadvantage are not an undifferentiated collection of individuals. And whether this is acknowledged or obscured in law holds significance. To explain why it is relevant to approach the situation of people living in poverty from the perspective of other positions and identities, let's take an old and famous case: *Airey v. Ireland*.[74] Mrs Airey claimed that she was unable to access the High Court to obtain a decree of judicial separation from her husband, as she could not afford the costs involved in legal representation and in the judicial proceedings. At the time, a separation decree was the only legal means of being relieved from a duty of cohabitation. The applicant had sought this remedy for years on the grounds of physical and psychological cruelty against her and their children. Although the parties could appear in person, in practice petitioners acted through legal representation because of the complexity of the proceedings. The Court found 'most improbable that a person in Mrs Airey's position can effectively present his or her own case'.[75] The Court described the applicant as a mother of four children, coming 'from a humble family background'.

---

73 See e.g. Laura T. Kessler, 'Getting Class', 56 *Buffalo Law Review* (2008) 915, at 917–918; Sheilagh Turkington, 'A Proposal to Amend the Ontario Human Rights Code: Recognizing Povertyism', 9 *Journal of Law and Social Policy* (1993) 134, at 181.

74 ECtHR, *Airey v. Ireland*, App. no. 6289/73, Judgment of 9 October 1979.

75 Ibid., para. 24.

She had a low wage at the time of the judgment and before that she had been in receipt of unemployment benefit, while her husband had ceased paying maintenance.[76] In view of this, and considering the high costs involved, the complexity of the proceedings and the lack of legal aid, the Court found a violation of Article 6 ECHR (access to a court). The Court's context-sensitive approach is remarkable. In fact, this is a landmark judgment for many reasons relevant to this book. The discussion will therefore come back to this case time and again. But for now, it suffices to highlight the Court's regard for the applicant's socio-economic situation.

Admittedly, lacking financial means was, in Ireland at the time, hindrance enough for any person seeking access to the High Court. But the fact that Mrs Airey was a woman suffering domestic violence allows raising some additional questions. How many victims of domestic violence could afford to petition for judicial separation? How many of those persons were women? Women are more likely to be both economically worse off and victims of domestic violence.[77] Hence, it is reasonable to think that among all persons who wished to separate and could not afford it women like Mrs Airey were particularly burdened. No statistics on this point were submitted to the Court in *Airey*. And luckily, the applicant did not need them to win her case. However, for the purpose of this analysis it is useful to reflect on how this gendered view of the applicant would have changed the arguments available to the parties and to the Court.

For instance, could that element have made it harder for the government to argue (as it did) that the problem at issue was a matter of personal circumstances for which the state had no responsibility? Could the integration of gender into the analysis have changed the Court's appreciation of the harm involved, or led it to examine the merits of the dismissed discrimination claim? Would those considerations have, at the same time, provided guidance to the state as to the kinds of civil proceeding for which legal aid could be required? There are reasons to think at least some of these questions should be answered in the affirmative. Alternatively, to make the point clearer, one may also assume that a woman like Mrs Airey who lacks financial means and wants to escape violence is complaining about the state's failure to ensure her effective access to temporary shelter or affordable housing. Would not the case miss a lot if such an applicant were characterised only in terms of her socio-economic needs? No doubt, it would. The risks of overlooking the

76 Ibid., para. 8. (The Court referred to this paragraph when considering the applicant's position.)

77 See e.g. UN Human Rights Council, Report of the Special Rapporteur on Violence Against Women, its causes and consequences, Rashida Manjoo, A/HRC/17/26, 2 May 2011, paras. 14, 38–39 and 74–75.

intersections between poverty and other social locations are further analysed below.

There are cases in which the need to take a compounded view of the applicant's socio-economic situation appears evident from the manner in which their rights are restricted by a given measure. Think, for instance, of statutory limitations imposed on account of people's migration status or nationality and which explicitly lead to economic hardship and/or adversely affect the worst off among foreign residents. Several regulations in the field of nationality and migration are accompanied by restrictions on working, moving or accessing social benefits. In such cases, it seems obvious that poverty cannot be detached from nationality or migration status. Examples are *O'Donoghue and Others v. the United Kingdom*, mentioned above, or *M.S.S. v. Greece and Belgium* and similar cases involving migrants and asylum seekers. In these judgments the Court has been keen to recognise, albeit to differing degrees and in different ways, the relationship between the applicants' socio-economic disadvantage and their migration/asylum status. In *M.S.S.* the Court attributed the applicant's extreme destitution to the deliberate omissions of the authorities in the reception of asylum seekers.[78] Under the right to marry (Article 12 ECHR), the Court in *O'Donoghue and Others* examined the financial limitations of the applicants in being able to afford the fee required to marry in view of the fact that persons subjected to migratory control were either not allowed to work or were likely to occupy the lowest economic positions.[79]

In many other cases, however, the links between the applicant's socio-economic circumstances and other identities or social locations were unstated aspects of the restrictions in question. Adopting a comprehensive approach then appears more challenging. Think, for instance, of cases dealing with the taking of children into care on account of their parents' poverty and with a view to protecting their wellbeing. As explained below, in examining these complaints the Court has tended to focus on the parents' destitution, while the interplay between poverty and power relations around gender, disability and/or ethno-cultural background has often been overlooked. Exceptions to this arose where the domestic authorities had explicitly relied on those other personal circumstances to justify the restrictions on family life.

A number of such cases concerning family separation have been brought to the Court. These cases have in common: (1) that the taking into care of children was motivated by the parents' situation of poverty; (2) that placement was ordered in the absence of evidence of abuse or mistreatment; (3) that none or

---

78 ECtHR, (GC) *M.S.S. v. Belgium and Greece*, App. no. 30696/09, Judgment of 21 January 2011, para. 250.

79 ECtHR, *O'Donoghue and Others v. the United Kingdom*, App. no. 34848/07, Judgment of 14 December 2010, para. 90.

little material support was provided to the families; and (4) that usually parents were additionally deprived of parental responsibility and denied all contact with their children. (5) Finally, in all these cases, family separation affected parents, notably mothers, and children, whose experience was marked by their socio-economic deprivation and their ethnic origin, gender and/or disability.[80] This case law reflects a broader problem, about which the European Council's Parliamentary Assembly (PACE) expressed concern in 2015. According to PACE, although statistics are lacking, evidence suggests that 'children from vulnerable groups are disproportionally represented in the care population of member states, whereas no evidence suggests that parents who are poor, less educated, belong to minorities or have a migration background are more likely to abuse or neglect their children'.[81] This problematic picture has furthermore unfolded in a context of economic crisis which may exacerbate the vulnerability of disadvantaged families to forcible separation. In fact, liberalisation trends may reinforce the 'privatisation' of childcare responsibilities while diluting the societal dimension involved in caregiving.[82]

Faced with these complaints, the Court has invariably found a violation of the right to family life (Article 8 ECHR) and recalled that unsatisfactory living conditions alone do not constitute sufficient justification for separating families. Cases in which poverty is easily conflated with neglect, in turn leading to child removal, can fairly be described as cases about parents and children living in poverty. Nevertheless, this poverty-centred account needs to be gendered. In the first place, women are overwhelmingly responsible for child upbringing and are also more frequently at risk of poverty.[83] In the second place, such economic

---

80 ECtHR, *Moser v. Austria*, App. no. 12643/02, Judgment of 21 September 2006; *Wallová and Walla v. the Czech Republic*, App. no. 23848/04, Judgment of 26 October 2006; *Havelka and Others v. the Czech Republic*, App. no. 23499/06, Judgment of 21 June 2007; *Savigny v. Ukraine*, App. no. 39948/06, Judgment of 18 December 2008; *A.K. and L. v. Croatia*, App. no. 37956/11, Judgment of 8 January 2013; *R.M.S. v. Spain*, App. no. 28775/12, Judgment of 18 June 2013; *N.P. v. the Republic of Moldova*, App. no. 58455/13, Judgment of 6 October 2015; *Soares de Melo v. Portugal*, App. no. 72850/14, Judgment of 16 February 2016 and *Barnea and Caldararu v. Italy*, App. no. 37931/15, Judgment of 22 June 2017. The case of *Gnahoré v. France*, submitted by an African immigrant father of three, also concerned child removal. But in this case, unlike the aforementioned ones, the separation was not solely based on material and educational grounds. ECtHR, *Gnahoré v. France*, App. no. 40031/98, Judgment of 19 September 2000.

81 PACE, Report on Social services in Europe: legislation and practice of the removal of children from their families in Council of Europe member States, 13730, 13 March 2015, para. 4.

82 Dorothy E. Roberts, 'The Dialectic of Privacy and Punishment in the Gendered Regulation of Parenting', 5(2) *Stanford Journal of Civil Rights & Civil Liberties* (2009) 191, at 192–93.

83 Both aspects, a disproportional share of care work and poverty are, in fact, interrelated. See UN General Assembly, Report by the Special Rapporteur on Extreme Poverty and Human Rights on unpaid care work and women's human rights, Magdalena Sepúlveda Carmona, A/68/293, 9 August 2013, paras. 6–17. In the same vein, Sandra Fredman and Beth Goldblatt, 'Gender Equality and Human Rights', 4 *UN Women Discussion Paper Series* (2014), at 19 and 44.

insecurity is significantly produced by the fact that care work enjoys little social support and recognition. This is reflected, *inter alia*, in a shortage of state-sponsored childcare institutions and in a job market that disapproves of and penalises flexible work schedules, as well as in the absence of public policies to pay for care work. It follows that a gendered approach to parents living in poverty does not only apply to women. It also covers the situation of men who may take the (gendered) role of caring for their children while also struggling to ensure material wellbeing, as in the case of *Havelka*.[84]

The situation of impoverished single mothers nonetheless merits special mention. Firstly, single mothers face greater obstacles in combining care and paid work, being more frequently in need of social welfare. Secondly, and related to the latter, since these women are mostly in charge of child-raising and more at risk of poverty, they may also be more exposed to forcible child removal on poverty grounds. In fact, cases such as *Moser v. Austria*, *A.K. and L. v. Croatia*, *R.M.S. v. Spain* and *Soares de Melo v. Portugal* all concerned child-mother separation.[85] Thirdly, it is not uncommon that underlying childcare orders against single poor mothers is a process of 'othering' that casts them as deviant. While their poverty is a major factor around which their 'otherness' is constructed, often that is intertwined with assumptions and value judgments concerning motherhood and sexuality.[86] As seen below, these assumptions are likely to be shaped by and combined with preconceptions related to disability and ethnic background.

In the aforementioned case of *Moser v. Austria*, the Court found a violation of the right to family life mainly on account of the state's failure to take positive actions to explore alternatives to child removal, including placement in a mother-child centre and regularisation of the applicant's residence status.[87] Aside from her migration status, the Court also approached her situation from the perspective of economic hardship and nationality, but in a quite limited fashion. When examining the discrimination claim on account of the fact that Austrian nationals and nationals from other EU member states would have been supported and placed in a mother-child home, the Court contented itself with noting that the legislation in question did not formally

84 The applicant in this case was a single father who struggled to provide for his six children. He had health problems, had difficulty in finding a job and could only engage in part-time paid work because he had to take care of the youngest children. Further on this case, see below this same section and *infra* section 3.1.3.

85 See also ECtHR, *Zhou v. Italy*, App. no. 33773/11, Judgment of 21 January 2014.

86 See among others, Emily Winograd Leonard, 'Expecting the unattainable: caseworker use of the "ideal" mother stereotype against the non-offending mother for failure to protect from child sexual abuse cases', 69 *NYU Annual Survey of American Law* (2013) 311, at 326–329; Martha Fineman, 'Images of Mothers in Poverty Discourses', (2) *Duke Law Journal* (1991) 274, at 291.

87 ECtHR, *Moser v. Austria*, App. no. 12643/02, Judgment of 21 September 2006, para. 70.

distinguish on the basis of nationality.[88] The question of how effective this was in practice was not addressed. The opportunities that were actually available to the applicant and her child could hardly be uncoupled from her position as a single mother of foreign origin without access to socio-economic aid or to a support network.[89]

Also, take the case of *R.M.S. v. Spain*,[90] which is in several respects representative of the way impoverished single women, and particularly those who belong to minorities or to other excluded groups, are portrayed as incapable of caring. In this case, the three-year-old daughter of a Spanish single mother of Guinean origin was taken into care after the mother had visited the social services, along with her daughter, seeking socio-economic support ('work, food and housing'). When the administrative and judicial authorities assessed her case, the fact that the applicant's two eldest children were looked after by her great-uncle while she was away working as a temporary worker was read simply as an act of child abandonment.[91] The applicant was depicted as a disinterested mother who, instead of staying close to her children, emigrated or moved around to work. In addition, she and her extended family were viewed as providing an inappropriate environment, and her sexual irresponsibility was pointed out (the father of her child was unknown and she was 'once again pregnant').[92] Further, the Spanish authorities blamed her for her own destitution, as they found that she had not made sufficient efforts despite her skills.[93] Finally, the fact that she complained against the taking of her child made her violent, maniac or mentally ill in the eyes of the authorities. These images about impoverished single mothers are not infrequent and have been documented elsewhere.[94] Yet, as further explained below, they remained unchallenged by the Strasbourg Court.

The interplay between gender, ethnic origin and poverty is likewise present in *Soares de Melo v. Portugal*, a case brought by a Muslim woman from Cape Verde.[95] Six of her ten children, aged between seven months and six years,

---

88 Ibid., para. 78.

89 The applicant and her three children were accommodated in the 40-square-metre apartment of a friend of hers but this was considered unsuitable and insufficient by the social services.

90 ECtHR, *R.M.S. v. Spain*, App. no. 28775/12, Judgment of 18 June 2013.

91 Ibid., para. 30.

92 Ibid., para. 34.

93 Ibid., para. 43.

94 Bruce Porter, Affidavit before the Superior Court of Justice, Ontario, Between Dale Broomer et al. and Attorney General of Ontario et al., 02-CV-229203 CM3, 2002, paras. 28–37; Emily Winograd Leonard, 'Expecting the unattainable: caseworker use of the "ideal" mother stereotype against the non-offending mother for failure to protect from child sexual abuse cases', 69 *NYU Annual Survey of American Law* (2013) 311, at 328–329; Shruti Rana, 'Restricting the rights of poor mothers: An international human rights critique of "workfare"', 33 *Columbia Journal of Law and Social Problems* (2000) 393, at 404–411.

95 ECtHR, *Soares de Melo v. Portugal*, App. no. 72850/14, Judgment of 16 February 2016.

were taken into care with a view to their adoption. The reason was, again, that she did not provide them with adequate material living conditions and neglected them. The domestic authorities considered that the applicant was incapable of performing her role as a mother and took into account that she persistently refused to undergo sterilisation, a condition stipulated in an 'agreement' reached with the social services. This aspect of the case shows that women living in poverty, especially when they belong to minorities, are more at risk of being victims of discrimination and violence, including that consisting of forced sterilisation.[96] Moreover, this and other affronts to the sexual and reproductive freedom of women in poverty usually rest on the assumption that poverty is caused by their sexual irresponsibility and that poor women are unfit to care for children.[97]

The maternal death case of *Şentürk v. Turkey*,[98] where the victims' socio-economic disadvantage was determinant, could similarly be engendered. In this case an eight-months-pregnant woman in great pain was not examined by doctors and was subsequently denied urgent medical attention because she was not able to pay the sum requested by the hospital. After wandering from one hospital to another in search of medical assistance, Ms Şentürk eventually died. According to the applicants, medical attention had been denied because they lacked financial means.[99] And this arguably also had an impact on the lack of response by the judicial system, although neither the applicants nor the Court said so. The Court notably found a substantive violation of the right to life (Article 2 ECHR) because medical care was subordinated to prior payment, despite the medical staff being aware of the risks involved, and because the legal framework in place was not capable of preventing this type of situation when a patient could not afford the fee.[100] A procedural violation, in turn, flowed from the excessive delays in the examination of the applicants' case and the failure to prosecute those who had endangered Ms Şentürk's life. Interestingly, however, none of these elements were linked to the victim's position as a woman and the fact that the healthcare denied is needed only by women. This contrasts with the perspective endorsed by the applicants and the CEDAW Committee in the case of *Pimentel v. Brazil*. Rejecting the

---

96 In its judgment the Court actually emphasised the gravity of forced sterilisation and recalled its jurisprudence on the matter. See e.g. ECtHR, *V.C. v. Slovakia*, App. No. 18968/07, Judgment of 8 November 2011, §§106–107; *N.B. v. Slovakia*, App. no 29518/10, Judgment of 12 June 2012, §80.

97 The applicant argued that the taking of her children was a way to punish her for not having been sterilised and having instead given birth to four children. ECtHR, *Soares de Melo v. Portugal*, App. no. 72850/14, Judgment of 16 February 2016, para. 79.

98 ECtHR, *Mehmet Şentürk and Bekir Şentürk v. Turkey*, App. no. 13423/09, Judgment of 9 April 2013.

99 Ibid., para. 84.

100 Ibid., paras. 95–97.

government's argument that the case was about medical negligence and had no link with gender equality, the Committee held that the victim's maternal death was compounded by her status as a woman of African descent and her socio-economic hardship.[101]

The importance of avoiding gender- and ethnicity-neutral assessment of welfare policies is further reaffirmed by *Garib v. the Netherlands*, a recent chamber judgment just confirmed by the Grand Chamber.[102] It concerned the refusal of a housing permit to a single mother living on social welfare on account of legislation imposing income requirements (in terms of level and source of income) on persons wishing to reside in a number of inner-city areas of Rotterdam. By virtue of this regulation, the applicant, who was already residing in a designated area, could not move to the new, more suitable accommodation she had found a few blocks away. The policy aimed at improving the quality of life of impoverished inner-city areas affected by 'unemployment, poverty, exclusion [...] antisocial behaviour, the influx of illegal immigrants and crime'.[103] The concentration of socio-economically disadvantaged groups placed 'greater demand on social security structures, reduced support for economic activities and services, hampered integration, threatened public safety and security, and led to increased crime'.[104]

Although primarily concerned with the applicant's source and level of income within the framework of a welfare policy, the case should not be examined in gender- and racially-neutral terms. As the applicant noted, the Dutch Council of State had expressed its concern not only about the burdens imposed on low-income groups, but also about 'the implicit distinction based on income, which might lead to indirect distinctions on grounds of race, colour or national or ethnic origin'.[105] Arguing along similar lines, the Equal Treatment Commission had posited that 'persons with non-Western European immigrant roots, such as persons of Turkish, Moroccan, Surinamese or Netherlands Antilles descent (*afkomst*) and single-parent families (i.e. working mothers and mothers on social welfare) were overrepresented among the unemployed

101 The Committee held that the lack of appropriate maternal health services that failed to meet the specific, distinctive health needs and interests of women not only violated their right to health (Article 12 CEDAW) but also constituted discrimination against women. And although in this case the applicant was not formally denied attention for economic reasons, as was the case of Ms Şentürk, the Committee was of the view that Ms da Silva Pimentel was discriminated against not only on the basis of her sex, but also on the basis of her socio-economic background and her status as a woman of African descent. See Committee on the Elimination of Discrimination against Women (CEDAW), *Alyne da Silva Pimentel v Brazil*, Communication no. 17/2008, Views adopted on 25 July 2011, paras. 5.4–7.7.

102 ECtHR, *Garib v. the Netherlands*, App. no. 43494/09, Judgment of 23 February 2016 (referred to the Grand Chamber on 12 September 2016).

103 Ibid., para. 23.

104 Ibid., para. 94.

105 Ibid., para. 20.

and among those earning less than 120 per cent of the statutory minimum wage'.[106] The Court, however, failed to consider these aspects as well as the applicant's specific circumstances.[107] Instead, it applied a lenient standard of review that validated any general social policy that the legislature judges to be in the 'public' or 'general' interest 'unless that judgment is *manifestly* without reasonable foundation'.[108] In doing so, the Court did not examine the proportionality of the measure in view of its application to a single mother on social benefits who resided in the designated area and had no criminal record. Nor did it consider the specific impact the refusal of housing permit had on her and her family, who were already in a vulnerable situation. The Court simply concluded that this fact and her 'good behaviour' 'cannot by itself suffice to outweigh the public interest which is served by the consistent application of legitimate public policy'.[109] At the same time, existing material casting doubt on the ability of the policy to accomplish its stated aims was overlooked.[110] This line of reasoning was fully endorsed by the Grand Chamber in 2017.[111]

Further cases demonstrate the importance of being sensitive to the interplay between poverty, gender and other non-privileged traits and positions, such as having a disability or a non-dominant ethno-cultural background. Take, for example, *Havelka and Others*,[112] *Savigny v. Ukraine*,[113] *A.K. and L. v. Croatia*[114] and *Barnea and Caldararu v. Italy*.[115] As in the family separation cases mentioned above, the children were also taken into care because of their parents' poverty. But their deprivations and the way the domestic authorities evaluated the applicants' parenting abilities were also closely linked to disadvantages attached to their disability, age or minority background. Contesting the authorities' assertion that he had not made enough effort to find a job, the applicant in *Havelka* argued that he was in a highly

---

106 Ibid., para. 42.

107 Ibid., para. 113. The Chamber held that '[i]n order to determine the proportionality of a general measure, the Court must primarily assess the legislative choices underlying it' and that 'the more convincing the general justifications for the general measure are, the less importance the Court will attach to its impact in the particular case'.

108 Ibid., paras. 116(a) and 127 (emphasis added). For an analysis on the inadequacy of this reasoning, see written comments submitted by the Human Rights Centre, Ghent University and Equality Law Clinic, Université Libre de Bruxelles; Joint Third Party Interventions, <www.hrc.ugent.be/wp-content/uploads/2017/01/Garib-tpi-hrc-ugent-ulb.pdf>, at 1–3.

109 ECtHR, *Garib v. the Netherlands*, App. no. 43494/09, Judgment of 23 February 2016, para. 133.

110 Ibid., paras. 47–48, 53 and 57(b)(c).

111 ECtHR, (GC) *Garib v. the Netherlands*, App. no. 43494/09, Judgment of 6 November 2017, paras. 137–158.

112 ECtHR, *Havelka and Others v. Czech Republic*, App. no 23499/06, Judgment of 21 June 2007.

113 ECtHR, *Savigny v. Ukraine*, App. no. 39948/06, Judgment of 18 December 2008.

114 ECtHR, *A.K. and L. v. Croatia*, App. no. 37956/11, Judgment of 8 January 2013.

115 ECtHR, *Barnea and Caldararu v. Italy*, App. no. 37931/15, Judgment of 22 June 2017.

disadvantaged position in the labour market due to his age, partial disability, lack of education and the fact that he was the sole caretaker of his three minor children.[116] Likewise, the applicants in *Savigny* claimed that they could not provide their children with better conditions due to their blindness and the discrimination they encountered.[117] In their view, 'their family was unique among blind couples due to the number of their children. Furthermore, none of the families registered with the USB [Ukrainian Society of the Blind] had such an unsuitable housing situation.'[118] For the applicants, 'their very special situation required more efforts from the State authorities to ensure their dignity and equality with healthy people'.[119]

Considering these applicants in their complexity, that is, beyond their situation of poverty, is not just about the outcome of the case. In fact, in the child removal cases discussed above a violation of their right to family life was found. Approaching rights holders as a whole helps to bring to light the specific barriers and harms encountered by women, minorities or people with disability who live in poverty, whether they are considered from the perspective of substantive Convention rights (particularly in terms of proportionality) and/or equality (Article 14 ECHR). Such a comprehensive approach also draws attention to the possible roots of violations, including entrenched inequalities and the use of compounded stereotypes. The next subsection turns to this.

3.1.3. *Addressing Intersecting Stereotypes and Indirect Discrimination*

As discussed in the previous chapter, stereotypes are generalised views or preconceptions about the attributes of members of a particular group or about the roles they should perform in society.[120] Similarly to CEDAW's condemnation of gender stereotypes, such as those that depict women as the home and child carer, the UN Guiding Principles on Extreme Poverty and Human Rights and other mechanisms underscore the need to protect persons living in poverty from stigmas attached to conditions of poverty.[121]

---

116 ECtHR, *Havelka and Others v. Czech Republic*, App. no 23499/06, Judgment of 21 June 2007, para. 46.

117 ECtHR, *Savigny v. Ukraine*, App. no. 39948/06, Judgment of 18 December 2008, para. 25.

118 Ibid., para. 64.

119 Idem.

120 Rebeca J. Cook and Simone Cusack, *Gender Stereotyping: Transnational Legal Perspectives* (University of Pennsylvania Press, 2010), at 9–13. See also Alexandra Timmer, 'Toward an anti-stereotyping approach for the European Court of Human Rights', 11(4) *Human Rights Law Review* (2011) 707.

121 UN Office of the High Commissioner for Human Rights, Guiding Principles on Extreme Poverty and Human Rights, Adopted on 27 September 2012 in Resolution 21/11 (OHCHR, 2012), Principle 21.

Typical preconceptions about people living in poverty portray them as lazy, irresponsible, indifferent to their children's health and education, dishonest and undeserving.[122] The fact that in some cases socio-economic disadvantage is not recognised as a legally relevant aspect of rights holders, as discussed earlier, makes it all the more difficult to tackle the incidence of poverty-related stereotypes in human rights violations. A first step in that direction is therefore to make socio-economic disadvantage visible in the way litigants and the Court approach the rights holders' situation. Once this is done and the door is open to scrutinising the state's reliance on poverty-based stereotypes, it is important to bear in mind that often different harmful stereotypes intersect. In so doing, they assign characteristics to members of subgroups of people.[123] As seen above, young mothers living in poverty are, for example, often perceived as incarnating a combination of the characteristics accorded to their gender roles and to their socio-economic disadvantage.

When care orders are implemented without evidence of child neglect or harm and certain caregivers (those who live in poverty, who have a migrant background, single-parent families, and parents with disabilities) are simply regarded as unfit for child-rearing, judges should closely scrutinise whether harmful stereotypes or other informal ways of disciplining social deviance are at stake. For this, an integrated rather than a unidimensional view of rights holders is needed.

The Court has adopted reasoning conducive to challenging the specific violations of family life suffered by parents living in poverty, including the use of unfounded assumptions about them. In both *R.M.S.* and *Soares de Melo*, as in virtually all other similar cases, the Court has noted that the domestic authorities lacked evidence supporting the social services' assertions regarding parents' irresponsibility or inability.[124] In *R.M.S.*, the Court also considered that the applicant was forced to prove that she was a good mother, while no evidence submitted to that effect could overcome the judicial authorities' assumptions.[125] In *Soares de Melo*, it found unacceptable that parental rights were made conditional upon sterilisation. Failure to undergo sterilisation,

---

122 CESCR, General Comment No. 20: Non-discrimination in economic, social and cultural rights (art. 2, para. 2, of the International Covenant on Economic, Social and Cultural Rights), E/C.12/GC/20, 2 July 2009, para. 35; UN Office of the High Commissioner for Human Rights, Guiding Principles on Extreme Poverty and Human Rights, Adopted on 27 September 2012 in Resolution 21/11 (OHCHR, 2012), Principle 21; UN General Assembly, Report of the Special Rapporteur on Extreme Poverty and Human Rights, Magdalena Sepúlveda Carmona, A/66/265, 4 August 2011, para. 7.

123 Rebeca J. Cook and Simone Cusack, *Gender Stereotyping: Transnational Legal Perspectives* (University of Pennsylvania Press, 2010), at 29–31.

124 ECtHR, *R.M.S. v. Spain*, App. no. 28775/12, Judgment of 18 June 2013, paras. 87–89; *Soares de Melo v. Portugal*, App. no. 72850/14, Judgment of 16 February 2016, para. 108.

125 ECtHR, *R.M.S. v. Spain*, App. no. 28775/12, Judgment of 18 June 2013, para. 89.

even if informed and voluntarily accepted, should not have been held against the applicant.[126] Moreover, the Court approached her situation in a most comprehensive manner. In finding a violation of Article 8 ECHR, it ascertained the lack of response from the social services to the material distress of the applicant, the mother of a large family who was parenting practically alone. The Court also took into account that the domestic courts had failed to consider the cultural differences involved in her case while adding to the pressure exerted on the applicant to undergo sterilisation.[127]

While conducive to the exposition and scrutiny of stereotypes, this line of reasoning has not fully unfolded. In the aforementioned cases, the Court could have pinpointed the state's use of negative compounded stereotypes and social expectations concerning the applicants' gendered roles, ethnic background and socio-economic status. And the same goes for the integration of other markers of difference, such as disability. As noted in previous chapters, one way in which stereotypes could be tackled is through the prohibition of discrimination. Of note, the EU Parliamentary Assembly has acknowledged the link between discrimination, the over-representation of vulnerable groups in the care population and the incidence of stereotypes and prejudice.[128] When it comes to intersecting stereotypes, in particular, usually the question will be one of indirect discrimination. However, this has not been scrutinised by the Court.

As seen above, people often perceive their situation as discrimination because of their experience as women, as a person with a disability and/or as having a migrant background rather than because of their socio-economic precariousness. This may be a strong indication that poverty-related disadvantage is a precondition or even a proxy for other socially devalued and subordinated social positions. Such an indication should lead the Court to examine more closely the links between these social identities or locations and poverty-related claims. Doing so is all the more important insofar as distinctions and disadvantages imposed by policies, regulations or practices relying on economic factors are likely to be regarded as reasonable.

---

126 ECtHR, *Soares de Melo v. Portugal*, Judgment of 16 February 2016, paras. 110–111. Remarkably, the Court found an additional violation of Article 8 ECHR (aside from the one stemming from child removal) on account of the pressure exerted on the applicant to undergo sterilisation. See para. 121 of the same judgment.

127 Ibid., para. 118.

128 PACE, Report on Social services in Europe: legislation and practice of the removal of children from their families in Council of Europe member States, 13730, 13 March 2015, para. 54. See also Council of Europe, Committee of Ministers; Recommendation Rec(2005)5 of the Committee of Ministers to Member States on the Rights of Children Living in Residential Institutions, Adopted on 16 March 2005, basic principle on the prohibition of discrimination in decisions concerning child placement.

As happens with the cultural expressions discussed in Chapters 2 and 3, such as dress, modes of living and language, it is easy for socio-economic considerations to be functionally connected to a legitimate social aim. This may take the form of a presumption of legitimacy or of the dismissal of any causal link between the contested measure and the resulting harm or exclusion. The consequence is that economic measures or criteria receive less scrutiny than they deserve. Take the Court's decision in *Haydarie and Others v. the Netherlands*.[129] The applicant, an Afghan woman who lived in the Netherlands with one of her children and her disabled sister, was denied family reunion with her three other children, who stayed behind when their mother fled the country. The reason for denial was that the applicant did not meet a minimum income requirement set by the law. Instead, she relied on social benefits. Upholding the government's argument, the Court did 'not consider unreasonable a requirement that an alien who seeks family reunion must demonstrate that he/she has sufficient independent and lasting income, not being welfare benefits [...].'[130] The Court subsequently turned to the applicant's efforts to find a paid job (which were regarded as insufficient) and evaluated her supposed choices (which were seen as wrong). At no point was there any examination of the justification for subjecting the applicant's family reunification to such an income requirement. The state did not explain it and the Court did not miss this information. The reasonability of the measure is just a given, especially in migration law. Against this, the principle that family separation cannot be justified solely on economic grounds and the best interest of children had no role to play. Cases such as *Haydarie* as well as *O'Donoghue and Others* (discussed earlier) nonetheless demonstrate how socio-economic requirements affect with particular intensity immigrants with non-European backgrounds, which raises an issue of indirect discrimination.[131]

The *Garib* case also provides an interesting example of the disparate effects of policy regulations based on supposedly general and rational economic criteria, such as level or source of income. The Dutch Inner City Problems Act restricted the right of welfare recipients to take up residence in some deprived areas with the aim of reducing the concentration of socio-economically disadvantaged people in those neighbourhoods. The level or source of income is thereby revealed as a criterion functionally related to the aim sought

129 ECtHR, *Haydarie and Others v. the Netherlands*, App. no. 8876/04, Decision of 20 October 2005.

130 Ibid., at 13.

131 For a discussion of indirect discrimination against migrants in the context of socio-economic criteria laid down for family reunification and in integration tests, see Sarah Ganty, 'Civic Integration Tests Under the Control of the European Court of Justice: A Perilous Tightrope Walk between Margin of Appreciation of the Member States and Protection of Third Country Nationals', 1 *European Journal of Human Rights* (2016) 32, at 32.

by the Act. Moreover, according to the Court, 'the restriction complained of [...] does not target any particular individual or individuals but is of general application in discrete areas (namely, circumscribed areas within the city of Rotterdam)'.[132] The abstraction of the account is remarkable, though. For one thing, the contention that the restriction did not target any particular individuals is at best artificial. The measure actually targeted persons relying on unemployment social benefits and households with an income under 120 per cent of the statutory minimum wage.[133] A similar pretence of neutrality is conveyed by the assertion that the application of such a housing policy was limited to discrete areas. These discrete areas actually happened to be rather deprived neighbourhoods, populated by socio-economically disadvantaged residents, mostly immigrants.[134]

For these reasons, the housing policy in question was problematic from the perspective of both direct discrimination against socio-economically disadvantaged people and indirect discrimination against the women and migrants among them. Nevertheless, these issues were not part of the analysis carried out under the right to choose one's residence, while the prohibition of discrimination was not examined.[135] Against this, the argumentation offered by Judge Pinto de Albuquerque (joined by Judge Vehabović) when dissenting from the majority in the Grand Chamber judgment in *Garib* is particularly remarkable. On the basis of extensive reasoning, they contend that the case gave rise to both an issue of direct discrimination on the basis of the applicant's 'social and economic situation', and of 'indirect' and 'intersectional discrimination' on account of her status as a woman in socio-economic precariousness.[136]

Related concerns may apply to cases involving the imposition of fees and other forms of economic requirement. Consider cases such as *Airey*, *Gnahoré*, *Şentürk*, *O'Donoghue* and *Ponomaryovi*. The conventional thinking is that service providers may set prices according to the market and other objective considerations. Claiming that these measures amount to direct discrimination on the basis of social condition or, alternatively, indirect discrimination against socio-economically disadvantaged people would therefore lead the Court into dealing with those economic justifications which, by their very nature, seem beyond the scrutiny of the law. These examples suggest that socio-economic

---

132 ECtHR, *Garib v. the Netherlands*, App. no. 43494/09, Judgment of 23 February 2016, para. 106.

133 Ibid., paras. 34 and 42.

134 Ibid., paras. 23, 28, and 94.

135 Article 14 ECHR was not invoked by the applicant before the Chamber and while it was raised before the Grand Chamber, the latter declined to have competence to examine it. See ECtHR, (GC) *Garib v. the Netherlands*, App. no. 43494/09, Judgment of 6 November 2017.

136 ECtHR, (GC) *Garib v. the Netherlands*, App. no. 43494/09, Judgment of 6 November 2017, Dissenting opinion of Judge Pinto De Albuquerque, joined by Judge Vehabović, paras. 27–39.

grounds, similarly to cultural requirements, are likely to be perceived as reasonably connected to a legitimate policy goal. This means that it is usually easier for states to defend, and for judges to accept, that the measure or conduct under scrutiny has not been based on any questionable ground or aimed at any particular category of people.[137] As seen in Chapter 2, the restriction of rights encountered by Muslim women was not, so goes the argument, because of being Muslim or because of religion. Nor were they based on the sex of the applicants. Rather, the Court stated, the restrictions stemmed from their failure to comply with an organisation's dress code. Similarly, in the cases discussed in the present chapter, the lack of access to courts, to marriage or to choose one's place of residence were not because of being poor and a single mother and/or a non-EU immigrant. Rather, those restrictions are said to have resulted from the fact that the person concerned did not pay, did not institute the required proceeding or did not comply with the income requirement set by law.

Ironically, though, there is nothing – legally speaking – preventing judges from closely scrutinising the above measures. In fact, human rights law and its mechanisms already deal with economic justifications. Take for example, the monitoring of the progressive realisation of socio-economic rights or the standard of reasonable accommodation. What is more, the prevailing principle on the matter says that economic considerations are not acceptable as justification for the restriction of human rights, at least for those that qualify as civil and political.[138] Irrespective of this, an argument of indirect discrimination that draws attention to the impact that such measures have on (single) women, migrants and people with disabilities, to mention some, introduces an additional and strong normative insight. When the complaint is examined from an intersectional perspective and the question turns, for example, to the specific risks and burdens faced by some minority and poor women, it is easier to have the claim of economic difference more seriously examined.

---

137 In this vein see The Equal Rights Trust, 'Combating Poverty through Equality Law – Possibilities and Pitfalls: ERT talks with Sandra Fredman and Margarita Ilieva', 3 *The Equal Rights Review* (2009) 83, at 87 (discussing the difficulties of enforcing a prohibition of direct and indirect discrimination on the ground of poverty. 'In such cases there may be a risk the judges would try to deal with such claims by tarnishing the test for rebuttal of a causal link between treatment and the protected ground. […] respondents to defend allegations by saying that the treatment was not because the person was poor, but because they were unable to pay.').

138 Traditionally, budgetary considerations have not been deemed to be permissible grounds for the limitation of civil and political rights. UN General Assembly, Report of the Special Rapporteur on Extreme Poverty and Human Rights, Magdalena Sepúlveda Carmona, A/66/265, 4 August 2011, para. 22 (recalling that 'economic reasons are …. outside the range of limitations permissible under human rights law.').

3.1.4. *Addressing Intersecting Disadvantages and Privileges*

Not everything is about stereotypes, though. Intersectionality, like discrimination, is not just about stereotyping. Taking seriously the specific harms and disadvantages that are placed on certain persons is crucial. For example, in *Garib*, the problem that intersectionality illuminates is that the income requirement exacerbated the subordination already experienced by the applicant on account of social precariousness *and* gender inequalities,[139] that is, those inequalities which are likely to explain that most single mothers like her had to rely on social benefits and had difficulty in finding a paid job while also securing the care of their children. In the case of Ms Garib, the heightened disadvantages were substantial. She was not just unjustly associated with criminality and antisocial behaviour. She also lost autonomy, was prevented from improving her and her children's life conditions and experienced further socio-economic deprivation.[140] The child removal cases, as well as the lack of access to judicial separation of Ms Airey and the maternal death of Ms Şentürk, similarly show the particular ways in which socio-economic disadvantage puts at risk and harms women, even more so when they belong to minorities or have a disability. In any event, in order to truly grasp the specific forms of subordination that socio-economic disadvantage places on differently situated individuals, it is important to appreciate that the issue is not merely one of overlapping identities or subgroups. Rather, it is about how those who occupy a racialised or gendered position are accorded disadvantages resulting from hierarchies that privilege those who do not.[141]

Conversely, seeing the individual as a whole may also enable the Court to recognise that the fact that a person is economically better off does not preclude the possibility of being discriminated against or illegitimately deprived of her rights as a result of inequalities attached to gender, ethnicity or other differences. As explained in Chapter 1 an intersectional perspective is attentive to the individual's multiple social locations, which may simultaneously signal both disadvantage and privilege. Consider, for example, complaints such as that of *de la Cierva Osorio de Moscoso and Others v. Spain*, which concerned male

---

139 Or, as Brodsky and Day put it: 'Poverty exacerbates and deepens the inequality of members of already disadvantaged groups. Poor women get sex inequality writ large.' See, Gwen Brodsky and Shelagh Day, 'Denial of the means of subsistence as an equality violation', *Acta Juridica* (2005) 149, at 162.

140 ECtHR, *Garib v. the Netherlands*, App. no. 43494/09, Judgment of 23 February 2016, para. 81. (The applicant argued that 'she had been forced to live in uncongenial conditions for a protracted period. She also argued that the outlay of EUR 1,000, all of which she lost, was considerable in comparison with her income.')

141 In this vein, Catherine MacKinnon, 'Intersectionality as Method: A Note', 38 *Sign* (2013) 1019, at 1023–1024; Sandra Fredman, Intersectional discrimination in EU gender equality and non-discrimination law, Report prepared for the European Commission (2016), at 31.

primacy in the lines of succession of the nobility.[142] While the Court did not address the applicant's claim of discrimination against women (because it does not deal with the merits of the case),[143] the state's arguments and the decisions adopted by other monitoring bodies in similar cases disclose difficulties in ascertaining the allegations of rights holders who are socio-economically powerful and nonetheless disadvantaged by gender relations. The Spanish government raised the inequality involved in the institution of peerages as a reason to dismiss the claims of those noblewomen.[144] Similarly, the UN Human Rights Committee has asserted that 'article 26 [ICCPR] cannot be invoked in support of claiming a hereditary title of nobility, an institution that [...] lies outside the underlying values behind the principles of equality before the law and non-discrimination protected by article 26'.[145]

Although such a system of social hierarchy is indeed objectionable from a human rights perspective, the above decisions failed to examine the applicants' experience as a whole. They were defined solely from the viewpoint of their socio-economic status, which was in fact one of power and privilege. A more comprehensive view, however, would problematise that account by integrating their experience as women. This requires acknowledging, as a dissenting member of the CEDAW Committee puts it, 'the element of discrimination against women that takes place in the distribution of social privileges using the law and legal processes'.[146] In so doing, the applicants' cultural affiliation (as members of Western customary elites) and contestations of nobility traditions would also be exposed. Neither these nor the underlying inferiority that nobility laws ascribe to women should be eclipsed by the applicants' socio-economic advantage.

Having said this, the next section will turn to another aspect of rights holders that is too often addressed through an either/or approach in cases concerning socio-economic disadvantage, namely their agency. As in cases regarding cultural difference, when it comes to economic difference individual agency

142 ECtHR, *De la Cierva Osorio de Moscoso, Fernandez de Cordoba, Roca y Fernandez Miranda and O'neill Castrillo v. Spain*, App. nos. 41127/98, 41503/98, 41717/98 and 45726/99, Decision of 28 October 1999.

143 The Court found that the subject matter of the complaint did not come under the scope of the ECHR since, according to the Court, the applicants' complaints under Articles 8 and 1 Protocol No. 1 were incompatible with the Convention *ratione materiae*. Accordingly, the complaints under Article 14 taken together with those provisions were likewise incompatible *ratione materiae*.

144 Ibid., at 8. See also the observations of the Spanish government in HRC, *Isabel Hoyos Martinez de Irujo v. Spain*, Communication no. 1008/2001, Decision adopted on 30 March 2004, para. 4.4.

145 Ibid., para. 6.5; see also HRC, *Mercedes Carrión Barcaiztegui v. Spain*, Communication no. 1019/2001, Decision adopted on 30 March 2004, para. 6.4.

146 CEDAW Committee, *Cristina Muñoz-Vargas y Sainz de Vicuña v. Spain*, Decision adopted on 9 August 2007, Dissenting opinion of Mary Shanthi Dairiam, para. 13.8.

and choices are crucial, contested features of rights holders. Questions about individual autonomy are in fact particularly strong in legal discourses concerning socio-economic disadvantage. On account of this, and in line with previous chapters, the following lines explores the extent to which the litigants and the Court fall into the trap of a dichotomist view of individual autonomy.

3.2. PROBLEMATISING THE 'EITHER/OR' VIEW OF INDIVIDUALS' AUTONOMY AND CHOICE

An either/or view of autonomy in the cases examined here is the kind of view that portrays impoverished individuals as having at one extreme little or no agency, while fully endowed with free choices at the other. Though in a different context, Fredman explores this paradox in terms of what she calls 'the relationship between agency and structure' in normative debates about poverty. She argues that 'the agency approach to poverty is based on the central assumption that, on the whole, people can be regarded as responsible for their own poverty'.[147] At the other extreme, 'the structural approach recognises that poverty is based on forces beyond the control of any one individual. However, there is a risk that such an approach leads to policy prescriptions which denude individuals of any agency.'[148] In what follows, it will be seen that this fragmentary understanding of autonomy has played out in the Strasbourg case law involving claims of socio-economic difference. We will start by exploring the reductionism that posits destitute individuals as fully free, autonomous and thus responsible for their grief. Then we will turn to the other pole, that of impoverished individuals lacking agency and needing guidance or supervision.

3.2.1. The Autonomous, Unconstrained Side of Impoverished Rights Holders

The idea that socio-economic disadvantage and its accompanying rights interferences are the result of the individual's choice and personal responsibility is an old one.[149] Arguably, this is fed by the belief that one's socio-economic position, unlike one's ethnic origin, colour of skin and sex, is changeable. One notable consequence of this narrative is that when confronted with rights

---

147 Sandra Fredman, 'The Potential and Limits of an Equal Rights Paradigm in Addressing Poverty', 3 *Stellenbosch Law Review* (2011) 566, at 579.

148 Ibid., at 580.

149 For a genealogy of the idea of poverty as an individual fault, see Emilio Santoro, 'A Historical Perspective: From Social Inclusion to Excluding Democracy', in Council of Europe, *Redefining and Combating Poverty: Human Rights, Democracy and Common Goods in Today's Europe*, Trends in Social Cohesion, No. 25 (Council of Europe, 2012), at 21–26.

claims related to poverty, judges may be more reluctant to afford protection for a circumstance that – supposedly – could have been avoided. Thus, in *Airey* the government argued that the applicant was 'free to go before [the High Court] without the assistance of a lawyer'.[150] Moreover, 'the alleged lack of access to court stems not from any act on the part of the authorities but solely from Mrs Airey's personal circumstances, a matter for which Ireland cannot be held responsible under the Convention'.[151] The Court's response in *Airey*, however, conveyed the message that even if states assume that individuals are responsible for their own economic fate, this does not authorise them to adopt a hands-off conduct when that situation encroaches upon human rights. In fact, in this case the Court recalled that factual hindrances to the enjoyment of rights could equally contravene the Convention, regarding which states needed to take positive action. They 'cannot simply remain passive'.[152]

Still, the idea of poverty as self-inflicted continues to be common among states. In *Wallova and Walla*, for instance, the applicants were regarded as responsible for their situation. According to the authorities, they had not made enough effort to overcome their destitution.[153] The same goes for virtually all cases of poverty-based child removal examined by the Court. The applicants in *Havelka and Others*, *Savigny* and *R.M.S.*, for example, were depicted at the domestic level and/or before the Strasbourg Court as simply having failed to accomplish better socio-economic conditions.[154] This view of impoverished rights holders furthermore seems to stand in every context. Even in *M.S.S.*, a case concerning the extreme destitution of an asylum seeker, 'the applicant had chosen to invest his resources in fleeing the country rather than in accommodation'.[155] For the Greek government, 'it was up to the applicant to come forward and show an interest in improving his lot'.[156] The logical consequence of this narrative is that any interference with the rights of those rights holders becomes a matter of choices beyond the reach of the law.

While the above rhetoric is more common in states' arguments than in the reasoning of the Strasbourg Court, the latter has not always remained

150 ECtHR, *Airey v. Ireland*, App. no. 6289/73, Judgment of 9 October 1979, para. 24.
151 Ibid., para. 25.
152 Idem.
153 ECtHR, *Wallová and Walla v. the Czech Republic*, App. no. 23848/04, Judgment of 26 October 2006, paras. 16, 18 and 60.
154 See *inter alia*, ECtHR, *Havelka and Others v. the Czech Republic*, App. no. 23499/06, Judgment of 21 June 2007, para. 40; *Savigny v. Ukraine*, App. no. 39948/06, Judgment of 18 December 2008, paras. 44–45 and 63; *R.M.S. v. Spain*, App. no. 28775/12, Judgment of 18 June 2013, para. 43.
155 ECtHR, (GC) *M.S.S. v. Belgium and Greece*, App. no. 30696/09, Judgment of 21 January 2011, para. 240.
156 Ibid., para. 242.

distant from it. Reductive accounts of individual autonomy and the conditions in which this unfolds have sometimes been left unchallenged, when not actually upheld by the Court. The case of *Haydarie*, mentioned above, is illustrative. In declaring the complaint inadmissible, the Court, like the domestic authorities, found that the applicant did not have the minimum income required to support her family because she had not made 'serious efforts' to find 'gainful employment'. Instead, she had 'preferred to care for her wheel-chair bound sister'.[157] The Court did not respond to the applicant's claim that the authorities had 'given insufficient weight to her [...] unpaid care work'.[158] Nor did it consider any other difficulties or limitations confronting the applicant's choices. Although her attempts to improve her chances in the labour market were noted (she successfully followed Dutch and sewing courses), these do not seem to have carried weight in the Court's analysis. Finally, the meaning assigned to her presumed choices was decisive. The fact that she 'preferred' to care for her sister instead of entrusting that to an aid-providing agency signified that she was not willing to undertake a 'real' job whereby she could improve her socio-economic situation. Her claim under Article 8 ECHR was therefore manifestly ill-founded.

Another problematic account of agency is offered by *Ponomaryovi v. Bulgaria*.[159] The Court found that requiring the applicants to pay fees for their secondary education on account of their nationality and immigration status was discriminatory, mainly because no provision for requesting exemptions was envisaged and no regard had been had for the applicants' specific circumstances. But the circumstances considered by the Court were all indications of the exceptionality of the applicants' situation in terms of their 'innocence' and lack of choice as immigrants. They were not like those 'individuals arriving in the country unlawfully and then laying claim to the use of its public services'.[160] And while they found themselves 'inadvertently' lacking residence permits, the authorities had no objection to their remaining.[161] They did not try to abuse the state education system, nor was it their choice to settle in Bulgaria, as they arrived very young.[162] Admittedly, the Court's assessment of autonomy in this case refers more to the applicants' choices as immigrants rather than to their socio-economic position. Nevertheless, both aspects were closely related and many of the remarks on their autonomy as immigrants could easily be transposed to social precariousness.

157 ECtHR, *Haydarie and Others v. the Netherlands*, App. no. 8876/04, Decision of 20 October 2005, at 13–14.

158 Ibid., at 12.

159 ECtHR, *Ponomaryovi v. Bulgaria*, App. no. 5335/05, Judgment of 21 June 2011.

160 Ibid., para. 60.

161 Idem.

162 Ibid., para. 61.

3.2.2. The Constrained, Passive Side of Impoverished Rights Holders

At the other side of the spectrum, rights holders in an underprivileged economic situation appear deprived of agency. They are depicted as unable to make 'right' choices, being in need of supervision and guidance. Put simply, others know better what is good for them. This discourse has resonance in the case law studied. In *Airey*, for instance, the government argued that 'the applicant has nothing to gain from a judicial separation',[163] challenging her entitlement to exercise her rights the way she deemed best. The Court, however, did not accept this approach and showed respect for the applicant's agency.

> The Court rejects this line of reasoning. Judicial separation is a remedy provided for by Irish law [...] It is for the individual to select which legal remedy to pursue; consequently, even if it were correct that Mrs. Airey's choice has fallen on a remedy less suited than others to her particular circumstances, this would be of no moment.[164]

Regrettably, this remarkable perspective went missing when a similar issue of agency was considered in *Garib v. the Netherlands*, referred to above.[165]

As a result of the gentrification policy applied in this case, the applicant, who had managed to obtain more suitable accommodation than what she had in the designated area, was prevented from improving her family situation in the way she saw fit. In spite of this, no violation of Article 2 of Protocol No. 4 (right to choose one's residence) was found by the Chamber. Nor did the latter acknowledge this curtailment of autonomy. In fact, the denial of agency was reinforced at Strasbourg. Both the government and the Chamber were of the view that the applicant had to justify why she wanted to move. For the government, it had not been shown 'that the applicant's dwelling in A. Street was in especially poor condition'.[166] And the Court, for its part, held that the applicant had 'stated no reason, cogent or otherwise, for wishing to live in Tarwewijk'.[167] The dissenting judges rightly pinpoint the paternalism underlying this approach. They reminded the majority that 'the applicant has the right to choose her residence, and she is not obliged to justify this choice'.[168]

The Court's reasoning appears even more striking given that the measure hinged on what was mainly an autonomy right, namely the freedom to decide where to take up residence. Of course, restricting this freedom does not make the regulation *per se* incompatible with the ECHR. Nevertheless, one cannot

---

163 ECtHR, *Airey v. Ireland*, App. no. 6289/73, Judgment of 9 October 1979, para. 19(b).

164 Ibid., para. 23.

165 ECtHR, *Garib v. the Netherlands*, App. no. 43494/09, Judgment of 23 February 2016 (referred to the Grand Chamber on 12 September 2016).

166 Ibid., para. 99.

167 Ibid., para. 131.

168 Ibid., Joint Dissenting Opinion of Judges López Guerra and Keller, para. 19.

but note that the intervention was addressed to one specific segment of the population only, that is, those who were socio-economically disadvantaged, such as the unemployed and recipients of social benefits. The selectivity of the policy matters because these persons are particularly at risk of having their agency severed, as recognised by the UN Guiding Principles on Extreme Poverty and Human Rights. These explicitly call for people living in poverty to be treated as autonomous agents, entitled to have their decisions respected.[169]

The Grand Chamber judgment in *Garib* ultimately confirmed the Chamber's view on this matter by holding:

> The corollary of the applicant's position that she is not required to justify her preference for a particular residential area, if accepted, would be that both the Court itself and the domestic authorities (...) would be deprived of the possibility of weighing the interest of the individual (...) an unspecified personal preference for which no justification is offered cannot override public decision-making (...).[170]

The Grand Chamber seems, however, to have conflated the autonomy protected by Article 2 Protocol 4 with the account that the applicant could have provided as to the harm caused by the restriction. To appreciate this, take another autonomy right, such as freedom of assembly and association (Article 11 ECHR). It would go against the essence of this right to require an individual to justify why she or he wanted to join an assembly or association at any particular place and time in order to determine the degree of protection afforded. A different matter is what this person could submit as regards the prejudice or disadvantage experienced as a result of being prevented from freely engaging in a peaceful assembly or association. The same goes for this case. The degree of protection afforded by the Convention cannot be made conditional upon the content of Ms Garib's choice to accept her landlord's offer to move to a dwelling a few blocks away.

Against this background one may wonder: why is the agency of people in a precarious socio-economic situation so commonly denied? It is submitted that this may have to do, at least in part, with stigmatising views about the supposed inability, irresponsibility or incapacity of people living in poverty, which is further discussed *infra* section 4.2.1. In this vein, it is convenient to bear in mind that being patronised, like being stereotyped or discriminated against, is a harm in and of itself.

The above examples demonstrate the importance of embracing the complexity of individuals' autonomy and its relational character, which, also

---

169 UN Office of the High Commissioner for Human Rights; Guiding Principles on Extreme Poverty and Human Rights, Adopted on 27 September 2012 in Resolution 21/11 (OHCHR, 2012), Principle 36.

170 ECtHR, (GC) *Garib v. the Netherlands*, App. no. 43494/09, Judgment of 6 November 2017, para. 166.

with regard to the question of socio-economic resources, does not stand as an either/or issue. Poverty may affect the exercise of autonomy but does not take it away. And while individuals are in many ways 'self-made', this does not mean that they have control over their destitution. Nor does this remove the state's responsibility for rights violations associated with their poverty. By the same token, it is a sterile task to try to resolve the cases examined by distinguishing poverty from unchangeable traits or from valued identities. Even if being on social benefits is something that should be changed or ended as soon as possible, as the government argued in the Grand Chamber hearing in *Garib*, the question will remain whether the state's aim of putting an end to a situation of disadvantage is a reason to deny legal protection.[171] Thus, while it is possible to argue that poverty is rather immutable (given the little social mobility that actually takes place in many societies), the point is rather why any fixed view of individuals' social positions should be seen as providing a conclusive legal basis for human rights protection. In what follows, another aspect of the relational self is explored, namely that of interaction and interdependence among rights holders.

3.3. A BROAD VIEW OF RIGHTS HOLDERS

In real life, the applicants of the cases studied are in constant interaction with other people. As a consequence, some of these other persons will usually be affected, for good or for bad, by the exercise or restriction of the applicant's rights. There is nothing revolutionary about this idea. This is basically what judges and policy-makers have in mind when setting conditions and limitations to rights. They normally care about 'the rights of others'. But while in this context the discourse of judges and policy-makers often focuses on the normative entities themselves (i.e. rights restrictions, obligations and regulatory frameworks), the discussion here focuses on the rights holders exercising them.

As explained in previous chapters, the fact that the Strasbourg Court operates on the basis of an individual justice model makes it difficult for it to look beyond the parties to the case. It was also explained, however, that the Court itself has demonstrated that doing so is possible and useful. Even when

---

171 In this vein, see Valeska David, 'Improving neighborhoods by preventing welfare recipients to take up residence: The Grand Chamber hearing in Garib v. the Netherlands', *Strasbourg Observers*, 2 February 2017, <strasbourgobservers.com/2017/02/02/improving-neighborhoods-by-preventing-welfare-recipients-to-take-up-residence-the-grand-chamber-hearing-in-garib-v-the-netherlands/>.
The hearing on the case is available at <www.echr.coe.int/Pages/home.aspx?p=hearings&w=4349409_25012017&language=en&c=&py=2017>.

the Court cannot declare violations with respect to individuals other than the applicant, it can and does consider who else is being affected by the measure in question. One evident way in which the Court does this is, as we have seen, by examining whether the rights restriction aims at the 'protection of the rights of others'. Here, the Court normally needs to analyse who these others are and how their rights are secured or undermined. To recall this is relevant because while in cases about cultural difference interferences are frequently justified on the grounds of protecting the rights of others (e.g. women, children, users of public services, private owners, other users of land, etc.), that is not so common in cases dealing with socio-economic disadvantage. In fact, many measures interfering with the rights of destitute people are based on public interest grounds, rather than on the need to protect others.

Still, protection of the rights of others is at the core of some poverty-related cases. Those concerning the taking into care of children on account of the parents' poverty are a paradigmatic example. State authorities claim that they take these children away to protect them. In addition, these cases attest to the need to have regard for the interests of rights holders other than the applicants who are nonetheless similarly prejudiced by the family separation. This is why this section primarily deals with child removal cases. Although most of these cases were submitted by the parent(s) who lost the care of their child(ren), the Court has routinely examined the interests of the child concerned, irrespective of the child's procedural standing before the Court. In this way the Court has rightly recognised that the rights of both parent(s) and child are involved. Moreover, in most of the cases studied, it has endorsed the principle (enshrined in the Convention on the Rights of the Child) according to which the best interests of the child must be a primary consideration in all decisions and actions concerning children, which obviously extends to family separation.[172] Yet, it is interesting to note that the judicial regard for children affected by family separation for reasons of poverty seems to fade when it comes to refusals of family reunification for economic reasons. In fact, the inadmissibility decision in *Haydarie* upheld the state's refusal to reunite a single mother with her children merely for lack of gainful income and without any reference to the children's interests. One may then wonder why the lack of financial means that is considered insufficient to justify the forcible separation of families with a deprived economic background is, on the other hand, enough justification to deny family reunification. And further, whether the framing of the case as being solely about family reunification allows the principles developed in cases of family separation to be done away with.

---

[172] Convention on the Rights of the Child, Articles 3 and 9; ECtHR, *Wallová and Walla v. the Czech Republic*, App. no. 23848/04, Judgment of 26 October 2006, paras. 70–72; *R.M.S. v. Spain*, App. no. 28775/12, Judgment of 18 June 2013, para. 71.

Nevertheless, it is also worth mentioning that the Court has not always taken its analysis of the children's interests to its fullest potential in cases of family separation, in particular by applying an interpretation attuned to the existing child rights framework. This is noticeable, for example, in cases in which the Court has overlooked the question of child participation in the decision-making process leading to family separation.[173] As further discussed below, the judgments in *R.M.S.* and in *Soares de Melo* attest to this oversight.

But we should also bear in mind that often the children and parent(s) concerned are not the only family members affected, which is particularly evident in the context of an extended family. This means that other rights holders, such as other next of kin or putative relatives, whose rights are prejudiced in a similar way as those of the applicant, may need to be considered. People living in poverty are actually more prone to live in and rely on an extended family than those who are better off.[174] The broadness of caregiving relations finds some normative recognition in the international corpus of children's rights. Reflective of this is the standard according to which effective judicial review of child removal requires that *all interested parties* be heard in the proceedings.[175] In *R.M.S. v. Spain*, however, the applicants' extended family was not allowed to take part in the judicial proceedings. The Court did observe that the applicant's great-uncle, who also opposed the child's removal, had not had an opportunity to express his views in the judicial proceedings. Nevertheless, this was not explicitly framed as a flaw in the decision-making process. In this vein, one may also note that references to the family ties between siblings do not abound in the judgments studied. Consequently, the siblings of the children who are taken away often disappear from sight. In *Gnahoré v. France*, the examination of the right to family life simply did not include the ties between

---

173 According to the CRC, children are entitled to participate and be heard in administrative and judicial proceedings affecting them, having due regard to their age and maturity. See Convention on the Rights of the Child, Article 12; Committee on the Rights of the Child, General Comment No. 12: The Right of the Child to be heard, CRC/C/GC/12, 20 July 2009.

174 In this vein, see e.g. Laura Stock *et al.*, Personal Relationships and Poverty: An Evidence and Policy Review – A Report prepared for the Joseph Rowntree Foundation by the Tavistock Institute of Human Relations (The Tavistock Institute, 2014), at 4 and 36 (explaining that extended family members play a key role in mitigating the risk of poverty for vulnerable individuals and groups); Organisation for Economic Co-Operation and Development, The Future of Families to 2030: Projections, Policy Challenges and Policy Options – A Synthesis Report (OECD, 2011), at 31–32.

175 Convention on the Rights of the Child, Article 9(2) (emphasis added). See also Article 5: 'States Parties shall respect the responsibilities, rights and duties of parents or, where applicable, *the members of the extended family* or community as provided for by local custom, legal guardians or other persons legally responsible for the child, to provide, in a manner consistent with the evolving capacities of the child, appropriate direction and guidance in the exercise by the child of the rights recognized in the present Convention.' (Emphasis added.)

the children. Meanwhile, in *Wallová and Walla* the Court remained silent on the applicants' claim that the authorities had not considered the need to keep the children together, as they had been placed in two different institutions.[176]

But what difference, if any, would it make to consider the situation of those other children? After all, the judgment in *Wallová and Walla*, for example, nonetheless found a violation of the right to private and family life on account of the disproportionality of the measure. Against first impressions, the question does hold relevance. For instance, by ignoring the issue of separation between siblings, the Court missed the opportunity to oversee and give guidelines on the implementation of care orders. Siblings' separation runs against existing standards on the rights of children that most member states have subscribed to. Moreover, leaving this question out of the discussion does not do justice to the lived experience of the whole family and especially of children, who also suffer because of their separation from brothers and sisters. This also affects the possibility of satisfaction awards for non-pecuniary damage. If the harm resulting from splitting the children between themselves is not seen, it will not be repaired by the Court.

Against this background, the Court's approach in *Savigny* and *Soares de Melo* is praiseworthy. In both cases, the Court explicitly took into account the breaking of family ties between siblings. In *Savigny* the Court noted that 'not only were the children separated from their family of origin, they were also placed in different institutions. Two of them live in another city, away from Romny where their parents and siblings reside, which renders it difficult to maintain regular contact.'[177] Of note, the Court took this approach in spite of the fact that none of the children were applicants in the case. In *Soares de Melo*, where the applicant's children were placed in three different homes, the Court also assessed the harm they experienced because of their separation and found, on this basis, that 'the measure went against the best interest of the children'.[178]

Finally, the Court has also adopted a broad view of rights holders to the extent that it has distinguished among applicants to bring into light those who are most likely to remain invisible, or those whose interests can easily be diluted among others' interests. This is usually the case with children. Thus, in *Tarakhel v. Switzerland*,[179] a case concerning the expulsion from Switzerland to Italy of a family of asylum seekers, including six minors, who had left Italy due to the poor living conditions of reception, the Court was willing to recognise the

---

176 ECtHR, *Wallová and Walla v. the Czech Republic*, App. no. 23848/04, Judgment of 26 October 2006, para. 63.

177 ECtHR, *Savigny v. Ukraine*, App. no. 39948/06, Judgment of 18 December 2008, para. 59.

178 ECtHR, *Soares de Melo v. Portugal*, App. no. 72850/14, Judgment of 16 February 2016, paras. 80 and 114.

179 ECtHR, (GC) *Tarakhel v. Switzerland*, App. no. 29217/12, Judgment of 4 November 2014.

risk of violation of Article 3 ECHR (prohibition of torture and inhuman or degrading treatment) resulting from destitution, mostly because of the threshold of suffering that it applied to children.[180]

As will be seen below, the attention to the children affected by the measures discussed in poverty-related cases has frequently led the Court to apply stringent standards as well as to integrate socio-economic rights. This and other aspects of normative integration are analysed below.

4. INTEGRATED RIGHTS: CROSS-THINKING ABOUT HARMS AND NORMS

Irrespective of the definitional troubles around the notion of poverty, and admitting the multidimensionality of the concept, it is safe to say that poverty is heavily determined by resource deprivation. Questions of redistribution and socio-economic rights are therefore frequently at issue in poverty-related complaints. The ECHR was, however, primarily conceived to secure civil and political rights, which undoubtedly feeds the adoption of a fragmentary approach to the rights contained therein.

4.1. A PRELIMINARY NOTE ON THE INDIVISIBILITY OF RIGHTS

Though the idea of indivisibility, as a theoretical and normative device, may still be contested, its practical implications are manifest in people's lives. In the case of those living in poverty, in particular, rights regarded as socio-economic and as civil and political are in practice all too interconnected. What follows from this is, as noted by Brodsky and Day, 'that it does not serve the interests of justice or logic to take a categorical approach to the protections that people living in poverty need'.[181]

Cases concerning child removal provide a clear example of the unsuitability of a categorical approach. Without aspects of socio-economic protection, the right to family life has little relevance for those parents and children forcibly separated. And rejecting family separation on account of poverty alone necessarily invokes states' positive obligations, with resource implications. According to the vast majority of applicants, the domestic authorities failed to help them to improve their living conditions effectively in terms of, for example,

---

180 Ibid., paras. 119–122.

181 Gwen Brodsky and Shelagh Day, 'Poverty is a Human Rights Violation', paper prepared for the December 2001 consultation of The Poverty and Human Rights Project (Canada), at 7.

housing, jobs and childcare. They mostly limited themselves to monitoring the family situation, eventually taking the children away.[182] In most of these cases, the Court has been inclined to affirm the indivisibility of rights, although in a very careful manner. For example, when the Court has concluded that the state should have supported families to overcome material hurdles instead of adopting the most drastic measure envisaged to protect children,[183] it has been very cautious in characterising that endeavour. The Court has generally used the verbs 'to help', 'to inform', 'to guide' and 'to advise' with respect to options for obtaining social housing, benefits and other means of overcoming the family's difficulties. So, instead of requiring the provision of socio-economic support, the Court has adopted a procedural review in the framework of the less restrictive means test. The issue is whether the authorities explored alternatives for keeping the family together, such as informing, advising and guiding the parents on the social assistance available to them.[184] By contrast, 'it is not the Court's role to determine whether the promotion of family unity in the case entitled the applicants' family to a particular standard of living at public expense'.[185]

In *Havelka*, however, the Court appears to go a step further. Although it used a careful and procedurally oriented language, it regarded the financial assistance provided by the state as insufficient. What it is more, it suggested that more concrete and focused socio-economic steps should have been taken. Interestingly, the Court referred, 'for information purposes, to the Committee of Ministers' Recommendation (2006) 19 on policies to support positive parenthood, according to which families in difficult socio-economic situations should be granted attention, more specific support and a more focused approach'.[186] But a real shift came with *Soares de Melo*. Here, the Court not only took a more substantive perspective, it also engaged more with the applicant's experience. She survived on a family allowance of 393 euros per month and obtained food and clothing for her large family by relying on donations and

---

[182] ECtHR, *Wallová and Walla v. the Czech Republic*, App. no. 23848/04, Judgment of 26 October 2006, paras. 63–64; *Havelka and Others v. the Czech Republic*, App. no. 23499/06, Judgment of 21 June 2007, paras. 60–61; *R.M.S. v. Spain*, App. no 28775/12, Judgment of 8 June 2013, paras. 73 and 86.

[183] ECtHR, *Wallová and Walla v. the Czech Republic*, App. no. 23848/04, Judgment of 26 October 2006, para. 73; R.M.S. v Spain, App. no. 28775/12, Judgment of 8 June 2013, para. 86.

[184] ECtHR, *Moser v. Austria*, App. no. 12643/02, Judgment of 21 September 2006, para. 70; *Wallová and Walla v. the Czech Republic*, App. no. 23848/04, Judgment of 26 October 2006, paras. 74–75; *Savigny v. Ukraine*, App. no. 39948/06, Judgment of 18 December 2008, para. 58; R.M.S. v. Spain, App. no. 28775/12, Judgment of 8 June 2013, para. 86; *N.P. v. the Republic of Moldova*, App. no. 58455/13, Judgment of 6 October 2015, para. 79.

[185] ECtHR, *Savigny v. Ukraine*, App. no. 39948/06, Judgment of 18 December 2008, para. 57; *N.P. v. the Republic of Moldova*, App. no. 58455/13, Judgment of 6 October 2015, para. 80.

[186] ECtHR, *Havelka and Others v. the Czech Republic*, App. no. 23499/06, Judgment of 21 June 2007, para. 61.

food stamps. The authorities were well aware of the family's deprivation. Yet, the Court states, they failed to alleviate its hardship through 'additional financial assistance to cover the basic needs of the family (e.g. in food, electricity and running water) and the daily care of the younger children to allow the applicant to exercise a paid job'.[187] Unlike previous judgments, the Court in *Soares de Melo* did not shy away from specifying the state's duty to support families instead of splitting them apart. In this reading, the right to family life enshrined in Article 8 ECHR got remarkably close to its socio-economic counterpart. It is interesting to note that these cases, where the Court has also adopted a relatively broad view of rights holders and of the relevant norms, have been defined as being about interferences with the right to family life and not about welfare or social policy, as have other cases studied here.

As will be further seen below, socio-economic provision or claims of assistance underlie several other cases studied here. But more often than not the Court is very cautious (more than in the cases discussed above) or even reluctant to derive socio-economic entitlements from Convention rights. Without downplaying this question of indivisibility, the following discussion will not elaborate further on the socio-economic rights dimension of poverty-related cases. Since this book is interested in what can be gained from looking at cases in a cross-thinking manner, the subsections below concentrate on harms and rights not immediately connected to socio-economic rights, which are the usual focus of attention in normative discourses about poverty and rights.

4.2. INTEGRATING RECOGNITION AND STRUCTURAL ISSUES INTO REDISTRIBUTION WRONGS

As mentioned at the outset, the experience of poverty usually involves a recognition dimension that cannot be underestimated. In the theoretical chapter of this book, it was seen that Fraser describes recognition harms as those rooted in cultural patterns and which impede equal participation in social life. These take different forms, such as being subjected to cultural values that are alien and/or hostile to one's own, being rendered invisible and being routinely disrespected, maligned or stereotyped.[188] While often these harms are mostly

---

187 ECtHR, *Soares de Melo v. Portugal*, App. no. 72850/14, Judgment of 16 February 2016, para. 106 (author's translation). The original text in French reads: 'les autorités internes n'ont pas essayé de combler ces carences au moyen d'une aide financière supplémentaire afin de couvrir les besoins primaires de la famille (par exemple en matière d'alimentation, d'électricité et d'eau courante) et les frais d'accueil des enfants les plus jeunes dans des crèches familiales pour permettre à l'intéressée d'exercer une activité professionnelle rémunérée (…)'.

188 Nancy Fraser and Axel Honneth, *Redistribution or Recognition? A Political-Philosophical Exchange* (Verso, 2003), at 13 and 29–30.

associated with claims concerning, for example, ethno-cultural, gender and sexual differences, they are also at issue in cases marked by poverty or socio-economic disadvantage.

The recurring link between recognition harms and rights claims related to poverty is well reflected in the Guiding Principles on Human Rights and Poverty and in the views of the several stakeholders that were involved in their drafting. Explicit reference is made, for example, to the need to recognise the human rights claims of people living in poverty, as well as address their stigmatisation, stereotyping, discrimination and lack of legal recognition.[189] The good news is that, in principle, for a human rights court like the Strasbourg Court, it is easier to deal with these harms than with those more connected to maldistribution. As scholars have noted, courts in general feel more comfortable in addressing issues of discrimination, humiliation and stigmatisation, than in touching socio-economic concerns.[190] Despite this, it will be seen that the Court has only partially, and at times timidly, dealt with recognition harms linked to socio-economic difference. In the cases examined, at least three types of recognition harm are discernible, namely (1) stereotyping, (2) humiliation and (3) invisibility. The following sub-sections explore the way the Court has (not) taken them aboard.

4.2.1. Addressing the Stereotypes and Humiliation Involved in the Experience of Poverty

As discussed earlier, stereotyping is a key aspect in most cases dealing with the taking of children for reasons of poverty. Many administrative and judicial decisions leading to family separation relied explicitly or implicitly on negative preconceptions about parents, especially mothers, living in poverty.[191] Portrayed as unable or unfit for parenting, lazy, uninterested in their children or irresponsible, they saw the care orders enforced despite the lack of evidence of abuse or neglect. We have seen that in all of these cases, one or more violations were found. However, as explained above the Court did not name or scrutinise those stereotypes and stigmas. Most of them were compounded, intersecting assumptions regarding not only economic status, but also gender and body-ability. But none of them was integrated into the analysis of the right to private

189 UN Office of the High Commissioner for Human Rights, Guiding Principles on Extreme Poverty and Human Rights, Adopted on 27 September 2012 in Resolution 21/11 (OHCHR, 2012), preface and paras. 18, 21 and 69. See also, UN Human Rights Council, Analytical compilation of the submissions received in writing and made at the consultation on the progress report on the draft guiding principles on extreme poverty and human rights – Report of the Office of the United Nations High Commissioner for Human Rights, A/HRC/19/32, 16 December 2011, at 3 and 6.

190 Sandra Fredman, 'Redistribution and Recognition: Reconciling Inequalities', 23 *South African Journal on Human Rights* (2007) 214, at 219–220 (mostly referring to judges in South Africa and Canada, but her analysis on this point also holds for judges at the supranational level).

191 See *supra* sections 3.1.2 and 3.1.3.

and family life (Article 8) or of equality and non-discrimination (Article 14). These forms of misrecognition were thus side-lined.

True, the Court's assessment of the applicants' procedural rights (framed as a matter of Article 8 and/or Article 6 ECHR) might appear to have taken heed of the aforesaid preconceptions to the extent that the absence of supporting evidence was criticised. Yet, this falls short of taking stereotyping and stigma seriously. Leaving them unnamed and unweighted, the Court failed to challenge them and foster transformation of the cultural patterns that were at the root of the violations. The lack of engagement with the stereotypes accorded to poverty is also apparent in the case of *Garib v. the Netherlands*. It is not uncommon that welfare measures, while aiming at alleviating poverty, rely on harmful assumptions about people living in poverty. However, the need or urgency of socio-economic intervention must not lead to further stereotyping or stigmatisation.[192] This also holds true for migration policies which appear primarily concerned with restricting the rights of a subset of immigrants, such as those with a precarious economic background and with non-European roots, as the case of *O'Donoghue and Others* demonstrates.

Overall, misrecognition associated with the experience of poverty has yet to be challenged by courts such as the ECtHR.[193] The relevance of remedying this should not be underestimated. The implications of failing to identify and condemn this type of injury go beyond the applicant and the case at hand. Since law is performative, as noted in Chapters 2 and 3, whatever meaning or assumption attached to words used by law to capture the experience of poverty will remain 'unstated but everpresent'[194] That is, those stereotypes will be internalised, reproduced and eventually used to justify socio-economic difference and its consequences. Ultimately they will also frustrate efforts aimed at redistribution.[195] This confirms the idea that 'struggles for recognition

192 See e.g. Sheilagh Turkington, 'A Proposal to Amend the Ontario Human Rights Code : Recognizing Povertyism', 9 *Journal of Law and Social Policy* (1993) 134, at 146. ('In a welfare state, the poor will always be subject to legal naming and categorization. […] The purpose of this project is not to eliminate the naming but to challenge the assumptions and values implicit in them.')

193 Similar concerns have been raised with regard to domestic courts. See for example Colleen Sheppard, '"Bread and roses": Economic justice and constitutional rights', 5 *Oñati Socio-legal Series* (2015) 225, 235–237; Michele Benedetto, 'Socio-economic bias in the judiciary', 61 *Cleveland State Law Review* (2013) 137, at 146 and ff.

194 Sheilagh Turkington, 'A Proposal to Amend the Ontario Human Rights Code: Recognizing Povertyism', 9 *Journal of Law and Social Policy* (1993) 134, at 146; Martha Minow, *Making All the Difference. Inclusion, Exclusion and American Law* (Cornell University Press, 1990), at 52, 56–74.

195 Wendy R. Williams, 'Struggling with Poverty: Implications for Theory and Policy of Increasing Research on Social Class-Based Stigma', 9(1) *Analyses of Social Issues and Public Policy* (2009) 37, at 42 (explaining why 'whether "outsiders" view social class as either achieved or ascribed has serious consequences for the allocation of resources'). From another

can aid the redistribution of power and wealth'.[196] For example, addressing poverty-related stereotypes in cases of child removal is necessary not only to overcome status subordination – and ensure recognition – but also to challenge the social structures that personalise – 'privatise' – both individual or family material well-being and the 'failure' to accomplish it.[197]

Many instances of stigmatisation or stereotyping like the ones discussed above carry humiliation. But humiliation in connection with an experience of poverty may also arise independently and lead to a violation in itself. This is aptly demonstrated by *M.S.S. v. Greece and Belgium*. Noting that the applicant was living on the street, prevented from having a livelihood and had no resources and access to basic services, the Court weighed up the humiliation suffered by the applicant. His experience of severe poverty was thereby framed as a denial of dignity. In the words of the Court, 'the applicant has been the victim of humiliating treatment showing a lack of respect for his dignity (...) this situation has, without doubt, aroused in him feelings of fear, anguish or inferiority capable of inducing desperation.'[198] On account of this and of the prolonged uncertainty in which the applicant remained, a violation of the prohibition of degrading treatment (Article 3 ECHR) was found. This line of reasoning was, notably, confirmed in the case of *V.M. and Others v. Belgium*, concerning a family of asylum seekers of Roma origin who endured extreme destitution while staying for three weeks in a railway station in Brussels, after being expelled from reception facilities and denied permission to stay.[199] In the Court's view, the Belgian authorities failed to satisfy their obligation not to expose the applicants to conditions of extreme poverty that breached their dignity and aroused in them feelings of fear or inferiority capable of inducing desperation, which amounts to degrading treatment.[200]

---

perspective, Bruce Porter also argues that the denial of a space for the adjudication of socio-economic rights is related to pervasive and rooted prejudices, stereotypes and discrimination against the poor. See Bruce Porter, 'Claiming Adjudicative Space: Social Rights, Equality, and Citizenship', in Margot Young *et al.* (eds.), *Poverty: Rights, Social Citizenship, and Legal Activism* (UBC Press, 2007), at 80–81 (providing examples of stereotypes that make the sole idea of having poor people in the courtroom problematic).

196 Nancy Fraser, 'Rethinking Recognition', 3 *New Left Review* (2000) 107, at 109.

197 Valeska David, 'Caring, rescuing or punishing? Rewriting RMS v Spain (ECtHR) from an integrated approach to the rights of women and children in poverty', in Eva Brems and Ellen Desmet (eds.), *Integrated human rights in practice* (Edward Elgar, 2017), at 166.

198 ECtHR, *M.S.S v. Greece and Belgium*, App. no. 30696/09, 21 January 2011, para. 263. The first time the Court adopted this line of interpretation was in the case of *Moldovan and Others v. Romania*, App. nos. 41138/98 and 64320/01, 12 July 2005, paras. 103 and 110. The Court had previously accepted the possibility of an Article 3 violation on similar grounds in *Volsem v. Belgium*, App. no. 14641/89, Decision of 9 May 1990, and in *Budina v. Russia*, App. no. 45603/05, Decision of 18 June 2009; but ultimately rejected it in both.

199 ECtHR, *V.M. and Others v. Belgium*, App. no. 60125/11, Judgment of 7 July 2015.

200 Ibid., paras. 162–163; ECtHR, *V.M. and Others v. Belgium*, App. no. 60125/11, Judgment of 7 July 2015, paras. 159–160. It should be noted, however, that after being referred to the Grand Chamber at the request of the government, this case was eventually struck out of its list of

There is no reason to think that only humiliation can lead to suffering and degradation capable of breaching Article 3 ECHR. The physical suffering resulting from lacking food or medical assistance, for instance, could also amount to inhuman and degrading treatment.[201] But given the caution with which the Court normally deals with questions of socio-economic assistance, tackling the humiliation resulting from dehumanising living conditions seems to facilitate responsiveness towards the applicant's destitution while avoiding entering into contested socio-economic terrain. In fact, proscribing the humiliation resulting from severe poverty as contrary to Article 3 ECHR is not totally free from material implications. If states are to comply with the prohibition of inhuman and degrading treatment as applied in *M.S.S.* and *V.M.*, they should assure some socio-economic conditions allowing a dignified life, such as shelter and food, at least for asylum seekers.[202] For this, however, the threshold of suffering and denigration is very high. This, as well as the very specific circumstances underlined by the Court in cases such as *M.S.S.* and *V.M.*, make it difficult to extend this line of reasoning to the severe destitution and vulnerability faced by other persons (who are not under the state custody).[203] The Court's decision in *Hunde v. the Netherlands* also supports this interpretation. Confronted with the same kinds of issue raised by the cases discussed above, but with regard to an undocumented migrant, the Court in *Hunde* departed from *M.S.S.* Key among the considerations for doing so was

---

cases on account of the lack of contact between the applicants and their legal representative before the Court. Importantly, once a request for referral has been accepted by the Grand Chamber, the Chamber judgment in question does not become final. See, ECtHR, (GC) *V.M. and Others v. Belgium*, App. no. 60125/11, Judgment (Striking Out) of 17 November 2016. Other factors considered by the Court were the long duration in which the applicant in *M.S.S.* had lived in a state of the most extreme poverty; that the uncertainty experienced by the applicant was different from *M.S.S.* in that it was not linked to the Netherlands authorities' assessment of his asylum request; and that the Netherlands authorities had not shown ignorance or inaction towards the applicant's situation because they had given a four-week grace period with state-sponsored entitlements, after which the applicant could have applied for reception facilities at a centre where his liberty would be restricted.

201 In this vein, Colm O'Cinneide, 'A modest proposal: destitution, state responsibility and the European Convention on Human Rights', 5 *European Human Rights Law Review* (2008) 592, at 588–589.

202 Other cases in which the Court has found a violation for the failure to provide in the face of destitution are e.g. ECtHR, *Nencheva and Others v. Bulgaria*, App. no. 48609/06, Judgment of 18 June 2013 (but here the state failed to protect children in the care of a state-run institution whose risk to life as a result of lack of food, heat and medicines, was known or should have been known to the state authorities).

203 With regard to persons under state custody the Court has generally accepted that Articles 2 and 3 ECHR requires the state to ensure certain minimum living conditions. See e.g. Janneke Gerards, 'The ECtHR's Response to Fundamental Rights Issue related to Financial and Economic Difficulties. The Problem of Compartmentalisation', 33(3) *Netherlands Quarterly of Human Rights* (2015) 274, at 284–285.

that the applicant in the former case was a 'failed asylum seeker'.[204] On this basis, the Court also rejected the applicant's plight to rule similarly to the European Committee of Social Rights (ECSR) in similar cases against the Netherlands, thus deviating from the normative weight that in *V.M. and Others* the Court itself had accorded to decisions issued by the ECSR in similar cases against the respondent state.[205] This indicates that only in exceptional circumstances, so far mostly limited to asylum seekers, can the humiliation and degradation associated with extreme poverty be covered by Article 3 ECHR (prohibition of torture, inhuman and degrading treatment) and convey some duty of socio-economic support. It is yet to be seen whether a different conclusion might be reached under Article 8 ECHR (right to private and family life). Having said this, it is time to turn to the third kind of recognition injury referred to above. This is invisibility, which basically translates into exclusion from legal protection.

4.2.2. *Addressing Invisibility: Indifference and Discrimination on Account of Poverty*

A person is invisible to the legal order, for our purposes to human rights law, insofar as the latter does not recognise or react to his or her grief.[206] In domestic legal orders this is typically reflected in those cases where the harm perpetrated

204 ECtHR, *Gadaa Ibrahim Hunde v. the Netherlands*, App. no. 17931/16, Decision of 5 July 2016, paras. 55–59. Other considerations were that the applicant's uncertainty was not linked to the Dutch authorities' assessment of his asylum request; that he failed to cooperate for his return to Ethiopia; and that he was given a four-week grace period with state-sponsored accommodation. The Court reiterated that 'that there is no right to social assistance as such under the Convention and to the extent that Article 3 requires States to take action in situations of the most extreme poverty – also when it concerns irregular migrants.'

205 Ibid., paras. 53–54. Of note, similar cases to those discussed in this section keep reaching the Court. Recently, for example, the Court issued a decision in a case concerning the return of an Eritrean single mother and her child from Switzerland to Italy, where she had been granted refugee status but had been living for more than a year in appalling conditions and without accommodation. The Court found that the applicant's complaint under Article 3 was manifestly ill-founded with regard to both Switzerland and Italy, basically in view of a letter submitted by the Italian government confirming that the applicant would be accommodated in a reception facility and seeing that, as a refugee, the applicant was legally entitled to social assistance. To some extent, the reasoning offers a rather formalistic and hypothetical assessment of the risks of humiliation and degrading treatment resulting from extreme poverty. See ECtHR, *E.T. and N.T. v. Switzerland and Italy*, App. no. 79480/13, Decision of 30 May 2017.

206 On the invisibility of people living in poverty, see e.g. Oscar Vilhena Vieira, 'Inequality and the Subversion of the Rule of Law', in Thomas Pogge (ed.), *Freedom from Poverty as a Human Right. Volume 2: Theory and Politics* (UNESCO Publishing, 2010), at 228. ('Invisibility means here that the human suffering of certain segments of society does not cause a remedial moral or political reaction from the most advantaged and does not trigger an adequate legal response from state officials.')

on some people, such as women, ethnic minorities and the destitute, does not trigger a response, or at least not a serious one, from the justice system. Claims against this sort of indifference can be seen in the maternal death case of *Şentürk v. Turkey*, mentioned earlier, insofar as the grief of the applicants and the deceased victim were invisible to both the health and the justice personnel.[207] Another example is provided by cases in which people living in poverty had obtained judicial orders to be re-housed or provided with basic services, which nonetheless remained unenforced by the local authorities.[208] In these cases, the Court has notably rejected arguments of economic limitations and found violations for the failure to enforce final judgments.[209] It has also acknowledged applicants' heightened distress and frustration for the authorities' indifference and awarded compensation accordingly.[210]

But invisibility also manifests itself at the international level. The cases studied show, for example, how claims of discrimination on poverty-related grounds are left without legal response, not only by domestic systems but also by the Strasbourg Court. This amounts to another form of invisibility. So long as the Court does not react to the claims, the applicants in these cases undergo two instances of misrecognition: one before the domestic authorities and another before the Court. The problem is not that they risk losing their cases at Strasbourg. Rather, the point is that their discrimination claims are legally invisible, for the Court regularly declines even to examine them, irrespective of how well applicants articulate them on the basis of Article 14 ECHR.

To approach this matter, it is relevant to start by pointing out that a large proportion of the cases involving claims related to socio-economic disadvantage posited allegations of discrimination based on Article 14 ECHR in conjunction with substantive provisions, such as Articles 6 and 8 ECHR (right of access to a court and right to private and family life, respectively).[211] Within this universe,

207 ECtHR, *Mehmet Şentürk and Bekir Şentürk v. Turkey*, App. no. 13423/09, Judgment of 9 April 2013.

208 ECtHR, *Tchokontio Happi v. France*, App. no. 65829/12, Judgment of 9 April 2015; *Gerasimov and Others v. Russia*, App. nos. 29920/05, 3553/06, 18876/10, 61186/10, 21176/11, 36112/11, 36426/11, 40841/11, 45381/11, 55929/11 and 60822/11, Judgment of 1 July 2014.

209 A breach of Article 6 ECHR (access to justice and fair trial) was found in both cases, while a violation of Article 1 Protocol 1 no. 1 was only found in *Gerasimov and Others*.

210 ECtHR, *Gerasimov and Others v. Russia*, App. nos. 29920/05, 3553/06, 18876/10, 61186/10, 21176/11, 36112/11, 36426/11, 40841/11, 45381/11, 55929/11 and 60822/11, Judgment of 1 July 2014, para. 193.

211 ECtHR, *Airey v. Ireland*, App. no. 6289/73, Judgment of 9 October 1979; *Moser v. Austria*, App. no. 12643/02, Judgment of 21 September 2006; *Wallová and Walla v. the Czech Republic*, App. no. 23848/04, Judgment of 26 October 2006; *Savigny v. Ukraine*, App. no. 39948/06, Judgment of 18 December 2008; *A.K. and L. v. Croatia*, App. no. 37956/11, Judgment of 8 January 2013; *R.M.S. v. Spain*, App. no. 28775/12, Judgment of 18 June 2013; *Lacatus v. Switzerland*, App. no. 14065/15, Case communicated on 11 February 2016; *O'Donoghue and Others v. the United Kingdom*, App. no. 34848/07, Judgment of 14 December 2010;

however, only some complaints were explicitly framed as discrimination on grounds of poverty, 'social origin' or 'property'.[212] Socio-economic disadvantage may not have been the primary driver of the discrimination complained of in some cases, despite being a relevant aspect of the rights restrictions in question. Yet, socio-economic difference was missing in a number of allegations of discrimination that actually had much to do with the applicants' financial resources. Perhaps anticipating the lack of legal cognisance of such claims before the Strasbourg Court, these discrimination complaints, instead of referring to social origin or property, were based on other categories, such as nationality, disability and race.[213] As the Court declined to examine poverty-based allegations of discrimination, it naturally made no attempt to explore this possibility in cases in which discrimination was not litigated in those terms.

As early as in the *Airey* case, the applicant argued that it was discriminatory to make judicial separation more easily available to those with the financial resources to pay for a lawyer than to those who, like her, could not afford to do so. This amounted, in her view, to discrimination in the exercise of the right to access to a court on account of property (Article 14 taken jointly with Article 6.1 ECHR).[214] In response, the Court held that there was no need to examine this claim. This followed from the fact that in its opinion – for some inexplicable reason – inequality in the enjoyment of Article 6 was not a fundamental aspect of the case.[215] The conclusion was not unanimous, though. Among the dissenters, Judge Evrigenis, notably, explained why discrimination on the basis of property should have been examined. First, 'there can be no doubt that in making the claim in question the applicant was complaining of a "clear inequality" of treatment which is based on property and is a "fundamental aspect" of the case'. Second, 'the fact that the Court had found a violation of Article 6 para. 1 taken alone did not dispense it from examining the case under Article 14'.[216] It is noteworthy that by the end of the 1970s part of the Court was already eager to tackle discrimination on economic grounds. Equally notable is however that up to now the Court has not come back to that reasoning.

Ponomaryovi v. Bulgaria, App. no. 5335/05, Judgment of 21 June 2011; *Loncke v. Belgium*, App. no. 20656/03, Judgment of 25 September 2007; *Garib v. the Netherlands*, App. no. 43494/09, Judgment of 23 February 2016 (pleadings before the Grand Chamber on 25 January 2017).

212 ECtHR, *Airey v. Ireland*, App. no. 6289/73, Judgment of 9 October 1979, para. 29; *Wallová and Walla v. the Czech Republic*, App. no. 23848/04, Judgment of 26 October 2006, para. 86; and *Loncke v. Belgium*, App. no. 20656/03, Judgment of 25 September 2007, para. 55.

213 See e.g. ECtHR, *Moser v. Austria*, App. no. 12643/02, Judgment of 21 September 2006, para. 78; *Savigny v. Ukraine*, App. no. 39948/06, Judgment of 18 December 2008, para. 64; *R.M.S. v. Spain*, App. no. 28775/12, Judgment of 18 June 2013, para. 95.

214 ECtHR, *Airey v. Ireland*, App. no. 6289/73, Judgment of 9 October 1979, para. 29.

215 Ibid., para. 30.

216 Ibid., Dissenting Opinion of Judge Evrigenis, at 26, para. 1.

The Court reached the same conclusion in *Loncke v. Belgium*, another case concerning court fees.[217] The applicant argued, to no avail, that the inadmissibility of his appeal as a result of his inability to pay the requested fee constituted discrimination on the basis of property and financial resources.[218] For the Court, however, the issue had been settled in its analysis of the right of access to a court (Article 6 ECHR).[219] The same approach was taken in child removal cases. The applicants in *Wallová and Walla* alleged that the attitude of the authorities reflected 'a discriminatory approach to them, motivated by their social origin and poverty'.[220] A similar, although more implicit, complaint was raised in *R.M.S. v. Spain*, where the applicant alleged discrimination in the enjoyment of family life on the grounds of, *inter alia*, her physical appearance and lifestyle.[221] In both family separation cases, the Court's answer was the same. Given its findings under Article 8 ECHR, there was no need to go into Article 14 ECHR.

More recently, an analogous claim resurfaced in the applicant's pleadings in *Garib* before the Grand Chamber,[222] a legal complaint not formally raised in the Chamber's proceedings. The Grand Chamber acknowledged that it was the master of the legal characterisation to be given to the facts of the case; that it could apply the *juria novit curia* principle limited to the Chamber's decision on admissibility of a complaint, understanding that such a complaint 'is characterised by the facts alleged in it and not merely by the legal grounds or arguments relied on'.[223] The Grand Chamber also took note of the fact that the complainant had advanced the discrimination claim at the domestic level.[224] Eventually, however, the Grand Chamber declined to examine her Article 14 allegation. The main reason advanced for this was that 'it was not open to the applicant (especially after having been legally represented throughout) to change her legal characterisation of the facts before the Grand Chamber'.[225] This 'new' criterion appears to be somewhat in contradiction with the Court's

217 ECtHR, *Loncke v. Belgium*, App. no. 20656/03, Judgment of 25 September 2007.

218 Ibid., para. 55.

219 Ibid., para. 59.

220 ECtHR, *Wallová and Walla v. the Czech Republic*, App. no. 23848/04, Judgment of 26 October 2006, para. 86.

221 ECtHR, *R.M.S. v. Spain*, App. no. 28775/12, Judgment of 18 June 2013, para. 95.

222 The hearing on the case is available at <www.echr.coe.int/Pages/home.aspx?p=hearings&w=4349409_25012017&language=en&c=&py=2017>. For an overview of the arguments raised at the hearing before the Grand Chamber, see Valeska David, 'Improving neighborhoods by preventing welfare recipients to take up residence: The Grand Chamber hearing in Garib v. the Netherlands', *Strasbourg Observers*, 2 February 2017, <strasbourgobservers.com/2017/02/02/improving-neighborhoods-by-preventing-welfare-recipients-to-take-up-residence-the-grand-chamber-hearing-in-garib-v-the-netherlands/>.

223 ECtHR, (GC) *Garib v. the Netherlands*, App. no. 43494/09, Judgment of 6 November 2017, paras. 98 and 101.

224 Ibid., para. 99.

225 Ibid., para. 101.

own principle that a complaint is characterised by the facts and not by the legal characterisation given to them, regarding which the last word is with the Court and not with the parties.

What reasons could explain the Court's reluctance to scrutinise, through the prohibition of discrimination, those regulations and practices which are allegedly directed at or adversely impact on the socio-economically disadvantaged? Clearly we need to look beyond the Convention, since Article 14 ECHR provides the normative basis for doing so. The grounds of social origin, property and even 'any other status' are, at least on paper, perfectly suited to the task. At the same time, however, it cannot be denied that Article 14 ECHR still remains undeveloped in the Court's general case law. As noted by O'Cinneide, the Court has the tendency 'to shy away from the complexities of Article 14 preferring instead to base its decisions on other articles of the Convention'.[226] Cases involving alleged discrimination on the basis of socio-economic disadvantage would thus be exemplary of such a practice of deferring to substantive provisions.

Yet there are good reasons to think that, over and above this tendency, there are obstacles quite specific to the subject matter. It is likely that the Court, like other supranational and domestic courts, encounters particular difficulties in addressing discrimination questions related to class, poverty or similar grounds.[227] A first reason for this lies with the strong identity group ascendancy in discrimination grounds.[228] Fineman, for example, explains that 'poverty, denial of dignity, and deprivation of basic social goods are "lack-of-opportunity categories" that the current framework of identity groups does not recognize'.[229] Indeed, this chapter started by underscoring how issues of socio-economic disadvantage do not lend themselves to legal discourses on identity and group difference. And here we see one of the consequences of that disconnection. A second but related complication concerns the understanding of the unfairness targeted by anti-discrimination law. Unfair discrimination

226 Colm O'Cinneide, 'The Right to Equality: A Substantive Legal Norm or Vacuous Rhetoric?', 1 *UCL Human Rights Law Review* (2008) 80, at 83–84.

227 In the context of the US Supreme Court, see e.g. Julie A. Nice, 'Whither the Canaries: On the Exclusion of Poor People from Equal Constitutional Protection', 60 *Drake Law Review* (2012) 1023, at 1039 and ff.; Mario L. Barnes and Erwin Chemerinsky, 'The Disparate Treatment of Race and Class in Constitutional Jurisprudence', 72 *Law and Contemporary Problems* (2009) 109, at 110–116.

228 Which echoes the idea that anti-discrimination law protects 'insular discrete minorities', as advanced by the United States Supreme Court. On the latter, see Kenji Yoshino, 'The New Equal Protection', 124 *Harvard Law Review* (2011) 747, at 758.

229 Martha Albertson Fineman, 'The Vulnerable Subject: Anchoring Equality in the Human Condition', 20(1) *Yale Journal of Law and Feminism* (2008) 1, at 17. In a similar vein, see Mario L. Barnes and Erwin Chemerinsky, 'The Disparate Treatment of Race and Class in Constitutional Jurisprudence', 72 *Law and Contemporary Problems* (2009) 109, at 125 ('Class is much more elusive to define than race, gender, alienage, or legitimacy.').

is too often associated with situations which the person affected has not contributed to creating and for which, therefore, he or she cannot be 'blamed'. As discussed *supra* section 3.2.2, poverty is usually seen through the opposite prism. Destitution is avoidable, as it is the result of personal conduct and choice. Therefore, those who experience it are responsible for it and the law has little or nothing to do about it.

This line of argument is likely to affect the standard of review and the width of the margin of appreciation applicable to poverty-related discrimination claims, whether advanced on grounds of 'social origin', 'property' or 'other status'. One may think of a number of scenarios where poverty-based discrimination could be presented as discrimination on the basis of 'other status'. In fact, it is unlikely that policies or regulations that negatively affect people living in poverty will be explicitly addressed to the poor or the socio-economically disadvantaged. Nor will they normally rely on 'social origin' or people's possessions as such. Rather, they will usually refer to related factors, such as income and being on social assistance, or will simply subject the enjoyment of rights to compliance with financial obligations. In *Garib v. the Netherlands*, for example, the government argued that 'source of income' does not qualify as a status prohibited under Article 14 ECHR.[230] This leads to two important observations. First, so long as economically oriented criteria are assumed to be rational, objective or legitimate in themselves (as already discussed *supra* section 3.1.3), the scrutiny of allegations of direct discrimination on poverty-related grounds will tend to be lenient. As such, litigants need to reinforce the substantiation of these claims by, for example, underscoring the interplay between financial criteria, such as type or source of income, and the disparate harms inflicted on women, ethnic minorities and other persons who are already subjected to exclusion and misrecognition. Second, it is important that when considering the application of the prohibition of discrimination on account of 'social origin', 'property' or 'other status', the Court embraces a flexible understanding of what this means. Or, in other words, an understanding that encompasses grounds closely related to poverty or economic precariousness, such as being in receipt of social assistance, unemployment and the like.[231] An otherwise essentialist and static view of poverty or of people in socio-economic disadvantage would be of little practical assistance.

While in a number of cases the Court has adopted a flexible approach to the question of what falls within 'other status', in others it has required that

230 ECtHR, Grand Chamber hearing in *Garib v. the Netherlands*, held on 25 January 2017 (Case referred on 12 September 2016).

231 In this vein, although in the context of the judiciary in Canada, see Martha Jackman, 'Constitutional Contact and the Disparities in the World: Poverty as a Prohibited Ground of Discrimination under the Canadian Charter and Human Rights Law', 2(1) *Review of Constitutional Studies* (1994) 76, at 108.

these be based on personal or objective characteristics 'by which persons or groups are distinguishable from one another'.[232] The restrictive interpretation applied to discrimination based on immigration status in *Bah v. the United Kingdom* is quite illustrative of the hurdles that poverty-related allegations may face if so examined by the Court:

> Given the element of choice involved in immigration status, therefore, while differential treatment based on this ground must still be objectively and reasonably justifiable, the justification required will not be as weighty as in the case of a distinction based, for example, on nationality. Furthermore, given that the subject matter of this case - the provision of housing to those in need - is predominantly socio-economic in nature, the margin of appreciation accorded to the Government will be relatively wide.[233]

Against this backdrop, even if addressed as a matter of 'social origin' or 'property', the elements of choice, objectivity, personal characteristics and the link to socio-economic policies may, at the very least, expose the discrimination claim to a lenient review.

Another route towards tackling the discrimination experienced on account of poverty is to recognise people living in poverty as a vulnerable group. According to the Court, very weighty reasons (as required by 'suspect categories') are needed to justify a restriction of the rights of a vulnerable group. These are groups which have suffered a history of prejudice and social exclusion or stigmatisation.[234] However, as noted at the outset, it is far from clear whether the Court will in the near future endorse the view that socio-economically disadvantaged people are a vulnerable group.

Assuming that the Court eventually agrees to examine the recognition injury involved in alleged acts of discrimination for reasons of poverty, a finding of violation does not seem easy. In addition to the challenges exposed above, there are further indications of the hesitance with which the Court approaches the role of socio-economic disadvantage in rights restrictions. For example, though the Court has regularly found that taking children into care because of the family's material circumstances alone violates Article 8 ECHR, it has not always

[232] ECtHR, *Clift v. the United Kingdom*, App. no. 7205/07, Judgment of 13 July 2010, para. 55. Cited in Oddný Mjöll Arnardóttir, 'The Differences that Make a Difference: Recent Developments on the Discrimination Grounds and the Margin of Appreciation under Article 14 of the European Convention on Human Rights', 14(4) *Human Rights Law Review* (2014) 647, at 659.

[233] ECtHR, *Bah v. the United Kingdom*, App. no. 56328/07, Judgment of 27 September 2011, para. 47.

[234] ECtHR, *Alajos Kiss v. Hungary*, App. no. 38832/06, Judgment of 20 May 2010, para. 42; *Kiyutin v. Russia*, App. no. 2700/10, Judgment of 10 March 2011, para. 64 (people living with HIV are a vulnerable group with a history of prejudice and stigmatisation).

taken a categorical stance on the matter. The standard, in keeping with the rights of children, should be clear-cut: poverty can never be the sole ground for separating children from their families,[235] just as the Convention on the Rights of People with Disabilities prohibits separation on the sole ground of children's or their parents' disability.[236] Nevertheless, the Court has at times called into question the seriousness, duration or other aspects of the applicants' economic circumstances, rather than the legitimacy of separating families because of poverty.

In *Havelka*, for instance, while the Court held that separating the family on account of financial deprivation was contrary to the best interests of the child,[237] it is interesting to note the main factors leading to that conclusion. These were that eviction was not imminent and that according to the national courts the applicants should have been provided with shelter as a precondition for proceeding with eviction.[238] In other words, instead of directly challenging the forcible separation for reasons of poverty, the Court disputed whether the material difficulties had been as extreme as the government claimed. The judgment in *R.M.S.* discloses a similar ambiguity, inasmuch as the Court emphasised the improvement of the economic situation of the applicant. It pointed out that the applicant had simply been faced with a shortage of funds and that the authorities had refused to take into account subsequent changes in her financial circumstances.[239] Having to prove a change in the circumstances from which the childcare order originated implies that the decision in question was sufficient to justify the separation, which could then be reversed when such sufficient reasons no longer existed. But the point is that the sole socio-economic situation of the applicant could not be considered sufficient justification. The conclusion therefore had to stand irrespective of whether the applicant's financial conditions had improved or not. In this vein, it is interesting to note the more appropriate approach taken in *Achim v. Romania*.[240] Here the Court, in finding a non-violation of Article 8 ECHR, took into account that domestic authorities had given consideration not only to the improvement in the family's material conditions, but also to the applicants' parental role.[241] What is more, the Court

---

235 In this vein, Committee on the Rights of the Child, General Comment No. 14: The Right of the Child to have his or her best interests taken as a primary consideration (art. 3, para. 1), CRC/C/GC/14, 29 May 2013, paras. 61–63.

236 Convention on the Rights of People with Disabilities (CRPD), Article 23 (4).

237 In this case the applicants did not raise a discrimination claim, although they contended, like other applicants in similar cases, that separation on the sole ground of financial deprivation was unjust.

238 ECtHR, *Havelka and Others v. the Czech Republic*, App. no. 23499/06, Judgment of 21 June 2007, para. 59.

239 ECtHR, *R.M.S. v. Spain*, App. no. 28775/12, Judgment of 18 June 2013, paras. 85–86.

240 ECtHR, *Achim v. Romania*, App. no. 45959/11, Judgment of 24 October 2017.

241 Ibid., para. 112.

weighted the concrete steps adopted by the national authorities to provide the applicants with guidance and financial assistance.[242]

All in all, though, the Court does not seem to deal comfortably with rights claims grounded in poverty. Whether because the identity group paradigm and the liberal creed of individual autonomy are too embedded in the Court's legal culture, or because of the idea that anything related to socio-economic conditions pertains to politics and not to law,[243] the result is that even recognition harms related to poverty are often overlooked. Reversing this certainly requires legal mobilisation on the part of litigants and third-party interveners. Still, more could be done by the Court. As concerns stereotypes and stigma, for example, just naming them would be a step forward. Moreover, while the lack of substantiation of poverty-based discrimination makes it difficult for the Court to examine such allegations, it does not seem to completely preclude their examination. The Court has repeatedly stated that it is the master of the legal characterisation to be given to the facts of a case. And recently it had no problem in applying Article 14 ECHR *motu proprio* in a judgment involving gender-based discrimination.[244]

4.2.3. Integrating Social Structures into the Legal Analysis of Economic Disadvantage

It is relevant to point out that, in some cases, the applicants' demands for socio-economic support are framed as being necessary to cope with structural barriers. Challenging the governments' charges of passivity or negligence, the Court has been invited to examine the role of social structures and institutions in producing their destitution. In *Havelka*, for example, the applicant – a lone father caring for six children – alleged that he was in a highly disadvantaged position in the labour market due to his age, partial disability, lack of education and caring responsibilities.[245] He had in fact managed to find temporary jobs only. As regards his accommodation (which was municipal property), he explained that his rent debt had increased dramatically as a result of the very high default interest (around 91 per cent per year). For him, all these institutional deficits meant that the state was in a position to do more.[246] In its

---

242 Ibid., paras. 121–125.

243 Sandra Fredman, 'Redistribution and Recognition: Reconciling Inequalities', 23 *South African Journal of Human Rights* (2007) 214, at 216–217.

244 ECtHR, *Bălşan v. Romania*, App. no. 49645/09, 23 May 2017, para. 72 (Having regard to the particular circumstances of this case and the nature and substance of the applicant's complaints, the Court considered it appropriate to communicate of its own motion a complaint under Article 14 of the Convention read in conjunction with Article 3).

245 ECtHR, *Havelka and Others v. the Czech Republic*, App. no. 23499/06, Judgment of 21 June 2007, para. 46.

246 Ibid., para. 47.

judgment, the Court took note of the relevance of these arguments. Notably, it discarded the argument that the problem lay with the applicant's lack of effort, as the government claimed. *R.M.S.*, for its part, discloses the harm that may result from an institutional design or practice that denies parents, children and other family members living in poverty participation in decision-making processes affecting them. In this case, domestic regulations did not guarantee a prompt judicial review,[247] and the domestic authorities allowed neither the applicant's extended family nor her child to intervene in the judicial proceedings. The Court noted only the lack of participation of the applicant's great-uncle, but still did not explicitly treat this as a flaw in the decision-making. The question was all the more important, though, since persons living in poverty face systemic obstacles in claiming their rights and accessing justice in both administrative and judicial settings.[248]

The applicant and third-party interveners in *M.S.S.* similarly brought to light the link between the violations denounced and the institutional arrangements for asylum seekers in Greece. And this time the Court examined more closely the structural problems explaining the applicant's destitution. It held:

> The reports consulted reveal that in practice access to the job market is so riddled with administrative obstacles that this cannot be considered a realistic alternative [...]. In addition, the applicant had personal difficulties due to his lack of command of the Greek language, the lack of any support network and the generally unfavourable economic climate.[249]

These factors were among those that led the Court to conclude that the applicant's vulnerability had not been considered and that the Greek authorities had to be held accountable for their inaction.[250]

An approach more attentive to structural issues does not require the Court to pronounce on substantive provision, as the above examples demonstrate. However, taking that path holds potential from an integrated perspective on human rights. In the first place, a greater concern for the relationship between social structures and rights violations helps in accounting for real-life complexity. As seen above, it places individuals' options and choices within

247 On the requisite of speediness of judicial review of administrative child removal, see Article 9 Convention on the Rights of the Child (CRC) interpreted in the light of Articles 8 and 12 therein. See also, Travaux Préparatoires (UN Doc. E/1982/12/Add.1, C), at 49–55 reproduced in Sharon Detrick (ed.), *The United Nations Convention on the Rights of the Child. A Guide to the Travaux Préparatoires* (Martinus Nijhoff, 1992), at 168.

248 UN General Assembly; Report of the Special Rapporteur on Extreme Poverty and Human Rights, Magdalena Sepúlveda Carmona, A/67/278, 9 August 2012.

249 ECtHR, (GC) *M.S.S. v. Belgium and Greece*, App. no. 30696/09, Judgment of 21 January 2011, para. 261.

250 Ibid., para. 263.

a specific social context, taking the analysis beyond people's characteristics and personal circumstances. In the second place, looking at social structures may reveal how policies and institutions produce or aggravate inequality and socio-economic disadvantage. This is not trivial. By pinpointing those structures, the Court would, at the very least, signal the need for social reform. This might facilitate mobilisation around strategies that aim at transforming the situation of many rights holders affected by the problems discussed in these judgments.

4.3. AVOIDING NORM REDUCTIONISM AND PROMOTING AWARENESS OF LEGAL PLURALISM

As seen in Chapters 2 and 3, a comprehensive approach to the norms that are relevant to dealing with the cases may be useful in a number of respects. In this vein, and with respect to the conventional norms, several provisions of the Convention have been employed in the cases studied. Among them are the right to access justice (Article 6), the prohibition of torture and inhuman treatment (Article 3) and the right to private and family life (Article 8). Although the Court's case law discussed in this chapter is not anchored in one Convention provision, as seen in Chapter 2, a few provisions have been too easily discarded. One is the prohibition of discrimination (Article 14), whose use, as already explained, is almost non-existent. The subsections above have proven that the latter is an unfortunate normative reductionism. But it is not the only one, and this is what shall be discussed now. The case law on Roma and Travellers living in irregular settlements and facing eviction discloses, as already noted in Chapter 2, the scant attention paid to the rights to property and education (Articles 1 and 2 Protocol No. 1). In what follows, the discussion shall concentrate on the displacement of the right to property, given its particular implications for accounting for the needs and interests of people living in poverty.

4.3.1. A More Comprehensive Approach to Convention Norms: The Right to Property of People in Poverty

Impoverished Roma and Travellers who have been deprived of the few possessions they had have frequently invoked a violation of their right to property (Article 1 Protocol No. 1 ECHR).[251] The Court, however, has

[251] In some cases the claim is having been denied the right to live peacefully on their own land. In others, they complain against the removal and destruction of belongings. See e.g. ECtHR, (GC) *Lee v. the United Kingdom*, App. no. 25289/94, Judgment of 18 January 2001, paras. 118–121; *Winterstein and Others v. France*, App. no. 27013/07, Judgment of

systematically declined to examine the application of this norm to their plight. The consequence is not just that a range of legally sound arguments may be unnecessarily overlooked, that is, the economic losses and proprietary interests vested in one's home and belongings, which are different from the interests protected under the right to respect for the home (Article 8 ECHR). The question also arises as to the extent to which the right to property is being defined and applied in a way that is not inclusive of diverse proprietary interests, particularly of those with fewer possessions.

Noting that the question of compensation for the loss of houses and belongings following eviction has been left unanswered in these cases, Gerds argues that 'the Court should consider the importance of the home – however poor it may be – as being often the only possession of people in extreme poverty and the only safeguard against homelessness'.[252] To be fair, though, the Court has not been wholly unresponsive to the protection of impoverished dwellers' possessions. The Grand Chamber judgment in *Öneryildiz v. Turkey*, a case that does not involve Roma people, is proof of that. The applicants' home, placed in an illegal slum, had been destroyed by a landslide caused by a methane explosion that also killed their relatives. In spite of the irregularity of their tenure, the Court confirmed the Chamber's finding that the applicant's proprietary interests in his dwelling and movable goods constituted 'possessions'.[253] What is more, a violation of the right to property was found. The authorities had acted negligently, failing 'to do everything within their power to protect the applicant's proprietary interests'.[254]

In the light of *Öneryildiz*, the Court's reluctance to recognise Roma's and Travellers' proprietary interests in their mobile or makeshift homes and in their household effects appears puzzling. The divergence is addressed by the Court in its most recent judgment (at the time of writing) on the forced eviction and demolition of irregular Roma dwellings: *Bagdonavicius and Others v. Russia*.[255] There were three main elements that, according to the Court,

---

17 October 2013, para. 66; *Yordanova and Others v. Bulgaria*, App. no. 25446/06, Judgment of 24 April 2012, paras. 91 and 150–151; *Connors v. the United Kingdom*, App. no. 66746/01, Judgment of 27 May 2004, paras. 99–100 (in this last case the authorities eventually returned the applicant's belonging).

252 Johannes Gerds, 'Human Rights of People Experiencing Poverty in Europe: Standards, Obstacles and Perspectives of Protection in Council of Europe Instruments. Part 1: The European Convention on Human Rights', in Council of Europe, *Redefining and Combating Poverty: Human Rights, Democracy and Common Goods in Today's Europe*, Trends in Social Cohesion, no. 25 (Council of Europe, 2012), at 123–124.

253 ECtHR, (GC) *Öneryildiz v. Turkey*, App. no. 48939/99, Judgment of 30 November 2004, para. 127. One of the main factors taken into account by the Court was that 'the authorities also acknowledged *de facto* that the applicant and his close relatives had a proprietary interest in their dwelling and movable goods'.

254 Ibid., para. 135.

255 ECtHR, *Bagdonavicius and Others v. Russia*, App. no. 19841/06, Judgment of 11 October 2016.

justified the difference in the approach to Article 1 Protocol No. 1 regarding the applicants' interests in their dwellings. First, in *Öneryildiz* the state authorities had failed to act in good time on the serious risks arising from a dangerous economic activity. Second, the applicants in *Bagdonavicius and Others* had not paid taxes, nor had they been connected to public services, as had the applicants in *Öneryildiz*. Third, in *Bagdonavicius and Others* there had not been legal uncertainty, in a way similar to *Öneryildiz*, about the application of the law on illegal settlements that would have given the applicants hope that their houses would not fall under its scope.[256] The Court thus clarified that without one or more of those elements, the length of tolerated possession was not enough to constitute a 'sufficiently recognised and important' patrimonial interest.[257] As a result, the proprietary complaint in *Bagdonavicius and Others* was inadmissible *ratione materiae*.

The line-drawing appears unconvincing. Leaving aside the fact that the Court seemed to enlarge the number of factors that actually informed its approach to Article 1 Protocol No. 1 in *Öneryildiz*,[258] the reasoning in *Bagdonavicius and Others* is too casuistic and does not shed much light from a normative perspective. Taking into account the wide set of economic interests and goods protected by Article 1 Protocol No. 1, it seems quite artificial to affirm that the actual loss of economically valuable materials such as homes, furniture and other items does not even qualify as loss of 'possessions'. Read this way, the right to property would hardly cover the very few possessions of those who live in poverty. As to the destruction of movable property in *Bagdonavicius and Others*, the Court declared the applicants' claim inadmissible because they had neither submitted a complaint nor applied to the domestic courts for compensation. Hence, there may be greater chances for people in similar situations to obtain recognition of their possession over their movable goods. But for that to be a real prospect and not illusory, applicants would need support from legal aid agencies or non-governmental organisations to access the justice system of their countries in order to bring their claims for compensation.

Having said this, it is now time to enquire: how do international and regional norms play out in the cases studied?

---

256 Ibid., paras. 116–117.

257 Ibid., para. 117.

258 The relevant paragraph in this case reads: '*It is sufficient in this connection* for the Court to refer to the reasons set out above, which led it to conclude that *the State authorities had tolerated the applicant's actions* (see paragraphs 105–06 above). *Those reasons are plainly valid in the context of Article 1 of Protocol No. 1* and support the conclusion that the authorities also acknowledged de facto that the applicant and his close relatives had a proprietary interest in their dwelling and movable goods.' ECtHR, (GC) *Öneryildiz v. Turkey*, App. no. 48939/99, Judgment of 30 November 2004, para. 127 (emphasis added).

4.3.2. *Integrating International and Regional Norms*

The Court's practice of resorting to extra-Convention norms in the cases reviewed here is varied. While some judgments, such as those on child placement and the forced eviction of Roma and Travellers living in informal settlements, refer to several international and European instruments, others do not. Cases concerning fees and costs are among those disclosing little use of comparative and international legal material. Judges Tulkens and Loucaides actually regretted the lack of this material in *Gnahoré v. France*. Departing from the majority, they criticised the scheme of legal aid envisaged for appeals on points of law for its detrimental effects on the least well-off members of society. They even suggested, as pointed out earlier, less restrictive alternatives for organising appeals and legal aid that could have equally ensured cost-saving. Noting that legal aid was an issue in all member states, with different proposals being under discussion at the time, the dissenters went on to hold that 'a detailed comparative-law examination could prove particularly helpful'.[259]

This remark discloses the utility of considering comparative and international law for the purposes of evaluating the proportionality of a restriction, particularly from the viewpoint of less restrictive means. The laws and practices from other states help in illuminating the alternatives that are, in fact, out there. While such analysis may be needed in a wide range of scenarios, it may have specific added value when the restrictions largely fall on socio-economically disadvantaged people or on others in non-dominant positions. Economic hardship and class bias are too often neglected in a legal discourse that, at the same time, easily takes for granted the reasonability and effectiveness of policies that rely on socio-economic criteria or aims. The logic of less restrictive alternatives, similar to that behind reasonable accommodation in disability rights, forces public power to justify why things could not have been arranged differently, thus contrasting dominant views of what is normal or acceptable with reasonable alternatives. Exposure to different regulations and policies may then reveal that the criteria or policies in question (e.g. fees and legal aid systems) are not necessary, effective or based on accurate premises, as other states may have accomplished the same legitimate goals through less restrictive means.

From this perspective, the reasoning of the Grand Chamber in its recent judgment in *Garib* is puzzling. For one thing, the Court included a section on 'Practice elsewhere' where it referred to the law of one member state (Denmark),[260] whose regulation actually happened to be substantially different

---

259 ECtHR, *Gnahoré v. France*, App. no. 40031/98, Judgment of 19 September 2000, Dissenting Opinion of Judges Tulkens and Loucaides, at 2.

260 ECtHR, (GC) *Garib v. the Netherlands*, App. no. 43494/09, Judgment of 6 November 2017, paras. 87–92.

from the one contested in *Garib*. But the Grand Chamber did nothing with this information; it drew no conclusion. Importantly, it failed to acknowledge that the Dutch gentrification measure was rather isolated within the Council of Europe, which was a reason to narrow the state's margin of appreciation. The Grand Chamber, however, remained silent about the lack of common practice or consensus. Furthermore, the Court completely ruled out the relevance of 'less restrictive means' for the purpose of assessing the necessity of the Act.[261]

In *Ponomaryovi v. Bulgaria*, which dealt with the imposition of fees for secondary education on non-European nationals, the Court undertook a comprehensive normative review. It examined laws and judicial decisions from other member states and even from the United States on the use of fees in education. It observed that out of 26 member states, 'it appears that in seventeen States primary and secondary education is free of charge and accessible to all persons living or residing in the country regardless of their immigration status or that of their parents'.[262] Only in a few countries were certain categories of aliens required to pay fees for upper secondary schooling. The judicial decisions cited by the Court also opposed the exclusion of foreigners (regardless of their residential status) from post-compulsory education.[263] In addition, the Court referred to international treaties other than the ECHR that had been ratified by Bulgaria, namely, the Convention on the Rights of the Child; the International Covenant on Economic Social and Cultural Rights, and the European Social Charter.[264] Nevertheless, these insights were not used in the judgment, which ultimately relied on a number of exceptional circumstances. More concretely, as noted previously, the finding of violation was based on the applicants' exceptionally blameless situation. In light of the previous account of comparative and international norms, however, one may wonder why the Court did not consider those norms from the perspective of a regional or international consensus and/or from the viewpoint of existing less restrictive measures to achieve the state's goals. These considerations would have provided a much stronger normative basis for its decision, being mindful of the margin accorded to states in both socio-economic policy and migration law.

When it comes to child removal cases, in turn, the Court has been particularly attentive to external instruments and decisions. Among those more frequently cited are the CRC, the concluding observations of its monitoring Committee (the Committee on the Rights of the Child – CRC Committee) and resolutions adopted by the Committee of Ministers of the Council of

261 Ibid., para. 157.
262 ECtHR, *Ponomaryovi v. Bulgaria*, App. no. 5335/05, Judgment of 21 June 2011, para. 36.
263 Ibid., paras. 38–39.
264 Ibid., paras. 33–35.

Europe. Many of these sources are not explicitly incorporated into the merits analysis. Yet, to different degrees they appear relevant in three particular ambits: 1) in the contextualisation of the case; 2) in determining what the principle of the best interests of the child requires (including child participation); and 3) in interpreting the scope of the state's positive duties to support families.

In referring to the CRC Committee's concluding observations, the Court has taken note of the concerns and findings of that body as to the extent and nature of the problems denounced by the applicants. Most observations point to the disproportionate use of child placement by social services dealing with families in social and economic difficulty and to the lack of social support available to them.[265] This allows the case to be contextualised while also benefiting from the appreciation of a specialised body. Moreover, viewing the best interests of the child in light of Article 9 CRC, the Court has consistently upheld the exceptionality of child removal. Sometimes it has also considered, under Article 12 CRC, the right of the child to be heard in judicial and administrative decisions affecting her/him.[266] Finally within this child rights framework the Court has integrated, as mentioned earlier, a number of regional sources concerning social rights and positive measures to enable child-rearing and family life.[267] It is interesting to observe, however, that neither the case of *A.K. and L. v. Croatia* nor that of *Savigny* contain any reference to the UN Convention on the Rights of Persons with Disabilities (CRPD), which enshrines an express provision prohibiting child separation on account of the child's or parents' disability and other norms of relevance to those cases.[268] The review made thus far nonetheless confirms the view, already advanced in previous chapters, that considering rights holders in their different identities and social positions may have a direct impact on the range of norms through which the case is examined.

---

265 See e.g. ECtHR, *Wallová and Walla v. the Czech Republic*, App. no. 23848/04, Judgment of 26 October 2006, para. 46; *Savigny v. Ukraine*, App. no. 39948/06, Judgment of 18 December 2008, para. 34; *N.P. v. The Republic of Moldova*, App. no. 58455/13, Judgment of 6 October 2015, para. 43 and *Soares de Melo*, App. no. 72850/14, Judgment of 16 February 2016, paras. 57 and 98. Of note, in this last case the Court incorporated this material into its merit analysis as a 'preliminary issue'.

266 See e.g. ECtHR, *Havelka and Others v. the Czech Republic*, App. no. 23499/06, Judgment of 21 June 2007, para. 62; *Savigny v. Ukraine*, App. no. 39948/06, Judgment of 18 December 2008, para. 59.

267 Notably, among them: Council of Europe, Committee of Ministers, Recommendation Rec(2006)19 of the Committee of Ministers to Member States on Policy to Support Positive Parenting, Adopted on 13 December 2006; Recommendation Rec(2005)5 of the Committee of Ministers to Member States on the Rights of Children Living in Residential Institutions, Adopted on 16 March 2005.

268 Convention on the Rights of Persons with Disabilities [2007] UKTS 13919 (2007), Articles 23(4) and 28.

4.3.3. *Reflecting on the Integration of Non-State-Generated Norms*

As we may expect rights claims of cultural difference to involve tradition-based or community norms, in cases concerning economic difference we may also find non-state-generated norms playing a relevant role. One particular type of non-state-sanctioned norm that is of particular interest for this chapter is that generated by international financial institutions. In a complaint against Greece on austerity measures affecting public servants and which was declared inadmissible, the Court noted (as a matter of fact) that the contested salary cuts were introduced as a result of the commitments to which the government had subscribed with European financial institutions.[269] The Court eventually found the measure to be proportional, mostly because it did not apply to low-income persons and the applicants had not been exposed to difficulties of subsistence.[270] Aside from that reference to international financial agreements, however, this type of normativity has been rather absent from the case law studied here.

Yet, one might expect international financial commitments to feature more often in the future, including in cases like those discussed in this chapter. For one thing, economic commitments of the sort and their problematic human rights implications (which were once typical of developing countries) are now a reality in Europe.[271] For another, economic crises and structural reforms promoted by international financial institutions risk impacting more adversely on low-income households and others in socio-economic vulnerability. In fact, some specific policy choices that run to their detriment are often dictated by international financial commitments. A notable example is the imposition of user fees to access social services, upon which loans from international institutions that advocate the application of market-oriented rules are sometimes made conditional.[272] Therefore, though international financial agreements do not seem to have been at play in the cases reviewed, the issue merits some reflection. From a normative perspective, it is worth considering,

---

269 ECtHR, *Koufaki and ADEDY v. Greece*, App. nos. 57665/12 and 57657/12, Decision of 7 May 2013. For a brief overview of the ECtHR case law on austerity measures, see European Parliament, Directorate General for Internal Policies, Policy Department Citizens' Rights and Constitutional Affairs, The Impact of the Crisis on Fundamental Rights across Member States of the EU: Comparative Analysis – Study for the LIBE Committee (European Parliament, 2015), at 152.

270 ECtHR, *Koufaki and ADEDY v. Greece*, App. nos. 57665/12 and 57657/12, Decision of 7 May 2013, paras. 46–47.

271 This has become particularly evident in the last decade, given the debt crises that have affected European countries such as Iceland, Greece, Ireland, Portugal and Spain.

272 As to their impact on the provision of health services, see e.g. Margaux J. Hall *et al.*, 'Answering the Millennium Call for the Right to Maternal Health: The Need to Eliminate User Fees', 12 (1) *Yale Human Rights and Development Journal* (2009) 62, at 68–69.

for example, the desirability of going beyond the usual arguments about state budgetary constraints to incorporate the role of international financial and debt-relief rules in the adjudication process when they are in fact at stake.

Making the impact of international financial norms visible in the judicial setting may be seen as something mostly useful to states wishing the Court to either exclude the matter from its competence or temper their liability under the Convention. But this is not the only aspect for which it could be useful to consider these norms. To appreciate this, one may take an example from another human rights jurisdiction. Consider *Federation of employed pensioners of Greece (IKA-ETAM) v. Greece*, a complaint brought to the European Committee of Social Rights (ECSR).[273] Against allegations of violations of the European Social Charter resulting from austerity measures, the Greek government argued, *inter alia*, that changes to the social protection afforded to pensioners were required by other international obligations, namely 'those deriving from a financial support mechanism agreed upon by the Government together with the European Commission, the European Central Bank and the International Monetary Fund ("the Troika")'.[274] Yet, as the reasoning of the ECSR in that case shows, the argument may not so easily discharge states from compliance with human rights conventions. The ECSR took the view that the fact that the policy in question was part of Greece's financial legal obligations did not, in the first place, remove the matter from the ambit of the Charter.[275] Secondly, it held that when preparing and implementing the adoption of binding economic measures, states should 'take full account' of their human rights commitments.[276] Thirdly, and admitting the difficulties created by the economic crisis, states must ensure a certain level of effective satisfaction of human rights. In this connection, the criteria applied by the ECSR to oversee compliance with the Charter included the adequacy of the reforms in that 'care had been taken to ensure that the burden of these reforms did not weigh too heavily on the economically most vulnerable households'.[277] Finally, the ECSR stated that even taking heed of the particular economic and normative constraints faced by Greece, 'the government has not conducted the minimum level of research and analysis into the effects of such far-reaching measures that is necessary to assess in a meaningful manner their full impact on vulnerable groups in society'.[278]

---

273 ECSR, *Federation of employed pensioners of Greece (IKA-ETAM) v. Greece*, Complaint no. 76/2012, Decision on the merits of 7 December 2012.

274 Ibid., paras. 10 and 66. The argument raises both a matter of admissibility and considerations for the merit analysis.

275 Ibid., para. 50.

276 Ibid., para. 51.

277 Ibid., para. 73.

278 Ibid., para. 79.

The reasoning followed by the ECSR allows to reflect on the importance and utility of according more attention to a wide range of norms potentially relevant to dealing with cases concerning, for example, fees and social cuts affecting the worst off, including normative commitments laid down in international economic agreements. Of course, if the European Court of Human Rights were to consider member states' financial obligations, the review would obviously have a very different scope to that undertaken by the ECSR, for the two bodies have substantially different subject-matter jurisdictions. However, the above case illustrates that the consideration of norms generated by financial institutions or other non-state actors may provide useful insights. In the first place, it may allow 'a holistic approach to human rights focusing on both the causes and context within which human rights violations occur'.[279] A holistic approach also means that the Court would not only take into account the Convention alongside the relevant financial international obligations, but also by virtue of Article 53 ECHR, regard would be had to existing human rights obligations under other treaties, with a view to ensuring that any interpretation of the Convention did not derogate from such obligations. Against this background and in giving precedence to human rights obligations, the UN expert Alfred Maurice de Zayas has specifically referred to the European Court's case law. He has advanced the view that 'as the European Court of Human Rights decided in its 1989 judgment in the case of *Soering v. the United Kingdom*, the obligations under the European Convention on Human Rights prevail over those under extradition treaties, *mutatis mutandis* over bilateral investment treaties and free trade agreements'.[280]

---

279 UN Human Rights Council; Report of the Independent Expert on the effects of foreign debt and other related international financial obligations of States on the full enjoyment of all human rights, particularly economic, social and cultural rights – Guiding Principles on Foreign Debt and Human Rights, Cephas Lumina, A/HRC/20/23, 10 April 2011, para. 7 (referring to the divide between the states that were in favour of addressing the issue of foreign debt from a human rights perspective and those which believed that human rights bodies should not deal with this matter. Those in favour called for a 'holistic approach to human rights'). It is to be noted, however, that the vast majority of European states that participated in the discussion of Resolution 20/10, through which the Human Rights Council endorsed the Guiding Principles referred to above, voted against it.

280 UN Human Rights Council; Report of the Independent Expert on the promotion of a democratic and equitable international order, Alfred Maurice de Zayas, A/HRC/30/44, 14 July 2015, para. 40. This case concerned the potential extradition to the USA by the UK of a German national charged with murder. He alleged that if extradited and sentenced to death, he would experience the 'death row', which was contrary to Article 3 ECHR. The judgment did not explicitly affirm the supremacy of the human rights obligations enshrined in the ECHR over the extradition treaties in question. But the Court did provide support for such a conclusion in the concrete case. It held, for example, that what other international treaties stipulated 'cannot, however, absolve the Contracting Parties from responsibility under Article 3 (art. 3) for all and any foreseeable consequences of extradition suffered outside their jurisdiction. In interpreting the Convention regard must be had to its special character as a treaty for the collective enforcement of human rights and fundamental freedoms.'

A second reason for highlighting the role of the norms dictated by international financial institutions in the restriction of human rights is that doing so brings to the surface a real-life dimension that remains downplayed under a state-centred view of international law. In this context, just naming financial agreements and their interplay with human rights norms may contribute to (1) bringing to the surface structural barriers and root causes of violations, while also (2) bolstering normative developments in the field of human rights obligations for non-state actors and state extraterritorial responsibility for human rights violations. One path that could evolve in this context is, for example, that of the responsibility of member states which act as lenders or as supervisors of private actors imposing conditions that lead to violations in the subscribing country.[281] Thirdly, a broad and inclusive normative spectrum like the one suggested here may help in refining states' human rights obligations *vis à vis* international financial commitments by way of specific substantive or procedural standards. Governments and rights holders may benefit from, for example, the application of an impact assessment-like requirement similar to

---

The Convention provisions must 'be interpreted and applied so as to make its safeguards practical and effective' and such interpretation 'has to be consistent with "the general spirit of the Convention, an instrument designed to maintain and promote the ideals and values of a democratic society"'. Likewise, the Court took into account the absolute nature of Article 3 ECHR. Further, it pointed out that 'the fact that a specialised treaty should spell out in detail a specific obligation attaching to the prohibition of torture does not mean that an essentially similar obligation is not already inherent in the general terms of Article 3 (art. 3) of the European Convention. It would hardly be compatible with the underlying values of the Convention, that "common heritage of political traditions, ideals, freedom and the rule of law" to which the Preamble refers, were a Contracting State knowingly to surrender a fugitive to another State where there were substantial grounds for believing that he would be in danger of being subjected to torture, however heinous the crime allegedly committed.' See ECtHR, *Soering v. the United Kingdom*, Plenary, App. no. 14038/88, Judgment of 7 July 1989, paras. 86–89.

According priority to human rights norms in the balancing of states' legal commitments appears to be the solution generally advocated by UN mechanisms. A key consideration is the fact that virtually all states subscribing to financial bilateral or multilateral obligations are already bound by major international instruments of human rights. See e.g. UN Human Rights Council; Report of the Independent Expert on the effects of foreign debt and other related international financial obligations of States on the full enjoyment of all human rights, particularly economic, social and cultural rights – Guiding Principles on Foreign Debt and Human Rights, Cephas Lumina, A/HRC/20/23, 10 April 2011, para. 6 (Foundational principles: 'Ensuring the primacy of human rights').

281 In this vein, see for example the analysis of legal avenues for holding Euro Area Member States accountable for the debt situation in Greece as explained by Olivier De Schutter and Margot E. Salomon, Legal Brief Prepared for the Special Committee of the Hellenic Parliament on the Audit of the Greek Debt (Debt Truth Committee) – Economic Policy Conditionality, Socio-economic Rights and International Legal Responsibility: The Case of Greece 2010–2015, 15 June 2015, at 6–8. (Although the arguments advanced by the authors are mainly grounded in UN-based human rights provisions, similar or other arguments might well be articulated in the framework of the European Convention system.)

that applied by the ECSR and to be carried out prior to subscribing to binding economic measures.[282] Finally, from the point of view of states' multiple international commitments, explicit references in the Strasbourg case law to the overlaps between states' human rights obligations and their international financial undertakings may provide normative grounds for governments seeking to prioritise their human rights obligations and having to defend doing so in other forums of dispute resolution. Thus, if the Court is to adjudicate on restrictions directed at or mostly affecting people in socio-economic disadvantage and which are driven by international financial commitments, it may be worthwhile integrating this layer of normativity into the judicial analysis. To that end, it is first and foremost for the parties and interveners in the case to bring those norms to the Court's attention.

5. CONCLUDING REMARKS

The range of cases studied in this chapter confirms the premise that although poverty and questions of socio-economic disadvantage can easily be isolated or side-lined in legal discourses, in reality they are better addressed from a relational and integrated perspective. Take the cases in which applicants could not afford fees to access justice, secondary education or health services or to marry; or those concerning child removal and restrictions on the right to choose one's residence and to security in tenure. Or consider the complaint against a criminal ban on begging in public places. In most of these cases, the various rights holders affected found themselves at the intersection of several identities and hierarchies. Equally, their grievances involved different categories of rights, touching upon maldistribution and misrecognition. Moreover, in most of them the applicants' position was depicted as arising out of individual choice or personal circumstances, while in reality this had a lot to do with broader social relations and institutions. More often than not, the idea that they deserved less or no legal protection was rooted in compounded stereotypes or social values that made them responsible for the rights interference complained of. Hence, in practice, these experiences speak of interdependence and complexity between rights holders and norms.

This chapter has provided an overview of different ways in which the above complexity has, however, been disaggregated in the Court's judgments and decisions, while also highlighting where and how the Court has engaged in a more integrated analysis of poverty-related cases. This has been done with

282 The use of impact assessment in this field is already a practice. However, its consideration in the context of a procedural judicial review may provide more concrete guidelines on what such analysis should entail from the perspective of human rights.

regard more often to the applicable norms than to rights holders. In this connection, it is relevant to observe that the Court's restrictive accounts of rights holders are not marked by an emphasis on an identity or group defined by socio-economic disadvantage. While some judges of the Court are advocating for recognition of people living in poverty as a vulnerable group, this is still resisted. One could nonetheless argue that the lack of identity/group frames of analysis even offers an advantage. It could be an opportunity to shift the Court's attention towards social structures and relations and thus towards a comprehensive analysis, a shift largely missed in the resolution of cultural identity cases. However, things do not appear to be working in that direction. Paradoxical as it may be, it seems that while too much of a concern with groups or identity is problematic, so is the total absence of a group or identity frame of analysis. It appears that without recourse to this, the Court does not have some of the reasons or means to examine relations of inequality and the socio-economic experience of rights holders. When this happens, the analysis of the case is partial or fragmented. But this is not the only way in which the examination of claims of economic difference may become fragmentary.

In this chapter it was also noted that defining the case as one about the state's socio-economic policy and budgetary management may also lead to an abstract review and to an emphasis on the latitude of domestic authorities that loses sight of the specific rights holders and interests at stake. An example of this was found in the different reasoning and outcomes offered by rulings that are relatively similar as to the actors, norms and interests at stake but that differ as to the centrality accorded to the state's socio-economic policies. Take the cases defined as being about child removal, family separation and the right to family life and compare them with those that are framed from the perspective of the state's migration policy and its socio-economic limitations in that context. While in all those cases children were among the main affected rights holders and the right to family life was a key common interest, these aspects are substantially displaced once the case fell into the 'box' of the state's socio-economic policies. Similarly, it was seen that examining a case through the framework of the state's general social policies, as happened in *Garib v. the Netherlands*, triggers the application of an extremely abstract and deferential review.

Even when the Court has taken into account the applicants' socio-economic disadvantage, it has rarely examined this from an intersectional approach so as to recognise the different faces of poverty. The Court often overlooks the specific way in which the gender, racial/ethnic and body-ability position of the applicant shapes or exacerbates the rights interferences related to poverty. This has a number of normative consequences that include, but are not limited to, the analysis of proportionality and discrimination. It was seen that identity-neutral readings of poverty tend to obscure the particular barriers and harms encountered by women, minorities or people with disabilities who live in poverty, such as higher risks of discrimination and violence (as in *Soares de Melo v. Portugal*), maternal death (as in *Şentürk v. Turkey*) and denials of autonomy rights (as in *O'Donoghue and Others* and *Garib v. the Netherlands*).

Another problematic area of the Court's approach to rights holders in the cases studied is that concerning their autonomy and choices. The Court has only occasionally challenged assumptions that posit poverty as the result of individuals' exercise of free will, while at times upholding actions that impinge on their agency. The Court's appreciation of the range of rights holders affected in the cases is, however, more comprehensive, notably when it comes to children. Especially in some cases, such as those on family separation, the Court has taken a broad view that is more aligned with people's lived experience. On this basis, the Court has, for example, reinforced the socio-economic dimension of rights, specified certain obligations in a way more attuned to the persons involved and placed the issue of poverty and the ensuing rights restrictions within a concrete social context.

Similar insights have been gained through normative integration. Although still cautious about intruding into the socio-economic field, the Court has nonetheless affirmed the indivisibility of rights in certain cases. This has been particularly so in cases of exceptionally acute destitution and in cases which have not been framed as being mainly about social policy. With regard to harms that are not typically socio-economic, the Court has recognised, in limited circumstances, the humiliation and debasement endured as a result of extreme destitution. However, 'recognition' harms of stereotyping, stigma and general discrimination have yet to be integrated into the Court's legal analysis of poverty-related claims. This appears particularly true for cases perceived as being about positive duties of economic assistance.

As regards the range of Convention and extra-Convention norms that illuminate the resolution of cases, a variety of Convention provisions have been mobilised in relation to socio-economic disadvantage. Yet, the application of the prohibition of discrimination and the right to property, despite their relevance to the cases, has been too easily discarded. As to regional and international norms, the examination of comparative material and the idea of consensus has only occasionally been adopted, and not necessarily with a clear end. Cases of family separation for reasons of poverty notably expand more in the use of regional and international sources, deriving specialised guidelines regarding children's rights and socio-economic support for families. Finally, it might be worth exploring the role played by other international norms, such as those concerning financial agreements by states and private actors. The Court has already taken some steps in that direction, but more could be done in the future by just making this additional layer of norms and actors more visible.

CHAPTER 5

AN INTEGRATED APPROACH TO ECONOMIC DISADVANTAGE IN THE INTER-AMERICAN COURT OF HUMAN RIGHTS

1. INTRODUCTION

The Inter-American Court and the Commission are familiar with issues of poverty and inequality. They work in a region well known for its stark socio-economic contradictions. Poverty levels are alarmingly high and the region features as the most unequal in terms of income distribution.[1] Even though a big part of the Court's case law consists of cases involving gross and systematic violations perpetrated by dictatorships or authoritarian regimes, over the years an increasing number of cases have been brought about claims of inequality, some of them for reasons related to socio-economic disadvantage. The importance that the issue has attained in the region today is aptly reflected by the process of consultation that the Commission recently concluded on the topic of poverty and human rights.[2] It is therefore not surprising that the Court, following in many respects the Commission's drive, has been rather sensitive to questions of poverty and socio-economic difference. Nevertheless, while poverty is in the background of a number of cases, it should be pointed out that very few of them involve rights claims directly grounded in socio-economic disadvantage.

---

1 See e.g. United Nations, ECLAC, Inclusive social development: The next generation of policies for overcoming poverty and reducing inequality in Latin America and the Caribbean (ECLAC, 2015), at 18–20 ('Estimates for 19 Latin American countries indicate that in 2014, there were 167 million people living in conditions of poverty, of whom 71 million were facing extreme poverty' … 'Latin America and the Caribbean represent the world's most unequal region in terms of income distribution. That structural feature has remained largely unchanged over a lengthy time, even at times of high economic growth.').

2 A Preliminary Report on Poverty and Extreme Poverty and Human Rights in the Americas was published by the Inter-American Commission in 2016 on the basis of a consultation process among different stakeholders. During 2017 a platform was opened for receiving comments. See <www.oas.org/en/iachr/media_center/PReleases/2016/193.asp>.

It is against this backdrop that the present chapter aims, as the previous one did with regard to the Strasbourg Court, to explore first whether and how the Court accounts for claims of economic difference. Or, in other words, rights assertions that reflect the needs and concerns of those who are regarded as different and deviant from a socio-economic point of view. These are mostly people living in poverty or otherwise socio-economically disadvantaged. Secondly, this chapter explores how the Court accounts for those claims from a particular point of view, namely from an integrated and relational approach to human rights. In this way, the discussion that follows seeks to offer a complex understanding of the cases, one that better reflects the lived reality of rights holders and contemporary forms of normative interaction. Since prevailing approaches to issues of social difference and equality are often quite compartmentalised or narrowly framed, a comprehensive perspective may provide relevant insights for dealing with claims of socio-economic disadvantage, which, as seen in the first part of this book, pose a number of interesting challenges to human rights courts.

To undertake this analysis, this chapter concentrates only on those judgments where the Court accords some normative significance to claims of socio-economic disadvantage. This also means that, as in the previous chapter, the discussion is more concerned with cases in which socio-economic disadvantage is seen as leading to or facilitating violations, rather than those in which poverty appears to be one of the consequences of any kind of violation. It must be noted, though, that because of the types of case brought to the Court and the scarcity of complaints centred on poverty-related claims as such, the chapter discusses cases that concern not only issues of social inclusion and recognition, but also protection from acts of violence. This makes the sample of cases analysed here broader than that considered in previous chapters.

The discussion is divided into three main parts. Following the introduction (section 1), the first part (section 2) briefly examines how individuals' socio-economic disadvantage has come to be considered something normatively relevant in the Court's case law. This section also examines the role played by group identity and group vulnerability frameworks, as well that by other frames leading to compartmentalised thinking. Building upon this analysis, the second part of the discussion (section 3) examines who are, according to the Court, those persons raising claims of socio-economic disadvantage, taken from the perspective of their identities and social locations as well as their autonomy. In examining how an integrated view of rights holders is helpful in poverty-related cases, the situation of individuals other than the applicants is also examined. The third and last part of the discussion (section 4) focuses on the harms and norms taken into account when dealing with claims of socio-economic disadvantage. This part explores, *inter alia*, whether the Court has addressed, in addition to questions of socio-economic rights, the stereotypes and invisibility associated with an experience of poverty, as well as the incidence of structural inequalities. Further, the chapter revises the conventional and extra-conventional norms which are or could be used by the Court to address some of the challenges posed by the cases studied.

2. ECONOMIC DISADVANTAGE, GROUP IDENTITY QUESTIONS AND LEGAL COMPARTMENTS

2.1. FACING SOCIO-ECONOMIC DISADVANTAGE

As in the European Court's case law, rights claims grounded in people's economic reality, especially in socio-economic disadvantage, were first raised with regard to legal aid and access to justice.[3] It was in this context that the need to consider the material deprivation of rights holders was brought to the Inter-American Court almost three decades ago. But unlike the trajectory followed in Strasbourg, the issue was not introduced in an individual case. Rather, it arose out of a Commission request for an advisory opinion concerning the obligation to exhaust domestic remedies in order to access the Inter-American system.[4] The Commission had received petitions in which complainants alleged that they had not been able to comply with the requirement of exhaustion of remedies because they could not afford legal representation or court fees.[5] Against this background, the Commission asked the Court (1) whether the rule of exhaustion of domestic remedies should nonetheless be applied to those indigent applicants; and (2) whether refusing to exempt them from that obligation would not raise an issue of discrimination based on 'social condition' under Article 1.1 ACHR.[6]

Of course, the Convention provision governing the matter, Article 46 ACHR, makes no reference to indigence. The exceptions to the rule on exhaustion of remedies only provide for being 'denied access' to the remedies or being 'prevented from exhausting them'.[7] Nevertheless, these exceptions, according

---

3 ECtHR, *Airey v. Ireland*, App. no. 6289/73, Judgment of 9 October 1979. See Chapter 4, sections 3. 2 and 4.1.

4 IACtHR, Advisory Opinion OC-11/90 on the Exceptions to the Exhaustion of Domestic Remedies (Articles 46(1), 46(2)(a) and 46(2)(b) American Convention on Human Rights), Adopted on 10 August 1990.

5 Ibid., para. 3. The Commission also pointed out that it was 'aware that some States provide free legal assistance to persons who qualify because of their economic status. However, this practice does not obtain in all of the countries and even in those countries where it exists, it often covers only highly urbanised areas.'

6 Idem.

7 Article 46 ACHR, in its relevant parts, reads as follows:

1. Admission by the Commission of a petition or communication lodged in accordance with Articles 44 or 45 shall be subject to the following requirements:
   a. that the remedies under domestic law have been pursued and exhausted in accordance with generally recognized principles of international law; [...]

to the Court, covered impediments flowing from both legal and factual circumstances.[8] Hence, 'if it can be shown that an indigent needs legal counsel to effectively protect a right which the Convention guarantees and his indigence prevents him from obtaining such counsel, he does not have to exhaust the relevant domestic remedies'.[9] The same held for the payment of court fees. Additionally, the Court stated that if a person was prevented from seeking the protection of the law to assert her or his Convention rights because she or he, as a result of indigence, could not afford legal representation or the costs of the proceedings, then 'that person is being discriminated against by reason of his economic status'.[10] In that case, he or she 'is not receiving equal protection before the law'.[11] Both interpretations – on legal aid and court fees, on the one hand, and on economic discrimination, on the other – were later transposed to contentious cases. Nevertheless, as will be seen below it took much longer for the prohibition of discrimination for reasons of poverty to be applied in a case.

It is worth mentioning that the Commission has, through reports and decisions on individual petitions, further addressed domestic problems of access to justice on account of poverty.[12] Meanwhile, the Court has dealt with the provision of free legal aid to people without means (notably, irregular migrants), although more in advisory opinions than in contentious cases.[13]

---

2. The provisions of paragraphs 1.a and 1.b of this article shall not be applicable when:
   a. the domestic legislation of the state concerned does not afford due process of law for the protection of the right or rights that have allegedly been violated;
   b. the party alleging violation of his rights has been denied access to the remedies under domestic law or has been prevented from exhausting them; or
   c. there has been unwarranted delay in rendering a final judgment under the aforementioned remedies.

[8] IACtHR, Advisory Opinion OC-11/90 on the Exceptions to the Exhaustion of Domestic Remedies (Articles 46(1), 46(2)(a) and 46(2)(b) American Convention on Human Rights), Adopted on 10 August 1990, paras. 17 and 20.

[9] Ibid., paras. 30–31.

[10] Ibid., para. 22.

[11] Idem.

[12] See the reports and individual petitions summarised in IACommHR, Access to Justice as a Guarantee of Economic, Social, and Cultural Rights: A Review of the standards adopted by the Inter-American System of Human Rights, OEA/Ser.L/V/II.129 Doc. 4, 7 September 2007, paras. 48–80. See also, Ariel E. Dulitzky, 'Pobreza y derechos humanos en el sistema interamericano. Algunas aproximaciones preliminares', 48 *Revista Instituto Interamericano de Derechos Humanos* (2008) 107, at 128–132.

[13] IACtHR, Advisory Opinion OC-16/99 on the The Right to Information on Consular Assistance in the Framework of the Guarantees of Due Process of Law, Adopted on 1 October 1999, para. 119 (holdings that 'the judicial process must recognize and correct any real disadvantages that those brought before the bar might have [...] [which] necessitates countervailing measures that help to reduce or eliminate the obstacles and deficiencies that impair or diminish an effective defense of one's interests'); Advisory Opinion OC-18/03 on the Juridical Condition and Rights of the Undocumented Migrants, Adopted on 17 September 2003, para. 126 (referring specifically to free legal aid); Rights and guarantees of children

In *Cantos v. Argentina*, however, the Court examined a related issue: the imposition of court fees and its impact on the right to access courts.[14] Interestingly enough, however, the applicant in this case was far from facing socio-economic difficulties. He was the owner of an important holding, the principal shareholder of two companies and the owner of urban and rural lands. Following a series of searches carried out on his premises and the seizure of several important items, he initiated legal actions for the ensuing damages and losses. He had paid the filing fees and had requested litigation without incurring costs, which the domestic courts refused. Eventually the applicant was required to pay more than 83 million US dollars, which corresponded to a fixed fee of 3 per cent of the total amount of damages claimed. On top of that, a fine of 41 million US dollars was imposed for failure to pay the said fee.

The Commission argued that these amounts, coupled with other charges, were a disproportionate burden and thus incompatible with the right to access justice.[15] The Court agreed. It found that even though the sum was arithmetically proportional to the amount claimed by the applicant, it was 'unreasonable' and 'disproportional'.[16] As such, it amounted to a violation of the applicant's right of access to justice (Article 8.1 ACHR) regardless of the fact that he had not paid it and the proceedings had concluded with a final judgment. This was so because 'those participating in the proceeding must be able to do so without fear of being forced to pay disproportionate or excessive sums because they turned to the courts'.[17] Surprisingly, at no point did the Court (or the Commission) discuss the applicant's financial resources, which played no role in the proportionality analysis.[18] This strong procedural protection suggests that extremely high fees or economic requirements for the purpose of exercising fundamental rights such as access to justice would not be acceptable no matter the economic capacity of the person in question. But this is not self-evident, especially in a time when human rights are

in the context of migration and/or in need of international protection; Advisory Opinion OC-21/14 on the Rights and guarantees of children in the context of migration and/or in need of international protection, Adopted on 19 August 2014, paras. 124, 130–132, 204 and 248–251 (referring to free legal assistance of an interpreter and of a legal representative throughout the proceedings). The Court has nonetheless briefly addressed the right of migrants to free legal aid in contentious cases. See, for example, IACtHR, *Vélez Loor v. Panama*, Judgment of 23 November 2010, paras. 136–139.

14 IACtHR, *Cantos v. Argentina*, Judgment of 28 November 2002.

15 IACommHR, Written arguments submitted to the IACtHR in the case of *Cantos v. Argentina*, 9 March 1999, at 36–37.

16 IACtHR, *Cantos v. Argentina*, Judgment of 28 November 2002, para. 54.

17 Ibid., para. 55.

18 It appears that the Court attached importance to the amounts involved and possibly as well to the authorities' alleged acts of persecution and hostility towards the applicant. See ibid., paras. 7(e) and 35.

tending to expand and cover an increasing number of fields. A more concrete analysis of proportionality would therefore have been helpful.

The above rulings and judgments, alongside others such as *Uzcátegui et al. v. Venezuela*,[19] show that the applicants' socio-economic disadvantage is identified as something legally relevant. It can at the very least, and regardless of other identities and disadvantages, affect the proportionality analysis. Unlike the judgment in *Cantos*, the assessment in *Uzcátegui* is considerably less abstract. This case concerned the extrajudicial execution, by police officers, of a young man from a humble family who had been seeking justice for the death of his brother. As usual in this type of case, several violations were found, including the prohibition of torture and inhuman treatment (Article 5) and the rights to life (Article 4), to liberty (Article 7), privacy (Article 11) and freedom of expression (Article 12) ACHR. Additionally, and in view of the way the police broke into the victim's home, damaging its structure and household items, the victims' representative asked the Court to declare a violation of their right to property (Article 21 ACHR). In doing so, the Court held:

> Given the circumstances in which the action took place and, in particular, the socioeconomic status and vulnerability of the Uzcátegui family, the damage to their property during the raid had a far greater impact than it would have had for other family groups with other means. In this regard, the Court considers that States must take into account that groups of people living in adverse circumstances and with fewer resources, such as those living in poverty, experience an increase in the extent to which their rights are affected, precisely because of their more vulnerable situation.[20]

Although the Court did not say it, the question appears to be one of proportionality. The right to property may be restricted and some interference may be inherent in police raids. In the case at hand, though, the arbitrary nature of the operation had compromised the legality and legitimate aim of any ensuing restriction of the applicants' right to property. The Court could have focused on that and, by the same token, it could also have opted to subsume this wrong under a violation of the rights to privacy and liberty, for example. But it did not. The Court thus seems interested, as will be seen later (section 4.2.1), in recognising as a distinctive harm the excessive impact that the inflicted material losses had on a family living in poverty. The same words on the greater harm that damage to property causes to people living in poverty were restated shortly after, in the *Massacre of Santo Domingo* case.[21] The remark, however, hardly found application in this judgment, since the vast majority of

---

19 IACtHR, *Uzcátegui et al. v. Venezuela*, Judgment of 3 September 2012.

20 Ibid., para. 204.

21 IACtHR, *The Santo Domingo Massacre v. Colombia*, Judgment of 30 November 2012.

interferences with the applicants' possessions (looting and damage to homes, crops and animals) could not be attributed to the state.[22]

Following a similar logic, the applicants' economic hardship has additionally been identified as normatively relevant for the purpose of granting reparations. It has been seen that reparation orders geared to the victims' socio-economic needs are not uncommon in the Court's case law. These typically include measures of a social and redistributive character. Several of these were examined in Chapter 3 when discussing some reparation awards in indigenous land cases. Among them are the restitution of land, the creation of development funds, the construction of public facilities and the provision of social services. But in addition, the Court has also considered the victims' situation of poverty for the purpose of determining the damage and the extent of the remedies. The underlying rationale resembles that of poverty as a factor that intensifies or aggravates the rights interferences. Just as this weighs in the proportionality analysis, the heightened harm would also affect the extent of the reparations for the ensuing violations. Judgments such as those in '*the Juvenile Reeducation Institute*' and *Yakye Axa*, both against Paraguay, attest to that.[23]

Having clarified that the Court has generally been sensitive to questions of economic disadvantage, which has been regarded as something legally relevant, it is time to enquire about the place of the identity group framework and the vulnerability of people living in poverty. Questions of identity, group and vulnerability usually hold great significance in the way litigants and courts frame and address complaints of social difference and inclusion, as explained in Chapter 1. It was seen that this also holds true for claims grounded in cultural difference. When it comes to socio-economic disadvantage, however, the previous chapter demonstrated that such a framework does not seem to apply easily, at least in the context of the ECtHR. And while the lack of that sort of compartmentalisation may offer some opportunities, the total lack of reference to group identity or vulnerability may give rise to further difficulties, some of which were analysed in Chapter 4. That is why it is worth exploring, as does the following subsection, the questions whether people living in poverty are regarded as a vulnerable or otherwise protected 'group'; and whether their experience is evaluated through the frames of 'identity' and 'difference' or through other categories that foster compartmentalisation.

---

22 Ibid., paras. 273–282. (Evidence indicated, in line with the government's argument, that most of the damage to property complained of had been caused by members of the FARC – The Revolutionary Armed Forces of Colombia.)

23 IACtHR, *The Yakye Axa Indigenous Community v. Paraguay*, Judgment of 17 June 2005, para. 202; *'Juvenile Reeducation Institute' v. Paraguay*, Judgment of 2 September 2004, para. 262. ('In determining reparations in the instant case, the Court must consider the fact that there were children involved who were very poor and whose human rights were grievously violated.')

2.2. THE SOCIO-ECONOMICALLY DISADVANTAGED AS VULNERABLE

While it is not possible to assert that poverty in the Inter-American system, and more particularly in the Court, is regarded and mobilised in the same way as any other group identity claim, the difference is not as sharp as one would expect. This can be appreciated, in the first place, in the relative visibility of people's socio-economic disadvantage in the arguments of the applicants and the Commission, as well as in the Court's judgments. In the second place, and perhaps more crucially, it should be noted that because of the attention that the Inter-American system has devoted to group identity discrimination and to substantive or structural equality, poverty has been addressed in close connection with all of these elements namely, groups, vulnerability and discrimination.

The Court has not explicitly stated that people living in poverty as such constitute a vulnerable group requiring special protection. But it should be recalled that the Court, rather than talking about 'vulnerable groups', usually refers to groups in a vulnerable situation or in aggravated vulnerability. In this sense, the Court has indeed moved towards the recognition of people living in economic precariousness as being in a condition of vulnerability entitled, as such, to special measures of protection. Already in the Paraguayan cases dealing with indigenous communities living in deplorable socio-economic conditions, the Court, in keeping with the applicants' allegations, explicitly linked the concept of vulnerability with destitution.[24] Thus, in *Sawhoyamaxa* it notably held:

> From these general [state] obligations [enshrined in Articles 1.1 and 2 ACHR] *special duties are derived* that can be determined according to the *particular needs of protection* of the legal persons, whether *due to* their personal conditions or because of the specific situation they have to face, such as *extreme poverty*, exclusion or childhood.[25]

The above standard was recently reiterated in the case of *Hacienda Brasil Verde*, which is so far the judgment that most directly and extensively deals with rights claims of poverty.[26] In this case, the Court characterised the

---

24 IACtHR, *The Sawhoyamaxa Indigenous Community v. Paraguay*, Judgment of 29 March 2006, paras. 182 (on the arguments submitted by the victims' representatives) and 154; *The Xákmok Kásek Indigenous Community v. Paraguay*, Judgment of 24 August 2010, paras. 259 and 273 (characterising the lack of access to water, food, sanitation and education as conditions of 'extreme vulnerability').

25 IACtHR, *The Sawhoyamaxa Indigenous Community v. Paraguay*, Judgment of 29 March 2006, para. 154 (emphasis added).

26 IACtHR, *The Hacienda Brasil Verde Workers v. Brazil*, Judgment of 20 October 2016, para. 337.

victimisation of the applicants (85 workers rescued from slave-like work) mostly in terms of poverty.[27] What is more, on this basis, and in view of the passivity of the state authorities, the Court found that the state 'did not consider the vulnerability of the 85 rescued workers (...) by virtue of the discrimination on account of economic status they were subjected to'.[28] A similar analysis of group vulnerability on the basis of poverty can be seen in the cases of *Gonzales Lluy and Others v. Ecuador* (concerning the discrimination and social exclusion faced by a girl with HIV) and *Ramírez Escobar et al. v. Guatemala* (dealing with the placement and irregular adoption of children for reasons of poverty).[29] Besides asserting that people with HIV, and children in particular, are groups in greater vulnerability, the Court explicitly situated the vulnerability of the applicants and their families in their socio-economic precariousness.[30] In its view, the applicants' situation of vulnerability put the state under an 'exceptional duty of due diligence'.[31]

So, as will be further seen below, the Court has conceived poverty as a factor of vulnerability or risk to human rights violations that may reinforce state obligations.[32] Further, the Court, in line with the Commission, has developed a frame of analysis that is particularly attentive to the situation of groups historically subject to exclusion and discrimination which, as a matter of fact, are also disproportionally affected by poverty.[33] Thus, where applicants are identified as belonging to one of these groups or the case is mainly defined as dealing with the rights of children, indigenous people, Afro-descendants or others, the Court views their socio-economic disadvantage mostly as a side effect of their ethnic origin, age vulnerability or other status group discrimination. In these cases, poverty appears as an element that exacerbates their disadvantage as members of those groups or subgroups.[34] Finally, in the

---

27 Ibid., para. 339. The other judgment directly dealing with poverty-based claims is *Ramírez Escobar et al. v. Guatemala*, Judgment of 9 March 2018.

28 Ibid., para. 341.

29 IACtHR, *Gonzales Lluy et al. v. Ecuador*, Judgment of 1 September 2015. To some extent, this analysis is also present in *Cuscul Pivaral et al. v. Guatemala*, Judgment of 23 August 2018, which concerns people with HIV too. See also, *Ramírez Escobar et al. v. Guatemala*, Judgment of 9 March 2018.

30 Paras. 193 and 216 and footnote 349 (stating that when people are in conditions of vulnerability because of their economic situation and other factors aggravate this vulnerability, such as living with HIV, the state should provide them free legal assistance to exercise their rights in proceedings of particular importance to preserve the integrity of persons with HIV. This would be the case, for example, in proceedings to request medicines). See also *Ramírez Escobar et al. v. Guatemala*, Judgment of 9 March 2018, paras. 240 and 304.

31 Ibid., para. 311.

32 For a fuller discussion see *infra* in section 3.1.4.

33 See e.g. IACommHR, Preliminary Report on Poverty, Extreme Poverty and Human Rights in the Americas (2016), para. 262. ('The Inter-American system has a strong focus on poverty and discrimination, tackling in particular the situation of groups frequently affected by poverty, ongoing discrimination and historic exclusion in their countries.')

34 For a fuller discussion see *infra* in sections 3.1.1 and 3.1.3.

cases of *Hacienda Brasil Verde* and *Cuscul Pivaral et al. v. Guatemala* cited above, the Court was willing to apply the prohibition of discrimination for reasons of poverty (on grounds of 'economic status'), as provided by Article 1.1 ACHR. This last move has allowed the Court and litigants to place questions of socio-economic disadvantage as an issue of difference and inequality, that is, as something that can be seen as relational to the privilege and wealth of others.

The openness to considering people living in poverty as a group in need of heightened protection seems to reflect the increasingly flexible way in which groups who are discriminated against or placed in vulnerability are envisaged by the Inter-American system. The Commission's position appears to be quite influential in this respect. In its recent report on Poverty and Human Rights, the Commission points out:

> 'Groups in a vulnerable situation' or 'groups that historically suffer discrimination' will vary from one society to the next and from one point in history to another. Therefore, every State has a duty to determine who those groups are in order to devise appropriate inclusive policies that ensure them the free and full exercise of their rights.[35]

Viewed from this perspective, it is understandable why people living in poverty have come to be considered a social group in need of protection. Yet, the question will arise as to whether the legal approach to the group will remain flexible and contingent enough to avoid some of the difficulties with identity/group frameworks studied in the previous chapters. Part of this question is addressed in the section below, which discusses how much complexity is acknowledged in the experience of rights claimants living in poverty. Before turning to this, though, a final clarification is required as to the role played by other possible forms of fragmentary thinking.

2.3. A WORD ON LEGAL COMPARTMENTS

Unlike what was seen in the ECtHR's case law studied in Chapter 4, the IACtHR has not devised any specific set of principles for cases defined as concerning socio-economic policy. To understand this, it is necessary to recall an important difference between the two regional courts that was mentioned in Chapters 1 and 3: so far the Inter-American Court does not apply the doctrine of the state's margin of appreciation. True, for a long time the IACtHR took care not to adjudicate directly socio-economic rights whose enforcement was not explicitly

[35] IACommHR, Preliminary Report on Poverty, Extreme Poverty and Human Rights in the Americas (2016), para. 111.

authorised – or so interpreted – by the Additional Protocol to the American Convention on Human Rights in the area of Economic, Social and Cultural Rights ('Protocol of San Salvador'). But in general the Court does not seem to avoid questions of socio-economic disadvantage or insulate cases that touch upon socio-economic policies by means of a particularly lenient review. This means that, in principle, the IACtHR's approach to claims of economic disadvantage is relatively free from some important drivers of fragmentary thinking. Nevertheless, it remains to be seen how integrated the Court's approach is to the rights holders as well as to the norms involved in cases of economic disadvantage, and with what consequences. Sections III and IV below deal, respectively, with these questions.

3. WHOLE HUMANS: LOOKING THROUGH AND ACROSS RIGHTS HOLDERS

In discussing the case law of the European Court, it was explained that on several occasions the applicants' socio-economic circumstances were overlooked by litigants and the Court alike. It was also seen that when applicants claim socio-economic deprivation as a relevant factor of disadvantage compromising their rights, a two-fold difficulty arises. First, it may be that this aspect is not regarded as legally relevant by the Court or if considered, is subsumed under another marker of diversity. Second, it is also possible that when people's socio-economic circumstances are taken into account, other relevant social positions and identities get displaced. In the context of the Inter-American Court, however, both scenarios need revision.

3.1. LOOKING BEYOND THE APPLICANTS' POVERTY

To start with, it is important to reiterate that the Commission – which for a long time has acted as a litigant before the Court – and the victims' representatives usually give some visibility to the applicants' experience of poverty. The Court, for its part, has proceeded similarly. In paying attention to the applicants' economic precariousness, it has mostly conceived of this as a relevant contextual element that facilitates, results from or reinforces the violations discussed in a case. In other words, the Inter-American Court generally does take into account, albeit often briefly, the economic hardship of rights holders. The question of economically neutral readings is therefore not as much an issue as it is in the European Court's case law. As discussed below, the Inter-American Court has for the most part tended to examine the applicants' situation of poverty through other grounds of difference. By this it is meant, more specifically, integrating the applicants' socio-economic disadvantage as one of the elements characterising their experience as members of a discriminated or otherwise vulnerable group. This is the first dimension of integration to be discussed in this section.

The next question explored in the following lines concerns the reverse question, in other words, the extent to which the litigants and the Court have been keen to transcend a poverty-based reading of cases to integrate other dimensions of the life of rights holders. As explained in the previous chapter, thinking of people's poverty alone and detached from gender, ethnic origin, age or from other social locations ignores how these positions substantially change the experience of poverty and the rights deprivations associated with it. This also means overlooking the different responses and justifications available in each case. To explore whether the Court adopts an integrated perspective to the experience of poverty, however, a further clarification is in order. The Inter-American Court has hardly examined cases whose main discourse goes to socio-economic disadvantage as such. As mentioned above, the large majority of cases incorporate issues of economic status as an aspect related to other traits of difference and disadvantage. The most notable exceptions so far are the 2016 case *The Hacienda Brasil Verde Workers v. Brazil* and the 2018 case of *Cuscul Pivaral et al. v. Guatemala*. The former is nonetheless the landmark judgment on the matter, which led the Court to focus on poverty as the sole and main ground of the applicants' disadvantage.[36] Therefore, this case is the main object of analysis in the second part of the present section.

3.1.1. Socio-Economic Disadvantage through Other Grounds of Difference

Many of the cases decided by the Court are framed as cases concerning identity groups discriminated against or otherwise people in vulnerable situations. In these cases, the main narrative is that of being prejudiced in the enjoyment of rights mainly because of the applicants' position as, for example, children, indigenous, disabled, migrant and/or Afro-descendant. Within this discourse, the question arises: do the litigants and the Court integrate the socio-economic location of these persons? And if so, what does their socio-economic disadvantage add to the identity group rights claims? What advantages and risks does this form of integration entail? These are some of the questions discussed hereunder.

The Court started to develop an approach to applicants' poverty through the lens of other differences in the so-called '*street children*' case.[37] This concerned the police arrest, ill-treatment and execution of five adolescents aged between 15 and 20, who lived in the streets of deprived areas in the City of Guatemala.

---

36 IACtHR, *The Hacienda Brasil Verde Workers v. Brazil*, Judgment of 20 October 2016.

37 IACtHR, *The 'Street Children' (Villagrán-Morales et al.) v. Guatemala*, Judgment of 19 November 1999.

Their murders were part of a larger pattern of police violence against children living on the streets, as a measure to counter juvenile delinquency and vagrancy.[38] The Commission alleged violations of the rights to personal liberty, life, the prohibition of torture and the right to measures of protection as children. It was within the framework of this last right (enshrined in Article 19 ACHR) that 'the Commission described the three child victims of the facts of this case as persons who lived in extremely precarious socio-economic conditions and who fought to survive alone and fearful of a society that did not include them'.[39] The Commission's arguments then pointed not only to the state's failure to protect the children against violence, and to investigate and prosecute the crimes perpetrated against them, but also to the steps that the state should have adopted to prevent or alleviate the deprivation and social exclusion of 'street children', given the risks that this condition entailed for their development and life and which were known to the state.[40]

The state's obligation of protection under Article 19 ACHR also encompassed, according to the Commission, the protection of social and economic rights.[41] This suggests that the poverty experienced by the victims, to the extent that it was not remedied by the state and fell on children, contravened Article 19. The Court adopted a similar stance. It found that the children suffered a double aggression. Besides the violations to their lives and physical integrity, they were victimised because the state did 'not prevent them from living in misery, thus depriving them of the minimum conditions for a dignified life'.[42] In taking this view, the Court interpreted Article 19 ACHR in light of the Convention on the Rights of the Child, particularly the provisions that bind states to secure children's socio-economic well-being.[43]

This line of reasoning was further developed in *Servellón García v. Honduras*, where the Court returned to the encounter between juveniles living in poverty and state policies of crime prevention.[44] Similarly to the '*street children*' case, the victims in *Servellón García*, including two minors, had been arbitrarily detained, tortured and killed by police agents. The crimes took place in the course of collective detention operations targeting youth in poverty who were presumed to be linked with the so-called *Maras* or gangs in Honduras. The judgment elaborated on the destitution and social risk faced by juveniles like the victims.[45] And against this background, it reiterated

---

38 Ibid., paras. 59(c), 79 and 190.
39 Ibid., para. 184.
40 Ibid., paras. 180–181.
41 Ibid., para. 185.
42 Ibid., para. 191.
43 Ibid., paras. 195–196.
44 IACtHR, *Servellón García et al. v. Honduras*, Judgment of 21 September 2006.
45 Ibid., paras. 37, 79(1) and 110–111.

the state's duty to address the socio-economic deprivation of children at risk, which was identified as the main reason for the harm inflicted on them.[46] Moreover, this time the Court also considered, with regard to equality and non-discrimination, the stigmatisation of children and youth living in poverty who are portrayed as criminals.[47] This is discussed in section 4.1.1 below.

The socio-economic disadvantage of rights holders has likewise been considered to be a contextual element associated with their ethnic origin. Underpinning this view is what the Commission has explained thus: 'being indigenous seems of itself to be a cause of poverty and extreme poverty.'[48] The correlation has to do with the historical discrimination against indigenous peoples and their lack of self-determination and access to their ancestral lands and natural resources.[49] Examples are cases brought by indigenous communities of the Paraguayan Chaco, which were previously examined in Chapter 3; here, the Court observed that mostly as a result of land destitution, the members of the indigenous communities of *Yakye Axa*, *Sawhoyamaxa* and *Xákmok Kásek* lived in appalling conditions.[50] Under the right to life (Article 4 ACHR), read as entitlement to a dignified life, their lives were characterised, *inter alia*, by unemployment, malnutrition, lack of access to basic services and infrastructure and high rates of preventable diseases.

Also mentioned earlier in this book, the situation of these community members has been further distinguished by the Court. The experience of children, pregnant women and the elderly among the communities was examined as regards their lack of access to adequate nutrition and to appropriate and timely medical care, which resulted in their premature death. In the case of *Sawhoyamaxa*, for example, the Court examined the lack of access to health care and the ensuing death of mostly children of the indigenous community whose mothers could not afford the medicines prescribed. In the words of the victims: 'there are no medicines for the poor'.[51] The applicants had

46 Ibid., para. 117. ('The facts of the present case occurred in reason of the victims' condition of people in situations of social risk, which proves that the State did not provide Marco Antonio Servellón García or Rony Alexis Betancourth Vásquez with an environment that would protect them from violence and abuse, nor did it allow them access to basic services and goods, in such a way that said absence without doubt deprived the minors of their possibility to emancipate, develop, and become adults that could determine their own future.')

47 Ibid., paras. 112–116. See also the concurring opinion of Judge Cançado Trindade, paras. 28–32.

48 IACommHR, Preliminary Report on Poverty, Extreme Poverty and Human Rights in the Americas (2016), para. 302.

49 Ibid., para. 305.

50 IACtHR, *The Yakye Axa Indigenous Community v. Paraguay*, Judgment of 17 June 2005; *The Sawhoyamaxa Indigenous Community v. Paraguay*, Judgment of 29 March 2006; and *The Xákmok Kásek Indigenous Community v. Paraguay*, Judgment of 24 August 2010.

51 IACtHR, *The Sawhoyamaxa Indigenous Community v. Paraguay*, Judgment of 29 March 2006, para. 174, fn. 220.

argued that the state was partly responsible for the death of children and other ill members of the community who contracted preventable diseases while living in deplorable conditions at the side of a road. The state, by contrast, argued that public health services had been made available to them and it was their own responsibility to approach the health centres and make use of medical assistance.[52] The Court noted that while the children were entitled to free medical care in public health centres and had been treated there, they could not obtain the prescribed medicines. Shortly after, they had died because their families could not pay for them. In view of these economic impediments, the judgment concluded that the health care provided to those children was insufficient and untimely for securing their right to life (Article 4 ACHR).

Since the state had been aware of the extremely precarious situation of these persons, the Court attributed the children's death to the state's lack of diligence. It had failed to adopt the positive measures that were reasonable to expect to prevent or mitigate the life-threatening situation of those indigenous children.[53] Similar analyses were applied to the destitution of the elderly, women and children of the other indigenous communities who brought cases against Paraguay. With regard to all of them the Court applied heightened state obligations aimed at alleviating their destitution and providing them with assistance, food and access to basic services. While in the case of indigenous children those duties were grounded in Article 19 (Children Rights), in the case of pregnant women and the elderly, the Court simply concluded that ensuring their right to life (Article 4 ACHR) required 'special measures of protection'.[54]

In other cases, however, the socio-economic disadvantage associated with membership of a discriminated group is mostly included as part of the general context of the case. The judgment in *Yean and Bosico* is an example.[55] This case, already examined in Chapter 3, concerned two Dominican girls of Haitian descent who were denied birth registration. As a consequence, they could not enrol in school and access other services, nor could they have their names formally recognised. The Commission linked the violations at stake mostly to the applicants' origin (Haitian descent) and the migration status of their parents.[56] And so did the Court. The applicants' poverty, which was substantial, formed

---

52 IACtHR, *The Sawhoyamaxa Indigenous Community v. Paraguay*, Judgment of 29 March 2006, para. 147(a).

53 Ibid., paras. 175–178.

54 IACtHR, *The Xákmok Kásek Indigenous Community v. Paraguay*, Judgment of 24 August 2010, paras. 232–233 (regarding pregnant women) and 257–260 (regarding children); *The Sawhoyamaxa Indigenous Community v. Paraguay*, Judgment of 29 March 2006, paras. 159, 171 and 175–178; *The Yakye Axa Indigenous Community v. Paraguay*, Judgment of 17 June 2005, paras. 172–176.

55 IACtHR, *The Girls Yean and Bosico v. Dominican Republic*, Judgment of 8 September 2005.

56 Ibid., para. 112.b.

part of the general context within which the Court situated the case. Poverty was one of the features that marked the living conditions of most Haitians and Dominicans of Haitian origin in the Dominican Republic.[57] Likewise, lack of financial resources was one of the factors explaining why most mothers of Haitian origin gave birth at home and resorted to late birth registration.[58] It was also suggested that poverty was one of the effects of denying birth registration to children of Haitian origin, as this compromised their education and prospects of employment.[59] The Court's attention to a life context of poverty has also featured, albeit with varying levels of thoroughness, in other cases involving gender and racial violence against Afro-descendants and women.[60]

It is interesting to note that the judgment in *Yean and Bosico* ultimately did not go into the specific socio-economic deprivations encountered by the applicants and their families. The Court did not really address the human rights impact of the costs of administrative proceedings imposed on impoverished migrant children and their families. Addressing this aspect might seem unnecessary, though, particularly in the face of what their racialised and migratory positions already entailed for them. Yet, looking into the applicants' economic hardship might have been useful in responding to the claim that the state should have set limits to the cost of birth registration proceedings. In fact, the Commission had pointed out the expenses involved in complying with the requirements imposed on the applicants (including obtaining abundant documentation) as one of the elements hindering the exercise of their rights.[61] What is more, the victims' representatives asked the Court to order the state, as a reparation measure of satisfaction and non-repetition, 'to reduce the birth registration costs'.[62] But this was left unanswered. The Court did not make any finding either on the merits or in the reparations awards regarding the costs of administrative proceedings. The omission is not trivial. Even if the state sets out clear criteria for birth registration and ensures their non-arbitrary application, the exclusion of children of Haitian origin like the applicants will continue if the costs of the proceedings are beyond their means.[63]

---

57 Ibid., paras. 109(2) and 109(3).

58 Ibid., para. 109(10).

59 Ibid., para. 169 (referring to conclusions of the UN Committee on the Rights of the Child).

60 See e.g. IACtHR, *Expelled Dominicans and Haitians v. Dominican Republic*, Judgment of 28 August 2014, paras. 256–258; *Rosendo Cantú et al. v. Mexico*, Judgment of 31 August 2010, para. 201; *González et al. ('Cotton Field') v. Mexico*, Judgment of 16 November 2009, paras. 277 and 282.

61 IACtHR, *The Girls Yean and Bosico v. Dominican Republic*, Judgment of 8 September 2005, para. 111(c). See also para. 29(b) concerning the Commission's merit report in the case.

62 Ibid., para. 232(h).

63 On how the costs of these proceedings constitute a significant barrier to accessing birth registration for Dominican children of Haitian descent, see Amnesty International, Dominican Republic: A life in transit – The plight of Haitian migrants and Dominicans of Haitian descent (Report, March 2007), at 23.

To tackle this, either on the merits or in the reparations, it would have been necessary to explore the applicants' economic difficulties *vis-à-vis* their access to birth registration.

Finally, applicants' socio-economic disadvantage has been briefly considered from the perspective of disability. First, this was taken as part of the background to cases where disability appeared to be one of the consequences of poverty. Thus, in *Ximenes Lopes v. Brazil* the Court emphasised that those who lived in poverty and social exclusion faced greater risks of becoming disabled.[64] It was thereby implied that since states should take steps to prevent disability, they should also address people's poverty. Later, the disability approach to poverty received a more concrete application in the case of *Furlan and Family v. Argentina*, where the linkage was incorporated into the assessment of the harm faced by the alleged victims. The case concerned an excessive delay in resolving a civil action to ensure medical treatment for a child who became disabled at the age of 14, following an accident on army property. The Court examined the procedural guarantees that assisted him in light of a vulnerability that it defined in terms of the 'negative effects produced by the combination of his disability and his and his family's very limited financial resources'.[65] This, according to the Court, 'meant that his impoverished circumstances had a disproportionate impact on his condition as a person with disabilities'.[66]

A similar view of socio-economic disadvantage from the perspective of disability was advanced in a more recent case against Costa Rica involving a general ban on *in vitro* fertilisation techniques.[67] In this judgment, however, the issue of socio-economic disadvantage was not really subsumed within the disadvantages accorded to disability. As further discussed below, here the issue of the 'greater impact' resulting from lacking resources took the form of indirect discrimination in the enjoyment of the rights to humane treatment (Article 5), personal liberty (Article 7) and private and family life (Articles 11 and 17) ACHR. The argument basically posited that preventing people with a reproductive disability from accessing medically available *in vitro* fertilisation treatment in the respondent country put an excessive burden on those who did not have the economic resources to seek treatment elsewhere.[68] The reasoning resonates with some of the arguments usually put forward with regard to the disparate impact that abortion bans place upon poor women.[69]

---

64 IACtHR, *Ximenes Lopes v. Brazil*, Judgment of 4 July 2006, para. 104.

65 IACtHR, *Furlan and Family v. Argentina*, Judgment of 31 August 2012, para. 243.

66 Idem.

67 IACtHR, *Artavia Murillo et al. ('In vitro fertilization') v. Costa Rica*, Judgment of 28 November 2012.

68 Ibid., para. 303.

69 See e.g. Charles G. Ngwena, 'Inscribing Abortion as a Human Right: Significance of the Protocol on the Rights of Women in Africa', 32 (4) *Human Rights Quarterly* (2010) 783, at 820

They, unlike women of means, are overwhelmingly driven into unsafe abortion. In the alternative, they are forced to bear the heightened risks and hardships of unviable or unwanted pregnancies.

Now, what are the advantages and drawbacks of viewing applicants' socio-economic disadvantage through the lens of discriminated against or vulnerable identity groups?

While the Court's limited analysis of poverty-related claims from the perspective of the different identities discussed above makes it difficult to draw definite conclusions, some preliminary inferences are possible. First, in most cases where the applicant's poverty is incorporated as part of his or her already disadvantaged group, the insight plays out as a factor that magnifies the rights interferences, whether considered as a matter of general context or as something concretely experienced by the applicant. In some cases, this translates into more specific or heightened state obligations. A second important advantage of incorporating poverty within the group context in which the case takes place is that by doing so the Court avoids reducing the experience of socio-economic disadvantage to an isolated and individual matter. Besides the significance of this at the discursive level, it may also alleviate the burden of proof for applicants and facilitate the prospect, depending on the case, of allegations of discrimination in connection with poverty.

It is also possible, however, to discern some risks in this approach. A first potential drawback is that by defining socio-economic disadvantage as a contextual characteristic of certain groups, the Court may end up overlooking an individualised evaluation of how the specific rights holders in question experience this. Another danger of viewing poverty through other identity groups is conveying the message that poverty stems from certain personal/group characteristics or that these by themselves put people at risk of poverty. This may lead to a reduced understanding of poverty, one in which the group identity framework obscures the role of social structures. Finally, the Court should be careful not to bypass claims of socio-economic disadvantage from those who in principle would not seem to fall into one of those groups historically discriminated against. Think of the rights of urban white men living in poverty, for example. Their plight also deserves attention and should not be dismissed simply because their other identities or social locations are relatively privileged.

Up to here the analysis provides a fair account of what could be gained or illuminated by examining people's disadvantaged identities and positions in a manner that is sensitive to their socio-economic differences. Now, the reverse

---

and 826; Pamela Bridgewater, 'Gonzales v. Carhart: Continuing the Class Critique of the Reproductive Rights Doctrine and Movement', 59(4) *South Carolina Law Review* (2008) 827 (discussing limitations on access to abortion from the perspective of women in poverty in the context of the United States).

question arises. What if the Court were also mindful of enriching its account of people's poverty and its relationship with the enjoyment of human rights?

3.1.2. Integrating the Different Faces of Poverty

As mentioned earlier, so far the Court has placed the experience of poverty at the core of two cases: *Hacienda Brasil Verde v. Brazil* and *Ramírez Escobar y otros v. Guatemala*, ruled in 2016 and 2018, respectively.[70] But since the former was the case that broke new ground on the matter, this will be discussed first and more in depth. *Hacienda Brasil Verde* concerned the lack of state prevention and response regarding the slave labour conditions of 85 workers, some of them children, in the privately owned estate 'Hacienda Brasil Verde'.[71] In its fact-finding considerations, the Court identified poverty, alongside the concentration of property and deregulation, as one of the structural causes that made possible the continuation of slave labour in Brazil after its legal abolition. In this context, the Court also characterised the problem in terms of the features shared by the people affected by it. The persons recruited to work in slavery-like conditions were mostly workers from the poorest regions of the country and with the highest rates of illiteracy. Moreover, the majority were young, poor, Afro-descendant men.[72] This also held true for the 85 rescued workers from *Hacienda Brasil Verde*, where they were held in deplorable conditions.[73]

In its merit analysis the Court focused on poverty. It noted that the main characteristics of victimisation shared by the 85 rescued workers related to destitution. They lived in poverty, came from the poorest regions of the country, lacked education and were illiterate, which made them prone to recruitment into slavery by fraud and deceit. This was constitutive of 'a situation of imminent risk for a determinate group of persons with identical characteristics and who

70 IACtHR, *The Hacienda Brasil Verde Workers v. Brazil*, Judgment of 20 October 2016; *Ramírez Escobar et al. v. Guatemala*, Judgment of 9 March 2018.

71 This is a landmark judgment for several reasons. Among others, it is the first ruling on slavery and human trafficking in the region, which therefore sets standards, so far undeveloped, under Article 6 ACHR (Freedom from Slavery). The ruling further elaborates on the state's duties of due diligence regarding human rights abuses perpetrated by private actors, extending standards developed in the framework of violence against women to other forms of private exploitative violence. For our purposes, however, the discussion will concentrate on the equality and non-discrimination dimension of the case, which is where the Court deals with poverty and socio-economic inequality.

72 IACtHR, *The Hacienda Brasil Verde Workers v. Brazil*, Judgment of 20 October 2016, paras. 111–113.

73 Armed guards prevented the workers from escaping their slavery and subhuman living conditions. Attempting or expressing the wish to leave was punished with threats and mistreatment.

came from the same regions of the country'.[74] Such a risk had historical roots and had been known to the state for years. Stressing that poverty was the main factor leading to the workers' recruitment into slavery and forced labour, the Court concluded that the rescued workers were discriminated against in their right to be free from slavery (Article 6 ACHR in conjunction with the prohibition of discrimination enshrined in Article 1.1 ACHR). And the same went for their rights to access justice (Articles 8 and 25 ACHR, also in combination with the prohibition of discrimination). With regard to both sets of rights, the Court found that they were discriminated against on account of their (low) economic status.[75] The Court's reasoning on economic-based discrimination will be closely examined *infra* section 4.1.2. For now, this discussion is interested in the following questions. Does this poverty-centred analysis account for what had happened to the recruited workers? And is this single aspect – poverty – the one most relevant to their experience? How would a more situated view of poverty change this and other similar cases?

The victims' representatives had argued that most victims in this case were Afro-descendants or *morenos* men aged between 17 and 40 and living in extreme poverty and vulnerability; this, in their view, disclosed an issue of 'structural discrimination'. Further, the representatives claimed that the state had failed to remove the obstacles to accessing justice on the basis of their ethnic, race and socio-economic position.[76] The Commission, for its part, alleged *de facto discrimination* against a 'determinate group of persons' without grounding this in their poverty.[77] But importantly, the Commission's report on the case had recommended that Brazil adopt measures to combat racism, which was reiterated in its reparations request before the Court.[78] The same concern about racial discrimination appeared in the Commission's claim of structural discrimination in the applicants' inability to access to justice. In support of this claim, the Commission recalled that the conciliation agreement between the domestic authorities and the owner of Hacienda Brasil Verde stipulated a fine for each worker found in slavery-like conditions 'whether they were white or black'.[79] Even the Court admitted, as a matter of fact, that the workers who were more exposed to forced labour and slavery in Brazil were

---

74 IACtHR, *The Hacienda Brasil Verde Workers v. Brazil*, Judgment of 20 October 2016, para. 339. (Author's translation. At the moment of writing this chapter the judgment in question is available in Spanish only.)

75 Ibid., paras. 340–343. It is worth noting, however, the ambiguity of the Court's wording. Literally, the Court holds that 'it notes the existence of a situation based on the economic status of the rescued victims […] which characterized a discriminatory treatment'. (Author's translation. No official English version available at the time of writing.)

76 Ibid., para. 226.

77 Ibid., para. 216.

78 Ibid., para. 463.

79 Ibid., para. 349.

not only poor, but also men of African descent.[80] And yet the Court, strikingly, addressed the applicants' economically-based discrimination on its own, as something unrelated to other grounds.

In fact, an intersectional approach is missing in the legal analysis, which is unfortunate. For one thing, the element of racial discrimination was overlooked, despite being at the root of the commodification and hence, slavery, of Afro-descendant people. For another, the fact that most victims were men also merited recognition. Some men and boys experience greater risks of specific forms of trafficking and slavery aimed at rural labour exploitation. Yet, their grievances are too often neglected.[81] The way in which economic structures and racial hierarchies in Brazil oppressed mostly young, rural, Afro-descendant men living in poverty was therefore obscured. An intersectional approach to the applicants' poverty and slave labour would have done justice to their real-life experience, exposing the specific risks and harms they encountered. This, in turn, would have allowed adequate responses to be devised, guiding state action in terms of prevention and remedies. If the specificities of the victims' experience are obfuscated and collapsed into poverty, the message could in fact be misleading. Legal and policy interventions that aim at improving the material conditions of the poor, for example, but do not really tackle racism and the concentration of property are likely to fall short of redressing the situation. There is, furthermore, added value in tackling the interplay between poverty and not just their identity as men of African descent, but racism.

First, by connecting poverty to racial discrimination, that is, by regarding poverty as something mostly experienced by people of African descent, the recognition and redistribution injustices at play are integrated. This is important as it allows a distancing from widely held discourses that posit that all the problems of those communities arise from poverty and not racism.[82] Secondly, intersectionality provides stronger and more precise grounds for the Court's interpretation of pervasive poverty as discrimination affecting the right to be free from slave labour. In fact, this part of the judgment is exposed to important challenges, which Judge Sierra Porto's dissenting opinion represents well. He pointed out that although in general the workers subjected to

---

80 Ibid., para. 113 (discussing proven facts regarding 'the characteristics of slave work in Brazil').

81 UN, Report of the Special Rapporteur on trafficking in persons, especially women and children, Joy Ngozi Ezeilo, A/HRC/26/37 (Thematic report, 1 April 2014), para. 45. ('The Special Rapporteur has regularly raised concerns about the lack of appropriate assistance to men and boys who have been trafficked. [...] Many States have been slow to recognize the issue of trafficking in men, a situation that is explained, at least in part, by the continuing strong focus on trafficking for sexual exploitation at the expense of trafficking for labour exploitation.')

82 Ariel E. Dulitzky, 'A region in Denial: Racial Discrimination and Racism in Latin America', in Angela P. Harris (ed.), *Race and Equality Law* (Ashgate, 2013), at 97.

slavery-like conditions had some common (poverty-related) characteristics, 'these characteristics are also shared by a large number of people in Brazil who live in poverty and are uneducated'.[83] He noted that the Court did not have sufficient evidentiary elements to conclude that the whole population of Piauí (the victims' region of origin) suffered historical structural discrimination on the basis of poverty. Nor did the Court have the elements to declare the existence of such historical discrimination against the workers rescued from *Hacienda Brasil Verde*.[84]

In other words, the issue is that not all or not even most illiterate people living in poverty in the poorest regions of Brazil were victims of trafficking, forced labour or slavery. Nor does it seem plausible to say that all or most of them, solely by their material circumstances or place of residence, were victims of discrimination. By the same token, one could add that not all Afro-descendant people were poor, nor were all of them subject to forced labour. All this reminds us of the difficulties typically faced by litigants 'falling between the cracks' of discrimination grounds, as Crenshaw put it when criticising the same line of reasoning in the case of the black women who brought a lawsuit against General Motors.[85] An intersectional approach, however, underscores the fact that nearly all the poorest people in Brazil are black and nearly all those working in slavery-like conditions are black. And this does say something. The Court's finding of structural discrimination would therefore have stood on firmer ground if it had relied on intersectionality.

An additional and related objection posited by the dissenter in *Hacienda Brasil Verde* concerns the socio-economic context of the country and the limitations on its ability to deal with poverty. Indeed, locating poverty as the sole and central ground of historical structural discrimination in a country like Brazil raises legitimate questions about the state's capacity to comply with what may be perceived as unrealistic human rights standards. But holding the state accountable for widespread poverty is not quite the same thing as doing so for creating or sustaining, through its institutions and norms, the historical racial discrimination that has kept Afro-descendants overrepresented among the poor and, in the case of rural men, poor and exposed to forced labour and other forms of labour exploitation. This nuances

83 IACtHR, *The Hacienda Brasil Verde Workers v. Brazil*, Judgment of 20 October 2016, Dissenting Opinion of Judge Sierra Porto, para. 10. (Author's translation. No official English version available at the time of writing.)

84 Ibid., paras. 7–10.

85 Kimberle Crenshaw, 'Demarginalizing the Intersection of Race and Sex: A Black Feminist Critique of Antidiscrimination Doctrine, Feminist Theory, and Antiracist Politics', 140 *University of Chicago Legal Forum* (1989) 139, at 41 (the issue was that black women were not hired by the company prior to 1964 and later, when they were hired, all of them lost their jobs as a result of a seniority layoff).

the idea of state responsibility for poverty. Due to the way racism and concentration of property put young Afro-descendant men from rural areas in extreme poverty and at the mercy of slavery and trafficking, and because this was known to the state, the latter had specific duties of prevention and protection. Failure to do so would have revealed discrimination in a similar way as the failure to prevent and respond to violence against women amounts to discrimination. While this may have entailed some socio-economic steps, the state's obligation was not one of general socio-economic provision and poverty alleviation, but one that was much more targeted.

The case of *Ramírez Escobar et al. v. Guatemala*, for its part, does offer a more integrated account of the applicants' poverty as the latter is approached in relation to other social positions, in particular, gender. This is the Court's first judgment dealing with family separation, including illegal international adoption, for reasons of poverty. It concerns the removal and placement of two siblings aged eight and two who were subsequently surrendered for adoption in the United States. Like similar cases decided by the Strasbourg Court, the administrative and judicial authorities' main ground to justify those extreme measures was the family's socio-economic precariousness. Also similar to those cases, here too the issue at stake needed to be gendered. In fact, *Ramírez Escobar et al. v. Guatemala* reveals, once again, how poor single women and their children are particularly vulnerable to arbitrary forced separation.

Whilst the Court paid great attention to how the applicants' experience of poverty had led to preconceptions and barriers that irreparably severed the family ties, it also examined the way all this was shaped by gender relations and stereotypes. The Court, in fact, identified and condemned the use of gender stereotypes regarding the children's mother and father. As regards Ms Ramírez (who was the main child carer), the Court observed the national authorities' remarks about her supposed inability to fulfil her 'maternal role', 'feminine role' and her alleged irresponsibility for abandoning her children to go out for work.[86] In addition, the Court explained that the authorities' exclusive focus on the children's mother and the total lack of interest in the role of the father not only prejudiced Ms Ramírez (as she was placed as the only bearer of child-caring responsibilities), but also Mr Tobar, the children's father. Although living abroad, he had maintained the relationship with his children and yet at no point in the domestic proceedings was he contacted or considered as an alternative to the children's placement. This indicated that, so argued the Court, the authorities had acted upon the gender stereotype that a father does not have the same obligations, abilities and love to care for

86 IACtHR, *Ramírez Escobar et al. v. Guatemala*, Judgment of 9 March 2018, paras. 296–297.

his children than a mother.[87] As further explained below, the judgment states that this amounts to gender discrimination, which in the case of Ms Ramírez is furthermore compounded by her economic status.

The subsections above show that a more holistic view of rights holders that incorporates their socio-economic position and links it to other dimensions of their lives entails important normative consequences. As already noted, many but not all of them concern equality and non-discrimination. Consideration should therefore first be given to what an intersectional view has meant or could mean for the application of equality and non-discrimination. Thereafter, it is convenient to turn to what an intersectional approach to rights holders, *lato sensu*, has or could add in other areas of adjudication.

3.1.3. An Intersectional Approach within the Antidiscrimination Review: Intersectional, Indirect and De Facto Discrimination

The case law examined thus far provides a fair sample of the possible connections between an integrated approach to people's socio-economic differences and the prohibition of discrimination. The most notorious and extended linkage in the Court's jurisprudence is that of poverty as an expression and consequence of entrenched forms of group identity discrimination. This understanding builds upon a conception of 'structural' or substantive equality that transcends a formal notion of discrimination centred on individual wrongs arising from arbitrary treatment.[88] The paradigm of equality embraced by the Court (and by the Commission before it) – already introduced here and in Chapter 4 – is sensitive to social context and the different forms of exclusion and disadvantage that persist among certain groups. In order to redress their subordination, this structural equality fosters an active state and the adoption of a wide range of positive measures.

This conception of equality underpins the framing and handling of most of the cases examined above, albeit not necessarily leading to the application of anti-discrimination provisions. Observing that one of the entrenched disadvantages that women, indigenous peoples, children, people with disabilities and others encounter in most countries of the American region is

87 Ibid., para. 298.

88 See e.g. Valeska David, 'The Inter-American concept of structural equality and discrimination', 2 *Anti-Discrimination Law Review* (2017) 5, at 11–12; Oscar Parra Vera, 'Derechos humanos y pobreza en el Sistema Interamericano. El rol del análisis estructural a partir de informes y siete escenarios estratégicos basados en la responsabilidad internacional', 56 *Revista Instituto Interamericano de Derechos Humanos* (2012) 273, at 300–301. For a fuller discussion of structural discrimination and its relationship with socio-economic disadvantage, see *infra* section 4.1.2.

poverty and social exclusion, the Court has taken this as one of the harmful effects of a history of discrimination. While in several judgments this translates into an emphasis on the applicants' vulnerability and exclusion in the context of substantive provisions, in others that normative conception leads the Court to scrutinise issues of socio-economic disadvantage as a matter of indirect and *de facto* discrimination as well as intersectional discrimination. The following discussion will start by examining the latter.

People's economic disadvantage has been integrated as a matter of multiple and intersectional discrimination in recent cases concerning access to health care and education. A significant step in this direction was taken in *Artavia Murillo et al ('In vitro fertilization') v. Costa Rica* (hereinafter, 'IVF case'), which was introduced above.[89] A number of couples with fertility problems complained against a blanket ban imposed on all in vitro fertilisation (IVF) practices with the aim of protecting the right to life of embryos in Costa Rica. The Commission argued that the ban raised equality issues, among which were the specific and disproportionate impact it had on women.[90] The victims' representative, in turn, framed the problem in compounded terms. He argued that the ban discriminated against the applicants on the basis of their reproductive incapacity – which amounted to a disability – *and* on the basis of their financial resources, since better-off couples could access IVF techniques abroad.[91] Having found several violations of the applicants' rights, including their rights to private and family life, the Court, remarkably, examined whether the ban had 'a disproportionate impact in relation to disability, gender and socio-economic situation'.[92] It found that it had. The ban amounted to indirect discrimination against the applicants due to disability (encompassing reproductive incapacity), gender and, for some couples, their financial situation.[93]

The Court discussed each of these grounds. Building upon the Convention on the Rights of Persons with Disabilities and the 'social model' it propounds, the Court posited that the applicants' infertility, in the context of the case, constituted a disability regarding which the ban further limited their autonomy and social inclusion.[94] With regard to gender, the judgment stated that prohibiting techniques which are mostly performed on women's bodies had a distinctive negative impact on them. Yet, men were harmed too. The Court stressed that a significant part of the harm and suffering endured by both

89 IACtHR, *Artavia Murillo et al. ('In vitro fertilization') v. Costa Rica*, Judgment of 28 November 2012.
90 Ibid., para. 265 *in fine*.
91 IACtHR, *Artavia Murillo et al. ('In vitro fertilization') v. Costa Rica*, Judgment of 28 November 2012, para. 267.
92 Ibid., para. 287.
93 Ibid., paras. 287–316.
94 Ibid., para. 293.

infertile women and men flowed from being unable to conform to gender stereotypes and social expectations regarding motherhood, fertility and maleness.[95] Finally, the judgment addressed the applicants' experience from the perspective of the limitations associated with their lack of financial means. The ban had a disparate effect on those who could not afford seeking treatment abroad, like many couples with means had done.[96]

To some extent, the approach in this case is more representative of multiple than intersectional discrimination. Distinguishing between these two concepts is not always easy. Nevertheless, the dividing line could be explained as follows: multiple discrimination does not involve much of a qualitative change in the experience of discrimination, but rather 'a double burden and additive discrimination'.[97] The ban on IVF techniques had a disparate impact on persons with fertility problems – which the Court regarded as disability – irrespective of their financial situation. Its impact, however, was further aggravated in the case of those who had fewer resources. In other words, the latter experienced essentially the same discrimination as better-off victims but in a more acute way.

The second judgment of relevance here is the 2016 case of *Gonzales Lluy et al. v. Ecuador*, where the Court explicitly applied for the first time the concept of intersectional discrimination.[98] Talía Gonzales Lluy, a three-year-old girl, was infected with HIV in the course of blood transfusion from the Ecuadorian Red Cross. Aside the damage to her health, she was barred from the kindergarten she attended because of her health status. By then the family were already in a modest economic situation. They had to be granted a waiver of court fees in order to file civil actions for damages. Following the girl's infection, they faced repeated loss of employment and were forced to move every time the girl's condition was discovered, which aggravated their economic hardship. All this was accounted for in the judgment, which even contained a section entitled 'situation of poverty faced by the Lluy family'.[99] Normatively, this aspect played out in the analysis of the right to personal integrity of the girl's family, which is further discussed *infra* section 4.1.1, and in the examination

95 Ibid., paras. 298–302. Of note, the Court acknowledged that this reasoning was problematic insofar as it rested on the same kinds of stereotype that arguably it sought to challenge. As such, the Court introduced the following 'disclaimer': 'The Court emphasizes that these gender stereotypes are incompatible with international human rights law and measures must be taken to eliminate them. The Court is not validating these stereotypes and only recognizes them and defines them in order to describe the disproportionate impact of the interference caused by the Constitutional Chamber's judgment.'

96 IACtHR, *Artavia Murillo et al. ('In vitro fertilization') v. Costa Rica*, Judgment of 28 November 2012, para. 303.

97 Nicholas Bamforth *et al.*, *Discrimination Law: Theory and Context. Text and Materials* (Sweet and Maxwell, 2008), at 541.

98 IACtHR, *Gonzales Lluy et al. v. Ecuador*, Judgment of 1 September 2015.

99 Ibid., para. 155.

of the girl's right not to be discriminated against in her access to education. It is in this last context that the applicant's poverty seems to have given rise to a violation in itself, although in combination with other grounds.

The Court examined the allegations of discrimination in the light of the social model of disability, since persons with HIV have historically encountered 'social and attitudinal barriers' preventing their equal access to rights.[100] Several violations were found in this case, including, for the first time, the right to education (Article 13 Protocol of San Salvador),[101] alone and in combination with intersectional discrimination. In this regard, the Court held that 'numerous factors of vulnerability and risk of *discrimination intersected* that were associated with [the girl's] condition as a minor, a female, a person living in poverty, and a person living with HIV'.[102] The Court explained why it regarded this as 'a specific form of discrimination that resulted from the intersection of those factors'. As regards poverty, it contended that this had an impact on the low quality of health that was accessible to the girl (which resulted in her HIV infection). Moreover, 'the situation of poverty also had an impact on the difficulties to gain access to the education system and to lead a decent life'.[103] The Court then addressed discrimination from the perspective of being a child with HIV and found that she faced obstacles to accessing education that 'had a negative impact on her overall development'.[104] As a child with HIV, she also required greater support from the state. Finally, as a woman she faced specific dilemmas and difficulties related to intimate relationships and future maternity.[105] According to the Court, the case illustrated that the impact of HIV stigmatisation 'is more severe on members of vulnerable groups'.[106] The application of intersectional discrimination thus allowed the Court to account for the specific and qualitative experience of discrimination encountered by the girl in her position as a female minor, living in poverty and with HIV.

This line of reasoning has been confirmed in another recent case concerning 49 persons with HIV who alleged several violations as a result of inadequate medical attention. In *Cuscul Pivaral et al. v. Guatemala*,[107] the Court recalled that people living in poverty are often under greater risks of infection and death as a result of unequal access to health services and information.[108]

100 Ibid., para. 236.
101 Protocol of San Salvador, Article 13 ('Right to Education').
102 IACtHR, *Gonzales Lluy et al. v. Ecuador*, Judgment of 1 September 2015, para. 290 (emphasis added).
103 Idem.
104 Idem.
105 Idem.
106 Idem.
107 IACtHR, *Cuscul Pivaral et al. v. Guatemala*, Judgment of 23 August 2018.
108 Ibid., para. 131.

It further noted that such vulnerability is increased in the case of women and those pregnant among them, which requires states to adopt special measures of protection. The Court thus focused on the situation of the female victims who were pregnant prior to and after their diagnosis with HIV. It found that the denial of antiretroviral treatment to a pregnant woman and the refusal to carry out a preventive c-section to another amounted to gender intersectional discrimination (in violation of the right to health implied in Article 26 together with the prohibition of discrimination enshrined in Article 1.1. ACHR). Their position as pregnant women living with HIV meant, according to the Court, that different factors of vulnerability converged to their detriment. The Court added that states must recognise and address these forms of interrelated discrimination and their negative impact upon the women concerned through laws and policies.[109]

The prohibition of intersectional discrimination has been further applied in the case of *Ramírez Escobar et al. v. Guatemala*, where the Court found that the discrimination suffered by the first applicant (a single mother living in poverty who had been forcibly separated from her children) was 'intersectional'.[110] The violations she experienced were the result of the vulnerabilities encountered as a single mother living in poverty placed against a context of irregular adoptions. Interestingly, though, the finding of discrimination based on poverty and gender combined does not appear to have any specific impact on the reparations orders.

In addition, it is possible to scrutinise poverty-related rights allegations through the prohibition of indirect discrimination, which is quite relevant if one considers the reasonability that usually clothes economic criteria. As pointed out in the previous chapter, one of the reasons why measures and policies that rely on economic considerations and which undermine the rights of destitute people often go unchallenged is that their neutrality and functionality is generally accepted. They are not aimed at any group in particular and are reasonably related to the achievement of a legitimate aim. The notion of indirect discrimination, however, is one of the mechanisms whereby the prejudicial effect of policies and practices that are apparently neutral can be scrutinised. This is precisely what the judgment in *IVF v. Costa Rica* does – similarly to the Court's advisory opinions on questions of access to domestic and international justice.[111] These rulings show that setting

109 Ibid., paras. 137–138.

110 IACtHR, *Ramírez Escobar et al. v. Guatemala*, Judgment of 9 March 2018, para. 304.

111 As seen earlier (*supra* section 2.1) the Court has taken the view that facially neutral regulations on access to domestic and international courts may have an unequal impact on persons in economic disadvantage. For that, positive or corrective measures may be required, including exemptions from standard rules (e.g. that on exhaustion of domestic remedies) and provision of free legal aid in administrative proceedings. See e.g. IACtHR, Advisory Opinion OC-11/90 on the Exceptions to the Exhaustion of Domestic Remedies (Articles 46(1), 46(2)(a)

economic requirements, such as fees, or precluding the provision of social services, such as certain medical treatment, can have a disparate prejudicial effect on people with fewer economic resources in general and therefore, also on those specific groups that are overrepresented among the poor.

The Court has, moreover, relied on the concept of *de facto* discrimination to examine rights claims associated with an experience of poverty which are not dictated by specific regulations, but appear to be the result of social, institutional and cultural practices. The sections above and the previous chapter discussed the Court's finding of *de facto* discrimination against the members of the *Xákmok Kásek* indigenous community. While the Court did not specify any discrimination ground, nor did it refer to poverty as such, it implicitly seems to have conceived the dire living conditions of the applicants as constitutive of *de facto* discrimination against indigenous peoples. That would be to say that poverty amounts to *de facto* discrimination on the grounds of race or ethnic origin. This follows from the elements upon which the Court concluded that there had been *de facto* discrimination against the members of the *Xákmok Kásek* community. These notably included the situation of extreme vulnerability they experienced, the lack of institutional support and the absence of socio-economic services in the area, alongside a system of ownership which privileged the rights of private owners over those of indigenous communities.[112] The judgment in *Hacienda Brasil Verde* gives the impression of heading in a similar direction, albeit here the legal categorisation is one of structural and not *de facto* discrimination. In practice, though, it is not clear what scope of application these two forms of discrimination have and in fact both notions seem conflated in the Court's case law.[113] Nonetheless, as already mentioned, the discrimination analysis in *Hacienda Brasil Verde* focused on the workers' poverty, while neglecting an intersectional approach. Consequently, this judgment is further discussed *infra* section 4.1.2, which examines the prohibition of discrimination on the grounds of economic status.

Still, as mentioned above the effects of an intersectional approach to rights holders alleging socio-economic disadvantage as a matter of human rights need

---

and 46(2)(b) American Convention on Human Rights), Adopted on 10 August 1990, paras. 30–31; Advisory Opinion OC-18/03 on the Juridical Condition and Rights of the Undocumented Migrants, Adopted on 17 September 2003, para. 126.

112 IACtHR, *The Xákmok Kásek Indigenous Community v. Paraguay*, Judgment of 24 August 2010, paras. 273–275.

113 This is strongly suggested by the Court's reasoning not only in this case, but also in an advisory opinion regarding immigrants in which it held: 'this situation of vulnerability [...] is maintained by *de jure* (inequalities between nationals and aliens in the laws) and *de facto* (structural inequalities) situations.' IACtHR, Advisory Opinion OC-18/03 on the Juridical Condition and Rights of the Undocumented Migrants, Adopted on 17 September 2003, para. 112.

not to be restricted to equality and non-discrimination. This is explored in the next subsection.

3.1.4. An Intersectional Approach Beyond the Antidiscrimination Review

A more holistic view of rights holders and their socio-economic circumstances entails various normative consequences beyond the question of discrimination. At the very least, it holds relevance for the analysis of proportionality and the award of reparations, insofar as it calibrates the type and extent of the harm at stake. Moreover, when the Court addresses economic disadvantage as an aspect of belonging to an excluded or otherwise vulnerable group, the normative effect is mostly one of reinforcing and specifying state obligations under the ACHR. These obligations, further discussed *infra* section 4.2.2, are generally interpreted in the light of other instruments with a specific focus on those groups and on their socio-economic needs. Some of these instruments contain substantive and procedural guarantees that are quite closely tailored to the people concerned. As such, those standards may provide helpful and concrete guidance to the Court.

Interestingly, a significant part of the rationale according to which state obligations are enhanced or specified in the face of poverty seems to rest on a view of international responsibility based on the risks of human rights violations created by poverty when they have been known or should have been known to the state. These are, in other words, risks created, aggravated or otherwise tolerated by the state. According to Abramovich, the Inter-American Court has adopted a doctrine of risks to deal with the state's responsibility for imminent and particular risks created by non-state actors and which were known or ought to have been known by the state, provided that the state could reasonably prevent or mitigate their materialisation.[114] A variant of this doctrine is that of 'created risks', which is conceived for cases where the state has not just failed in its duties of protection but has rather contributed to the objective creation of risks of violation.[115] This situation gives rise to stringent state obligations.

So, once poverty is conceived as a factor of risk of and vulnerability to rights violations known to the state, the Court could inquire into what the latter has done to prevent and protect people from the materialisation of those risks. As some authors have observed, a key question for that purpose is what can be reasonably demanded of the state.[116] While an intersectional perspective

---

114 Víctor Abramovich, 'Responsabilidad estatal por violencia de género: comentarios sobre el caso "Campo Algodonero" en la Corte Interamericana de Derechos Humanos', 6 *Anuario de Derechos Humanos* (2010) 167, at 174.

115 Ibid., at 175.

116 Fernando A. Chinchilla *et al.*, 'Pobreza y Derechos Humanos: hacia la definición de parámetros conceptuales desde la doctrina y acciones del sistema interamericano', in Instituto

on rights holders may not by itself answer that question, it may at least indicate when different risks or vulnerabilities accumulate. For example, besides the vulnerability to violations resulting from poverty, an applicant may also face risks associated with gender and racial hierarchies. From this perspective, it follows that the more that factors of risks or disadvantage occur alongside poverty (such as disadvantages associated with age, disability, gender and racial hierarchies), the stronger will be the response expected from the state. This could therefore have an impact on what the Court finds to be reasonable to demand from states in poverty-related violations.

In what follows, another dimension of rights holders is examined, namely autonomy. It is worth exploring what place this element has had in the Court's case law; whether the Court and/or litigants conceive of autonomy as a process or as something dichotomistic; and the implications that result from this.

3.2. PROBLEMATISING THE 'EITHER/OR' VIEW OF INDIVIDUALS' AUTONOMY AND CHOICE

Previous chapters have stressed that normative recognition of individual autonomy and choice should not lead to these becoming detached from the network of social relations in which they take place; nor should the law assume the meaning of one's choices. In other words, it is important to acknowledge that 'people often adapt their choices to their circumstances' and the fact that certain choices are made 'should not imply that there is no further need for legal intervention'.[117] This is particularly relevant in cases involving claims of economic disadvantage, since the accompanying rights interferences are prone to be attributed to people's choices.

Along these lines, scholars have noted that 'economic deprivation is coercive and that it is difficult to be self-sufficient and to implement individual choice when one does not have the resources to do so'.[118] This suggests, in keeping with the capability approach propounded by Sen,[119] that for individuals to exercise their autonomy and pursue what they value, some socio-economic security is needed. The Inter-American Court has explicitly endorsed this view in the

Interamericano de Derechos Humanos, *¿Quién responde por los derechos humanos de las poblaciones más pobres en América Latina y El Caribe? Democracia vs desigualdad 2007–2011* (Instituto Interamericano de Derechos Humanos, 2012), at 110.

117 Sandra Fredman, 'Substantive equality revisited', 14(3) *International Journal of Constitutional Law* (2016) 712, at 730.

118 Athena D. Mutua, 'Introducing ClassCrits: From Class Blindness to a Critical Legal Analysis of Economic Inequality', 56(4) *Buffalo Law Review* (2008) 859, at 895 (referring to Angela Harris's and Martha Fineman's comments about autonomy).

119 Amartya Sen, *Development as Freedom* (Oxford University Press, 1999), at 87–110 ('Chapter 4. Poverty as Capability Deprivation').

street children cases, where a direct correlation was established between the destitution experienced by those children and the encroachment on their project of life and opportunity for self-development.[120] At the same time, though, not everything is about coercion. The agency of those living in poverty should not be reduced to victimhood or passivity.

Unlike what was seen in several cases ruled on by the Strasbourg Court, in the Inter-American Court's case law the autonomy of impoverished rights holders is something seldom discussed. While in the *IVF case*, for example, the Court elaborated on the autonomy of the applicants, this analysis was not so much connected to their socio-economic disadvantage. In that judgment, the connection between this and autonomy was that lacking financial means reinforced the limitations imposed on the applicants' reproductive autonomy and life choices.[121] Yet, a few other cases provide some insights into how the Court has approached the autonomy of impoverished rights holders, and whether or not this is seen in a dichotomistic way. As will be seen below, in the few instances where a discussion of autonomy has arisen, the Court has generally tended to consider the coercive effects of poverty without denying the agency of the individuals affected by it.

As mentioned in Chapter 4, the idea that the cause and remediation of destitution lies with individuals' autonomy was taken up by Paraguay in cases such as the *Yakye Axa* and *Sawhoyamaxa* communities. The state argued that these indigenous communities, guided by their leaders, had freely decided to undergo the harsh living conditions they complained of. It was their choice to place themselves at the side of a road where they could not cater to their needs or have access to health services, education, water and sanitation.[122] The Court rejected this line of reasoning in both cases. In *Sawhoyamaxa*, this was done in a particularly direct way. Here, the Court considered that

> there were powerful reasons for the members of the Community to abandon the estates where they lived and worked, due to the extremely hard physical and labor conditions they had to endure [...] Likewise, this argument is not enough for the State to disregard its duty to protect and guarantee the right to life of the alleged victims.[123]

---

[120] IACtHR, *The 'Street Children' (Villagrán Morales et al.) v. Guatemala*, Judgment of 19 November 1999, para. 191 (holding that the state had prevented street children 'from "the full and harmonious development of their personality", even though every child has the right to harbor a project of life that should be tended and encouraged by the public authorities so that it may develop this project for its personal benefit and that of the society to which it belongs.').

[121] IACtHR, *Artavia Murillo et al. ('In vitro fertilization') v. Costa Rica*, Judgment of 28 November 2012, para. 150.

[122] See IACtHR, *The Yakye* Axa *Indigenous Community v. Paraguay*, Judgment of 17 June 2005, paras. 159(d) and 170; and *The Sawhoyamaxa Indigenous Community v. Paraguay*, Judgment of 29 March 2006, para. 147(b)(c)(d).

[123] IACtHR, *The Sawhoyamaxa Indigenous Community v. Paraguay*, Judgment of 29 March 2006, para. 163.

The Court conceded that the state had not placed the indigenous community at the side of the road to endure poor living conditions, but finds it true that the state 'did not adopt the adequate measures, through a quick and efficient administrative proceeding, to take them away and relocate them within their ancestral lands, where they could have used and enjoyed their natural resources'.[124] The Court thereby seemed to uphold the autonomy of the applicants without making them responsible for the ensuing material difficulties. To that end, the Court firstly took into account the concrete circumstances of the applicants, the social imbalances that shaped their choices and, somewhat implicitly, their limited opportunities to make their demands heard. Secondly, the Court also considered that compliance with human rights obligations was not conditional upon the behaviour or decisions attributed to rights holders, an argument that was reinforced by the normative framework used in the case namely, the right to life.

The Court's approach in *Yakye Axa* was slightly different, since the agency argument was challenged more indirectly. The Court first observed that 'the members of the Community decided to settle alongside a national road [...] as part of the struggle to claim their territory'[125] and that the alternatives of relocation offered by the state were declined because 'they were not duly consulted, bearing in mind the significance for them of remaining on those lands, or because there could be conflicts with other indigenous communities'.[126] Following these remarks, the Court immediately turned to 'highlight the special gravity of the situation of the children and the elderly members of the Yakye Axa Community'.[127] This sequence of arguments has an interesting effect. It appears as if instead of directly challenging the relevance of the applicants' choices to freeing the state from responsibility for their deprivation, the Court drew attention to the situation of those who arguably did not have much of a say on the decision to settle next to a highway, that is, children. In other words, no matter what the community leaders or adult members had opted for, the fact was that many children had no food and no water and had lost the school year because they were ill. In the face of this, the Court recalled that the state had the obligation, based on Article 19 ACHR (Rights of the Child), to adopt special measures of protection to ensure children's development, in accordance with the principle of the best interests of the child.[128] Thereafter, the Court referred to 'the special consideration required by the elderly'.[129]

124 Ibid., para. 164.
125 IACtHR, *The Yakye Axa Indigenous Community v. Paraguay*, Judgment of 17 June 2005, paras. 170–171.
126 Ibid., para. 171.
127 Ibid., para. 172.
128 Ibid., paras. 172–174.
129 Ibid., para. 175.

Particularly worrying was the impact of the lack of access to food and basic services on their health, which was already life-threatening in some cases.

To some extent, this emphasis on the needs of children and the elderly resonates with the tendency of laws and policies to focus on 'innocent' victims who are worthy of assistance in situations of poverty.[130] Evoking the image of 'innocent victims' as a way to counter the argument that rights do not assist those who have allegedly contributed to their own destitution has its downsides, though. Notably, (1) it may obscure the role of social structures and policies which have shaped and limited the choices of all the persons affected; (2) it may convey the idea that human rights and the corresponding state obligations are reserved for individuals with a certain degree of 'moral purity'; (3) it may unnecessarily associate certain rights holders – such as children and the elderly – with notions of disempowerment, vulnerability and passivity; and finally, (4) focusing on the blameless rights holder may also legitimise the lack of state intervention in cases where the persons affected do not fit that image. However, it must be noted that these drawbacks were considerably mitigated in the aforementioned judgment. The Court did contextualise the community's decision to settle at the side of the road by pointing to the struggles and difficulties resulting from, *inter alia*, land regulations and the length of restitution proceedings.[131] Additionally, by directing attention to the situation of indigenous children and elderly people, the Court was in a better position to distinguish the reinforced or particular duties that the state owed some rights holders, in this case some members of the indigenous community. This brings us to the normative relevance of seeing and weighting the situation of a broad range of rights holders, which is further analysed in the next subsection.

Before turning to that, a final remark is in order. It is possible that the generally limited attention devoted to questions of autonomy in the cases studied could be due, at least in part, to a judicial review that is often too

---

130 In this vein, see e.g. Wouter Vandenhole, 'Child Poverty and Children's Rights: An Uneasy Fit?', 22 *Michigan State International Law Review* (2014) 609, at 633 (problematising the image of children as 'the prototype of "deserving poor"'); Jeanne M. Woods, 'Justiciable Social Rights as a Critique of the Liberal Paradigm', 38 *Texas International Law Journal* (2003) 763, at 790 (noting that in the Treatment Action Campaign case before the South African Constitutional Court, 'the beneficiaries of constitutional relief were not the infected mothers, but the innocent – hence "deserving" – infants to whom the disease was transmitted in *utero*'); Leroy H. Pelton, 'Welfare Discrimination and Child Welfare', 60 *Ohio State Law Journal* (1999) 1479, at 1479 (showing that welfare programmes regard poor elderly and children as more worthy than other categories of people, such as single parents and other non-elderly adults).

131 IACtHR, *The Yakye Axa Indigenous Community v. Paraguay*, Judgment of 17 June 2005, paras. 50.13–50.16 and 171. See also, *The Sawhoyamaxa Indigenous Community v. Paraguay*, Judgment of 29 March 2006, paras. 164–166.

concerned with excluded groups and their contextual situation, sometimes at the expense of individualised assessments. Still, the absence of a narrative of poverty that conceives of this as the result of people's free will may change the imaginable spectrum of normative responses to socio-economic disadvantage. Conceiving socio-economic difference and poverty as something created that needs to be tackled not simply by intervening in the lives of those affected by it redirects attention to social institutions and inequalities. This, in turn, underscores the role of the state and other actors in addressing poverty and the violations associated with it. It opens the door to the setting of standards and frameworks of state responsibility for poverty-related violations (which in the future could perhaps extend to other actors).[132] In this vein, taking distance from autonomy-based explanations for restricting the rights of people living in poverty also challenges the idea that 'chosen' characteristics or circumstances attain less or no legal protection. This promotes the recognition of people living in poverty as worthy of legal attention, irrespective of the 'mutability' of their condition.

So far, the discussion has focused mostly on whether applicants are considered as whole individuals, in terms of their identities and social positions as well as in their exercise of autonomy. But, as mentioned in previous chapters, individuals do not stand in isolation. Accordingly, an integrated view of human rights is also attentive to other rights holders potentially affected by the measures disputed in the cases. This is the next question explored in this chapter.

3.3. A BROAD VIEW OF RIGHTS HOLDERS

This book has already explained that one of the main reasons for human rights courts to consider the situation of rights holders other than the applicant is the fact that some restrictions are made for the protection of the rights of others. In such cases, courts need to pay attention to the effects that the measure discussed in the case has on those persons, even if they are not a party to the case. From this perspective, it is important to point out that, probably as a result of the types of poverty-related case brought to the Inter-American Court, the issue of the protection of the rights of others has not had much salience.

[132] See, for example, the liability frameworks discussed by Fernando A. Chinchilla *et al.*, 'Pobreza y Derechos Humanos: hacia la definición de parámetros conceptuales desde la doctrina y acciones del sistema interamericano', in Instituto Interamericano de Derechos Humanos, *¿Quién responde por los derechos humanos de las poblaciones más pobres en América Latina y El Caribe? Democracia vs desigualdad 2007–2011* (Instituto Interamericano de Derechos Humanos, 2012), at 104–116.

In some cases, states have not substantiated the rights interferences at all, have not considered the rights of others to that effect, or have acknowledged their responsibility for the violations. Moreover, at times the restrictions discussed in the cases barely allow justification in the light of the rights of others (e.g. summary executions of children and slavery and forced labour). There are, however, some judgments in which this element of analysis does feature. Among these are indigenous cases in which the deprivations experienced by the applicants were attributed to the need to ensure the rights of private owners. Likewise, in *Gonzales Lluy* the state claimed that the restrictions of the applicant's right to education sought to protect other children from the risks of HIV infection. A similar line of argument featured in the *IVF v. Costa Rica* case, where the state claimed that the blanket ban on IVF techniques aimed at protecting the life of embryos. Probably it is the case of *Ramírez Escobar et al. v. Guatemala* where the protection of the rights of others appears more clearly addressed, for the taking into care of children on account of the mother's poverty was done with a view to protect the children concerned. Save for this judgment, though, the analysis conducted in relation to other rights holders does not seem to have been connected to the claims of socio-economic disadvantage involved in the cases.

So here the discussion will first turn to another, although more implicit way in which the protection of other rights holders appears at issue in the cases studied, namely through arguments of budgetary limitation. In *Sawhoyamaxa*, for example, the state posited that it had done what it could within the limitations of its financial resources.[133] Usually, the Court has not analysed these arguments in depth, nor have states developed their claims of economic capacity from the perspective of the rights of other rights holders. Yet, the situation faced by persons other than the applicants is frequently in the background of resource scarcity justifications. For instance, in order to satisfy the needs and rights of the whole population, certain economic disadvantage may be imposed on some to the benefit of others. A regulation that causes or aggravates the applicants' socio-economic disadvantage may thus do so with the aim of attending to the needs of others who are worse off. An argument like this would obviously need careful examination in the context of the concrete case, but it is certainly a relevant normative ground. Importantly, as will be seen below, it may lead the Court and litigants to consider the situation of other rights holders whose interests are likely to remain invisible, namely those with fewer resources.

133 IACtHR, *The Sawhoyamaxa Indigenous Community v. Paraguay*, Judgment of 29 March 2006, para. 147 (c).

3.3.1. Protecting Impoverished Others against the Prohibition of Retrogression in Social Rights

Social policies and legal reforms aimed at restricting social rights are particularly prone to raise issues of retrogression and redistribution. The case of *Five Pensioners v. Peru* is illustrative of this.[134] The case concerned the modification and reduction of the pension regime of five former public servants, a measure that for the state was justified by legal reforms seeking to adjust pensions in light of the cost of living and the economic resources of the country.[135] According to the Commission, however, the cuts amounted to a violation of the applicants' right to property (Article 21 ACHR). The victims' representative additionally contested what they regarded as a 'regressive measure' in violation of the 'progressive development' of social rights, as protected by Article 26 ACHR.[136] Eventually, the Court found a violation of the right to property (Article 21 ACHR) and ruled out the question of Article 26. Leaving aside the debate on the justiciability of social rights through (the now fully enforceable) Article 26 (which was introduced in Chapter 3 and is further discussed below), it is interesting to ask how the argument of retrogression could have played out for the integration of rights holders other than applicants.[137] How would the prohibition of retrogression in social and economic rights be balanced with an arguable claim of redistribution? This question implies an examination of whether the measure in question affected the pensions of the better-off with a view to improving the situation of the poor, while elucidating the normative weight this carries. Bringing these other rights holders, those potentially benefiting from the pension reform, could thus have changed the understanding of what was at stake in the *Five Pensioners* case. It could have led the Court to consider, *inter alia*, the extent to which or the conditions under which redistributive measures could

---

134 IACtHR, *'Five Pensioners' v. Peru*, Judgment of 28 February 2003.

135 Ibid., paras. 92 (f)(g).

136 Ibid., para. 143 (d).

137 The concept of retrogression was introduced by the UN Committee on Economic Social and Cultural Rights. According to its General Comment No. 3, 'any deliberately retrogressive measures … would require the most careful consideration and would need to be fully justified by reference to the totality of the rights provided for in the Covenant and in the context of the full use of the maximum available resources.' CESCR, General Comment No. 3: The Nature of States parties' obligations (art. 2, para. 1, of the Covenant), E/1991/23, 1 January 1991, para. 9. General Comment No. 19 further clarifies: 'There is a strong presumption that retrogressive measures taken in relation to the right to social security are prohibited under the Covenant. If any deliberately retrogressive measures are taken, the State party has the burden of proving that they have been introduced after the most careful consideration of all alternatives and that they are duly justified by reference to the totality of the rights provided for in the Covenant, in the context of the full use of the maximum available resources of the State party.' CESCR, General Comment No. 19: The Right to Social Security (art. 9), E/C.12/GC/19, 4 February 2008, para. 42.

be frustrated by the obligation of progressive realisation and its correlative prohibition of retrogression. This is an important question for a human rights approach sensitive to the interests of people living in poverty. In fact, according to Landau (who relies on a comparative study of several constitutional courts), negative injunctions like those grounded in the prohibition of retrogression tend to favour more affluent groups instead of the poorest.[138]

The Inter-American Commission has, in the meantime, addressed claims of retrogression and redistributive policies aimed at low-income people. In doing so, it has accorded the protection of these persons' significant normative weight. Reviewing a similar case against Peru and within the scope of Article 26 ACHR, the Commission took into account, for example, the fact that 'the majority of pensioners in the public sector did not enjoy the benefit'; that the pensioners affected were 'not representative of the development stage of the right to social security' in the country; and that the suppressed equalisation of the pensions 'constituted a privilege' that made 'difficult the progressive improvement of the conditions of pensioners who were not beneficiaries of the equalization'.[139] On this basis, the Commission found that the pension reform was not retrogressive and therefore not incompatible with Article 26 ACHR.[140] As already noted, the Court's judgment in *Five Pensioners*, which relies on the rights to property and to judicial guarantees, did not deal with these issues.[141] However, these might at some point come

138 David Landau, 'The Reality of Social Rights Enforcement The Reality of Social Rights Enforcement', 53 *Harvard International Law Journal* (2012) 402, at 445–453 (arguing that these negative injunctions, closely related to the international law concept of non-retrogression are 'likely to have a strong tilt in favor of more affluent groups [...] who tend to have pensions, decent health care, and other subsidies. These benefits can be attractive targets for governments that urgently need to cut budget deficits and which may be under international (IMF, World Bank, etc.) pressure to do so.' These injunctions 'may prevent or slow necessary structural reforms', giving rise to a 'middle class' jurisprudence. As such, he suggests that 'the Committee [on Economic Social and Cultural Rights] should deemphasize or abolish the non-retrogression principle').

139 IACommHR, *National Association of ex-Employees of the Peruvian Social Security Institute et al. v. Peru*, Admissibility and Merits, Report no. 38/09, Case 12.670, 27 March 2009, para. 142. In this case the state had specifically argued that 'the fiscal saving generated by the application of the new pension rules would be used to increase the lowest pensions.' Further, the increases in the savings generated by the reform had made it possible to increase the pensions for widowhood and those of persons with disabilities. See paras. 55–58.

140 Ibid., paras. 143–147. The Commission 'finds that the reduction affected a reduced number of pensioners with the aim of improving the conditions of the exercise of the right by the rest of the beneficiaries. Thus this part of the reform did not constitute a regression as prohibited by article 26 of the Convention.'

141 The Court ultimately rejected the examination of the issue of progressive realisation and the prohibition of retrogression on the basis of a brief and somewhat confusing reasoning. It held: 'Economic, social and cultural rights have both an individual and a collective dimension. This Court considers that their progressive development, (...) should be measured in function of the growing coverage of economic, social and cultural rights in

before the Court, since the justiciability of Article 26 ACHR (Progressive Development) is now fully in force.[142] Moreover, even if the right to property would appear inadequate for holding that discussion, framing the problem as one of consideration for other affected rights holders could arguably facilitate this.

3.3.2. *Impoverished Rights Holders Among or on the Same Side as Applicants*

A comprehensive approach to rights holders also has another side. This is, as explained in previous chapters, the side of those who are affected in a similar way as the applicants. Thinking of these rights holders in a broad perspective means, in the context of this book, looking beyond the applicants or, at least distinguishing among them so as to bring to light those who may be less visible. This is especially relevant for people living in poverty, for reasons similar to those discussed above. People living in poverty have more difficulty in accessing justice. Litigants, therefore, often do not represent the experience of those of lower socio-economic status. Consequently, courts may end up delivering a rather middle-class-oriented justice. Against this backdrop, the judgment in *IVF v. Costa Rica* shows how looking at rights holders comprehensively and distinguishing among them helps to counteract that risk. Out of the nine plaintiff couples in this case, four were not socio-economically disadvantaged, while five had been unable to undergo treatment abroad for lack of economic resources.[143] Despite a middle- or upper-class perspective being a dominant point of reference, the Court was able to differentiate the situation of those applicants who had less means. What is more, this motivated a more attuned finding that grasped their specific experience *vis à vis* the rest of the applicants, namely, indirect discrimination on account of their financial situation. By doing so, the Court avoided issuing a ruling that would have been responsive to a very limited segment of rights holders potentially affected by the ban.

---

general, and of the right to social security and to a pension in particular, of the entire population, bearing in mind the imperatives of social equity. It is evident that this is what is occurring in the instant case; therefore, the Court considers that it is in order to reject the request to rule on the progressive development of economic, social and cultural rights in Peru, in the context of this case.' IACtHR, *'Five Pensioners' v. Peru*, Judgment of 28 February 2003, paras. 147–148.

142 See IACtHR, *Lagos del Campo v. Peru*, Judgment of 31 August 2017; *Cuscul Pivaral et al. v. Guatemala*, Judgment of 23 August 2018; and *Muelle Flores v. Peru*, Judgment of 6 March 2019.

143 IACtHR, *Artavia Murillo et al. ('In vitro fertilization') v. Costa Rica*, Judgment of 28 November 2012, para. 303. (Also see para. 86, where the Court notes, for example, that one of the couples had already applied for loans and mortgages; they had mortgaged their home and sold some of their belongings in order to cover the costs of insemination.)

A similar kind of awareness is particularly needed when the applicants are a collectivity, such as an indigenous community. Chapter 3 showed that although the Court has, until recently, repeatedly stated that the applicants in indigenous cases are the individual members of the community, their specific position could easily be diluted in the concern for the community. In addition, although these indigenous communities are internally diverse, they are likely to be represented by those members who hold relatively dominant positions, as happens with most collectivities. Nevertheless, in *Yakye Axa, Sawhoyamaxa and Xákmok Kásek*, the Court was willing to examine the alleged violations not only from the perspective of the communities' leaders, or the adult males of the communities concerned. In those cases, the Court also accounted for the way less visible community members, such as children, women and the elderly, were affected by land destitution and poor living conditions. In so doing, it made it clear that specific, more stringent standards were at play. In fact, children and other individuals are entitled, by virtue of specialised provisions or rights regimes, to differentiated protection.[144] Moreover, a significant part of this differentiated protection includes duties of socio-economic assistance, as further explained below. This therefore confirms that taking into consideration social locations other than economic conditions, such as age and gender, may nonetheless provide useful insights for dealing with claims of socio-economic disadvantage. At the same time, the aforesaid judgments show that a comprehensive view of rights holders helps in identifying different normative frameworks that may be applicable to different applicants in a single case.

In the aforementioned indigenous cases, those less visible rights holders (children, women and the elderly) were formally applicants. Yet, it may well be possible that in other cases only some amongst an indigenous community, or any other group of people, act as plaintiffs. One may furthermore think of other communities who endure similar deprivations on account of measures being examined in a Court case in which they are not a party. In all these cases, it would be equally counterproductive to adjudicate in disregard of those other persons and the specific rights and obligations that could potentially apply to them.

Finally, it is worth mentioning that in *Ramírez Escobar et al. v. Guatemala*, the Court rightly recognised that the rights of both parents and children were adversely affected by their forcible separation while also taking into account the role of other family members. The Court examined the case through the perspective of children's rights and found their removal and

---

144 In this vein, Eva Brems, 'Should Pluriform Human Rights Become One? Exploring the Benefits of Human Rights Integration', 4 *European Journal of Human Rights* (2014) 447, at 460–461.

adoption to be against the protection of their best interest and their right to be heard, as provided by the CRC.[145] As seen below, these are not the only child-specific standards used in the judgment. The Court furthermore noted that the grandmother, who was not a party to the case, was discarded as an alternative to child placement for discriminatory reasons (based on her sexual orientation) which amounted to discrimination against the child Osmín Tobar.[146] And although the latter was the only sibling who was a party to the case and granted reparations accordingly, the Court did recognise the interests of the child who did not want to take part in the Court's proceedings.[147]

Having explored whether and how the litigants and the Court address people's socio-economic disadvantage in a manner sensitive to their complexity as persons with multiple social positions, who stand alongside other individuals and try to make choices while embedded in social relations and institutions, it is time to discuss how all these affect the normative assessment of poverty-related cases. To this the remainder of the chapter now turns.

4. INTEGRATED RIGHTS: CROSS-THINKING ABOUT HARMS AND NORMS

As in the previous chapter, this section aims at thinking comprehensively about the harms and norms involved in cases of socio-economic disadvantage. This means, in particular, paying attention to those harms and norms that are usually side-lined by the way certain claims are framed. In the case of rights claims related to poverty or socio-economic disadvantage, it is likely for the adjudicator and other actors to put the emphasis on material distress and marginalisation. Against this backdrop, the first section below (4.1) explores whether other types of harm and wrong, such as disrespect and stigma, as well as structural inequalities, have been considered. This analysis not only seeks to provide a more complex understanding of what is at stake in the cases studied, but also to identify what can be gained from such an understanding.

The second section below (4.2) is devoted, as in previous chapters, to the Court's practice of normative integration as regards Convention and extra-Convention provisions. The premise underlining this discussion is that avoiding norm reductionism and promoting awareness of legal pluralism are helpful.

145 IACtHR, *Ramírez Escobar et al. v. Guatemala*, Judgment of 9 March 2018, paras. 173 and 182–183.

146 Ibid., para. 302.

147 Ibid., paras. 46–48.

The analysis will examine why this is so. It should be pointed out, however, that while in principle cross-thinking about the norms involved in cases of economic disadvantage would not lead to much emphasis on socio-economic rights (since the socio-economic dimension of rights is usually underlined in this type of case), this category of rights will nonetheless be discussed. The reason for this is that in the particular case of the Inter-American Court's case law, the Court's awareness of legal pluralism and its ensuing practice of normative integration in the cases studied here has been closely linked to the indivisibility of rights. In fact, the litigants and the Court have generally endeavoured to integrate extra-Convention norms and standards while also using several Convention provisions with a view to dealing with the socio-economic rights dimensions of the cases. That is why section 4.2 below discusses the Court's awareness of legal pluralism in relation to indivisibility.

But before exploring this, the following lines will first analyse cases of socio-economic disadvantage from the perspective of harms and norms that are not so easily seen and weighted, such as stereotype, stigma and the prohibition of discrimination on account of poverty.

4.1. INTEGRATING RECOGNITION AND STRUCTURAL ISSUES INTO REDISTRIBUTION WRONGS

4.1.1. Addressing Poverty-Related Stigma and Stereotypes

It is not contested that people living in poverty or who are identified with a low socio-economic status are all too often rendered invisible. The Commission itself has underlined the seriousness of this problem.[148] And, as seen in the previous chapter, stereotypes and stigmas are very often at the root of the problem. As early as in the 1999 case of *Villagrán Morales (Street children)*, it was clear that the violence and murders perpetrated by state agents against adolescents living on the street, as well as the lack of institutional response, were the result of a generalised view that portrayed those children as criminals and undeserving. The Court hinted at the incidence of these stereotypes when it held that if the state had evidence for believing that the children were involved in criminal acts, it should have taken measures of prevention and rehabilitation.[149] However, the Court did not acknowledge this harm as such and no normative consequence was attached to it.

---

148 IACommHR, Preliminary Report on Poverty, Extreme Poverty and Human Rights in the Americas (2016), para. 5.

149 IACtHR, *The 'Street Children' (Villagrán-Morales et al.) v. Guatemala*, Judgment of 19 November 1999, para. 197.

This was amended in the similar subsequent case of *Servellón García v. Honduras*, where the Court recognised the stigma suffered by the victims as children living in poverty. It even noted that this very stigma placed them at risk of serious violations.[150] Yet, the judgment did not clarify the normative grounds compromised. It suggested that this contravened Article 19 ACHR (children's rights) and while it recalled the relevance of non-discrimination standards, no violation of this provision was found. In this connection, it is important to bear in mind that the stigma of the poor as criminal continues to be a determinant factor for the disparate levels of violence against some segments of the population, such as Afro-descendants, something with which the Court continues to be confronted.[151]

A somewhat similar oversight appears in the *Cotton Field* case mentioned above, whose ruling acknowledged that most women victims of violence had a precarious socio-economic situation. In its commendable review of equality and non-discrimination, the Court condemned the gender stereotypes that had facilitated the violence and the passivity of state authorities. Interestingly, however, the Court seemingly missed the fact that those stereotypes were linked to or compounded by preconceptions based on the victims' socio-economic position. In fact, it was a particular subgroup of women, namely those who were young, immigrant and *poor*, those who were seen as disposable and less deserving of protection by the authorities.[152]

Against this background, the most recent judgments of the Court represent a significant step forward in seeing and weighing, as a separate harm, the stigma and disrespect attached to the experience of poverty. The case of *Gonzales Lluy et al. v. Ecuador* admittedly focused on the stigma associated with an HIV condition, rather than with poverty. But in doing so, the Court also underscored how such stigmatisation led to poverty, while the latter, in turn, exacerbated the stigma and impeded resilience.[153] Importantly, stigma

---

150 IACtHR, *Servellón García et al. v. Honduras*, Judgment of 21 September 2006, paras. 112 and 116.

151 For a recent example, see IACtHR, *Favela Nova Brasília v. Brazil*, Judgment of 16 February 2017, para. 2.II.(g) on the recommendations made by the Inter-American Commission in its merits report on the case, which included providing training to police agents on how to deal with people from a socially vulnerable background, including residents of the *favelas*, so as to overcome the stigma that all people in poverty were criminals.

152 In a similar vein, but with regard to the assessment of the CEDAW Committee on the state response to the crimes against women in Ciudad Juarez, see Rebecca J. Cook and Simon Cusack, *Gender Stereotyping: Transnational Legal Perspectives* (University of Pennsylvania Press, 2010), at 214–215 (arguing that the Committee failed to name the compounded stereotypes at play and which affected poor and young migrant women).

153 The Court recalls the following excerpt from Mrs Lluy's (Talías's mother's) testimony: 'the most difficult times have related to financial problems since the legal actions were filed, the loss of my job, the social rejection owing to the absence of opportunities, […] education, house rental expenses and frequent moves, [being discriminated against by] the home owners.' She was dismissed several times, had to sell her household items and worked in

was addressed within the framework of both the right to personal integrity (Article 5) and the prohibition of discrimination (Article 1.1).[154] The judgment in *Hacienda Brasil Verde*, however, provides the most direct and clear response to the recognition harm resulting from poverty. As will be seen below, the Court applied the prohibition of discrimination on the grounds of economic status to the invisibility of the workers in the eyes of law enforcement officials. In the Court's view, the officials' passivity and lack of diligence and the little importance attached to the workers' grievances reflected a lack of condemnation of what had happened to them. The Court attributed this to prevalent preconceptions about workers from the poorest regions. Although it did not specify the content of these preconceptions, the Court explained them as perceptions that 'normalised' the treatment dispensed to the workers and which, consequently, made them less deserving of protection.[155] Interestingly, no specific statements or actions of the authorities were singled out in this respect, which suggests that the Court's conclusion rested on the general context of the case.

Considering the normative developments allowed by the ACHR, it may come as a surprise that stereotypes, preconceptions and the invisibility accorded to poverty were not really tackled until recently. The recent case law, however, is promising and attests to the importance of integrating those harms into the legal analysis. Even in cases that are first and foremost about destitution and economic exploitation, there is a dimension of recognition that needs to and can, normatively speaking, be integrated. Doing otherwise exposes those in poverty to further invisibility while leaving untouched some of the underlining causes of the violations.

4.1.2. *Discrimination on Account of Poverty and the Integration of Social Structures into the Legal Analysis*

Linked to questions of stigma and misrecognition, although not limited to them, is the consideration of the harm derived from discrimination for reasons of poverty. As mentioned in previous chapters, proponents of substantive

---

the informal sector, while her attempts to obtain social assistance were unsuccessful. Meanwhile her eldest son aged 15 had to drop his studies and start working, suffering discrimination and social isolation too. See IACtHR, *Gonzales Lluy et al. v. Ecuador*, Judgment of 1 September 2015, para. 215.

154 Ibid., paras. 216–229. The Court found a violation not only with regard to the girl who lived with HIV, but also with regard to her mother and brother. The Court observed that mother and son devoted most of their physical, economic and material efforts to ensure survival and a decent life for Talía. This carried health problems, severe stress and depression. Relying on expert reports, the Court concluded that their afflictions were related to the stigma and discrimination derived from their association with a person living with HIV.

155 IACtHR, *The Hacienda Brasil Verde Workers v. Brazil*, Judgment of 20 October 2016, paras. 418–419.

equality conceive of anti-discrimination norms as having the potential to tackle issues of poverty and socio-economic exclusion.[156] For one thing, substantive equality presupposes an active state and a commitment to redress social group disparities.[157] For another, this conception of equality, at least in its transformative strand, is arguably equipped to address the stereotypes and social arrangements behind measures that negatively impact on destitute people. In practice, though, supranational adjudicatory bodies and more particularly, the European Court of Human Rights have rarely used antidiscrimination laws to scrutinise stereotypes and disparate disadvantages on the basis of poverty.[158] Until recently, this was also true for the Inter-American Court.

At the outset of this chapter it was noted that the Court long ago recognised, in the framework of an advisory opinion, that discrimination on economic grounds is prohibited by the ACHR.[159] Yet, it took a while before this was applied in contentious cases. After some failed attempts, the Court eventually examined the existence of discrimination for socio-economic reasons in the cases of *IVF v. Costa Rica* and, shortly after, in *Gonzales Lluy v. Ecuador*. In both, poverty was taken jointly with other grounds, as pointed out earlier. Also of note, these rulings on economically-based discrimination did not have much to do with the stigmatisation and stereotypes associated with the experience of poverty. Rather, what amounted to discrimination in both cases was the disparate impact and particular burdens confronted as a result of lacking economic resources. The prohibition of discrimination based on 'economic status' as such was subsequently applied in the cases of *Hacienda Brasil Verde* and *Ramírez Escobar*, ruled in 2017 and 2018 respectively and further discussed below.

In the case of *IVF v. Costa Rica*, the Court concluded that the ban on IVF techniques constituted indirect discrimination based on economic status,

---

156 Bruce Porter, 'Expectations of Equality', 33(2) *Supreme Court Law Review* (2006) 23, at 27; Sandra Fredman, 'Providing Equality: Substantive Equality and the Positive Duty to Provide', 21(2) *South African Journal on Human Rights* (2005) 163, at 166.

157 Ibid. See also, Gwen Brodsky and Shelagh Day, 'Beyond the Social and Economic Rights Debate: Substantive Equality Speaks to Poverty', 14 *Canadian Journal of Women and the Law* (2002) 184, at 205–206.

158 Few existing examples include: CEDAW Committee, *Alyne da Silva Pimentel v. Brazil*, Communication no. 17/2008, Views adopted on 25 July 2011, para. 7.7; ECSR, *International Planned Parenthood Federation–European Network v. Italy*, Complaint no. 87/2012, Decision on the merits of 10 September 2013, paras. 190–194. For an example of the lack of application of the prohibition of discrimination to scrutinising poverty-based stereotypes in the European Court of Human Rights, see Valeska David, 'Caring, rescuing or punishing? Rewriting RMS v Spain (ECtHR) from an integrated approach to the rights of women and children in poverty', in Eva Brems and Ellen Desmet (eds.), *Integrated human rights in practice* (Edward Elgar, 2017), at 164–167.

159 IACtHR, Advisory Opinion OC-11/90 on the Exceptions to the Exhaustion of Domestic Remedies (Articles 46(1), 46(2)(a) and 46(2)(b) American Convention on Human Rights), Adopted on 10 August 1990, paras. 22 and 31.

given the 'disproportionate impact on the infertile couples who did not have the financial resources to undergo IVF abroad'.[160] The disproportionate impact the Court referred to was not based on statistical data indicating that a much larger number of least well-off couples were affected by the ban. Rather, the disparate impact seemed to refer to the much-reduced capacity those people had to cope with the ban. While people with financial means had at least the chance to seek alternatives to circumvent the ban and obtain treatment, those who lacked resources did not. Although the Court's reasoning was concise, it marked an important step forward in protecting socio-economically disadvantaged people against unequal access to rights and services. The distributive potential of the finding was furthermore amplified by the reparation orders. The Court requested the inclusion of IVF within the Social Security Scheme of Costa Rica, so as to make it available without discrimination.[161]

For its part, as seen earlier, the case of *Gonzales Lluy* addressed the applicant's poverty as a ground of (direct) discrimination intertwined with her HIV condition, age and gender. Stigmatisation was a key component of the discrimination experienced by the girl and the family, but this mostly concerned her HIV condition. Discrimination against her for reasons of poverty was situated in the differentiated, less favourable conditions that the lack of resources had for her access to health services and her options for coping subsequently with social barriers associated with a life with HIV. In the following similar case of *Cuscul Pivaral et al. v. Guatemala*, the Court noted that people living in poverty were more vulnerable to contracting HIV and experiencing health inequalities. However, these considerations are not reflected in the finding of discrimination, which is mostly grounded in gender.

In sections 3.1.1 and 3.1.3 above it was said that the line of reasoning adopted in the cases of *IVF v. Costa Rica* and *Gonzales Lluy et al. v. Ecuador* provided a situated account of poverty that accounted better for the applicants' lived experiences, including the specific burdens and harms that they encountered. But there is another notable aspect of these two judgments that is of great importance to the present discussion, that is, how the Court, in addition to emphasising the overlapping identities or social positions of the victims, underscored the role of social barriers and institutions.

This was mainly done, as noted above, through the lenses of the so-called 'social model of disability'.[162] Since this model is built upon a structural

160 IACtHR, *Artavia Murillo et al. ('In vitro fertilization') v. Costa Rica*, Judgment of 28 November 2012, para. 303.

161 Ibid., para. 338.

162 On the paradigm shift brought about by the CRPD, see e.g. Colin Barnes, 'Understanding Disability and the Importance of Design for All', 1(1) *Journal of Accessibility and Design for All* (2011) 55–80; Rosemary Kayess, and Philip French, 'Out of Darkness into Light?

understanding of disability, its use with regard to the interplay between disability, poverty and other axes of disadvantage allows for a structural notion of intersectionality. As discussed in previous chapters, intersectionality is too often misconceived as concerned with the interplay between multiple identities.[163] Yet, its added value does not lie in recognising an ever-increasing number of sub-groups or identities in need of protection. One of its greatest potentials is rather to illuminate the synergetic way in which structures of power work.[164] Thus, the Court's attention to 'attitudinal and social barriers' in the *IVF* and *Gonzales Lluy* cases has two important effects. One is that it makes the structural perspective behind the social model of disability suitable for approaching the rights deprivation associated with poverty and other social differences besides disability. Second, by doing so, it paves the way for the law to interrogate social structures instead of singling out people's traits, thus directing laws and policies toward the roots of violations. These are in fact some of the important insights that ended up being downplayed in *Hacienda Brasil Verde*. This is the other case that merits close analysis in this section.

The prohibition of discrimination on the grounds of economic status alone was applied for the first time in the recent case of *Hacienda Brasil Verde*, which offers a number of interesting aspects. Since some of them have already been discussed, here the discussion shall focus on two questions. The first is how the Court regarded poverty as an issue of 'structural discrimination'. The second is how the Court applied the prohibition of discrimination with regard to both the material conditions of deprivation experienced by the applicants and the lack of recognition and disrespect endured.

Although in *Hacienda Brasil Verde* the Commission had alleged *de facto discrimination*,[165] the Court followed the representatives' argument that the slavery and forced labour experienced by the workers reflected 'structural discrimination'.[166] In rather obscure language, the analysis started by considering extreme poverty or marginalisation as a source of vulnerability that gave rise to positive obligations of protection from the state.[167] According to

Introducing the Convention on the Rights of Persons with Disabilities', 8(1) *Human Rights Law Review* (2008) 1, at 6 and ff. See also Chapter 2, section 4.2.3.

163 For a critique of intersectionality anchored in identity, see Joanne Conaghan, 'Intersectionality and the Feminist Project in Law', in Emily Grabham *et al.* (eds.), *Intersectionality and Beyond. Law, power and the politics of location* (Routledge Cavendish, 2009), at 29.

164 Catharine Mackinnon, 'Intersectionality as a Method: A Note', 38(4) *Signs* (2013) 1019, at 1023–1024; Ben Smith, 'Intersectional Discrimination and Substantive Equality: A Comparative and Theoretical Perspective', 16 *The Equal Rights Review* (2016) 73, at 77.

165 IACtHR, *The Hacienda Brasil Verde Workers v. Brazil*, Judgment of 20 October 2016, para. 216.

166 Ibid., para. 336.

167 Ibid., para. 337.

the Court's case law, every person who finds herself in a situation of vulnerability is the holder of 'a special protection'.[168] The Court applied this to poverty. The scope of the state's positive obligations depended on the particular needs for protection arising from the applicants' condition of extreme poverty.[169] From here, and without defining structural discrimination, the Court went on to hold that when there was structural discrimination, the state incurred international responsibility if it failed to take specific measures to alleviate the victimisation suffered by the individuals concerned as a result of their particular situation of vulnerability.[170] These measures were lacking in *Hacienda Brasil Verde*. But since the right to be free from slavery enshrined in Article 6 ACHR also entails positive obligations which, in this case, demanded, among others, an adequate and effective oversight of the estate in question and a prompt response once the crimes were reported to the police, one may wonder what positive actions were to be taken on the basis of the workers' poverty. Could the state have been required to provide goods and services so as to redress or alleviate poverty, the main source of their vulnerability to slavery? Also implicit in the statement that the state should have reacted to existing structural discrimination seems to be the view that the fact that people like the rescued workers were disproportionally affected by poverty in itself amounted to structural discrimination. The judgment, however, left these questions open.

The Court instead looked at the risks created by poverty. It was not contested that poverty was the main factor leading to the workers' recruitment into slavery-like labour, which also held true for the 85 rescued workers from *Hacienda Brasil Verde*. They lived in poverty, came from the poorest regions of the country, lacked education and were illiterate, which made them prone to recruitment into slavery by fraud and deceit. This was, according to the Court, 'a situation of imminent risk for a determinate group of persons' which was known to the state for years. The state, however, had failed to act duly upon it. The Court thus attributed the slavery and trafficking suffered by the applicants to their economic status, which gave rise to discrimination, in violation of Article 6 taken in conjunction with Article 1.1 ACHR. Moreover, this discrimination on the basis of economic status (Article 1.1 ACHR) was, in the Courts' view, 'structural' and 'historical'. The conclusion was that 'the State did not consider the vulnerability of the 85 rescued

168 Ibid., para. 337; IACtHR, *The Sawhoyamaxa Indigenous Community v. Paraguay*, Judgment of 29 March 2006, para.154; *The Xákmok Kásek Indigenous Community v. Paraguay*, Judgment of 24 August 2010, para. 233.

169 IACtHR, *The Hacienda Brasil Verde Workers v. Brazil*, Judgment of 20 October 2016, para. 337.

170 Ibid., para. 338.

workers [...] by virtue of the discrimination on the grounds of economic status to which they were subjected'.[171]

Turning to the applicants' discriminatory denial of access to justice, which was examined within the framework of Article 25 ACHR (right to an effective remedy) instead of Article 8 ACHR (right to a fair trial), the Court followed the Commission's and representatives' claim that the judicial passivity and investigative shortcomings revealed 'structural discrimination' against the workers.[172] Emphasising that the abuses disproportionally affected uneducated people from the poorest regions, such as the 85 workers, the Court ascribed the impunity and lack of judicial diligence to a 'normalisation' of the working conditions to which those people were subjected.[173] In other words, the victims' discriminatory access to justice was the result of existing 'preconceptions' that turned their harsh working conditions into something socially accepted. Hence, while the finding of discrimination regarding the right to be free from slavery related to redistributive wrongs consisting of the most severe forms of economic exploitation, this economic discrimination in access to justice exposed the misrecognition harms – invisibility, devaluation – caused by poverty.[174]

But the Court not only directly applied the prohibition of discrimination on the ground of 'economic status' listed in Article 1.1 ACHR.[175] It also found, as just mentioned, 'structural discrimination' in the enjoyment of the rights to be free from slavery and to access justice. This is not the first time the Court has referred to 'structural discrimination'.[176] However, in *Hacienda Brasil Verde* it went beyond the recognition of a context of structural discrimination, as previously done in the gender violence case of *Cotton Field*.[177] This time the Court held Brazil accountable, albeit with hesitant

171 Ibid., para. 341.

172 Ibid., paras. 349 and 355.

173 Ibid., paras. 417–419.

174 Valeska David, 'The Inter-American concept of structural equality and discrimination', 2 *Anti-Discrimination Law Review* (2017) 5, at 23.

175 IACtHR, *The Hacienda Brasil Verde Workers v. Brazil*, Judgment of 20 October 2016, para. 335.

176 On the concept of structural discrimination in the Inter-American system, see Valeska David, 'The Inter-American concept of structural equality and discrimination', 2 *Anti-Discrimination Law Review* (2017) 5–27. The Committee on the Rights of People with Disability (CommRPD) has recently conceptualised 'structural discrimination' in the context of the rights of women with disabilities: 'Structural, or systemic, discrimination is reflected in hidden or overt patterns of discriminatory institutional behaviour, discriminatory cultural traditions and discriminatory social norms and/or rules. Harmful gender and disability stereotyping, which can lead to such discrimination, is inextricably linked to a lack of policies, regulations and services specifically for women with disabilities.' CRPD, General Comment No. 3: Women and girls with disabilities, CRPD/C/GC/3, 25 November 2016, para. 17(e).

177 IACtHR, *González et al. ('Cotton Field') v. Mexico*, Judgment of 16 November 2009, paras. 399–402.

wording, for (not reversing) the historical structural discrimination endured by the rescued workers.[178] The hesitation in the wording appears to reflect the judges' disagreement on the point. On the one hand, Judge Ferrer Mac-Gregor argued that this was the first case where the Court expressly found that a state was internationally responsible for 'perpetuating a historical situation of structural exclusion'.[179] On the other, though, Judge Vio Grossi declared that the judgment's reference to 'historical structural discrimination' did not imply a declaration of the state's international responsibility on that ground. Instead, it could only be considered the context in which the facts of the case took place.[180] Meanwhile, Judge Sierra Porto criticised the judgment for suggesting that the state was solely responsible for the existence of poverty and slavery in Brazil. Against this, he argued that 'the existence of structural social problems does not automatically generate Brazil's international responsibility'.[181]

The trouble with the finding of structural discrimination is furthermore compounded by the lack of clarity that surrounds the application of the concept. For example, in one case the Court took into account the 'structural discrimination' suffered by the group to which the applicant belonged but without holding the state accountable for structural discrimination.[182] Meanwhile, in *Nadege Dorzema v. Dominican Republic* the Court referred to abundant material documenting widespread discrimination against Afro-descendants. And yet it decided, contrary to the arguments of the Commission and the representatives, that it was unnecessary to make a ruling on the alleged context of structural discrimination. Likewise, the Court in *Xákmok Kásek*, as mentioned above, spoke of *de facto* discrimination and not of structural discrimination. So, it is actually uncertain when structural discrimination is a matter of context, as in *Cotton Field*, and when a violation in itself, as in *Hacienda Brasil Verde*.

The Court's reasoning regarding structural discrimination in the right to be free from slavery on account of the victims' economic status in *Hacienda Brasil Verde* is, moreover, not entirely clear as to the specific conduct or effect that amounts to discrimination. Arguably, the most feasible interpretation is to consider that the workers' economically based discrimination lies with the fact that people like them, living in severe poverty, were overwhelmingly exposed and subjected to rural slavery, forced labour and trafficking. Judge Ferrer Mac-Gregor also advanced this view in his

---

178 IACtHR, *The Hacienda Brasil Verde Workers v. Brazil*, Judgment of 20 October 2016, para. 343.

179 Ibid., Concurrent Opinion of Judge Ferrer Mac-Gregor, para. 84.

180 Ibid., Concurrent Opinion of Judge Vio Grossi, paras. 1 and 4.

181 Ibid., Partially Dissenting Opinion of Judge Sierra Porto, paras. 11–12.

182 IACtHR, *Atala Riffo and daughters v. Chile*, Judgment of 24 February 2012, para. 92.

concurring opinion.[183] However, as already pointed out, the Court's argumentation also hints at the state's liability for inaction in the face of existing poverty. While the first line of reasoning implies that the state is obliged to adopt measures to prevent and protect people living in poverty from being exploited, enslaved or trafficked, the second line of reasoning goes further. It conveys the idea that entrenched poverty may be conceived as discrimination, at least in this case.

In any event, in order for both interpretations (which are not mutually exclusive) to stand, a more intersectional approach to the rights holders affected is needed, that is, as explained earlier, an approach that integrates into the discrimination analysis the applicants' position as young Afro-descendant men. Or, in other words, an approach that incorporates racism. One important reason for this is that doing otherwise may frustrate the transformative potential of the notion of 'structural discrimination' as applied to poverty. As the term 'structural' suggests, one of the most promising features of structural equality should be shifting the focus from group traits to the social structures and institutions producing inequality. In the case at hand, this required going beyond the workers' characteristics of poverty repeatedly emphasised by the Court.

Even regarding poverty as discrimination may not be as far-fetched as it may appear at first sight if the problem is presented in terms of the way poverty is entrenched and concentrated in one specific sector of the population that has suffered long-lasting discrimination. Thinking of poverty this way resonates with the view of other human rights monitoring mechanisms, including the Inter-American Commission.[184] According to the United Nations Special Rapporteur on contemporary forms of racism, the intersection between poverty and racism can be seen in the legacy of *de jure* and *de facto* discriminatory regimes that 'have left a large number of racial and ethnic groups [...] trapped in conditions of "chronic deprivation of resources" with limited choices and vulnerable to multiple violations of their rights'.[185]

183 Ibid., Concurring Opinion of Judge Ferrer Mac-Gregor, para. 75 (stating that the Court concluded that there had been discrimination on the basis of economic status due to the fact that people living in poverty were more prone to be victims of trafficking).

184 'The situation of poverty endured by Afro-descendants in the region can be perceived in terms of the standards of the inter-American human rights system as a situation of structural racial discrimination, understood as the set of both de jure and de facto standards, rules, routines, patterns, attitudes, and behavioral guidelines that make way for a generalized situation of inferiority and exclusion against a group of persons, which are perpetuated over time and even from one generation to the next, meaning that this is not a situation of isolated, sporadic, or episodic cases but rather discrimination that arises as the consequence of a historic, socioeconomic, and cultural context.' IACommHR, Preliminary Report on Poverty, Extreme Poverty, and Human Rights in the Americas, 2016, para. 324.

185 UN General Assembly, Report of the Special Rapporteur on Contemporary Forms of Racism, Racial Discrimination, Xenophobia, and Related Intolerance, Mutuma Ruteere, A/68/333, 19 August 2013, para. 20.

Along similar lines, the Committee on the Elimination of Racial Discrimination has explained:

> Racism and structural discrimination against people of African descent, rooted in the infamous regime of slavery, are evident in the situations of inequality affecting them and reflected, inter alia, in the following domains: their grouping, together with indigenous peoples, among the poorest of the poor [...] [and in the] additional difficulties they face in access to and completion and quality of education, which results in the transmission of poverty from generation to generation; [and] inequality in access to the labour market [...].[186]

It is somewhat surprising that this line of international normative sources was not incorporated by the Court into its judgment in *Hacienda Brasil Verde*, considering its increasing and expansive use of international sources. Doing so could have helped it to assess the role of racial discrimination, on which it was eventually silent. This silence, alongside the confusions around the notions of 'structural' and '*de facto* discrimination', complicates the Court's ability to provide an adequate legal response to structural inequality, or to some forms of structural inequality. At least, this seems to be the case for racism, in particular, bearing in mind that this is not the first time that the Court has disregarded structural racial discrimination in the face of evidence of it.[187]

A year later, the Court issued again a judgment concerning poverty-based discrimination. As pointed out earlier, *Ramírez Escobar et al.* asserts the impermissibility of family separation on account of poverty and regards this as discrimination based on economic status, in violation of Article 1.1 read in conjunction with the rights to family life (Articles 11.2 and 17.1) and child protection (Article 19) ACHR. The Court not only found that the removal and illegal adoption of children for economic reasons amounted to discrimination, it also found that the applicants' inability to afford the fees to avail themselves of judicial remedies constituted an additional breach of the prohibition of discrimination on account of economic status. What is more, the assessment weighted the existence of a general context of illegal

---

186 CERD, General Recommendation No. 34: Racial discrimination against people of African descent, CERD/C/GC/34, 3 October 2011, para. 6.

187 For example, in cases involving Haitians and Dominicans of Haitian origin living in the Dominican Republic, the Court has declined to pronounce on structural racial discrimination against them, despite acknowledging the existence of multiple materials on their historical exposure to discrimination and subjection to racism. In both cases the Court prefers to speak of discrimination on the basis of their migration status or simply their condition as Haitians and Dominicans of Haitian descent. See IACtHR, *Expelled Dominicans and Haitians v. Dominican Republic*, Judgment of 28 August 2014, para. 404; *Nadege Dorzema et al. v. Dominican Republic*, Judgment of 24 October 2012, paras. 232–238.

adoptions affecting the worst-off families in Guatemala and known to the state authorities.[188]

4.2. AVOIDING NORM REDUCTIONISM AND PROMOTING AWARENESS OF LEGAL PLURALISM

4.2.1. A More Comprehensive Approach to Convention Norms: The Right to Property of People in Poverty

In cases concerning economic difference or disadvantage, several Convention norms have been mobilised before the Inter-American Court. As noted in Chapter 4, given the multidimensionality of poverty and the lack of provisions specifically aimed at dealing with this feature, it is natural that a myriad of rights are involved in cases of socio-economic disadvantage. In the Inter-American Court's case law, those include the Convention rights to life (Article 4); to humane treatment (Article 5); to freedom from slavery (Article 6); to fair trial (Article 8); to family life (Articles 11.2 and 17.1) and to a lesser extent, the prohibition of discrimination (Articles 1.1 and 24) and the right to property (Article 21). The availability of such a broad spectrum of Convention norms facilitates a comprehensive analysis of the cases studied here. Yet, as noted above the prohibition of discrimination was until recently underutilised. Chapter 4 reached a similar conclusion with regard to this and the right to property. Against this background, it is worth asking what has the right to property, as interpreted by the Inter-American Court, offered to those with fewer possessions in the Americas?

Albeit briefly, the Court has taken into account the applicants' experience of poverty from the perspective of the right to property. This is noteworthy if one thinks of the difficulties that sometimes arise when it comes to protecting the possession of those who have little property. Difficulties particularly affect those whose life circumstances involve situations of precarious legality. Recall the cases of Roma and Traveller eviction discussed in the previous chapter. The destruction and loss of their belongings has not attracted, for the most part, the protection of the right to property. At the Inter-American Court, however, the judgment in *Uzcátegui et al. v. Venezuela* offers a different approach. As noted earlier, in this case the Court found a violation of the right to property for the material losses caused in a poor household during a police operation. The ruling, notably, rested on the severe impact that the damage and destruction of the household structure and mobile

[188] IACtHR, *Ramírez Escobar et al. v. Guatemala*, Judgment of 9 March 2018, paras. 288–291.

goods had on the applicants – the family of the deceased victim, given their socio-economic disadvantage.[189]

Of note, the Inter-American Commission has also endeavoured to grasp the pecuniary losses, however small they may be, of impoverished individuals in legally precarious situations. In its merit report in the case of *Expelled Dominicans and Haitians* (also known as *Benito Tide Mendez and Others*), the Commission was willing to declare a violation of the right to property of documented and undocumented Haitians and Dominicans of Haitian descent who, as a result of their expulsion from the country, lost their belongings and personal items without being compensated.[190] Interestingly, however, this line of reasoning was not upheld by the Court. Once the case reached San Jose, the Court adopted a Strasbourg-like approach to the proprietary complaint (Article 21 ACHR). Leaving aside those allegations that fell outside its temporal jurisdiction, the Court was of the view that there was no need for a separate ruling on the loss of household items, personal effects, clothing, livestock, cash and wages. In its opinion, these allegations were related to facts addressed under other provisions.[191]

It remains to be seen how this issue will evolve. What is clear though is that the stakes can be higher than usually recognised. Even when the above proprietary claims appear as accessory aspects of the cases, they may have devastating consequences for the persons concerned. In the aforesaid case of *Expelled Dominicans and Haitians*, for example, the Court itself observed that people like the applicants were usually 'dropped at the border', often arriving in Haiti 'with nothing more than the clothes on their back. They may have to beg for food and for a place to sleep'.[192] This also held true for the victims in that case. In fact, their representative asked the Court to take into account the fact that following their expulsion, the applicants 'were placed in [...] circumstances of extreme poverty'.[193]

4.2.2. Integrating International and Regional Norms with a View to the Indivisibility of Rights

When it comes to norms outside the ACHR, the Court's practice of cross-referencing encompasses growing and varied sources. They include binding

189 IACtHR, *Uzcátegui et al. v. Venezuela*, Judgment of 3 September 2012, paras. 204–206. See also, *The Santo Domingo Massacre v. Colombia*, Judgment of 30 November 2012, para. 274.

190 IACommHR, *Benito Tide Mendez and Others v. The Dominican Republic*, Merits, Report no. 64/12, Case 12.271, 29 March 2012, paras. 329–332.

191 IACtHR, *Expelled Dominicans and Haitians v. Dominican Republic*, Judgment of 28 August 2014, paras. 442–443.

192 Ibid., para. 169.

193 Ibid., para. 122. (The victims' representative asked the Court to take into account these circumstances for the purpose of applying more flexible procedural and evidentiary rules.)

and non-binding instruments, with a general and specialised focus on different areas of regulation, as well as national and international judicial decisions. The references in the cases studied here include, for example, the International Covenant on Civil and Political Rights; the Convention on the Rights of the Child; the International Covenant on Economic, Social and Cultural Rights; UN Committees' General Comments; resolutions from the UN Human Rights Council; the International Guidelines on HIV/AIDS; the Slavery Convention and the Supplementary Convention on the Abolition of Slavery; judgments from the International Criminal Court for the former Yugoslavia and other international criminal courts; judgments from the European Court of Human Rights; decisions from the African Commission on Human and Peoples' Rights; and pronouncements and reports of UN Special Rapporteurs. The list is actually much longer. In addition, especially in recent cases, the Court has increased its references to the laws and decisions of American states – even if mostly with a focus on Latin America and the United States.[194]

Having said that, it is convenient to point out that many of the international norms and rulings indicated above have not been used in direct connection with poverty-related violation claims. But this does not mean that the Court's practice of normative integration will not play a greater role in future cases dealing with socio-economic disadvantage.[195] This may well be the case. In fact, already a while ago it was suggested that 'one possible avenue for action to rejuvenate the system so that its institutions can begin to address issues of poverty is to develop the interrelationships among instruments, whether binding or hortatory'.[196] But for the time being, references to international norms on socio-economic rights and child rights have been the most relevant extra-Convention sources in the cases examined in this chapter. A good example of the latter is the judgment in *Ramírez Escobar et al.*, concerning family separation on account of poverty. This notably rests on similar rulings from the ECtHR examined in Chapter 4 and on several standards from the CRC. Among others, the Court took into account the best interest of the child, the exceptionality of family separation, the children's participation in decision-making affecting them, the subsidiarity of inter-country adoption

194 See e.g. IACtHR, *Artavia Murillo et al. ('In vitro fertilization') v. Costa Rica*, Judgment of 28 November 2012, paras. 185 (fn. 283), 255–256 and 262; *Gonzales Lluy et al. v. Ecuador*, Judgment of 1 September 2015, para. 256; *I.V. v. Bolivia*, Judgment of 30 November 2016, para. 197.

195 This was not just because of the Court's legal praxis, but also because of the way applicants and third-party interveners tend to bring more and more international and comparative norms before it.

196 Inter-American Institute of Human Rights, *Human rights from the perspective of poverty. A path unexplored in the Inter-American system* (Inter-American Institute of Human Rights, 2007), at 40.

and the prohibition of improper financial gain for those involved in it.[197] While reference is also made to child specific norms aimed at the socio-economic protection of the family, the Court does not really elaborate on the state's failure to provide material support to the applicants with a view to avoid taking the children away. Nevertheless, the Court's normative integration has often brought to light the socio-economic rights dimension of the cases.

The Court's embracing of indivisibility and interdependence has come hand in hand with awareness of legal pluralism. Indeed, a large part of the extra-Convention norms incorporated into the case law studied concern socio-economic rights. Several judgments attest to this. Already in the *Street children* case, for example, most references to the Convention on the Rights of the Child (CRC) were made with a view to connecting the state's obligation to adopt measures of protection under Article 19 ACHR with children's socio-economic wellbeing. According to the Court:

> The American Convention and the Convention on the Rights of the Child form part of a very comprehensive international *corpus juris* for the protection of the child that should help this Court establish the content and scope of the general provision established in Article 19 of the American Convention.[198]

On this basis, the Court resorted to, *inter alia*, the CRC obligation to protect children against discrimination (Article 2); the obligation to ensure to the maximum extent possible their survival and development (Article 6.2); the duty to afford special protection and assistance to children deprived of their family environment (Article 20.1); and the right of children to an adequate standard of living, including the provision of assistance and material support to parents and other caregivers (Article 27.1 and 3). The Court incorporated these CRC standards to define the scope of the protection measures envisaged by Article 19 ACHR, which thereby involved socio-economic rights. Given the seriousness of the crimes perpetrated by state agents against the child victims in this case, the Court obviously concluded that the state failed to comply with these obligations.[199] Although the Court did not explicitly say

---

197 IACtHR, *Ramírez Escobar et al. v. Guatemala*, Judgment of 9 March 2018, paras. 203–237.

198 IACtHR, *The 'Street Children' (Villagrán-Morales et al.) v. Guatemala*, Judgment of 19 November 1999, para. 194. The Court had already held that in interpreting a treaty, it should take into consideration (1) the agreements and instruments formally related to it, as required by Article 31.2 of the Vienna Convention; and (2) the system within which the Convention is inscribed, as indicated by Article 31.3 of the Vienna Convention. See IACtHR, Advisory Opinion OC-16/99 on the The Right to Information on Consular Assistance in the Framework of the Guarantees of Due Process of Law, Adopted on 1 October 1999, para. 113.

199 IACtHR, *The 'Street Children' (Villagrán-Morales et al.) v. Guatemala*, Judgment of 19 November 1999, para. 196.

so in the *Street children* case, it is interesting to note that its interpretation of the special measures of child protection appears closely related to its broad interpretation of the right to life. Despite the fact that the immediate violation of the right to life in that case arose from the execution of children, the judgment referred to the right to 'not be prevented from having access to the conditions that guarantee a dignified existence'.[200] Importantly, this reading yielded the foundation of the right to a dignified life under Article 4 ACHR, which has since served as an umbrella norm for the integration of socio-economic rights, particularly as defined by international sources.

As explained in Chapter 3, this normative framework has mostly been developed in indigenous cases where the appalling living conditions of the communities threatened the very survival of their members. These were the cases of *Yakye Axa*, *Sawhoyamaxa*, and *Xákmok Kásek v. Paraguay*. In all of them the Court found that the extreme poverty of the community members and the state's failure to ensure their access to basic services and goods such as water, sanitation, food, health and education fell short of enabling them to live with dignity, in contravention of the right to life (Article 4 ACHR).[201] The Court's attribution of responsibility for violation of the right to a dignified life in those cases followed a two-fold track. In the first place, the Court noted that the state bore responsibility for the land dispossession suffered by the communities, which deprived them of the means for a dignified existence. In the second place, once the communities settled at the side of highways and the state was aware of the concrete risks and deprivations faced by the community members, the Court considered that the state had failed to secure living conditions compatible with human dignity.

In order to define the minimum conditions for a life with dignity, the Court took into account the rights provided by other instruments ratified by Paraguay, such as the Additional Protocol to the American Convention on Human Rights regarding Economic, Social and Cultural Rights and ILO Convention No. 169.[202] In connection with the latter, the applicants' representatives argued in *Yakye Axa* that 'in light of ILO Convention No. 169 [...] protection of the right to life and integrity of the indigenous peoples cannot be disassociated from protection of economic, social, and cultural rights'.[203] On the other hand, it is worth mentioning that in *Xákmok Kásek*,

---

200 Ibid., para. 144.

201 IACtHR, *The Yakye Axa Indigenous Community v. Paraguay*, Judgment of 17 June 2005, paras. 161–176; *The Sawhoyamaxa Indigenous Community v. Paraguay*, Judgment of 29 March 2006, paras. 157–178; *The Xákmok Kásek Indigenous Community v Paraguay*, Judgment of 24 August 2010, paras. 194–217.

202 IACtHR, *The Yakye Axa Indigenous Community v. Paraguay*, Judgment of 17 June 2005, para. 163.

203 Ibid., para. 158 (f).

unlike the previous Paraguayan cases, the Court did not really examine the concrete obstacles to accessing social services and the ensuing harms experienced by the applicants. Rather, the Court appeared to focus on minimum deliverables. It basically applied indicators provided by other monitoring bodies such as the UN Committee on Economic Social and Cultural Rights and the World Health Organization, which it contrasted to the coverage and figures attained by the state.[204]

The commitment to indivisibility was taken a little further in *Gonzales Lluy et al. v. Ecuador*, where the Court undertook extensive normative considerations on the right to health. But neither the ACHR nor the provision of the Protocol of San Salvador, which authorises oversight of some social rights via the individual petition system established in the ACHR, refers to that right.[205] The Court nonetheless examined this within the framework of the rights to life (Article 4 ACHR) and to humane treatment (Article 5 ACHR). Invoking numerous regional, international and domestic sources (both binding and non-binding) on economic and social rights, the judgment scrutinised two kinds of obligation: the state's obligations to monitor the provision of private health care services; and the applicants' claims regarding the quality, accessibility and other aspects of the health care provided.

The Court explicitly recalled the indivisibility and interdependence of civil and political rights and socio-economic rights with a view to interpreting the obligation to secure both categories of rights as comprising several dimensions of the right to health. On this basis, the Court brought in standards on, for example, the 'accessibility' of health services, goods and facilities as developed by the Committee on Economic, Social and Cultural Rights and which, remarkably, included economic accessibility (or affordability).[206] Likewise, it asserted that the right to health of people living with HIV required a comprehensive approach that was inclusive of continuous prevention, treatment, care and support. In this vein, the Court also referred to international and comparative sources promoting the adoption of a comprehensive approach precisely because of the costs and financial difficulties

---

204 IACtHR, *The Xákmok Kásek Indigenous Community v. Paraguay*, Judgment of 24 August 2010, paras. 194–200.

205 Article 19.6. of the Additional Protocol to the American Convention on Human Rights in the Area of Economic, Social and Cultural Rights ('Protocol of San Salvador') reads as follows: 'Any instance in which the rights established in paragraph a) of Article 8 and in Article 13 [rights to form trade unions and to education, respectively] are violated by action directly attributable to a State Party to this Protocol may give rise, through participation of the Inter-American Commission on Human Rights and, when applicable, of the Inter-American Court of Human Rights, to application of the system of individual petitions governed by Article 44 through 51 and 61 through 69 of the American Convention on Human Rights.'

206 IACtHR, *Gonzales Lluy et al. v. Ecuador*, Judgment of 1 September 2015, paras. 171–173.

in accessing HIV treatment.[207] The issue of socio-economic disadvantage did not, however, take a prominent place in this part of the judgment, which, rather, elaborated on other aspects of the right to health. Though the judgment broke new ground in the field of the right to health – further advanced in the 2018 case of *Cuscul Pivaral et al. v. Guatemala*, the standards developed in this field will not be dealt with here.[208]

Instead, the discussion that follows looks at the judgment's method of analysis and conclusions regarding indivisibility. These more general issues can be of relevance in a number of cases concerning socio-economic disadvantage, since many of these are likely to involve socio-economic rights demands. From this perspective, a first noteworthy aspect of the judgment is that though the Court ultimately opted for infusing Convention rights with elements of social rights, as it usually does, the direct justiciability of the right to health was seriously considered. This is revealed by Judge Pérez Pérez's concurring opinion. He explained that the main motivation for writing his separate opinion was 'the constant proposals made during the deliberation of the case to cite the right to health as the main right violated by the State's action'.[209] He and Judge Sierra Porto rejected that possibility, which, as posited by the victims' representatives, would rely on the alleged justiciability of Article 26 ACHR (Progressive Development).

This provision refers to the progressive realisation of 'the rights implicit in the economic, social, educational, scientific, and cultural standards set forth in the Charter of the Organization of American States'.[210] As mentioned in Chapter 3, for quite a while Article 26 has been interpreted by some as allowing the Court to adjudicate on a broad list of socio-economic rights. This is despite the fact that the Protocol of San Salvador – the Inter-American

---

[207] Ibid., para. 197, fn. 230 (citing OHCHR and UNAIDS, International Guidelines on HIV/AIDS and Human Rights, 2006 consolidated version, and the Colombian Constitutional Court).

[208] Note that in *Cuscul Pivaral et al. v. Guatemala*, the Court asserted the autonomus and justiciable character of the right to health and declared its violation on the basis of Article 26 ACHR. See IACtHR, *Cuscul Pivaral et al. v. Guatemala*, Judgment of 23 August 2018, paras. 98–139. For a thorough analysis of the right to health in the Court's case law prior to *Gonzales Lluy*, see Oscar Parra Vera, 'The Protection of the Right to Health through Individual Petitions before the Inter-American System of Human Rights', in Ebenezer Durojaye (ed.), *Litigating the Right to Health in Africa. Challenges and Prospects* (Routledge, 2015), at 243.

[209] IACtHR, *Gonzales Lluy et al. v. Ecuador*, Judgment of 1 September 2015, Concurring Opinion of Judge Alberto Pérez Pérez, para. 1. See also Concurring Opinion of Judge Humberto Antonio Sierra Porto.

[210] The full provision reads as follows: Article 26 (Progressive Development): 'The States Parties undertake to adopt measures, both internally and through international cooperation, especially those of an economic and technical nature, with a view to achieving progressively, by legislation or other appropriate means, the full realization of the rights implicit in the economic, social, educational, scientific, and cultural standards set forth in the Charter of the Organization of American States as amended by the Protocol of Buenos Aires.'

treaty specialised in social, economic and cultural rights – explicitly establishes the judicial enforceability of only two social rights enshrined therein. In addition to the indivisibility of human rights, the pro-adjudication argument usually rests, *inter alia*, upon a *pro-personae* interpretation of the Convention and notably, upon the precedent laid down in the 2009 case of *Acevedo Buendía*.[211] Also referenced in Chapter 3, this judgment held that the Court had competence to examine the violation of all Convention rights, including those socio-economic rights flowing from Article 26 ACHR. It pointed out, *inter alia*, that since the provision was placed under the part entitled 'State Obligations and Rights Protected', it was 'subject to the general obligations contained in Articles 1(1) and 2',[212] that is, the obligations to respect, ensure and adopt legislative and other measures to give effect to Convention rights.

It is nonetheless interesting to observe that none of the conflicting positions around the justiciability of Article 26 ACHR have contested the indivisibility and interdependence of rights. The opposition to using the said provision to adjudicate social rights, as reflected in the position of Judges Sierra Porto and Pérez Pérez, posits that the best way to give application to indivisibility and interdependence is by examining the socio-economic rights dimensions implicit in Convention rights. Those who favour the direct application of Article 26 ACHR, like Judge Ferrer Mac-Gregor, argue conversely that this indirect

211 IACtHR, *Acevedo Buendía et al. ('Discharged and Retired Employees of the Comptroller') v. Peru*, Judgment of 1 July 2009. The case concerned 273 members of the Association of Discharged or Retired Employees of the Comptroller General of the Republic who challenged the reduction of their pension rights introduced by a legal reform. Prior to this, the applicants were entitled to a pension equal to the salary of an employee performing the same or similar function to the one he or she performed at the time of his or her retirement.

212 Ibid., para. 100. The Court's stance in *Acevedo Buendía* represented a notable shift away from its previous pronouncement on Article 26 in the *Five Pensioners* case. In this case, the Court refused to rule on the progressive realisation of the applicants' right to social security, as argued by their representatives, given that the progressive development of such rights 'should be measured in function of the growing coverage of economic, social and cultural rights in general, and of the right to social security and to a pension in particular, of the entire population, bearing in mind the imperatives of social equity'. In other words, the Court in *Five Pensioners* seemed to disregard the application of the general obligations contained in Articles 1.1 and 2 ACHR, confining the oversight of Article 26 to an evaluation of progressive and collective development. See the IACtHR, *'Five Pensioners' v. Peru*. Judgment of 28 February 2003, para. 147. Notwithstanding this, the remarks on Article 26 made in *Acevedo Buendía* were *obiter dicta*, as the case was decided from the viewpoint of the rights to property and the right to judicial remedies. The Court explains that 'considering that the analysis is not centered on some measure adopted by the State that hindered the progressive realization of the right to pension, but on the State's non-compliance with the payment ordered by the domestic courts, the Tribunal deems that the violated rights are those protected in Articles 25 and 21 of the Convention and it does not find ground to additionally declare the non-compliance with Article 26 of said treaty.' Ibid., para. 106.

approach does not sufficiently advance the indivisibility and interdependence of rights.[213]

While an exhaustive analysis of the debates surrounding Article 26 is beyond the ambition of this work, the integrated normative perspective adopted by the Court in this context deserves some attention. Of particular interest is the Court's appeal to a consensus-like argument with a view to supporting the possible adjudication of Article 26 ACHR. In fact, in *Acevedo Buendía* the Court revisited the debate among states' representatives during the *travaux préparatoires* of the ACHR in order to determine what kind of protection they intended to afford to social, economic and cultural rights. In doing so, it suggested that states were inclined to grant these rights as much protection as possible. However, as Judges Sierra Porto and Pérez Pérez observed in *Gonzales Lluy* – as did scholars before them – the Court referred to only four of the 23 states that participated in the Inter-American Specialized Conference of 1969. What is more, many of those countries which were not mentioned in the judgment were either reluctant or against enforcing Article 26 socio-economic rights through the individual petition system established in the Convention.[214] Nevertheless, it is plausible that the justiciability argument might fare better under a 'true' consensus framework. That would be the case, in other words, if the point of reference were the normative protection that the American states, especially Latin American countries, accord to social rights in their domestic legal orders. However, it was doubtful that this consensus argument could attain much weight when the question is more about competence than just interpretation. In any event, the justiciability of Article 26 ACHR has now been settled. In the 2017 case of *Lagos del Campo v. Peru*, whose analysis is beyond the scope of this book, the Court decided to apply Article 26 *ex officio* (based on the principle of *Juria Novit Curia*) and declare a violation of the right to labour stability.[215] The Court has since further

---

213 IACtHR, *Gonzales Lluy et al. v. Ecuador*, Judgment of 1 September 2015, Concurring Opinion of Judge Ferrer Mac-Gregor, para. 15. See also Separate concurrent opinion of Judge Ferrer Mac-Gregor in IACtHR, *I.V. v. Bolivia*, Judgment of 30 November 2016, para. 1. It is important to note that other judges before him also advocated for the justiciability of the social rights derived from Article 26 ACHR. See, in particular, Concurring Opinion of Judge Margarette Macaulay in IACtHR, *Furlan and Family v. Argentina*, Judgment of 31 August 2012.

214 IACtHR, *Gonzales Lluy et al. v. Ecuador*, Judgment of 1 September 2015, Concurring Opinions of Judge Humberto Sierra Porto, para. 27 and Judge Alberto Pérez Pérez, para. 19. See also, Laurence Burgorgue-Larsen and Amaya Úbeda De Torres, *The Inter-American Court of Human Rights. Case Law and Commentary* (Oxford University Press, 2011), at 633; Oswaldo Ruiz Chiriboga, 'The American Convention and the Protocol of San Salvador: Two Intertwined Treaties, Non-Enforceability of Economic, Social and Cultural Rights in the Inter-American System', 31(2) *Netherlands Quarterly of Human Rights* (2013) 159, at 170.

215 IACtHR, *Lagos del Campo v. Peru*, Judgment of 31 August 2017, paras. 141–154.

expanded its social rights jurisprudence based on the direct application of Article 26 ACHR.[216]

But for present purposes, it is relevant to reflect on the normative sources silenced in *Acevedo Buendía*. In opening adjudication space for socio-economic rights, the Court also 'forgot', as Judge Sierra Porto points out, the aforementioned Protocol of San Salvador.[217] The Court referred to the views of the UN Committee on Economic, Social and Cultural Rights,[218] but not to the Inter-American Instrument specialised in economic, social and cultural rights. This line of reasoning brings back one problematic feature of the Court's integrated perspective on human rights norms already discussed in Chapter 3, namely, its selectivity.

The Court's readiness to integrate a wide range of normative sources for the purpose of addressing socio-economic claims, including those that may arise in connection with poverty, has proven useful and even desirable. But to take real advantage of the opportunities offered by human rights integration, the Court should be more careful to remain inclusive and non-selective. This is particularly important when it comes to adjudicating on new, controversial or otherwise sensitive issues. At stake is not only the need to preserve the Court's legitimacy among different stakeholders and especially among member states, but also the opportunity to give sound and clear guidelines to those actors. The lack of consistency in the Court's normative integration as applied in *Acevedo Buendía* has been singled out because of its relevance to the way poverty-related claims could be handled in the future. However, the case law studied reveals further instances of 'cherry-picking' or insufficient justification in the Court's integrated approach to international normative sources.[219]

---

216 See IACtHR, *Cuscul Pivaral et al. v. Guatemala*, Judgment of 23 August 2018 and *Muelle Flores v. Peru*, Judgment of 6 March 2019.

217 IACtHR, *Gonzales Lluy et al. v. Ecuador*, Judgment of 1 September 2015, Concurring Opinion of Judge Humberto Sierra Porto, para. 10.

218 IACtHR, *Acevedo Buendía et al. ('Discharged and Retired Employees of the Comptroller') v. Peru*, Judgment of 1 July 2009, paras. 102–103.

219 For example, in *Hacienda Brasil Verde*, the Court conducted an exhaustive review of international law and case law on the prohibition of slavery and related practices, such as trafficking and servitude. Among different international and regional bodies, the Court, as usual, referred to the European Court's case law. But the Strasbourg Court, unlike other bodies, has not applied the figure of slavery as prohibited in Article 4 ECHR and has at best conflated the concept of slavery and trafficking, giving application only to the latter. Ultimately, the Inter-American Court took a different position. It endorsed a very broad interpretation of the element of property that defines the prohibition of slavery, which in fact allowed it to apply it to the case. In support of this view, the Court referred to e.g. international criminal courts and to the Court of Justice of the Economic Community of West African States. The Court in this part omitted the Strasbourg Court because indeed it departed from it on this matter. At the same time, though, the Court did rely on the ECtHR's conceptualisation of servitude. The divergence is certainly

Against this backdrop, it should be noted that the Court has recently attempted to clarify some elements of its integrated normative approach. For instance, in the *IVF* case, it explained that international human rights law was of particular relevance for its 'systematic interpretation' of the Convention, that is, pursuant to Article 31.2 of the Vienna Convention, with a view to interpreting the Convention norms within the legal system or legal context to which the ACHR belongs.[220] For its part, the Court accorded 'special relevance' to comparative law for the purpose of its 'evolving interpretation'. Based on Article 29 ACHR, this requires the Court to interpret the Convention in the light of present times, the latter being especially needed when it comes to issues that did not exist or were not envisaged at the time the Convention was drafted, such as *in vitro* fertilisation techniques.[221] This as well as further clarifications of the Court's method of integration are much welcome.

Thus far the chapter has discussed the normative frameworks within and outside the Convention that have been used most frequently in cases involving claims of socio-economic disadvantage. The remainder of the chapter turns to a reflection on the possible incorporation of other, less used norms which are nonetheless worth exploring.

4.2.3. *Reflecting on the Integration of Non-State-Generated Norms*

The case law analysed here also discloses the relevance of international financial agreements and other norms developed by state and non-state actors, whose rules certainly shape socio-economic differences across peoples and countries. The Court was confronted with this issue in *Sawhoyamaxa v. Paraguay*.[222] The state in this case had subscribed to a bilateral investment treaty with Germany that protected and promoted capital investments from both countries. The disputed land, whose restitution the community was demanding while settling along a highway, was in the hands of German private investors. Although the state authorities had supported the restitution claim of the indigenous community and invited the corporations to sell the land, they had

legitimate, but it appears puzzling. The Court did not provide any justification for this, despite it being its common practice to follow the ECtHR's case law. See IACtHR, *The Hacienda Brasil Verde Workers v. Brazil*, Judgment of 20 October 2016, paras. 259–272. The Court concretely refers to ECtHR, cases of *Siliadin v. France*, App. no. 73316/01, Judgment of 26 July 2005 and *Rantsev v. Cyprus and Russia*, App. no. 25965/04, Judgment of 7 January 2010. In this last case the Court reversed its previous position, according to which the definition of slavery corresponded to the classic meaning of slavery as exercised through legal ownership of a person. Yet, it did not apply the notion of slavery, instead mixing this with trafficking.

220 IACtHR, *Artavia Murillo et al. ('In vitro fertilization') v. Costa Rica*, Judgment of 28 November 2012, para. 191.

221 Ibid., paras. 245–246.

222 IACtHR, *The Sawhoyamaxa Indigenous Community v. Paraguay*, Judgment of 29 March 2006.

refused to do so. The state eventually argued that those private actors were protected by the investment treaty.[223] In response, the Court first attempted to reconcile the norms in tension. While noting that it had not been provided with the trade treaty in question, it observed that the government had conceded that the instrument in question allowed for capital investments made by a contracting party to be nationalised for a public interest. It followed, so argued the Court, that this could be used for the restitution of the land to the indigenous community. That said, priority was nonetheless accorded to the human rights obligations derived from being a party to the ACHR. The Court held that bilateral investment agreements could not be applied in contravention of the American Convention. In justifying this approach, emphasis was placed on the 'singularity' of the ACHR. As a multilateral treaty on human rights, this 'stands in a class of its own and that generates rights for individual human beings and does not depend entirely on reciprocity among States'.[224]

It is evident that in practice the problem addressed above is far more complex than would appear from a declaration of subordination to human rights law. So long as other states and, especially, non-states actors do not commit to respect human rights, violations like the ones addressed in *Sawhoyamaxa* will persist, given the increasing leverage and power of financial institutions and private corporations. The Court, however, did not refer to the conduct of these actors or to their (arguable) obligations to respect human rights, which is understandable. After all, the Court lacks jurisdiction to hold non-state actors and non-member states liable. Even so, more recently the Court has been inclined to highlight the emerging human rights norms moving in that direction. In the indigenous case of *Kalina and Lokono*, for example, the Court took 'note of the "Guiding Principles on Business and Human Rights", endorsed by the Human Rights Council of the United Nations, which establish that businesses must respect and protect human rights, as well as prevent, mitigate, and accept responsibility for the adverse human rights impacts directly linked to their activities'.[225] Although the rest of the analysis focused on the obligations of the respondent state, the fact that the Court 'took note' of those norms is remarkable.[226]

---

223 Ibid., para. 115(b).

224 Ibid., para. 140.

225 IACtHR, *The Kaliña and Lokono Peoples v. Suriname*, Judgment of 25 November 2015, para. 224.

226 For an argument in favour of integrating the human rights obligations of non-state actors into the Court's case law, see Lieselot Verdonck and Ellen Desmet, 'Moving human rights jurisprudence to a higher gear: rewriting the case of the Kichwa Indigenous People of Sarayaku v. Ecuador', in Eva Brems and Ellen Desmet (eds.), *Integrated human rights in practice* (Edward Elgar, 2017), at 467–473.

The fact that this kind of normativity is made visible and that the state is called upon to reconcile commercial and human rights helps account for the actual interaction taking place between different laws and actors. It also carries significance for political and legal mobilisation, while providing guidance and support to states wanting to uphold human rights. As noted in the previous chapter, incorporating international financial agreements and non-state actors into the picture may also illuminate the causes of poverty and inequality in a way that exposes the role of those actors and the law in creating it. This conversely reveals that the law can be used for challenging socio-economic disadvantage and the rights deprivations it engenders.

5. CONCLUDING REMARKS

So far there are very few rulings of the Inter-American Court in which questions of socio-economic disadvantage have had a protagonist role in the plight of litigants or in the Court's reasoning. Rather, this issue has been a contextual, supplementary consideration in several cases and in most of them the Court has shown a general sensitivity to the matter. Although usually addressed briefly, the Court has taken note of people's socio-economic disadvantage, which appears legally relevant. Thus, unlike what was seen in Chapter 4, in the Inter-American Court's case law economically neutral readings of cases are not really an issue. Poverty as such has furthermore been regarded as a factor that facilitates human rights violations and which affects the proportionality analysis and the reparation awards. The Court's predominant approach to poverty is that of something derivative from membership of a group historically discriminated against or rendered vulnerable. The Court thus frequently examines claims of socio-economic disadvantage through the angle of the rights of children, indigenous peoples, Afro-descendants, women and other disadvantaged groups. In the light of this and of its most recent judgments dealing with socio-economic disadvantage, it is possible to discern in the Court's discourse an openness to recognising people living in poverty as a group in a vulnerable situation, entitled to 'special protection'. Likewise, socio-economic disadvantage appears closely related to group discrimination. In addition, the IACtHR, unlike the ECtHR, does not show any particular deference or devise any particular categories of review for cases involving states' socio-economic policies. The compartmentalised analysis that often accompanies that line of reasoning before the ECtHR is not at issue either in this area of case law before the IACtHR.

An important consequence of the IACtHR's approach is that it helps to expose the elements of difference and inequality involved in the experience of poverty. Additionally, state obligations tend to be specified and subjected to stricter standards in that context. But while the Court has been able to integrate poverty within the experience of excluded identity groups; its judgment in *Hacienda Brasil Verde* shows that it has not done the same the other way around. Even so, the application of the prohibition of discrimination on the grounds of economic status represents a remarkable normative development. Moreover, the Court has taken important steps to bring to light the role of structural barriers and of what it has called 'structural discrimination'. Part of the transformative potential of the notion of structural discrimination as applied to poverty has, however, been diluted by the Court's oversight of racism and the lack of clarity on the content and scope of structural discrimination. This carries practical problems for both rights holders and state parties.

The Court's recent case law has nonetheless refined its analysis of socio-economic disadvantage from an intersectional perspective. This has led it to consider more closely the interaction between people's socio-economic disadvantage and other identities and social locations. Also of note is the fact that the Court has recently addressed, as a separate harm, the stigma, stereotypes and invisibility attached to the experience of poverty. This confirms that even in cases that are first and foremost about destitution and economic exploitation, there is a dimension of recognition that needs to and can be integrated. What is more, doing so helps to expose some of the underlying causes of violations.

While the issue of the protection of rights holders other than the applicants does not have much incidence in the case law studied here, it was possible to identify one area in which it may play an important role. This is the state's economic limitations and, more precisely, the prohibition of retrogression on socio-economic matters. Although this has not yet been discussed by the IACtHR, it was seen that taking into account a broad range of rights holders that is inclusive of those who are economically worst off may be helpful in illuminating whether and how the aforesaid prohibition (whether framed as such or as a limitation of Convention rights) is frustrating the state's redistributive efforts to improve the situation of people living in poverty. The Commission has undertaken this line of reasoning and it is possible that the Court may do so in future cases concerning socio-economic disadvantage.

An additional issue to highlight is that the Court has not always conducted an individualised assessment of proportionality where an integrated view of people living in poverty could play out significantly. This may partially explain the limited attention devoted to questions of autonomy in the cases studied. Nevertheless, where this has been discussed, it is remarkable that the Court has distanced itself from reductive narratives that depict impoverished people as fully autonomous or as denuded of agency. This allows a more comprehensive view of poverty and the rights violations it produces, while making it easier to build frameworks of international responsibility for poverty-related violations.

Unlike what was seen in cases concerning claims of cultural disadvantage, the normative repertoire used by the Court to deal with rights claims of socio-economic disadvantage is relatively broad. Besides reasons of treaty wording and litigation strategies, the variety of provisions used in this field may also have to do with the relative diffuse nature of poverty-related claims. Either way, the point is that these claims have been approached from different normative angles both substantively and procedurally. The Convention norms applied in this framework include the right to (a dignified) life (Article 4), the prohibition of slavery (Article 6) and the right to access justice (Articles 8 and 25), although these last provisions have been used more in the context of advisory opinions than in cases involving questions of socio-economic disadvantage. Only recently has the prohibition of discrimination (Articles 1.1 and 24) come to play an important role, while that of the right to property (Article 21) is still evolving. From the perspective of international law and also, gradually, comparative law, the quantity and variety of normative sources offered by the judgments studied is even larger. This is especially so in the most recent cases. Yet, the Court's holistic normative approach to claims of socio-economic difference offers some problematic aspects. In the first place, and similarly to what was seen in its case law on cultural difference, the Court still falls short of being sufficiently inclusive and non-selective. Further, while the comprehensive normative analyses undertaken by the Court have resulted in a proliferation of (at times, quite innovative) standards, these often lack clarity.

CONCLUSION

Given the complexities and concerns surrounding cases of cultural and economic disadvantage, it appears natural, so to say, to resort to the simplification offered by legal categories. Nevertheless, to differing degrees over-reliance on normative 'boxes' that bolster a unidimensional or fragmented analysis appears problematic for the handling of the cases studied and for similar future cases. In fact, approaching human rights norms and rights holders in a disaggregated fashion seems to exacerbate rather than alleviate the challenges identified in the Introduction and Chapter 1. However, the analysis conducted with regard to both the European and the Inter-American Courts of Human Rights also suggests that a degree of integration is already taking place and that moving further in this direction is both feasible and desirable. The trends, opportunities and challenges that have arisen along the way are discussed in this last chapter.

1. UNDERSTANDING COMMONALITIES AND DIVERGENCES BETWEEN THE REGIONAL COURTS

1.1. COMMONALITIES

The discussion in Part II (cultural difference) reveals that in a significant number of cases both courts adopt a normative approach centred on group ethno-cultural identity. This focus appears justified in several respects. Among these are the legal argumentation of the parties and the need to define who the applicant is in order to identify the set of rights and restrictions that are accordingly applicable. However, the culturally based legal framework also ends up mobilising a narrow set of legal arguments. Importantly, at times it overshadows the real-life experience of rights holders and a wider range of relevant harms and norms. This is particularly so in cases concerning a Roma way of life, the Islamic headscarf and indigenous/tribal culture. Thus, while the approach taken by the regional courts in these cases varies considerably, they share some interesting features.

One is that both courts undertake an appraisal of the value and meanings of those identities and cultures. In doing so, they essentialise them. They also, in different ways, overlook the circumstances of concrete individual applicants as well as those of other rights holders who are either similarly or differently situated *vis-à-vis* the applicants. Additionally, these judgments and decisions often address cultural harms and restrictions of civil and political rights, while making the socio-economic stakes of the cases more or less invisible. This is more acute in the case of the European Court than in the Inter-American Court. In cases where the normative salience of group identity is not accompanied by an emphasis on cultural affirmation or preservation, the normative oversights are less intense and integration is more present in both courts. Nonetheless, both courts display a more comprehensive stance at the level of the norms that are relevant to deciding the cases. They are quite keen on integrating international and regional norms. The tendency appears particularly strong in the case of the IACtHR, which in addition shows a readiness to consider customary or tradition-based norms.

Another remarkable commonality across the case law studied concerns something that was not really said or tackled: racism. Since the case law selection for claims related to cultural difference or disadvantage led to concentrating on ethno-cultural minorities (or non-dominant groups), it was anticipated that racism could be a problem at the background or the foreground of such cases. Questions of race and racism indeed underpin a large sample of cases concerning cultural difference, but both courts say little or nothing about this. With cases of socio-economic disadvantage, however, for which this book did not target any particular category of persons but a general segment of claimants in material hardship, the mediation of issues of racism was not so foreseeable. Yet, it turned out that several cases on economic difference examined by the two regional courts also involve ethno-cultural minorities, migrants, asylum seekers or persons with a migrant background. Taking an intersectional view of rights holders and cross-thinking about harms and norms in such cases brought to light, respectively, the applicants' racialised positions as well as risks of preconceptions and disparate effects based on race inequality. Interestingly, though, racism, a pervasive form of structural inequality, is left largely unchallenged, or not named at all by either of the regional courts. The question arises immediately: why? This book has been able to raise the question but not to offer an answer. The book's content and scope cannot provide an explanation of that oversight. What this book nonetheless suggests is, firstly, that the silence around race is irrespective of the integrated or fragmentary character of the legal analysis. Therefore, answers need to be found elsewhere. Secondly, this book also indicates that cultural and economic requirements or restrictions may be particularly burdensome for ethno-cultural minorities, migrants, asylum seekers or persons with a migrant background. And this, in turn, could mean that, at least in recent decades, racism may have been working more through cultural and economic measures than through blatant forms of racial exclusion.

The above, moreover, suggests that bringing together the examination of claims of cultural and economic disadvantage was worth doing. This book has shown that using the scholarship and normative developments regarding diversity and human rights provides interesting insights for dealing not just with people's cultural differences, but also with differences in economic position. It has been seen that both kinds of claim may have, as just noted, important commonalities. But the book also disclosed significant interactions. For instance, the legal approach developed in the context of one type of case may not work for the other (e.g. the identity focus applied to claims of cultural difference cannot easily be transposed to claims of economic disadvantage). Further, the harms and experiences that are typically associated with the realm of cultural rights claims can be relevant to cases dealing with socio-economic disadvantage and vice versa.

Similarly, it is interesting to observe that certain legal concepts or techniques (further discussed *infra* section 2.3) that are typically employed in one kind of case could well be useful for others. For instance, the use of participatory rights (such as prior consultation) that are usually associated with the handling of claims of ethno-cultural difference in indigenous cases may well serve in dealing with claims of economic disadvantage (such as those involving eviction or other serious restrictions affecting the rights of impoverished populations). Conversely, the concept of progressive realisation of rights and the related 'reasonability review', which are typically confined to dealing with socio-economic claims, could also assist in the resolution of cases concerning cultural difference. These cases may also raise issues of progressive change and review of public policy. At the same time, though, it was seen that both kinds of claims are understandably mobilised and addressed in different ways. Importantly, this book acknowledges that cultural aspects, especially those linked to cultural expression, are meaningful to people. They are part of people's sense of belonging and self-realisation. As such, it may be healthy to let normative assertions of cultural difference or identity flourish in a manner that does not apply to aspects of socio-economic difference, as the latter is most usually expressive of inequality and disadvantage.

1.2. DIVERGENCES

The discussion in Part III (economic disadvantage) shows more divergences than commonalities between the two courts. Firstly, the visibility and legal relevance of people's economic disadvantage are quite dissimilar. In the ECtHR both the applicants and the Court side-lined this on a number of occasions. But that was not so much the case at the Inter-American Court. Secondly, while the concept of group vulnerability appears unsuitable to people living in poverty for the ECtHR, the opposite holds true for the IACtHR. Thirdly, the legal discourses on autonomy and the degree of consideration given to socio-economic rights are also notably different. Although the IACtHR admittedly goes further in addressing discrimination and stigma for reasons of poverty, for a while the stance of the two Courts was not so different in this regard. Also less contrasting is their practice of normative integration as regards the incorporation of regional and international norms. Nevertheless, while the ECtHR shows substantial deference to states on socio-economic matters, the IACtHR does not. And while the ECtHR has not always used the normative insights provided by its consensus review, the IACtHR's reliance on comparative and regional law has been uneven.

A general salient difference is that the European Court appears more reluctant than the Inter-American Court to undertake a comprehensive analysis inspired by intersectionality and indivisibility. The Inter-American Court has also adopted an integrative stance that is more inclusive of customary norms and multiple international sources than the one applied by the European Court. However, the integration of regional norms by the Inter-American Court appears insufficiently systematic and inclusive. Moreover, its standard setting within the framework of extensive normative reviews lacks clarity in some cases. It is also worth mentioning that the ECtHR's emphasis on and deference to the state's identity or socio-cultural context does not seem to have been an issue at the Inter-American Court. The latter's jurisprudence lacks normative categories based on the state's characteristics. However, rather than a normative choice, this appears to be the likely consequence of not having much regard (deference) for the context or particularities of states parties.

It is fair to say then that the Inter-American Court has a general inclination to undertake a comprehensive review of the cases under examination and to respond to claims of cultural and economic difference. However, some caveats apply to this conclusion. First, one should bear in mind the relatively limited spectrum of cases dealing with cultural difference and economic disadvantage decided by the Court. As regards the former, they mostly concern indigenous or other persons and groups regarded as tribal, whose concerns and values happen to have attained broad international support. It has yet to be seen how the Court would address religious or other types of cultural claims, including those from unpopular minorities. As regards claims of economic disadvantage, the Court's responses need to be assessed in the context of a small sample of cases in which poverty-related violations have a prominent place in the arguments of the parties and/or the Court. Second, there are some aspects of the IACtHR's integrated approach that call for caution. For instance, it is important that the Court remains vigilant about the consequences of its preoccupation with groups, their characteristics and their disadvantages. In particular, it should be wary that this does not translate into an emphasis on the group, difference or disadvantage in itself (which amounts to essentialism) at the cost of individual circumstances and of social institutions. The Court also needs to review the limited inclusivity and lack of clarity in which it has often become embroiled in the pursuit of normative integration. Justifying why more weight is given to certain international or comparative sources and why departing from others, as well as clarifying the content and scope of standards set on the basis of extensive normative reviews, are required not only to preserve the Court's legitimacy. Doing so is also necessary to provide clear guidance to states and other stakeholders, which are confronted with an intricate multitude of relevant norms. This should also be seen in the context of judgments that are, on average, 120 pages long. This might sound trivial, but it is not. It makes the Court's profuse normative considerations, which are not always clear as to their value to the case at hand and to future cases, even less accessible.

Ultimately, the fact that the Inter-American Court is more inclined to engage in human rights integration has to do with the context in which the system developed. As explained in this book, an integrated approach to human rights tries to make law fit human beings and their reality, not the other way around. This effort was undertaken by the Inter-American Commission first and then by the Court when they started to monitor human rights in the region. This came from the need to respond to massive violations and to deal with recalcitrant states in a continent immersed in political conflict and widening economic inequality. As mentioned at the outset and further demonstrated by the case law discussed in this book, the Court's legal culture was significantly modelled on that reality. Or, to put it simply, it shaped its interpretations and working methods. Not by chance is the Inter-American Court used to conducting *in situ* visits to the affected areas/populations, engaging in extensive fact-finding work and receiving and hearing expert evidence from different disciplines. All these working methods facilitate a contextual and comprehensive view of the cases under examination. Take, for example, the *in situ* visits. To the extent that the Inter-American judges can verify for themselves the seriousness and the sorts of restriction complained of, it is easier for them to see the variety of actors, harms and norms involved in the cases. Had the European Court had the chance to visit the camping sites and the lands from which Roma and Travellers were evicted, for instance, would it have simply found, as it did, that alternative sites were available or that the claim about school disruption by the children was simply not substantiated?

Another factor that makes a difference is the role of the Inter-American Commission. The broad promotional powers enjoyed by this body, as explained in Chapter 1 have placed it in a position of proximity with the actual human rights problems of the region. The Commission is thus well familiarised with the context of the cases and the structural deficiencies leading to violations, both of which have been addressed through its monitoring activities. As a result of this, every time the Commission submits a case to the Court and intervenes before it, it brings to the latter a number of insights and claims based on its comprehensive view of the human rights situation in the respondent state and in the rest of the continent. It is not surprising, therefore, that the Commission has called upon the Court to declare the existence of structural discrimination; apply the notion of intersectionality; recognise the harm faced by rights holders other than the applicants; and address the links between poverty and rights violations.

Nevertheless, it is also important to point out that the regional context that forged both courts has changed. In the case of the Inter-American Court, most states now have (more or less consolidated) democracies, large-scale violations have receded and even the socio-economic landscape has improved in at least part of the region. The fact that the regional context has changed does not mean that the drive towards integration is no longer needed or useful – to the contrary. As seen in this book, 'new types' of human rights issues, such as claims concerning difference and inclusion, pose a number of challenges to human rights courts. Moreover, many of these claims raise complex issues such as structural violations, multiple identities and changing relations of power and disadvantage. To tackle these, the integrated framework proposed in this book retains utility. But at the same time, having more stable democracies and states willing to cooperate and dialogue about human rights implementation does reinforce the need to review the way the Inter-American Court engages in a project of human rights integration. This appears especially needed in view of the difficulties of consistency and inclusivity that the Court has displayed in its practice of resorting to a wide range of regional and international norms.

In light of the foregoing, it is also easier to understand the adjudication style of the European Court as well as the difficulties it faces in taking a more comprehensive and relational perspective on the cases. As noted in Chapter 1, the ECHR and the Court were set up in a very different scenario to that of the Inter-American system, one of mostly democratic states committed to human rights and with relatively similar political and historical traditions. For a while, the Court examined mostly isolated violations and fine-tuned human rights obligations. However, the European landscape has also changed significantly since the times of its origin. Notably, a number of member states are struggling with structural or even systematic violations and appear less cooperative. Likewise, older members face important changes and challenges after becoming much more plural and economically unequal than they used to be. Since the regional context has changed, so may the legal approaches to dealing with it. Thus, there is nothing fixed about the legal culture of the European Court of Human Rights that might impede its adaptation in a way that makes it more receptive to human rights integration than it is currently. In fact, the diversity of cultures coexisting in Europe makes changes in the Court's legal perspectives even more likely and legitimate.

In view of the distinct and common oversights and challenges that were identified in connection to the use of compartmentalised lines of reasoning, this book has found it to be desirable for the ECtHR and the IACtHR to take some distance from them. This does not mean that doing so is the only or even the main avenue for improving or enriching the adjudication of contested cases, such as those concerning cultural and economic difference. The analysis undertaken in this book nonetheless confirms that *one way* in which the European and Inter-American courts could do so is by embracing a more integrated approach to human rights law. While admittedly this could be interpreted as meaning a number of different things, this book has advanced one particular framework of analysis that could prove helpful. The following section first sums up the potential and actual opportunities, revealed by the case law studied, that make human rights integration helpful. Then, the discussion discloses the challenges and limitations that make human rights integration a difficult and ambitious enterprise.

2. OPPORTUNITIES, CHALLENGES AND TOOLS OF AN INTEGRATED APPROACH

2.1. OPPORTUNITIES OF AN INTEGRATED FRAMEWORK OF HUMAN RIGHTS LAW

A relational and integrated framework of human rights law such as the one applied in this book offers a number of opportunities for adjudicating claims about difference and inclusion. Notably, it has potential for (1) doing better justice to the lived experiences of rights holders; and (2) enriching the repertoire of relevant judicial arguments while illuminating alternative accounts of the cases. The opportunities created by 1 and 2 also mean that an integrated perspective holds potential for (3) delivering a context-sensitive justice and redirecting attention to the role of social relations and structures.

2.1.1. Doing Better Justice to the Lived Experiences of Rights Holders

The first level of integration applied in this book proposes to look holistically at the rights holders affected in a case. This means paying attention to their multiple social positions and the real-life conditions under which they exercise autonomy, while being attentive to rights holders other than the applicants. Doing this, as reflected by the case law analysis, has the potential to counterbalance the tendency to replace the concrete assessment of the applicants' experience with abstract and/or essentialist understandings of their identity. Likewise, it could lessen questionable assumptions about the agency of rights holders. By having a fuller picture of the rights holders and engaging in intersectionality analysis, courts could also render a more accurate account of the causes and effects of the restrictions and, in the case of the Inter-American Court, devise attuned remedies. Further, they could identify who are most disadvantaged and thus in need of differentiated responses or accommodation. Finally, such an understanding of rights holders could draw the courts' attention to customary and specific human rights norms tailored to the identities and social positions of those persons.

2.1.2. Enriching the Repertoire of Legal Arguments

The second level of integration applied in this book proposes to look holistically at the norms implicated in a case. By doing this, it has been seen that courts could open up the repertoire of available legal arguments, which would otherwise appear quite reduced in cases defined along relatively compartmentalised lines of reasoning. In addition, looking at harms and norms that are not immediately associated with the case (cross-thinking, as explained in the Introduction) has also proven to be useful. It could avoid displacing issues of socio-economic rights in cases of cultural difference and issues of stereotype or misrecognition in cases of economic disadvantage. For both kinds of case, such analysis could also bring to light structural inequalities and political marginalisation. A comprehensive normative approach could furthermore provide relevant grounds for justifying which rights claims are accommodated or granted heightened protection. Finally, by taking into account a broad set of norms, the courts could increase the normative interaction/dialogue with member states and with local communities in an inclusive and non-selective way, so as to embed contested decisions/ interpretations in regional and local reality. Along the way, courts could also gain insights that might help in assessing (usually in the context of a proportionality analysis) the use of less rights-restrictive alternatives to achieve legitimate goals.

2.1.3. Promoting Context-Sensitive Justice and Attention to Social Structures

Another positive aspect of using an integrated framework of human rights law to deal with complex or contested cases is its openness to divergent or 'unique' solutions that better fit the specific context of the case. This is to say that an integrated approach to human rights law, as understood here, is context-sensitive and does not aim at standardisation. In fact, at this point one may fairly argue that, eventually, all we have discussed thus far comes down to context. In other words, a view of human rights attentive to intersectionality and to other individuals and groups, as well as to related harms and norms, is all about context-sensitive adjudication. And indeed, it is.

Yet, it is submitted that the concepts and tools encompassed by the integrated framework applied here appear, in principle, to be more precisely defined and workable than the open-ended idea of context.

Moreover, it should be noted that each court has its specific ways of discussing questions of context. In the case of the European Court, for example, context-based arguments mostly concern a situation or climate prevailing in the respondent state. In dealing with claims of ethno-cultural difference, the ECtHR often refers to the state's commitment to equality, neutrality and secularism. Similarly, in cases involving economic disadvantage, the ECtHR pays attention to the state's budgetary constraints or to particular concerns behind its socio-economic policies. For the Inter-American Court, however, the preoccupation with context lies elsewhere. One of the main contextual issues considered by the IACtHR in both cultural and economic disadvantage cases is the history and social status of the group(s) to which the applicant allegedly belongs. The difference in approach is, again, more likely to be the result of historical and political factors than of legal considerations. Either way, the point is that context is not just about the political, cultural or socio-economic circumstances of the respondent state or the locality where the disputed events took place. But neither context needs to be reduced to the social status of any given group. Against this backdrop, acknowledging the multifaceted condition of rights holders and of the legal environment into which the cases are inserted promotes a context-sensitive view that is more inclusive and nuanced than the two versions just mentioned. The contextual impulse behind the integrated framework applied in this book has the advantage of not being too inclined towards any of those poles, while also considering the context of the individuals concerned.

In addition to context, the framework proposed has the potential to shift attention to social relations and structures, which may be some of the root causes of violations. This potential follows from several aspects of the framework. First, it starts from the perspective of rights holders, which makes it easier to pinpoint institutional exclusion and structural barriers. Second, the multiple positioning of rights holders is not examined from the angle of their identities as such, but from their social positions and the relations that attribute power and disadvantage to their identities. Looking at cases this way revealed, for example, the problems created by job and housing markets that penalise those (mostly women) undertaking care work; the incidence of racial discrimination and pervasive poverty in cases concerning Roma, Travellers and indigenous people; and institutional deficiencies in the reception of asylum seekers, to mention just some. Insofar as an integrated framework of human rights promotes a fuller understanding not just of the rights holders, but also of the norms and the harms at stake, it lessens the risk of reducing both the problem and the solution to the group or person concerned (more particularly, to her identity or personal autonomy) or to some normative category. If the problem and the solution are not reduced to that, then one may be inclined to look at social relations and institutions as well.

But many of the opportunities described above may not come to be realised. One reason for this is that, as this book suggests, an integrated approach to human rights law faces specific challenges and limitations.

2.2. CHALLENGES AND LIMITATIONS OF AN INTEGRATED FRAMEWORK OF HUMAN RIGHTS LAW

To start with, an integrated approach to human rights law such as the one applied in this book does not make the judicial task easy – to the contrary. Judges may not have the time, the resources or even the training to, for example, apply intersectionality or take into consideration a broad range of norms outside their material competence. This is the first big challenge. Hence, while the book has explored the potential offered by each dimension of integration advanced in this book, it does not seem realistic to expect human rights courts – or, for that matter, other courts of justice – to go into each and every 'layer' of integration. Yet, this book suggests that because of the relational character of the framework proposed, that is, because of the interaction between its different 'layers', it is likely that applying one of these 'layers' could lead to work with others, thus illuminating additional aspects of the case. For example, taking an intersectional approach to rights holders that exposes their multiple affiliations and social positions may reveal the relevance of international or tradition-based norms that are tailored to their specific experience or to which they feel bound. And this, in turn, will translate into a richer normative picture, thus reinforcing awareness of legal pluralism and normative integration.

Irrespective of the possibility that an integrated approach in one area may lead to its adoption in another, it is submitted that even doing a little bit of integration may be worthwhile. The analysis undertaken here suggests that any enlargement of the court's perception of complex cases could enrich the legal analysis, which would be a gain in itself. How much integration they undertake, however, cannot be answered only by reference to the courts' willingness or cultural predisposition to do so. As noted above, what this book has shown is that a satisfactory resolution of cases concerning cultural difference and economic disadvantage does not depend simply on the use of the model suggested in this book. In other words, it is not possible to say that the only or main explanation behind the normative perspectives applied by the two regional courts lies with the level of integration or fragmentation of human rights law. Nor can the explanation be exclusively situated in the legal traction of group identity arguments or other normative categories.

Extra-legal factors have proven to be of great importance. The political context and historical background in which human rights courts are embedded, as well as the working methods forged by those conditions, also play a decisive role, as already noted. Consequently, a move towards greater integration, in the sense advanced in this book, is not a success recipe for resolving difficult cases or for mitigating the anxiety they engender.

Up to this point the focus has been on the judges. However, there is no reason to think that judges are the only or main actors called upon to adopt an integrated human rights framework. Equally important is the role of litigants and third-party interveners. As seen in the previous chapters, the framing of the cases has depended to a large extent on the parties, so it is firstly up to them to present a fuller picture to the judges. It was also seen that third-party interveners may provide the courts with valuable empirical and normative material that helps judges to gain a richer understanding of the case at hand. Likewise, even if the integrated approach developed in this book fundamentally speaks to judges and litigants, several aspects of it may also be relevant for policy-making.[1]

But further challenges relate to the complexity that an integrated approach to human rights law adds to the adjudicatory task. In addition to questions of time, resources and expertise mentioned above, it should be noted that the application of an integrated approach to human rights may neither provide clear-cut answers to difficult cases nor lessen normative conflict or divergence. For one thing, such an approach distances itself from *a priori* formulas and category-centred reasoning to promote instead flexible and contextual decision-making. This might remove the concern about an endless proliferation of protected identities or categories, but it also removes handy forms of simplifying and anticipating the resolution of complex cases. For another thing, the endeavour to situate human rights norms in their broader normative environment (by integrating other relevant norms) and consider their interaction makes normative friction more, not less, visible and likely.

---

1 For an example of how an integrated approach like the one advanced here can be implemented in social policies, see e.g. Springtide Resources and United Way of Toronto, An Integrated Anti-Oppression Framework for Reviewing and Developing Policy. A Toolkit for Community Service Organizations (Toronto, 2008), at 4 and ff. ('Integrated anti-oppression looks at all the ways people can experience oppression and marginalization, and how those social locations intersect. This approach recognizes that individual contexts are different, and that people's lived realities are complex. It is integrated because it asks us to combine information and values from a range of people and sources in order to get a fuller, more inclusive result.') See also, United Nations Development Programme, *Humanity Divided: Confronting Inequality in Developing Countries* (UNDP, 2013), at 2 (noting that the complexity and multi-dimensionality of the drivers of inequality call for a complex and multi-dimensional response: one that involves e.g. social and fiscal policy, democratic institutions and anti-discrimination initiatives).

A third limitation has to do with the nature of litigation. Compared to other mechanisms for dealing with social conflict and disputes, litigation is probably one of the least suited to applying intersectionality and giving effect to the interdependence and indivisibility of rights. This follows from, among others, the intrinsic tendency of adjudication to categorise, the rigidity of evidentiary rules and the courts' limitations of material competence. For example, if in order to apply intersectionality courts were to require applicants to prove discrimination on each (intersecting) ground, it would be quite difficult to have intersectional discrimination legally enforced. Likewise, it is undeniable that for courts such as the ECtHR and until recently the IACtHR, which were originally entrusted with adjudicating civil and political rights, the ability to engage with the socio-economic rights dimension of cases is under permanent strain. From this perspective, it is always convenient to temper the expectations about what laws and tribunals can do while being encouraged to draw on the insights of human rights integration into social policy, politics and other fields.

Having said this, the following section will turn to a brief reflection on the legal techniques that were or could be helpful in developing an integrated approach to cases of cultural and economic difference or, for that matter, to other complex cases that may fall under a narrow frame of analysis.

2.3. SOME USEFUL LEGAL TOOLS AND CONCEPTS

The present book has elaborated on a few main avenues to promote an integrated analysis of cases that are often examined in a disaggregated fashion. Put simply, these avenues consist of intersectionality, indivisibility and normative interdependence. But the case law studied also provides interesting examples of specific mechanisms that foster an integrated analysis. These can be described as procedural and participatory tools. What is more, this book shows that while some legal concepts are taken as applying to claims of either cultural or economic difference, they may well serve to deal with the other. Making this mutual interaction visible may help human rights courts and other actors to use those legal concepts in a more integrated manner. The following lines thus provide a (non-exhaustive) overview of such procedural and participatory tools and legal concepts.

2.3.1. *Procedural and Participatory Tools*

Procedural tools: As already discussed, an integrated analysis has been facilitated not just by the substantive normative stance taken by the courts. In some cases, procedural mechanisms have played an important role. One notable example is the admission of third-party interventions. Particularly used in the practice of the ECtHR, these interventions have introduced a wide range of normative arguments while also providing contextual and empirical information about the rights holders involved in the cases. This has enabled the Court to access material that could significantly enrich its understanding of the cases and which might otherwise remain unknown to the Court. Third-party interventions are being increasingly used in the context of the Inter-American Court too.

A second and somewhat related tool is the use of expert evidence, which has been prominent in the practice of the Inter-American Court. It was seen that the insights of legal and non-legal experts from different disciplines have shed light on the living circumstances and harms faced by individuals and communities as well as on the political, historical and legal background of the cases. Again, this has allowed the Court to get a fuller picture of the cases in a way that probably would not have been possible without those experts' inputs.

A third notable tool is the opportunity to conduct *in-situ* visits or other working methods that ensure some proximity with the material reality in which the case takes place. The singular experience of the Inter-American Court reveals that first-hand contact with the context of a case makes it easier to develop a sense of the many actors and interests at stake. The practice is certainly uncommon for courts of justice and, as such, alien to the current options of many courts. Yet, it may be worth keeping it in mind, for working methods and evidentiary rules, like any other norm, evolve and change.

Participatory tools: The Inter-American jurisprudence on indigenous rights has shown the potential of legal tools for fostering people's participation. The Court has required states, at the least, to conduct informed consultation processes and, at best, to obtain the free prior and informed consent of indigenous communities on matters affecting them. By requiring states to undertake a process of dialogue, the Court has opened up a path that may bridge the abstract civil/political convention rights with indigenous people's cultural perspectives and economic needs. Participation can mitigate law's tendency to categorise and reify (cultural) identity claims. It may also bring to the surface a wider set of interests and concerns that may be relevant to resolving the dispute in question. While the European Court's case law studied here does not apply a consultation-like requirement, it does show that there are alternative ways to foster participation. One alternative is to assess, in the context of the proportionality analysis, the extent to which state authorities have attempted to engage in dialogue. In *Winterstein v. France*, for instance, the state authorities deliberately rejected the applicants' request to enter into mediation and participate in a study concerning their situation. In any case, it is important to bear in mind that, as mentioned earlier, there is no reason to think that participatory tools should be reserved for indigenous people or for cultural identity claims. Such mechanisms could well serve whenever the rights of otherwise unheard communities are threatened by regulations or decisions that overlook their specific needs, including economic ones. The requirements of consultation endorsed by other international bodies in the field of eviction and risk of homelessness (referred to in Chapter 2, section 3.2.2) attest to that.

2.3.2. Legal Concepts

Living instrument or dynamic interpretation: Seeking to update the respective human rights convention to current circumstances, both courts rely, although to differing extents, on normative sources derived from international, regional, national and even non-state law. This offers the courts a relatively comprehensive outlook on the cases. The concept of consensus also works along similar lines. Yet, for all these techniques it was seen that an important factor in getting the best out of those tools for integration is to avoid selectivity in the sources and arguments to be considered while being mindful of providing clear guidance and justifications about what weight is given to them.

Dignity: In the ECtHR's case law this concept appears to have been applied most frequently in relation to recognition and protection against humiliation. In the Inter-American Court's case law, however, the concept has been used in close connection with some level of socio-economic security, as reflected in the notion of dignified life. What these practices suggest is that although dignity may often be associated with either cultural/identity or socio-economic issues, it can actually be helpful for grasping both. Dignity is contingent and relational. As such, it lends itself as suitable for an integrated approach. This is also favoured by the concept's attention to rights holders and by its positive connotations, which arguably are more positive than those pertaining to the concept of vulnerability.

Vulnerability: In both areas of case law examined, the notion of vulnerability has appeared open to accounting not just for identity group disadvantages, but also for those resulting from economic precariousness. This was more notably the case with the IACtHR than the ECtHR. Previous chapters discussed some of the risks posed by the approach adopted by each court to the concept of vulnerability, so these will not be restated here. Instead, this reflection is interested in highlighting how this concept lends itself as suitable for an integrated analysis. Vulnerability appears to be comprehensive enough to account for varied and overlapping forms of risk and disadvantage, whether symbolic or material. It is also more flexible than other normative categories. It does not have clear boundaries and can be applied through substantive and procedural provisions. Notably, it may grasp issues of inequality without the constraints of equality law while bringing to light the role of social institutions in both producing and alleviating vulnerability.

Equality and non-discrimination: This legal concept has been interpreted, as seen in this book, in very different ways. As a result, it has produced quite disparate outputs. Nevertheless, the nature and normative place of equality and non-discrimination makes it, at least potentially, well suited to promoting an integrated view of human rights. In fact, the concept sits as a general principle of law that cuts across civil/political and socio-economic rights, as well as individual and group grievances. From the discussion in previous chapters, however, it appears that a substantive or structural reading of equality and non-discrimination provisions is more helpful to integration than alternative interpretations. Substantive equality enables the adjudicator to pinpoint structural, intersectional and *de facto* inequalities, including those on grounds of economic disadvantage. This might imply acknowledging, for example, that certain cultural patterns not only institutionalise cultural subordination but also socio-economic and political disadvantage, while the latter in turn reinforces cultural domination. An additional advantage of taking this perspective is that this does not require courts to define and protect any particular lifestyle or identity. From a substantive equality perspective, what matters is, rather, injustice and inequality, whether related to culture, identity, economic conditions or other circumstances.

Progressive realisation and reasonableness: The concept of progressive realisation has featured in the IACtHR's case law in relation to what has made it known, the legal enforcement of socio-economic rights. One of the main standards of review developed to operationalise the progressive realisation norm governing social rights is that of reasonableness. Although this concept was not applied as such in the case law reviewed, its underlying rationale was present in a few cases before both courts, mainly in relation to socio-economic policy. To determine whether states have discharged their obligations, courts apply reasonableness to scrutinise whether deliberate, concrete and non-discriminatory measures were adopted, as well as whether the disadvantaged position of certain groups were taken into account and situations of greater risk prioritised in the design and implementation of socio-economic policies. Through this concept they thus evaluate the adequacy, flexibility and aims of laws and policies, including related decision-making processes. So, one interesting feature of reasonableness is that it may facilitate the examination of the policies in place and thus the underlying institutional arrangements leading to violations. This, in turn, means analysing the case beyond legal categories and compartments, thus facilitating a more integrated approach to the issues debated. But here again one finds a useful legal concept that has been confined to one realm of rights claims, this time socio-economic issues. However, why not use this legal device to examine cultural/identity issues more comprehensively? After all, cultural/identity rights often require cultural change and thus time to be fully realised. In this respect, they are not so different from assertions of socio-economic rights. Further, cultural/identity disadvantages are usually institutionalised through norms and policies. Therefore, the review of social policies can also be of great assistance here.

Redefinition of legal concepts: The case law studied provided a number of examples of how redefining already established legal concepts made them flexible enough to integrate different interests and needs. This has been most notably achieved when the redefinition enlarges the array of human concerns and experiences underlying the concept. Examples are the reformulation of the right to property and the notion of 'injured party' (and thus, the concept of right holder) in the Inter-American Court's case law, as well as the inclusion of caravans and irregular houses within the notion of 'home' in the European Convention. Yet, often these redefinitions remain tailored to certain identities, as seems to be the case with collective property and collective rights holders for indigenous people. But why should these or other forms of conceptual expansion remain circumscribed to predefined categories or groups?

The above list is by no means exhaustive and aims more at opening rather than at closing the conversation. Just to give one additional example, one may well consider the potential for integration of the 'less restrictive means' test. In fact, it was seen that the rationale behind this tool is to question regulations or measures regarded as normal or acceptable from the viewpoint of reasonable alternatives. By doing this and forcing the state to explain why things could not be done differently, courts substantially enlarge their understanding of the case. This holds relevance for issues of both cultural and economic difference, which are particularly prone to be accepted or insufficiently scrutinised.

It is thus hoped that this book could encourage legal and non-legal actors involved in cases like those examined here to look beyond normative compartments and legal divides so as to interrogate whose and which rights are being considered or forgotten. This may, at the very least, increase the contextualisation of the cases and the crafting of more responsive, convincing rulings.

BIBLIOGRAPHY

Abramovich, Víctor; 'From Massive Violations to Structural Patterns: New Approaches and Classic Tensions in the Inter-American Human Rights System', 6(11) *SUR International Journal on Human Rights* (2009) 7–39.

——; 'Responsabilidad estatal por violencia de género: comentarios sobre el caso "Campo Algodonero" en la Corte Interamericana de Derechos Humanos', 6 *Anuario de Derechos Humanos* (2010) 167–182.

Acton, Thomas; Caffrey, Susan and Mundy, Gary; 'Theorizing Gypsy Law', 45(2) *The American Journal of Comparative Law* (1997) 237–249.

Addo, Michael K.; 'Practice of United Nations Human Rights Treaty Bodies in the Reconciliation of Cultural Diversity with Universal Respect for Human Rights', 32 *Human Rights Quarterly* (2010) 601–664.

Ajevski, Marjan; 'Fragmentation in International Human Rights Law – Beyond Conflict of Laws', 32(2) *Nordic Journal of Human Rights* (2014) 87–98.

Åkermark, Sia Spiliopoulou; 'Images of children in education: a critical reading of D.H. and Others v. Czech Republic', in Brems, Eva (ed.); *Diversity and European Human Rights. Rewriting Judgments of the ECHR* (Cambridge University Press, 2013).

Aktay, Yasin; 'European Values and the Muslim World: Turkish Cases at the European Court of Human Rights', 20(1) *Global Change Peace & Security* (2008) 99–108.

Alcoff, Linda Martín; Hames-Garcia, Michael; Mohanty, Satya P. and Moya, Paula M. L. (eds.); *Identity Politics Reconsidered* (Palgrave Macmillan, 2006).

Alcoff, Linda Martín and Mohanty, Satya P.; 'Reconsidering Identity Politics: An Introduction', in Alcoff, Linda Martin; Hames-Garcia, Michael; Mohanty, Satya P. and Moya, Paula M. L. (eds.); *Identity Politics Reconsidered* (Palgrave Macmillan, 2006).

Alexy, Robert; *Teoría de los derechos fundamentales* (Centro de Estudios Políticos y Constitucionales, 2008).

Allen, Anita L.; 'Coercing Privacy', 40(3) *William & Mary Law Review* (1999) 723–757.

Al Tamimi, Yussef; 'Human Rights and the Excess of Identity: A Legal and Theoretical Inquiry into the Notion of Identity in Strasbourg Case Law', 27(3) *Social and Legal Studies* (2018) 283–298.

Alvarado, Leonardo J.; 'Prospects and Challenges in the Implementation of Indigenous Peoples' Human Rights in International Law: Lessons from the Case of Awas Tingni v. Nicaragua', 24(3) *Arizona Journal of International & Comparative Law* (2007) 609–643.

American Anthropological Association, Executive Board; 'Statement on Human Rights', 49(4) *American Anthropologist* (1947) 539–543.

An-Na'im, Abdullahi A.; *Cultural Transformation and Human Rights in Africa* (Zed Books, 2002).

Anaya, S. James; *Indigenous Peoples in International Law* (Oxford University Press, 2004).

——; 'International Human Rights and Indigenous Peoples: The Move toward the Multicultural State', 21(1) *Arizona Journal of International & Comparative Law* (2004) 13–61.

Anderson, Carol; *Eyes off the Prize: the UN and the African American Struggle for Human Rights, 1944–1955* (Cambridge University Press, 2003).

Antkowiak, Thomas M.; 'Rights, Resources, and Rhetoric: Indigenous Peoples and the Inter-American Court', 35(1) *University of Pennsylvania Journal of International Law* (2013) 113–187.

——; 'A Dark Side of Virtue: The Inter-American Court and Reparations for Indigenous Peoples', 25(1) *Duke Journal of Comparative & International Law* (2014) 1–80.

Arnardóttir, Oddný Mjöll; 'The Differences that Make a Difference: Recent Developments on the Discrimination Grounds and the Margin of Appreciation under Article 14 of the European Convention on Human Rights', 14(4) *Human Rights Law Review* (2014) 647–670.

Arneil, Barbara; 'Recognizing Difference/Achieving Equality: Multiculturalism and Gender Justice', Paper Global Centre for Pluralism, Expert Roundtable on Canada's Experience with Pluralism (2008).

Ast, Frédérique; 'European legal frameworks responding to diversity and the need for institutional change. Indirect Discrimination as a means of protecting pluralism: challenges and limits', in Council of Europe; *Institutional Accommodation and the citizen: legal and political interaction in a pluralist society*, Trends in Social Cohesion No. 21 (Council of Europe, 2009).

Baer, Susanne; 'Dignity, liberty, equality: A fundamental rights triangle of constitutionalism', 59(4) *The University of Toronto Law Journal* (2009) 417–468.

——; 'A Closer Look at Law: Human Rights as Multi-Level Sites of Struggles over Multi-Dimensional Equality', 6(2) *Utrecht Law Review* (2010) 56–76.

——; 'Privatizing Religion. Legal Groupism, No-Go-Areas, and the Public-Private-Ideology in Human Rights Politics', 20(1) *Constellations* (2013) 68–84.

Bamforth, Nicholas; Malik, Maleiha and O'Cinneide, Colm; *Discrimination Law: Theory and Context, Text and Materials* (Sweet and Maxwell, 2008).

Banting, Keith G.; 'The Multicultural Welfare State: International Experience and North American Narratives', 39(2) *Social Policy & Administration* (2005) 98–115.

Barnes, Colin; 'Understanding Disability and the Importance of Design for All', 1(1) *Journal of Accessibility and Design for All* (2011) 55–80.

Barnes, Mario L. and Chemerinsky, Erwin; 'The Disparate Treatment of Race and Class in Constitutional Jurisprudence', 72(4) *Law and Contemporary Problems* (2009) 109–130.

Barry, Brian; *Culture and Equality: An Egalitarian Critique of Multiculturalism* (Polity Press, 2001).

Bartlett, Katharine T.; 'Feminist Legal Methods', 103(4) *Harvard Law Review* (1990) 829–888.

Baumgärtel, Moritz; 'Perspectives on the User: Unpacking a Concept for Human Rights Research', 8(2) *Human Rights & International Legal Discourse* (2014) 142–157.

Bazán, Víctor; 'El Control de convencionalidad: incógnitas, desafíos y perspectivas', in Bazán, Víctor and Nash, Claudio (eds.); *Justicia Constitucional y Derechos Fundamentales: El Control de Convencionalidad* (Fundación Konrad Adenauer, 2012).

Benedetto Neitz, Michele; 'Socioeconomic Bias in the Judiciary', 61 *Cleveland State Law Review* (2013) 137–165.

Benhabib, Seyla; *The Claims of Culture: Equality and Diversity in the Global Era* (Princeton University Press, 2002).

Berman, Paul Schiff; 'Global Legal Pluralism', 80 *Southern California Law Review* (2007) 1155–1237.

Bhamra, Meena K.; *The Challenge of Justice in Diverse Societies: Constitutionalism and Pluralism* (Ashgate, 2011).

Binder, Guyora and Weisberg, Robert; *Literary Criticism of Law* (Princeton University Press, 2000).

Bobbio, Norberto; *Igualdad y Libertad* (Paidós Ibérica, 1993).

Bomhoff, Jacco; '"The Rights and Freedoms of Others": The ECHR and its Peculiar Category of Conflicts between Individual Fundamental Rights', in Brems, Eva (ed.); *Conflicts Between Fundamental Rights* (Intersentia, 2008).

Bond, Johanna E.; 'International Intersectionality: A Theoretical and Pragmatic Exploration of Women's International Human Rights Violations', 52 *Emory Law Journal* (2003) 71–187.

Bossuyt, Marc; 'Is the European Court of Human Rights on a slippery slope?', in Flogaitis, Spyridon; Zwart, Tom and Fraser, Julie (eds.); *The European Court of Human Rights and Its Discontents: Turning Criticism into Strength* (Edward Elgar, 2013).

Bouchard, Johanne and Meyer-Bisch, Patrice; 'Intersectionality and Interdependence of Human Rights: Same or Different?', 16 *The Equal Rights Review* (2016) 186–203.

Brems, Eva; *Human Rights: Universality and Diversity* (Martinus Nijhoff Publishers, 2001).

——; 'Reconciling Universality and Diversity in International Human Rights: A Theoretical and Methodological Framework and Its Application in the Context of Islam', 5(3) *Human Rights Review* (2004) 5–20.

——; 'Reconciling Universality and Diversity in International Human Rights Law', in Sajó, András (ed.); *Human Rights with Modesty: The Problem of Universalism* (Springer, 2004).

——; 'Accommodating Diversity in International Human Rights: Legal Techniques', in Meerts, Paul (ed.); *Culture and International Law* (Hague Academic Press, 2008).

——; 'Human Rights as a framework for negotiating/protecting cultural differences: an exploration of the case-law of the European Court of Human Rights', in Foblets, Marie-Claire; Gaudreault-DesBiens, Jean-François and Dundes Renteln, Alison (eds.); *Cultural Diversity and the Law: State Responses Around the World* (Bruylant, 2010).

——; 'Introduction: rewriting decisions from a perspective of human rights integration', in Brems, Eva and Desmet, Ellen (eds.); *Integrated Human Rights in Practice. Rewriting Human Rights Decisions* (Edward Elgar, 2017).

——; 'Should Pluriform Human Rights Become One? Exploring the Benefits of Human Rights Integration', 4 *European Journal of Human Rights* (2014) 447–470.

—— (ed.); *The Experiences of Face Veil Wearers in Europe and the Law* (Cambridge University Press, 2014).

Brems, Eva and Desmet, Ellen; 'Studying Human Rights from the Perspective(s) of its Users', 8(2) *Human Rights and International Legal Discourse* (2014) 111–292.

Brems, Eva and Ouald Chaib, Saïla (eds.); *Fragmentation and Integration in Human Rights Law* (Edward Elgar, 2018).

Bribosia, Emmanuelle and Rorive, Isabelle; *Reasonable Accommodation beyond Disability in Europe?* (European Commission, 2013).

——; *Human Rights Tectonics* (Intersentia, 2018).

Bridgewater, Pamela; 'Gonzales v. Carhart: Continuing the Class Critique of the Reproductive Rights Doctrine and Movement', 59(4) *South Carolina Law Review* (2008) 827–840.

Brodsky, Gwen and Day, Shelagh; 'Poverty is a Human Rights Violation', paper prepared for the December 2001 consultation of The Poverty and Human Rights Project (Canada).

——; 'Beyond the Social and Economic Rights Debate: Substantive Equality Speaks to Poverty', 14 *Canadian Journal of Women and the Law* (2002) 184–219.

——; 'Denial of the means of subsistence as an equality violation', *Acta Juridica* (2005) 149–170.

Brooks, Peter; 'Narrative in and of the Law', in Phelan, James and Rabinowitz, Peter J. (eds.); *A Companion to Narrative Theory* (Blackwell Publishing, 2005).

Brown, Wendy; *Regulating Aversion Tolerance in the Age of Identity and Empire* (Princeton University Press, 2008).

——; 'Civilizational delusions: Secularism, tolerance, equality', 15(2) *Theory & Event* (2012).

Brubaker, Rogers; 'The Return of Assimilation? Changing Perspectives on Immigration and Its Sequels in France, Germany, and the United States', 24(4) *Ethnic and Racial Studies* (2001) 531–548.

——; 'Ethnicity without Groups', 43(2) *Archives Européennes de Sociologie* (2002) 163–189.

——; *Ethnicity without Groups* (Harvard University Press, 2004).

Bunting, Annie; 'Theorizing Women's Cultural Diversity in Feminist International Human Rights Strategies', 20(1) *Journal of Law and Society* (1993) 6–22.

Burgorgue-Larsen, Laurence; 'La Corte Interamericana de Derechos Humanos como tribunal constitucional', in Fix-Fierro, Héctor; von Bogdandy, Armin and Morales Antoniazzi, Mariela (coords.); *Ius Constitutionale Commune en América Latina. Rasgos, potencialidades y desafíos* (UNAM, 2014).

Burgorgue-Larsen, Laurence and Úbeda De Torres, Amaya; *The Inter-American Court of Human Rights. Case Law and Commentary* (Oxford University Press, 2011).

Burke, Roland; 'Confronting "Indivisibility" in the History of Economic and Social Rights: From Parity to Priority and Back Again', 12 *Human Rights and Human Welfare* (2012) 53–69.

Calabresi, Guido; *Ideals, Beliefs, Attitudes and the Law. Private Law Perspectives on a Public Law Problem* (Syracuse University Press, 1985).

Calder, Gideon and Ceva, Emanuela; *Diversity in Europe. Dilemmas of differential treatment in theory and practice* (Routledge, 2001).

Campbell, Fiona Kumari; *Contours of Ableism: The Production of Disability and Abledness* (Palgrave Macmillan, 2009).

Cançado Trindade, Antonio Augusto; 'Reflexiones sobre el Futuro del Sistema Interamericano de Protección de los Derechos Humanos', in Méndez, Juan E. and Cox, Francisco (eds.); *El Futuro del Sistema Interamericano de Protección a los Derechos Humanos* (IIDH, 1998).

Castilla Juárez, Karlos A.; '¿Control Interno o Difuso de Convencionalidad? Una Mejor Idea: la Garantía de Tratados', 13 *Anuario Mexicano de Derecho Internacional* (2013) 51–97.

Charlesworth, Hilary; 'Feminist Critiques of International Law and Their Critics', 13 *Third World Legal Studies* (1994) 1–16.

Chimni, Bhupinder S.; 'Third World Approaches to International Law: A Manifesto' 8 *International Community Law Review* (2006) 3–27.

Chinchilla, Fernando A.; Parra Vera, Oscar and Cáceres, Luis René; 'Pobreza y Derechos Humanos: hacia la definición de parámetros conceptuales desde la doctrina y acciones del sistema interamericano', in Instituto Interamericano de Derechos Humanos; *¿Quién* *responde por los derechos humanos de las poblaciones más pobres en América Latina y El Caribe? Democracia vs desigualdad 2007–2011* (Instituto Interamericano de Derechos Humanos, 2012).

Cho, Sumi; 'Post-Intersectionality. The Curious Reception of Intersectionality in Legal Scholarship', 10(2) *Du Bois Review: Social Science Research on Race* (2013) 385–404.

Choudhry, Sujit; 'Distribution vs. Recognition: The Case of Antidiscrimination Laws', 9(1) *George Mason Law Review* (2000) 145–178.

Choudhury, Tufyal; 'Muslims and Discrimination', in Amghar, Samir; Boubekeur, Amel and Emerson, Michael (eds.); *European Islam: Challenges for Society and Public Policy* (Center for European Policy Studies, 2008).

Chow, Pok Yin S.; 'Has Intersectionality Reached its Limits? Intersectionality in the UN Human Rights Treaty Body Practice and the Issue of Ambivalence', 16 *Human Rights Law Review* (2016) 453–481.

Clarke, Jessica A.; 'Beyond Equality? Against the Universal Turn in Workplace Protections', 86(4) *Indiana Law Journal* (2011) 1219–1287.

Clements, Luke and Read, Janet; 'The Dog that Didn't Bark: The Issue of Access to Rights Under the European Convention on Human Rights by Disabled People' in Lawson, Anna and Gooding, Caroline (eds.); *Disability Rights in Europe. From Theory to Practice: Essays in European Law* (Hart Publishing, 2005).

Collins, Dana; Falcón, Sylvanna; Lodhia, Sharmila and Talcott, Molly; 'New Directions in Feminism and Human Rights. An Introduction', 12(3–4) *International Feminist Journal of Politics* (2010) 298–318.

Collins, Hugh; 'Discrimination, Equality and Social Inclusion', 66(1) *The Modern Law Review* (2003) 16–43.

Collins, Patricia Hill; *Black Feminist Thought: Knowledge, Consciousness, and the Politics of Empowerment* (Routledge, 2000).

Collins, Patricia Hill and Bilge, Sirma; *Intersectionality* (Polity Press, 2016).

Conaghan, Joanne; 'Intersectionality and the Feminist Project in Law', in Grabham, Emily; Cooper, Davina; Krishnadas, Jane and Herman, Didi (eds.); *Intersectionality and Beyond: Law, power and the politics of subjectivity* (Routledge Cavendish, 2008).

Cook, Rebecca J. and Cusack, Simone, *Gender Stereotyping: Transnational Legal Perspectives* (University of Pennsylvania Press, 2010).

Coombe, Rosemary J.; 'Legal Claims to Culture in and Against the Market: Neoliberalism and the Global Proliferation of Meaningful Difference', 1(1) *Law Culture and the Humanities* (2005) 35–52.

Cooper, Davina; *Challenging Diversity: Rethinking Equality and the Value of Difference* (Cambridge University Press, 2004).

Council of Europe; *Institutional Accommodation and the citizen: legal and political interaction in a pluralist society*, Trends in Social Cohesion No. 21 (Council of Europe, 2009).

Cowan, Jane K.; Dembour, Marie-Bénédicte and Wilson, Richard A. (eds.); *Culture and Rights. Anthropological Perspectives* (Cambridge University Press, 2001).

Crenshaw, Kimberle; 'Demarginalizing the Intersection of Race and Sex: A Black Feminist Critique of Antidiscrimination Doctrine, Feminist Theory and Antiracist Politics', 140 *University of Chicago Legal Forum* (1989) 139–167.

——; 'Mapping the Margins: Intersectionality, identity politics and violence against women of Color', 43(6) *Stanford Law Review* (1991) 1241–1299.

Crooms, Lisa A.; 'Indivisible Rights and Intersectional Identities or, What Do Women's Human Rights Have to Do with the Race Convention', 40(3) *Howard Law Journal* (1996) 619–640.

Cusack, Simone and Pusey, Lisa; 'CEDAW and the Rights to Non-Discrimination and Equality', 14(1) *Melbourne Journal of International Law* (2013) 54–92.

Danchin, Peter G.; 'Islam in the Secular Nomos of the European Court of Human Rigths', 32(4) *Michigan Journal of International Law* (2011) 663–747.

David, Valeska; 'The Inauguration of the Inter-American Defenders' Era: Reflections after the *Furlan* Case', 7 *Inter-American and European Human Rights Journal* (2014) 245–268.

——; 'Caring, rescuing or punishing? Rewriting RMS v Spain (ECtHR) from an integrated approach to the rights of women and children in poverty', in Brems, Eva and Desmet, Ellen (eds.); *Integrated Human Rights in Practice: Rewriting Human Rights Decisions* (Edward Elgar, 2017).

——; 'The Inter-American concept of structural equality and discrimination', 2(2) *Anti-Discrimination Law Review* (2017) 5–27.

David, Valeska and Fraser, Julie; 'A Legal Pluralist Approach to the Use of Cultural Perspectives in the Implementation and Adjudication of Human Rights Norms', 23 *Buffalo Human Rights Law Review* (2017) 75–118.

Dembour, Marie-Bénédicte; *Who Believes in Human Rights? Reflections on the European Convention* (Cambridge University Press, 2006).

——; 'Critiques' in Moeckli, Daniel; Shah, Sangeeta and Sivakumaran, Sandesh (eds.); *International Human Rights Law* (Oxford University Press, 2014).

Desmet, Ellen; 'Analysing User's Trajectories in Human Rights: A Conceptual Exploration and Research Agenda', 8(2) *Human Rights and International Legal Discourse* (2014) 121–141.

——; 'Methodologies to Study Human Rights Law as an Integrated Whole from a Users Perspective: Lessons Learnt', in Brems, Eva and Ouald Chaib, Saïla (eds.); *Fragmentation and Integration in Human Rights Law* (Edward Elgar, 2018).

Detrick, Sharon (ed.); *The United Nations Convention on the Rights of the Child. A Guide to the "Travaux Préparatoires"* (Martinus Nijhoff Publishers, 1992).

Dhamoon, Rita; *Identity/Difference Politics. How Difference is Produced, and Why It Matters* (UBC Press, 2009).

Van Dijk, Pieter; Van Hoof, Fried; Van Rijn, Arjen; Zwaak, Leo and Flinterman, Cees (eds.); *Theory and Practice of the European Convention on Human Rights* (Intersentia, 2006).

Donders, Yvonne M.; *Human Rights: Eye for Cultural Diversity* (Amsterdam University Press, 2012). Inaugural Lecture delivered upon the appointment to the chair of Professor of International Human Rights and Cultural Diversity at the University of Amsterdam on 29 June 2012.

Donnelly, Jack; 'The Relative Universality of Human Rights', 29(2) *Human Rights Quarterly* (2007) 281–306.

Douzinas, Costas; 'The poverty of (rights) jurisprudence', in Gearty, Conor and Douzinas, Costas (eds.); *The Cambridge Companion to Human Rights Law* (Cambridge University Press, 2012).

Doz Costa, Fernanda; 'Poverty and Human Rights: From Rhetoric to Legal Obligations, a Critical Account of Conceptual Frameworks', 5(9) *Sur – International Journal of Human Rights* (2008) 81–107.

Duggan, Lisa; *The Twilight of Equality? Neoliberalism, Cultural Politics and the Attack on Democracy* (Beacon Press, 2004).

Dulitzky, Ariel E.; 'Pobreza y derechos humanos en el sistema interamericano. Algunas aproximaciones preliminares', 48 *Revista Instituto Interamericano de Derechos Humanos* (2008) 107–134.

——; 'When Afro-Descendants Became 'Tribal Peoples': The Inter-American Human Rights System and Rural Black Communities', 15(1) *UCLA Journal of International Law and Foreign Affairs* (2010) 29–81.

——; 'A Region in Denial: Racial Discrimination and Racism in Latin America', in Harris, Angela P. (ed.); *Race and Equality Law* (Routledge, 2013).

——; 'An Inter-American Constitutional Court? The Invention of the Conventionality Control by the Inter-American Court of Human Rights', 50(1) *Texas International Law Journal* (2015) 45–93.

Dworkin, Ronald; 'What is equality? Part 1: Equality of welfare', 10(3) *Philosophy & Public Affairs* (1981) 185–246.

——; *Sovereign Virtue. The Theory and Practice of Equality* (Harvard University Press, 2002).

Ehrenreich, Nancy; 'Subordination and Symbiosis: Mechanisms of Mutual Support Between Subordination Systems', 71(2) *UMKC Law Review* (2002) 251–324.

Eisen, Jessica; 'On Shaky Grounds: Poverty and Analogous Grounds under the Charter', 2(2) *Canadian Journal of Poverty Law* (2013) 1–33.

Eisenberg, Avigail; *Reasons of Identity: A Normative Guide to the Political & Legal Assessment of Identity Claims* (Oxford University Press, 2009).

——; 'Rights in the Age of Identity Politics', 50(3) *Osgoode Hall Law Journal* (2013) 609–636.

Engle, Karen; 'Culture and Human Rights: The Asian Values Debate in Context', 32(2) *NYU Journal of International Law and Politics* (2000) 291–334.

——; 'From Skepticism to Embrace: Human Rights and the American Anthropological Association from 1947–1999', 23(3) *Human Rights Quarterly* (2001) 536–559.

——; *The Elusive Promise of Indigenous Development: Rights, Culture, Strategy* (Duke University Press, 2010).

——; 'On Fragile Architecture: The UN Declaration on the Rights of Indigenous Peoples in the Context of Human Rights', 22(1) *European Journal of International Law* (2011) 141–163.

The Equal Rights Trust; 'Combating Poverty through Equality Law – Possibilities and Pitfalls: ERT talks with Sandra Fredman and Margarita Ilieva', 3 *The Equal Rights Review* (2009) 83–93.

Eskridge Jr., William N.; 'Some Effects of Identity-Based Social Movements on Constitutional Law in the Twentieth Century', 100 *Michigan Law Review* (2002) 2062–2184.

Evans, Carolyn; *Freedom of Religion Under the European Convention on Human Rights* (Oxford University Press, 2001).

——; 'The 'Islamic Scarf' in the European Court of Human Rights', 7(1) *Melbourne Journal of International Law* (2006) 52–73.

——; 'Individual and Group Religious Freedom in the European Court of Human Rights: Cracks in the Intellectual Architecture', 26(1) *Journal of Law and Religion* (2010) 321–343.

Evans, Malcolm and Petkoff, Peter; 'A Separation of Convenience? The Concept of Neutrality in the Jurisprudence of the European Court of Human Rights', 36(3) *Religion, State and Society* (2008) 205–223.

Farmer, Alice; 'Towards a Meaningful Rebirth of Economic Self-Determination: Human Rights Realization in Resource-Rich Countries', 39 *International Law and Politics* (2006) 417–473.

De Feyter, Koen; 'Localizing Human Rights', 2 *Discussion Paper*, Institute of Development Policy and Management, University of Antwerp (2006).

Fineman, Martha Albertson; 'The Vulnerable Subject: Anchoring Equality in the Human Condition', 20(1) *Yale Journal of Law & Feminism* (2008) 1–23.

——; 'Equality and Difference – The Restrained State', 66(3) *Alabama Law Review* (2015) 609–626.

Fiss, Owen M.; 'Groups and the Equal Protection Clause', 5(2) *Philosophy & Public Affairs* (1976) 107–177.

——; 'The Forms of Justice', 93(1) *Harvard Law Review* (1979) 1–58.

——; 'The Allure of Individualism', 78 *Iowa Law Review* (1993) 965–979.

——; 'Another Equality', 2(1) *Issues in Legal Scholarship*. Symposium: The Origins and Fate of Antisubordination Theory (2004).

Fludernik, Monika; 'A Narratology of the Law? Narratives in Legal Discourse', 1(1) *Critical Analysis of Law* (2014) 87–109.

Foster, Michelle; 'Non-Refoulement on the Basis of Socio-Economic Deprivation: The Scope of Complementary Protection in International Human Rights Law', 2 *New Zealand Law Review* (2009) 257–310.

Fournier, Pascale; 'Headscarf and burqa controversies at the crossroad of politics, society and law', 19(6) *Social Identities* (2013) 689–703.

Fournier, Pascale and Yurdakul, Gökçe; 'Unveiling Distribution: Muslim Women with Headscarves in France and Germany', in Bodemann, Y. Michal and Yurdakul, Gökçe (eds.); *Migration, Citizenship, Ethnos* (Palgrave Macmillan, 2006).

Fraser, Nancy; *Justice Interruptus: Critical reflections on the "postsocialist" condition* (Routledge, 1997).

——; 'Rethinking Recognition', 3 *New Left Review* (2000) 107–118.

——; 'Social Justice in the Age of Identity Politics: Redistribution, Recognition, and Participation', in Fraser, Nancy and Honneth, Axel; *Redistribution or Recognition? A Political Philosophical Exchange* (Verso, 2003).

Fraser, Nancy and Honneth, Axel; *Redistribution or Recognition? A Political Philosophical Exchange* (Verso, 2003).

Fraser, Nancy and Nicholson, Linda J.; 'Social Criticism without Philosophy: An Encounter between Feminism and Postmodernism', in Meyers, Diana Tietjens (ed.); *Feminist Social Thought: A Reader* (Routledge, 1997).

Fredman, Sandra; 'Beyond the Dichotomy of Formal and Substantive Equality: Towards a New Definition of Equal Rights', in Boerefijn, Ineke; Coomans, Fons; Goldschmidt, Jenny E.; Holtmaat, Rikki and Wolleswinkel, Ria (eds.); *Temporary special measures: Accelerating De Facto Equality of Women under Article 4(1) UN Convention on the Elimination of All Forms of Discrimination Against Women* (Intersentia, 2003).

——; 'Disability Equality and the Existing Paradigm', in Lawson, Anna and Gooding, Caroline (eds.); *Disability Rights in Europe: From Theory to Practice* (Hart Publishing, 2005).

——; 'Providing Equality: Substantive Equality and the Positive Duty to Provide', 21(2) *South African Journal on Human Rights* (2005) 163–190.

——; 'Redistribution and Recognition: Reconciling Inequalities', 23(2) *South African Journal of Human Rights* (2007) 214–234.

——; 'Facing the Future: Substantive Equality Under the Spotlight', *Oxford University Legal Studies Research Series Paper No. 57/2010* (2010).

——; 'Positive Duties and Socio-Economic Disadvantage: Bringing Disadvantage onto the Equality Agenda', 55 *University of Oxford Legal Research Paper Series* (2010).
——; *Discrimination Law* (Oxford University Press, 2011).
——; 'The Potential and Limits of an Equal Rights Paradigm in Addressing Poverty', 22(3) *Stellenbosch Law Review* (2011) 566–590.
——; 'Substantive equality revisited', 14(3) *International Journal of Constitutional Law* (2016) 712–738.
Fredman, Sandra and Goldblatt, Beth; 'Gender Equality and Human Rights', 4 *UN Women Discussion Paper Series* (2014).
Freeman, Alan David; 'Legitimizing Racial Discrimination Through Antidiscrimination Law: A Critical Review of Supreme Court Doctrine', 62 *Minnesota Law Review* (1978) 1049–1119.
Freitas Mohallen, Michael; 'Horizontal Judicial Dialogue in South America', in Müller, Amrei (ed.); *Judicial Dialogue and Human Rights* (Cambridge University Press, 2017).
Fuentes, Carlos Iván; Provost, René and Walker, Samuel G.; 'E Pluribus Unum – Bhinneka Tunggal Ika? Universal Human Rights and the Fragmentation of International Law', in Provost, René and Sheppard, Colleen; *Dialogues on Human Rights and Legal Pluralism* (Springer, 2012).
Ganty, Sarah; 'Civic Integration Tests under the Control of the European Court of Justice: A Perilous Tightrope Walk between Margin of Appreciation of the Member States and Protection of Third Country Nationals', 1 *European Journal of Human Rights* (2016) 32–56.
Ganty, Sarah and Vanderstraeten, Maxime; 'Actualités de La Lutte Contre La Discrimination Dans Les Biens et Les Services, En Ce Compris L'enseignement', in Bribosia, Emmanuelle; Rorive, Isabelle and Van Drooghenbroeck, Sébastien (eds.); *Droit de la Non-discrimination – Avancées et enjeux* (Bruylant, 2016).
García Bedolla, Lisa; 'Intersections of Inequality: Understanding Marginalization and Privilege in the Post-Civil Rights Era', 3(2) *Politics & Gender* (2007) 232–248.
Gerards, Janneke; 'Pluralism, deference and the margin of appreciation doctrine', 17(1) *European Law Journal* (2011) 80–120.
——; 'The ECtHR's Response to Fundamental Rights Issue related to Financial and Economic Difficulties – The Problem of Compartmentalisation', 33(3) *Netherlands Quarterly of Human Rights* (2015) 274–292.
Gerds, Johannes; 'Human Rights of People Experiencing Poverty in Europe: Standards, Obstacles and Perspectives of Protection in Council of Europe Instruments. Part 1: The European Convention on Human Rights', in Council of Europe, *Redefining and Combating Poverty: Human Rights, Democracy and Common Goods in Today's Europe*, Trends in Social Cohesion, No. 25 (Council of Europe Publishing, 2012).
Gerken, Heather K.; 'Larry and Lawrence', 42 *Tulsa Law Review* (2007) 843–856.
Golder, Ben; 'Beyond Redemption? Problematising the Critique of Human Rights in Contemporary International Legal Thought', 2(1) *London Review of International Law* (2014) 77–114.
Goldman, Robert K.; 'History and Action: the Inter-American Human Rights System and the Role of the Inter-American Commission on Human Rights', 31(4) *Human Rights Quarterly* (2009) 856–887.
Gómez Isa, Felipe; 'Cultural Diversity, Legal Pluralism, and Human Rights from an Indigenous Perspective: The Approach by the Colombian Constitutional Court and the Inter-American Court of Human Rights', 36(4) *Human Rights Quarterly* (2014) 722–755.

Goodhart, David; 'Too Diverse?', *Prospect*, February (2004).

Goodhart, Michael; 'Neither Relative nor Universal: A Response to Donnelly', 30 *Human Rights Quarterly* (2008) 183–193.

Grear, Anna; "Framing the Project' of international human rights law: Reflections on the dysfunctional 'family' of the Universal Declaration', in Gearty, Conor and Douzinas, Costas (eds.); *The Cambridge Companion to Human Rights Law* (Cambridge University Press, 2012).

Grillo, Trina; 'Anti-Essentialism and Intersectionality: Tools to Dismantle the Master's House', 10 *Berkeley Women's Law Journal* (1995) 16–30.

Gunn, T. Jeremy; 'The Complexity of Religion and the Definition of "Religion" in International Law', 16 *Harvard Human Rights Journal* (2003) 189–215.

Hall, Margaux J.; Ahmed, Aziza and Swanson, Stephanie E.; 'Answering the Millennium Call for the Right to Maternal Health: The Need to Eliminate User Fees', 12(1) *Yale Human Rights and Development Journal* (2009) 62–119.

Harris, Angela P.; 'Race and Essentialism in Feminist Legal Theory', 42 *Stanford Law Review* (1990) 581–616.

——; 'Theorizing Class, Gender, and the Law: Three Approaches', 72 *Law and Contemporary Problems* (2009) 37–56.

Harris, David J.; O'Boyle, Michael; Bates, Edward P. and Buckley, Carla M.; *Law of the European Convention on Human Rights* (Oxford University Press, 2014).

Harrison, Malcolm; Law, Ian and Phillips, Deborah; *Migrants, Minorities and Housing: Exclusion, Discrimination and Anti-Discrimination in 15 Member States of the European Union* (European Monitoring Centre on Racism and Xenophobia, 2005).

Henrard, Kristin; 'Fundamental Rights and Minorities', in Vertovec, Steven (ed.); *Routledge International Handbook of Diversity Studies* (Routledge, 2015).

Ho, Kathleen; 'Structural Violence as a Human Rights Violation', 4(2) *Essex Human Rights Review* (2007) 1–17.

Hooker, Juliet; 'Indigenous Inclusion/Black Exclusion: Race, Ethnicity and Multicultural Citizenship in Latin America', 37 *Journal of Latin American Studies* (2005) 285–310.

Honneth, Axel; 'Grounding Recognition: A Rejoinder to Critical Questions', 45(2) *Inquiry* (2002) 499–519.

Ignatieff, Michael; *Human Rights as Politics and Idolatry* (Princeton University Press, 2003).

Interights; *Non-Discrimination in International Law: A Handbook for Practitioners* (Interrights, 2011).

Inter-American Institute of Human Rights; *Human rights from the perspective of poverty. A path unexplored in the Inter-American system* (Inter-American Institute of Human Rights, 2007).

Jackman, Martha; 'Constitutional Contact and the Disparities in the World: Poverty as a Prohibited Ground of Discrimination under the Canadian Charter and Human Rights Law', 2(1) *Review of Constitutional Studies* (1994) 76–122.

Jørgensen, Marianne W. and Phillips, Louise J.; *Discourse Analysis as a Theory and Method* (SAGE, 2002).

Joshi, Yuvraj; 'The Trouble with Inclusion', 21(2) *Virginia Journal of Social Policy and the Law* (2014) 207–265.

Kabeer, Naila; 'Social Exclusion, Poverty and Discrimination. *Towards an Analytical Framework*', 31(4) *Institute of Development Studies Bulletin* (2000) 83–97.

Kapur, Ratna; 'Human rights in the 21st century: Take a walk on the dark side', 28(4) *Sydney Law Review* (2006) 665–687.

Kayaoglu, Turan; 'Trying Islam: Muslims before the European Court of Human Rights', 34(4) *Journal of Muslim Minority Affairs* (2014) 345–364.

Kayess, Rosemary and French, Philip; 'Out of Darkness into Light? Introducing the Convention on the Rights of Persons with Disabilities', 8(1) *Human Rights Law Review* (2008) 1–34.

Kennedy, David; 'The International Human Rights Movement: Part of the Problem?', 15 *Harvard Human Rights Journal* (2002) 101–125.

Kessler, Laura T.; 'Getting Class', 56 *Buffalo Law Review* (2008) 915–934.

Kingsbury, Benedict; 'Reconciling Five Competing Conceptual Structures of Indigenous Peoples' Claims in International and Comparative Law', 34 *NYU Journal of International Law and Politics* (2001) 189–250.

Koivurova, Timo; 'Jurisprudence of the European Court of Human Rights Regarding Indigenous Peoples: Retrospect and Prospects', 18(1) *International Journal on Minority and Group Rights* (2011) 1–37.

Koskenniemi, Martti and Leino, Päivi; 'Fragmentation of International Law? Postmodern Anxieties', 15(3) *Leiden Journal of International Law* (2002) 553–579.

Kovler, Anatoly; 'Human Rights in a Contemporary Society and European Values: Critique of Eurocentrism', *1 EU-Russia Paper*, Center for EU-Russia Studies, University of Tartu (2011).

Kymlicka, Will; 'The Rise and Fall of Multiculturalism? New Debates on Inclusion and Accommodation in Diverse Societies', 61 *International Social Science Journal* (2010) 97–112.

Kymlicka, Will and Norman, Wayne; *Citizenship in Diverse Societies* (Oxford University Press, 2000).

Landau, David; 'The Reality of Social Rights Enforcement', 53(1) *Harvard International Law Journal* (2012) 189–247.

Lavrysen, Laurens; 'Strengthening the protection of human rights of persons living in poverty under the ECHR', 33(3) *Netherlands Quarterly of Human Rights* (2015) 293–325.

Lawrence, Charles R. III; 'Each Other's Harvest: Diversity's Deeper Meaning', 31(4) *University of San Francisco Law Review* (1997) 757–778.

Leavy, Patricia; 'Introduction', in Leavy, Patricia (ed.); *The Oxford Handbook of Qualitative Research* (Oxford University Press, 2014).

Lentin, Alana and Titley, Gavan; 'More Benetton than barricades? The politics of diversity in Europe', in Titley, Gavan and Lentin, Alana (eds.); *The Politics of Diversity in Europe* (Council of Europe, 2008).

Lenzerini, Federico; *The Culturalization of Human Rights Law* (Oxford University Press, 2014).

Leonard, Emily Winograd; 'Expecting the unattainable: Caseworker use of the "ideal" mother stereotype against the non-offending mother for failure to protect from child sexual abuse cases', 69(1) *NYU Annual Survey of American Law* (2013) 311–356.

Letsas, George; 'The ECHR as a living instrument: Its meaning and its legitimacy', in Føllesdal, Andreas; Peters, Birgit and Ulfstein, Geir (eds.); *Constituting Europe. The European Court of Human Rights in a National, European and Global Context* (Cambridge University Press, 2013).

Lewis, Gail; 'Welcome to the margins: Diversity, tolerance, and policies of exclusion', 28(3) *Ethnic and Racial Studies* (2005) 536–558.

Liebengerg, Sandra; 'Engaging the paradoxes of the universal and particular in human rights adjudication: The possibilities and pitfalls of "meaningful engagement"', 12 *African Human Rights Law Journal* (2012) 1–29.

Lister, Ruth; 'Citizenship: Towards a Feminist Synthesis', 57(1) *Feminist Review* (1997) 28–48.

——; 'A politics of recognition and respect: Involving people with experience of poverty in decision-making that affects their lives', in Andersen, John and Siim, Birte (eds.); *The Politics of Inclusion and Empowerment. Gender, Class and Citizenship* (Palgrave Macmillan, 2004).

——; '(Mis)recognition, Social Inequality and Social Justice: A critical social policy perspective', in Lovell, Terry (ed.); *(Mis)recognition, Social Inequality and Social Justice. Nancy Fraser and Pierre Bourdie* (Routledge, 2007).

Littleton, Christine A.; 'Reconstructing Sexual Equality', in Meyers, Diana Tietjens (ed.); *Feminist Social Thought: A Reader* (Routledge, 1997).

Lynch, Kathleen and Walsh, Judy; 'Love, Care and Solidarity: What Is and Is Not Commodifiable', in Lynch, Kathleen; Baker, John; Lyons, Maureen; Feeley, Maggie; Hanlon, Niall; O'Brien, Maeve; Walsh, Judy and Cantillon, Sara (eds.); *Affective Equality. Love, Care and Injustice* (Palgrave Macmillan, 2009).

MacKinnon, Catharine A.; 'Substantive Equality: A Perspective', 96(1) *Minnesota Law Review* (2011) 1–27.

——; 'Intersectionality as a Method: A Note', 38(4) *Signs* (2013) 1019–1030.

Mahoney, Martha R.; 'Class and Status in American Law: Race, Interest, and the Anti-Transformation Cases', 76 *Southern California Law Review* (2003) 799–892.

Makkonen, Timo; 'Is Multiculturalism Bad for the Fight Against Discrimination?', in Scheinin, Martin and Toivanen, Reetta (eds.); *Rethinking Non-Discrimination and Minority Rights* (Institute for Human Rights Abo Akademi University, 2004).

Malhotra, Ravi and Rowe, Morgan; *Exploring Disability Identity and Disability Rights through Narratives. Finding a Voice of Their Own* (Routledge, 2014).

Malik, Maleiha; 'Religion and Minority Legal Orders', in Cohen, Jean L. and Laborde, Cécile (eds.); *Religion, Secularism and Constitutional Democracy* (Columbia University Press, 2016).

Mantouvalou, Virginia; 'Work and Private Life: Sidabras and Dziautas v. Lithuania', 30 *European Law Review* (2005) 573–585.

——; 'The Case for Social Rights', *Georgetown Public Law Research Paper No. 10–18* (2010).

Marcus, David; 'The Normative Development of Socio-Economic Rights Through Supranational Adjudication', 42 *Stanford Journal of International Law* (2006) 53–102.

Marshall, Thomas H.; 'Citizenship and social class', in Marshall, Thomas H. and Bottomore, Tom (eds.); *Citizenship and Social Class* (Pluto Press, 1950).

Marti, Urs; 'Social Rights in a Global Economy', in Merle, Jean-Christophe (ed.); *Spheres of Global Justice – Volume 2: Fair Distribution. Global Economic, Social and Intergenerational Justice* (Springer, 2013).

Martínez-Torrón, Javier; 'The (Un)protection of individual religious identity in the Strasbourg case law', 1(2) *Oxford Journal of Law and Religion* (2012) 363–385.

Matsuda, Mari J.; 'Besides my sister, facing the enemy: Legal theory out of coalition', 43 *Stanford Law Review* (1991) 1183–1192.

May Macaulay, Margarette; 'The relationship of English-Speaking Caribbean and the Inter-American Legal System of Human Rights', in García Ramírez, Sergio and Castañeda Hernández, Mireya (eds.); *Recepción nacional del derecho internacional de los derechos humanos y admission de la competencia contenciosa de la Corte Interamericana* (Universidad Autónoma de México, 2009).

McCall, Leslie; 'The Complexity of Intersectionality', 30(3) *Signs* (2005) 1771–1800.

McCluskey, Martha T.; 'How Equality became Elitist: The Cultural Politics of Economic from the Court to the "Nany Wars"', 35(4) *Seton Hall Law Review* (2005) 1291–1308.

McGarry, John; O'Leary, Brendan and Simeon, Richard; 'Integration or accommodation? The enduring debate in conflict regulation', in Choudhry, Sujit (ed.); *Constitutional Design for Divided Societies: Integration or Accommodation?* (Oxford University Press, 2008).

McGoldrick, Dominic; 'Multiculturalism and Its Discontents', 5(1) *Human Rights Law Review* (2005) 27–56.

McNay, Lois; *Against Recognition* (Polity Press, 2008).

Medina, Cecilia, 'Towards Effectiveness in the Protection of Human Rights in the Americas', 8(2) *Transnational Law and Contemporary Problems* (1998) 337–358.

——; *The American Convention on Human Rights. Crucial Rights and Their Theory and Practice* (Intersentia, 2016).

Mégret, Frédéric; 'The Disabilities Convention: Towards a Holistic Concept of Rights', 12(2) *The International Journal of Human Rights* (2008) 261–278.

——; 'The Human Rights of Older Persons: A Growing Challenge', 11(1) *Human Rights Law Review* (2011) 37–66.

——; 'Where Does the Critique of International Human Rights Stand? An Exploration in 18 Vignettes', in Beneyto, José María and Kennedy, David (eds.); *New Approaches to International Law* (TMC Asser Press, 2013).

Van Meijl, Toon, 'Anthropological Perspectives on Identity: From Sameness to Difference', in Wetherell, Margaret and Talpade Mohanty, Chandra (eds.); *The SAGE Handbook of Identities* (SAGE Publications, 2010).

Melish, Tara J.; 'The Inter-American Commission on Human Rights. Defending Social Rights through Case-Based Petitions', in Langford, Malcolm (ed.); *Social Rights Jurisprudence: Emerging Trends in Comparative and International Law* (Cambridge University Press, 2008).

——; 'The Inter-American Court of Human Rights. Beyond Progressivity' in Langford, Malcolm (ed.); *Social Rights Jurisprudence: Emerging Trends in Comparative and International Law* (Cambridge University Press, 2008).

Merry, Sally Engle; 'Human Rights Law and the Demonization of Culture (and Anthropology Along the Way)', 26(1) *Political and Legal Anthropology Review* (2003) 55–76.

Minow, Martha; *Making All the Difference. Inclusion, Exclusion and American Law* (Cornell University Press, 1990).

——; 'Identities', 3(1) *Yale Journal of Law & the Humanities* (1991) 97–130.

Modood, Tariq; 'Difference, Multi and Equality', in Seymour, Michel (ed.); *The Plural States of Recognition* (Palgrave Macmillan, 2010).

Molestina, Marisol; 'La Sentencia de Reparaciones del Caso Aloeboetoe y Otros: Un Punto de Vista Antropológico', 25 *Revista IIDH*, Comentarios sobre la práctica de los órganos del sistema interamericano de protección de los derechos humanos (1998) 109–123.

Moore, Sally Falk; 'Law and Social Change: The Semi-Autonomous Social Field as an Appropriate Subject of Study', 7(4) *Law & Society Review* (1973) 719–746.

Morondo Taramundi, Dolores; 'El principio de igualdad entre mujeres y hombres frente a la prohibición del velo islámico integral', 30 *Anuario de Filosofía del Derecho* (2014) 291–307.

Mutua, Athena D.; 'Introducing ClassCrits: From Class Blindness to a Critical Legal Analysis of Economic Inequality', 56(4) *Buffalo Law Review* (2008) 859–913.

——; 'Multidimentionality is to Masculinities What Intersectionality is to Feminism', 13(2) *Nevada Law Journal* (2013) 341–367.

Mutua, Makau.; *Human Rights. A Political and Cultural Critique* (University of Pennsylvania Press, 2002).

——; 'Human Rights in Africa: The Limited Promise of Liberalism', 51(1) *African Studies Review* (2008) 17–39.

Nash, Jennifer C.; 'Re-thinking intersectionality', 89 *Feminist Review* (2008) 1–15.

Nedelsky, Jennifer; 'Reconceiving Autonomy: Sources, Thoughts and Reflections', 1(1) *Yale Journal of Law and Feminism* (1989) 7–36.

——; *Law's Relations. A Relational Theory of Self, Autonomy, and the Law* (Oxford University Press, 2011).

Neuman, Gerald L.; 'Import, Export and Regional Consent in the Inter-American Court of Human Rights', 19(1) *The European Journal of International Law* (2008) 101–123.

Ngwena, Charles G.; 'Inscribing Abortion as a Human Right: Significance of the Protocol on the Rights of Women in Africa', 32(4) *Human Rights Quarterly* (2010) 783–864.

Nice, Julie A.; 'No Scrutiny Whatsoever: Deconstitutionalization of Poverty Law, Dual Rules of Law, and Dialogic Default', 35(3) *Fordham Urban Law Journal* (2008) 629–671.

——; 'Whither the Canaries: On the Exclusion of Poor People from Equal Constitutional Protection', 60 *Drake Law Review* (2012) 1023–1067.

Nickel, James W.; 'Rethinking indivisibility: Towards a theory of supporting relations between human rights', 30(4) *Human Rights Quarterly* (2008) 984–1001.

O'Brien, Wendy; 'Can International Human Rights Law Accommodate Bodily Diversity?', 15(1) *Human Rights Law Review* (2015) 1–20.

O'Cinneide, Colm; 'A modest proposal: destitution, state responsibility and the European Convention on Human Rights', 5 *European Human Rights Law Review* (2008) 583–605.

——; 'The Right to Equality: A Substantive Legal Norm or Vacuous Rhetoric?', 1 *UCL Human Rights Review* (2008) 80–102.

O'Connell, Paul; 'On Reconciling Irreconcilables: Neo-Liberal Globalisation and Human Rights', 7(3) *Human Rights Law Review* (2007) 483–509.

Odello, Marco; 'Indigenous peoples' rights and cultural identity in the Inter-American context', 16(1) *The International Journal of Human Rights* (2012) 25–50.

Okere, B. Obinna; 'The Protection of Human Rights in Africa and the African Charter on Human and Peoples' Rights: A Comparative Analysis with the European and American Systems', 6(2) *Human Rights Quarterly* (1984) 141–159.

Oomen, Barbara; 'The application of socio-legal theories of legal pluralism to understanding the implementation and integration of human rights law', 4 *European Journal of Human Rights* (2014) 471–495.

Oswin, Natalie; 'Producing Homonormativity in Neoliberal South Africa: Recognition, Redistribution, and the Equality Project', 32(3) *Signs* (2007) 649–669.

Ouald Chaib, Saïla; *Belief in Justice. Towards More Inclusivity in and through the Freedom of Religion Case Law of the European Court of Human Rights*, PhD Dissertation (Ghent University, 2015).

Palmer, Ellie; 'Protecting Socio-Economic Rights through the European Convention on Human Rights: Trends and Developments in the European Court of Human Rights', 2(4) *Erasmus Law Review* (2009) 397–425.

Parekh, Bikhu; 'Redistribution or Recognition: a misguided debate', in May, Stephen; Modood, Tariq and Squires, Judith (eds.); *Ethnicity, Nationalism and Minority Rights* (Cambridge University Press, 2004).

——; *Rethinking Multiculturalism. Cultural Diversity and Political Theory* (Palgrave Macmillan, 2006).

——; *A New Politics of Identity. Political Principles for an Interdependent World* (Palgrave Macmillan, 2008).

Parra Vera, Oscar; 'Derechos humanos y pobreza en el Sistema Interamericano. El rol del análisis estructural a partir de informes y siete escenarios estratégicos basados en la responsabilidad internacional', 56 *Revista Instituto Interamericano de Derechos Humanos* (2012) 273–320.

——; 'The Protection of the Right to Health through Individual Petitions before the Inter-American System of Human Rights', in Durojaye, Ebenezer (ed.); *Litigating the Right to Health in Africa. Challenges and Prospects* (Routledge, 2015).

Pelinka, Anton; 'Right-wing populism: Concept and Typology', in Wodak, Ruth; Khosravinik, Majid and Mral, Brigitte (eds.); *Right-Wing Populism in Europe. Politics and Discourse* (Bloomsbury Academic, 2013).

Pelton, Leroy H.; 'Welfare Discrimination and Child Welfare', 60(4) *Ohio State Law Journal* (1999) 1479–1492.

Peroni, Lourdes; *Opening Up the European Convention Human Rights Subject: An Inclusive Multilayered Framework for Adjudicating Religious and Cultural Claims*, PhD Dissertation (Ghent University, 2014).

Peroni, Lourdes and Timmer, Alexandra; 'Vulnerable Groups: The Promise of an Emerging Concept in European Human Rights Convention Law', 11(4) *International Journal of Constitutional Law* (2013) 1056–1085.

Petchesky, Rosalind P.; 'Human Rights, Reproductive Health and Economic Justice: Why They Are Indivisible' 8(15) *Reproductive Health Matters* (2000) 12–17.

Phillimore, Jenny; 'Diversity and Social Welfare. To restrict or include?', in Vertovec, Steven (ed.); *Routledge International Handbook of Diversity Studies* (Routledge, 2015).

Phillips, Anne; 'Equality, Pluralism, Universality: Current Concerns in Normative Theory', 2(2) *British Journal of Politics & International Relations* (2000) 237–255.

——; *Multiculturalism without Culture* (Princeton University Press, 2007).

——; 'What's wrong with Essentialism?', 11(1) *Distinktion: Scandinavian Journal of Social Theory* (2010) 47–60.

Pierik, Roland and Van der Burg, Wibren; 'What Is Neutrality?', 27(4) *Ratio Juris* (2014) 496–515.

Pieterse, Marius; 'Coming to Terms with Judicial Enforcement of Socio-Economic Rights', 20(3) *South African Journal on Human Rights* (2004) 383–417.

——; 'Finding for the Applicant? Individual Equality Plaintiffs and Group-based Disadvantage', 24(3) *South African Journal on Human Rights* (2008) 397–424.

Pogge, Thomas; 'Are We Violating the Human Rights of the World's Poor?', 14(2) *Yale Human Rights and Development Law Journal* (2011) 1–33.

Poulter, Sebastian; *Ethnicity, Law, and Human Rights: the English Experience* (Clarendon Press, 1998).

Porter, Bruce; 'The Crises of ESC Rights and Strategies for addressing it', in Squires, John; Langford, Malcom and Thiele, Bret (eds.); *The Road to a Remedy: Current Issues in the Litigation of Economic, Social and Cultural Rights* (UNSW Press, 2005).

——; 'Expectations of Equality', 33(2) *Supreme Court Law Review* (2006) 23–44.

——; 'Claiming Adjudicative Space: Social Rights, Equality, and Citizenship', in Young, Margot; Boyd, Susan B.; Brodsky, Gwen and Day, Shelagh (eds.); *Poverty: Rights, Social Citizenship, and Legal Activism* (UBC Press, 2007).

Quane, Helen; 'A Further Dimension to the Interdependence and Indivisibility of Human Rights?: Recent Developments Concerning the Rights of Indigenous Peoples', 25 *Harvard Human Rights Journal* (2012) 49–83.

Quinn, Gerard and Arstein-Kerslake, Anna; 'Restoring the "human" in "human rights": personhood and doctrinal innovation in the UN disability convention', in Gearty, Conor and Douzinas, Costas (eds.); *The Cambridge Companion to Human Rights Law* (Cambridge University Press, 2012).

Rajagopal, Balakrishnan; *International Law from Below: Development, Social Movements, and Third World Resistance* (Cambridge University Press, 2003).

——; 'Counter-Hegemonic International Law: Rethinking Human Rights and Development as a Third World Strategy', 27(5) *Third World Quarterly* (2006) 767–783.

Ramji-Nogales, Jaya; 'Undocumented migrants and the failure of Universal individualism', 47 *Vanderbilt Journal of Transnational Law* (2014) 699–763.

Rana, Shruti; 'Restricting the rights of poor mothers: An international human rights critique of "workfare"', 33 *Columbia Journal of Law & Social Problems* (2000) 393–438.

Rawls, John; *A Theory of Justice* (Harvard University Press, 1971).

Relis, Tamara; 'Human Rights and Southern Realities', 33(2) *Human Rights Quarterly* (2011) 509–551.

Remiche, Adélaïde; '*Yordanova and others v Bulgaria*: the Influence of the Social Right to Adequate Housing on the Interpretation of the Civil Right to Respect for one's Home', 12(4) *Human Rights Law Review* (2012) 787–800.

Rich, Camille Gear; 'Performing Racial and Ethnic Identity: Discrimination by Proxy and the Future of Title VII', 79(4) *NYU Law Review* (2004) 1134–1270.

Ringelheim, Julie; 'Diversity and Equality: an ambiguous relationship', in Titley, Gavan and Lentin, Alana (eds.); *The politics of diversity in Europe* (Council of Europe, 2008).

——; 'Chapman redux: the European Court of Human Rights and Roma Traditional Lifestyle', in Brems, Eva (ed.); *Diversity and European Human Rights: Rewriting judgments of the ECHR* (Cambridge University Press, 2012).

——; 'Rights, Religion and the Public Sphere: The European Court of Human Rights in Search of a Theory?', in Zucca, Lorenzo and Ungureanu, Camil (eds.); *Law, State and Religion in the New Europa: Debates and Dilemmas* (Cambridge University Press, 2012).

Rorty, Richard; 'Is "Cultural Recognition" a Useful Notion for Leftist Politics?', 1(1) *Critical Horizons* (2001) 7–20.

Roberts, Dorothy; 'The Dialectic of Privacy and Punishment in the Gendered Regulation of Parenting', 5(2) *Stanford Journal of Civil Rights & Civil Liberties* (2009) 191–200.

Rosen, Lawrence; *Law as Culture. An Invitation* (Princeton University Press, 2006).
Rubio-Marín, Ruth (ed.); *The Gender of Reparations. Unsettling Sexual Hierarchies While Redressing Human Rights Violations* (Cambridge University Press, 2009).
Ruiz Chiriboga, Oswaldo R.; 'The American Convention and the Protocol of San Salvador: Two Intertwined Treaties: Non-Enforceability of Economic, Social and Cultural Rights in the Inter-American System', 31(2) *Netherlands Quarterly of Human Rights* (2013) 159–186.
Saba, Roberto; '(Des)igualdad estructural', 11 *Derecho y Humanidades* (2005) 123–147.
Sadurski, Wojciech; 'Partnering with Strasbourg: Constitutionalization of the European Court of Human Rights, the Accession of Central and East European States to the Council of Europe, and the Idea of Pilot Judgments', 9(3) *Human Rights Law Review* (2009) 397–453.
Sagüés, Néstor Pedro; 'Obligaciones Internacionales y Control de Convencionalidad', 8(1) *Estudios Constitucionales* (2010) 117–136.
Sajó, András; *Human Rights with Modesty: The Problem of Universalism* (Springer, 2004).
Salomon, Margot E.; 'Why Should It Matter That Others Have More? Poverty, Inequality, and the Potential of International Human Rights Law', *LSE Law, Society and Economy Working Papers No. 15/2010* (2010) 1–21.
Sánchez, Rosaura; 'On a Critical Realist Theory of Identity', in Alcoff, Linda Martin; Hames-Garcia, Michael; Mohanty, Satya P. and Moya, Paula M. L. (eds.); *Identity Politics Reconsidered* (Palgrave Macmillan, 2006).
Sandland, Ralph; 'Developing a Jurisprudence of Difference: The Protection of the Human Rights of Travelling Peoples by the European Court of Human Rights', 8(3) *Human Rights Law Review* (2008) 475–516.
Santoro, Emilio; 'A Historical Perspective: From Social Inclusion to Excluding Democracy', in Council of Europe; *Redefining and Combating Poverty: Human Rights, Democracy and Common Goods in Today's Europe*, Trends in Social Cohesion, No. 25 (Council of Europe, 2012).
Santos, Boaventura De Sousa; 'Nuestra America reinventing a subaltern paradigm of recognition and redistribution', 18(2–3) *Theory, Culture & Society* (2001) 185–217.
——; 'Public Sphere and Epistemologies of the South', 37(1) *Africa Development* (2012) 43–67.
Sarat, Austin and Kearns, Thomas R.; *Cultural Pluralism, Identity Politics, and the Law* (The University of Michigan Press, 2001).
Saul, Ben; *Indigenous Peoples and Human Rights. International and Regional Jurisprudence* (Hart Publishing, 2016).
Sayer, Andrew; 'Essentialism, social constructionism, and beyond', 45(3) *The Sociological Review* (1997) 453–487.
Scheinin, Martin; 'International Human Rights Law and the Islamic Headscarf: A Short Note on the Position of the European Court of Human Rights and the Human Rights Committee', in Durhan Jr., W. Cole; Torfs, Rik; Kirkham, David M. and Scott, Christine (eds.); *Islam, Europe and Emerging Legal Issues* (Ashgate, 2012).
De Schutter, Olivier and Verstichel, Annelies; 'The Role of the Union in Integrating the Roma: Present and Possible Future', 2 *European Diversity and Autonomy Papers (EDAP)* (2005).
Sen, Amartya; *Inequality Reexamined* (Clarendon Press, 1992).
——; *Development as Freedom* (Oxford University Press, 1999).

——; 'Social Exclusion: Concept, Application, and Scrutiny', *Social Development Papers No. 1* (Asian Development Bank, 2000).

Sheppard, Colleen; 'Constitutional Recognition of Diversity in Canada', 30 *Vermont Law Review* (2006) 463–487.

——; '"Bread and Roses": Economic Justice and Constitutional Rights', 5(1) *Oñati Socio-Legal Series* (2015) 225–245.

Sijniensky, Romina I.; 'From the Non-Discrimination Clause to the Concept of Vulnerability in International Human Rights Law. Advancing the Needs for Special Protection of Certain Groups and Individuals', in Haeck, Yves; McGonigle Leyh, Brianne; Burbano Herrera, Clara and Contreras Garduno, Diana (eds.); *The Realisation of Human Rights: When Theory Meets Practice. Studies in Honour of Leo Zwaak* (Intersentia, 2013).

Sinclair, June; 'Giving Meaning to the Right to Social Assistance', 2 *Stellenbosch Law Review* (2012) 191–224.

Smis, Stefaan; Cambou, Dorothée and Ngende, Genny; 'The Question of Land Grab in Africa and The Indigenous Peoples' Right to Traditional Lands, Territories and Resources', 35 *Loyola of Los Angeles International and Comparative Law Review* (2013) 493–535.

Smith, Adam; *An Inquiry into the Nature and Causes of the Wealth of Nations* (Clarendon Press, 1975).

Smith, Anne and McLaughlin, Eithne; 'Delivering Equality: Equality Mainstreaming and Constitutionalisation of Socio-Economic Rights', 61(2) *Northern Ireland Legal Quarterly* (2010) 93–121.

Smith, Ben; 'Intersectional Discrimination and Substantive Equality: A Comparative and Theoretical Perspective', 16 *The Equal Rights Review* (2016) 73–102.

Stacy, Helen; 'International Human Rights in a Fragmenting World', in Sajó, András (ed.); *Human Rights with Modesty. The Problem of Universalism* (Martinus Nijhoff Publishers, 2004).

Stavenhagen, Rodolfo; *Peasants, Culture and Indigenous Peoples – Critical Issues* (Springer, 2013).

Steiner, Henry J.; Alston, Philip and Goodman, Ryan; *International Human Rights in Context: Law, Politics, Morals* (Oxford University Press, 2007).

Suárez-Krabbe, Julia; 'Race, Social Struggles, and 'Human' Rights: Contributions from the Global South', 6 *Journal of Critical Globalisation Studies* (2013) 78–102.

Tamanaha, Brian Z.; 'Understanding Legal Pluralism: Past to Present, Local to Global', 30 *Sydney Law Review* (2008) 375–411.

Taylor, Charles; 'The Politics of Recognition', in Taylor, Charles; *Philosophical Arguments* (Harvard University Press, 1995).

Thomas, Carol; 'Disability and diversity', in Vertovec, Steven (ed.); *Routledge International Handbook of Diversity Studies* (Routledge, 2014).

Thompson, Simon; *The Political Theory of Recognition: A Critical Introduction* (Polity Press, 2006).

Thompson, Simon and Yar, Majid (eds.); *The Politics of Misrecognition* (Routledge, 2011).

Timmer, Alexandra; 'Toward an anti-stereotyping approach for the European Court of Human Rights', 11(4) *Human Rights Law Review* (2011) 707–738.

Toivanen, Reetta; 'Is Multiculturalism bad for the fight against discrimination?', in Scheinin, Martin and Toivanen, Reetta (eds.); *Rethinking Non-Discrimination and Minority Rights* (Institute for Human Rights Åbo Akademi University, 2004).

Tomlinson, Barbara; 'To Tell the Truth and Not Get Trapped: Desire, Distance, and Intersectionality at the Scene of Argument', 38(4) *Signs* (2013) 993–1017.

Torbisco Casals, Neus; *Groups Rights as Human Rights* (Springer, 2006).

The Traveller Movement; *A Place to call home: Ethnicity, culture and planning for Traveller sites* (The Traveller Movement, 2014).

Tulkens, Françoise; *The European Convention on Human Rights and the economic crisis: The issue of poverty*, European University Institute Working Papers AEL 2013/08 (2013).

Turkington, Sheilagh; 'A Proposal to Amend the Ontario Human Rights Code: Recognizing Povertyism', 9 *Journal of Law and Social Policy* (1993) 134–191.

Twining, William (ed.); *Human Rights: Southern Voices: Francis Deng, Abdullahi An-Na'im, Yash Ghai and Upendra Baxi* (Cambridge University Press, 2009).

Vandenhole, Wouter; 'Child Poverty and Children's Rights: An Uneasy Fit?', 22(2) *Michigan State International Law Review* (2014) 609–636.

Verdonck, Lieselot and Desmet, Ellen; 'Moving human rights jurisprudence to a higher gear: rewriting the case of the Kichwa Indigenous People of Sarayaku v. Ecuador', in Brems, Eva and Desmet, Ellen (eds.); *Integrated Human Rights in Practice. Rewriting Human Rights Decisions* (Edward Elgar, 2017).

Vickers, Lucy; 'Religious Discrimination in the Workplace: An Emerging Hierarchy?', 12(3) *Ecclesiastical Law Journal* (2010) 280–303.

——; 'Promoting Equality or Fostering Resentment? The Public Sector Equality Duty and Religion and Belief', 31(1) *Legal Studies* (2011) 135–158.

Vieira, Oscar Vilhena; 'Inequality and the Subversion of the Rule of Law', in Pogge, Thomas (ed.); *Freedom from Poverty as a Human Right. Volume 2: Theory and Politics* (UNESCO Publishing, 2010).

Vojdik, Valorie K.; 'Politics of the headscarf in Turkey: Masculinities, Feminism, and the Construction of Collective Identities', 33(2) *Harvard Journal of Law and Gender* (2010) 661–685.

Waldron, Jeremy; 'Cultural Identity and Civic Responsibility', in Kymlicka, Will and Norman, Wayne; *Citizenship in Diverse Societies* (Oxford University Press, 2000).

West, Robin; *Narrative, Authority, and the Law* (The University of Michigan Press, 1993).

——; *Re-Imagining Justice: Progressive Interpretations of Formal Equality, Rights, and the Rule of Law* (Ashgate, 2003).

Whelan, Daniel J.; *Indivisible Human Rights. A History* (University of Pennsylvania Press, 2010).

Wiles, Ellen; 'Headscarves, Human Rights, and Harmonious Multicultural Society: Implications of the French Ban for Interpretations of Equality', 41(3) *Law & Society Review* (2007) 699–736.

Williams, Wendy R.; 'Struggling with Poverty: Implications for Theory and Policy of Increasing Research on Social Class-Based Stigma', 9(1) *Analyses of Social Issues and Public Policy* (2009) 37–56.

Woods, Jeanne M.; 'Justiciable Social Rights as a Critique of the Liberal Paradigm', 38 *Texas International Law Journal* (2003) 763–793.

Wrench, John; 'Diversity management', in Vertovec, Steven (ed.); *Routledge International Handbook of Diversity Studies* (Routledge, 2015).

Yoshino, Kenji; 'Assimilationist Bias in Equal Protection: The Visibility Presumption and the Case of Don't Ask, Don't Tell', 108(3) *The Yale Law Journal* (1998) 485–571.

——; 'The New Equal Protection', 124 *Harvard Law Review* (2011) 747–803.
Young, Iris Marion; 'Structural Injustice and the Politics of Difference', in Grabham, Emily; Cooper, Davina; Krishnadas, Jane and Herman, Didi (eds.); *Intersectionality and Beyond. Law, power and the politics of location* (Routledge-Cavendish, 2009).
——; *Justice and the Politics of the Difference* (Princeton University Press, 2011).
Yuval-Davis, Nira; 'What is Transversal Politics', 12 *Soundings* (1999) 94–98.
——; Anthias, Floya and Kofman, Eleonore; 'Secure borders, safe haven and the gendered politics of belonging: Beyond social cohesion', 28(3) *Ethnic and Racial Studies* (2005) 513–535.
Zempi, Irene and Chakraborti, Neil; *Islamophobia, Victimization and the Veil* (Palgrave Macmillan, 2014).

INDEX

ABOUT THE AUTHOR

Valeska David is an attorney, research affiliate at the Human Rights Centre of Ghent University, Belgium, and assistant professor of International Law at the University of Navarra, Spain. She has worked as a researcher, consultant and lecturer for human rights institutions and universities in Europe as well as Chile, where she has also been involved in human rights training programmes for judges, prosecutors and defenders from all over Latin America. She has had her work published in international journals, books and blogs and her areas of particular interest include equality law, international courts, minority rights, gender studies, cultural and economic rights, remedies and access to justice.

www.ingramcontent.com/pod-product-compliance
Ingram Content Group UK Ltd.
Pitfield, Milton Keynes, MK11 3LW, UK
UKHW051846100926
8556IPUK00005B/476

9 781780 688336